Sports

Other Books on Sports by Allen Guttmann

From Ritual to Record:
   The Nature of Modern Sports (2004)

The Olympics:
   A History of the Modern Games (2002)

Japanese Sports:
   A History (with Lee Thompson, 2001)

The Erotic in Sports (1996)

Games and Empires:
   Modern Sports and Cultural Imperialism (1994)

Women's Sports: A History (1991)

A Whole New Ball Game:
   An Interpretation of American Sports (1988)

Sports Spectators (1986)

The Games Must Go On:
   Avery Brundage and the Olympic Movement (1984)

Sports

THE FIRST FIVE MILLENNIA ALLEN GUTTMANN

UNIVERSITY OF MASSACHUSETTS PRESS Amherst and Boston

Copyright © 2004 by University of Massachusetts Press

All rights reserved

Printed in the United States of America

LC 2004013506

ISBN 1-55849-470-7

Designed by Richard Hendel

Set in ITC Charter and The Serif Black

by Graphic Composition, Inc.

Printed and bound by The Maple-Vail

Book Manufacturing Group

Library of Congress Cataloging-in-Publication Data

Guttmann, Allen.

Sports : the first five millennia / Allen Guttmann.

   p.   cm.

Includes bibliographical references and index.

ISBN 1-55849-470-7 (cloth : alk paper)

1. Sports—History.   2. Sports—Social aspects.

3. Sports—Cross-cultural studies.   I. Title

GV571.G88 2004

796'.09—DC22

   2004013506

British Library Cataloguing in Publication

data are available.

Title page photo by permission of Colorsport.

To Ommo Grupe

Action and representation merge and society's values and norms can be seen and experienced most definitely in sport.
—OTMAR WEISS

The ballpark is still the place to go if you want to see people as they are.
—THOMAS BOSWELL

Studies of sport which are not studies of society are studies out of context.
—NORBERT ELIAS

CONTENTS

Illustrations follow pages 144 and 272

PREFACE AND ACKNOWLEDGMENTS

"That's what literature is good for," says Henri in Simone de Beauvoir's novel *Les Mandarins* (1954), "it shows to others the world as we see it." *Sports: The First Five Millennia* is my attempt to do the same sort of thing, to show to others the history of the world's sports as I see it. I am well aware that others understand that history differently. I cannot prove that my interpretation of the history of sports is better than that offered by other scholars, but I *can* say that my interpretation is based on more than thirty years of research and that it has been tempered by the heated give-and-take of critical debate.

Some sections of this book are based on or revised from material originally presented in my earlier books and essays. A number of paragraphs are based on collaborative research into Japanese and Islamic sports history, research that originally appeared in *Japanese Sports: A History* (coauthored by Lee Thompson) and in "From Iran to All of Asia: The Origin and Diffusion of Polo" (coauthored by Houchang Chehabi). Neither Thompson nor Chehabi is responsible for what I have made of our joint efforts.

My research was generously supported by two grants from Amherst College. I wish also to acknowledge the assistance and encouragement that I have received from other scholars, but I am dismayed by the magnitude of my debts. When I attempted to list those to whom I am especially grateful, the list became longer—and longer—and longer. It began to resemble the directory published by the North American Society for Sport History (NASSH). Rather than naming a hundred scholars and omitting the names of a hundred others, I have decided to let my extensive endnotes tell the story of my innumerable debts to colleagues in NASSH and in several other organizations devoted to sports studies.

To that austere rule, there are three exceptions (in addition to Ommo Grupe, to whom this book is dedicated). I am especially grateful to Richard Mandell, whose *Nazi Olympics* (1971) tipped the balance when I was still undecided about whether or not to commit myself to the field of sports studies; to Clark Dougan, whose expertise as historian and as editor attracted me to the University of Massachusetts Press; and to Doris Bargen, whose steadfast love brings to mind a pair of lines from the poetry of Conrad Aiken:

> Music I heard with you was more than music.
> Bread I ate with you was more than bread.

CHINESE AND JAPANESE NAMES

Chinese family names ("Mao") appear before given names ("Zhedong") and are listed in notes and in bibliographies in that order. This convention is well understood and causes no problems. Japanese family names also appear before given names—*except* when the Japanese present themselves in the West. This means that Japanese authors appear family-name-first when they publish in Japanese and family-name-last when they publish in English. I follow this awkward convention in my notes. For example:

Tanaka Hideo, *Nihon no Spōtsu*" (Tokyo: Fumaidō, 1999), p. 69.

Hideo Tanaka, "Japanese Sports," *Journal of Sports History,* 15:4 (Fall 1999): 69–96.

Sports

INTRODUCTION
RULES OF THE GAME

Sports are a human universal, appearing in every culture, past and present. But every culture has its own definitions of *sport*. Quibbles about these definitions are tedious, but a lack of clarity can muddle one's research. You can't study sports if you aren't clear about what you want to study, which is why mixed-bag studies are confused by the inclusion of board games, card games, dancing, cycling to work, window-shopping, and sunbathing. England's General Household Survey, for example, classifies housewives as sports participants if they walk to the bakery and the greengrocer's shop.[1] This does not seem reasonable. My working definition of *sports* sites them within a paradigm that is quite specific about sport's relationship to *play, games,* and *contests.*

People work because they have to; they play because they want to. The pleasures of *play* are intrinsic rather than extrinsic to the activity. In a word, play is autotelic (from *auto,* "its own," and *telos,* "goal, end, or purpose"). In theory, play "evokes an activity without constraint but also without consequences for the real world."[2] (In practice, of course, there may be all sorts of consequences.) This activity can be divided into two types—spontaneous play and rule-bound or regulated play.

Spontaneous play is impulsive, voluntary, and uncoerced. Examples abound. A boy sees a flat stone, picks it up, and sends it skipping across the still waters of a pond. A Nobel laureate delivering an acceptance speech amuses herself and the audience with an impromptu pun. Neither action is premeditated, and both are at least relatively free of cultural constraint. They provide us with an ecstatic sense of pure possibility.

The second type of play has rules and regulations to determine which actions are acceptable and which are not. These rules transform spontaneous play into *games,* which can, accordingly, be defined as rule-bound or regulated play. Leapfrog, chess, "playing house," and basketball are all games, some with rather simple rules, others governed by lengthy sets of regulations. Do the constraining rules and regulations contradict my assertion that play is autotelic? Not really. Not if we willingly surrender spontaneity for the sake of playful order. We continue to remain outside the domain of material necessity and we don't expect our games to feed or clothe or shelter us. We freely obey the rules we impose upon ourselves because they—the rules—are what constitute the game.

Of my four examples, chess and basketball are obviously different from leapfrog and "playing house." The first pair of games involves competition, the second does not. One can win a game of chess or basketball, but it makes no sense to ask who has won at leapfrog or "playing house." In other words, chess and basketball are *contests.* Anthropologists who ignore this competitive–noncompetitive distinction have come, wrongly, to the conclusion that some cultures have no games.[3]

A final distinction separates contests into two categories: those that require physical prowess, i.e., *sports,* and those that do not. Football and shuffleboard are handy examples of the first category, while Scrabble and poker will do to exemplify the second. The sports that have most excited the passions of participants and spectators have required much more physical prowess than a friendly game of shuffleboard. For good reason, sports heroes commonly demonstrate uncommon strength, speed, stamina, agility, dexterity, and endurance. It must be understood, however, that physical prowess is a necessary but not a sufficient characteristic of sports. The simplest sports require *some*—but not very much—intellectual effort. "Stay in your lane" should suffice as the last-minute instruction to a slow-witted sprinter. Other sports, like baseball, call for a considerable amount of mental alertness.

To summarize: sports can be defined as *autotelic physical contests.* On the basis of this definition, I have more than once proposed a simple inverted-tree diagram.

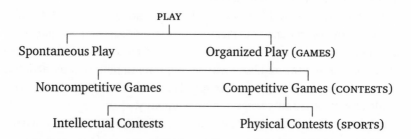

PLAY

Spontaneous Play   Organized Play (GAMES)

Noncompetitive Games   Competitive Games (CONTESTS)

Intellectual Contests   Physical Contests (SPORTS)

Despite the clarity of the definition, all sorts of questions arise. Some are easily answered. Is mountain climbing a sport? It is if one understands the activity as a strenuous contest between the climber and the mountain or as a competition among climbers eager to be the first to accomplish a difficult ascent. Are jogging and working out in a fitness studio sports? Here, too, it depends on whether or not the activity is done competitively. Automobile races present a different problem. Are the drivers in the *Le Mans Grand Prix* and the Indianapolis 500 really *athletes?* They are if one believes that physical skill and endurance are required to survive the grueling competition. What should one say about competitions in domestic activities such as weaving, sewing, and cornhusking? Although the amount of physical effort they require is not great, they fit my definition as clearly as do workplace competitions in logrolling, plowing, and calf-roping. The first group is seldom mentioned in histories of sports because men have almost always decided which physical contests are socially and culturally important and which are not. I am ready to welcome a history of sports that pays as much attention to women's contests—of all sorts—as it does to men's contests, but the source materials for this kind of radically revisionist history are not yet, and may never be, available.[4]

There is one question that threatens to upset my neatly arranged definitional applecart. Spontaneous play is autotelic, but reluctant children compelled by their parents or teachers to compete in a game of soccer are not really engaged in play for its own sake. Neither are the superstars of professional sports if their only motivation is a monthly million-dollar paycheck. "Radical autotelism" is an untenable position.[5] In the real world, as a practical matter, motives are usually mixed and often quite impossible to fathom. In the real world, people become involved in sports for all sorts of extrinsic reasons—for prestige, economic gain, course credit, improved cardiovascular fitness, stress reduction—as well as for the intrinsic pleasures of a physical contest. The psychological tests used to determine the motivations of today's athletes are blunt instruments, and they are obviously no help at all when we speculate about the motives of Roman gladiators or Heian-period Japanese archers. Unless we have evidence to the contrary, it is reasonable to give the players the benefit of a doubt and to assume that they really are motivated by at least a measure of intrinsic satisfaction, by the pleasure of finding, discovering, knowing, realizing, actualizing, and developing the self.[6] Michael Jordan, returning from retirement, did not *need* his paycheck. I believe him when he says that he loves basketball.

A number of theorists—mostly European—have analyzed sports to say what they *signify*, what they *mean*. Some have gone for essences. For Bernard Jeu, all sports were "a meditation on death and violence." For Michel Bouet, skiing suggested "the idea of spatial penetration." The ephemeral trail left upon the snow by the skier is "a mystification of the temporal by the spatial." The snow itself is "an embodiment of silence." I am fascinated by speculations like these, but—in the last analysis—I agree with anthropologists like

Ommo Grupe who conclude that a sport means whatever the participants, embedded in their cultures, say it means. In the last analysis, the attribution of significance is what Gunter Gebauer termed "an essentially arbitrary process." The influential Dutch psychologist F. J. J. Buytendijk asserted that kicking games are *essentially* masculine while throwing games are *essentially* feminine. This tells us something about the state of Dutch culture in 1952. It tells us nothing about soccer and baseball, then or now.[7]

Although my initial paradigm of play–games–contests–sports is unhistorical, in that it purports to define these concepts and their relationships one to another wherever and whenever they occur, what follows this introductory chapter is a cultural *history* of sports that attempts to relate sports to *some* of their political, economic, social, religious, and cultural contexts. My emphasis is on the forms and functions of a number of exemplary sports as they have appeared at different times and places. To play with a bit of ancient insight: *Tempora mutantur, mutantur ludi in illis* (Times change and sports are changed with them). A refusal to recognize this mutability of form and function lies behind the dogmatic assertions—"sports = capitalist exploitation = patriarchal domination"—that appear, much too often, in journals devoted to the study of sports.[8]

Although "grand narratives" are definitely out of fashion among those who believe that we live in "postmodernity," much of what follows consists of narration explicitly or implicitly organized within a comprehensive historical framework derived, in part, from Max Weber and from Norbert Elias. Basic to this famework are three convictions: (1) The formal–structural characteristics of modern sports are strikingly different from those of premodern sports. (2) Premodern sports have tended either to acquire the formal–structural characteristics of modern sports or to survive on the margins of the mainstream as what Raymond Williams called "residual culture." (3) The evolution from premodern to modern sports is an instance of what Elias called—somewhat tendentiously—"the civilizing process," in the course of which the members of a society internalize values that reduce the level of expressive (but not instrumental) interpersonal violence.

Modern (as opposed to premodern) sports can be defined by a set of seven interrelated formal–structural characteristics.[9] Preliminary discussion of them can be condensed, somewhat cryptically, into seven short paragraphs.

Secularism. Modern sports are not related to the transcendent realm of the sacred. Sports in premodern societies frequently occurred as an aspect of religious observance. The Olympic Games, for example, were sacred to Zeus, and Japanese *shinji-zumô* was performed at temple and shrine festivals.

Equality. Modern sports require, at least in theory, that everyone—including the elderly and the handicapped—be admitted to the game on the basis of his or her athletic ability. In addition, the rules must be the same for all contestants. Premodern sports frequently excluded people on the basis of social class, religion, ethnicity, or gender, and the rules for premodern sports often varied with variations in social status.

Specialization. Many modern team sports (rugby, soccer, and American football) have evolved from earlier, less differentiated games and many (baseball, cricket) have a gamut of specialized roles and playing positions. At the elite level, individual athletes rely on an ancillary team of supportive specialists. The Dutch Olympic swimmer Inge de Bruijn, for instance, arrived in Sydney with two coaches, two masseuses, two physiologists, a nutritionist, a sports psychologist, and a personal trainer.[10]

Bureaucratization. Local, regional, national, and international bureaucracies now administer every level of modern sports from Little League Baseball to the World Cup Final. Lacking this kind of administrative structure, premodern sports usually took place under the aegis of local political or religious authorities.

Rationalization. Modern sports are a prime example of what Max Weber called *Zweckrationalität* (instrumental rationality). Sports contests take place in built-to-purpose facilities where scientifically trained athletes compete with standardized equipment on the basis of constantly revised rules and regulations that are looked upon as means to an end. Rationalization leads also to abstraction, to what Georges Vigarello calls *déréalisation.*[11] The equestrian vaulter's whinnying, restlessly moving mount becomes the gymnast's quietly immobile "horse," and the backyard hurdler's leafy hedges are replaced by the track athlete's lightly constructed portable rectangles. In every way, premodern sports exhibited a much lower level of instrumental rationality.

Quantification. In modern sports, as in almost every aspect of our daily lives, we live in a world of numbers. At their panhellenic athletic festivals, the ancient Greeks measured neither the times runners ran nor the distances throwers threw (and they had no standardized units for temporal or spatial measurement in the unlikely event that they were concerned about the numbers).

Obsession with Records. The unsurpassed quantified achievement, which is what we mean by a sports record, is a constant challenge to all who hope to surpass it.[12] André Obey, a French athlete and man of letters, wrote lyrically of his hope that his daughter would "one day recite the litany, not of battles but of records, more beautiful than the labors of Hercules."[13] Without the prerequisite of a quantified achievement, premodern athletes were unable to set—and were perhaps unable even to imagine—sports records.

For each of these generalizations about the stark contrast between the present and the past, there are exceptions. For example, the achievements of ancient Roman charioteers and seventeenth-century Japanese archers *were* quantified. There were, in other words, anticipations of modernity in sports as in other institutions. Isolated examples, however, do not constitute a system. In considering the contrast between premodern and modern sports, one must bear in mind that the characteristics of modernity are not a random collection of arbitrary attributes. They fit together like the pieces of a puzzle.

Unfortunately, modernization theories have fallen into unwarranted disfavor. The paradigm of modernization can be misinterpreted to imply that the observed changes occurred as part of some uniform and inevitable process that must of necessity and by some preordained schedule transform each and every aspect of each and every society in precisely the same way—which is nonsense. The paradigm of modernization can also be misused as a facile instrument of ethnocentric ethical judgment—as if modern ways were somehow a *moral* as well as a technological advance beyond traditional folkways. Although nineteenth-century observers may have felt optimism about the future, their children and grandchildren have experienced the adverse effects as well as the benefits of modernization. Toxic wastes and the threat of thermonuclear catastrophe are as much a part of modernity as are laser surgery and electronic telecommunications.

If the disavowal of assumptions about the alleged inevitability, ubiquity, and desirability of modernization seems like an inadequate response to criticism, one may reasonably ask if there is a better way, in the domain of sports, to understand the contrast between a medieval game of folk-football and the globally televised spectacle of soccer football's World Cup Final? In the last analysis, the *usefulness* of the modernization paradigm is the best argument for its continued use.

Within this highly abstract theoretical framework with its focus on unfashionable "grand narratives," there is ample space for an eclectic array of less abstract approaches to sports history. Among them are the "cultural studies" approach, which draws upon the insights of Antonio Gramsci, and the not-yet-labeled approach of Pierre Bourdieu, which underlines the importance of habitus (the socially constructed behaviors that we take for granted). My cards are on the table. It's time to play the historian's game.

1 PRELITERATE PEOPLES

"War, " proclaimed Carl Diem, was "the noblest of sports . . . and the wellspring of all other sports."[1] This claim was as reckless as the Marxist assertion that "all sports were originally one with the means of production."[2] Another of Diem's lapidary generalizations was closer to the mark. "All sports," he wrote, "began as cult."[3] An overstatement, no doubt, but Diem was right to call attention to a remarkable fact about the sports of preliterate cultures (which must serve as our surrogate for the sports of prehistorical times). The sports of grown men and women were often—perhaps usually—embedded within or aspects of religious ritual. In the vast anthropological literature devoted to the lives of preliterate peoples, innumerable examples can be found to illustrate the myriad interactions of sports and religion. Summarizing the encyclopedic detail of his enormous compendium, *Games of the North American Indians* (1907), anthropologist Stewart Culin concluded that the games of adult men and women "appear to be played ceremonially, as pleasing to the gods, with the object of securing fertility, causing rain, giving and prolonging life, expelling demons, or curing sickness."[4] Religious significance can often be detected in sports that appear, on the surface, to be simple secular pastimes. Kite-flying, which was a passion during Thailand's Sukhothai period (1238–1347), was "part of the ritual of asking for the cool wind for the summer months."[5]

The Americas

Stickball games, from which modern lacrosse evolved, were common throughout nearly all of pre-Columbian North America. Among the most carefully studied of these games was the version played by the Choctaws and Cherokees of the southeastern United States.[6]

The Cherokee version of the game began with a lunar month (twenty-eight days) of sexual abstinence. At the end of this period, the players spent a night sequestered together in a sacred precinct under the supervision of shamans who scarified them with a seven-toothed comb made from the leg bone of a turkey. Sets of twenty-eight scratches each were made on the players' arms, legs, backs, and breasts. When the shaman was done with the scarification ceremony, each player bled from nearly three hundred gashes. The game itself took place upon a field whose boundaries were not strictly defined. The goals might be one hundred feet or several miles apart. There were no sidelines, and the number of players varied from as few as twenty to several hundred on a side. Some games lasted for only a few hours; others went on for several days. The game was often violent and serious injuries were common. A week after the game, there was a victory dance, after which the players were allowed to resume sexual intercourse. The purpose of the game seems to have been to ensure the fertility of plants and animals.

Like the stickball game, the relay races of the Jicarilla Apaches of the Southwest were originally part of a fertility rite. The track upon which adolescent boys raced was called "The Milky Way" (a reference to the heavenly path on which, according to Jicarilla myth, the sun and the moon had originally raced). The track connected the circle of the sun and the circle of the moon. Around the circumference of the solar and the lunar circles small holes were dug into which pollen was dropped. In each hole, a sapling was planted. The race itself took place on the third day of the festival, at which time a fire was ignited in each of the two circles. Painted, pollened, and adorned with feathers, the boys were led to their circles by two young girls who carried an eagle feather in one hand and an ear of corn in the other (symbolizing animal and vegetable sources of food). The runners ran in no particular order, and some ran more often than others. The outcome of the relay race was less important than the elaborate ceremony that contextualized the contest and endowed it with cultural significance.[7]

Another kind of relay race was central to the culture of the Tarahumara Indians of northern Mexico. Kicking a small wooden ball, young men ran for days back and forth along a course that stretched for miles north and south of the starting point. An ethnologist who witnessed a race in the 1920s was told that one of the men had covered six hundred miles in five days.[8] Another observer watched as a runner paused to be fed by a girl. Although he had already run fifty miles, he breathed as easily as if he had sauntered in from a stroll, but his eyes were glassy and he stared into space. After he continued on his way, the girl fed a rival runner. The men ran through the night, "as if in a trance," while the spectators sang, danced, and shouted "hysterically." It is probable that the ball originally symbolized the sun or the moon and that the relay was meant to acknowledge or to ensure cosmic order, but the Tarahumara relay race, emptied of its ritual significance, has now become an Internet-advertised touristic event.[9]

The "sports equipment" of the Timbira runners of Brazil consisted of logs that weighed as much as one hundred kilograms. Shifting their logs from shoulder to shoulder, runners covered distances of five to twelve kilometers. Although the culture of the Timbira was organized on the basis of a number of dualisms—sun and moon, dry season and rainy season, male and female—there was apparently little or no interest in the binary that bewitches modern sports fans: winner and loser. "In return for their extraordinary physical performance," wrote anthropologist Käthe Hye-Kerkdal, "neither the winning team nor the best runner receives any kind of recognition." The religious significance of the log race accounts for this lack of interest in the outcome. What exactly that significance was is hard to determine. Speculating that there was in Timbira culture an association between trees and the souls of the dead, Hye-Kerkdal conjectured that the race might have "originally comprised part of funeral games." She wondered also if the race might have been part of a fertility rite. Perhaps it was. It is suggestive that the log races of another Brazilian tribe, the Canela, allowed the winner sexual access to the maiden whose body, when measured before the start of the race, determined the length of the log he was to carry. The women were, in turn, eager to sleep with a winner and to bear his stalwart offspring.[10]

_____ Africa

Leni Riefenstahl, the famous (and controversial) German film-maker, lived among the Nuba of the Sudan and documented their ritual wrestling matches in a book of photographs accompanied by an extensive text. The matches, which are the only occasions during which the various Nuba villages come together, are "the expression of all that distinguishes the Nuba way of life." They are a manifestation "in the visible and social world of the invisible world of the mind and of the spirit."[11]

When the council of tribal elders decides that a match should take place, messengers are dispatched to invite the wrestlers to the ceremony. On the day of the ritual match described by Riefenstahl, several thousand Nuba walk as far as twenty miles to the site of the festival. Everyone is "decorated . . . with beads, ash, furs and calabashes." The wrestlers, wearing calabashes tied to the backs of their belts, are dusted with ash, which gives them a ghostly appearance appropriate for men who perform in the liminal space between life and death. The wrestlers also wear cumbersome _merre_ ("tails"), which hinder their movements even as they contribute to the symbolism of the ceremony by suggesting the connection between the men and the cattle that are the economic basis of Nuba culture. The connection becomes obvious when the wrestlers stamp their feet and "utter muffled sounds imitating the roar of a bull. . . . At this stage the wrestlers are identified with the 'spirit' of their herds of cattle." The wrestlers are no longer addressed by their human names.[12]

In an "aggressive crouch," the wrestler studies his opponent and decides whether or not to accept the challenge. Like Japanese sumo¯ wrestlers, the men may spend more time glaring than they do grappling. When they do charge, they "move together heaving and straining, huge muscles bulging, until with a gasp and . . . a roar from the crowd, one throws the other to the ground. A particularly powerful wrestler sometimes lifts . . . his opponent like a sack and simply lays him on his back." The loser leaves; the winner dances and utters sounds like the call of an animal. He is then carried from the ring on the shoulders of a male friend or relative. An older wrestler, often a maternal uncle, hands him a branch of acacia wood, "the only tangible prize a wrestler ever receives." This branch is taken home and burned. The ash is then carefully preserved. Half of it is kept in a horn, which is hung in the wrestler's house. It is to be used at the funeral ceremony that will mark his death. The rest of the ash is preserved in a gourd to be used to dust the wrestler when he is, once again, "in need of strength and protection."[13]

With nightfall, the feast begins. The wrestlers dance in groups, after which the women begin to pour marissa beer for everyone except the wrestlers. The men sit quietly now, eying but not approaching the young women. Sexual fulfillment will come with the rainy season, when there are no more wrestling matches.

When Riefenstahl returned to the Nuba after an absence of several years, she was horrified to discover that "the lovely calabashes that had adorned the backs of [the wrestlers'] belts were now frequently replaced with plastic bottles or even empty tin cans." Like the Melanesians who combined traditional rituals and modern sports to produce "Trobriand cricket," the Nuba have created a mix of premodern and modern elements. Ironically, the most "authentic" wrestlers are now found in Sudanese cities, where they perform for camera-wielding tourists.[14]

Although twentieth-century sociologists have described sports as a "masculine preserve" from which women have been excluded by male gamekeepers, many—perhaps most—African tribes had ritual sports for young women. Pubescent girls often wrestled as part of their ritual initiation into mature womanhood. Among the Diola of Gambia, for instance, adolescent girls wrestled one another, strongly motivated by the prospect of the winner's marriage with the winner of the boys' matches. In other tribes, such as the Yala of Nigeria and the Njabi of the Congo, the gods desired that young men and women wrestle one another.[15]

The imbrication of sports and religious ritual in the cultures of preliterate peoples should not be interpreted to mean that the sports of grown men and women were never secular affairs. In an activity known as *gusimbuka,* the Tutsi of Rwanda and Burundi demonstrated their prodigious ability as high-jumpers. A frequently reproduced photograph taken during Adolf Friedrich von Mecklenburg's 1907 ethnographic expedition shows a Tutsi jumper leaping far above Mecklenburg's head. In a brilliant book critical of Western misinterpretations of this phenomenon ("All representations can be read as deformations"), John Bale suggests that *gusimbuka,* which some anthropologists have read as a *rite de passage* for adolescent males, may have been a simple demonstration of physical superiority, a way to "normalize" Tutsi political domination of the Hutu majority.[16]

Before I leap backward, metaphorically, to ancient Egypt, I should note that traditional games are invariably stripped of their religious associations as they evolve into modern sports. The Choctaws still play stickball, but the pre-Columbian rituals have vanished with the Great Spirit who called them forth. When modern stickball teams compete, each side has the same set number of uniformed players. On a rectangular, bounded field, they play for a fixed number of minutes. Medicine men can still be seen on the sidelines, chanting their magic incantations, but it is the task of uniformed officials to enforce the rules and determine the penalty for their infraction. Stickball, which was once a constituent element in the tribal culture of the entire Southeast, has become a secularized ethnographical curiosity.[17]

BEFORE THE GREEKS

_____ **Egyptian Sports**

The oldest sports about which we have reasonably reliable information are those of ancient Egypt. Evidence from elsewhere in the ancient world is scattered and difficult to interpret. Sumerian seals depict wrestlers who may or may not have been engaged in sports rather than mortal combat, and there are Sumerian hymns in which King Sulgi boasts of his achievements as an archer, hunter, wrestler, and runner. (That he actually ran from Nippur to Ur and back in a single day must have been quite literally incredible except to those who meekly accepted priestly myths of royal prowess.) The Sumerian seals and hymns are typical of the problematic evidence cited by historians searching for the origins of sports in ancient Mesopotamia.[1]

The literary evidence from ancient Egypt is also scanty, but there are a few tales—such as *The Story of Sinuhe*—in which fact can be sifted from fantasy. (Sinuhe journeys to Syria and proves his mettle as a wrestler.) The archeological evidence is more abundant, thanks largely to the passionate desire of the pharaohs and their courtiers to bequeath to posterity visual records of their athletic accomplishments. Of the sports of ordinary men and women, much less is known.

It was a matter of political dogma that Egyptian rulers were physically powerful. The pharaoh's prowess as a runner, a hunter, and an archer manifested his ability to protect his people from the threats of human and divine enemies. To prove his physical fitness after thirty years on the throne, the pharaoh performed a ritual run across a course that symbolized the realm over which he ruled. Near the pyramid of Djoser, which was built in the middle of the third millennium B.C., the distance between the course's semicircular end markers was approximately fifty-five meters.[2]

Among the most fascinating depictions of this ritual is a temple relief in Karnak, from the middle of the second millennium B.C., in which Queen Hatshepsut, accompanied by the steer–god Apis, runs across the sacred precinct, thereby testifying that she, too, was physically fit to rule.[3] Whether she or any of the male pharaohs actually performed the depicted feats is questionable.

There is no need to question the fact that the pharaohs and their courtiers hunted for the excitement of the chase (and not because food was in short supply). A colorful relief from the tomb of Tutankhamen shows him with a drawn bow and arrow while his consort hands him another arrow and helpfully points to some birds in flight. This scene is charmingly realistic, but the pharaohs' fabulous exploits in the hunt for lions and other dangerous beasts may be just that—the stuff of fable. When we read on a stele that the eighteenth-dynasty monarch Thutmose III bent his bow and loosed arrows that killed one hundred twenty bulls and seven lions "in an instant," we are right to suspect, at the very least, exaggeration. Similarly suspect is the assertion, on another stele, that Thutmose slew one hundred twenty elephants, "an achievement hitherto unequaled by any who wore the white crown." Boasts of this sort are clearly contributions to the political myth that legitimated authoritarian rule. The pharaoh, explains Wolfgang Decker, was "the guarantor of the world's order, which he had to defend against the forces of chaos." Like the ceremonial run at the end of thirty years on the throne, the bodies of the slain bulls, lions, and elephants were visible proof that the pharaoh was fit for his superhumanly arduous task. [4]

The same political motivation lay behind the "records" set by Thutmose and his descendents as each of them shot arrows through a set of hammered copper sheets. Reading that each ruler surpassed his predecessor with an unprecedented achievement, one grows increasingly skeptical. Amenhotep II did more than send four arrows through four sheets (all thicker than the sheets penetrated by Thutmose). "One arrow shot at a copper target penetrated it and fell to earth on the other side." Decker—the world's foremost authority on Egyptian sports—takes these accounts of quantified achievements as an indication that the Egyptians anticipated the concept of the sports record, which he defines simply as "the surpassing of an achievement." It may be that Decker is right about the way the Egyptians conceptualized achievement, but it seems more likely that the fabulous numbers were fabricated in order to awe and astonish the pharaoh's subjects and thereby to contribute to the political myth. Of one thing we can be sure: No mesomorphic trooper stepped forward to bend a stouter bow than his ruler's and to send his arrow through a thicker set of copper sheets. Pharaohs were, by definition, invincible. [5]

Pharaohs asserted their superiority as archers; their soldiers proved themselves as wrestlers. In a temple frieze from the reign of Ramses III, Egyptian soldiers vanquish foreign wrestlers—apparently Nubians—and dismay their opponents' backers. Likening Ramses to Mon, the Egyptian god of war, a spectator congratulates him on his soldiers' prowess and attributes their success to divine favor: "On your behalf, Amun has thrown down the enemies who came here to distinguish themselves." The techniques used by the Egyptian wrestlers are depicted in great detail on the walls of an eleventh-dynasty tomb at Beni Hassan, on the Nile, the richest of all sources for Egyptian sports.[6]

Other paintings from Beni Hassan show young women, perched upon the backs of other women, tossing balls back and forth. E. Norman Gardiner assumed, on the basis of dress, that the women were professional entertainers. "Yet we can hardly suppose that the games thus represented were not popular also among the young of both sexes." If the ball game *was* popular, which seems plausible, if the young women turned the pastime into a contest, which seems equally plausible, then we have one of the earliest depictions of women's sports.[7]

From wooden spoons whose handles were formed by the slender extended bodies of nearly nude girls, historians have inferred that Egyptian women swam. For evidence that the girls were really swimmers, historians can point to the handle of a spoon whose bowl is formed by an elaborately carved duck, but there is no warrant to assume that girls swam competitively.[8]

There is no doubt, however, about the competitiveness of a seasonal aquatic sport that German scholars know as *Fischerstechen* ("fishermen's jousting"). Numerous paintings show boatmen (who are probably *not* fishermen) bringing in the harvest from the fertile delta of the Nile. While some use poles to propel their boats forward, others use *their* poles to strike the crewmen of the other boats, tumbling them into the shallow water.[9]

In the Hellenistic period, after the conquest of Egypt by Alexander the Great, ethnically Greek Egyptian athletes participated in the Olympic Games and in local festivals like the Basileia in Alexandria. In Roman times, the emperor Hadrian—known for his philhellenism—founded Greek-style athletic games in memory of his lost lover Antinoos, who had drowned in the Nile in 130 A.D. Participants in these games were as ethnically diverse as the polyglot Roman empire.[10]

Minoan and Mycenean Sports

Since the days of Heinrich Schliemann's discovery of "the Tomb of Agamemnon" at Mycenea and Arthur Evans' excavation of "the Palace of Minos" at Knossos, modern scholars have made some—but not very much—

progress in their effort to decipher the language of the Mycenean and Minoan cultures that appeared, prospered, and disappeared in southern Greece and on Crete during the second millennium B.C. Of the documents that can be translated from these two prehellenic cultures, none refers specifically to sports. Archeological evidence depicts a great deal of physical activity, but the precise nature and significance of the activity remains conjectural. Feminists in search of matriarchal societies have been gratified by indications that women seem to appear side by side with men in the representations of Mycenean and Minoan sports—if the activities represented *were* sports. This is an important qualification. Whether a spear is thrown by a hunter, a warrior, or an athlete depends "on the social definition of the situation . . . and the interpretation given that situation by the actors and those who observe them."[11] In the investigation of the origins of sports, a picture is definitely *not* worth ten thousand words.

Young men and women leaping over the horns of a charging bull are depicted in the spectacular fresco that Evans found in what he surmised to have been the palace of the legendary King Minos, constructed, most probably, around 1500 B.C. Girls (painted white) boldly grip the horns of the huge bull or wait to catch the boy (painted red) who is in flight over the bull's elongated back. It is possible that the painted figures represent acrobats performing for the amusement of the court, but it is more likely that they were engaged in an initiatory ordeal or a fertility ritual.[12] "The question," writes Thomas Scanlon, "should probably be not *whether* the bull games were religious, but *how* and *to what extent* the participants were conscious of a sacred dimension to the activity."[13] To say this is not to deny that the ritual may also have been a sports contest. Minoan cult may have been a combination of sports and religious worship similar to the Greek athletic festivals celebrated (much later) at Olympia, Delphi, and other sacred sites. Minoan athletes may have competed for the excitement of the contest *and* to pay homage to the gods. If that was so, the motivation for their feats was comparable to the motivation of a modern choral group singing Johann Sebastian Bach's *Christmas Oratorio*— for the glory of the music *and* as a celebration of the birth of Jesus.

Nearly as famous as the bull-leaper fresco are the three reliefs of the gold Vapheio Cup from Hagia Triada. They vividly depict boxers, wrestlers, and what seems to be a group of Minoan hunters. The boxers and wrestlers are clearly male. Were the hunters men or women? Evans thought that at least one of the figures was "certainly that of a girl in spite of the sinewy limbs that it displays." If Evans was right, if Minoan art showed female as well as male hunters, we are still left to wonder about the relationship between representation and reality. A recently discovered thirteenth-century Mycenean coffin from Tanagra depicts bull-leapers, sword-fighters, and charioteers, all apparently in conjunction with a procession of mourning women. Wolfgang Decker has interpreted these images as a representation of Mycenean funeral rites. Of a similar scene depicted in Mycenean fragments found at Tiryns in southern Greece, J. K. Anderson wondered, "Is the whole scene in fact legendary?"[14] The question arises maddeningly often.

GREEK ATHLETIC FESTIVALS

Although the *Iliad* is set in the Mycenaean age, its athletic contests mirror those of Homer's time, which was probably the eighth century B.C. Book XXIII includes a detailed account of the funeral games held by the invading Greeks in honor of Achilles' beloved friend Patroclos, slain by the Trojan Hector. Competing for valuable material prizes as well as for honor, the fiercely agonistic Greek warriors box, wrestle, run races, and ride their chariots at breakneck speed. Success or failure is determined less by the physical prowess of the contestants than by the will of the gods, the divine spectators who intervene to assist their favorites and to thwart those who have offended them. In the course of his beautifully crafted description, Homer scarcely mentions the human spectators, except to say that they were numerous and that they laughed, applauded, and "thundered approval." Nobody displays an anachronistic sense of good sportsmanship. Losers are mocked and mishaps occasion scornful laughter.

Sports also appear in Book VIII of the *Odyssey*, where Homer's hero, shipwrecked on his way home from Troy, is washed ashore among the Phaeacians. His hosts taunt their wave-battered, bedraggled guest with an insulting allegation, "You are no athlete." Odysseus, resenting the slur, demonstrates his physical prowess, awes the Phaeacians, and dazzles the young princess who had discovered him on beach. She "gazed upon Odysseus with all her eyes and admired him."

The Athletic Body

The organized sports contests of the Homeric age may have been limited to aristocrats, while the common people stood aside and watched, but such exclusivity had certainly vanished by the classical period, when the imperatives of Greek culture dictated that all male citizens had a moral obligation to defend their *polis* on the battlefield. Citizen–soldiers were expected to be athletically active in order to be physically fit. The historian Xenophon, writing in the fourth century B.C., relates in his *Memorabilia* that Socrates encountered a flabby youth and promptly rebuked him for his disgraceful failure to train his body at the gymnasium. Although Socrates seems in this instance to have been motivated by aesthetic considerations, by a widely shared conception of the ideal male body, the aesthetic ideal was the result of military imperatives. The muscular male body was ideal *because* it was the soldier's body, shaped by the rigors of combat, always ready to take up sword and shield in defense of the *polis*.[1]

We cannot know from anecdotes like Xenophon's, nor from the Olympic and Pythian odes of the poet Pindar, nor from countless figured vases commemorating victory at the Panathenaic Games, nor from the athletic statues of Polycleitos and Myron, just how many Greeks actually lived up to their cultural ideals of athletic excellence. We do know, from the comments of the second century A.D. travel-writer Pausanias, that every *polis* worthy of the name needed a gymnasium (just as every modern city needs a representative major-league sports team). At least 126 Greek cities had gymnasia that served—as Massimiliano Papini has noted—not only as sites for athletic encounters but also as "centers of cultural, religious, and political life." Hellenistic Pergamon had at least five gymnasia, while Athens in its heyday had nine public gymnasia and innumerable private ones. Before their workouts, as they rubbed their bodies with olive oil, and after they had trained, as they scraped the oily dirt from their weary arms and legs, ambitious young men dreamed of Olympic glory and imagined themselves cast in bronze in the form of victors' statutes.[2]

The images of these athletes painted on black-figured and red-figured vases are familiar to every museum-goer. They adorn the red-figured amphora that were filled with olive oil and given as prizes to the victors of the Panathenaic Games. (Over twelve hundred of these vases survive.) Athletic iconography is a vivid proof that the ancient Greeks valorized the human body to a degree that became unthinkable once Christianity, with its ascetic tradition of hostility to "the flesh," had triumphed over paganism. The valorization of the body, especially the male body, included an unabashed acceptance of the erotic dimension of sports. Black-figured and red-figured vases depict many scenes in which an older man appears as the lover (the *erastes*) of an adolescent athlete (the *eromenos*). Texts by Plato, Xenophon, and many other writers also describe the erotic attractiveness of the young male athlete. Eros was one of the gymnasium's tutelary deities and a sixth-century B.C. statue of Eros was the point of departure for the Panathenaic torch race.[3]

——— The Olympic Games

Olympia was unquestionably the grandest showplace for the athletic body. The athletic festival celebrated at that sacred site functioned as a quadrennial affirmation of cultural unity despite the political divisions that impelled the fractious Greeks to constant warfare, city against city. To the Olympics, which were until Roman times restricted to free male ethnic Greeks, came athletes from as far away as the western shore of the Mediterranean and the eastern shore of the Black Sea. Greeks came to watch as well as to compete. Their number can be conjectured from the size of the third stadium (constructed in the middle of the fourth century B.C.). It must have held some forty thousand spectators. The hippodrome, which lay a little to the south and east of the stadium, was two or three times as large.[4]

The Olympic Games were religiously as well as politically significant. Ludwig Deubner described them as "sacred games held at a sacred site at a sacred time, a cult performance in honor of the gods." On the basis of archeological evidence unearthed at the site, some historians believe that Olympia was originally sacred to Gaea, goddess of the earth, but there is no consensus about the prehistoric origins of the games. Since the rites in honor of Gaea did not include athletic contests, Ulrich Popplow concluded that the Olympic Games derived not from Gaea's fertility myth but from *Totenkult,* that is, from funeral rites. More specifically, the *Totenkult* from which the Olympic Games derived was that of the mythical hero Pelops. Not everyone agrees. Commenting on the sports that seem most clearly to betray an origin in funeral games, Michael Poliakoff argues that "one can better explain Greek combat sport without recourse to the cult of the dead."[5]

Whatever their origins, by classical times the Olympic Games were definitely syncretic—the altar of Gaea survived, not far from the temples dedicated to Zeus and to Hera, and the funeral rites of Pelops were commemorated on the second or third day of the games. Of all the gods and goddesses worshipped at Olympia, Zeus was clearly the most important. His temple was the largest structure at Olympia, and his monumental fifth-century B.C. statue by Phidias—one of the seven wonders of the ancient world—presided over the games.

Religious awe was quite compatible with sports-induced frenzy. Watching the runners sprinting from the starting blocks to the post at the far end of the stadium, the spectators were—as M. I. Finley and H. W. Pleket noted in their popular history of the ancient games—"as partisan, as volatile and as excitable as at any other period of time." Written evidence of the spectators' excitement, from Pausanias and a host of other ancient authors, is abundant.

When this passionate partisanship combined with searing heat and choking dust, crowd control was a problem for the *Hellanodikai,* who administered the games and were responsible for their conduct. Disorderly conduct did not, however, degenerate into deadly violence.[6]

Restraint was not a consequence of deference to women. Whether or not maidens were present at these sacred games as spectators remains unclear, but married women were definitely excluded. Pherenike, daughter of Diagoros of Rhodes, violated this rule, disguised herself as a trainer, and attended the games at which her son Pisidorus was competing. When he won, she rushed forward and was discovered. She was forgiven because her father, her brothers, and now her son were all Olympic victors, but a law was passed requiring trainers to appear as naked as the athletes.[7]

The exact year of the first Olympic Games is unknown. The traditional date for the first games, 776 B.C., was calculated from a list of victors prepared three centuries later by Hippias of Elis. His date was merely guesswork, but historians cannot agree on a better one. The time of the festival was as sacred to the Greeks as the place. The games occurred at the time of the second or third full moon after the summer solstice. Athletes and spectators took advantage of a very limited truce that guaranteed their safe passage to and from Olympia. (There is no truth to the sentimental modern myth that all warfare ceased for the duration of the games.) Thirty days before the contests began, the athletes gathered at the nearby town of Elis, which had responsibility for administering the games through most of their thousand-year history. At the end of this final period of preparation, there was a two-day procession, with much religious ceremony, to the actual site on the river Eurotas.[8]

The athletic program for the earliest Olympics was quite limited. The only contest—according to most historians—was a simple *stade* race (one length of the stadium).[9] In time, the program expanded to comprise a five-or-six-day festival with nearly a score of events for men, boys, and horses. The first expansions came in 724 and 720, with the introduction of the *diaulus* (to the end of the stadium and back) and the *dolichos* ("long race'"). These two races seem to have inaugurated a long period of Spartan dominance. From 720 to 576, forty-six of the eighty-one victors whose names we know were Spartans.[10]

Over the next five hundred years, the program continued to expand.

THE OLYMPIC PROGRAM

776 B.C. *Stade* race (one length of the stadium)

724 *Diaulos* (two lengths of the stadium)

720 *Dolichos* ("long race")

708	Pentathlon and wrestling
688	Boxing
680	Four-horse chariot race
648	Pankration and horse race
632	*Stade* race and wrestling for boys
616	Boxing for boys
520	Race in (partial) armor
384	Four-foal chariot race
368	Two-foal chariot race
396	Competition for heralds and trumpeters
256	Race for foals
200[11]	Pankration for boys

The pentathlon was composed of running, jumping, hurling the discus, throwing the javelin, and wrestling. Despite decades of abstruse controversy, no one has given a satisfactory answer to the deceptively simple question: How was the winner determined? Historians seem now to agree only that wrestling was the last event and that Roberto Petrucco was wrong to assert that there was "a point system." The pankration, introduced sixty years after the pentathlon, was an extremely brutal no-holds-barred combat. Biting an opponent and gouging his eyes were forbidden, but seizing him by his genitals seems to have been allowed.[12]

There is great disagreement about the sequence of events during the five or six days of the festival. While admitting that most speculation is "pure fantasy," Hans-Volkmar Herrmann conjectures that the first day was entirely devoted to religious ritual (until 396 B.C., when the competition for heralds and trumpeters was introduced). The second day was for the boys' contests, the third for equestrian events and the sacrifice to Pelops, the fourth for the worship of Zeus. The fifth day was set aside for all the other athletic contests, after which the victors received their olive branches, cut from the sacred grove of Zeus by a boy whose parents were still alive (presumably as a sign of divine approval). The entire athletic festival concluded with a feast at which the Olympian gods received their due in the form of libations.[13]

Whether the earliest Olympic athletes were aristocrats or commoners is unclear. The first victor was the runner Koroibos of Elis, variously identified as a cook or as a ritual sacrificer. Aristotle refers to another victor as a fishmonger, but Aristotle may have meant to mark him as an exception. Economic factors limited entries in the chariot races. Prominent among those able to afford the expense of transporting chariots and horses to Olympia were the tyrants who ruled the Greek cities of Sicily and southern Italy. (They entered the chariots but did not drive them.) The expense was worth it to men whose victories were taken as signs that they were "predestined to rule." Among the most famous Olympians was the boxer Theagenes of Thasos, active during the first half of the fifth century B.C. Theagenes was credited with over a thousand victories at hundreds of different athletic festivals. He won twice at Olympia, three times at Delphi, ten at Corinth, and nine at Nemea. Nearly as renowned was the runner Leonidas of Rhodes, victor at four successive Olympics (164 to 152 B.C.).[14]

This sort of enumeration—discussed at length by David Young—is the closest the Greeks came to the modern mania for quantification. They made no effort at their sacred games to time the races, which would have been very difficult, or to measure the distances, which would have been relatively easy. Whether or not the victor at Olympia threw his discus farther than the discus thrown four years earlier was apparently a matter of complete indifference, which explains why there was no attempt to standardize linear measurements or to regulate the size or weight of the discus. Why bother? The Olympic athlete's ambition was not to set records but to embody excellence (*arete*), not to compare his achievements abstractly to those of someone a thousand miles away, not to "make his name" in some list of memorable deeds, but to be gloriously present, visibly the best of all the Greeks assembled at Olympia.[15]

The date of the last Olympics is as uncertain as the date of the first. Until quite recently, the last known victor was the Armenian prince Varazdat, who won the boxing competition in 369 A.D., but an inscription discovered at Olympia in 1994 gives the names of several athletes whose victories came as late as 385 A.D. If Theodosius I decreed an end to the Olympics in 394, as some scholars believe, then the last games took place in 393. (The evidence for this belief comes from an eleventh-century manuscript by Georgios Kedrenos.) It is possible, however, that the games lingered on until 426, when Theodosius II ordered the destruction of all heathen temples. An "Olympic" festival celebrated at Antioch may have survived until 520.[16]

The Olympics were not the only panhellenic athletic festivals. Nearly as important were the games celebrated at Delphi, Corinth, and Nemea. "The true age of these and other competitions are unknown," wrote Hans-Volkmar Herrmann, but the games at Delphi and Corinth are conventionally dated from 582 B.C., those at Nemea from 573 B.C. The games at Delphi and Nemea were sacred to Apollo, those at Corinth were dedicated to Poseidon. These four panhellenic festivals constituted the *periodos,* and athletes who triumphed at all four gloried in the title of *periodonike* ("period" victor). For lesser athletes there were hundreds of local festivals ranging in importance from the Panathenaic Games, which rivaled those of the *periodos,* to minor events about which nothing is known beyond the fact of their obscure existence.[17]

Although the games of the *periodos* offered no immediate material prizes, winners were welcomed home with open arms and opened coffers. The sixth-century Athenian statesman Solon decreed that Olympic victors receive five hundred drachmas. The less prestigious festivals, like the one at Aphrodisias in Asia Minor, lured contestants with lists of prize money. The prize offered by Aphrodisias for the winner of the pankration was three thousand *denarii,* about the equivalent of eight years' wages for the ordinary workman. Although the material rewards for successful athletes were huge and the temptation to cheat must have been immense, the first recorded case of Olympic bribery—that attempted by the boxer Eupolos of Thessaly in 388 B.C.—occurred after nearly four centuries of Olympic competition.[18] Moderns take note.

_____ Women's Sports

The motivations for the institutionalization of men's athletics were so obvious to the Greeks that it did not occur to them to dwell upon it, but Sparta's encouragement of female athleticism was unusual and required explanation. It still astonishes modern historians such as Sarah Pomeroy, who comments, "There is more evidence . . . for athletics than for any other aspect of Spartan women's lives." According to Xenophon, the legendary Spartan lawgiver Lycurgus believed "that the highest function of a free woman was the bearing of children," which led Lycurgus to insist that young women train their bodies. He instituted "contests in running and feats of strength for women as for men. His belief was that where both parents were strong their progeny would be . . . more vigorous." That was also the opinion of Plutarch, looking back from the vantage point of the second-century A.D. He wrote that Lycurgus "ordered the maidens to exercise themselves with wrestling, running, throwing the discus, and casting the javelin, to the end that the fruit they conceived might, in strong and healthy bodies, take firmer root and find better growth."[19]

One striking example of the Spartan emphasis on female physical development was a race run by eleven girls as part of the annual festival of Dionysus Colonatas. The race may have been a way to select the priestesses of Dionysus, but, in light of the Spartan emphasis on eugenics, Thomas Scanlon believes it was a "a prenuptial initiatory trial."[20]

Although it was widely agreed throughout the ancient world that Spartan women were healthier but more beautiful than other women, Spartan practice was not emulated. Eugenic motives were trumped, elsewhere in Greece, by the conviction that respectable married women should lead sedentary domestic lives and that their daughters should not be violated by public scrutiny. Legendary Atalanta, competing against men as a runner, a wrestler, and a hunter, captivated the imagination of ancient artists, but ordinary maidens were no more likely to imitate her athletic feats than they were to seize a sword and emulate the equally mythical Amazons. If they longed to release their energy in the form of an athletic contest, their desires were thwarted by the norms of patriarchal culture.[21]

The exclusion of non-Spartan females from sports was not total. Shards from Attic vases and a few lines from a comedy by Aristophanes attest to a fifteen-mile race for girls—probably a prenuptial girlhood-to-womanhood ritual—from the temple of Artemis at Brauron to Athens. Thomas Scanlon remarks that the shards "may preserve unique visual evidence of girls' races in a cultic context, if indeed the running does represent races, and if the activity can be associated with festivals of Artemis." A third-century B.C. inscription records the boast of Cynisca, a Spartan princess, who claimed to have been the first woman to win an Olympic contest. Her claim was possible because victory in the chariot races was ascribed to the owner and not to the driver of the chariot. In a first-century A.D. inscription found at Delphi, Hermesianax of Tralles boasts of the victories of his three daughters in races run in the Pythian, Nemean, and Panathenaic games. Another first-century inscription refers to a contest for maidens at the Isthmian Games in Corinth. A more important exception to the rule of exclusion was the Heraia, an athletic festival in honor of the goddess Hera. The Heraia was contested at Olympia by girls from throughout the Greek world (but mostly, it seems, from Sparta).[22]

Literary evidence for the Heraia, which occurred quadrennially in the spring of the year, approximately a month before the men's games, comes—like so much of our knowledge of the Olympics—from Pausanias: "The games consist of foot-races for maidens. These are not all of the same age. The first to run are the youngest; after them come the next in age, and the last to run are the oldest of the maidens." Unlike the men and boys, the girls were not entirely nude. Pausanias was told that "a tunic reaches to a little above the knee, and they bare the right shoulder as far as the breast." The winners received "crowns of olive and a portion of the cow sacrificed to Hera."[23] The archeological evidence for the Heraia consists mainly of two statues of Spartan provenance. They show running girls clothed exactly as Pausanias described them.

What did it mean? One possible answer is that the Heraia was a fertility ritual that predated the Olympics. Writing in 1962, Erwin Mehl noted such a ritual in modern Greece: "During the sowing and the harvesting seasons, [barefoot] girls run across the fields in order to make them fruitful."[24]

_____ The Hellenistic and Roman Period

In the Hellenistic era, Greek athletics flourished throughout the vast empire created by Alexander the Great and ruled by dynasties founded by his generals. One sign of the spatial diffusion of Greek sports was the prominence among Olympic victors of ethnic Greeks from Egypt and Asia Minor. They outnumbered and outperformed their rivals from Greece proper. It is doubtful that athletics were very popular among the conquered Asians and North Africans ruled by the Greek-speaking minority in the Hellenistic period, but a number of Jews frequented the stadia and hippodromes of Palestine. Greek sports were even more popular after the Roman conquest of the eastern Mediterranean in the second and first centuries B.C. Encouraged by King Herod's accommodationist policies, young Jews scandalized their orthodox kinsmen by entering Jerusalem's gymnasium (under the eyes of Hermes, its patron deity), stripping themselves naked, oiling their bodies, and engaging in athletic contests. This may have been the first time that Jews demonstrated eagerness to adopt sports as an instrument of cultural assimilation. It was certainly not the last time.[25]

ROMAN SPORTS

_____ Etruscan Prelude

Historians of Etruscan sports confront a familiar problem. How can we interpret visual evidence from a culture whose written language remains a mystery? Were the painted charioteers whom we see on the walls of Etruscan tombs on their way to battle or off to the races? Did the hunters hunger for a taste of venison or for "an aristocratic *divertissement*"? One clue is the presence in Etruscan frescoes of spectators, who appear more frequently and in greater numbers than in Greek art. Athletic paraphernalia offer additional clues. A scene depicted on a seventh-century B.C. vase from Veie, for example, shows two male boxers, a chair or tripod, and vegetation that may be a cypress (symbolizing death) or a palm tree (signifying victory). Similarly, bronze figures from the sixth century can be reliably classified as wrestlers rather than warriors because they are accompanied by an official equipped with a baton.[1]

Although archeologists have yet to unearth an Etruscan stadium or gymnasium, the evidence gleaned from Etruscan tombs enabled Jean-Paul Thuillier, the unchallenged authority on Etruscan sports, to conclude that there was "an intimate liaison . . . between sports and the sacred" (despite the fact that the gods most closely associated with Greek athletics—Hermes and Apollo—were "not to be found in this role in Etruria").[2] The "liaison" was manifested principally in the form of funeral games. The athletes were probably slaves rather than free men, which is to be expected if the funeral games evolved from burial rites that included human sacrifice.[3]

In Etruscan tombs, archeologists have discovered many images of boxers. They appear also on vases and even on a belt buckle from Sienna. The boxers hold their arms high, which suggests that blows to the body were not allowed. They are often accompanied by flute players, which raises a question. Was Etruscan pugilism, like Brazilian *capoeira,* a fusion of music, dancing, and fighting, or did the flute players merely signal the start and the end of the match? We can only guess. Etruscan men also wrestled, but, if the evidence drawn from Etruscan tombs can be trusted to represent daily life, Greek-style athletics were not especially popular. Greek influence on Etruscan sports can be dated from the middle of the sixth century B.C., but the Etruscans were selective. There are few images of runners (except on ceramics imported from Greece), and the Etruscans "showed no great interest in the discus or the javelin."[4]

Chariot races were quite another matter. The *Tomba delle Bighe,* which took its name from the two-horse chariots painted on its walls, has elaborate frescoes showing wooden stands in which male and female spectators mingle to watch the races. In the *Tomba delle Olimpiadi,* which has nothing to do with the Olympics, a fresco illustrates a chariot race at which an accident has occurred. Three female spectators appear to be terrified by the sight of the overturned chariot and the driver who has been flung into the air.[5]

The presence of female spectators at chariot races and other sports events from which Greek custom excluded them shocked Greek observers of Etruscan life. The gossipy traveler Theopompus reported in dismay that Etruscan women exercised (and were also scandalously free to eat and drink in the company of men and to reveal more of their bodies than was proper).[6] Etruscan gender equality, if it existed outside the febrile imagination of Greek travelers, did not extend to participation in sports. In scenes of Etruscan art, women appeared as spectators for chariot racing, boxing, and wrestling, but the charioteers, the boxers, and the wrestlers were all men.

Men figure actively in other frescoes that raise an important question. Did the Etruscans, whose kings ruled Rome before it became a republic in 510 B.C., bequeath the *munera*—the gladiatorial games—to the Romans? Livy and other Roman historians thought they did, but modern researchers are doubtful that the *munera* had Etruscan origins. The best evidence for the older supposition is the *phersu* game. The name of this mysterious Etruscan activity is taken from a word inscribed on two murals from the Tomb of the Augurs. The first pictures a masked man who seems to be disguised as an animal. He confronts a dog in what Jean-René Jannot called "a bloody game with chthonic connotations." The other mural shows a man in flight. If the *phersu* game had any direct influence on Roman sports, it was probably upon the *venationes,* in which men were matched against wild animals.[7]

_____ Republican Festivals

The Romans of the republican era were unimpressed by the Greek athletic festivals that they encountered when they subjugated the Greek colonies of southern Italy and Sicily. The poet Horace reacted typically when, in his *Second Satire,* he scornfully contrasted effeminate Greek sports to rough Roman military drill.[8] In Roman eyes, the gymnasium was a poor substitute for the battlefield. Observing the Greeks at their games, Roman spectators grudgingly acknowledged that the wrestlers and the boxers had the stuff from which soldiers might be made, but the sight of a naked runner struck them as ridiculous.

In place of the Greek gymnasium, the Romans had their baths, thousands of them. They were as multifunctional as a modern sports complex. The grander baths included not only sports facilities but also shops, refreshment booths, gardens, libraries, and conference rooms. Despite the Horatian rhetoric about rough and tough masculinity, afternoons at the Baths of Caracalla frequently included a friendly game of *harpastum* or *trigonaria* with slaves to retrieve the balls and keep the score. The activity was not strenuous and "the words 'victory' and 'defeat' do not appear in connection with [Roman] ball games."[9]

The Romans celebrated a number of annual festivals that were known, collectively, as *ludi.* The Latin term is usually translated as "games" because these festivals typically included sports events as well as theatrical performances and a grand procession (*pompa*) of carts that transported images of the Olympian gods to the site where sacrifices were made to them. (From the Latin singular, *ludus,* we derive the useful adjective "ludic.") Among the earliest of these festivals was one in honor of Jupiter. When the temple of Jupiter was dedicated, early in the sixth century B.C., there were chariot races (*circenses*) in the *Circus Maximus.* By the middle of the fourth century, this event seems to have evolved into annual games known as the *Ludi Romani.* During the prolonged struggle of the Punic Wars (264–202 B.C.), when invading Carthaginian armies threatened Rome's continued existence, a number of important annual festivals were introduced into the Roman calendar. Typical of these were the *Ludi Apollinares,* dedicated to Apollo. First celebrated in 212 B.C., these games became an annual event in 208. Between the sixth and the thirteen of July, there came six days of theatrical performances and a day of chariot races. At the *Ludi Ceriales* of 42 B.C., gladiatorial games (*munera*) replaced chariot races for the first time.[10]

In addition to the annual *ludi* there were votive games to mark special occasions—a military victory, a political triumph. Typical of the votive festivals of the late Republic were the *Ludi Victoriae* staged by Julius Caesar in July of 45 B.C. to celebrate his military defeat of Pompey at Pharsalus. From the twentieth to the thirtieth, Caesar offered the *populus* a grand program of theatrical performances, Greek-style athletic contests, gladiatorial combats, and chariot races.[11]

_____ **Imperial Spectacles**

By the end of the Republic, the calendar included sixty-six days of _ludi_, of which fourteen were devoted to chariot races. By middle of the fourth century A.D., there were one hundred seventy-five regularly scheduled holidays (_feriae_)—ten with _munera_, sixty-four with chariot races, and one hundred and one with theatrical performances.[12] The grandest of these annual _ludi_ were overshadowed by the extravagant games that commemorated special events. In 80 A.D., for instance, the emperor Titus offered one hundred days of games to dedicate the Colosseum.[13]

In addition to the regular and the votive _ludi_, a number of emperors founded quadrennial athletic festivals modeled on the Olympic Games. Augustus began the _Actia_ in 28 B.C. to commemorate his naval victory over Antony and Cleopatra at Actium. The most successful of these quadrennial festivals was probably the _Capitolia_, inaugurated by Domitian in 86 A.D. In addition to all the agonistic and musical events common to the major Greek athletic festivals, the _Capitolia_ had races for women.[14] The least successful of the new festivals was probably the one that the megalomaniacal Nero named for himself in 60 A.D. The _Neronia_ did not outlast its founder's death in 68 A.D. Nero's faith in himself as an artist and as an athlete also motivated him to tour Greece and compete in all the major athletic festivals, some of which were rescheduled for his imperial convenience. He drove his own chariot at Olympia and was declared the victor despite the awkward fact that he fell from his chariot before it crossed the finish line. After returning to Rome with 1,808 crowns and wreaths, Nero commemorated his achievements by awarding himself a triumphal procession.[15]

Apart from Greek-style athletic festivals such as the _Capitolia_ and the _Neronia_, most of the performers at imperial sports spectacles were slaves or freedmen rather than freeborn Roman citizens, but a number of free men, driven by boredom or exhibitionism, did volunteer to risk their lives in gladiatorial combat. Incomplete inscriptions from Venusia refer to a gladiatorial _familia_ consisting of eighteen slaves and ten free men, but that was probably an atypical proportion. Volunteers signed a contract (_auctoratio_) and took their chances. Although Augustus refused to let senators and knights become _auctoratii_, later emperors allowed—and sometimes ordered—these aristocrats to descend into the arena and engage in mortal combat. In private, the depraved emperor Commodus fought as a gladiator and invariably won. What might have happened to an opponent foolish enough to vanquish and humiliate him?[16]

Slave or free, gladiators should not be confused with common criminals who were dragged to the arena for a public execution nor with Christian martyrs, like Saint Placida, who perished in the same place for their faith. When Christians sentenced to die *ad bestias* were torn to shreds by wild beasts, the statues of the gods were veiled.[17]

Paradoxically, gladiators and charioteers from the very bottom of the social hierarchy, men who were legally stigmatized as *infama,* were nonetheless idolized by the Roman masses. For many women, the gladiators' erotic appeal was irresistible. The excavated ruins of Pompeii had a graffito proclaiming that the gladiator Celadus was *suspirium et decus puellarum,* which might be freely translated as "the hero and heart-throb of all the girls." In the quarters where Celadus and his fellow gladiators were housed, archeologists discovered the skeleton and the jewels of a wealthy woman whose weakness for athletic virility must have overcome her fears of volcanic eruption. These women drew the wrath of moralists such as the second-century A.D. poet Juvenal, who satirized a senator's wife for her adoration of a blood-spattered brute.[18] It is doubtful that his scintillating poetic barbs shone as brightly as her gladiatorial lover's gleaming sword.

Venereal rewards of the sort condemned by Juvenal were among the compensations for a short career. Although some gladiators fought and won dozens of duels, inscriptions indicate that most survived less than a year. According to Keith Hopkins, those who survived for five years were given their freedom. Gladiators acclaimed by the crowd for exceptional bravery were sometimes freed on the spot; signs of cowardice were as abruptly fatal.[19]

If historians are now more hesitant than they once were to attribute the *munera* entirely to Etruscan influence, they are on safer grounds when they date and locate the first gladiatorial combat. In 246 B.C., in Rome's cattle market, six gladiators fought in honor of the deceased father of Marcus and Decius Brutus. Like the retainers who had in earlier times been buried with their masters in order to render posthumous service, gladiators acted in a bloody drama in which the *virtus* of the fighters symbolized a triumph over death, This may explain why the *munera* came to an end when Christianity offered an alternative triumph.[20]

In the centuries that followed the first combats, Livy and a number of other Roman historians recorded (and frequently lamented) an apparently irreversible tendency toward the spectacular. The number of gladiators increased exponentially, and the arenas in which they battled grew to colossal dimensions. Candidates for office eschewed "reasoned analysis or discourse" and competed recklessly "to put on a show."[21] In 22 B.C., the Senate, worried about the manipulation of the populace by means of these magnificent and deadly entertainments, enacted an ancient equivalent of campaign-finance reform. The Senate limited the *munera* to two a year, each with no more than one hundred twenty gladiators, but the effort was futile. In imperial times, politically adroit emperors competed in increasingly grandiose efforts to divert the masses with sadistic entertainment. The *munera* became more and more spectacular. The emperor Claudius, who followed the notoriously stingy Tiberius, entertained Rome with massive nautical combats—*naumachia*—on an artificial lake. Nineteen thousand men were involved. His reign, which ended in 37 A.D., was the last during which private citizens were allowed to sponsor a *munus.* In 106 A.D., Trajan enlisted some eleven thousand gladiators to celebrate his victory over the Dacians with one hundred twenty-three days of games.[22]

Gladiators were highly specialized. Some were trained to appear in the *venationes,* the combats against wild animals. (Technically, these fighters were *bestiarii* and not gladiators, but most historians ignore the fine distinction.) At first, the animals were those native to Italy, but Marcus Fulvius Nobilior sought favor with the masses by staging combats, in 186 B.C., with North African lions and panthers. Many consider this event, which celebrated the successful conclusion of the Aetolian War, to be the first real *venatio.* In later centuries, exotic animals were imported to Rome from as far away as England and Egypt. Thousands of animals were slaughtered, some of them—if the poet Martial was credible—by women.[23]

When men fought men, rather than leopards and lions, there was no impulse to equalize the conditions of combat (as there was, for instance, in the introduction of weight classes in modern combat sports). The *retiarius* who strutted about the arena with a trident and a net was routinely matched against a *secutor* armed with sword and shield. Heavily armed "Thracians," who were said to be especially attractive to adolescent girls, advanced against opponents whose pikes marked them as "Gauls." (The designations in these cases refer to the style of combat, not necessarily to the ethnicity of the gladiators.)[24]

Gladiators were trained and they were valuable property. When a wealthy Roman decided to sponsor a gladiatorial spectacle, he—the *editor*—contracted with a *lanista* who provided the desired number of fighters. Wounded gladiators looked to the *editor* for an indication of their fate. As the *editor* considered whether to signal "thumbs up" or "thumbs down," compassion had an ally in economic calculation. The *lanistae* were canny entrepreneurs who demanded compensation for any gladiator put to death and dragged from the arena for disposal in the Tiber. When emperors replaced private citizens as sponsors of *munera,* the material costs of acquiring, training, and maintaining a gladiator continued to be a factor in life-or-death decisions. Economics sometimes played a role in martyrdom. In 177 A.D., contrary to custom, Christians were used in a *munus* staged in Lyon because they were "unpopular, cheap, and convenient."[25]

Since temporary stadia built of wood had an unfortunate tendency to collapse, killing thousands, they were replaced by monumental stone structures, the most famous of which, the Colosseum, still stands as an icon of Roman grandeur. This gigantic structure, begun by Vespasian and dedicated in 80 A.D. by his son Titus, seated fifty thousand. Smaller stadia were constructed at Nîmes and elsewhere throughout the empire. Increasingly, arena design catered to pampered spectators accustomed to ancient equivalents of today's luxury boxes. The arena in Pompeii, for example, offered awnings to shield spectators from the sun and sprays to cool them.[26]

In Roman stadia, social hierarchy took spatial forms. Different demographic groups were seated in different *cunei* (wedges) of the stadium. The Senate, prompted by Augustus, decreed that citizens be separated from slaves, soldiers from civilians, men from women, children (supervised by their tutors) from adults. The Senators reserved the front seats for themselves while Augustus was seated, or reclined, on the *pulvinar* (couch), where he was said to occupy himself with administrative paperwork.[27]

Calm demeanor was unusual. Most spectators seem to have reacted with frenzy. The philosopher–dramatist Seneca captured the mood in an epigram: *"Mane leonibus et ursis homines, meridie spectatoribus suis obiciunter"*: "In the morning they throw men to the lions and the bears; at noon, they throw them to the spectators." Seneca's show of compassion was exceptional. Most Romans shared Cierco's conviction that the *munera* provided the spectators with a wholesome image of manly fortitude. The poet Ovid was also upbeat about bloodshed, urging women to display their physical charms in the stadium, "where the sands are sprinkled with crimson." The Christian moralist Tertullian, no devotee of Ovid's erotic poetry, reacted rather differently. He was appalled by the spectators' sadistic passion: "Look at the populace coming to the show—mad already! disorderly, blind!"[28]

While Christian oppositon to the *munera* was undoubtedly motivated by an ethical revulsion at the spectacle of needless slaughter, theology also played a role. The *munera* were inextricably implicated in paganism. The eminent French historian Georges Ville denies this, insisting that the *munera* were "pure spectacles with no connection to the gods or the cult of the dead," but his own books provide the evidence to refute him. Although religion was not so obtrusive as it was at the *ludi* of the Republican era, the gladiatorial games of the imperial period preserved many vestiges of pagan cult. Images of the god Nemesis symbolized the gravity of the occasion. Slaves dressed as Mercury jabbed fallen gladiators with hot irons to make certain that death was not feigned; other slaves in the garb of the god Dis Pater dragged the corpses away. The priest of Jupiter offered the deity a cup filled with blood. The perils of ludic paganism were visible enough for the Christian theologian Novatian to wail, *"Idolatria . . . ludorum omnium mater est"*: Idolatry is the mother of all games.[29]

When the paganism of the games faded, when the Roman persecution of their religion ceased, Christians flocked to the *munera* and joined in the hysteria. In his *Confessions,* Augustine bewailed the weakness of a young disciple who ventured into the stadium and became "intoxicated with the bloody pastime." Over time, opposition mounted and Christian moralists demanded an end to the *munera.* Nevertheless, it was not until late in the fourth century or early in the fifth that the emperor Honorius acceded to their insistence and finally closed the gladiatorial schools. The *munera* may have gone on for another generation. Stripped of threatening pagan images, the *venationes* lingered on for at least another century, but Christian concern reduced the level of violence done to and by the hunted beasts. The heavy armor and the shields of the *venator* disappeared, "replaced by a variety of devices designed to protect the combatants, both human and animal." In their concern for the animals, some Romans went beyond protection to compassion. In a Tunisian mosaic, carousing drinkers are scolded for disturbing the slumber of bulls who face a hard day in the arena: *"Silentium, dormiant tauri"*: "Quiet! The bulls are sleeping."[30]

By this time, the *circenses* had probably become more popular than the *munera.* The Circus Maximus in Rome, which lay in the valley between the Palatine and Aventine hills, may have accommodated as many as one hundred fifty thousand spectators. It was nearly a mile in length. At the Circus Maximus, at several other *circenses* within the city, and at smaller venues throughout the empire, races were contested by charioteers divided into four teams, invariably identified by their colors: red, white, blue, and green. Some charioteers raced for more than one team. The second-century charioteer Gaius Appuleius Diocles went from the Whites to the Greens to the Reds. In the Byzantine era, the Reds and Whites were absorbed by the Blues and the Greens.[31]

Although novices raced in *bigae* drawn by two horses, experienced charioteers drove hard-to-manage *quadrigae* to which four horses were harnessed. The track was elliptical, and rounding the turn required considerable equestrian skill. Accidents were frequent, but their number was reduced by the installation of a "spine" (*spina*) that prevented chariots that had already rounded the turn from colliding with those that had not yet reached it. On the *spina* of the Circus Maximus, to mark the laps, were seven "eggs" (*ova*), replaced in 33 B.C. by seven bronze dolphins from whose mouths water cascaded.[32]

There were a number of anticipations of modernity. There were starting gates (*carceres*) to prevent "jumping the gun," and the line of chariots at the gates was slanted like the line of sprinters in a modern 400-meter race. This egalitarian device assured that the distance to the turn was approximately the same for all chariots. There was also a level of quantification otherwise unattained in ancient sports. Lacking stopwatches, lacking standardized temporal units, the Romans were unable to time their races accurately, but it was easy for them to count the number of first-place, second-place, and third-place finishes. An inscription to Gaius Appuleius Diocles credits him with 1,462 victories in 4,257 starts. He was second in 861 races and third in 576. No Roman statistician thought to calculate and compare winning percentages (dividing MCDLXII by MMMMCCLVII would have been a challenge), but Gaius Appuleius Diocles does seem to have set and claimed an authentic sports record.[33]

The tendency to quantify extended to the horses as well. Those with a hundred victories were called *centenarii*. Gutta Calpurnianus owned a horse named *Victor* (how appropriate!) who finished first in 429 races.[34]

These intimations of modernity should not be interpreted as a sign that the *circenses* were completely secular affairs. Images of the gods were carried in the *pompa circensis* just as they were in other ritual processions. The *quadrigae* were considered sacred to the sun, the *bigae* to the moon. An obelisk originally erected at Heliopolis by Ramses II in honor of the Egyptian god of the sun was removed to the Circus Maximus by Augustus and placed in the middle of the *spina*. At the Temple of the Sun, which was probably placed a short distance away, at the finish line, sacrifices were performed.[35]

In a detailed study of 229 charioteers active from the first century B.C. to the fifth century A.D., Gerhard Horsmann was able to determine the social status of ninety-four of them: sixty-six slaves, fourteen freedmen, thirteen who were probably one or the other, and one man—Gutta Calpurnianus—who was certainly free. Since Roman slaves were normally allowed to keep a portion of their earnings, some of these fourteen freedmen may have bought their freedom with their prize money. That may have been the case with the famously successful Gaius Appuleius Diocles, who regularly earned more in a single day than a procurator earned in a year.[36]

All charioteers were legally *infama,* but the wealth amassed by Gaius Appuleius Diocles and the magnificent funerary monument of Gutta Calpurnianus are indications that the complaints of the poets were not unfounded: charioteers were adored by the populace who expected the emperor to provide—in Juvenal's sarcastic phrase—bread and circuses (*panem et circenses*). The most celebrated and admired charioteer of the later empire was Porphyrius, who flourished in early-sixth-century Constantinople. In addition to the usual mosaics, glassware, ceramics, and statuettes that signaled a charioteer's popularity, a monument in the city's hippodrome commemorated his achievements. Grandly ensconced, the stone figure of Porphyrius towers over his four horses and the tiny spectators. He was also honored by no fewer than thirty-two epigrams collected in the *Greek Anthology*. He was, moreover, known for more than his athletic ability. The chronicler John Malalas, a contemporary, relates that Porphyrius led a mob of Greens that burned a synagogue in Antioch and a murdered a number of Jews.[37]

At the races as at the gladiatorial games, one's social status determined one's seat so that "the circus was . . . a microcosm of the Roman state." In the Circus Maximus, the emperor Claudius provided stone seats for senators; his successor, Nero, provided them for the equestrian class. Plebians seem to have jostled one another for the "nonreserved" seats. In Rome, it is probable that the "circus factions" sat in their own sections, very like the fans of modern soccer teams. In Constantinople, Antioch, and other Byzantine cities, this was clearly the mode.[38]

Men and women sat together, which provided ample opportunity for flirtation. In his erotic poetry, Ovid offered advice to young men in search of sexual adventures. One might, for instance, try this seductive opener: "You watch the races, and I watch you—what a wonderful system! / Each of us feasting our eyes on the delights that we prize." Juvenal was, as usual, acerbic; he satirized "the tarts who display their wares at the Circus." Lustful Romans who preferred predictable cash transactions to the uncertainties of seduction made their way to minibrothels conveniently located in the arcades of the Circus Maximus.[39]

In the absence of the political parties characteristic of modern parliamentary democracies, Roman sports became a mechanism for the expression (and manipulation) of public opinion. Under the Caesars, the races became—

in Traugott Bollinger's words—a "safety-valve for dissatisfaction and a substitute for democratic assembles." In an age that lacked modern mass communications, the hippodrome became the locus of whatever direct interaction occurred between the emperor and his subjects. Although the emperor and his consort sat, surrounded by officials, in the imperial box, he was apparently accessible to petitioners. He was also exposed, despite the presence of his guards, to outbursts of discontent. If an emperor was known to favor the Greens, spectators with a political grievance cheered loudly for the Blues. (This was sometimes dangerous. When some spectators jeered Caracalla's favorite charioteer, that notoriously cruel emperor dispatched soldiers to slay the offenders.) The second-century historian Dio Cassius reported a day at the races when political protest took the form of an eerie silence followed by cries for peace. Dio Cassius also described a riot that began at the races when a maiden accused an unpopular official, Cleander, of creating famine by hoarding grain. The excited crowd took to the streets, threatened the emperor's villa, and "persuaded" the emperor, Commodus, to dismiss Cleander.[40]

At times, the circus factions did more than threaten. Arsonists burned Constantinople's wooden stands in 491, 498, 507, and 532, after which the emperor Justinian prudently invested in a hippodrome built of stone. History's worst case of sports-related spectator violence began on January 13, 532, when supporters of the Blues and the Greens joined forces in order to rescue a number of criminals sentenced to be executed in the hippodrome. Unplacated by Justinian's promise of additional races, the rioters continued their rampage. On the fourteenth, the emperor agreed to dismiss John of Cappodicia and other unpopular officials, but the rioters' rage had become too intense for easy appeasement. By the eighteenth, the unpacified mob proclaimed a new empeor to whom a number of frightened senators paid hasty homage. Their capitulation was premature. Justinian was restored to power by the army—at the cost of an estimated thirty thousand lives.[41] In comparison to this carnage, the death of thirty-eight spectators at Brussels' Heysal Stadium, in 1985, seems almost trivial.

Despite this evidence of politically motivated disorder, the foremost authority on the circus factions has denied that the factions played any role at all in Byzantine politics. Alan Cameron argues that they were "simply supporters' clubs." During the civil war of 609–10, he comments, "the political conflict became a convenient façade for the colors to fight each other openly and with impunity." The factions, he concludes, "deserve no prominent mention in any history of popular expression." Although Cameron's argument is a valuable correction of earlier historians' description of circus factions as functioning like modern political parties, Cameron is too narrow in his definition of politics. He concedes that the Blues and the Greens may have differed "in behaviour and even in social class."[42] In the modern world, differences in social class always have political consequences. It is difficult to believe that this Marxist truism was not valid in Byzantine times.

The political aspects of the circus were, however, secondary. The addictive thrill of a dozen chariots rounding the turn and racing pell-mell to the finish line surely mattered more to the average spectator than the occasional opportunity for political protest. The historian Ammianus Marcellinus assumed this when he wrote scornfully of fans who "declare that the country will be ruined if . . . their . . . champion does not come first off the starting-gate and keep his horses in line as he brings them round the post." Life certainly became meaningless for a certain Felix Rufus when his favorite charioteer died. Inconsolable, Felix Rufus—unlucky despite his name—threw himself on his idol's funeral pyre and perished with him. Engaged partisanship was not, however, the same as informed appreciation. In a letter, Pliny the Younger condemned the "childish passion" of ignorant fans who cheered mindlessly for the Blues or the Greens, but cared little for "the speed of the horses or the drivers' skill."[43] The complaint is a familiar one.

The last known chariot race in the city of Rome took place in 549, but the sport continued, for nearly seven hundred years, in Constantinople, Antioch, Alexandria, and other Byzantine cities.

Women's sports were even more marginal in the Roman world than they had been in the Greek. The historian Suetonius and the poet Statius both refer to female gladiators active during the reigns of sadistic emperors such as Nero and Domitian. These women were probably enslaved captives. Two female gladiators, aptly named Achillia and Amazon, are carved in relief on a stele found at Halicarnassus. If the *Satyricon* of Petronius Arbiter is a reliable indicator of what the fans wanted, then they were excited by girls who fought from chariots. It is improbable, however, that female gladiators with "breasts Amazon-naked" ever faced wild boars (as Juvenal claimed in his *Satires*).[44]

We know little about the sports of ordinary women. There were foot races for them at some of the *ludi* that were inaugurated in late-republican or early-imperial times on the model of Greek athletic festivals. Women competed, for example, in the *Capitolia* in Rome and at the *Augustalia* and the *Sebasteia* in Naples. The most famous evidence of Roman women's sports comes, however, from a villa in Sicily. Ten young, bikini-clad women, whose vigorous movements are forever immobilized in the tiles of a splendid mosaic, run, jump, throw the discus and the javelin, play ball, and flourish the palm branches that they have won as prizes. Who were they? Sheltered daughters of wealthy aristocrats at play in the walled gardens of their fathers' villas? Proletarian women displaying their athletic skills (and their sinewy bodies) at the *Augustalia* or the *Sebasteia*? No one knows.[45]

5 TRADITIONAL ASIAN SPORTS

_____ China

Chinese physical culture has always oscillated between two poles: at one extreme, violent competition; at the other, the peaceful quest for spiritual harmony. Boxers, wrestlers, and other athletes embody the first extreme; the second can be represented by devotees of *tai ji,* known in the West as *tai chi,* a combination of gymnastic exercise and philosophy. Chinese sports, which fall by definition into the first category, have often been modified by influences from the second category, which has meant that Chinese sports competitions have often been gentler than the agonistic combats typical of European sports through most of their history. Good form has often been prized above competitive success.[1]

Throughout Chinese history, aristocrats obsessed with the quest for spiritual harmony tended to disdain sports, a tendency strengthened by the arrival of Buddhism during the Han dynasty (206 B.C.–220 A.D.) In the moralistic eyes of Confucian sages, playing ball games was a sign of weak character, little better than drinking, gambling, and womanizing. Yet even Confucian scholars succumbed to the seduction of archery and granted that sport a half-hearted endorsement. When mandarins bent the bow, however, it was certainly not with the warrior's deadly serious intent nor even with the earnestness encountered at European crossbow matches. Archery was a ceremonial activity in which social status counted for more than athletic performance. "Even the way they contend," said Confucius of the archers, "is gentlemanly."[2]

Archery was also a sport practiced by ladies of the imperial court. And for men and women who found archery too strenuous a pastime, there was *touhou,* which required the player to toss an arrow into a vase. In time, this courtly game was refined to the point where nine officials were required for a two-person match.[3]

Parallel to the tradition of gentle sports practiced in a spirit of harmony ran the more bellicose traditions of the armed and unarmed martial arts, known collectively as *wushu*. The earliest extant references to sports occur in conjunction with military preparation. In the Zhou period (1122–256 B.C.), for instance, soldiers ran, jumped, threw objects of various sorts, wrestled, and practiced their skills as archers, swordsmen, and charioteers. They also demonstrated their prowess as weight lifters. *Kangding* (tripod lifting) was popular as early as the Qin dynasty (221–206 B.C.). These sports seem not to have been closely associated with any religious cult.

By the time of the Han dynasty, foot soldiers and mounted warriors had replaced charioteers as the mainstay of the army, and the practice of *wushu* was highly developed. Although *wushu*'s unarmed techniques were especially prized, archery, too, had numerous devotees, and the sport was immensely popular during the Northern Song (960–1126) and Southern Song (1126–1279) periods. An eleventh-century district survey found 588 archery societies enrolling 31,411 members, nearly 15 percent of the local population.[4]

The overthrow of the Ming dynasty (1358–1644) by tribesmen from the northeast initiated a new phase in the history of Chinese sports. The ethnically Manchu rulers of the Qing dynasty (1644–1911) were enthusiasts for equestrian sports, including mounted archery, but they preferred that their Chinese subjects not practice the armed martial arts. Unarmed *wushu* survived, however, and experienced a surge in popularity during the nationalistic reaction to the Chinese defeat by the British in the Opium War of 1839–1842.

Ball games, played with carefully sewn stuffed skins, with animal bladders, or with found objects as simple as gourds, chunks of wood, or rounded stones, were popular in China as they have been in every known culture. Exactly when Chinese ball games began, no one knows, but stone balls, which may have been used for some kind of game, have been dated as far back as the sixth millennium B.C. *Cuju*, which resembled modern soccer football, is mentioned in the *Shiji*, one of the oldest extant Chinese texts. During the Han dynasty, football was the subject of a twenty-five-chapter handbook. It also figured in a short poem by Li Yu (50–136).

A round ball and a square wall,
Just like the Yin and the Yang.
Moon-shaped goals are opposite each other,
Each side has six in equal number.[5]

In the version of *cuju* played during the Wei dynasty (220–265), the football field seems to have symbolized the earth while the ball represented a heavenly body. The players were twelve in number because there are twelve signs in the zodiac. In the Tang period (618–907), according to Hans Ulrich Vogel, there were societies formed to play the game, which now included goalposts through which the balls were kicked. Vogel also believes that Chinese women played the game, emitting "erotic signals" all the while. (Vogel does not offer to decode the signals.) During the Qing dynasty, Confucianism gained ground and football lost its appeal.[6]

Through most of China's recorded history, racket games were popular among women. A Ming-dynasty scroll painting, *Grove of Violets,* depicts five elegantly attired ladies playing *chuiwan,* a game combing elements of modern billiards and golf. According to a thirteenth-century text, the *Wanjing,* the players took turns striking a wooden ball and sending it into holes marked with colored flags. The ethos of the game stressed fairness and harmony among the players.[7]

In China as in southeast Asia, adults and children flew kites, some of which were fanciful works of art in paper and wood. This form of ludic amusement, known as early as the twelfth century B.C., became a national obsession during the Tang dynasty (618–907). In the competitive version, contestants sought to maneuver their kites so that they cut the strings of their opponents' kites and sent them crashing to earth. Another ancient sport, dragon-boat racing, elicited a similar mix of aesthetic and agonistic impulses. This sport evolved from impromptu races among boats decorated with talismanic dragons in order to protect their crews from storms. Eventually, races were held to commemorate the drowned. The most famous of these races was in memory of the poet Qu Yuan, who perished in 278 A.D. By the Tang period, there were fixed dates and strict rules for the races, which had become major events. Some of the dragon boats had female crews.[8]

Harmony was definitely not foremost among the values of the Mongols who invaded Sichuan and Yuan provinces in 1252 and concluded their conquest of China in 1279. During the period of Mongol rule, the martial arts flourished and mounted archers were the backbone of the army. If the Italian traveler Marco Polo can be believed, the Mongol dynasty produced at least one physically fit and feisty heroine. Princess Aiyaruk was said to have owned more than ten thousand horses, acquired one hundred at a time as she out-wrestled a long line of doomed suitors. Marco Polo was notoriously gullible, and Aiyaruk's athletic exploits were probably as imaginary as those of Atalanta, but the story testifies to the Mongol admiration for physically strong women.[9]

Although Mongol emperors like Kublai Khan (1215–1294) were passionate about hunting, that sport's golden age seems to have come and gone several centuries later, during the Qing dynasty. There was a seventeenth-century revival of sorts. The emperor Kangxi (1654–1722) was said to have hunted with a retinue of seventy thousand horsemen and three thousand archers. The numbers—like those recorded for Egypt's pharaohs—were doubtless exaggerated in order to magnify the stature of the royal hunter.[10]

Polo was widely played in the Chinese army, and the most skilled player of the entire Tang period may have been General Xia. During the reign of Dezong (r. 779–805), Xia is said to have placed a stack of twelve coins in the middle of the polo field and then to have struck them, at full gallop, one by one, twenty meters into the air. There was a downside to the popularity of polo among military men. When the Mongols invaded their homeland, the Chinese generals were said to have been "more competent at polo than at war."[11]

Li Guo was among the many Tang poets who wrote about polo. In his eyes, "The tip of the polo stick curves like a crescent moon." Another Tang poet, Wang Jian, wrote of the somatic benefits to court ladies who had taken up polo: "Since the ladies of the court have learned to play polo, they ride with slender hips." These women were definitely not isolated examples of female participation in the game. Many Tang statuettes show women riding and wielding polo sticks. Photographs of six of these statuettes are reproduced in Carl Diem's *Asiatische Reiterspiele*.[12]

Polo continued to be played during the Song dynasty (960–1279). Women of the court, including the empress, played the game as they had during the Tang era. A painting by the eleventh-century Song artist Li Kung-lin depicts sixteen polo players, of whom five are female. During this period, polo matches for mixed male-and-female teams were apparently common. There was even a report of a game played "in drag" by young men dressed as girls. (In tune with the travesty, they rode donkeys instead of ponies.) There were also nocturnal polo games played by torchlight. On the whole, however, enthusiasm for polo was less intense and less widespread than it had been in the Tang period. Members of the court no longer rode horses, and polo seems to have been "largely limited to professional players in the army and to court entertainers."[13]

If that was the case, then Taizong (r. 976–997) was an exception. That emperor staged a national polo tournament and participated in it as an active player. It was he who began play and resumed play after a goal was scored. By Taizong's time, it was customary to have two goals rather than one and to have them defended by goalkeepers. The east and west goals were bedecked with flags and surmounted by a golden dragon. The "Easterners" wore yellow, the "Westerners" wore red. Gongs were sounded to signal that a goal had been scored. To some observers, Taizong's enthusiasm seemed excessive.

One of his advisers warned him that his imprudent participation in the game was creating an awkward political dilemma. When his team won, his subjects were shamed by the defeat; when his team lost, his subjects grew haughty and forgot their place. In either event, time spent in play was time not spent on pressing imperial duties.[14]

The Southern Song emperor Xiaozong (r. 1163–1189) was also devoted to the game. His ministers warned him that he risked injury, but he stubbornly ignored their sage advice. He joined a game of polo and "lost control of his pony. The animal bolted under a veranda, the eaves of which were very low; there was a crash, and the terror-stricken attendants crowded around to help. The pony had got through, and his Majesty was left hanging by his hands to the lintel." He was rescued and play resumed. The spectators cheered.[15]

Daoist priests frequently objected to the game. As early as the Tang period, one of them complained that "polo hurts the vitality of the players and it also hurts that of the horses." During the Song dynasty, Confucian scholars articulated their doubts about polo: "From the standpoint of strict Confucian morality, polo was akin to heavy drinking, gambling, popular music, licentious conduct, and other forms of immoral activity." Criticisms of this sort may have had some effect. Polo went into an irreversible decline during the Ming and the Qing dynasties. According to James T. C. Liu, Xiaozong (r. 1163–1189) was the game's last imperial enthusiast; after him, "not a single Chinese emperor or prince has ever played polo."[16]

India

The warriors of India's Vedic Age (2000–1400 B.C.) fought their battles and hunted their animal prey with bows and arrows and with spears. We can safely conjecture that their sports involved the same equipment as their wars and their hunts. Like the warriors of other cultures, they also hardened their bodies and tested their skills in running, jumping, throwing, and wrestling contests. If the *Ramayana* (composed 500–300 B.C.) and the *Mahabharata* (composed 400 B.C.–400 A.D.) can be taken as guides, swimming, weight lifting, wrestling, archery, and sword fighting were hallmarks of the Epic Age (1400–1000 B.C.). The epic hero Arjuna successfully relies on meditation to enhance his skills in archery. Instructed by Lord Krishna, Arjuna has a commitment to ethics that sets him apart from his brother Bhima, who is merely an athlete.[17]

Meditation and yogalike techniques to control and even to deny the reality of the body gained in importance after the Epic Age. This ascetic tendency was intensified in the fifth century B.C. when the spread of Buddhism challenged Hindu religious dominance of the subcontinent. For devout Buddhists, the quest for spiritual enlightenment took priority over physical fitness and military prowess. Although wrestling remained popular among students at the University of Nalanda, Buddhist influence was very strong. Among the students' other "sports" were hopping nimbly over diagrams drawn on the ground and guessing other people's thoughts.

The Islamic conquest of the northwestern part of the Indian subcontinent began in 711. Muslim rule reached a culmination in the Mughal Empire established by Tamerlane's descendant Babur. Polo arrived with the Islamic invaders. The first sultan of Delhi, Qutbuddin Aimak (r. 1206–1210) died prematurely during a polo game when he fell from and was then crushed by his horse. Emperor Akbar (r. 1556–1605), the most famous of the Mughal rulers, was, like his contemporary Shah Abbas of Iran, renowned for his polo skills and for his love of the game, which he also played at night, using luminous balls made from the wood of the palas tree. His adviser Abu l-Fazl (1551–1602) wrote a lively defense of Akbar's favorite pastime:

> Superficial observers regard the game as a mere amusement, and consider it mere play; but men of more exalted views see in it a means of learning promptitude and decision. Strong men learn, in playing the game, the art of riding; and the animals learn to perform feats of agility and to obey the reins. It tests the value of a man and strengthens bonds of friendship. Hence His Majesty is very fond of this game.[18]

Scenes of polo appear frequently in Mughal literature and art, which reached their apogee in the seventeenth century. A number of illuminated manuscripts represent Akbar's son Jahangir (r. 1605–1627) as a polo player. The text of one manuscript urges him to strike the ball boldly. Hindu princes were not encouraged to do likewise. In fact, their Muslim rulers tried to prevent Hindus from drinking and from playing polo, two activities liable to make them unruly—if not rebellious—subjects. Mughal art sometimes included female polo players, but we cannot be sure that the scenes depicted contemporary customs. Some paintings are obviously the products of fantasy. An anachronistic miniature from the court of Akbar, for instance, shows us Queen Homây (mother of King Darius of Persia) playing the game centuries before its invention.[19]

Adherence to Hinduism or Islam was quite compatible with a passion for wrestling and the martial arts. In fact, these activities were, and still are, perceived by Indians as manifestations of the religious life. The traditional sports *Bharatiya kushti* (Indian wrestling) and *kalarippayattu* (exercises in an open pit), both of which are still practiced, are representative examples of the Indian melding of sports and religion. Neither sport seems to have been radically changed by two centuries of British rule.

_____ Japan

Sumō wrestling is the most distinctive of Japan's traditional sports. The earliest reliable accounts are from the eighth century A.D., when annual matches were performed at the imperial court in Nara. These matches took place on the seventh day of the seventh month of the lunar calendar. A garden adjacent to the *Shishinden* (Hall for State Ceremonies) was strewn with white sand for the occasion. Announced by the sound of drums and gongs, thirty-four wrestlers entered the garden. They were followed by officials, musicians, and dancers. The "left" team wore paper hollyhocks in their hair; the "right" team wore paper calabash blossoms. After each match, musicians beat their drums, struck their gongs, and performed a ritual dance. The annual event was political rather than religious.[20]

Serving as a vivid demonstration of imperial authority, the matches continued after the court's removal from Nara to Heian-kyō (modern Kyoto) in 794. After the Heian period ended in 1185, political power shifted to Kamakura, near modern Tokyo, and *sumō* was rarely performed at the imperial court in Heian-kyō. *Sumō* survived, however, as *shinji-zumō* ("the gods' *sumō*"), performed as part of festival celebrations at Buddhist temples and Shinto shrines. In *karasu-zumō* ("crow wrestling"), for example, boys representing the god Takemikazuchi wrestled against other boys representing the mundane world. There was also *onna-zumō* ("women's wrestling"). The debased motivation for this activity is suggested by the names of the wrestlers: "Big Boobs," "Deep Crevice," "Holder of the Balls."[21]

During the Tokugawa shogunate (1600–1868), when Japan was ruled by the military (*shōgun* = "general"), *sumō* became an urban phenomenon. In woodblock prints of street-corner *sumō* we can study not only the massively muscled wrestlers but also the ordinary citizens of Osaka and Edo (modern Toyko) who jostled one another for a glimpse of their outsize heroes.[22]

As *sumō* migrated from the countryside to Japan's urban centers, the sport experienced a concurrent rise in status. Thanks largely to the organizational efforts of Yoshida Zenzaemon, *sumō* wrestlers were invited, in 1791, to exhibit their skills before the Shogun Tokugawa Ienari. It was Yoshida who introduced the *dohyō matsuri* (ring ceremony) that is performed at the beginning of each *sumô* tournament. The shogun gave Yoshida's efforts a significant boost when he awarded a bow to the great wrestler Tanikaze Kajinosuke. Tanikaze broke into a spontaneous dance, the basis for the *yumitorishiki* (bow-dance ceremony) that is now an indispensable part of every *sumō* tournament. "Shogunal sumo lifted the sport out of the vulgar world of entertainment," wrote Patricia Cuyler, "and imparted to it a sense of ritual that later became its major characteristic."[23]

The kimono-clad courtiers of Heian-kyō were fond of watching *sumō* matches, but for exercise they chose *kemari*. The game was played outdoors on a square earthen court with sides about six or seven meters in length. At each of the corners was a pine, willow, cherry, or maple tree. The eight players were stationed two to a tree. The object of the game was to keep a deerskin ball aloft. The number of times a player kicked the ball before he passed it on was not fixed, but three was considered most appropriate—one kick to bring the ball under control, one to propel it high above the player's head, and one to pass it to another player. Players were not judged by the number of successful kicks but rather by the "three virtues of the ball," which were proper posture, swiftness and skill, and mastery of strategy. From the twelfth century to the nineteenth, *kemari* was a popular aristocratic pastime.[24]

Toughened warriors of the samurai class were no more likely to spend their time at *kemari* than they were to compete in bouts of *sumō* against nearly naked peasants. Warriors preferred to demonstrate their physical prowess as archers and fencers. Archeologists have found obsidian arrowheads from the Stone Age—and "heavenly-feathered arrows" were a token of the mythical Jimmu's right to rule the Japanese islands—but the earliest historical documents relating to archery as a sport date from late in the seventh century. Although the Japanese gripped the bow in the Mongol fashion, with the thumb wrapped over the bowstring, they used the long bow derived from southeastern Asia rather than the much shorter Mongol bow. The long bow, which measures over two meters, is still used and is still gripped as it was in the Heian period, with two-thirds of the bow's length above the archer's hand.[25]

Archery, like *sumō*, was incorporated into the annual calendar of ceremonies performed at the imperial court. Cameron Hurst notes that the contests were "designed to preserve harmony between Heaven and Earth and secure the political order." In the *Dairishiki*, which chronicles court ceremonies from 646 to 930, archery matches far outnumbered all other ceremonies. The light bows used at court were probably more effective as symbols of authority than as weapons of war.[26]

Jarai was typical of the many kinds of target archery performed at the imperial court. *Jarai* matches were held at the *Burakuin* ("Court of Abundant Pleasures") in the middle of the first lunar month. Twenty noblemen, including imperial princes, were selected to participate. Standing on mats made of calfskin, aiming at deerskin targets, the nobles shot first. A gong rang once to indicate that an arrow had hit the target's outer ring. The gong rang twice if the arrow lodged in the middle ring, three times if the innermost ring was struck. Members of the imperial family aimed their arrows at a target some 20 percent larger than the one provided for the nobility. Heralds announced the results along with the contestant's name, rank, and office. In accordance with the culture's hierarchical caste of mind, the archer's rank influenced the prize he received.[27]

A courtier's performance at the rather gentle sport of *jarai* was no predictor of his battlefield prowess. *Yabusame,* which required equestrian as well as toxophilic skills, was more like the real thing. In *yabusame,* the contestants drew their bows and loosed their arrows while galloping down a straight track some 220 to 270 meters long. The archers were required to shoot in quick succession at three small targets (c. 55 centimeters square) placed on meter-high poles 7 to 11 meters from the track and spaced at intervals of 72 to 90 meters. In a second pass, the archers shot at tiny clay targets a mere 8.2 centimers in diameter. The heyday of the sport ran from 1187 to 1484.[28]

During the Tokugawa era, the importance of archery as a battlefield skill declined. The samurai continued to practice with bow and arrow, but the motivation was not what it had been when the accuracy of one's aim made a life-or-death difference. Archery became a form of spiritual training. Throughout the Tokugawa period, schools of archery proliferated as *kyūjutsu* ("techniques of the bow") became *kyūdō* ("the way of the bow"). When the spokesmen of the various schools codified the rules and techniques of their particular styles, they tended to express their thoughts in the religious terminology—Shinto, Buddhist, or Confucian—that was the common currency of learned men. Zen Buddhism contributed significantly to the idea of archery as a spiritual activity, but it was only one of several influences.[29]

For the most part, fencers trod the same path as archers and *kenjutsu* ("techniques of the sword") became *kendō* ("the way of the sword"). Hundreds of masters founded schools in which they taught the techniques and styles revealed to them—they alleged—by the gods. Fencers were in general slower than archers to move from mortal combat to sports competition to spiritual exercise. During the relatively peaceful Tokugawa period, deadly encounters were still common. The legendary Miyamoto Musashi, for instance, fought in the battle of Sekigahara (1600), in the Shimabara Rebellion (1637), and in a number of duels, the most famous of which was against Sasaki Kojirō on the island of Ganryō-jima.[30] Musashi's classic *Book of Five Rings (Gorin no sho),* which he completed just before his death in 1645, was utilitarian rather than philosophical. "To master the virtue of the long sword," he wrote, "is to govern the world and oneself." He did, however, allow himself this enigmatic epigram: "By knowing things that exist, you can know that which does not exist. That is the void."[31]

When archers moved from *kyūjutsu* to *kyūdō,* there was no need to transform weaponry into sports equipment. Bows used in battle functioned just as well when the target was a set of concentric circles rather than the armored enemy's unprotected throat. Fencers, however, had to modify their equipment to avoid the deadly damage inflicted by the Japanese sword (which was a much sharper instrument than its European counterpart). Bamboo swords, which dated from the sixteenth century, were not so dangerous, but they still caused serious pain and injury. In response to the challenge, enthusiasts for *kendō* developed a variety of protective gear to make their sport safer: *kote* (gloves for the hands and lower arm); the *men* (a cotton helmet with a metal protector for the face); the *dō* (a chest protector); and the *tare* (armor for the waist and groin). This equipment was not devised all at once, but gradually over time. By the beginning of the eighteenth century the mask, gloves, and trunk padding had achieved something like their present form and were widely used for simulated combat. "Protective gear represented a dramatic step forward in the transformation of military techniques into the sport forms that we know today."[32]

Along with the adoption of protective gear came an emphasis on repetitive exercises known as *kata.* Constant repetition of *kata* led all too frequently to "an extreme formalism that emphasized . . . outward elegance." This emphasis, which went beyond the *politesse* of Renaissance fencers, tended to degenerate into theatrical display of complicated *kata* that were useless in a real contest.[33]

The predictable lament of the traditionalists was that protective gear and a fixation on *kata* distanced the sport too far from the conditions of manly combat. Early in the eighteenth century, Matsushita Kunitaka complained about effeminate samurai who plucked their eyebrows and powdered their faces. He "noted wryly that the hand techniques of a swordsman looked like those of a Noh dancer who had simply exchanged a sword for his fan." The swordsman's nimble feet moved as if he were engaged in a game of courtly *kemari.*[34]

Traditionalists had another reason to despair. Although the right to bear real swords was limited to the samurai, commoners were permitted to wield *kendō*'s bamboo implements. "Late Tokugawa fencing," writes Cameron Hurst, "became an activity in which samurai and commoner were brought together, helping to further blur the class distinctions between lower-ranking samurai and upper peasants or merchants." It was a small but important step on the path to ludic equality.[35]

_____ Islamic Asia

Throughout the Islamic regions of western and central Asia, from Turkey through the entire Arab world to Iran and Pakistan, hunting was "the sport of kings." Iranian poetry makes innumerable references to the pasttime. Allusions link Iranian sportsmen to their distant pre-Islamic Persian ancestors, whose passion for the hunt was chronicled by the Greek historian Xenophon. Colorful hunting scenes, crowded by depictions of rulers, courtiers, attendants, and an assortment of panicky prey, are among the most common themes of sixteenth- and seventeenth-century Indian art.

Closely associated with the hunt was the sport of archery. The mounted hunters who brought down their quarry with bow and arrow honed their skills at archery, shooting not at abstract targets but at natural objects like gourds (_qabaq_) or baskets filled with sand (_qighaj_). Accuracy was not the only mark of a good archer. Among the Turks, "flight shooting" (for distance) was a favorite sport. The fifteenth-century sultan Muhammad II constructed an archery ground north of recently captured Constantinople. Stones were placed on the field to mark the longest shots. Composite bows made of wood and horn enabled Turkish archers to outperform their European contemporaries. In 1798, Selim III sent his arrow 972 yards—to the astonishment of Sir Robert Ainslie, the British ambassador.[36]

Archery was the Turkish rulers' favorite sport. Their subjects wrestled. The importance of both sports—and of equestrian skill—is suggested by an episode in _The Book of Dede Korkut,_ an oral epic that took written form in the sixteenth century. Prince Beyrek seeks the hand of Lady Chichek, an athletic damsel who will not accept a husband who is her physical inferior. Disguised as a servant girl, she challenges Beyrek. "Come let us ride out together. We shall shoot our bows and race our horses and wrestle. If you beat me in these three, you will beat [Lady Chichek] too." Beyrek accepts the challenge. "They both mounted and rode out. They spurred their horses, and Beyrek's horse passed the girl's. They shot their bows and Beyrek's arrow split the girl's arrow. Said she, 'Well young man, nobody has ever passed my horse or split my arrow. Come now, let us wrestle.' At once they dismounted and grappled; they stood as wrestlers do and grasped each other. Beyrek picked the girl up and tried to throw her, then she picked him up and tried to throw him." Astonished and fearful of humiliation, Beyrek "made a supreme effort, grappled with the girl and . . . seized her slender waist, held her tight and threw her on her back."[37]

The prince gets the princess. Historically, the most skillful wrestlers were rewarded with a summons to Istanbul, the renamed capital. There they fought in 1524 to celebrate the wedding of Ibrahim Pasha and in 1582 to celebrate the circumcision of the sultan's son. In villages throughout the Ottoman realm, men formed wrestling guilds and frequented "houses of strength," where Allah was invoked to secure a wrestler's victory and poets were enlisted to celebrate it. Similar "houses of strength" (*zûrkhânah*) are still an important part of Iranian culture, where they continue to emhasize the ideals of traditional masculinity. Open only to Muslims, the *zûrkhânah* is a place of worship as well as a sports site. While the wrestlers prepare for their match, a *morshed* chants and drums and reminds them of the deeds of the greatest *pahlavan* of all, the fourteenth-century poet Mahmud Kharazmi.[38]

Turkish and Persian wrestlers made an indelible impression upon the Arab invaders who swept through the Middle East in the seventh century. "After the Arabs made contact with the Persians and the Turks, they began to imitate their customs. Cosmopolitan cities [like Baghdad and Damascus] began to have troupes of wrestlers, many of them Persians or Turks."[39]

Equestrian games were popular throughout Asia. In all probability, polo, the most widely diffused, evolved from *buzkashi* and other traditional games played by the nomadic peoples of Central Asia. In the Afghan form that survived into the twentieth century, *buzkashi* was characterized by a dusty melee in which hundreds of mounted tribesmen struggled to seize the headless carcass of a goat. The winner was the hardy rider who managed to grab the animal by a leg and drag it clear of the pack. Polo may be considered a refined version of this rough contest.[40]

Polo was played in Iran from at least the beginnings of Sasanian rule in the third century A.D. The Saffarid ruler 'Amr b. Layth (r. 879–901) played the game despite the fact that he was blind in one eye. The Samanid prince 'Abd al-Malik (r. 954–961) unintentionally sacrificed his life to polo when he was thrown from his horse and broke his neck.[41]

The Turkic and Mongol dynasties that ruled Iran from the mid-eleventh century onward continued the royal patronage of polo. Sultan Mahmud of Ghazna (r. 998–1030), played it, and one of his court poets, Farrukhi, documented his feats for posterity. "There are four things for kings to do," the poet wrote, "To feast, hunt, play polo, and make war."[42]

The fourteenth-century Turkish conqueror Timur (1336–1405), known and feared in the West as Tamerlane, seems to have promoted polo as well as Islam in his domains, which extended from Russia through Iran and Central

Asia to India. His contemporary, the Iranian poet Hafiz, drew upon Timur's knowledge of the game when he wished him luck: "May the heads of your enemies be your polo balls."[43]

As the quotation from Hafiz suggests, the imagery of polo pervaded Iranian poetry. In the *Book of Kings* (*Sh hn meh*), the national epic of Iran written by the tenth-century poet Hakim Abu l-Q sem Ferdowsi, royalty are forever playing polo. Some of the regal players were placed by Ferdowsi in periods that antedated the first historically attested mention of polo by many centuries. The lack of archeological, historiographical, or numismatic evidence for polo in the days of Darius and Alexander the Great hardly matters. The poets worked with metaphors. When they lauded their royal patrons (or their patrons' distant ancestors), the polo ball represented the earth and the mallet that propelled it symbolized kingly authority. When poets wrote of love, the same images had other meanings. "For lovers the heart is like a ball and their back is curved like a polo stick." (An odd image, but love is an inexplicable emotion.) Polo also found its way into the metaphors of mystical poetry, where the highest bliss was likened to being driven back and forth by a divine polo mallet.[44]

The centrality of polo to court life meant that it became, together with hunting, a favorite subject for Iranian (and later Turkish and Indian) miniature painters. An illustration for the thirteenth-century poet Sa'di's *Gulistan*, for instance, depicts "a prince waylaid as he rides to the polo ground."[45]

After the Arab conquest of what is now Syria and Iraq, polo was played in the Umayyad capital of Damascus under the second Umayyad caliph, Yazid I (r. 680–683), and in Baghdad during the reign of the Abbasid caliph Harun al-Rashid (r. 786–809), the famed contemporary of Charlemagne. The caliph is better known in the West as the presumed listener to Sheherazade's *Thousand and One Nights*, a series of tales in which polo makes several appearances. The founder of Egypt's Ayyubid dynasty, Salah al-Din (r. 1169–1193), more familiar in the West as the Crusaders' chivalrous opponent Saladdin, was also a polo enthusiast—as was the Mamluk ruler Baibar I (r. 1260–1277), a man renowned for his physical prowess. Baibar was said to have played polo in both Cairo and Damascus in a single week.[46]

In the course of their conquest of the Byzantine Empire, the Seljuk and Ottoman Turks also found time to play polo, but the game was less popular among the Turks than it was in Iran.

6

EUROPEAN SPORTS FROM THE MIDDLE AGES TO THE RENAISSANCE

Tournaments

The connection between sports and warfare has seldom, if ever, been closer than in the Middle Ages. For the medieval knight, the line between tournament and battlefield, between mock and real warfare, was thin and often transgressed. As the French diplomat–historian Jean Jusserand wrote in 1901, "The union of warfare and games was so close that it is frequently difficult to decide if a given activity ought to be classified under one rubric or the other." The warlike features of the tournament were especially pronounced in the twelfth century, when the typical tournament was a confused melee composed of dozens of knights simultaneously fighting, capturing one another, seeking not only glory but also ransoms. A contemporary, celebrating the life of the famed twelfth-century knight-errant William Marshal, wrote that "the fracas was such that God's thunder couldn't have been heard." The armored knights who entered the lists full of *ira et odium* (anger and hatred) were hardly the embodiments of chivalry envisioned by Sir Walter Scott and the Pre-Raphaelite painters. Violence frequently exceeded the limits established by the rules. At a tournament held in Neuss in 1240, scores of knights perished, more than were killed on the typical medieval battlefield. At Châlons-Sur-Marne in 1274, when Edward I of England was seized in contravention of the rules, a brawl ensued during which several people were killed. At Boston in 1288, one side was dressed as monks and the other was costumed as canons of the church, but clerical garb did little to tame lay passions; a riot broke out and much of the town was reduced to ruins.[1]

Realizing that it was impossible to ban tournaments, Richard I of England, in 1194, authorized them at five sites and issued regulations to minimize the mayhem. The *Statuta Armorum* issued by Edward I in 1292 decreed that "they who shall come to see the Tournament, shall not be armed with any Mannor of Armour, and shall bear no Sword, or Dagger, or Staff, or Mace, or Stone." When the Holy Roman Emperor Friedrich II gave the town of Lübeck the right to hold a tournament, in 1230, he warned the townspeople against rape (*violationes matronum et virginum*). In general, regulations were ineffective. Swiss historians record that a bloody tumult occurred at a tournament in Basel, in 1376, when bourgeois spectators, trampled by mounted noblemen, reacted violently and slew several of the offending knights.[2]

Dicta issued by the Roman Catholic Church were as ineffective as the regulations promulgated by medieval monarchs. Appalled by the violence of early tournaments, the Roman Catholic Church banned them five times between 1130 and 1179. To no avail. And when kings ignored ecclesiastical prohibitions, the Church was powerless to stop them. In the course of time, clerical leaders gave up their efforts to ban tournaments and joined their secular counterparts, viewing the processions, watching the jousts, and gorging themselves at the banquets that concluded the festivities. Although the addiction to tournaments was never so severe in Italy as in northern Europe, jousts took place in St. Peter's Square in 1471.[3]

Nature rather than civilization provided the typical site for early tournaments. "The contests," wrote Francis Henry Cripps-Day, "seem to have been held in open country, featured perhaps with little woods, a bridge and a stream." Since the early tournament was not meant as a spectacle, there was little provision for spectators nor was there a strict division in social roles. Knights who came merely to watch sometimes decided, on the spur of the moment, to join in the fun. Philip, Count of Flanders, took advantage of this custom. He waited unobtrusively on the sidelines until he saw an opportunity to seize some exhausted, unwary combatant and bear him off for ransom. On one occasion, the tables were turned. William Marshal waited patiently, *hors de combat,* until he saw a chance to capture Count Philip, which he did.[4]

In the course of time, from the twelfth to the sixteenth century, bellicose tournaments became a form of theater, an occasion for pageantry and dramatic performance. Eventually, they were "little more than a spectacle."[5] The joust between two mounted knights separated by a wooden barrier replaced the wild free-for-all clash of groups. Weapons were blunted to minimize injuries. Jousts were decided by a complicated system of points. A lance broken against an opponent's helmet, for instance, was worth more than one splintered against his breastplate.[6]

A tally of points scored facilitated the selection of a champion, but his bright burst of glory was often overshadowed by the pomp and circumstance that framed the combat. When a tournament was organized to welcome Queen Isabelle into Paris, in 1389, Jean Froissart's account of the event dwelled longer upon the elaborate pageantry than upon the jousts. When an allegorical castle was constructed with a recumbant figure of St. Anne, when twelve chaplet-crowned maidens wandered among symbolic animals (a hart, a lion, and an eagle, symbolizing vulnerability and two forms of protective strength), when an effigy of Saladin's castle was attacked and defended by costumed knights, it must have been obvious to Isabelle and her court that demonstrations of aptitude for battle were less apropos than the accompanying dramatic folderol. At the famous *Pas de la Bergère* that René d'Anjou staged at Tarascon in 1449, knights dressed as shepherds rode forth from pavilions designed to look like cottages. The chivalric combat was all but lost in the stage sets that Sydney Anglo described as "the fanciful disguising orginally devised as an adornment to it." René's own account of the tournament is a compulsively detailed etiquette book regulating exits and entrances, appropriate attire, and proper behavior. Jousting is scarcely mentioned. As historian Jean Verdon notes, René "adored sumptuous festivals [and] was mainly interested in ceremony and costume."[7]

English tournaments were similar. When the Duke of Buckingham staged a tournament at Westminster in 1501, the pageant cars—like modern Rose Bowl floats—were a phantasmagoria of dwarves, giants, savages, and allegorical animals. The jousts were inept. In the letters of the Lisle family we learn of a tournament at Brussels in 1538 during which there were injuries—at the banquet, where "some took more hurt with the cups than at the barriers with cutting of the sword"[8] This comment should remind us that Renaissance pomp and pageantry were always liable to disruption.

The best illustration of theatricality may be the thirty-six vellum membranes of the Great Tournament Roll of Westminster, a splendid pictorial representation of a grand and immensely costly tournament given by Henry VIII in 1511 to celebrate the birth of a son by Catherine of Aragon. The first membrane contains a heraldic device; the last contains another device and a poem. Membranes 24–27 show Henry tilting before the pavilion in which the queen is seated. Thirty membranes depict the colorful entry and exit processions.[9] If the modern Olympics were staged with this ratio of pageantry to athletic competition, we would have a week of opening ceremonies followed by two days of sports and a week of closing ceremonies.

The tamer the tournament, the greater the pressure to open the lists to urban patricians enchanted by the prospect of aristocratic make-believe. Philippe VI of France acceded to the pressure and gave permission to the bourgeoisie of Paris to *faire joustes contre les bourgoiz du royaulme.* German noblemen, for whom "tournaments served . . . as a wall of separation between themselves and the bourgeoisie," were more obdurate than their French counterparts. They thought that the wealthy urban merchant's proper role was to help defray the immense costs of the pageantry and the combats. The urge to exclude those of baser birth was so extreme among the German nobility that knights sometimes had to prove that they had sixteen, or even thirty-two, noble ancestors. When Nuremberg's burghers attempted, in 1434, to participate in a knightly tournament, they were attacked and severely beaten. A similar fate befell the knight Heinrich von Ramstein at Schaffhausen in 1436 simply because he had married a commoner. German rules also excluded knights who abducted nuns from their convents.[10]

Illuminated manuscripts, such as Robert de Borron's *Histoire du Graal,* sometimes pictured medieval women engaged in jousts, but the jousters— mounted on goats or rams and wielding distaffs and spindles—inhabited an imaginary topsy-turvy world in which women astride notoriously lustful mounts enacted forbidden roles. Women did not compete in tournaments. Historians who claim they did were misled by verbal or visual depictions of a *Frauentournier,* in which the female combatants were really men "in drag" disguised as women, just as other knights in other tournaments were disguised as Moors or Saracens.[11]

As the tournament's function as a demonstration of military prowess faded to insignificance, its function as a political statement came to the fore. The tournament became an awesome theater of power in which rulers such as Henry VIII, François I, and Maximilian I, personally or through their knightly representatives, enacted a fantasy of total control over real or imagined dangers. Unlike the fierce encounters of the early tournament, the mock assault on "Saladin's castle" was always successful; the threatening "giants" were always subdued. The spectators—and perhaps the actors as well— were awed, excited, thrilled, and reassured. It was not necessary for politically astute monarchs actually to don their armor, be hoisted to their saddles, and position their lances for a potentially fatal encounter. Henry VIII's daughter, Elizabeth I, safely seated in the royal box, sponsored eight tournaments in the first seven years of her enormously successful reign.[12]

Tournaments were a form of propaganda. They were, in the words of Alan Young, a "microcosm of the realm" in which social status determined passive as well as active participation. At the tournament at Smithfield in 1467, for which a public holiday was proclaimed, there was a special "grandstand" for the mayor of London and assorted dignitaries. The seats for knights and squires and others of noble birth rose in three tiers. Commoners unable to crowd into the enclosure climbed trees to obtain a glimpse of the marvelous pageantry and the unimpressive combats. When a tournament was held in a treeless urban square, which was often the case in the fifteenth and sixteenth centuries, city dwellers crowded into windows overlooking the site. The more adventurous among them clambered to the rooftops of adjacent buildings. The stands, windows, and roofs were carefully delineated in a print, dated 1570, which commemorates the 1559 tournament at which Henri II of France was fatally wounded. J. J. Jusserand quotes Henri's moving epitaph: *"Quem Mars non rapuit, Martis imago rapit"* (He whom Mars did not seize is seized by the image of Mars.) [13]

Women became an important presence at tournaments, but it is impossible to say when women first appeared among the spectators. The long biography of William Marshal describes his participation in a dozen tournaments, but female spectators are mentioned only once. They occur occasionally in the romances of Chrétien de Troyes and Wolfram von Eschenbach. Writing of a tournament held in 1389, the poet Eustache des Champs urges his knightly protagonist to "look sweetly" toward "the angels of paradise" sitting in the stands. Women were certainly present at the Smithfield tournament of 1467, where there were galleries for ladies. [14]

In poetry and in the prose romance, in painting and in tapestry, ladies are not only present, they are the focus of attention. It is impossible to assess the historical accuracy of these representations, but medieval tournaments— like King René's—did enact the fantasies of Arthurian romance. To the degree that the late medieval tournament followed the script of courtly love, an erotic function supplemented (and perhaps overshadowed) the tournament's military and political functions. The love-smitten knight knotted his beloved's scarf around the tip of his blunted (but still presumably phallic) lance and then displayed his courage and military skills. The prize for victory at a tournament in Merseburg in 1226 was "a nicely dressed young girl" *(puellam decoram valde),* but fifteenth-century chivalry seems to have settled for a kiss. The romantic stereotype of the knight and his lady has enough basis in historical reality for Maurice Keen to have detected "strong erotic undercurrents" at tournaments and for Louise Olga Fradenburg to have perceived tournaments as a way to dramatize "the masculinity of the warrior." In her view, tournaments were an arena in which knights soughts to ward off suspicions of effeminacy and to "constitute themselves as 'men.'" German historians agree that the tournament was, among other things, a "marriage market." [15]

Eventually, to eliminate totally the possibility of accidents like the one that killed Henri, "ring tournaments" were introduced. The lance was sharp, but the target was "nothing more than geometric space." In a 1623 print by Chrispyn de Passe the Younger, a gorgeously costumed knight in a plumed hat is guided by a foppish courtier as he thrusts his lance through a ring dangling from a cord. The symbolism is sexual rather than martial. [16]

Fencing

Dismounted swordplay, which had often been a feature of the early tournament, evolved in the same manner as the mounted joust. There was a shift from brute strength to agility and finesse. The difference between the vertical slash of the heavy two-handed sword and the rapid horizontal thrust of the light rapier signaled a transformation in aristocratic culture. Inevitably, traditionalists lamented the loss of rough and manly ways. Mere women might have—although they normally did not—wielded a rapier. Observing the newest fashion in swordplay, George Silver complained in 1599 about the decadent influence of "these Italianate weake, fantasticall and most divellish and imperfect fights."[17] His complaints were ineffectual. The young noblemen of England and northern Europe rushed to take lessons from masters who had learned their elegant art in Italy and France.

As fencing became increasingly rationalized, with rules to govern every move, treatises emphasized its aesthetic appeal. At royal courts throughout the continent, the correct performance of the ceremonial bow, the *révérence,* seemed as important as the proper way to execute a thrust. "For the Renaissance fencer," writes Henning Eichberg, "the charm of his sport clearly lay in exhausting every spatial and positional possibility." Fencers' manuals such as Camillo Agrippa's *Trattato di Scientia d'Arme* (Treatise on the Science of Arms) of 1553 and Girard Thibault's *L'Académie de l'espée* (The Academy of the Foil) of 1628 were illustrated with diagrams of the appropriate positions to take before, during, and after the match. Such manuals resembled textbooks in geometry.[18]

For his copperplate print, *The Fencing Hall of Leiden University* (1608), Willem Swanenburgh arranged his figures within a complicated geometrical pattern imposed upon the straight lines of a tiled floor. The picture is an epitome of elegance. Despite traditionalists' sneers at "effeminate" fencers, the sport remained as much a "masculine preserve" in the seventeenth century as it had been in the twelfth. There are no female intruders in Swanenburgh's *Fencing Hall.*[19]

Hunting and Hawking

When we turn to hunting and hawking, we see an altogether different picture. Inclusion and exclusion were determined by social status rather than by gender. Field sports were an aristocratic passion. Gaston III, Comte de Foix, wrote in his *Livre de chasse* that he took "special delight in three things: arms, love and hunting." John I of Portugal thought bear hunting "comparable to experiencing the glory of God," and Francesco Sforza of Milan—surely no softy—wept at the death of his favorite falcon. Throughout Europe, rulers set aside vast tracts of forested land as game reserves. The Earls of Northumberland had twenty-one such reserves in Northumberland, Cumberland, and Yorkshire. Restrictive game laws prevented starving peasants from stalking the woods for food but allowed aristocratic lords and ladies to mount their horses and gallop after deer, trampling fields of grain in their heedless pleasure. From 1390 to 1830, commoners "not having in lands 40 shillings *per Annum*" were threatened with imprisonment "for one whole yeare" if they hunted deer or any other animal reserved for "gentlemen." In 1831, one sixth of all convictions in English courts were for infractions against the game laws.[20] By then, the poacher's punishment was usually a fine rather than an imprisonment.

The medieval social hierarchy was, of course, much more subtle than a crude division between commoners and gentlemen. Hierarchy was complicated and it was signaled in many ways. Status was revealed, for instance, in the types of falcon with which one hunted. Royalty sported with the gerfalcon, earls with the peregrine, ladies with the merlin, servants with the lowly kestrel. The rules for the hunt were codified in treatises like the *Boke of St. Albans* (1486), a widely admired work attributed (wrongly) to Dame Juliana Berners.[21]

It was not that aristocratic women were reluctantly permitted to participate in field sports—they were welcomed. Léon Gautier's *La Chevalerie* (1884) noted that medieval knights in search of a bride preferred maidens who knew how to ride and to hawk. Joseph Strutt claimed in *The Sports and Pastimes of the People of England* (1838) that "the ladies had hunting parties by themselves," but this seems improbable. If gentlewomen were unable to find gentlemen who were inclined to spend an afternoon in pursuit of game, there were always male retainers to accompany, assist, and protect them.[22]

Medieval art attests to women's passion for the chase. Illuminated manuscripts such as Marguerite de Bar's *Breviary* and the "Tenison Psalter" abound with images of noblewomen pursuing stags or handling falcons. In the beautifully illustrated *Très Riches Heures du Duc de Berry,* the scene for the month of August includes richly attired mounted ladies with their falcons against a background of peasants working their fields. Scenes like this constituted an iconography of hierarchy.[23]

The passion for field sports seems to have intensified during the Renaissance. The chase was a primary motive for the construction of royal châteaux at Fontainebleau and throughout the Loire Valley. (On a smaller scale, every German prince had to have his *Jagdschloß.*) It was inevitable that the walls of

Chenonceaux, Chambord, and other palaces should be decorated with tapestries and paintings that showed François I, Henri II, and their successors as hunters. And it was just as inevitable that their wives and mistresses expected the same kind of iconographic attention. Henri's mistress, Diane de Poitiers, loved to pose with bow and arrow; her portrait, by an anonymous painter of the School of Fontainebleau, presents her as "the ancient goddess [of the hunt] whose name she bore."[24]

Elizabeth I was notorious for her lifelong inability to withstand the temptation of field sports. George Turberville's *Book of Falconrie or Hawking* (1575) depicted the queen as huntress. Rowland White, writing to another member of her court, noted that Elizabeth was "exceedingly disposed to hunting, for every second day she is on horseback, and continues the sport long." Visiting Kenilworth Palace in the queen's company, Robert Dudley, Earl of Leicester, sent the same message in a letter to William Cecil, Lord Burghley: "Her Majesty is going to the forest to kill some bucks with her bow, as she hath done in the park this morning. God be thanked, she is very merry and well-disposed now."[25] In England and Scotland, as on the continent, the royal hunt was clearly a political act as well as a sport. It was a deadly display of privilege and power.

Ordinary men and women, deprived of the opportunity to hunt, turned to animal sports of a different kind.[26] In England, cockfights were common and bearbaiting was a special treat. In a typical baiting, dogs were set upon a bear chained to a post, but Thomas Platter, a German visitor to England, observed a *berenhatz* that climaxed when the bear, old and blind, was beaten by men wielding sticks. Although Joseph Strutt asserted that "blood sports" attracted only "the lowest and most despicable part of the people," there is ample evidence that cockfights, bearbaiting, and bullbaiting were as popular among the high and mighty as among the lowly. Henry VIII was fond enough of cockfights to add a pit to Whitehall, and Elizabeth I prohibited theaters from opening on Thursdays because they interfered with "the game of bear-baiting, and like pastimes, which are maintained for her Majesty's pleasure."[27] If such majestic "pastimes" had a purpose other than the provision of sadistic delight, they were—perhaps—felt by the Elizabethans as reassuring demonstrations of humankind's domination of other animals. In that sense, they were close to Roman *venationes* and somewhat more distantly related to modern circus acts.

_____ Archery Matches

While medieval lords and ladies found amusement at tournaments and in the pursuit of game, while kings and queens and commoners delighted in the taming and torture of animals, members of the nascent bourgeoisie reveled in archery contests. In a swath of territory from Picardy in the west through Flanders and Brabant to Holland, archery guilds were formed early in the fourteenth century. By century's end, they were found throughout northern France and German-speaking central Europe. In England, where yeomen were required by law to maintain their skills with the long bow, there were archery meets, some of which drew thousands of participants, but the sport never flourished among the urban middle classes there as it did on the continent.[28]

Although the members of a late-medieval crossbow guild were a welcome cadre for a last-ditch urban defense, when all citizens were urgently needed on a besieged city's walls, the raison d'être of the guild was recreational, and membership was usually quite restricted. Abbeville's guild, for instance, was limited to fifty members. Ironically, the archer with the keenest eye and the steadiest hand—the _Schützenkönig_ (king of the archers)—was usually exempted from the night watch. In fourteenth-century Paris, _all_ the members of the archers' _Confrérie_ enjoyed this privilege as well as exemption from certain taxes.[29]

Noblemen were usually welcome at bourgeois archery meets, but they were few in number and seldom the center of attention that they were at a tournament. In addition to the fundamental social distinction between the nobility and the bourgeoisie, there were subtle hierarchical gradations within the latter group. The crossbowmen, whose patron was frequently St. George, were of relatively high status; they tended to be civic officials, merchants, and master craftsmen. The longbowmen, under the patronage of St. Sebastian, tended to come from the same social strata but were somewhat less affluent. They were often from villages rather than towns. Last of all in the march from the guildhall to the fields adjacent to the city's walls came the _nouveaux riches_ with their firearms and images of St. Barbara. Although the archery guilds were primarily manifestations of bourgeois life, aristocratic archers sometimes competed among themselves in socially exclusive contests like the one held at Prague in 1585, at which "not only the participants but also the spectators had to be members of the nobility."[30]

Over time, the _Schützenfeste_ (archery meets) evolved into major urban festivals, combining a number of different sports with pageants, banquets, dances, drunkenness, buffoonery, and the randy pleasures of illicit sex. At the grand archery match held in Augsburg in 1509, on the occasion of a visit by Holy Roman Emperor Maximilian I, the ancillary entertainments included footraces for male and female attendants and servants, ninepin contests, horse races, and a tournament for mounted knights. Footraces held in conjunction with archery meets were widely accepted as ways for young women to display their athleticism for men's admiration or mockery. There were, for instance, women's races at Munich in 1448, at Augsburg in 1470, at Herrenburg in 1478. In Flanders there were also ball games for women.[31]

At major matches, there were scores of men employed as clerks to certify that the archers' names were clearly inscribed upon their arrows, as spotters to record the number of hits and misses, as jurymen to resolve disputes, and as overseers of the lotteries that were an additional attraction of German archery festivals. In German-speaking central Europe there was usually a *Pritschenkönig* ("king of the whip") who combined the roles of police chief and poet laureate. He was expected to keep order and to provide festive verses. When the excitement of competition was intensified by the consumption of excellent local beer, the *Pritschenkönig* was not always equal to his task of quelling the rowdies. In 1458, quarrels that began at a meet in Konstanz culminated in a war against the nearby city of Zurich.[32]

While medieval tournaments were usually one-time events staged to celebrate royal marriages and other special occasions, archery matches were somewhat more likely to occur at set times. Typically, an archery guild had its grandest match on the day of its patron saint. The spring of the year customarily brought the annual competition to select the *Schützenkönig*. At this contest, the target was mimetic rather than abstract. Rather than aiming at the paper disk used for ordinary matches, the contestants for *Schützenkönig* shot at wooden birds—popinjays—perched high atop a pole. Female archers were sometimes invited to compete for the title of *Schützenkönigin,* an indication that this vernal competition might once have been a fertility ritual. Isabella of the Netherlands, daughter of Philip II of Spain, shot at the popinjay in Brussels in 1615 and at Ghent in 1618. Elsewhere in Flanders—at Kappelen, Hoogerheyde, and Olen—bourgeois *gildezusters* (sisters of the guild) competed for the title of *köningin.*[33]

The grandest meets, to which archers from distant cities were invited, frequently occurred in conjunction with important religious festivals. They were planned months in advance and the letters of invitation were extremely detailed. The typical letter announced the date of the meet, the number of matches, the dimensions of the target, the distance from the line of archers to the targets, and the many valuable prizes to be awarded. Since medieval units of measurements were not standardized, it was customary for the letter of invitation to indicate the size of the target with a circle and the length of the local "foot" with a line printed on the letter's margin or with an attached piece of cord.[34]

Targets were simply paper disks, small ones for crossbow contests and larger ones (at a much greater distance) for arquebus competitions. The disks were commonly attached to a post or a butt by a large wooden nail (hence: "to hit the nail on the head"). Spotters waved flags to signal a hit or a miss. The number of hits determined who qualified for a second round. At Augsburg in 1509, for instance, three of the forty-two archers had eleven hits each. Those three shot again, and the arrow closest to the central nail took the prize.[35]

At some late-sixteenth-century matches in Cologne and other German towns, concentric-ring targets were used, which may have permitted the officials to score matches in the modern manner. We can be definite about seventeenth-century scorers; they made their calculations on the basis of a complicated point system. In this sense, German archery matches anticipated "the elementary characteristics of 'modern' sports meets."[36]

Chroniclers of archery meets named the winners, but they provided much less information on the achievements of the contestants than on the variety and value of the prizes. The hosts supplied the prizes, which were carefully listed in the letters of invitation, but their costs were offset by entrance fees. For a fee of one gulden, a lucky craftsman might win the equivalent of a year's income.

Apart from the fascination with the prizes, there were other indications that toxophilic skills were not always uppermost in the spectators' minds. The most memorable occurrence at a match in Strasbourg, in the spring of 1576, was the bravado delivery of a kettle of porridge to win a wager. The legendary pottage, whisked downstream from Zurich to Strasbourg in a mere nineteen hours, was still warm enough to be eaten with gusto. The bravado event was celebrated in a jolly poem by Johannes Fischart.[37]

—— Court Tennis

In the later Middle Ages, the complicated game of court or royal tennis came into favor, first among royalty, who forbade servants and laborers to play the game, and then among the urban bourgeoisie. Originally known as *le jeu de paume*—because the ball was struck by the palm of the hand—the sixteenth-century form of the game was played with raquets on courts divided by a cord from which ribbons dangled. The ball's trajectory was especially unpredictable when it bounced from the court's irregularly shaped walls or from the roof of the low gallery that extended along three sides of the court. Unpredictability seems to have been part of the fun.[38]

The diary of Jean Héroard, the doctor responsible for the health of young Louis XIII, noted no fewer than three hundred forty-four games of court tennis. Louis XIV had ball courts at four of his palaces—and this was at a time when the game had begun to lose favor. Sixteenth-century Paris had no fewer than two-hundred-fifty ball courts that provided employment for some seven thousand persons. There were also ballhouses in many provincial towns. Most of the players were men, but the *Journal d'un Bourgeois de Paris* noted the exploits of an exceptional woman. Writing in 1427, the Parisian diarist noted that a certain Margot, a twenty-eight-year-old from the town of Hainault, had come to Paris and had outplayed the men at their favorite game. After her moment of fame, somewhat longer than the fifteen minutes allotted by Andy Warhol, Margot disappeared forever from the historical record.[39]

From France, court tennis spread to England, where Henry VIII was so enthralled by the game that he played it in at least a dozen different ballhouses. The palace at Winchester had four of them. When Charles V visited London in the summer of 1522 in order to discuss an alliance between England and the Holy Roman Empire, Henry took him as doubles partner in a game against the Prince of Orange and the Marquis of Brandenburg. Cambridge's colleges had a number of tennis courts and Londoners also played the game. In 1616 or 1617, Thomas and Henry Cornwallis received the right to license fourteen tennis courts (plus thirty-one bowling alleys and forty gaming houses). Elizabethan plays, including Shakespeare's *Henry V*, were enlivened with references to court tennis. In *Microcosmographie* (1625), John Earle complained of students whose "marks . . . of seniority" were the worn velvet of their gowns and their "proficiency at tennis." (Earle was not keen on bowls either: "No antic screws men's bodies into such strange flexures.")[40]

From France, court tennis went south and east as well as west. Florence had a ballhouse in 1618, and Turin had one in 1700. *Ballhäuser* also became a part of the urban landscape throughout German-speaking Europe. Of Austria's eighteen known courts, Vienna's—constructed in 1525—was the first. At least fifty-two other courts were built elsewhere in Germany. When the game died out, in the eighteenth century, many of the *Ballhäuser* were turned into theaters—like the one in Salzburg frequented by Mozart.[41]

The Basque ballcourt game of *pelota,* which seems also to have had roots in the *jeu de paume* from which court tennis grew, survives as a popular outdoor game in southern France and in parts of Hispanic America as well as in northern Spain.[42]

Football and Street Fights

Since historians have traditionally emphasized the deeds of the high and the mighty rather than the "short and simple annals of the poor," we know relatively little about the pastimes of the medieval peasantry. The sport about which we are best informed is folk-football (known in France as *soule*).

The rules were simple. Kicking, throwing, and carrying the ball, villagers made their way across fields, through hedges, over streams, and down narrow streets until they were able to propel the ball into the portal of the opposing villagers' parish church. Everyone was involved: male and female, young and old, rich and poor, clergy and laity. There was no effort to equalize the number of players on each side, and the separation of roles characteristic of modern sports was totally absent. As a contemporary observer noted, "Neyther maye there be anye looker on at this game, but all must be actours."[43]

Folk-football may have begun as a fertility rite, a lively way to mark the vernal equinox and to celebrate the rebirth of vegetation after winter's death. In northern France, *Mardi-Gras* was likely to include a lively game of *soule* between the bachelors and the married men. This game, like British Shrove Tuesday contests that pitted the married men (or women) against the unmarried, underlined the difference between those who were and those who were not (officially) sexually active. At Boulogne-la-Grasse, the rituals accompanying the game played on *le jour de Mardi-Gras* survived into the nineteenth century. The sexually suggestive paraphernalia of the day included a basket of eggs and a phallic staff from which a beribboned leather ball was suspended.[44]

Football's function as a fertility ritual did little if anything to diminish its violence. In Michel Bouet's vivid description, the participants in the game of *soule* were engaged in "a veritable combat for possession of the ball," for which they fought "like dogs battlling for a bone." Writing of British football, Eric Dunning and Kenneth Sheard describe "savage brawls" engendering "excitement akin to that aroused in battle." Appalled by such disorder, Edward II, Edward III, Richard II, Henry IV, and Henry V all tried to prohibit folk-football. Between 1314 and 1414, the game was banned nine times. On the continent, as in England, folk-football "seemed to trouble municipal, judicial, and religious authorities." In 1369, Charles V of France joined the long list of monarchs who prohibited the game.[45] These as well as subsequent prohibitions were widely ignored.

During the Renaissance, the game became somewhat more civilized, but there was still enough violence to worry humanists such as Sir Thomas Elyot.

In *The Boke of the Governour* (1537), he condemned football for its "beastely fury." His Puritan contemporary, Philip Stubbes, dissected the game in his *Anatomy of Abuses* (1583) and found it conducive to "fighting, brawling, contention, quarrel picking, murther, homicide, and great effusion of blood." Even James I, outspoken in defending traditional English sports from Puritans who wanted to abolish them, worried that folk-football was "meeter for mameing than making able the [players] thereof." By the time that James expressed his concern, a passion for football was no longer confined to the peasantry. Although Oxford and Cambridge had both forbidden the game, Sir Thomas Overbury lamented that the typical student, contemptuous of scholarship, prided himself on "the excellency of his Colledge (though but for a match at football)."[46]

In time, football became tamer and slightly more "civilized" (in the sense that internal restraint reduced the level of interpersonal violence). Players separated themselves from mere spectators. When the youths of twelfth-century London took to the surrounding fields to play ball, their elders were content to observe and to indulge in nostalgia. In the words of William fitzStephen, the city's fathers came "on horseback to watch the contests of the younger generation, and in their turn recover their lost youth." Rural football was considerably less urbane. As late as the eighteenth century, folk-football brought "disorder, fighting, bloodshed, broken limbs, and the occasional death."[47]

The "civilizing process" was more evident in Renaissance Italy, where fashionable young aristocrats transformed the rough-and-tumble sport of folk-football into the highly formalized game of *calcio,* described in 1580 by Giovanni de' Bardi in his *Discorso sopra il Gioco del Calcio Fiorentino* (Discourse on the Game of Florentine Football). Early commentators were as quick as modern journalists to liken *calcio* to a *battaglia,* but sixteenth-century *calcio* was actually a highly regulated contest played by disciplined teams of twenty-seven men on a rectangular field exactly twice as long as it was wide. The ball was kicked and batted but not thrown. The game was normally preceded by a grand procession. A contemporary print showing the commencement of a game of football in the Piazza di Sante Croce in Florence depicts the church and the square, the surrounding buildings, the stands (divided into a pavilion for honored guests and "bleachers" for the less favored), the playing field (marked by a low fence), and a series of pikeman to prevent disorder in the event that internal restraint proved insufficient. The contestants, wrote de' Bardi, should be "gentlemen from eighteen years of age to forty-five, beautiful and vigorous, of gallant bearing and of good report." The physical beauty of the players disturbed the clergy. They thought it sinful that handsome young men skipped the Sunday sermon in order to preen, cavort, and revel in "maidenly attention."[48]

De' Bardi urged also that every gentleman player wear "goodly raiment and seemly, well fitting and handsome." In contemporary accounts of *calcio,* descriptions of the players' clothes were "more detailed than the account of the game." It is easy to imagine that the players of *calcio* were also readers of Baldesar Castiglione's manual of courtly behavior, *Il Cortigiano* (1528). A much-mocked adage might actually have been valid for these young men: It was not whether they won or lost but how they played the game. There has rarely been as much emphasis on decorum and good form in the practice of sports.[49]

The emphasis upon the aesthetic aspect of the game is precisely what one expects of Renaissance sports, but there were also political ramifications. The French artist Jacques Callot dedicated his illustrations of *calcio* to Lorenzo de' Medici. In poetry and in the visual arts, the *calcio* ball was associated with the sun and with the six golden balls of the Medici coat of arms. The game was frequently staged as a choreographed symbolic statement of that family's political power. When power was secured by marital alliance, a game of *calcio* was just what the family ordered. There were, for instance, two games of *calcio* played in the summer of 1558 to celebrate the marriage of Lucrezia de' Medici and Alfonso II d'Este.[50]

While aristocratic youths in silken uniforms entertained the patricians of Florence with exhibitions of their skill at *calcio,* there were rougher *cittadini* who preferred traditional folk pastimes. In Perugia, for instance, it was customary for a thousand or more men and women to join in the annual stone fight. In these battles "fatal accidents were extremely numerous," which motivated the skittish authorities to moderate the mayhem, in 1273, by threatening that those who killed their opponents would henceforth be tried for murder.[51]

Nearly as violent were the *battagliole sui ponti* (little battles on the bridges) that provided pugnacious Venetians with an opportunity to pummel one another. There were individual and collective versions of the sport, both of which took place on the bridges linking rival neighborhoods. The individual version—the *mostra*—began with a challenge and ended when one of the fighters drew first blood or tumbled his opponent into the canal. Posters and poems celebrated the winners and ridiculed the losers. Rivalry among neighborhoods was so intense that there was a tendency for the individual *mostra* to turn into a collective *frotta,* in which throngs of men battled for control of the bridge. Winners of a *frotta* were allowed three nights of celebratory bonfires, fireworks, banquets, and dances.[52]

During a *frotta,* passions ran high, injuries were inevitable, and deaths were common. After witnessing the "little battle on the bridges" in 1574, Henri III of France wittily remarked that the event was "too small to be a real war and too cruel to be a game." If Henri's remark was meant to imply that the French at play were more civilized than the Italians, he was mistaken. Writing about the young unmarried men of sixteenth-century Artois, Robert Muchembled commented, "Whether individual or collective, play in all its forms . . . was a prelude to violence and murder."[53] The level of expressive and instrumental violence varied from country to country and from class to class, but the ludic house of cards was always in danger of collapse.

"MADE IN ENGLAND"
THE INVENTION OF MODERN SPORTS

_____ **A Paradigm Shift**

At the risk of radical simplification, one can say that the cultural difference between the Renaissance and modern times can be read from the changing meaning of a single word: *measure*. To the readers of Henry Peacham's popular handbook, *The Compleat Gentleman* (1622), *measure* was a noun that implied proportion, balance, decorum, and moderation. The connotations of the word were geometric. A century later, *measure* was much more likely to be used as a verb, and the connotations were definitely arithmetical. There was a similar shift in German linguistic usage, where a concern for the proper *Maß* (measure) was increasingly replaced by a mania for an accurate *Messen* (measurement). Throughout Europe, science supplanted the arts as an embodiment of the *Zeitgeist*. The semantic shift can also be observed in the ways that Europeans talked about their sports. The Renaissance vocabulary of aesthetic response gave way, although never completely, to the modern language of quantified achievement. Unlike *Maß,* which was a balance to be maintained, *Messen* was meant to be surpassed. Measurement, wrote André Obey, a French man of letters, became "the marrow of sports."[1] Traditional sports and pastimes became modern or they became marginal.

Robert Malcolmson's history of English "popular recreations" from 1700 to 1850 traces the gradual transformation or extinction of dozens of activities that once enlivened the otherwise dreary life of the rural English. Annual parish "wakes" in Protestant England were very like carnivals in Catholic countries. They offered opportunities for eating, drinking, singing, dancing—and courting. They featured wrestlers, boxers, cudgellers, and runners, but there were also wheelbarrow races, sack races, bullbaiting, badgerbaiting, cockfights. There were additional contests to discover who was best at gobbling scalding hot portions of hasty pudding, at grinning through a horse collar, or at chasing a greased pig. Like the continental carnival, English wakes had erotic overtones. The playwright Thomas Parkyns noted that wrestlers attracted "young Women, who come not thither to choose a Coward, but the Daring, Healthy, and Robust Persons fit to raise an Offspring from." The cultural contrast between a wake at the start of the century and a game of cricket at the end was not absolute, but it was pervasive and profound.[2]

This transition from traditional to modern sports took place in England much earlier than in the rest of Europe.[3] In this sense, the English can be said to have invented modern sports. And while the English were about it, the French and the Germans—obsessed perhaps with the intellectual challenges of the Age of Reason?—lost interest in sports. When Heinrich von Watzsdorf visited England in 1786, he was puzzled by the sight of grown men playing cricket, a recreation "suitable only for schoolboys."[4]

Periodization is a problem. The shift of emphasis from traditional to modern sports took place over generations, but 1660 is a convenient temporal marker for the beginnings of the transit from measure to measurement. The end of the Puritan Commonwealth and the restoration of the monarchy, in the person of Charles II, signaled a move from narrow piety to expansive hedonism. While in exile in France and Flanders, Charles had spent his time at golf, tennis, archery, and other sports. In the Restoration's rush to active and passive sports participation, Charles led the way. He was an enthusiast for court tennis, at which—according to Samuel Pepys—he "did play very well and deserved to be commended." Having developed a passion for sailing in the Dutch *jaght schip,* he had built for him no fewer than fourteen yachts. Charles also shared the enthusiasms of his subjects. *The Loyal Protestant* reported wrestling and "Cudgel-playing before His Majesty at Windsor." The same journal noted that Charles was present at "a great Match of boxing" and that he "received great satisfaction" from cockfights. Charles was also an avid patron of the horse races at Newmarket. During his reign, in search of swifter horses, the British began to import stallions from North Africa and the Arabian peninsula.[5]

Equestrian Sports

The shift of emphasis from measure to measurement was especially notable in equestrian sports. From the prehistorical moment when horses were tamed and mounted, their riders must have raced. Evidence of horse races certainly appears in the history of Sumer and other ancient civilizations. In the seventeenth century, European courts sponsored the development of a distinctly different kind of equestrian competition. "The equestrian ballet [*Reiterballett*]," wrote Henning Eichberg, "was derived from courtly dance, accompanied by music, and choreographed on the basis of fixed geometrical patterns." The handbook of this equestrian ballet was Antoine de Pluvinel's *Manège royal* (1623), in which the author urged an elegant human–equine partnership in which *l'adresse* was substituted for *la force*. This baroque form of equestrianism survives today, anachronistically, among modernity's moneyed elite in the form of a subjectively quantified aesthetic competition: the Olympic sport of dressage.[6]

The contrast between the *Reiterballett* and a horse race is hard to overstate. The former charmed a coterie of aristocrats; the latter aroused the passions of everyone from the realm's royal elite to its rabble of vagrants. (The stallion *Eclipse,* foaled in 1769, was probably the century's most famous "athlete.") More important than mere popularity was the fact that English horse races were among the first sports events to take on the characteristics of modernity. Distances were standardized. Weights were added to equalize competition by handicapping lighter riders. When wagers of a thousand pounds or more were at stake, times measured to the minute were not good enough. In the early 1730s, stopwatches were used to time the races to the second. This drive to attain precise chronological measurement occurred in an era when many Europeans still kept time as the ancient Romans had, by dividing the day into twelve diurnal and twelve nocturnal hours, which meant that the length of an hour changed from day to day.[7]

The "sport of kings" was modernized in other ways as well. Early in the 1750s, gentlemen meeting informally at Richard Tattersall's London tavern began to describe themselves as the Jockey Club. By 1758, they controlled the races at Newmarket. In 1773, James Weatherby, the Jockey Club's secretary, treasurer, solicitor, and stakeholder, began publishing his *Racing Calendar.* The calendar soon included a series of annual events that are still among the highpoints of the sporting season: the St. Leger (1776), the Oaks (1779), and the Derby at Epsom (1780). The first of these events was named for Colonel Barry St. Leger, who organized a sweepstakes for three-year-olds that made the one-against-one race more or less obsolete. In 1791, in an effort to breed stock rationally, James Weatherby, a nephew of the Jockey Club's secretary, produced the *General Stud Book.* Yesterday's thoroughbred stallions and mares were distant prototypes of tomorrow's genetically manipulated athletes.[8]

Many of the changes in equestrian sports (and in other sports as well) were driven as much by the gambler's desire to have an unambiguous outcome as by a dispassionate scientific quest for quantified precision. "If the Restoration carried a maypole in one hand," wrote Dennis Brailsford, "it also carried a purse full of stake money in the other." The desire for an unambiguous outcome led to more than the introduction of stopwatches and the colored "silks" that enabled the crowd to identify the jockeys. Professional gamblers, who have always preferred a sure thing to the whims of Lady Luck, bribed jockeys and bet on "dark horses" whose color came from the nocturnal application of a paint brush.[9]

The obsession with horses and the compulsion to bet on them was not restricted to men. Colonel Thomas Thornton of Falconer's Hall in Yorkshire had a young wife, twenty-two-years old in 1804, who raced her brother-in-law for a stake of a thousand pounds. She lost that race but won seven hundred guineas and the applause of a hundred thousand spectators when she defeated a professional jockey in a two-mile race at the York track. She was the toast of the town until it was discovered that Colonel Thornton's lovely "wife" was actually the unmarried daughter of a Norwich clockmaker.[10]

As the Jockey Club extended its control over the sport—a process that took decades—there were intermittent efforts to end corruption. As early as 1791, the club was influential enough successfully to blacklist Sam Chifney; he was the favorite rider of the Prince of Wales (who then comforted his protégé with a generous annuity). In 1844, the Jockey Club, presided over by Lord George Bentinck, published strict rules to prevent deception, but the drive to cleanse the sport was hampered by the fact that Lord George was himself a notorious cheat. The Jockey Club issued somewhat more effective rules in 1870, but it was another eighty years before horse races became comparatively honest.[11]

_____ Pedestrianism

From the late-seventeenth into the early-nineteenth century, the mania for running and walking contests—"pedestrianism"—developed along with the passion for horse races. English aristocrats employed "forerunners" who ran ahead of their coaches to clear the road of men and animals that might impede their carriages. For amusement, lordly employers wagered on their servants' swiftness and endurance. Large sums of money changed hands and large numbers of ordinary Englishmen with extraordinary limbs and lungs saw pedestrianism as an opportunity to make their fortunes. The London–York–London race was a standard test (Foster Powell did it in 1773 in six days), but James Pellor Malcolm's eighteenth-century compendium of odd events includes mention of a poulterer who walked 202 times around Upper Moorfields "to the infinite improvement of his business, and great edification of hundreds of spectators." The passion for pedestrian contests grew to the point where *The Sporting Magazine* for April 1822 reported that some fifteen thousand spectators had assembled in Newcastle to cheer fifty-six-year-old George Wilson as he successfully walked 90 miles in 24 hours. Three mutton chops enabled him to prevail despite wind, rain, sleet, and snow. The greatest pedestrian of all was Allardyce Barclay. Among his achievements were a 6-mile walk in 60 minutes (in 1796) and a 1,000-mile walk in a 1,000 hours (in 1809). "It was reckoned," reported Dennis Brailsford of the second feat, "that £100,000 had been bet on the outcome."[12]

Pedestrian races, which foreign travelers like J. B. LeBlanc and Zacharias Konrad von Uffenbach saw as typically English, were not limited to men. Busy Londoners also found time to gawk at and place bets on female walkers and runners. In 1667, Pepys watched girls race across a bowling green. In May of 1749, an eighteen-month-old girl earned her backers a considerable sum of money when she toddled the half-mile length of Pall Mall in 23 minutes, 7 minutes faster than required. In 1806, a forty-six-year-old woman defeated a twenty-six-year-old man over a two-mile course. In 1822, a seventy-eight-year-old woman covered 180 miles in 5 days. The *Stirling Journal* reported in 1829 that the Scots of Falkirk were in "complete uproar" in 1829, when a sixty-year-old woman undertook to walk 15 miles in 3 hours.[13] The presence of gamblers and the circuslike atmosphere of pedestrianism eventually doomed such races and inhibited rather than encouraged the evolution of modern track-and-field sports.

_____ Pugilism

The prize-ring was illegal, but it was nonetheless a favorite venue for demonstrations of virility. Bare-knuckle boxing flourished in eighteenth-century England. The *True Protestant Mercury* for January 12, 1681, reported a bout between a butcher and a footman in service to the Duke of Albemarle, one of many newspaper reports of pugilism. (The butcher won, "though but a little man.") A more renowned aristocratic patron was the Duke of Cumberland, a son of George II, who allegedly lost £10,000 in 1750, when an out-of-shape, forty-six-year-old Jack Broughton, England's champion, succumbed to Jack Slack.[14]

Odd as it seems to us, eighteenth-century Englishmen spoke of boxing as a *scientific* sport. They pointed to Broughton's 1743 rules for pugilism as evidence that "pugs" were not simply brawlers. Pugilists agreed that it was not really fair to hit below the waist, to seize an opponent by the hair, or to batter him after he had fallen to his knees.[15]

Parliament outlawed pugilism in 1750, but London's press continued to pay serious and sustained attention to "the manly art." When *Bell's Life in London* began its run as the world's first sports weekly, in 1822, boxers were celebrated as national heroes in Pierce Egan's lively prose. That pugilism was illegal mattered little to the "fancy" who pushed and shoved for a glimpse of the fighters nor to the titled aristocrats who patronized the sport. Moulsey Hurst, the residence of the Duke of Clarence, the future William IV, was a favored venue.[16]

Pugilism seemed distinctively British. Visitors from the continent expressed amazement that noblemen stripped to the waist and avenged insults with their fists instead of with their swords. The British, for their part, responded with scorn for the effeminate foreigners who relied on metal instead of mettle. Champion boxers were patronized by the aristocracy, lionized by the masses, and immortalized by Thomas Rowlandson and other artists. In 1810 and 1811, Tom Cribb was celebrated as a national hero when he twice defeated Tom Molineaux, an African American who had crossed the Atlantic in order to challenge him. Contrary to several accounts of the first fight, Carl Cone has persuasively argued that "eyewitness accounts . . . do not support [the] allegation that Molineaux was cheated of victory." Cribb owed his decisive victory in the second bout to his out-of-shape opponent's heavy breakfast of "a boiled fowl, an apple pie, and a tankard of beer."[17]

In his collection of "boxiana," Pierce Egan assumed that pugilists were representative figures. Of course, the English favored Cribb against Molyneaux. Of course, they backed Matthew Weeping over Jack Langan. It was, after all, "a kind of war between England and Ireland." Less prejudiced than the "fancy" and the "yokels" whom he vividly described, Egan expressed sympathy for the Jewish boxer Daniel Mendoza, "an intelligent and communicative man."[18]

Throughout the eighteenth century lower-class women flocked to ringside to see the fights at popular venues like James Figg's "Amphitheatre," which opened in 1743. Women were relatively rare *in* the ring, but Pierce Egan quoted a popular ditty that referred to Figg's establishment as a place where "cocks, and bulls, and Irish women fight." The German traveler Zacharias Conrad von Uffenbach encountered a rowdy female spectator who claimed that she herself "had fought another female in this place without stays and in nothing but a shift. They had both fought stoutly and drawn blood, which was apparently no new sight in England." The *Daily Post* for October 7, 1728, published a notice from Ann Field, an ass-driver, who challenged Elisabeth Stokes to fight for a stake of ten pounds. Stokes was more than ready: "I do assure her I will not fail meeting her for the said sum, and doubt not that the blows which I shall present her with will be more difficult for her to digest than any she ever gave her asses."[19]

────── Cricket

Of all the sports played and watched in early modern England, the most typically English—in the retrospective view—was cricket, a very old game whose origins are quite obscure. The earliest documentary evidence of the game derives from the late thirteenth century, during the reign of Edward I, when expenses for a prototype of cricket seem to have been responsible for an item in his son's wardrobe accounts for 1299–1300. The amount disbursed for *"Creag' et alios ludos"* was most probably spent for "cricket and other games." More certain is a reference from 1598, when John Derrick of Guildford, then fifty-nine years old, testified that "he and diverse of his fellowes [at school] did runne and play there at creckett and other plaies." Allusions to cricket became frequent in the seventeenth century. When Oliver Cromwell sought to extend English power over Irish Catholics, he behaved in accordance with our stereotypes of Puritanism and pleasure; the invading army's depredations included the destruction of Dublin's cricket equipment. After the demise of Cromwell and the ascetic Puritan Commonwealth he ruled, after the sports of "merry England" had made their comeback, members of the Restoration court amused themselves at "the cricket match at Dicker."[20]

Of the details of the match at Dicker we know almost as little as we do about the medieval game of "creag." Specific information about the rules of cricket dates from the eighteenth century, when, for instance, the dimensions of the bat and the pitch were determined, and niceties such as the leg-before-wicket prohibition were mentioned. The first complete set of rules appeared in 1744, which was also the year that the size of the pitch was fixed and the first year from which we have records of a fully scored match. Cricket's first recorded gate money, collected at the Artillery Ground in Finsbury, also dates from 1744. This innovation reduced the number of impecunious troublemakers, but it did not eliminate disorderly behavior on the part of players and spectators. It was not until 1787 that the rules of cricket specifically forbade interference with a fielder attempting a catch.[21]

From southeastern England, from Surrey, Kent, and Sussex, the game spread to the north and west. By midcentury, the game was played on great estates, where the squire bowled and his tenants batted, and on village greens, where parsons bowled to local farmers. "The cricket pitch, nestling among mature trees with the Norman church and half-timbered pub nearby," writes John Bale, "is, to many, the quintessence of rural England." By the middle of the eighteenth century, cricket had become a standard trope in English literature. It seemed natural that a lovesick lord—John Frederick Sackville, third Duke of Dorset—turned to cricket to express his sorrow: "What is human life but a game of cricket?—beauty the bat and man the ball."[22]

Rationalization intruded upon the pastoral scene in 1785, when the *Daily Universal Register* reported that the White Conduit Fields at Islington were now enclosed (to prevent disruptions of play). At about this time, players began to specialize and to maximize their skills as batsman or bowler. Behind its protective fence, the White Conduit Club evolved into the Marylebone Cricket Club (1787), which became the game's most hallowed, most authoritative institution. The MCC's games were played at private grounds provided by Thomas Lord, first in Dorset Fields, then in Regent's Park, and—finally, from 1814—in St. John's Wood.[23]

Although the titled aristocrats who controlled the MCC were status-conscious enough to distinguish "gentlemen" cricketers from mere "players," they were egalitarian enough to allow the latter to join the former on (but not off) the field. Less discriminatory than the Victorian "amateur rule," the gentleman–player distinction lasted until 1963.[24]

Early in the nineteenth century, John Nyren, cricket's first great player–chronicler, reported crowds of twenty thousand spectators. Of Hampshire's legendary Hambledon team, he wrote, "Half the county would be present, and all their hearts with us." Cricket was popular among rural Englishmen of every social class. The game was played not only on village greens and urban grounds but also at the "public schools" to which the nobility and the *haute bourgeoisie* sent their sons.[25] Timothy Chandler has shown that the game became "a regular part of the life of Etonians, Wykehamists, and Westministers." In 1805, Lord Byron, then a student at Harrow, played in the first recorded match against Eton. In 1820, Charles Wordsworth, then an undergraduate at Harrow, lamented that the school had used a professional coach for that year's game against Eton. Seven years later, he arranged for the first Oxford–Cambridge match (in which no professionals participated).[26]

Before the end of the eighteenth century, a number of women's teams were formed. On Godsden Common, near Guilford in Surrey, on July 26, 1745, eleven maids of Bramley met a team from Hambleton. The *Reading Mercury* reported the details: "The Bramley maids had blue ribbons and the [Hambleton] maids red ribbons on their heads. The Bramley girls got 119 notches and the Hambleton girls 127 . . . . The girls bowled, batted, ran and catched as well as most men could do in that game." Only two years earlier, the *London*

General Advertiser for July 14 referred to a tournament at the Artillery Ground, Finsbury, to which women's teams from several Sussex villages were invited. In the decades that followed, *The Times* and *The Sporting Magazine* reported numerous cricket matches between the women of neighboring villages or between the married women and the maidens of a single country town.[27]

CRICKET FOLLOWS THE FLAG

In the eighteenth and nineteenth centuries, the British expelled the French from Canada and from India, replaced the Dutch who had begun to colonize Australia, and extended their rule over much of the African continent. Cricket followed the flag. Early in the twentieth century, P. F. "Plum" Warner, president of the Marylebone Cricket Club, affirmed that cricket was more than a game: "It is an institution, a passion, one might say a religion. It has got into the blood of the nation, and wherever British men and women are gathered together there will the stumps be pitched."[1] Warner was right. From the remnants of wickets and bats, future archeologists of material culture will be able to reconstruct the boundaries of the British Empire. They will, however, have to rely on historians to chart the rise and fall of cricket as a badge of nationhood.

_____ Canada

"The game of the English landed aristocracy," wrote Alan Metcalfe, was "transmitted to the 'colonial' elite."[2] British soldiers had played the game in the eighteenth century and continued to take wickets and score runs throughout the nineteenth. In 1829, British soldiers stationed in Montréal, the heart of French Canada, joined the city's ethnically British civilian upper class to form the Montreal Cricket Club. It may well be that consciousness of their minority status intensified the anglophones' desire to flaunt their ethnic identity with an unmistakably English game.[3]

The Montreal Amateur Athletic Association (1881), which brought together several single-sport clubs founded in the 1840s and 1850s, was for decades truly the "powerhouse of Canadian sport" that Don Morrow called it, but cricket's most secure Canadian foothold was in Toronto and the other culturally British cities of Ontario. Toronto played the town of Guelph in 1834, and the *Toronto Patriot* for July 13, 1836, proudly proclaimed that the Canadian cricketer "detests democracy and is staunch in his allegiance to his King." Edward Thring, the games-mad headmaster of England's Uppingham School, assured his equally games-mad Canadian counterpart, George Parkin, that cricket was "the greatest bond of the English-speaking race." Elite schools like Toronto's Upper Canada College made sure that the boys were—in the words of their collegiate newspaper—"taught to play what, as British subjects, we regard as our national game!" The boys must have been taught to play reasonably well; the year the college's team was formed it defeated eleven adults representing the Toronto Cricket Club (which had been founded two years earlier). In 1847, the school's team, which now included a number of alumni, vanquished an eleven composed of "gentlemen" from the entire Province of Upper Canada.[4]

Québec's francophone majority eyed cricket—and most other sports—with suspicion. The game's ethnic associations were not the only problem. As late as 1934, Roman Catholic prelates like Cardinal Rodrigue Villeneuve condemned sports as a "pagan" cult of the body, dedicated to "sensual pleasure . . . and the development of the human animal." In the parochial schools of Québec and Montréal, physical educators preached the virtues of military drill (for boys) and noncompetitive gymnastic exercises (for boys and girls). Montréal's Catholic schools did not include interscholastic sports in their extracurricular program until nearly a century after the city's Protestant schools had done so. Poverty was another obstacle. Most of the French Canadians were poor, and the poor have always been underrepresented in modern sports.[5]

Québec's resistance was not the only sign that cricket's place in Canadian culture was less than secure. As a summer pastime, cricket lost ground to lacrosse, adapted by members of the Montreal Lacrosse Club (1856) from games that the Montreal Snow Shoe Club (1843) had played against the Caughnawaga Indians. Canada's lacrosse players were not ingrates. In 1876, when they revised the constitution of their National Lacrosse Association (1867), they made a concession to their indigenous teachers: "No club in the Association shall play for a money challenge except with Indians." Lacrosse, incorporated into Canada's Dominion Day celebrations, was promoted by an appropriately nationalistic motto: "Our country and our game." Lacrosse spread so rapidly throughout Canada that the game became, for a brief time, the nation's most popular sport. Excitement spilled across the border. John R. Flannery of Montréal's Shamrock Club organized several teams in the United States, enough of them for a National Amateur Lacrosse Association to be formed in 1879.[6]

Baseball, too, made inroads, especially among the Canadian working class. The first team, the Hamilton (Ontario) Young Canadians, appeared in 1854. Within a few years, Hamilton had seventeen baseball teams. A short-lived Canadian Association of Baseball Players was formed in 1864, and a somewhat more robust Toronto-based Canadian Base Ball Association was formed twelve years later. The Montréal *Gazette* reported in 1869 that baseball was "gradually getting to be very popular amongst our young men." In the 1870s and 1880s, Canadian teams such as the London Tecumseh Redmen and the Guelph Maple Leafs joined their American counterparts as members of the International Base Ball Association. The impetus for these minor-league forerunners of the Montreal Expos (1969) and the Toronto Blue Jays (1977) came less from expansionist American dreams of "manifest destiny" than from what Don Morrow and his coauthors admit to have been "mutual consent and Canadian solicitation." Between 1900 and 1920, baseball ousted lacrosse as the country's most popular sport. It is often said that Canadian baseball appealed to every ethnic group and to every social class, but the habitus of the game was clearly working-class. Colin Howell notes that the Philadelphia Cricket Club was given red-carpet treatment by the political and social elite of Halifax on the occasion of a visit in 1874. "No such treatment was ever accorded touring baseball clubs."[7]

Canadian baseball reached an apogee of sorts in 1992 and 1993, when the Blue Jays won back-to-back World Series. Most Canadians experienced a surge of national pride, but there were some who dismissed the team as representatives of a colonial power. The Blue Jays had no Canadian players or coaches, they were owned by a Belgian brewer, and they played their home games in the SkyDome, which was owned by an American corporation. "To what extent is a community stunted," asks Bruce Kidd, "when its children play another country's national pastime?"[8]

The United States

Canadians were not the only North Americans to whack away at cricket balls. Culturally as well as materially, New England was stony ground on which to sow the seeds of cricket, but Hartford, Connecticut, had cricket matches as early as 1767. The Middle Colonies were a more likely field. Eighteenth-century New York was, in fact, quite hospitable to immigrant cricketers. There were reports of cricket in 1751, and a 1766 advertisement in James Rivington's *Gazette* announced that cricket balls were available for purchase (along with battledores, shuttlecocks, and tennis rackets).[9]

The southern colonies were an even better market for cricketing equipment. In his diary, the Virginian planter William Byrd recorded a number of matches. The entry for February 20, 1710, is noteworthy: "We played at cricket and I sprained my backside." Although unable to run, Byrd limped back to defend his wicket. When the game was over, he mounted his horse "by a chair" and rode home for dinner and a friendly game of cards. In his diary for April 30, 1741, William Stephens noted that the residents of Savannah, Georgia, had spent that Easter Monday "at cricket and divers other athletick sports." Benjamin West's group portrait, *The Cricketers* (1763), depicts five young aristocrats from Virginia and South Carolina, all five presumably proud to play a game that marked them as culturally English.[10]

The end of British rule over the thirteen colonies and the emigration of thousands of "Loyalists" to Canada greatly hampered but did not entirely halt the spread of cricket. The St. George Cricket Club was founded in Manhattan in 1838, and the frontier town of Chicago had three clubs by 1840 and thirty-two in 1866. The Newark Cricket Club was organized in 1845, and San Franciscans found time to establish a club in 1852, in the midst of the gold rush, but Pennsylvanian fields were the most receptive.[11]

Although English immigrants working in Philadelphia's textile industry played the game in the 1830s, the "take-off" came a decade later when the city's mercantile class was introduced to the game. Robert Waller, an English merchant who had helped to found Manhattan's St. George Cricket Club, moved to Philadelphia and organized the Union Club in 1843. At a postgame banquet, he offered a toast: "Cricket, a sturdy plant indigenous to England; let us prove that it can be successfully transplanted to American soil." Waller did more than swing a mean bat and lift a hopeful glass. He encouraged young William Rotch Wister to organize a cricket club for his fellow students at the University of Pennsylvania. The students hired an Englishman, William Bradshaw, to coach them. In 1854, after leaving the university, Wister organized the Philadelphia Cricket Club. That same year, he encouraged the formation of a club in nearby Germantown. Mischievous younger boys, whom the older ones excluded from play, pelted the Germantown cricketers with apples and then, more constructively, begged to have a club of their own. All went well, and the Young America Cricket Club was born in 1855.[12]

Most of the bowlers and batsmen on the greens of New York and Philadelphia were English immigrants or their descendants. Their enthusiasm peaked in 1859 when an All-England Eleven toured the United States, playing games in New York, Hoboken, Philadelphia, and Rochester. A year later, Frederick Lillywhite proclaimed, in *The English Cricketers' Trip* that "cricket in Philadelphia has every prospect of becoming [America's] national game."[13] The bright prospects dimmed. Within a decade, Americans had fallen in love with baseball.

One reason for cricket's failure to hold its ground was the game's prominent ethnic imprint. The English aura that made the game especially attractive to immigrants from East Anglia and Yorkshire and to the anglophiles of Philadelphia sullied it in Irish-American and German-American eyes. The social pretensions of the mostly upper-middle-class cricket players also detracted from the game's popularity. Newark's cricketers were blue-collar workers, but Philadelphia's clubs were dominated by merchants and professional men. In 1870, 57.3 percent of the members lived in the posh Rittenhouse Square area and 17.6 percent in Germantown and Chestnut Hill. All four of the most prestigious cricket clubs—the Philadelphia, the Germantown, the New Merion, and the Belmont—were located in Philadelphia's affluent suburbs, far from the madding (i.e., baseball-playing) crowd.[14]

_____ The British West Indies

The British, who never constituted more than a small fraction of the islands' population, brought modern sports to the Caribbean for their own amusement. The Kingston (Jamaica) Cricket Club (1863) was the creation of the colony's colonial secretary, assistant colonial secretary, and lieutenant-governor. Black Jamaicans constructed and maintained—but did not play on—the island's cricket grounds. The island's racially exclusive clubs were annoyed rather than pleased by the prospect of black batters and bowlers. Pride, however, goeth before a defeat. The pressures of competition persuaded some Jamaican clubs to recruit black players whose superior skills carried the teams to victory. On Barbados, at the "public schools" that attended to the education of the island's elite, black as well as white, British teachers were less exclusionary. Like schoolmasters elsewhere in the empire, they were dazzled by the vision of sports as character-builders. They propagated the "games ethic" and made cricket into a hallmark of the island's habitus. When the black lower classes took up the game in the twentieth century, "The codes and standards to which they aspired were those established and maintained by the culturally dominant cricketing products of the elite schools."[15]

No contest mattered more than Tests (international cricket matches) against English, Australian, and South Asian elevens. The selection committee bowed to necessity and began to name black players, such as Learie Constantine, to the representative British West Indian team. When Constantine emigrated and played league cricket for the English town of Nelson, he enjoyed "the adulation of the local white population,"[16] but, back home, racially motivated resistance to the inclusion of nonwhites lingered well beyond the middle of the twentieth century. Long after white players had become a minority on the West Indian cricket team, they insisted on reserving the captaincy for one of their own. Black men, they felt, were good chaps with a bat but not quite up to the demands of leadership.

The social tensions of the West Indian game were brilliantly analyzed in C. L. R. James's autobiography, *Beyond a Boundary* (1963). Born into Trinidad's black middle class, James claimed "Puritanism and cricket" as his twofold inheritance. By the time he passed the entrance examination and was admitted to Government College, it had been drummed into him by his parents and teachers that hard study was the ladder to higher status, but the "first temptation was cricket and I succumbed without a struggle." James had no reason to regret his youthful ardor for cricket, nor did his subsequent conversion to Marxism shake his faith in the game. Orthodox Marxists ridiculed the liberal commitment to the "rules of the game," which they saw as a fetish and a distraction from the revolutionary task of changing capitalism's inherently unfair rules. James disagreed. "I learnt [the code of fair play] as a boy, I have obeyed it as a man and now can no longer laugh at it." Visiting the United States, James was astonished and dismayed at the lack of sportsmanship he witnessed. H. Addington Bruce bragged in *Outlook* of American baseball fans whose hearts were "full of fraternity and good will," but James "heard the howls of anger and rage and denunciation . . . hurled at the players as a matter of course." James had a similar reaction when he learned how widespread bribery and fixed games were in American intercollegiate basketball: "These young people had no loyalties to school because they had no loyalties to anything."[17]

Although West Indian efforts to form a postcolonial political union foundered on the reef of insular nationalism, the former colonies were able to field a unified cricket team, one that represented racial rather than national pride. That pride was enhanced in 1960, when Frank Worrell, after much controversy, became the first black to captain a representative West Indian team. When a quarter-million Australians cheered Worrell through the streets of Melbourne, James glowed with optimism and evoked the names of Thomas Hughes and other English apostles of "muscular Christianity."[18]

Worrell's captaincy came ten years after a racially mixed West Indian team defeated the English in a Test. He was followed as West Indian captain by Garfield St. Aubrun "Gary" Sobers, hailed by Brian Stoddart as "the greatest all-round player in cricket history." It was, however, a full twenty-four years before a Jamaican mulatto, Allen Rae, became the first nonwhite chairman of the West Indian Cricket Board of Control.[19] Considering the slow pace of racial justice, younger and more militant Marxist scholars have been less charitable than James about the progress of West Indian cricket. Commenting on crowd disturbances at Georgetown's Bourfda Ground, Port-of-Spain's Queen's Park Oval, and Kingston's Sabrina Park, Orlando Patterson noted that "only in matches against the English have riots taken place." The reason was obvious. "In the West Indies a test match is not so much a game as a collective ritual." It is not, however, the ritual of racial integration celebrated by James, but rather "a social drama in which almost all the basic conflicts of the society are played out symbolically." The drama is complicated. When West Indians play India, ethnically East Indian cricket fans cheer for the visitors.[20]

Despite the successes of young players like Brian Lara, who scored a record-shattering 375 runs against England in one inning, the black lower class of Trinidad has turned from cricket to basketball, a sport once popular among islanders of Asian descent, and made it into a vehicle for class and racial pride. Largely indifferent to the disorganized and inefficient Trinidad and Tobago Basketball Federation, black players follow National Basketball Association games broadcast from the United States, adopt NBA team and player names, and mimic the moves of NBA stars. The point is less to express admiration for the United States than to mark the difference between basketball and cricket, a sport that has maintained its upper-class aura even after shedding many of its British associations. As played by the "Lakers" and "Celtics" of Trinidad and Tobago, basketball has become "an activity of [black] empowerment."[21]

_____ Australia

If ethnicity is one of the key factors in the process of ludic diffusion, then one might expect cricket to have flourished "down under," where a majority of Australians claim British ancestry. Cricket has, indeed, despite the popularity of Australian Rules football, not only flourished but also contributed importantly to a sense of national identity. Cricket, which many Americans consider to be a rather effete, upper-class, tea-and-crumpets pastime, was celebrated by Aussies as a symbol of egalitarian male vigor. Australians discarded the gentleman–player distinction that divided English cricket teams along class lines. It would, in any event, have been difficult to concoct dignified visions of strict social hierarchy when farmers and their cows shared the rustic atmosphere of the Australian cricket pitch.[22]

In attaining its place in the sun as the national game, cricket overshadowed the sports of Australia's racial and ethnic minorities. The traditional sports of the aboriginals had almost no influence on the white population.[23] Nineteenth-century German immigrants to South Australia brought with them their passion for bowling, target-shooting, and performing the distinctive form of gymnastics known as *Turnen,* but their children and grandchildren, reluctant to live in ethnic enclaves, turned to the sports of the British majority.[24]

Australian cricket history began in Sydney in 1804, seventeen years after the creation of the penal colony, when the officers and crew of the *Calcutta* indulged themselves in some landlubberly amusement. Cricket in Sydney became firmly rooted when the Australian Cricket Club was organized in 1826, but it was not until 1838 that viable clubs were planted in both Melbourne and Adelaide. Rivalry among these three cities contributed to the diffusion of the game throughout New South Wales, Victoria, and South Australia. Rivalry also led to disorder, well studied by Richard Cashman in *'Ave a Go, Yer Mug!* "Huge attendances, plebeian spectators and . . . limited crowd control techniques created law and order problems right from the start of major cricket."[25]

When Adelaide's St. Peter's College opened its doors in 1847 to the sons of the colonial gentry, it was cricket—not hunting and certainly not horse racing—that was emphasized. Interest in scholastic sports became a mania after 1854, when Cambridge-educated George Farr took the helm as headmaster. At St. Peter's as at the other colonial counterparts to Great Britain's "public schools," cricket seemed to be the ideal means for inculcating the rugged doctrines of "muscular Christianity." When the "All England Eleven" visited Adelaide in 1877, the boys at St. Peter's were given two half-holidays so all could see the game.[26]

By the end of the century, Adelaide's girls' schools—Unley Park (1855), Hardwicke (1882), St. Peter's Collegiate School for Girls (1894), Tormore House (1898)—also had cricket teams. Upper-class girls in Sydney and Melbourne were similarly instructed in bowling, batting, fielding, and sharply discriminating between what was and what was *not* cricket. At Melbourne's Methodist Ladies' College, for instance, the young women were divided, in 1891, into two teams, the "Kangaroos" and the "Possums," for intramural cricket. A Victorian Ladies' Cricket Association was founded in 1905, presided over by women's-rights activist Vida Goldstein.[27]

In the gold fields of New South Wales, adult women may have played the game as early as 1855. A better attested game was played in 1886 between the Siroccos, led by Nellie Gregory, and the Fernleas, captained by her sister Lily. Although the encounter was staged to raise money for charity, the *Sydney Mail* lamented the indecent spectacle and deprecated the possibility of a repetition. There were other matches, but female cricketers were not taken seriously. The reason, of course, was the conviction that *serious* sports are a masculine domain. Male opposition retarded but failed to halt the growth of women's cricket.[28]

If the ability unflinchingly to defend one's wicket was indeed indicative of one's virility, all the more reason to challenge the English, who were not above disparaging comments on the physical decadence of colonial populations. International matches began when English professional teams, led by H. H. Stephenson (in 1861–1862) and George Parr (in 1863–1864), toured Australia. Both visiting teams vanquished their hosts and left them with renewed determination to master the sport. The Australians received another lesson and the game another boost in 1873–74, when W. G. Grace toured Australia with a group of English cricketers. Large crowds gathered to see the man who was, then as now, the most famous cricket player of all time.[29] (About him, more later.)

The first cricket team to venture home to the British Isles was composed of thirteen aborigines. Although their departure was illegal, they left Lake Wallace in Western Victoria in the summer of 1868, evaded the colonial authorities, sailed to England, and challenged all comers. Johnny Mullagh and his teammates won fourteen games, lost fourteen, and drew nineteen. The British public was favorably impressed. Although the aborigines gave exhibitions of prowess with spears and boomerangs, the *Times* thought these exhibitions less noteworthy than the visitors' cultural attainments. Flattered by emulation, the editors opined that the aborigines "are perfectly civilised, and are quite familiar with the English language."[30]

Although the aboriginal cricketers have been forgotten by most Australians, collective memory has enshrined another antipodean team. In 1882, four years after a team led by Charles Bannerman defeated the Marylebone Cricket Club at Lord's, its home grounds, another group of Australian invaders duplicated the feat and provoked London's *Sporting Times* to add a legend to the history of sport. The newspaper printed a mock obituary:

> In Affectionate Remembrance of English Cricket
> Which died at the Oval on 29th August, 1882,
> Deeply lamented by a large circle of sorrowing
> friends and acquaintances.
> **R.I.P.**
> N.B. The body will be cremated and the ashes taken to Australia.

Ever since, the "Ashes," physically represented by a large wooden urn, have symbolized victory in a Test between England and Australia.[31]

"Beating them at their own game" became a tradition, and great players able to accomplish the feat—like Victor Trumper and Donald Bradman—

became heroic names in the history of Australian sports. As William Mandle has astutely noted, cricketing victories over the English were prized above other triumphs because they simultaneously affirmed Australia's membership in the British Empire ("we play the same game you do") and flaunted Australia's superior prowess ("we're better at it than you are").[32]

The emotional stakes involved in a Test Series were never more obvious than during the "bodyline controversy" of 1932–1933 when the team sent to Australia by the Marylebone Cricket Club was led by Douglas Robert Jardine, a fanatic competitor who allegedly instructed the players to bowl *at* the opposing batsmen rather than *to* them. Hearing that Jardine had been appointed captain, the ace bowler Rockley Wilson commented lugubriously, "Well, we shall win the Ashes—but we may lose a Dominion." Pelham Warner, the manager of the MCC's team, complained of Jardine, "When he sees a cricket field with an Australian on it, he goes mad." The tour did not go well. After several Australian batsmen had been struck by English bowlers, the Australian Cricket Board formally protested, only to receive a dismissive response from the MCC: "We . . . deplore your cable message and deprecate the opinion that there has been unsportsmanlike play." The controversy raged in the press of both countries, and the Secretary of State for South Australia personally visited with the Secretary of State for the Dominions in an effort to calm the waters. Before the series was concluded, the prime minister had been forced to intervene.[33]

Australian cricket survived the political crisis, but the game has had to struggle to keep its status as the national game. An Australian football code was created in Melbourne in 1858 by Thomas Wills, a Rugby graduate who was serving as secretary of the Melbourne Cricket Club. He devised Australian football as a way to keep cricketers fit during the winter months. The inaugural game, which Wills umpired, pitted Scotch College against Melbourne Grammar School. In 1877, a seven-club Victoria Football Association was founded. Although the rules were amended in 1869, 1872, 1872, 1874, and 1875, the level of on-the-field violence remained high. Players still threw their opponents to the ground, commented Robin Grow. They "tripped, charged, punched, kicked, 'rabbited' and jumped on them . . . . The rougher the game, the more the crowds liked it." Liked it they did. At a time when England's Cup Final drew six thousand spectators, ten thousand crowded into the Melbourne Cricket Grounds to watch Australian Rules Football. In 1897, the professional game was launched by the Victorian Football League (later renamed the Australian Football League). In the 1930s, the game drew crowds far larger than those for cricket. The 1938 final between Carlton and Collingwood was contested before 96,834 spectators. Today, Australian Rules Football is the most popular men's game in every state except New South Wales and Queensland, where the Rugby Football Union is now dominant.[34]

In the 1950s, cricket's hold on its fans was probably weaker than that of tennis. Harry Hopman, who led the Davis Cup team to fifteen victories between 1950 and 1969, produced a series of "Grand Slam" winners, including Frank Sedgman, Ken Roswall, and Lew Hoad.[35] Australian swimming and athletics also reached their international apogee in the 1950s. At the 1956 Olympics, which took place in Melbourne, gold medals went to swimmers Dawn Fraser and Lorraine Crapp and to runners Betty Cuthbert and Shirley Strickland. Interest in these sports faded when Australians lost their momentary hegemony, but it revived during Sydney's "Millennium Olympics," when Cathy Freeman and Ian Thorpe ran and swam their way to glory.[36]

His glory was undisputed; hers was not. Many aborigines had called upon her to boycott the games. That she carried both the Australian and the aboriginal flags when she took her 400-meter victory lap failed to placate her critics. Freeman was also condemned for wearing the Nike-manufactured uniform that Jennifer Hargreaves termed "a symbol of the commodification and corporate appropriation of a hugely talented sportswoman."[37]

Cricket's ground was also eroded by the growing popularity of soccer football, which, by the 1990s, was the second most popular football code in every state. Soccer is the sport of choice for immigrants from southern and eastern Europe who numbered in the hundreds before World War II and now number in the hundreds of thousands. The Australian Soccer Federation has ordered them to rename their clubs so that they are no longer ethnically marked, but new names are not enough to erase old biases. Soccer pitches remain a favorite venue for Serb-versus-Croat hostilities. The Croatian fans of Sydney United idolize the World War II Nazi collaborator Ante Pavelic, which infuriates Serbian fans.[38]

Australian baseball poses another problem for Australian cricket. Popularly believed to have been inspired by the presence of American servicemen stationed in Queensland during World War II, baseball actually arrived in the mid-nineteenth century. A decade after the discovery of gold at Sutter's Mill in California, a number of "Forty-Niners" hastened to Australia to try their luck in another gold rush. Some of them were foresighted enough to pack a few balls and bats along with their picks and shovels. Two teams of Americans, who may or may not have been miners, laid out a baseball diamond in Sydney's Moore Park in 1882. They played the first historically attested game of Australian baseball.[39]

Australians were exposed to a more professional version of the game in 1888, when Albert G. Spalding took the Chicago White Sox and the "All-Americans" on a round-the-world tour, in the course of which he planted the seeds of several baseball leagues. Britain's league did not flourish. "To lovers of rattle, boisterousness and hysterical excitement," opined the *Birmingham Daily Post,* "baseball may have attractions; but as a spectacular game it is incomparably inferior to cricket." Spalding had much better luck in Australia, where his teams performed in Sydney, Melbourne, Adelaide, and Ballarat. One member of Spalding's entourage, Harry H. Simpson, stayed behind to test this belief in baseball's potential. He organized teams in Victoria and South Australia. Play began in the spring of 1889, and there were soon a dozen or more active teams. In 1912, the Australian Baseball Council was launched, but the game remained a marginal activity until 1989, exactly a century after Spalding's tour, when an eight-team professional Australian Baseball League was formed.[40]

American involvement in the ABL was direct and indispensable. In addition to an infusion of American players (four to a team), each of the eight franchises was able to rely upon financial and administrative support from an American major-league club. Additional support came from Pepsi-Cola, which signed a three-year sponsoring deal worth $500,000. Channel Nine TV helped by purchasing the rights to the 1990–91 final series and by telecasting major-league games from North America.[41]

Channel Nine, owned by entrepreneur Kerry Packer, also played a role in cricket's survival as "a diminished thing." In 1977, when the Australian Cricket Board rejected Packer's bid for television rights, he organized and televised one-day matches under the rubric World Series Cricket. When the International Cricket Council banned Packer's players from the ICC's version of the game, he sued and won. Fifty thousand largely working-class spectators paid to see the first night game at Sydney Cricket Ground. In addition to cricket under the lights, Packer marketed his product with a white ball, colored uniforms, televised interviews with players, lively songs, colorful logos, and "honey shots" of sexually attractive female spectators. World Series Cricket lost money, but Packer persevered until 1979, when he was able to clinch a deal with the Australian Cricket Board for ten years of exclusive rights. In its Americanized format, Australian cricket seems likely to survive if not to prevail.[42]

THE INSTITUTIONALIZATION OF MODERN SPORTS IN GREAT BRITAIN

_____ Schoolboy Cricket

When Victoria was crowned, in 1837, British sports were still, for the most part, relatively informal occasional affairs sponsored by the rural gentry, the parish church, or the local publican.[1] When she was succeeded by Edward VII, in 1901, the typical sports contest was a regularly scheduled event sponsored by a sports club with membership in a national sports federation. Folk-football came once a year, to mark the winter equinox or celebrate the arrival of spring. Attendance at a Saturday afternoon game of soccer football was part of a workman's weekly routine. This transformation, this institutionalization of modern sports, was to a remarkable degree the work of the masters, the students, and the graduates of Eton and other "public schools" established to educate the sons of the British elite.

During Victoria's long reign, the notion that amateur sports—especially team sports, especially cricket—were the foundation of "character" had become an article of faith more firmly maintained than the doctrines of the Church of England. "Muscular Christianity," that unstable partnership of piety and athleticism, was actually rather slow to develop. English educators were initially reluctant to accept sports as the mainstay of their curriculum. When the boys at Westminster School discovered the pagan gratifications of cricket and crew, their teachers were horrified rather than pleased. In 1796, the headmaster of Eton flogged eleven pupils for playing cricket against Westminster in defiance of his orders. The boys were not dissuaded. Pampered sons of the aristocracy were, on the contrary, indignant when their socially inferior teachers tried to block their play. When Westminster's headmaster interfered with rowing, the lads reviled him as a "cowardly, snivelling, ungentlemanlike, treble damnable shit."[2]

A half-century later, harassed middle-class schoolmasters decided to accept and celebrate what they were unable to prevent. After all, they reasoned, sports might be prove to be a useful substitute for the poaching, drinking, and whoring that were among the preferred leisure activities of their upper-class pupils. Although Thomas Arnold, headmaster of Rugby from 1828 to 1842, has been glorified and vilified as the man who put sports at the center of elite education, G. E. L. Cotton at Marlborough and Edward Thring at Uppingham were actually the first headmasters to value skill with a cricket bat above the ability to parse verses from the *Aeneid*. In his diary for September 10, 1853, Thring wrote, "I entered on my Headmastership with very appropriate initiation of a whole holiday and a cricket match in which I . . . got 15 by some good swinging hits to the great delight of my pupils."[3]

Cotton, Thring, and their counterparts at the other "public schools" invested time and treasure in sports because of their unquestioned conviction that athletics were a nursery of manly character and Christian piety. They inculcated their convictions in generations of young Englishmen and they imprinted it upon the English landscape. Harrow had 8 acres for games in 1845 and 146 acres in 1900.[4] Other schools invested less expansively in space for games, but goalposts and boathouses often went up next to dormitories and classrooms that threatened to fall down.

Eventually, some masters had second thoughts. J. A. Mangan observes that Thring, like Cotton, "was a piper whose tunes provoked a frenzy he failed to contain." Was it right that cricket at Harrow claimed fifteen or twenty hours a week and that boys at Uppingham were beaten if they were too slow at timed runs? Critics were, however, fewer than self-satisfied proponents of the system who argued that leaders forged in the crucible of sports were just what Her Majesty needed to secure her empire. Mangan has satirized the proponents' creed as "Stoicism making bland use of Christian phraseology," but even he admits that the dogma was effective. Relating "the games ethic" to British imperialism, he comments, "Once the Empire was established, the public schools sustained it."[5] In addition to the way team games prepared young men for imperial rule, they were—as the masters fondly thought but never said aloud—an antidote to the masturbation and adolescent homosexuality that were fostered by claustrophobic, single-sex, public-school life.[6]

——— Bulls, Bears, Cocks, and Foxes

Animal sports, which had been condemned and forbidden during the Puritan Commonwealth, were revived during the Restoration, but they never regained the popularity they had enjoyed in Tudor times. After watching a bullbaiting, Samuel Pepys wrote in his diary that it was "a very rude and nasty pleasure." John Evelyn complained in *his* diary that he was "forc'd to accompanie some friends to the Bear-garden," where he witnessed bearbaiting, bullbaiting, and cockfights. It was "a famous day for all these butcherly Sports, or rather barbarous cruelties." A century later, when young James Boswell paid a visit to a cockfight, he was upset by the "uproar and noise" and by the lack of pity for the "poor cocks . . . mangled and torn in the most cruel manner."[7]

Credit for the organized campaign against animal sports goes to the Methodists and the Quakers. "How dreadful," wailed Methodism's founder John Wesley, in his journal, "are the concomitant and the consequent vices of these savage routs." Evangelical opposition to barbaric custom was the force behind the Society for the Prevention of Cruelty to Animals (founded in 1824). Middle-class religious sentiment finally prevailed in the form of prohibitive legislation. The Cruelty to Animals Act (1835) banned bullbaiting and bearbaiting, and cockfights were outlawed in 1849. To pass such laws was difficult; to enforce them was even harder. At Stamford, for instance, a local order to halt the annual bullrunning was issued in 1788, but twelve regular constables, forty-eight special constables, and a troop of dragoons failed to keep the populace from chasing bulls through the town and down to the river. The battle of wills between the authorities, who were determined to prevent the disorderly festival, and the townspeople, who refused to be deprived of it, lasted until 1840, when 670 "respectable" citizens pledged to end the custom.[8]

One by one, other animal sports were outlawed—with a major exception. Foxhunts had become fashionable in the previous century, thanks largely to the chases organized by Hugo Meynell as Master of the Quorn (from 1753 to 1800) and to the seal of social approval granted by Peter Beckford's *Thoughts on Hunting* (1781). More prestige accrued when the Dukes of Beaufort and Rutland took up the sport and the Prince of Wales switched from deer to foxes (in 1793). Between 1810 and 1854, the number of subscription packs rose from twenty-four to over one hundred.[9]

Foxhunters seemed deaf to complaints about the cruelty of their sport. Henry Alken's very popular *National Sports of Great Britain* (1825) lamented that "animal misery" had formerly been "a grand and favorite source of pleasure." He opposed bearbaiting but saw no great harm in foxhunts that began with the stirring sound of the horn and ended when the hounds tore their quarry to bloody bits. That the fox was inedible made its death an especially appropriate sign of conspicuous nonconsumption. As a class, foxhunters were influential—and they were arrogant. Richard Sutton, Master of the Quorn (1847–1856), dismissed a suggestion to relocate his hunt to avoid devastating farmers' crops: "Gentlemen, I have but one hobby; it costs me £1,000 a year—and I go where I like." When British diplomatic or military personnel were posted abroad in foxless regions, they hunted a man disguised as a fox.

The clues he dropped gave us the phrase "paper chase." As for the chase after real foxes, animal-rights advocates have not yet been able to persuade Parliament to outlaw it.[10]

——— Horse Races

Nineteenth-century horse races were an epitome of English life. "It is our fixed and firm belief," announced the novelist Anthony Trollope, "that the Turf, as it existed from 1800 to 1850, was the noblest pastime in which any nation, ancient or modern, has ever indulged." Trollope's great rival, Charles Dickens, was fascinated by the sight of "all London" en route to Epsom in "barouches, phaetons, broughams, gigs, four-wheeled chaises, four-in-hands, Hansom cabs, cabs of lesser note, chaise-carts, donkey-cars, titled vans made arborescent with green boughs and carrying no end of people." The colorful multitude conveyed to Epsom by these vehicles was painted by William Powell Frith in his panoramic *Derby Day at Epsom.* The crowd was depicted figuratively in the *Times,* which marveled at the presence of singers, dancers, boxers, thimble-riggers, performing dogs "and tender infants turning somersaults."[11]

Annual festivals of this sort overshadowed but did not eliminate odd challenges. In 1831, George Osbaldeston won a thousand guineas by riding fifty times around Newmarket's four-mile track in eight hours and twenty-four minutes. The feat required twenty-nine horses. Osbaldeston was also renowned for his flair as a flat-race and steeple-chase horseman and for his prowess as a boxer, cricket-player, oarsman, and foxhunter. His shortcomings, noted Dennis Brailsford, "included aggressiveness, arrogance, snobbery, profligacy and bad judgement, the last of which, on the turf alone, cost him at least £200,000 of his vast inherited wealth."[12]

The nationalization of the sport was accelerated in the 1840s when railroad cars replaced horse-drawn vans as vehicles for transporting thoroughbreds (and spectators) from track to track. Modern means of transportation also facilitated the movement of men and horses between England and the continent, where special trains linked Paris with the race tracks at Chantilly and Compiègne. The telegraph probably did even more than the railroad to popularize the sport. First used in 1847 to wire the results of the Derby and the St. Leger to London, the telegraph made race results instantly available and less liable to falsification by dishonest gamblers.[13]

There were also changes at the track. To control (and exploit) unruly crowds, promoters built enclosed courses and charged entry fees. Sandown

Park (1875), capitalized at £26,000, was the first. It was not simply that promoters wanted to sell tickets (although, of course, they did); it was also—as Wray Vamplew has explained—that "sports promoters . . . had a lot to lose if disorderly crowds got out of hand and destroyed valuable property." The tracks were only partially successful in their attempts to keep order. As long as "the uninhibited holiday atmosphere" included "the ready availability of sex, alcohol and gambling," a certain amount of tumult was unavoidable. The seamy side of the sport is nowhere to be seen in the art of Edgar Degas, who spent countless days at Longchamps in order to paint the horses, the riders, and the elegant *belle époque* spectators. Were French tracks more civilized or did Degas filter his impressions?[14]

Successful jockeys became wealthy celebrities who hobnobbed with the Prince of Wales and other high-born sportsmen (who did not seem to mind the racetrack's sordid reputation). Fred Archer, who won an astonishing 31 percent of his 8,004 races, earned £8,000 a year (when a workman's family might survive with £50). In the last years of the century, the diminutive American jockey James Forman "Tod" Sloan threatened to eclipse Archer's fame. In 1898 he won 55 percent of his races. Sloan's example persuaded British riders, who had ridiculed the crouched American style as "the monkey seat," to drop their prejudices and to move their center of gravity forward. Sloan, who was notoriously dishonest, was denied a license to race in 1901, but Britons who saw his disgrace as an American phenomenon were disingenuous. Bribed jockeys, drugged horses, and uncollectible debts had long been part of the game.[15]

Notoriously keen on gambling, the British were slow to adopt the *parimutuel* system that the more rational French had devised in 1868. (The technique set the odds by the total amount bet; those who backed the winners divided the money bet on the other horses minus a percentage for the track.) Although Americans switched to pari-mutuel in 1872, the system, known in Britain as the "tote" (from "totalizator"), was not introduced in Britain until 1929. A generation later, after the courts struck down a number of laws prohibiting various kinds of gambling, Parliament passed the Betting and Gaming Act (1960), which officially sanctioned ready-money betting shops. By decade's end, Britons patronized over fifteen thousand offtrack shops, where they were able to lose their money honestly. Subsequent relaxation of the law allowed the shops to provide television screens and refreshments.[16]

Purchasing social prestige rather than a chance to beat the odds, owners of thoroughbreds have always lost money. In 1980, 53 percent of the horses earned less than £100 a year and only 6 percent of them brought their owners enough to cover the immense costs of a racing stable.[17] It seems appropriate that wealthy Arabs now own many of the thoroughbreds whose blood lines can traced back to *Godolphin* and other stallions imported from the Near East.

_____ Boxing

In the second half of the century, special trains transported the "fancy" to the prize ring. Among the fans, notes Dennis Brailsford, were criminals who "picked pockets, harassed, jostled, stole tickets, and created general mayhem." Criminal or not, boxing fans were active and intrusive. In 1860, when the British champion Tom Sayers was about to be beaten by an American challenger, John C. Heenan, he was rescued from defeat by a patriotic mob that broke through the ropes, stopped the fight, and proclaimed Sayers the winner. The steamship *Vanderbilt* carried two tons of British newspapers to New York, where the *Herald* ran a seven-column report (in which Heenan was named the victor). *The Spirit of the Times* printed an extra one hundred thousand copies, and Currier & Ives distributed an unrealistic, but appropriately chauvinistic, print.[18]

Recognizing that pugilists like Sayers were shunned by respectable citizens, John Graham Chambers persuaded John Sholto Douglas, Marquis of Queensberry, to lend his name to a set of rules designed to modernize the sport and make it acceptable to gentlemen. Weight classes were introduced, an innovation that allowed a modicum of equality and a profitable increase in the number of official champions. (Today, with seventeen weight classes and four organizations claiming jurisdiction over professional boxing, boxing fans are faced with the mathematical possibility of sixty-eight reigning world champions.) Modernization also appeared in the form of timed rounds. (Rounds had previously ended with a knockdown. If the felled fighter managed to regain his feet and stagger to "scratch," a new round began.) Padded gloves, another modernizing innovation, became the norm after 1892, the year that John L. Sullivan donned them to defend and lose his heavyweight title against James Corbett.[19] That padded gloves greatly increase the danger of brain damage is a twentieth-century discovery.

_____ Rowing

Water-borne races must have begun in prehistoric times, but rowing as a modern sport is conventionally traced back to 1715, when Thomas Doggett, an Irish actor, offered a coat and a badge to the quickest of the watermen who ferried Londoners across the Thames. The excitement generated by this and other contests was so great that the sons of England's elite began to imitate the watermen. There were boat races at Eton as early as 1793, but the modern version of rowing received its strongest impetus on June 10, 1829, when Charles Wordsworth and Charles Merivale, two former Harrovians studying at Oxford and at Cambridge, organized a boat race on the Thames. Timothy Chandler's generalization about nineteenth-century English sports is unquestionably true for rowing: "Without the unifying influence of the universities, which acted as a 'relay station,' organized games could not have emerged in the schools with the same speed or to the same degree that they did in the years 1830–80." The famed Henley Regatta, which dates from 1839, was originally an Oxford–Cambridge affair. In 1845, its course was fixed at 4 miles and 374 yards—from Putney Bridge to Chiswick Bridge. During the 1840s and 1850s, boathouses were constructed on the banks of the Thames, the Tyne, and every other major river.[20]

The rationalization of the equipment occurred rapidly during the middle decades of the nineteenth century, but, as Christopher Dodd admitted, "There are rival claims to the inventions." Harry Clasper seems to deserve credit for the first workable iron outriggers (1845), which increase an oarsman's leverage. After that success, Clasper built the first keel-less boat (1847). In 1865, Robert Chambers, champion of the Tyne, is said by some historians to have used a sliding seat when he rowed against Harry Kelley, champion of the Thames. An American, J. C. Babcock, devised a more efficient sliding seat that was used by Yale in its 1870 race against Harvard. By then, the clumsy boats of the previous century had been lightened and streamlined to the point where they were useless for any purpose other than racing.[21]

Lighter boats were also easier for women to row. The *Gentlewomen's Book of Sports* (1880) told its upper-class readers that it was "essential that every English girl should learn to row." The girls whom the editors had in mind were those newly admitted to Oxford and Cambridge, girls who might have encountered the Chaucerian scholar F. J. Furnivall. "He will ask you," remembered Jessie Currie, "if you can scull. If you say 'No,' he will take you up the river to teach you. If you say 'Yes' he will take you up the river to keep you in practice." The acceptance of hardy female scullers did not mean the complete abandonment of stereotypes about gender. The Evesham Regatta had a women's coxed race, in 1909, for which the first prize was a sewing machine.[22]

The acceptance of women—up to a point—contrasted with the total exclusion of working-class men. The Isthmian Club described itself as a "Social Club, to be also a rendezvous for Gentlemen interested in rowing & other sports." Working men were not welcome. In 1879, the Henley Regatta promulgated an amateur rule that made this point in the crassest terms. Henley's definition of amateurism excluded not only anyone who rowed for money but also anyone who had ever been employed in manual labor of any sort whatsoever. *The Times* agreed that competition with "artisans, mechanics, and such like troublesome persons" amounted to the "social degradation" of amateur sports." Three years later, when the upper-middle-class oarsmen of the Metropolitan Rowing Association reconstituted their organization as the Amateur Rowing Association, they copied Henley's exclusionary rules. When it came to social class, women's rowing was as discriminatory as the men's. The 1896 winner of Oxford's "ladies' sculls" was disqualified because she was the sister of a waterman.[23]

The determination to exclude the lower classes may have been motivated, in part, by envy. Professional oarsmen attracted huge crowds and basked in their adulation. Their sport was thoroughly international. Australia's Edward Trickett defeated the English champion Joseph Henry Sadler in 1876. Trickett was dethroned four years later by Canada's hero, Ned Hanlan, who signaled his superiority by blowing kisses to and pausing to chat with the spectators congregated on the banks of the Thames. In those days, stakes were high, £2,000 or more for a single race, and morals were often distressingly low. An unknown malefactor diminished Charles Courtney's chance to defeat Hanlan by sawing Courtney's boat in two the night before the race.[24]

Professor Furnivall and a group of like-minded liberals tried to steer a middle course between fanatically exclusionary amateurism and the pervasive dishonesty that marred the professionals' contests. Establishing a National Amateur Rowing Association (1890), they accepted working-class oarsmen—but not those who received cash payment for their efforts. The leaders of the Amateur Rowing Association were not moved by the NAR to liberalize their rules. In 1930, the Australian oarsman Bobby Pearce—an Olympic champion—won the Henley Diamond Sculls only to be disqualified because he was a carpenter.[25]

For a short period, it seemed as if rowing were destined to become Europe's most popular sport. The aura of the Henley Regatta and the energetic example of British businessmen in Hanseatic seaports inspired thousands of middle-class and upper-class Germans to become oarsmen. The word spread quickly. In 1836, only six years after the English formed the Rowing Club of Hamburg, the *Hamburger Ruderclub* was founded. A regatta on the Alster followed in 1844. In the 1860s, Germans were to be seen rowing on the Rhine, the Main, the Spree, and nearly every other German river. When the rowers organized their *Deutscher Ruderverband* in 1883, they far outnumbered the soccer players. British influence accounted for Denmark's first rowing club (and first cricket match) in 1866. The Slavic bourgeoisie lagged behind, but anglophile Poles established rowing clubs in Warsaw (1882) and Krakow (1884), and enthusiasm for amateur rowing finally reached Czarist Russia in 1892, the inaugural year of the *Fédération Internationale de Sociétés d'Aviron*. Although the British amateurs had inspired the mania for rowing, the Amateur Rowing Association remained proudly aloof, not joining the *Fédération Internationale* until 1947.[26]

_____ **Athletics**

The sport that the British call "athletics" and Americans refer to as "track and field" includes throwing and jumping as well as running and walking. Professional pedestrians like Allardice Barclay were unquestionably among the metaphorical ancestors of the amateur athletes who helped to found the Mincing Lane Athletic Club in 1863, but the sport also received a powerful impetus from Scotland's Highland Games. These games, in which throwing figured prominently, experienced an important revival in 1832, when members of the Braemar Royal Highland Society began putting the stone, throwing the hammer, tossing the caber, and running races. In fact, the Highland Games provided British athletics with an attractively romantic past. "'Tossing the caber' was the image of Scottish sport that appealed to the English, who liked to think Scotsmen spent their lives eating porridge in kilts and hurling tree trunks around deserted glens."[27]

For most amateur athletes, however, the romantic past was less vivid than the precisely measured present. Pedestrianism's anecdotes of bizarre accomplishments—such as walking on stilts from London to Bristol—were less inspirational than the thought of a precisely measured record. The cinder track dates from 1837, when surveyors marked off exactly one-third of a mile at Lord's cricket grounds. Histories of athletics began to include lists of names, dates, places, times, and distances. "Firsts" were meticulously registered. On March 8, 1862, G. G. Kennedy of Trinity College, Cambridge, was the first to run the mile in 4:50. On April 3, 1868, at Beaufort House in London, J. P. Tennent was the first 100-yard sprinter to be timed at 10 seconds flat.[28]

Mincing Lane AC sponsored its first (*nota bene*) meet the following year at the Brompton grounds in West London. That same year Oxford and Cambridge inaugurated their track-and-field rivalry at Oxford's Christchurch Cricket Ground. Since English newspapers, which had lengthy reports on Derby Day and other equestrian events, were not especially interested in human runners and jumpers, *The Athlete,* which began to appear in 1867, provided the quantified results of track-and-field competition. According to Montague Shearman, the sport's contemporary chronicler, the first "modern championship meeting" occurred at the London AC's Stamford Bridge grounds on July 3, 1886. Shearman reported that the 100-yard dash was won in 10 seconds and the 440-yard race in 49.8 seconds, but he, personally, thought that the focus on quantified records "has demoralised the whole of the present generation of runners." Imagine, he suggested, how perverse a medieval tournament might have been if the champion were not "he who kept the ring against all comers, but he who knocked down with his lance twenty 'dummies' in the quickest time."[29]

In addition to the mania for records, which Shearman peevishly deplored, modernity was evident in the drive to equalize the conditions of competition. The drive was taken to an extreme in France, where the Cartesian tradition was supposedly regnant. At some French track-and-field meets, contestants were handicapped on the basis of age. Older runners were moved back from the start, one meter for every six months over the age of sixteen. Runners younger than sixteen were moved forward, one meter for every four months younger.[30] This experiment in equality now seems bizarre, but handicaps on the basis of weight are still taken for granted in horse races.

Shearman was eccentric in his abhorrence of quantification, but he was quite representative of his social class in his conviction that mechanics, artisans, and laborers lacked "sportsmanlike feeling" and a sense of fair play. When the Mincing Lane AC became the London AC, in 1866, the club's charter was quite specific about the relationship of athletics to social class. The founders wished to compete among themselves "without being compelled to mix with professional runners." When tradesmen—who were hardly ditch-diggers or factory hands—were admitted to the club in 1872, sixty indignant members resigned in protest. The Amateur Athletic Association, founded in 1880, continued the exclusionary tradition.[31]

The defenders of amateurism had other motives as well. Convinced that sports should be an avocation rather than a vocation, they condemned specialization. Looking down on American sports "from an English point of view," H. J. Whigham announced, in 1909, that it was essentially "the mark of a bourgeois mind to specialize."[32] Ironically, this comment might have come from Karl Marx—surely no hero to Whigham and his peers, nearly all of whom were the products of Britain's "public schools."

It should be said, in retrospect, that the class bias of the Amateur Athletic Association (AAA) and similar middle-class organizations was not entirely groundless. As a French Marxist noted, the ethos of amateurism and the code of fair play "were quite unable to excite the imagination of a population trapped in a world of constraint and without much prospect of escaping from it." As athletes, factory hands and miners were less able than their employers to afford the high-minded luxury of strict adherence to the rules. As spectators, they were less constrained by the code of good sportsmanship. Vociferously partisan, they were unconcerned—perhaps even pleased—that middle-class spectators were upset by what the *Birmingham Daily Mail* called their "disgusting language and shouting.[33]

In the Victorian era, social class was a higher barrier than race. African-born Arthur Wharton, who later played football for Preston North End and a number of other teams, participated in the the AAA's 1886 championships and won the 100-yard dash. He seems to have been accepted as a bona fide amateur athlete.[34]

Their reluctance to recruit working-class athletes certainly damaged British track-and-field teams when they competed internationally. By the turn of the century, British teams had lost ground to their more egalitarian American rivals. This was quite obvious at the Olympic Games celebrated in London in 1908. That many of the American stars were anglophobic Irish Americans grated on British nerves to the point that the officials—all of whom were British—acted with egregious bias. After the officials disqualified an American runner for allegedly elbowing Wyndham Halswelle, two other Americans refused to compete in the 400-meter final. Halswelle—the only contestant—won in a walkover. When the Italian marathoner Dorando Pietri collapsed a short distance from the finish line, British officials rushed forward, and Clerk of the Course J. M. Andrews dragged Pietri across the finish line. The Italian flag was hoisted, American officials protested, Pietri was disqualified, the Irish-American runner Johnny Hayes was awarded the gold, and the British press excoriated the Americans for their poor sportsmanship. Although Pierre de Coubertin thought the American attitude *déplorable,* the International Olympic Committee wisely decided that future officials should be international.[35]

In the 1920s, Finnish distance runners left the British in the dust. Paavo Nurmi, running like a metronome, outpaced the field at every distance from 1,500 meters to the marathon. In ten Olympic starts, he won seven gold and three silver medals. British track-and-field athletes were not wholly eclipsed. At the 1924 games, Harold Abrahams (100 meters) and Eric Liddell (400 meters) were victors memorable enough to inspire the sentimental film *Chariots of Fire* (1981). By the 1930s, however, British athletes trailed far behind American men (e.g., Jesse Owens) and German women (e.g., Gisela Mauermayer).[36]

There was a resurgence of athletic glory in the late 1970s and early 1980s when Sebastian Coe and Steve Ovett took turns as record-breakers over 800 and 1500 meters. These men—and women like Dorothy Hyman and Mary

Peters—were great athletes, but the archetypical English track-and-field star was Roger Bannister, the slender, self-trained Oxford medical student who ran the first sub-four-minute mile. His record of 3:59.4, set on May 6, 1954, was quickly broken, but Bannister survives as an anachronistic symbol of fair play. "No athlete," he wrote in his autobiography, "is content to take a prize accruing from a rival's misfortune."[37] Oxford, they say, is the home of lost causes.

——— Golf

The game of golf is inextricably associated with images of sand dunes, heather-lined fairways, and Scotsmen in tartan kilts. While Scots can claim most of the credit for golf's British development and global diffusion, the origins of the game can be traced back to the medieval Dutch game of *kolf,* played on Holland's frozen canals. The first Scottish reference is from 1457, when "futbawe" and golf were both forbidden. Perhaps the best way to settle the argument about origins and priority is to conclude, as Herbert Warren Wind did, that "the Scots were the first to play a game in which the player used an assortment of clubs to strike a ball into a hole dug in the earth."[38]

Scotland may have to abandon its claim to have invented the game, but it is undeniably true that the rules for golf were codified in 1744, when the Edinburgh Town Council asked to see them before agreeing to donate a silver cup to players from Leith. For its first tournament, the Royal and Ancient Golf Club of St. Andrews (1754) produced a more authoritative list of thirteen rules. In 1764, several Scottish clubs agreed that eighteen holes would be just the right number. (Leith had five holes and later seven; St. Andrews had twenty-two.)[39]

By the 1820s, Scots resident in England had introduced the game in Manchester and a number of other cities. The North Devon Golf Club was established in 1864, and there were clubs at Oxford and Cambridge by 1875. (The first intercollegiate match followed in 1878.) The Royal Liverpool Golf Club sponsored an amateur championship in 1885. A Ladies' Golf Union was formed in 1893. The social status of the players was obvious. The first three national women's titles were won by Lady Margaret Scott.[40]

Technology reshaped golf as it has reshaped all sports. Balls were originally made of wood or feather-filled leather. Gutta-percha balls arrived in 1848 and were supplanted early in the twentieth century by rubber-cored balls dimpled to steady their flight. The size of the ball was standardized in 1930. Hickory shafts were replaced by tubular steel ones in 1926 (over the objections of Scottish traditionalists). The clubs used in the 1920s are now, of course, obsolete. This rationalization of the balls and the clubs has not, however, been extended to the lengths of the fairways or to the configuration of the wooded patches, sandtraps, and ponds. Golf is notable among modern sports for its resistance to what John Bale has described as "rule-bound, ordered, enclosed and predictably segmented forms of landscape."[41] Every golf course is unique.

In twentieth-century competition with American golfers, Henry Cotton was among the rare British males to do well. Joyce Wethered had a better record in transatlantic competition. In 1929, at St. Andrews, she defeated Glenna Collett, the best American female golfer of the interwar period. Britain experienced a golfing boom in the 1970s, when public courses in new towns like Milton Keynes provided easier access for the middle classes, but the rise in the number of golfers has failed to break foreign domination of the British Open and the Ryder Cup.[42]

_____ **Tennis**

Apart from the fact that both games require the players to propel a ball across a net by means of a strung racquet, modern lawn tennis has very little in common with "royal" or "court" tennis, the quirky indoor game once popular among Renaissance noblemen. The game's terminology reveals its French ancestry. *L'œuf* signals scorelessness as neatly as "goose egg," the English-speaker's metaphorical analogue. Credit for the invention of lawn tennis is customarily given to Major Walter Wingfield, who received a patent for his portable hour-glass-shaped court on February 23, 1874. (The rectangular court dates from 1877.) The unfortunate name Wingfield chose for his invention charmed students of Greek and mystified everyone else, but common sense prevailed and "Sphairistike" quickly became lawn tennis. The game may have set a record with the rapidity of its diffusion. The game reached the United States and Canada before Wingfield's patent was ten months old. A year later it was played in India. In 1876, there was a remarkable sign of the game's acceptance among weekenders at English country houses: Oscar Wilde, the mauve decade's symbol of flaccid aestheticism, tried his hand at it. Students at the women's colleges at Oxford and Cambridge began intercollegiate doubles competition in 1878.[43]

The following year, the All-England Croquet Club, located in Wimbledon, staged its first tennis tournament (men only). Spencer Gore won. He later predicted, rather ungraciously, that tennis was not likely to occupy a place "among our great games." Tennis had a more positive representative in William Renshaw, the Wimbledon winner from 1881 to 1886. In 1884, nineteen-year-old Maud Watson, serving overhead, defeated her twenty-six-year-old sister Lillian to become the first women's champion. She managed this while wearing a bustle and a floppy hat. Moving nimbly, wearing short skirts, teen-aged Lottie Dod won the national championship in 1887 and 1888, spent the next two years yachting, and then won three more championships. She retired from tennis at twenty-two and went on to win a golf championship (1904) and a silver medal in Olympic archery (1908). She also found time to row, ride, and captain the national field-hockey team.[44]

In 1877, Britons in Paris began to play tennis at *Le Decimal-Club.* In the 1880s, the British took the game to Bad Homburg, Deauville, and other venues frequented by the European leisure class. For decades, British supremacy was assumed, but, in the 1920s, the French displaced the British as the leading players. Jean Borotra, René Lacoste, and Henri Cochet dominated the men's game as Suzanne Lenglen did the women's. Lenglen, famed for exotic attire and flamboyant behavior as well as for athletic skill, was the first sportswoman to become an international celebrity. She was the Wimbledon champion in 1919 and returned in 1920 with bobbed hair and "two yards of brightly coloured silk chiffon wound tightly around her head." Her dress was designed by Jean Patou. In seven years of singles play, she lost two sets. Although Lenglen was definitely *une jolie laide,* she radiated sexuality as she pirouetted across the court and she capitalized on her temperamental charisma. "Suzanne," explained her mother, *"est coquette toujours."* Her 1926 match against the American phenomenon, Helen Wills, was hyped as allegory: the Old World versus the New. Lenglen won. The British did not have a comparable Wimbledon winner until Virginia Wade came through for the Queen in 1977.[45]

_____ **Field Hockey**

In addition to their participation in golf and tennis, which was considerable, middle-class and upper-class British women were active and enthusiastic field-hockey players. In all probability, the rules for the women's version of the game were codified in 1887 at the Molesey Ladies' Hockey Club, but the students at Oxford's Lady Margaret Hall must have played an earlier verison of field hockey because the college's administration banned the game in 1885. Oxford's other college for women, Sommerville, banned the game in 1887. In both colleges, the ban was in force until 1893. A year after play resumed at Oxford, a team from Cambridge's Newnham College was invited to Ireland by Dublin's Alexandra College, which had founded its first club in 1892. The Newnhamites lost every match but continued to be enthusiasts for the game. The women's colleges of London were also hospitable to female hockey players. King's College for Women had a club in 1895. That year, its president, Lillian Faithfull, became the first president of the Ladies' Hockey Association, formed when the women were rebuffed by the all-male Hockey Federation. The LHA retaliated, stipulating that men not be permitted to hold office. The LHA, renamed the All England Women's Hockey Association, began publishing *Hockey Field* in the fall of 1901. It was "the first periodical devoted entirely to women's sport."[46]

The LHA scheduled its practices and matches on weekdays rather than weekends, "which excluded working women; and club subscription fees and the cost of uniforms and travel to matches were an additional guarantee of class distinction." There was also an effort to exclude spectators who were neither members nor guests of the association. This was not unusual, but the LHA went a step further. To obviate exposure to what feminists now refer to as "the male gaze," most games took place "away from the prying eyes of the public."[47]

In its earliest years, LHA was decidedly middle-class, recruiting members from the elite girls' schools as well as from the women's colleges. At Roedean School, in 1897, there were ten hockey teams (and eight cricket teams) for a student population of approximately one hundred. Field hockey was also played by working-class women on pre–World War I teams organized through the sports programs sponsored by Cadburys, Rowntrees, and other industrial firms.[48]

Inevitably, there were some who thought the game entirely too rough for young ladies. "Let women play violent and confused games," wrote G. K. Chesterton, "if you think it will do them any good to be violent and confused." Other critics expressed dismay that the game created coarse hands, unsightly muscles (quadriceps and biceps femoris), a grim visage, and a disinclination to become mothers. Troglodyte opposition is fun to quote, but most opinion was actually positive. The mainstream journal *Womanhood* cheered the players on: "Vigorous, vivacious young womanhood is certainly seen at her athletic best when taking part in some keen struggle with the sticks between the goals."[49]

The women persevered, and the game went global. In distant New Zealand, high school girls enjoyed "the opportunity to get dirty [and] sweaty and to engage in rough play." In the United States, British-born Constance Applebee introduced the game at a number of elite women's colleges, including Vassar, Mount Holyoke, Smith, Radcliffe, and Bryn Mawr (where she coached until her retirement in 1928). An international federation was formed in 1927.[50]

County and Test Cricket

By the end of the nineteenth century, everyone agreed that cricket was England's summer game and that W. G. Grace, a Gloucestershire physician, was the game's greatest player. William Henry Grenfell was unquestionably a more accomplished athlete. Grenfell played cricket for Harrow. He ran and rowed for Oxford. He fenced, climbed mountains, and hunted big game. Grenfell was admired, Grace was idolized. Grace was big, burly, bearded, and prodigiously talented. He intimidated the officials, was greedy and deceitful, and went "well beyond the boundaries of sharp practice . . . to avoid defeat," but the public adored him, perhaps because he was almost childlike in the obvious pleasure that he derived from the game of cricket.[51]

In 1864, just before Grace began to play first-class matches, bowlers were allowed to throw "over-arm" rather than "round-arm," which made the ball harder to hit, but Grace, undaunted, scored thousands of runs a season. First-class county cricket began in 1873, and players were expected—even required—to play for the counties of their birth, a restriction that Kent and Yorkshire maintained until 1900. Grace was happy to be closely identified with his home county, Gloucestershire, and he was lucky to play in an era when the line between amateurism and professionalism in cricket was much less distinct than in other sports. When he toured Australia in 1873–1874, he pocketed huge sums without jeopardizing his amateur status. Between 1870 and 1910, benefit matches and reimbursements for expenses brought him approximately £120,000.[52]

Grace's fifty-eight-year career coincided with and certainly contributed to cricket's apogee as *the* archetypical English sport. The game was—in Jack Williams' apt phrase—"a metaphor for England and for Englishness." The glow lasted through the interwar period, scarcely dimmed by a steady decline in the ratio of amateurs to professionals. Professionals had been prominent ever since William Clarke organized the first touring team in 1846, but the amateurs still ran the show. In 1933, for instance, nearly two-thirds of the MCC Committee members were titled and all twenty-one of them had attended Eton, Harrow, or some other "public school." There was hysterical opposition to the thought of professional captains. Said Lord Hawke, "Pray God no professional will ever captain England!" He prayed in vain. A number of county teams hired professional captains, and Jack Hobbs, a professional, captained England in a Test against Australia at York's Old Trafford ground. One reason for the amateurs' grudging acceptance of the professionals was that the latter seldom objected to a game characterized, in Ric Sissons' words, by "paternalism, dependence, deference and strict discipline." The professionals shared the upper-class myth of cricket as the ludic embodiment of what it meant to be English.[53]

The myth included women. There seems to have been a hiatus in women's cricket during the early part of the nineteenth century, but there was a strong revival in the 1860s and 1870s, when girls' schools and the newly founded women's colleges of Oxford and Cambridge adopted the game. Indeed, the spread of cricket among the women was rapid enough for *Punch* to speculate with weak humor that it was "all over with men. They had better make up their minds to rest contented with croquet, and afternoon tea, and sewing machines, and perhaps an occasional game at drawing-room billiards." *Cricket,* a magazine whose readership probably came from the same echelons of British society as *Punch,* managed to be more supportive: "The New Woman is taking up cricket, evidently with the same energy which has characterized her in other and more important spheres of life." Aristocratic women who played the game at their country houses formed the White Heather Club in 1887. Their daughters and granddaughters founded the Women's Cricket Association in 1926 and ventured to Australia and New Zealand for matches against their antipodean relatives. By the end of the twentieth century, women's cricket had lost ground to field hockey and to netball—the British adaptation of basketball—but the game continues to be played by at least a few women wherever English is spoken.[54]

During the latter half of the twentieth century, the number of recreational players probably increased in absolute terms, but cricket's share of the nation's active and passive sports participation decreased. Between 1947 and 1981, attendance at first-class matches dropped by more than 90 percent. The remaining fans of county cricket are considerably older than the supporters of soccer football's Premier League. In 1977, only 6 percent of the population watched cricket, and more than half of this group was over forty-five years old. English cricket may also have been harmed by the reluctance of its players to support the International Cricket Council's opposition to South African apartheid. (There were many "rebel tours," and approximately a quarter of England's county cricketers spent their winters playing in South Africa.) Crowds of upper-class and upper-middle-class spectators still arrive at Lord's to support England in Test matches against Australia and other traditional rivals, but they come with the realistic expectation that their team will be badly outscored.[55]

In 1963, in an attempt to expand the number of cricket fans, the Cricket Council began actively to seek commercial sponsors. The Gillette Company was induced to bankroll one-day cricket with a grant of £6,500. In 1977, the UK's twelfth-largest insurance company, Cornhill, allotted a million pounds to save Test and county cricket, and Cadbury Schweppes added £360,000. It was a good deal for Cornhill, whose name recognition increased from 2 percent of the population to 17 percent, and it is likely that the newly insured also upped their consumption of Cadbury's chocolates. Six years later, the Test and County Cricket Board had a surplus of £3 million, but sponsorship brought in only a trickle of income compared to the torrent poured into football. Commercial sponsorship and the sale of television rights guarantee that cricket will survive, but the game's glory days as an undisputed emblem of Englishness are gone forever. Ironically, the game is now, at the recreational level, more popular among Britons of Indian and Pakistani origin than it is among the "authentic" English.[56]

_____ Soccer Football

In its modern form, soccer football began as a middle-class pastime, a nineteenth-century adaptation of folk-football (which survived, in some parts of England and Scotland, well into the twentieth century). The game was codified in one seven-hour session by fourteen students of Trinity College, Cambridge. The "Cambridge Rules" of 1848 created one football game from the many that had been played at Eton, Harrow, Rugby, Winchester, and other schools. Initially, the "old boys" had little influence on the first football club for adults, which was founded in Sheffield in 1857. Seventeen of the first fifty-seven club members were graduates of Sheffield Collegiate School, and only one had been educated at an elite "public school." At first, Sheffield FC, Sheffield Wednesday FC, and Sheffield United FC all played their home games at the Yorkshire County Cricket Ground at Bramall Lane. Cricket clubs everywhere midwifed football clubs and were then dwarfed by them.[57]

The name "soccer" (abbreviated from "Association") derives from the fact that the sport was nationally organized by the Football Association, founded on October 26, 1863, a day that scholars agree was "the most important date in the modern history of football." The London-based founders, mostly graduates of Oxford and Cambridge, thoughtfully limited the duration of the football season (September 1 to April 30) so that it did not conflict with cricket. In the short run, the Sheffield FC was much more influential than the Football Association, especially in the north of England, and Sheffield's rules were more often adopted by the Londoners than the other way around, but the FA was more or less in control of the game by the end of the 1870s.[58]

In 1867, the FA introduced the first of its many versions of the "off-sides" rule. The corner kick came in 1871, the year that goalkeepers were permitted to handle the ball. Adroit passing rather than clever dribbling was recognized as the most effective tactic, but not everyone conformed. When faulted for not passing the ball at the 1877 England–Scotland match, Alfred Lyttleton replied, like a good amateur, that goals were not his goal. "I am playing purely for my own pleasure!"[59]

Surveying British sports and pastimes in 1868, Anthony Trollope—a good novelist and a bad prophet—predicted that soccer had no future. In fact, the game spread with astonishing rapidity. Birmingham had one club in 1874, twenty in 1876, one hundred fifty-five in 1880. Liverpool had two in 1878 and over one hundred fifty in 1886. The "old boys" wanted to keep the game for themselves, but it was quickly diffused downward through the social strata. Aston Villa FC and the Bolton Wanderers, both founded in 1874, were typical of the many clubs whose first members stepped forward from the congregations of churches and chapels. Within a few years, other clubs destined to figure grandly in the annals of English sports were organized by the employees of industrial enterprises. Manchester United began as Newton Heath FC, founded in 1880 by railroad workers, and Coventry City FC had its start as a club organized by the workers at Singer's bicycle factory. In 1895, laborers at the Thames Iron Works founded a team that became West Ham United FC.[60]

By that time, the class balance in English soccer had already tipped. In 1883, a team of Lancashire workmen—Blackburn Olympic FC—defeated the Old Etonians to win the FA Cup Final. Blackburn's team included three weavers, a spinner, a cotton operator, an ironworker, a plumber, and a dental assistant. These workers were probably amateurs, but other working-class players were fully professional in that football was the focus of their lives even when it was not their main source of income.[61]

Working-class players brought different attitudes to the game. John Hargreaves lists some of them: "vociferous partisanship, a premium on victory, a suspicion of and often a disdain for, constituted authority, a lack of veneration for official rules, mutual solidarity as the basis of team-work, a preference for tangible monetary rewards for effort and a hedonistic 'vulgar' festive element."[62] To which one should add: pride in the "manly" roughness of the game.

Confronted on the field by men whose purpose in life was to play football, many middle-class amateurs decided to be good losers. The strictly amateur Corinthians "never trained and refused even to meet as a team before a game." When penalty kicks were introduced in 1891, the Corinthians refused to accept them or to defend against them, a stand on principle that hastened their demise as contenders.[63]

By the late nineteenth century, there was a solid economic basis for soccer's working-class popularity. The Factory Act (1850) and subsequent legislation shortened Saturday hours for industrial workers. Unionization and a series of strikes brought a significant rise in real wages during the second half of the century. There was, in other words, more time and more money for soccer and other forms of amusement and recreation. Wray Vamplew has documented a subtle change overlooked by other historians: As real income rose, workers were better fed and therefore more able to expend their energy in strenuous sports.[64]

Their economic situation had not, however, improved to the point where they were able to leave work and travel to matches in distant cities. Reluctantly, the FA agreed that clubs might reimburse needy players for their travel expenses, but believers in amateurism drew the line at payments for "broken time" (time lost from work). It was a lost cause. Under-the-table payment became so common and so embarrassing that the FA's middle-class directors felt themselves forced, in 1888, to accept the establishment of openly professional teams, a decision that shocked the more conservative Scottish Football Association. (When the SFA did accept professionalism, in 1893, 50 clubs immediately registered 560 men, which suggests a certain degree of pre-1893 subterfuge.)[65]

The openly professional Football League began with twelve teams, six from the North of England and six from the Midlands. At the urging of Aston Villa's William McGregor, it was agreed that there should be a fixed schedule of home and away games to replace the unpredictable sequence of challenge matches. Success came swiftly. Four years after its birth, Football League expanded into a First and a Second Division. Teams from the Midlands and the North, Britain's most industrialized areas, dominated the early years of Football League.[66]

The working-class soccer club was an important social phenomenon. Its announced *raison d'être*—to play football—was often less important than the opportunities for social interaction and identity formation. As John Lowerson observed, "The design of a club uniform or badge and membership and event cards created an iconography which then passed further into team and club photographs."[67]

The habitus of working-class fans was often offensive to the sensibilities of the middle class. "The multitude flock to the field," wrote Charles Edwardes, "in their workaday dirt, and with their workaday adjectives very loose on their tongues." It was not just the adjectives that offended men like Edwardes. Working-class spectators were seldom restrained by the canons of good sportsmanship that required one to applaud a jolly good play by the opposing team. Fans cheered for their home team and shouted insults at the visitors (a sorry lot, no doubt). Rough play on the field or a bad call by an official was occasionally followed by a barrage of rocks and bottles or by a "pitch–invasion." "Earth, small stones, rubbish of all sorts . . . began flying about our heads," wrote the victim of an attack by Aston Villa fans who were angered by their lopsided 5–1 loss to Preston North End. "Thicker and faster came the stones, showers of spittle covered us; we were struck at over the side [of our van] with sticks and umbrellas." Although disorder of this sort greatly worried proper Victorians, there was no need for a moral panic. After the inauguration of the annual FA Cup Final in 1872, football crowds swelled from a few thousand to a 1905–1914 average of nearly eighty thousand, but there were very few disturbances of any magnitude. Indeed, for all Football League games between 1894 and 1914, the average number of recorded physical assaults—for the entire league—came to 1.2 a week, hardly a sign of a descent into anarchy.[68]

If turn-of-the-century working-class fans behaved well, it may have been because they saw soccer football as *their* game. In his exploration of football and early twentieth-century English society, Nicholas Fishwick writes that the connection between soccer and the working class was so strong and the feelings for the game were so intense that "it was no exaggeration for some to describe football . . . as a 'religion.' The football grounds of England were the Labour Party at prayer." Others have used religious metaphors to describe the increasingly capacious stadia erected in early in the twentieth century. They were often dubbed "modernity's cathedrals." The epithet became even more appropriate in 1927, when the Anglican hymn "Abide with Me" was introduced into the Cup Final program.[69]

As Fred Inglis noted, the "cathedrals" constructed for turn-of-the-century soccer were as much a part of "the industrial landscape [as] pitheads, steel rolling mills, the massive walls and windows and lintels of waterfront warehouses." Twenty-five of these stadia were built by the Scottish engineer Archibald Leitch. He had a formula that called for a full-length, two-tier grandstand, with seats in back and an enclosure in front, plus three open terraces where working-class spectators stood to watch (and occasionally join) the action. Only the wealthiest teams—e.g., Glasgow's Celtics and Rangers, Manchester United, Sheffield Wednesday—had grandstands on two sides of the field. Many of these early-twentieth-century facilities, the most famous of which was Wembley Stadium, were still in use seventy-five or eighty years later.[70]

Soccer fans came to love these places and to exhibit all the signs of affection that geographers now call "topophilia." But love of place is never inexhaustible. Comfortless facilities and a series of catastrophic accidents, the worst of which occurred at Sheffield Wednesday's Hillsborough ground on April 15, 1989, when ninety-five spectators were crushed to death, led to the renovation of old stadia and the construction of new ones. The new facilities were a contribution to what Niels Nielsen has termed the "rationalization of the landscape." In this rationalized landscape, the ideal sports complex shimmering dreamlike behind the blueprints for Britain's new stadia is Toronto's Skydome. That complex, built on the site of an abandoned railroad yard at a cost of $580 million Canadian, has 4 McDonald's, a number of full-menu restaurants, a 118-seat cinema, a 348-room hotel, 5 squash courts, a fitness club, and a field that can be used for baseball, football, and rock concerts. "The Dome," quipped John Bale, "is to a British football ground what a wine bar is to a pub."[71]

If British football grounds were, until quite recently, rather shabby in comparison with the domed stadia that dot the North American landscape, the main reason is that Football League was a limited-liability enterprise with a fairly narrow economic base. Teams were financed by thousands of fans who purchased inexpensive shares in their local clubs. In the 1890s, strong clubs such as Aston Villa and Sheffield United sold £5 and £10 shares, while weaker clubs such as Croyden Common, Dartford, and Southport Central offered them for as little as 5 shillings.[72] It was relatively easy, in those days, to sell inexpensive shares because there were strong ties between soccer players and average "blokes." Soccer players not only came from the same class as miners and dock workers, they remained members of their class of origin. They lived in the same row houses and drank their ale at the same pubs.

Grateful supporters often raised additional money for improved facilities. The clubs' directors, who were for the most part unpaid local dignitaries, were also tapped for contributions to acquire a much-needed goalie or to stave off imminent bankruptcy. The directors were often patronizingly dismissive of the supporters, whose financial contributions they took for granted, but they were not cynical about the community. To move a team from one city to another in search of greater profits, which is common practice in the United States, was nearly unthinkable in the United Kingdom.[73]

The players did move, but the club decided when and where. Rule 18, enacted in 1890, read, "No bona fide player of a League club shall be allowed to join another League club without the written consent of the Secretary of the club with which he was last engaged."[74] Transfers were arranged by the clubs and money earned from the sale of players went into the clubs' coffers. The "retain-and-transfer" system effectively bound a player to his club for as long as the club felt he was useful.

Football League exploited the retain-and-transfer system in order to keep wages low. In 1900, the league imposed a maximum wage of £4 a week. For star players, there were also bonuses, under-the-table payments, and quite a few bribes from gamblers, but professional footballers were, on the whole, not paid significantly more than other skilled workers—and their careers were painfully short. (Of 250 new players signed by the FL in 1893–1894, 91 never played, 111 played for a single year, and only 11 played for longer than five years.)[75]

A players' union, originally formed in 1898, was reconstituted in 1907 and reluctantly recognized by the FA in 1909, but it was totally ineffective. Frustrated players went to court to ameliorate their lot, but the laws were biased against them. In *Kingaby vs. Aston Villa FC* (1912), the courts upheld the retain-and-transfer system even when the club intentionally set an impossibly high transfer fee to prevent a player's move.[76]

Like the owners of American sports teams, directors of British clubs claimed that the restraints on the player's economic freedom were justified in order to prevent wealthy clubs from dominating the game. It is true that the standard deviation of the teams' won–lost percentages was much greater in cricket, where players were relatively free, than in soccer, but the main effect of the retain-and-transfer system was to keep wages low (and players docile). Some economic historians—like Wray Vamplew—argue that soccer was the only major sport run by profit-maximizers. Others—like Nicholas Fishwick—maintain that the directors were utility-maximizers, who "soldiered on when, commercially, any sane capitalist would have closed the club down." The refusal to move to greener pastures, as the Brooklyn Dodgers and the New York Yankees did in 1958, suggests that the directors as well as the supporters of professional football clubs really were utility-maximizers who felt a genuine bond with their team and the community it represented.[77]

The downside of the emotional bond between the supporters and their representative team is the hostility focused on rival teams. Through the first half of the twentieth century, this hostility was kept in check. Crowd disorders actually became *less* frequent as working-class football fans internalized middle-class notions of proper decorum. In the 1960s, however, a number of young working-class male fans began to use soccer matches as occasions to indulge in "aggro" (aggression) and to act out their alienation from British society.

Ian Taylor, a sympathetic observer, argued that these "football hooligans" were proletarian victims of economic circumstance, but even he acknowledged that they were given to "fascist displays and violence." Brian Holland and other unsympathetic observers were horrified by what looked very much like a bond between the hooligans and right-wing political extremists. In the 1980s, for instance, hooligan supporters of Leeds United adopted the Nazi salute and "the terrace supporters of West Ham, Chelsea, Brentford, and Millwall [were] notorious for their pathological displays of fascist regalia."[78] Tottenham Hotspur FC, a club which has considerable support among London's Jews, was the target of anti-Semitic chants ("Spurs are on their way to Belsen, Hitler's gonna gas 'em again"). When John Barnes took the field for Liverpool in 1988, Everton fans chanted, "Niggerpool!"[79]

The permutations of racism were, however, complex. Tony Witter, who played for Millwall, recalls a moment when the Millwall fans who were shouting racist abuse at Ian Wright, assured him that *he*, Witter, was "all right." Witter concluded that "they just see a blue shirt when they look at me. But with Ian Wright they see a red shirt, then they see a black face. But do they not see my colour?"[80] In a sense, they did not. Team loyalty trumped racism, just as nationalism does for most of the United Kingdom when black Britons like Daley Thompson and Tessa Sanderson mount the Olympic victory stand.

In the 1990s, there was a drop in the level of sports-related violence and a return of *in situ* spectators to football grounds. There had been a decline in attendance from over 40 million in 1948–1949 to 16.5 million in 1985–1986, a decline attributable in part to television, in part to the perceived danger of hooligan violence. By 1998, attendance was approaching 25 million. It seems reasonable to assume that a perception of greater safety played a role in this turnabout. It is uncertain whether the decline in hooliganism can be explained by supporters' clubs calling for civility or by all-seater stadia being stripped of their antagonizing perimeter fences or by the government's taking countermeasures, such as the drastic increase in the extent and the swiftness of police intervention. Media pundits and academic analysts, nevertheless, agree that there really was less mayhem in 2000 than there had been. Whatever multifactor regression formula one devises, it is likely that most of the variance can be explained by the appearance of the all-seater stadium. It is much harder to be a real "nutter" while seated.[81]

By the year 2000, there was also full freedom of contract. For players older than twenty, the average annual salary in English football's Premier League was over £400,000. Munificence had not been obtained without a struggle. As late as the early 1960s, clubs were still able to retain players indefinitely and to demand payment for their transfer. Skilled laborers then earned roughly £800 a year; first-division soccer players earned less than a thousand. It was not until 1961 that Football League agreed to abolish the maximum wage—in order to avert a strike. The retain-and-transfer system survived legally until 1963, when it was successfully challenged by George Eastham in *Eastham vs. Newcastle United Football Club.*[82]

Million-pound annual salaries are no small item when directors must also find the money for a new all-seater stadium. One way to square the economic circle is to sell the right to telecast the game. In 1992, two years after British Satellite Broadcasting merged with Murdoch's Sky Television to form BSkyB, the new media giant proposed that Football League's top teams form a new league. The inducement was a five-year contract (1993–1997) for £304 million. The contract signed in 1996 brought the Premier League £670 million. One might have thought that largesse of this magnitude would have allowed the directors to hold ticket prices steady. Nevertheless, between 1989 and 1993, the price of a Manchester United ticket more than tripled. Inflated prices had two advantages (from the directors' perspective): They increased revenue and they reduced the influx of impecunious troublemakers.[83]

A predictable consequence of million-pound salaries and increasingly costly tickets was the estrangement of many of the game's traditional supporters. The typical hero of the 1930s was a thin, slightly hunched, bony-kneed "mate" such as Stanley Matthews, a working man from Staffordshire who starred for Stoke City and Blackpool. "He came," wrote an admiring Arthur Hopcraft, "from that England which had no reason to know that the twenties were Naughty and the thirties had Style." The typical hero of the 1960s had plenty of Style. George Best symbolized—for Richard Ford—an era that was "youth-oriented, creative, impudent, classless and undisciplined." Best was an icon to be pinned to a teenager's bedroom wall along with Mick Jagger and the Beattles. By century's end, the average English worker was in a position to envy David Beckham's skill (and his marriage to Spice Girl Victoria Adams), but Beckham was a commodified celebrity rather than a "mate," and football—popular once again with the middle classes—was no longer the fixed center of a working man's life. The apogee for *in situ* spectatorship came in 1948–1949, when 41,250,000 fans trudged to the grounds to be there, fair weather or foul. Football attendance has rebounded from its nadir in the 1980s, but most of the millions who follow "footie" today are content to follow it while sprawled on the parlor sofa, a posture that signals something less than passionate emotional involvement.[84]

Perhaps it is different in Scotland, where "football took its place alongside the Church of Scotland [and] Scottish regiments . . . as the newest, and perhaps the most emotionally charged, symbol of the Scottish nation." In addition, ethnic and religious differences intensify the excitement of matches between the Celtics, who are perceived as representatives of immigrant Irish Catholicism, and the Rangers, who are seen as the champions of Scottish Protestantism. When Celtics fans wearing Irish Republican Army scarves are greeted by Rangers fans singing "Billy Boy" or "Boyne Water," Ibrox Park might as well be located in Belfast as in Glasgow. Meanwhile, Aberdeen supporters sing "Flower of Scotland" and keep their religious commitments, if any, to themselves. Scottish soccer is obviously "more than just a game."[85]

The challenge for women's football is to convince football fans that it really *is* a game. Late in the nineteenth century, a few hardy women began to invade the pitch as players. The first official women's team seems to have been formed by the Crouch End AC in 1894. There is some question about the Crouch Enders' opponents. Were there other women's teams against whom they took the field? More sustained involvement began during World War I, when Grace Sibbert formed a women's team from among the employees of Dick, Kerr & Company, an engineering firm. After the war, the Dick, Kerr's Ladies hosted a series of four matches against a combined team formed from nine French sports clubs. The force behind the French players was Alice Milliat, of the *Fémina Sports Club* (1911), a remarkable woman who founded the *Fédération des Sociétés Féminines Sportives de France* (1917) and the *Fédération Sportive Féminine Internationale* (1921). Twenty-five English teams formed an oddly named Ladies' Football Association—did *ladies* play the game?—at Blackburn in 1921, but the FA banned use of its grounds. In neither the United Kingdom nor in France did the women's game flourish until the very end of the twentieth century.[86]

_____ Rugby

Radical feminist sociologists, male as well as female, have condemned sports as an instrument of "hegemonic masculinity," a blanket condemnation that muffles the difference between the click of a croquet mallet and the thud of two colliding *sumō* wrestlers. More discerning sociologists, sensitive to the differences among sports, have identified rugby as a "masculine preserve." The stoic acceptance of the game's inevitable abrasions, fractures, and concussions is as much a part of rugby culture as the hedonistic postgame revelry. Wherever English is spoken, rugby ranks among the macho male's favorite sports. In Victorian "public schools," it was a rite of passage from boyhood to manhood. Exported to France, New Zealand, South Africa, and Japan, rugby served as a test of virility. The United States is an exception to the rule. The typical American rugby player is now likely to be a female collegian strenuously engaged in the "deconstruction" of gendered stereotypes.[87]

The game began in 1823 at Rugby School, where William Webb Ellis was said to have carried the ball in bold disregard of the rules of football as it was then played. A credible story except for the total lack of evidence. No one knows when or why rugby football players first went their separate way. The initial set of written rules was produced by sixth-form boys in 1845 and slightly modified a year later. The rules allowed for a much rougher game than the versions of football played at the other "public schools." It was not until 1871, for instance, when Rugby Football Union (RFU) was formed, that "hacking" was prohibited (despite the protests of "old boys" convinced that kicking another player in the shins was half the fun).[88]

In terms of social class, rugby's history was similar to soccer's. As the game spread through the British Isles and beyond, it began to attract miners, dockers, and factory hands. In the 1880s, some northern clubs recruited working-class players and paid them small sums of money from the rather large sums of money the clubs received at the gate. (Bradford took in as much as £2,500 a year.) RFU's response was fanatical adherence to the amateur rule. Eric Dunning and Kenneth Sheard noted that the agument, "couched largely in sport-specific terms," was actually "based, to a considerable extent, on class hostility." In the late 1880s and early 1890s, Huddersfield, Leigh, Salford, Wigan, and a number of other clubs were punished for clandestine infractions of the amateur rule. There was bitter dissension at RFU's 1893 annual meeting when delegates from Yorkshire proposed to open the door for working-class participation by allowing reimbursement for "broken time." The proposal was voted down. Two years later, the annual meeting tightened the definition of an amateur and expelled or suspended players who had played or practiced on the pitch of a professional club. At this point, eleven clubs from Yorkshire, nine from Lancashire, and two from Cheshire withdrew from RFU and formed the Northern Rugby Football Union, which allowed compensation for wages lost when players missed time at work. RFU's reaction was to expel clubs whose members dared to play with or against a Northern RFU club.[89]

After the break from RFU, the far-from-radical Northern RFU clung to its version of the amateur rule. It was a full decade before the northerners accepted players for whom rugby was their sole employment. Minor infractions of petty rules were strictly punished. "A Hull player was banned for a month for not telling [Northern Union] that he had changed jobs." It was not until

1922 that Northern RFU changed its name to Rugby League and acknowledged that it was a fully professional organization.[90]

Why was the division between RFU and Northern RFU accompanied by such bitter strife while Football League managed to remain under the organizational umbrella of the Football Association? Why were rugby amateurs hysterically concerned about contamination by professionals while amateurs and professionals had for more than a century competed together on cricket teams? The answer offered by Eric Dunning and Kenneth Sheard is that RFU attracted socially insecure men who, unlike upper-class sportsmen, felt "seriously threatened by contact with social subordinates." If this was the case, RFU paid a high price. In the face of competition from Rugby League, membership in RFU plummeted from 481 clubs (in 1892) to 244 (in 1903).[91]

RFU experienced a different kind of loss during World War I. Fifty-three British "internationals" were killed. Of the sixty men who played for London Scottish RFC in 1913–1914, only fifteen survived the war. If the game flourished between 1919 and 1939, despite the decimation of its players, it was largely because of its adoption in British secondary schools. In the post–World War II era, RFU compromised its principles and accepted "knock-out" competition (1971–1972), but the organization remained—in the words of Dunning and Sheard—"isolated as a proponent of pure amateur principles" in a world "increasingly characterized by cups, leagues and more or less open 'shamateurism.'"[92]

While faltering in England, RFU flourished in Wales. With clubs like Cardiff FC, Wales has a proud tradition of soccer football, but manly, anglophobic nationalism is more strongly expressed through rugby. Ever since eleven clubs formed Welsh RFU in 1881, the game has been an emblem of nationhood, if not a substitute for religion. When Llanelli defeated Newport in the final game of the 1886 South Wales Challenge Cup, the *Llanelly* [sic] & *County Guardian* exulted, "Torches burned, houses were illuminated, coloured lights flared, an election victory paled before it." Matches against the New Zealand All-Blacks, inaugurated in 1905, were even more momentous than the Cup Final because of "the final, ineradicable identification of these two countries . . . with rugby football." Cardiff Arms Park, which held seventy thousand spectators, became a fortress of national sentiment and—in the words of David Smith and Gareth Williams—a "shrine of working-class communion." Welsh rugby is as ethnically marked as the poetry and choral music of the National Eisteddfod Society (which was born the year before Welsh RFU).[93]

The persistence of the Eisteddfod in an age when the world's teenagers download hip-hop from Internet sites is a reminder that traditional sports do not simply disappear from the cultural screen with the tap of a computer key. For decades after the arrival of modern sports, traditional games remained popular in isolated rural regions of the British Isles. Fifty years after the foundation of the Football Association, Northumberland miners still expressed their sense of community by means of potshare bowling. It was, said Alan Metcalfe, "the only sport played solely by miners." Traditional sports survived, but they did not prevail, not even in Northumberland. By 1914, football clubs, of which Newcastle United (1892) was the most important, "dominated the lives of males, young and old."[94]

10

THE INSTITUTIONALIZATION OF
MODERN SPORTS IN THE UNITED STATES

_____ **Puritans as Spoilsports**

Sports historians have portrayed the Puritans who colonized New England as a dour lot for whom frolic was akin to sacrilege, as ascetic ministers and magistrates who were unrelentingly hostile to the traditional sports of "merrie England." "The Puritan," wrote Thomas Babington Macaulay, "hated bearbaiting, not because it gave pain to the bear, but because it gave pleasure to the spectators."[1] Foster Rhea Dulles saw the American Puritans in a similar (rather dim) light. He admitted that the Puritans had their playful impulses and that they "failed to eradicate the early Americans' natural urge for play," but their influence on American culture was ostensibly so baleful that subsequent generations had to *learn* what animals and children know instinctively, that is, how to play.[2]

Evidence of repressive attitudes is plentiful. The Court of Assistants of Massachusetts Bay reacted severely in 1630—the year the colony was founded—when it ordered that John Baker "be whipped for shooteing att fowle on the Sabbath day." In 1647, the General Court outlawed the gentle sport of shuffleboard. Connecticut also banned "the Game called Shuffle Board, in howses of Common Interteinment, whereby much precious time is spent unfruitfully." Bowling was prohibited in 1650. Vermonters who ran, rode, jumped, or danced on Sunday were subject to ten lashes and a forty-shilling fine. At "Plimouth Plantation," Governor William Bradford was confronted in 1621 by a number of men who thought that Christmas should be a time of revelry rather than labor. (Christmas was not a Puritan holiday.) Bradford found them "in the street at play, openly; some pitching the bar, and some at stool-ball and such like sports." He stopped them in their tracks and informed them that it was contrary to his conscience "that they should play and others work." Nearly a century later, when Puritan asceticism had lost some of its rigor, Judge Samuel Sewall commented in his diary that he had ventured out that day and done the Lord's work: "Dissipated the players at Nine-Pins at Mount-Whoredom."[3]

But the picture of the Puritan as spoilsport has been too darkly painted. Puritan theologians acknowledged the need for what they termed "lawful" recreation. Cotton Mather—the prototypical Puritan minister—admitted that constant prayer exhausted the mind and the body. The Elect required moments of "Diversion." If sports did not become occasions for drinking, gambling, and whoring, if they did not interfere with keeping the Sabbath, then they "fit us for Service, by enlivening and fortifying our frail Nature." The bottom line was drawn by Richard Baxter, whom American clerics revered: "All sports are unlawful which take up any part of the Time, which we should spend in greater works." His tepid affirmation of "lawful sport or recreation" came with eighteen qualifications.[4]

By the end of the seventeenth century, folk-football, which Boston had banned in 1657, was tolerated if the players refrained from breaking one another's bones and were careful not to disturb the peace of more meditative colonists. John Dunton, an English visitor to Rowley, Massachusetts, came upon "a great game of Foot-Ball to be play'd with . . . bare feet, which I thought was very odd; but it was upon a broad Sandy Shoar, free from Stones, which made it more easy." By 1714, the *Boston Newsletter* announced the happy availability of a bowling green. A decade later, New Englanders were game for horse races. Although Boston was not ready to rival Newmarket, the *Gazette* did announce a three-mile race on Cambridge Common for a silver punch bowl worth £10.[5]

None of the contests that we commonly classify as sports was thought suitable for women. Their sports were limited to husking bees, quilting contests, and other competitions directly related to women's domestic labor. When the militia trained, men ran, wrestled, and fired at targets, and women brought the day to a happy conclusion by serving "a feast that included a special desert known as training cake."[6]

In the course of the eighteenth century, the "Protestant ethic" delineated by Max Weber merged with the "spirit of capitalism" to create a more secular, less puritanical culture. New England prospered materially and evolved culturally. Ministers such as Cotton Mather indulged themselves with powdered wigs and became members of the Royal Society for the Advancement of Science. New England was hardly sports-mad, but its sober magistrates were ready to condone "lawful" sports—so long as they did not disturb the Sabbath.

Southern Sportsmen

Sports historians have made much of the symbolic cultural opposition of New England and the South. In its most exaggerated form, the contrast takes the form of a parody in which Puritans are too fearful of damnation to indulge in a game of darts, while aristocratic planters are too absorbed in horse races and cockfights to worry about the state of their souls. The parody distorts the facts, but Virginians and Marylanders *were* more likely than other British colonists to indulge in sports. Outdoor sports *were* more various, more popular, and more socially acceptable in the South than in the North.

In a book entitled *Carolina Sports* (1859), William Elliott was lyrical about "the healthful, generous, and noble diversion of hunting." Southern hunters roamed the woods long before Elliott's time (as they will, forever, in the novels of William Faulkner), but there is, nonetheless, reason to be somewhat skeptical about Elliott as a representative Southerner. His forebears seem to have been keener about watching than about doing. "The common planters," wrote Hugh Jones in *The Present State of Virginia* (1724), "leading easy lives, don't much admire labor or any manly exercise except horse-racing, nor diversion except cock-fighting."[7] Jones was a shrewd observer. Southerners enjoyed the pursuit of game, but they were infatuated with cockfights and horse races.

John Brickell's *Natural History of North Carolina* (1737) noted that the passion for cockfights impelled the colonists to "implore Masters of Ships, and other Trading Persons" to supply birds from England and Ireland. The first known cockfight in Virginia was advertised in the *Virginia Gazette* for February 19, 1751. A generation later, Philip Vickers Fithian, tutor to the aristocratic Carter clan, observed the passion for cockfights at both ends of social spectrum. Ignoring the fact that mains had been illegal in Virginia since 1740, the Carters witnessed them, wagered upon the outcomes, and granted their slaves a holiday to attend "Cock Fights through the County." On another occasion, Fifthian wrote, "Before Breakfast, I saw a Ring of Negroes at the Stable, fighting Cocks." The Southern mania for these fights disgusted visiting New Englanders such as Elkanah Watson. He was "sickened" by the sight of plantation owners "promiscuously mingled with the vulgar and debased" as they watched wounded birds die from "the cruel gaffles [steel spikes] . . . driven into their bodies." It was, he concluded, a "barbarous sport . . . . I was much better entertained, in witnessing a voluntary fight between a wasp and a spider." Cockfights continue to be illegal and they continue to occur in the rural South as "a form of cultural defiance."[8]

Horse races, common in the South as early as the seventeenth century, were often scenes of rowdy disorder. Thomas Ashe, an English traveler, watched in horror when a backwoods race spawned a rough-and-tumble fist-fight. With alacrity, the delighted spectators transfered their bets from the horses to the humans and "shouted with joy" when one of the combatants gouged out the other's eyes. In contrast to the barbarism of backwater cock-fights and horse races in the hinterlands, tidewater equestrian sports were quite civilized. After observing the races at Williamsburg, which was Virginia's colonial capital, the British actor John Bernard wrote that he had never seen "better order and arrangement . . . at Newmarket." Similar praise came from Thomas Anburey, another traveling Englishman, who thought the track "a very excellent course" and opined somewhat condescendingly that the horses "would make no contemptible figure at Newmarket." South Carolinians boasted of Charleston's York Course (1665) and Blake Track (1760), fashionable venues for the colony's planters, merchants, and—one assumes—gamblers.[9]

Early in the nineteenth century, horse races were a popular passion in New Orleans, the only Southern city to contribute importantly to the development of modern sports. The first track was laid out in 1814 or 1815 on Wade Hampton's plantation, a short distance from town. The Metairie Course was built in 1837. The most influential horse-race promoter of the antebellum South was, however, a transplanted Northerner of Dutch ancestry. Albany-born Richard Ten Broeck, moved to New Orleans, modernized the Metairie Course, and ordered the jockeys to wear the owners' colors. Another Northerner, James O. Nixon, purchased the *New Orleans Crescent* and used that newspaper to advocate and publicize modern sports. Along with John Egerton, a New York banker, Nixon helped to found the Southern Yacht Club in 1849.[10]

The greatest excitement, the largest crowds, and the biggest bets were generated by intersectional horse races, the first of which occurred in 1823. Colonel William R. Johnson of North Carolina accepted a northern challenge and took *Sir Henry* to New York to race for a stake of $20,000. Newspapers reported that sixty thousand spectators crowded the Union Course on Long Island for a three-heat race against *Eclipse,* owned by Cornelius W. Van Ranst of New York. *Eclipse* won and Van Ranst pocketed the $20,000. The largest antebellum sports crowd—perhaps as many as one hundred thousand—assembled at the Union Course in 1843 to watch *Peytona* outrun *Fashion.* A famous Currier & Ives print celebrates the North's great victory. In the long run, however, the South's claim to superiority was vindicated. After the Civil War, the center of racing gravity shifted to the more densely populated North, but the annual derby at Churchill Downs, in Louisville, Kentucky, has been the highlight of the racing calendar since the inaugural run of 1875.[11]

With their white suits and their mint juleps, Southern aristocrats liked to imagine that an afternoon at Churchill Downs was like Derby Day at Ascot. (They did not dwell on the fact that their first and most successful jockey was Isaac Murphy, an African American.) The Kentucky Derby was and is a grand event, but the American turf was like the British in ways that the white-suited julep-drinkers preferred not to emphasize. The racing subculture was a seedy place of "fraud and deceit . . . . There was no control over what food, drink, or drugs might be given [the horses], with or without their owners' permission. They were sometimes stolen or mutilated on the eve of races."[12] Dishonest jockeys dismissed from one track found quick employment at another.

Honest or dishonest, more and more of them rode on northern tracks such as Saratoga Springs (1863), home of the American Jockey Club (1894). We have no idea how many nineteenth-century Americans opted for a day at the races, but they probably outnumbered those who preferred an afternoon of baseball or football. In our own time, *in situ* horse tracks definitely outdraw other sports venues. In 1977, for instance, eighty-two million fans spent time at American racetracks, while the combined attendance at intercollegiate and openly professional football was only forty-four million. It is likely that most of the eighty-two million were motivated by the chance to place a bet on a long shot (*Pied Lourd*) or a sure thing (*Secretariat*).[13]

_____ Boxing

For most of the nineteenth century, pugilism in the United States was an Irish-American specialty. It was part of a bachelor subculture whose prominent figures included saloonkeepers, gamblers, and prostitutes. In that milieu, pugilists represented an ethical advance. "The manly stand-up fight," affirmed *The Spirit of the Times* (August 22, 1837), "is surely far preferable to the insidious knife—the ruffianly gang system—or the cowardly and brutal practice of biting, kicking or gouging now so prevalent." Within the bachelor subculture, John C. Heenan was a hero. His apogee of glory—his epic battle against Tom Sayers—was one of the century's most memorable sporting events. Heenan died in poverty, but John Morrissey's career resembled that of John Gully, the British pugilist who became a Member of Parliament. Morrissey, whom Elliott Gorn characterized as "a distinctly working-class version of the American dream," was famed for his defeat of "Yankee Sullivan" (who was actually an Englishman named James Ambrose). Morrissey whipped Heenan in 1857 and invested his winnings in a New York gaming house and then in a Saratoga Springs racetrack. He hobnobbed with Cornelius Vander-built, brought thoroughbred racing to Saratoga Springs in 1863, and was elected to Congress in 1866.[14]

Even more famous was John L. Sullivan, the "Boston Strong Boy." Sullivan was a braggart and he may have been—in the words of the *New York Times* (September 8, 1892)—"a mean and cowardly bully," but he was also a devastating slugger. "When Sullivan struck me," moaned Paddy Ryan, "I thought that a telephone pole had been shoved against me endways." The sexual image is appropriate: Sullivan was undeniably an icon of masculinity. And he was an incarnation of Hibernian ethnicity. Irish-American eyes shone at the sight of Sullivan as he strode to the ring in shamrock-colored tights with an American flag wrapped about his waist. "Gentleman Jim" Corbett, who dethroned Sullivan in 1892, was a different kind of boxer, one who trained carefully and mastered the finer points of the "sweet science." Corbett was never idolized as Sullivan had been, but Irish Americans identified with him because he, too, had suffered from—and opposed—the slings and arrows of condescension and discrimination.[15]

Had they not been stopped by the "color bar," African-American boxers might have pushed the Irish Americans out of the ring, but neither Sullivan nor Corbett gave black boxers a chance at the title. Jack Johnson took the heavyweight title in 1908—from a Canadian fighting in Australia—and defended it successfully against Jim Jeffries, "the great white hope," in 1910. Jeffrey Sammons concedes that Johnson alienated middle-class African Americans (and infuriated white racists) with "his fondness for fast cars, fancy clothes, glib talk, and, most of all, white women," but his defiant behavior endeared him to the "black urban masses." Johnson was framed by the police and unjustly convicted of a felony. He fled to Europe, and it was another generation before Joe Louis introduced a second era of black domination. Between Johnson and Louis, the only American fighter to achieve iconic status was another heavyweight, Jack Dempsey. The lower ranks were dominated by American Jews and by Italian Americans. (In 1933, half the champion boxers were Jews, ethnic rather than national models of tough working-class masculinity.)[16]

From 1937, when Louis defeated James Braddock, to the present, there have been only five years without a black heavyweight champion. Unquestionably the most famous of these champions—perhaps the most famous American athlete of his time—was Muhammad Ali. It was his misfortune and his good luck also to have been the most controversial athlete of the era. His 1964 bout with Sonny Liston seemed like an allegory. As a young, radiantly handsome, verbally adroit ("float like a butterfly, sting like a bee") challenger,

Cassius Clay confounded the experts. He danced around the ring, outboxed the stolid, menacing, heavily favored title-holder, and stood over Liston's supine body as if he were an exultant Roman gladiator. Arriving as he did after decades of criminal control of the sport, Clay seemed to be a dark angel of good tidings. And then, as the newly crowned champion, Clay announced his conversion to Islam. He changed his name and—in 1967—refused military service ("I ain't got no quarrel with the Viet Cong"). In court, he asserted his right to a draft exemption on religious grounds, but his plea was rejected by a jury that debated the case for all of twenty minutes. Three hours later, the New York State Athletic Commission, which had issued licenses to at least ninety convicted felons, stripped him of his title. Other states followed New York's lead. In a fit of petty vindictiveness, the Nixon administration revoked Ali's passport. Journalists rash enough to defend him received death threats. Then, in the course of the next three years, the American public turned against the lost war in Vietnam, the federal courts reversed the unjust conviction (albeit on technical grounds), and Ali regained his title, which he then lost and recovered in several of the sport's most memorable fights.[17]

In retirement, Ali became a spokesman for a racially tolerant Islam. His long battle with Parkinson's disease, which he seems to have fought to a draw, has made him an even more sympathic figure. He is the embodiment of a sport that—in the words of Joyce Carol Oates—"celebrates the physicality of men even as it dramatizes the limitations, sometime tragic, more often poignant, of the physical." Ali's detractors were not all converts to magnanimity. "Ali's eyes are shiny and vacant," wrote Gary Smith, "two rain-streaked windows in an abandoned builting." Most Americans have been more positive. Paradoxically, the nation's most sordid and criminally tainted sport has produced one of the nation's most revered athletes.[18]

_____ Track-and-Field Sports

For a brief period, pedestrianism was America's most popular sport. In the spring of 1835, New Jersey sportsman John Stevens offered $1,000 for anyone able to run ten miles in less than an hour. Henry Stannard bested eight other men on Long Island's Union Race Course and finished in a jovial mood: "It is fun to run," he said, "I had rather run a race than eat my dinner." Nine years later, Stannard competed in a series of thousand-dollar races at the Beacon Race Course near Hoboken. He won the first race and was defeated by John Gildersleeve in the second. Forty thousand spectators flocked to the third race. It was won by John Barlow, an English runner, in record time (54 minutes, 21 seconds). From then until the outbreak of war in 1861, pedestrianism in the United States was dominated by another Englishman, William Jackson, who lowered the 10-mile record to 51:20.[19]

Despite a reputation for dishonesty, pedestrianism continued to be popular after the Civil War. The announced stakes, which were seldom paid in full, were as much as $100,000. Daniel O'Leary collected enough of his winnings to turn promoter and stage six-day pedestrian races in New York's Madison Square Garden. To be eligible for one of O'Leary's prizes, a runner had to cover at least 480 miles.[20]

Female pedestrians were also prominent in postwar America. In the 1870s, German-born Bertha von Hillern was among the most successful, defeating male as well as female rivals. Newspaper opinion was generally positive. The *Worcester Evening Gazette* described von Hillern as "an apostle of muscular religion" and "a true evangel to her sex."[21]

When runners began to race on designed and measured tracks rather than on dirt roads, when throwers and jumpers began to use standardized equipment rather than blacksmith's hammers and conveniently located hedges and fences, the challenge matches for high stakes and the informal contests associated with county fairs and local holidays evolved into modern track-and-field sports. Scottish Americans created an American equivalent of the Oxford–Cambridge athletics meets. The Highland Society of New York held a track-and-field meet in 1836, and Caledonian clubs were founded in Boston in 1853 and in New York four years later. When American colleges began to stage track-and-field meets, they borrowed from the Caledonian Games. Students at Williams College were pole-vaulting in 1873, fifty years before Oxford and Cambridge competed in that Scottish event. The Caledonian games were also an influence on the New York Athletic Club, founded in 1868, and on the Amateur Athletic Union that the NYAC midwived twenty years later.[22]

The NYAC was an important institution. William B. Curtis, the most influential of its founders, was editor of *The Spirit of the Times,* the nineteenth-century analogue to *Sports Illustrated.* When he quit competing in 1880, at forty-three, Curtis had already won hundreds of contests in a number of different sports. From 1860 to 1872, he was undefeated at the 100-yard dash. He was also a track-and-field modernizer. He advocated standardized distances and stopwatches that measured to the tenth rather than to the fifth of a second. In other ways, however, he resisted the inner logic of modern sports. He adamantly rejected the notion of equal access to sports. Working-class athletes were not welcomed at the NYAC (nor at the Chicago Rowing and Athletic Club that he helped to found in 1871). The NYAC remained racially segregated through its first hundred years.[23]

The most famous runner of the Victorian era competed for the NYAC's rival, the Manhattan AC. Between 1878 and 1888, Laurence Eugene "Lon" Myers set American and world records over distances from 50 yards to a mile. In 1880, he won the national championships for 100, 220, 440, and 880 yards—in a single day. A year later, he ventured abroad and lowered the English quarter-mile record to 48.6 seconds. In 1886, he traded accolades for money and turned professional.[24]

In the United States as in the United Kingdom, the word "amateur" signaled that an organization catered only to the middle and upper classes. In America as in Europe, members of the leisure class wished to compete among themselves without the unwelcome intrusion of the "lower orders." Writing in 1895, Caspar Whitney, the influential editor of *Outing,* was blunt: "The laboring class are all right in their way; let them go their way in peace, and have their athletics in whatsoever manner best suits their inclinations . . . . Let us have our own sport among the more refined elements, and allow no discordant spirits to enter into it."[25]

Within a decade of Whitney's snobbish remarks, however, a win-at-all-costs approach to sports began to topple the exclusionary barricades. The stellar athletic achievements of working-class Irish Americans shone too brightly to be overlooked when an Olympic team had to be assembled. A baseball umpire can call them as he sees them; it is difficult for a biased official to differ with a stopwatch. Collegians from relatively affluent "Anglo-Saxon" homes, were to continue for another fifty years to play a role in American track-and-field sports, but the future of men's and women's track-and-field was definitely working-class, multiethnic, and multiracial.

Irish Americans such as marathoner Johnny Hayes dominated athletics at the 1908 Olympics. Four years later, Jim Thorpe, a Fox and Sac from the Carlisle (Pennsylvania) Indian School, entered the pentathlon and the decathlon and overwhelmed his opponents. He was congratulated by King Gustav of Sweden, who called him the world's greatest athlete. To this regal praise, Thorpe politely replied, "Thanks, King." When the International Olympic Committee discovered that he had played semiprofessional summer baseball while a student at Carlisle, he was forced to return his medals. He became a symbol of victimization. What the IOC did not know, what Thorpe's defenders are reluctant to admit, is that Thorpe had long been a professional according to the rules as they were then understood. Football coach Glenn Scobie "Pop" Warner had paid him (and others) to compete for Carlisle.[26]

The star of the 1932 Olympics was Mildred "Babe" Didrikson, the Texas-born Norwegian American, whom a disparaging reporter described as a "thin, muscular girl with a body like a Texas cowpuncher." (He failed to add that she had a vocabulary to match.) Didrikson entered eight events at the Amateur Athletic Union's 1932 national championships. In three hours, she won six of them, set four world records, and scored more points than the twenty-two women of the second-place Illinois Athletic Club. At the 1932 Olympics in Los Angeles, she won gold medals in the 80-meter hurdles and the javelin and a silver medal in the high jump. (Later, as a professional golfer, she won national open championships in 1948, 1950, and 1954.) Three years later, at the Big Ten championships in Ann Arbor, Michigan, Jesse Owens, in the space of an hour, set three world records and tied a fourth. He and another African-American runner, Ralph Metcalfe, dominated the sprints at the 1936 Olympics and spoiled Adolf Hitler's afternoon. By the end of the twentieth century, African-American women (Florence Griffith-Joyner and her sister-in-law Jackie Joyner-Kersee) had joined the men (Carl Lewis, Edwin Moses) as Olympic icons. By the century's end, the amateur rule was gone (except in the hypocritical world of intercollegiate sports).[27]

By then, elite track-and-field athletes, richly rewarded for their amazing performances, had their counterparts in the lowly joggers, the fifty-year-old yuppies who did their three miles a day in return for improved cardiovascular function and a cherished sense of moral superiority. Somewhere in the middle, between the Olympians and the plodders, were the tens of thousands competing in the Boston and the New York Marathons.[28]

_____ Baseball: Origins and Organization

If Abner Doubleday is still remembered as the mythic progenitor of a game that he may never have played, the misinformation can be credited to one of baseball's greatest entrepreneurs—Albert Goodwill Spalding. As a former player, coach, manager, and owner, as a manufacturer of equipment and publisher of guidebooks, Spalding had a financial and emotional stake in baseball. In order to scotch rumors that America's "national game" derived from traditional British children's games (which, in fact, it did), Spalding, in 1905, named a six-man investigatory commission headed by his friend Abraham G. Mills. Relying on the memory of elderly Abner Graves, a man who was subsequently diagnosed as criminally insane, Mills dutifully reported in 1907 that Doubleday was the man and Cooperstown, New York, the place. The legendary event occurred, according to Mills, in 1839 when the inventive Doubleday was still a child. The gospel of a purely American genesis was announced in Spalding's *Official Baseball Guide* for 1908 and was repeated in his book, *America's National Game,* published three years later (and still in print). Baseball, proclaimed Spalding, was "a game too lively for any but Americans to play." How absurd to imagine that stolid John Bull was capable of inventing Uncle Sam's lively pastime![29]

Careful readers of *America's National Game* will, however, come upon the names of Alexander Joy Cartwright and the Knickerbocker Base Ball Club, which Cartwright helped to organize on September 23, 1845. Historians agree that the Knickerbockers played an intraclub ballgame on October 6 and that they lost an interclub match to the "New York Nine," by the embarrassing score of 23–1, on June 19, 1846. Were these the first baseball games? Perhaps not. Melvin Adelman has called attention to references in the *New York Herald* to earlier interclub games between the "New York Club" and the "Brooklyn Club." It is impossible to pinpoint the evolutionary moment when traditional bat-and-ball games became baseball, but it seems probable that the Knickerbockers' rules were, after all, different enough from earlier rules to credit them with the invention of the game.[30]

The Knickerbockers, unlike the Cooperstown urchins of cherished myth, were urbane men of the mercantile class. And they were "more expert with the knife and fork at post-game banquets than with bat and ball on the diamond." This comment by Harold Seymour may explain their sorry performance in the match against the New York Nine.[31]

No matter that baseball's founding fathers turn out to have been gourmets and that they were soon overshadowed by other teams. The Knickerbockers deserve the laurels posthumously awarded to Abner Doubleday. The rules of their "New York game" spread quickly and those of the rival "Massachusetts game" were forgotten. The New York Gothams (1850), originally dubbed the Washington Club, were followed by the Excelsiors (1854) and a number of other middle-class teams. The first viable plebeian clubs seem to have been the Eckfords of Greenpoint and the Atlantics of Jamaica, both founded in 1856. It was they—the dockworkers, teamsters, bricklayers, and carpenters, not the merchants and young professionals—who became the new sport's typical players. The game's pre-Civil War popularity among the working class can be conjectured from an 1857 song, "The Baseball Fever":

> Our merchants have to close their stores
> Their clerks away are staying,
> Contractors too, can do no work,
> Their hands are all out playing.[32]

The urban worker at play was an annoyance to his employers and fair game for vote-hunting politicians. Office-seekers began to scramble aboard the ludic bandwagon. They sponsored baseball teams whose "players were ostensibly city employees in the coroner's office or the sanitation department, but they were actually . . . subsidized to play baseball." The New York Mutuals, organized in 1857 by the volunteer firemen of the Mutual Hook and Ladder Company, were directed by Boss William Marcy Tweed, who subsequently used the team as a cog in his Tammany Hall political machine. Not every aspiring alderman had his own team, but he still could be there to cheer from the bleachers and toast the team's unparalleled accomplishments at post-game festivities. Despite its claim to be the "national game," despite its hold on an extraordinary number of poets and novelists, baseball's appeal, after its first decade, has always been to the masses rather than the classes.[33]

By 1858, baseball was popular enough for twenty-two clubs to form a National Association of Base Ball Players. Among the organization's contributions were the nine-inning format and the called strike. Contrary to what one might have expected, the Civil War, rather than hindering the diffusion of the game, actually advanced it. What better way was there to alleviate the boredom of life in a military camp? Thanks to the enforced spatial mobility of war, soldiers from the Northeast were able to teach the game not only to the men of Midwestern regiments but also to Confederate troopers with whom they fraternized in prisoner-of-war camps. Ironically, it was often immigrants born in County Kerry or in Brandenburg who explained the rules of the new "national game" to fellow citizens whose ancestors had arrived on the *Mayflower*.[34]

After the war, progressive Southerners such as Atlanta newspaperman Henry Grady promoted modern sports as a way to put the past behind them. Grady placed a charter-member team in the Southern League (1884), and other minor-league teams were formed throughout the South. There was, however, considerable ambivalence in sectors of the "Bible Belt" where evangelical Protestantism was (and still is) a strong force. In 1891, for instance, the Little Rock *Arkansas Baptist* condemned baseball as the chief evil of the day.[35]

In the post–Civil War years, baseball occasionally crossed racial lines as well as state borders. African Americans were active in teams such as Philadelphia's Pythian Base Ball Club. It was common, even in the nineteenth century, for naïve believers to seize on such facts and then to describe baseball as the most democratic of games. "The bleachers are equally cordial," wrote Frederick W. Cozens and Florence Scovil Stumpf, "to coal-miners, politicians, and bank presidents." In fact, African-American baseball remained racially segregated long after the Pythian Base Ball Club had come and gone.[36]

Openly professional baseball began in 1869, when Harry Wright's Cincinnati Red Stockings were paid $9,400 for a series of on-the-road games contested in a number of northeastern cities. The team vanquished the New York Mutuals and went on to play for a year without losing a single game. Despite success on the field, the Red Stockings' 1870 net profit of $1.39 suggested to Wright that barnstorming was not the path to great wealth. His response was to enroll the Red Stockings in the National Association of Professional Base Ball Players, which began play in 1871. There was no gate-sharing, and the rationalization of the game was not far enough advanced for the teams to agree on a fixed schedule. Although each team agreed to play every other team five times, there were no games between Troy and Chicago. The league's teams were so unequal that Boston won seventy-one games in 1875 while Brooklyn won only two. The unbalanced league lasted a mere five years.[37]

Baseball's organizational problems were finally solved in 1876, when group of canny entrepreneurs, led by William A. Hulbert, A. G. Spalding, and the ever-hopeful Harry Wright, banded together to create an eight-team National League of Professional Base Ball Clubs. Their rationalization of the game called for restricted membership, territorial monopoly, a regular schedule with a set number of games against a set number of opponents, and strict contractual control of the players. The National League served as a model of successful commercialization. Success inspired competition. The American Association, for instance, was formed in 1881 by a group of midwestern entrepreneurs—mostly German-American brewers—who enticed crowds with twenty-five-cent tickets, Sunday games, and foaming mugs of beer.[38]

It is a historical commonplace that the tempo of industrialization was quicker in the United States than it had been in England. We can trace a similar acceleration in the evolution of American sports. If one dates the "invention" of soccer football from 1848, when the Cambridge Rules were drafted, then baseball was born three years before "the people's game." Baseball's national association of amateur players preceded soccer's by six years. When overtly professional soccer began in England, with the creation of Football League in 1888, baseball's developmental lead had risen to twelve years. Baseball's more rapid march toward modernity might have been interpreted by the prescient as an omen of Great Britain's eventual displacement by the United States as the premier exporter of modern sports.

In economic terms, the National League functioned as a cartel. Competition occurred within a cooperative framework. It was in no team's long-term interest to force another team into bankruptcy and it was in every team's interest to maintain something close to competitive equality. Acting as a cartel, the league solved the problem of star players who "jumped" from team to team in search of better pay. After the 1879 season, the owners agreed to allow each team to "reserve" five players who were required to renew their annual contracts or face blacklisting by major-league baseball. (The number of "reserved" players was gradually increased to cover the whole roster.) In 1885, in response mainly to this contractual restriction, nine aggrieved New York Giants players, led by John Montgomery Ward, met in a tavern and formed the Brotherhood of Professional Ball Players.[39]

When the owners refused to negotiate in good faith with the Brotherhood, the players organized a rival league administered jointly by them and a set of wealthy "contributors." Although the National League's owners quickly raised salaries, many of their stars deserted to the Players National League of Base Ball Clubs, which quite pointedly did *not* include a reserve clause in its three-year contracts. In its inaugural season, the upstart league drew more fans than the established National League. Despite this initial success, the players were betrayed by the "contributors." "By January 16," explains David Stevens, "all but one major backer had cut deals." The rebellious players returned to their former teams—and were paid, on average, even less money than before their abortive challenge.[40]

After the 1891 season, the National League came to an agreement with the American Association, absorbed four of its teams, and used its monopolistic power to raise ticket prices and reduce players' salaries. The pattern established by the American Association's challenge to the National League was repeated dozens of times in many different sports over the course of a century. Of the one hundred and three North American team-sport franchises operating in 1991, forty began in rival leagues, many of which were established expressly in order to break into an established league.[41]

After its absorption of the American Association, the National League became increasingly profitable. Between 1901 and 1911, for instance, the Chicago White Sox earned over $700,000 for the notoriously tight-fisted owner Charles Comiskey. The Philadelphia Athletics did well enough for the Shibe family to invest $301,000 in a steel and concrete baseball stadium: 23,000-seat Shibe Park opened in 1909.[42]

Comiskey's profitable franchise was part of the American League (1900), the creation of Byron Bancroft "Ban" Johnson, who had renamed the Western League (1878) and moved several of its teams into cities where the National League had enjoyed a monopoly. The American League took in three teams dropped from the National League. After the new league outdrew the old one by a quarter of a million fans, it was reluctantly recognized, in 1903, as an equal partner. To regulate cooperation between the two leagues, a three-person National Commission was established. Each league had one representative and the two of them chose the third member.[43]

Up to this point, baseball had been in constant flux. By Harold Seymour's

calculation, "From 1876 to 1900 no fewer than twenty-one cities were represented in the National League at one time or another." The sixteen teams
party to the 1903 agreement stayed where they were for the next half-century.
Stability was not the only benefit. The 1903 pact allowed for a "World Series"
between the champions of the two leagues. Boston upset Pittsburgh in the
first postseason encounter. There was no World Series in 1904 because the
irascible New York Giants owner John McGraw, consumed by his vendetta
with "Ban" Johnson, refused to play the American League winners. Inter-
league play resumed in 1905, when McGraw deigned to play Connie Mack's
Philadelphia Athletics. The Giants took the series four games to one.[44]

The rationalization of sports journalism paralleled the rationalization of
the organizational frame. Newspapers published regular sports sections
whose main function was to glorify the exploits of the local baseball team and
to provide, in the form of box scores, the results of the previous day's games.
The box score, like the batting average, was the ingenious invention of
British-born Henry Chadwick, a sportswriter whose contributions to the
game earned him a place in the Baseball Hall of Fame.[45]

Chadwick was also determined to improve the morals of the players, a
more difficult task than his invention of the box score. As *Spalding's Guide*
lamented in 1889, "The two great obstacles in the way . . . of the majority of
professional ball players are wine and women. The saloon and the brothel are
the evils of the baseball world." Spalding might have had in mind the game's
most popular player, Michael "King" Kelly, "a free spender, a fancy dresser,
and an avid pursuer of night life." Kelly was also a womanizer and a resourceful cheater. No matter—Arthur Soden paid $10,000 to acquire him for
the Boston Braves.[46]

⸻ Baseball: Gender

Although the years that followed the Civil War were the heyday of
the "cult of domesticity," a surprisingly large number of young women acquired the ability to wield a bat and field a line drive. In Bordentown, New
Jersey, the Belle Vue and Galaxy clubs were playing baseball in 1867. Another
pair of teams—the Laurels and the Abenakis—were formed a year earlier at
Vassar College. In 1875, Vassar had three humorously named teams: the Sure-
Pops, the Daisy-Clippers, and the Royals. "The public . . . was shocked," recalled one of the players for readers of *Popular Science Monthly*, "but in our
retired grounds . . . we continued to play." That same year, at Smith College,
Minnie Stephens and her friends organized a team. When their attempt to
steal a bat from a group of Northampton boys failed, they did the proper thing

and bought one. Girls at nearby Mount Holyoke College formed their first baseball team in 1884. "The athletic, robust, healthy, competitive woman," writes Gai I. Berlage, "was the antithesis of the [era's] ideal and yet . . . sports for women—and especially baseball—were part of college life." Softball, which Chicagoan George Hancock invented in 1887, eventually replaced baseball as a recreational sport, but the young women had already proven that they were able to play hard ball.[47]

The privileged students at elite women's colleges were obviously not typical of their sex, but there were scattered indications that other women were hardy enough to play the national game. In the 1880s, an entrepreneur named Harry H. Freeman sponsored a short-lived team of female professionals, and a number of women had brief careers as semiprofessionals. The invention of softball more or less halted the growth of women's baseball, but a decade of glory commenced in 1943, when Philip Wrigley, owner of the Chicago Cubs, enlivened the wartime doldrums of major-league baseball with an All-American Girls' Baseball League. The league, which inspired the film *A League of Their Own* (1992), lasted for nearly a dozen years.[48]

_____ **Baseball: Ethnicity and Race**

"King" Kelly was worth the $10,000 that Arthur Soden paid for him because he was an Irish American. In every ethnically diverse society, the sports of the majority tend to act as agents of acculturation and—eventually—assimilation, but baseball was especially attractive to outsiders who longed to be insiders. Irish-American players were the first to cross the line. British-American players like Chicago's Adrian C. "Cap" Anson had their ardent admirers, but "Hibernian" players seemed to have a special place in the vernacular imagination. Songs like "Slide, Kelly, Slide" (for Boston's hero) and poems like "Casey at the Bat" (for Mudville's fall guy) commemorated the triumphs and the fiascos of real and fictional Irish-American players. A generation after Kelly went to Boston, eleven of the sixteen managers in major-league baseball were Irish Americans, among them the New York Giants' legendary John J. McGraw.[49]

African-American athletes were doubtless as eager and talented as the Irish Americans. By the turn of the century they were jockeys, boxers, and even cyclists—Marshall Taylor was the world's champion 1898–1900—but they were not major-league baseball players. Talented black players had seemed on the verge of a significant breakthrough in 1884, when Oberlin-educated Moses Fleetwood Walker and his brother Weldy played for Toledo in the American Association. Unfortunately, men like "Cap" Anson felt that the presence of black players was an intolerable affront. African-American players were forced from major-league baseball, and Anson was doomed to be remembered less for his great skills than for his infamous shout, "Get that nigger off the field!" Given no other choice, African Americans formed their own professional teams, of which the "Cuban Giants" (1885) was among the first. Launched at the Argyle Hotel in Babylon, Long Island, the team traveled about the country, competing against collegiate teams, among them Amherst, Yale, and Princeton.[50]

By the end of the century, the African Americans were gone, and the German Americans, including the great John Peter "Honus" Wagner, had arrived. As Larry Gerlach tells it, "German and Irish players so dominated some rosters that teams on St. Patrick's Day staged intrasquad games between the two ethnic groups." Ironically, the greatest German-American player was never painted in ethnic colors. Well on his way to a criminal career, young George Herman Ruth revealed a saving talent for baseball that took him first to the Boston Red Sox and then to the New York Yankees. By the 1920s, the process of assimilation had gone far enough for his ethnic origins to be wholly ignored. As the "Babe," the "Bambino," and the "Sultan of Swat," Ruth was worshiped as a representative American rather than as an ethnic hero.[51]

He was also a *deus ex machina* who appeared just in time to divert attention from baseball's worst-ever scandal. The "Black Sox" were a clique of Chicago White Sox players, who—resentful that Charles Comiskey grossly underpaid them—conspired successfully with a group of New York gamblers to throw the 1919 World Series to the Cincinnati Reds. The sequence of events is hard to reconstruct because the bribe-givers and the bribe-takers double-crossed each other in an intricate minuet of dishonesty. Comiskey, the Chicago newspapers, and some members of the district attorney's office all managed to ignore, suppress, or "misplace" incriminating evidence. Several of the players confessed, then retracted their confessions. After a trial that should have been made into a Marx Brothers movie, the guilty players were acquitted. And then they were banished from the game by baseball's new commissioner, Judge Kenesaw Mountain Landis, a man whom Jules Tygiel castigated for bringing "to baseball a disdain for law and due process characteristic of his judicial career." He was a mentally unstable despot whom even a friendly biographer, J. G. Taylor Spink, characterized as "vain, autocratic and easily offended." His arbitrary rulings nevertheless reassured the uneasy public.[52]

As did Babe Ruth's play. Had he not been the greatest batter the game has ever known, he might have become one of its greatest pitchers. His ability to swat balls into right, left, and center field was prodigious. His record of 714 career home runs lasted until 1974. His 154-game record of 60 home runs was not broken until 1961—and Roger Maris needed an extra eight games to do it. Ruth's demeanor was uninhibited and his speech was demotic. To the nation's president he remarked, on a bright summer day, "Hot as hell, ain't it, 'Prez,'?" Journalists conspired to conceal his drinking and his whoring from jazz-age fans who would probably have adored him even more had they known the truth about his nocturnal escapades. "Anybody who doesn't like this life," he said, while caressing two women in a Philadelphia brothel, "is crazy!" Millions mourned him when he succumbed to cancer. Decades later, when Hank Aaron and Mark McGwire threatened to surpass the records that document Ruth's immortality, they had to cope with death threats.[53]

When Ruth retired from active play, his place was taken, literally as well as symbolically, by Joe DiMaggio, an Italian American from San Francisco, whom the Yankees acquired in 1936. DiMaggio's ethnicity was emphasized for a few years and then more or less ignored. Unlike Francesco Stefano Pezzolo, who played for Chicago as Ping Bodie, DiMaggio didn't have to change his name to win acceptance as an athlete. Briefly married to Marilyn Monroe, he reminded her in a famous exchange that he, too, was a star. "Joe," she told him after she had sung for the American troops in Korea, "You never heard such cheering," "Yes I have," he replied.[54]

In baseball's ethnic succession, Jews were next in line. Jewish fans identified proudly with Hank Greenberg (Detroit Tigers) and Sandy Koufax (Brooklyn Dodgers), but it is doubtful if many other Americans thought of them as anything other than gifted athletes.

Had racial prejudice not blinded them, the owners might have stocked their teams with players from the Negro National League, which lasted, with a two-year hiatus, from 1920 to 1948, after which it was absorbed by the Negro American League (1937–1960). The most celebrated African-American teams—Cumberland Posey's Homestead Grays and William A. "Gus" Greenlee's Pittsburgh Crawfords—lit the sporting landscape with bright constellations of black stars: Leroy "Satchel" Paige, Oscar Charleston, Josh Gibson, James "Cool Papa" Bell, and Julius "Judy" Johnson. The Crawfords, amply financed by Greenlee's numbers racket, might truly have been what Rob Ruck called them: "the best baseball team ever assembled for regular season play." Asked how he played Josh Gibson, Satchel Paige, one of baseball's finest pitchers, replied, "You look for his weakness and while you lookin' for it he liable to hit forty-five home runs."[55]

Tantalized by such obvious talent, Branch Rickey of the Brooklyn Dodgers decided to break the owners' "gentleman's agreement" on racial exclusion. In *Baseball's Great Experiment* (1983), Jules Tygiel characterized Rickey as a devout Methodist and as a modernizer for whom baseball "represented a science in which one researched, experimented, and refined techniques for maximum results." Although the other owners opposed him, fifteen to one, Rickey persevered in his plan to integrate the game. On April 15, 1947, seven years before the Supreme Court concluded in *Brown v. Board of Education* that racially segregated education was unconstitutional, Jackie Robinson came to bat for the Dodgers. It was not quite the end of an era. The Boston Red Sox remained an all-white team until 1959. By then, however, Willie Mays and other black stars were a major presence in major-league baseball.[56]

Two years after Robinson's debut with the Dodgers, major-league baseball's first Cuban-born star, Saturnino Orestes Arrieta Minoso Armas, donned the uniform of the Cleveland Indians (and had his name reduced to "Minnie Minoso"). By the end of the century, Hispanic players were among the game's brightest stars, and the Dominican Republic, on a per capita basis, was the prime source of baseball talent. Hispanics are not likely to be outnumbered by the Japanese and Korean players who are the most recent ethnic newcomers.[57]

Racial integration did not mean instant equality. Gerald Scully proved in 1974 that black baseball players suffered salary discrimination despite the fact that they earned, on average, more than white players. Regression analysis showed clearly that they were paid less than white players who performed at the same level. Fifteen years later, Scully replicated his original study and found that salary discrimination was gone. Subsequent research has come to the same conclusion.[58] Other forms of discrimination lingered on. For decades after baseball was racially integrated, black players tended to be "stacked" in the outfield. They seldom played the infield positions from which coaches and managers were recruited, which meant, as a consequence, that they were (and still are) underrepresented in those roles and in the front office.[59]

Baseball: Economic and Legal Aspects

If the market for baseball was large enough for two major leagues, why not for three? The Federal League competed with the two older circuits in 1914 and 1915. Events unfolded as they had during the brief life of the "Brotherhood League" and as they were to do in American basketball and football. Thanks to opportunities created by the establishment of the Federal League, players were able to escape the monopolistic restrictions of the "reserve clause." Of the 264 players recruited by the new league, only 43 were not under contract to major-league or minor-league teams. Competition for players also raised salaries for those who did not break their contracts. Average pay went from $1,200 to $2,800, and underpaid Tyrus "Ty" Cobb's salary soared from $12,000 to $20,000. The Federal League failed, but some of its owners were allowed to acquire major-league franchises.[60]

The owners of Baltimore's Federal League team were not happy with the offer of a franchise in the International League. Citing the "reserve clause" as their prime evidence, the Terrapins' lawyers accused organized baseball of unlawful and monopolistic restraint of interstate commerce in clear violation of the Sherman Act (1890) and other antitrust legislation. In 1922, Oliver Wendell Holmes, speaking for the majority, delivered the Supreme Court's opinion adjudicating Baltimore's case. The court considered the facts and then ignored them. Baseball, concluded the learned jurists, was not interstate commerce. Although baseball teams traveled from state to state, baseball games were merely "exhibitions" of talent and they were always played within the boundaries of a single state. This bizarre interpretation of the law was reaffirmed fifty years later in *Flood v. Kuhn*. In that decision, written by Harry A. Blackmun, the justices admitted that their predecessors had made a mistake, but they refused to correct the "established aberration." Since the Supreme Court *had* ruled that basketball and football games *were* instances of interstate commerce as defined by the Sherman Act, it was difficult to understand the court's reluctance to follow its own logic. The solution to the puzzle lay in baseball's mythic appeal. Blackmun's majority opinion quoted from "Casey at the Bat" and cited the fiction of Ring Lardner. Blackmun intoned "the many names . . . that have sparked the diamond and its environs and that have provided tinder for recaptured thrills, for reminiscence and comparisons, and for conversation and anticipation in-season and off-season." He recited the names of Ty Cobb, Babe Ruth, and eighty-six other legendary players. Confronted with economic injustice and legal absurdity, the justices wallowed in nostalgia.[61]

It was, finally, unionization that brought organized baseball into the twentieth century. The Major League Ball Players Association, which had been founded in 1954, was stirred from its lethargy in 1966 by Marvin Miller, an aggressive lawyer who had represented the United Steelworkers. Miller became the MLBPA's activist executive director. The 1972 season was interrupted by a nine-day strike, after which the owners agreed to arbitration for the 1974 season. Between 1976 and 1980, the average salary tripled. An unexpected statistical consequence of arbitration was that players' salaries were more closely correlated to their performance.[62]

In 1975, when the arbiter sided with two aggrieved players, the irate owners fired him. The players—Andy Messersmith of the Dodgers and Dave

McNally of the Expos—sued and won their case. Faced with the risk that the Supreme Court might recover its wits and terminate the "established aberration" upon which baseball's monopoly depended, the owners compromised and allowed veteran players to become free agents (subject to certain restrictions). Players were free to market themselves, with the help of their agents, to the highest bidder.[63]

The owners tried to recapture their advantage by means of collusion. They simply refused to offer contracts to players who opted for free agency. After the 1985 season, sixty-two players filed for free agency, and none received a new offer. The union filed a series of grievances, the owners were eventually fined $280 million, and noncollusive bargaining sent salaries rocketing even higher. Comparisons with the salaries of ordinary workers illustrate this dramatically. In 1947, the average baseball player earned four times as much as the average American worker; in 1999, he earned fifty-six times as much. Free agency also increased the degree of inequality among the players. The Gini coefficient, the standard statistical technique for measuring inequality, rose from 0.354 (for 1965–1974) to 0.505 (for 1986–1990). The coefficient is much larger in baseball than it is in U.S. family income and U.S. individual income.[64]

The supply-and-demand equations have had other effects. The demand for franchises is far greater than the supply, which means that the competition for them has become increasingly intense and astronomically expensive. In 1991, eighteen groups in ten cities bid for two National League expansion franchises, each of them going for $95 million. (The winners were the Colorado Rockies and the Florida Marlins.)[65]

No bid is really credible without the lure of a new ballpark. This means that stadia costing hundreds of millions of public dollars are constructed on the basis of an owner's promise to relocate to a community or his threat to abandon one. Between 1962 and 1971, new ball parks were built—all of them adjacent to expressways, all of them with vast parking lots, all of them at public expense—in Atlanta, Cincinnati, Houston, New York, Oakland, Philadelphia, Pittsburgh, San Diego, St. Louis, and Washington. In 1990–1991, the Astros, the Brewers, the Giants, the Indians, the Mariners, the Tigers, and the White Sox were all threatening to move. Not all the threats were credible, but the White Sox were offered a fine new home in Tampa–St. Petersburg, which motivated Illinois to create the Illinois Sports Facilities Authority. The ISFA then authorized $150 million for a new stadium plus payments to displaced Chicagoans plus an agreement to share 50 percent of any losses on the stadium (up to $10 million a year) plus $2 million a year for maintenance plus an agreement to buy 300,000 tickets a year. In return for their generosity, the taxpayers were offered not only enhanced pride but also the opportunity to rent 82 "skyboxes" at a bargain-basement rate of $90,000 a year. (Toronto's luxury suites went for $225,000, and the price did not include the cost of tickets.) Of the 113 franchises in the four major team sports, 31 of them acquired new stadia between 1989 and 1997—all at public expense. Government largesse of this magnitude in a supposedly market economy stands in ironic contrast to the situation in France, where a *dirigiste* socialist government coaxed private investors into paying 53 percent of the costs of the new stadium constructed for the 1998 World Cup Final.[66]

Taxpayers who routinely refuse to support bond issues to finance public education are moved to such uncharacteristic generosity toward franchise owners, because urban political and economic elites persuade them that cities without a major-league sports team are provincial backwaters. (Los Angeles, a city without a center, seems to have an insatiable lust for sports teams that can confer identity and generate a sense of community.)[67] Appeals to local pride and community spirit are invariably seconded by claims of economic benefit, but these claims are almost always bogus. Opportunity costs are discreetly ignored. The reduction in income—because public property is not taxed—is seldom mentioned. The revenue generated by a sports complex rarely matches the amortized costs of the facility and the vision of thousands of new jobs is a mirage. It also happens that the public officials who commit cities, states, or metropolitan areas to an economically ruinous contract sometimes depart from public service in order to work for the very franchises they had so generously benefitted.[68] There are, however, few signs that the taxpayers, reveling in the psychic benefit of "big time" sports, are disturbed.

The owners of sports franchises routinely assert that they, too, revel in psychic benefits. They claim to be utility-maximizers rather than profit-maximizers. They publish economic data indicating that they are hovering on the brink of bankruptcy. "It seems to be an annual ritual," comments Andrew Zimbalist, "that no matter how bountiful the year [major-league baseball] proclaims that eight to twelve teams suffered losses." Skepticism about alleged unprofitability is, indeed, in order. The New York Mets, purchased in 1962 for $3.75 million, were sold in 1986 for $100 million, which is more than most businesspeople are willing to pay for the opportunity to lose money.[69]

Actual profits can be transformed into ostensible losses by means of a few simple manipulations. Owners can form a corporation to issue the bonds they use to acquire the franchise—and claim the interest they pay to themselves as an expense. They can also pay themselves huge salaries, which drastically reduces the franchise's profits. Best of all, they can claim the players as depreciable assets—like oil wells—so that the flow of millions of dollars is transformed by economic sleight of hand into a pool of red ink. In short, New York Yankees owner George Steinbrenner can have his cake (i.e., profits) and eat it too (i.e., have all the fun). The fans who are outraged at his mistreatment of managers and players are meekness personified when he comes to them for a handout.[70]

_____ Why Baseball?

Why was baseball, for more than a century, perceived as "our national game"? It is nonsensical to argue that Americans opted for baseball rather than soccer because baseball is a democratic game. It is equally nonsensical to maintain that baseball is more suitable than other sports for the display of masculinity. And it is absurd to explain that fans flock to the bleachers in order to munch a "totem feast" of peanuts and popcorn, during which the batter participates in an Oedipal effort to slay the "primal father."[71] My best answer to the question is that baseball was and to some degree still is a paradoxical combination of premodern and modern characteristics, a blend of myth and history.[72]

In its spatial configuration, baseball differs from most modern ball games. Soccer, rugby, basketball, volleyball, team handball, lacrosse, field hockey, and even cricket—baseball's nearest ludic relative—are all characterized by a back-and-forth movement. Baseball is different. When a player hits safely, he takes off on a circular course that ends exactly where it began. The motion is cyclical, as in the eternal return of myth, rather than linear, as in history's one thing after another. There is a second spatial difference. Most modern ball games are played within a rectangular bounded space of standardized dimensions. Baseball's field of play is bounded on two sides by lines that radiate, in the mind, to infinity. If the batter hits the ball between these two lines, he cannot hit it too far.

Baseball's temporal pattern is also different from that of most other modern sports. Generalizing about all sports, Michael Real observed that they "overlie the sacred cycle of mythic time to provide a needed psychic relief from the tedium of western linear time."[73] Most sports are, in fact, seasonal (and therefore cyclical), but most modern ball games also follow the dictates of "linear time." The game ends when the clock runs out. Baseball is different. In a very real sense, play is timeless. With sufficient inequality of skill, the game might go on forever as the weaker team tries vainly to retire the opposing side. As it is, no one can tell when a game is likely to end, an uncertainty that annoys television programmers but pleases those who feel that the game is never over until the last man is out.

Spatially and temporally premodern, baseball was nonetheless perceived by the men who played it as an eminently modern game. Steven Gelber argues that the players' "day to day work lives created a set of values that included a scientific world view [and] an appreciation for rationality." Another way to describe this aspect of baseball is to say that the game shared all the defining characteristics of modern sports. Specialization, for instance, was present from the beginning in that the defensive side was divided into nine separate playing positions. Bureaucratic organization came with the establishment of the National League. Rationalization appeared in many forms. The impromptu challenge match, for example, was replaced by a regular 154-game season in which every team played every other team a fixed number of times at scheduled times and places. There was also constant revision of the rules. Between 1876 and 1889, for instance, the base-on-balls rule was altered seven times. Equipment was standardized and then subjected to constant experimentation. Baseball was, moreover, marked from the start by quantification and by the proliferation of records that quantification makes possible. Appreciation of baseball does not require *literacy;* appreciation demands what Patricia Cline Cohen calls *numeracy,* the ability to work with numbers. "Baseball," wrote Roger Angell, is "the most intensely and satisfyingly mathematical of all our outdoor sports." The quantified action, which includes four balls, three strikes, three outs, and nine innings, leads to an abstract world of batting averages, fielding averages, earned-run averages, and all the other spectral numbers that haunt the ballpark, flicker on the borders of the television screen, crowd the columns of *The Sporting News,* and come to rest in the hallowed pages of *The Baseball Encyclopedia.* The mania for quantification grips the modern fan even more tightly than it did the nineteenth-century "crank."[74]

And from the numbers we extract the records. Baseball's cornucopia of quantified information makes it absurdly easy to calculate records, which can be as memorable as Ruth's 60 home runs or as forgettable as the computer-generated numbers cited by television commentators whose flow of distracting anecdotes has momentarily run dry.

Decade by decade, there has been a steady diminution of baseball's premodern characteristics and a constant accentuation of its modern characteristics. Baseball was once a summer afternoon's pastime, played on sunny green fields that *seemed*—even when they were not—distant from the factories and offices of the industrial landscape. Today, more often than not, the final game of the season is played at night, in late October, under artificial illumination. The vast majority of the spectators sit at home or in a sports bar and follow the action on an electronic screen that provides them, in rapid sequence, with a pitcher's-eye view of home plate, the batter's lifetime "stats," and a series of fast-paced advertisements for SUVs, diet pills, and other necessities of modern life. It is not what Alexander Cartwright had in mind, and it is certainly not the pastoral game attributed to Abner Doubleday.

_____ American Football: Origins and Evolution

Although intercollegiate sports began with an 1852 regatta on New Hampshire's Lake Winnipesaukee and with an 1859 "Massachusetts rules" baseball game between Amherst and Williams, it was football that permanently changed the culture of American campuses. Football games became the center of a complex autumnal ritual, a saturnalian "time out" from study, a series of parades and parties reminiscent of the pageantry and the drunken revelry of a medieval archery meet. In the nineteenth century, the seasonal climax came at Thanksgiving, the holiday that most vividly expresses America's sense of itself as an "imagined community." The twentieth century corroborated, a thousand times over, what the *Yale Literary Magazine* asserted in 1864: Sports championships are "sacredly connected with the glory of Alma Mater herself." And football championships are unquestionably the most glorious. "You are now going out to play football against Harvard," intoned Yale's coach, "Never again in your whole life will you do anything so important."[75]

A brief retrospect is necessary. Eighteenth-century Harvard students played a version of folk-football. By the early nineteenth century, at the latest, Yale students did the same. David Hackett Fischer has reprinted an 1807 engraving showing Yale "students in beaver hats and swallow-tailed coats playing football on New Haven Common, while an elder who closely resembled college president Timothy Dwight looked on with an air of disapproval." In 1858, Winslow Homer drew *Class Day at Harvard University,* showing a freshman–sophomore football match. At many antebellum colleges, the faculty, like their predecessors at Oxford and Cambridge, banned folk-football as a threat to piety and a danger to life and limb. The faculty won many battles. On July 2, 1860, students at Harvard College, with mock solemnity, buried "Football Fightum," a casualty of professorial disapproval. In the long run, however, the students prevailed. Compulsory chapel attendance has vanished from most American campuses. Edwin Cady is right; the heathenish festivities of the "football weekend" have become "the most vitally folkloristic event in our culture."[76]

Celebrators of American football sometimes cite the Princeton–Rutgers contest of November 6, 1869, as the first intercollegiate football game, won by the latter with a score of 6–4. That historic game was an approximation of soccer football. Something akin to modern rugby was brought to the United States on May 15, 1874, when students from Montreal's McGill University competed against a novice squad from Harvard. This contest, which occurred only two years after Oxford and Cambridge inaugurated their rugby rivalry, ended in a scoreless tie.[77]

Rugby was immensely attractive to upper-class youths seeking to demonstrate the manly courage that their fathers and older brothers had recently proved on the bloody battlefields of the Civil War. The game spread from school to school. On November 26, 1876, representatives from Harvard, Columbia, Princeton, and Yale met in the Massasoit House at Springfield, Massachusetts, founded the Intercollegiate Football Association, and formally adopted rules similar to those of Rugby Football Union.[78]

In a famous essay entitled "Football in America: A Study in Culture Diffusion," sociologists David Riesman and Reuel Denney described the transformation of British rugby into American football as a "procedural rationalization" that "fitted in with other aspects of . . . industrial folkways." The process required a quarter of a century. By 1895, Caspar Whitney was able to dismiss rugby as "an elementary game," clearly not on a level with American football's "scientifically developed play."[79]

To a remarkable degree, the impetus behind the evolution of American football came from a single man. Walter Camp, who played the game for Yale, was for forty-six years the dominant force on the Rules Committee that—step by step, year by year—turned rugby into American football. Camp, an engineer who worked for a clock manufacturer, approached the game from "what is essentially a managerial and technocratic perspective."[80] His approach to sports revealed an obsessive commitment to instrumental rationality.

Camp was responsible for the reduction of the team from fifteen men to eleven. More important, he conceived the static line of scrimmage that replaced the chaotic shoving and pushing of the rugby scrum. Both innovations were introduced in 1880. After dogged possession of the ball turned the 1882 Yale–Princeton game into a scoreless tie, Camp required the offensive team to gain five yards in three tries (called "downs") or to surrender possession of the ball. That rule, in turn, required a field marked with lines of chalk. (The look of the lined field gave the game its nineteenth-century name: gridiron football.) In 1883, Camp revised the scoring system.

Like a good engineer, Camp understood the advantages of specialization. "Division of labor," he wrote, "has been so thoroughly and successfully carried out on the football field that a player nowadays must train for a particular position." Yale's team specialized and trained and became an engine of destruction that steamrollered Ivy League rivals. From the middle of 1885 to the end of the 1899 season, Yale won 46 straight games, outscoring hapless opponents by 2,018 to 29. In 1914, Yale inaugurated a 75,000-seat stadium, an architectural tribute to Camp's effectiveness.[81]

Realizing that Harvard's teams were no match for Yale's, President Charles William Eliot overcame his doubts about the educational value of football and hired William Reid as a coach. He paid him $7,000 a year, 30 percent more than Harvard's best-paid professor. In strictly economic terms, it was a good deal. Hundreds of students attended class to hear William James lecture on pragmatism; 38,000 packed Harvard's grand new stadium to see Reid's squad in action. President William Rainey Harper of the University of Chicago, founded in 1891, was another educator who recognized football's contribution to a school's prestige. He hired Amos Alonzo Stagg to coach the team, gave him professorial status, and told him to put the fledgling university on the academic map. "I want you to develop teams which we can send around the country and knock out all the colleges." Stagg complied.[82]

Not every president was enchanted by the prospect of athletic glory. Cornell's Andrew D. White rejected out of hand the football team's request for an "away" game: "I will not permit thirty men to travel four hundred miles merely to agitate a bag of wind." The University of Wisconsin's John Bascom suggested that colleagues addicted to intercollegiate sports hire "a few persons, as we do clowns, to set themselves apart to do this work." Bascom's sarcastic analogy seems also to have occurred to a dissatisfied parent who complained to Princeton's James McCosh "that he had sent his boy to college to become a scholar but . . . what he had learnt there only fitted him for a position in a circus."[83]

Although Southern students were desperately eager to get into the game, Southern educators, many of whom taught at church-related schools, had doubts more profound than Andrew White's worry about a waste of time and money. Speaking for the region's Methodists, the *Wesleyan Christian Advocate* complained that the game's violence unleashed "the lower impulses of the physical man" and encouraged young males to "find their pleasure in mere sensual energy." Football was an ominous reversion to "Olympic Greece and her barbaric ideals." The religious opposition to intercollegiate football was so adamant that Trinity College (now Duke University) abandoned the game in 1894 and did not resume play until 1920. The complaints about physicality were not mere hysteria. Within the tight confines of its procedural rationality, football also allowed for bravado demonstrations of rugged masculinity. While Walter Camp—ever the rationalist—explained to the upper-class subscribers of *Outing* that the "instrumentality of sport [introduced] a certain amount of modern discipline" into a young man's life, W. Cameron Forbes,

Amenhotep as an archer. Stele, Eighteenth dynasty (fifteenth century B.C.).
Photograph from the collection of Wolfgang Decker.

Brygos Painter, gymnasium scene. Attic red-figured two-handled cup, ca. 480 B.C.
Photograph © 2004 Museum of Fine Arts, Boston.

Archaic Greek bronze
statue of a running girl,
probably Spartan.
© The British Museum.

Gladiator
mosaic from
Leptis Magnus,
North Africa,
second century
A.D. From
Vera Olivová,
*Sport und
Spiel im Altertum*
(Munich: Copress,
1985).

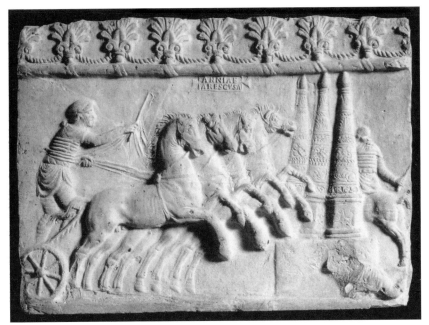

Roman chariot race. Terra-cotta plaque, first half of first century A.D.
© The British Museum.

Japanese archery at the Kitano Shrine, Kyoto. Kamakura period, 1219 A.D.
From *Bijutusu ni miru Nihon no supōtsu* (Nagoya: Tokugawa Bijutsukan, 1994).

Richard, Earl of Warwick, jousting at Calais, January 1414.
British Library Cott.Jul.E.IV art 6 f15v. By permission of the British Library.

Pol de Limbourg, falconing scene from
Les Très Riches Heures du Duc de Berry,
early fifteenth century. Musée Condé, Chantilly, and
Bridgeman-Giraudon/Art Resource, New York.

A crossbow match in Zurich, August 12, 1504. Woodblock print.
Photograph from the collection of Kusada Kazuhiko.

Chrispyn DePasse le Jeune, *Baroque Ring-Tournament*, 1612.
Bildarchiv de Schweizerischen Sportmuseum.

Michael Sweerts, *Roman Wrestlers*, ca. 1650. Staatliche Kunsthalle, Karlsruhe.

Persian polo match from an illuminated manuscript, late sixteenth century.
Photograph from the collection of the author.

The Game of Cricket, ca. 1790. Oil on canvas by an anonymous artist.
The Marylebone Cricket Club, London, UK/Bridgeman Art Library.

Ludwig Friedrich Jahn on the Hasenheide Turnplatz. Lithograph by Gottfried Kühn, ca. 1858. Heimatmuseum, Neu Kölln.

J. Jackson, *Tom Cribb, Champion of England*. Engraving by J. Moore, 1842.
Collection of the author.

William Powell Frith, *The Fair Toxophilites*, 1872. Royal Albert Memorial Museum, Exeter, Devon, UK/Bridgeman Art Library.

Cycling in the Bois de Bologne. *Harper's Weekly*, December 19, 1868.

The first Australian cricket team to tour England, 1878.
National Library of Australia.

Senda Berenson teaching basketball at Smith College, 1904.
Sophia Smith Collection, Smith College.

21. RAMBOUILLET — Foot ball dans le parc

Youths playing soccer in the Parc de Rambouillet, ca. 1900.
Collection of Serge Laget.

Herzog Adoph Friedrich von Mecklenburg and a Tutsi jumper,
German East Africa, 1907. Deutsches Sportmuseum.

Suzanne Lenglen, 1925. AP/Wide World Photos.

A soccer team in Cameroun, 1927. Spiritains Arch. Photo Paris.

Ville Riota (Finland), Paavo Nurmi (Finland), and Edvin Wide (Sweden)
vie in the 10,000-meter race at the 1928 Olympics in Amsterdam.
Photograph from the collection of Ronald Smith.

writing in the same journal, described football as "the expression of the strength of the Anglo-Saxon. . . . It is the dominant spirit of a dominant race." The football stadium was a forum where privileged young men demonstrated their manliness. The *Police Gazette,* a periodical that catered to the working class, highlighted football's "brutality and sexual interest." The *Gazette's* coverage of the game demonstrated clearly that "masculinity" and "manliness" were often euphemisms for "virility." The erotic theme was underlined when—in the disapproving words of Michael Messner—the "bare and vulnerable bodies" of female cheerleaders were inserted into the "text" of a football game, but the theme was there from the start.[84]

Amateur football's move toward today's unacknowledged professionalism began when the players themselves, driven by a desire to win at all costs, secured the temporary services of husky young farmhands and steelworkers whose only connection with the college was the hard labor performed on Saturday afternoons. In 1894, for example, seven of Michigan's eleven starters "neither enrolled in school nor attended any classes."[85] Shenanigans of this sort moved indignant faculties to take control of the game. Professors quickly realized, however, that time spent supervising intercollegiate sports was time not spent teaching and doing research. They gladly surrendered control to professional coaches such as Harvard's Reid and Chicago's Stagg.

One of the most serious problems faced by nineteenth-century coaches was the game's deadly violence. Eighteen players were killed in 1905, and one hundred fifty-nine were seriously injured. Stanford and the University of California dropped football in 1906 and did not return to the game until 1919. Columbia and the University of Chicago also gave up on the game. From the White House, Theodore Roosevelt, a great believer in football as a school of masculinty, anticipated these departures and delivered an ultimatum to Reid and his Ivy League colleagues at Yale and Princeton: Reform the game before the "mollycoddles" abolished it altogether. When the Ivy League failed to act, New York University Chancellor Henry McCracken took the lead. Several conferences at New York's Murray Hill Hotel climaxed in January 1906 with the birth of the thirty-eight-school Intercollegiate Athletic Association. Renamed the National Collegiate Athletic Association (NCAA), the organization eventually claimed—and nearly attained—monopolistic control over all intercollegiate sports.[86]

The NCAA attempted to reform the game. New rules specified that ten yards were required for a first down (instead of five), and four downs were allowed (instead of three), but changes of this sort did little to achieve the diminution of violence that was the organization's original raison d'être. In fact, the number of those fatally injured rose, in the fall of 1909, to thirty.

Meaningful reform came when the Rules Committee decided the following spring to remove the fifteen-yard penalty for an incomplete forward pass. This encouraged throwing the ball rather than running with it. Biomass ceased to be decisive.[87]

As the strategy of the game became more important, the coach's role—as recruiter, game-planner, motivator, and publicist—came to overshadow the player's. In the 1920s, journalists made pilgrimages to Notre Dame University to interview Knute Rockne and quoted him as if he were an oracle. Metaphors drawn from religion are appropriate. As one of Rockne's colleagues, Father John O'Hara, said, "Notre Dame football is a spiritual exercise because it is played for the honor and glory of God and the exaltation of his Blessed Mother." Stories about Rockne's uncanny power to inspire the team ("Win one for the Gipper!") captivated worshipful fans, including young Ronald Reagan, and continue to circulate through the world of popular culture.[88]

During and after the decade of Rockne's glory—1921–1931—the NCAA was involved in a bitter organizational struggle with the Amateur Athletic Union. The AAU's ace in hand was its close ties to the International Olympic Committee; the NCAA's trump card was its tight control of intercollegiate football. The balance of power tipped in 1962, when the AAU lost control of amateur baseball, gymnastics, and track and field. The coup de grace to the AAU came when Congress passed the Amateur Sports Act of 1978. By then, the NCAA was locked in another jurisdictional conflict, this time with the Association of Intercollegiate Athletics for Women (AIAW). The NCAA's control of intercollegiate football was, once again, a decisive factor in its drive to control *all* major intercollegiate sports.[89]

The AIAW was created in 1971 to oppose the grotesque inequality between men's and women's intercollegiate sports. At that time, programs for female athletes at NCAA Division I schools received approximately 2 percent of the money budgeted for sports. At the University of New Mexico, for instance, the men received $527,000, the lion's share allotted to football, and the women had to be content with $9,150.[90] With legal support from Title IX of the Education Act of 1971, which mandated an end to sexual discrimination in federally funded education, the AIAW attempted to create an alternative to the NCAA's model.[91] The NCAA's response to implementation of Title IX was to beg Congress for an exemption for "revenue-producing sports," a code phrase for football and men's basketball. Congress refused to comply, and the AIAW seemed to have a clear field. The number of women involved in intercollegiate sports increased exponentially (and their graduation rates and academic profile began to replicate the men's patterns).[92]

The NCAA, led by Walter Byers, decided to absorb the AIAW. The women, who wanted desperately to remain in control of their own sports, resisted, but the huge economic inequality between the AIAW and the NCAA stacked the deck against them. Fighting the NCAA bankrupted the AIAW, which, in its tenth and last year, devoted 41.7 percent of its total income to legal costs and only 9.4 percent to its national championships. Control of women's sports passed from the impoverished AIAW to the affluent NCAA.[93]

The affluence was crucial. In 1951, the hitherto impecunious NCAA discovered television's electronic cornucopia and began, hesitantly, to sell the right to televise its football games. The price for eleven games shown on NBC during the 1952 season was over a million dollars, and the NCAA was on its way to wealth beyond the dreams of its high-minded reformist founders. George Sage pointed out, correctly, that television contracts turned the NCAA into "a business organization which is part of the entertainment industry whose product is competitive intercollegiate sports events." Determined to exercise control over the sale of rights, NCAA began to behave like a cartel. When the University of Pennsylvania dared to negotiate on its own, the NCAA Council intervened and forced the university to refund the $80,000 advance it had received from ABC television.[94]

Inevitably, in a ludic landscape where some football teams played before a few hundred students and professors while others performed in stadia filled with tens of thousands of spectators, there were disagreements over the division of the spoils. The NCAA's 1977 television contract with ABC brought in $116 million, a sum which Notre Dame University and sixty other "football powers" thought too meager to be shared with smaller schools. They formed the College Football Association (CFA). Two members of the CFA, Oklahoma and Texas, sued the NCAA, charging that its monopolistic control over television money violated federal antitrust law. Without waiting for the Supreme Court's decision, the CFA confidently negotiated (but did not sign) a four-year, $180-million television contract with NBC. The NCAA then experienced a rare setback. The Supreme Court found for the plaintiffs and held that the NCAA's monopoly endangered amateur football. (That seven of the nine justices thought the NCAA played "a critical role in the maintenance of a revered tradition of amateurism in college sports" was another sign of the court's distance from reality.) Acting for schools that consented to its representation of their economic interests, the NCAA then negotiated a four-year contract with ABC and CBS for $263.5 million and another with TNT for $17.7 million. This was good enough to persuade the CFA to drop its plan to sign with NBC, but the organization nonetheless decided to break away for the 1984 season. The CFA signed with ABC and ESPN for $35 million. Eventually, Notre Dame found the restraints of the CFA irksome and negotiated its own arrangements with the media. Notre Dame sold the rights for 1991 through 1995 to NBC for $38 million.[95]

Despite sums of this magnitude, contrary to conventional wisdom, intercollegiate football is not a profitable industry. Very few football programs are economically viable. In 1995–96, the sports program at NCAA Division I schools had a net loss of $245 million. Athletic success was no guarantee of solvency. The University of Michigan is a case in point. The athletics department, which is a legally separate entity, packed its 100,000-seat stadium to capacity for 97 consecutive games, received additional income from television and from postseason play, and ran a deficit.[96]

Money is not the only problem. Long before the advent of television raised the economic stakes to astronomical levels, presidents of colleges and universities discovered that they had created the equivalent of Frankenstein's monster. They watched helplessly as football coaches recruited analphabetic young men whose primary purpose was definitely not to tackle the books. The presidents were powerless to stop the clandestine flow of hard cash and expensive gifts from wealthy alumni and boosters' clubs to "amateur" athletes from economically strapped families. A 1929 report issued by the Carnegie Commission lamented that "a system of recruiting and subsidizing has grown up, under which boys are offered pecuniary and other inducements to enter a particular college." "Athletic scholarships" mocked the ideals of higher education.[97]

The commission's sharp criticism created a momentary flurry in the nation's newspapers, most of which sprang to the defense of the status quo in intercollegiate sports. The *Atlanta Constitution* was typical. The editors commented that "the layman cannot see why it is destructive to the morals of a boy who can play football to help him through school." Better a robust athlete than a narrow-chested bookworm with "an aptitude for Greek verbs and botany." The Carnegie study was quickly forgotten, which has been the fate of subsequent studies documenting the same (and much worse) abuses. By the last quarter of the twentieth century, critics of intercollegiate sports had reason to despair. Some of the nation's most successful football teams consisted of some of the nation's least-engaged students enticed to campus by some of the nation's most unscrupulous coaches. President A. Whitney Griswold of Yale admitted that intercollegiate football had gone "professional in disguise." John Underwood, writing for *Sports Illustrated,* complained, "The fundamental illogic of sending functional illiterates into college classrooms has not yet dawned on educators and administators."[98]

Distorted ideals led to grotesque misallocations of resources. On the threshold of the twenty-first century, the University of North Carolina granted almost $3.2 million in scholarship aid to 690 athletes and less than one-fifth that amount to its other 15,000 students. Despite the financial aid (and clandestine payments) received by the nation's "scholar–athletes," graduation rates at NCAA Division I schools are dismal. Five years after their matriculation, only 52 percent of white athletes graduate and only 26 percent of black athletes. Graduation rates at the nation's elite private colleges and universities are better, but, even there, varsity athletes tend to fall short of their academic potential and commit more than their share of mayhem.[99]

It has not been at all unusual for a president who clashed with the football coach to discover that it was he, not the coach, whom the trustees dismissed. John Abercrombie, on leaving the University of Alabama, commented bitterly: "I have no ambition whatever to preside over a corruptly conducted athletic club." In a world where status is determined mainly by money, differences in income are culturally significant. At Texas A&M, President Frank E. Vanidiver's 1992 salary of $90,000 marked him as an educational ancillary compared to Jackie Sherrill, whom the trustees offered $287,000 to coach the football team. When the chairman of the board of trustees was questioned about Sherrill's salary, he defended the extravagance with an unanswerable argument: "Higher education is a business." Vanidiver clarified the chairman's remark: "The people want a major football program." When Sherrill's subsequent misconduct caused the NCAA to place Texas A&M on probation, the trustees provided him with a cash settlement of $648,000. Sherrill moved on to become head coach at Mississippi State.[100]

An episode at Southern Methodist University requires a few more words. SMU's priorities took brick-and-mortar form when it constructed its football stadium in 1926 and its library in 1939. The priorities were expressed in fiscal terms when SMU cut faculty salaries in order to pay the mortgage on the stadium. The NCAA penalized the school for various infractions in 1958, 1974, 1976, 1981, and 1985. The most serious penalty was imposed in 1987 after the NCAA learned of a secret $400,000 slush fund that allowed SMU to pay individual players as much as $25,000 each. (Some players were dissatisfied with their share of the loot. They broke into an office and stole the monthly payroll. No one dared inform the police.) When the corrupt system was exposed, the naïve, outraged, underpaid SMU faculty petitioned vainly for the "immediate, unconditional and permanent abolition of quasi-professional sports." President Donald Shields, who tried and failed to eliminate the corruption, was forced to resign by the SMU Board of Governors. The head coach moved on to the openly professional National Football League—with severence pay of $556,272. The NCAA ordered cancellation of the school's 1987 season, but a new president and a new football coach promised a quick return to SMU's glory days.[101]

After the passage of Title IX of the Education Act of 1971, there were additional new reasons to worry about the costs of intercollegiate football. Since the Supreme Court refused to overturn a 1995 ruling by the First Circuit Court of Appeals, Title IX now requires that the proportion of male athletes in varsity sports must not be significantly larger than the proportion of the school's male students. If Brown University's student body was 51 percent female, which no one disputed, then it was illegal for only 38 percent of of Brown's intercollegiate athletes to be female.[102] Unfortunately, the number of women who want to be involved in intercollegiate sports almost never equals the number of men. This means that the number of men must be reduced. The elimination of football, which requires an enormous number of players, is one way to bring a school into compliance with the law (and simultaneously to balance its athletic budget), but this solution is rarely, if ever, acceptable. Gender parity has, instead, been achieved at many schools by eliminating men's teams in "minor sports" such as gymnastics, water polo, and wrestling.

There is at least one other problem created by the desire to field winning football teams. Empirical data corroborate the gory anecdotal evidence. Football players are more likely than other students to commit rape and other violent assault.[103] At the University of Oklahoma, for example, Coach Barry Switzer moaned, "I never thought I needed to post rules against committing felonies."[104] This was in response to players arrested for raping coeds, selling cocaine, and shooting one another. The explanations for the criminal behaviors vary: socialization in a violent adolescent subculture, a sense of privilege and virtual immunity from punishment, a frustrated realization of academic inadequacy, bitterness at failure to become stars or even starters, or rancor occasioned by racism.

It is, no doubt, possible to become *too* cynical about academically unqualified football players and the coaches who recruit them to represent institutions of higher learning. For many football players, perhaps for most of them, varsity sports are what they are supposed to be: an educational experience. Of his time as a student–athlete at Notre Dame, sports historian Michael Oriard has written, "I read Latin and Greek and Shakespeare, discovered the fundamentals of chemistry and physics, studied history and religion. But through football I discovered myself."[105] Oriard cannot be the only football player to have had a transformative experience.

Whatever one's final assessment of the pros and cons of intercollegiate football, one has to understand that most Americans cherish the entertainment provided by intercollegiate sports and cannot be expected to endure an autumn in which Nebraska, Florida State, and other Division I football powers do not do battle for the imaginary national championship.[106] For them, abolition is unthinkable. There may, however, be a way out of the ethical cul-de-sac. Recent critics of Division I sports have suggested that the obvious way to end the hypocrisy about intercollegiate "amateurism" is to pay collegiate athletes a fair salary and allow them to enroll in a degree program as an optional fringe benefit. The entire system of subterfuge might then be transformed, argues John Rooney, into "an honest business operation designed to entertain the university community, alumni, and other interested parties." The NFL, which exploits the College Football Association as its minor league, might even be induced to subsidize such a system.[107]

_____ High School Football

No account of the game, however brief, should omit mention of high school football. One version of the story begins, innocently enough, in 1885, at Chicago's Hyde Park, North Division, and Lake View high schools, where the students formed their own football teams. They soon had reason to complain about their teachers' unreasonable demands: "Who can hope for success in Foot-Ball when most of the players are weighed down daily by a long Cicero lesson, or some other mark of tyranny?" Bostonian adolescents continued the story in 1888, when students at four high schools organized the Interscholastic Football Association. (Whether or not they read less Cicero is unknown.) By the turn of the century, high schools from coast to coast had teachers who divided their time between the classroom and the football field, dissecting frogs or discussing the Battle of Gettysburg until three o'clock, coaching the team until November's early dusk. The story of high school football came to a climax, but certainly not to an end, a century later, in Texas, where the football coach's budget siphons funds from the already underfunded classrooms, where the football stadium is often capacious enough to seat the entire town, where teenaged football players are idolized by their parents and teachers as well as by their classmates, where football separates manly young Texans from allegedly effeminate soccer-playing Mexican Americans, where the "rites of autumn" are celebrated with the obsessive intensity of a pagan cult.[108]

In Dallas, young Gary Edwards acted as if he owned Carter High. "You walk around, you break all the rules. The teachers and administrators, they see you, they just don't say anything to you." At exam time, Edwards expected his teachers to provide him with answer sheets, which most did. When his algebra teacher did not, Edwards received a midterm grade of 68.75, at which point the school's principal transferred Edwards to a more compliant teacher. The Dallas Superintendent of Schools ruled, however, that Edwards had played while ineligible and that Carter High had to forfeit three games, which meant that Carter High could not compete for the state championship. The citizens of Dallas were enraged, and the superintendent quickly reversed himself, but the State Commissioner of Education ruled that Edwards had indeed been ineligible and that Carter High had no right to be in the playoffs. Carter High and the Dallas School District went to court, and Judge Paul Davis promptly issued an injunction that allowed the school to compete for the state championship, which it won. Will Bates, the scrupulous teacher who thought algebra more important than football, was suspended without pay and then transferred to another school (where he was not allowed to teach mathematics). Shortly after this, the cash-strapped Dallas Independent School District fired 245 teachers rather than reduce the budget for interscholastic football.[109] The whole sorry story can be read as a gloss on a popular slogan coined in Texas: No child left behind.

_____ NFL Football

The National Football League arrived on the scene, in 1920, as a rather bedraggled collection of small-town teams scattered through the Middle West. For some years, the league was little more, in John Allen Krout's words, than "a sorry counterfeit of the great spectacle of the campus." The NFL's first serious challenge to the intercollegiate game was mounted in 1925, when George Halas persuaded Harold "Red" Grange, the era's greatest football player, to withdraw from the University of Illinois in order to play for the Chicago Bears. Grange had amazed the nation a year earlier. Before a home-game crowd of nearly seventy thousand, he scored against Michigan with runs of 95, 67, 56, and 45 yards. He then completed a forward pass for a fifth touchdown. When he joined the NFL, hundreds of thousands of fans rushed to see the newest god in the pantheon of sports. President Calvin Coolidge was not among them. Informed that Grange was with the Chicago Bears, the president replied enigmatically, "I've always liked animal acts."[110]

For the next forty years, NFL games attracted fewer spectators than intercollegiate contests. And the nation's newspapers were distinctly less likely to ballyhoo their games. In the 1960s, the league emerged from the shadows. Whether or not the increased popularity of this physically violent game was related to American military involvement in Vietnam is an unanswerable question. It is certain, however, that the demand for professional football exceeded the supply offered by the NFL.

Television offered a solution to the supply-and-demand equation. NFL Commissioner Alvin "Pete" Rozelle was instructed by the league's owners to negotiate a national contract, one that allowed the league to block telecasts that threatened to interfere with ticket sales. To do this, the NFL required an exemption from federal antitrust law, which Congress obligingly granted. The Sports Broadcasting Act of 1961 allowed the NFL to negotiate as a league and to blackout home games.[111]

The bright prospect before the NFL was somewhat darkened by the appearance, in 1960, of the American Football League. After a complicated corporate dance in which television networks and sports leagues walzed from one partner to another, the AFL was able to arrange a marriage with the NFL. The dance began in 1961, when the NFL signed with CBS television for $4,500,000. Having lost the NFL to its major rival, NBC television signed a five-year contract with the AFL. The $42-million largesse resuscitated the faltering AFL. After several years of head-to-head economic competition, the NFL offered a merger. Since the prospect of a merger raised the spectre of monopoly, Congress was initially skeptical, but Rozelle courted Senator Russell Long and Representative Hale Boggs, both of Louisiana. They arranged for the NFL to receive an exemption from federal antitrust legislation. Shortly thereafter—was it a coincidence?—New Orleans received an NFL franchise. In begging for the exemption, the NFL owners had promised Congress not to move from any of the stadia in which their teams played. Within a decade, there were moves by Boston, Chicago, Cincinnati, Dallas, Kansas City, Oakland, Philadelphia, Pittsburgh, St. Louis, and San Francisco. Congress seemed not to notice.[112]

Football teams were, of course, not the only nomads. In 1997, of 113 teams in the four major team sports, only 28 had been in the same place since 1950. In the high-stakes game of franchise location, the owners had the upper hand and they knew it. As Robert Irsay said when he moved the Colts from Baltimore to Indianapolis: "This is my team. I own it, and I'll do whatever I want with it." Congress did not play the spoilsport. When the NFL's monopoly was threatened, in 1994, by an antitrust bill, Senator Dennis DeConcini (R–Arizona) made certain that it died in committee. Two years later—was this, too, a coincidence?—the Phoenix Cardinals took to the field.[113]

The enlarged NFL decided to end its season with the "Super Bowl," a "mega-event" that routinely rates as one of the world's most watched sports spectacles. An indirect indication of the event's popularity is the amount of money advertisers will pay to interrupt it with a thirty-second commercial: In 2003, the price tag was two million dollars.[114]

Among the major television networks, ABC was the first to profit significantly from the bonanza created by advertisers eager to have their commercials aired before, during, and immediately after a football game. In the 1960s, ABC Sports, imaginatively guided by Roone Arledge, was a dynamo of innovation. Arledge emphasized slow motion, instant replay, multiple cameras, the split screen, and "honey shots" of sexually attractive spectators. For the immensely popular "Wide World of Sports," which premiered in 1961, Arledge hired O. J. Simpson, admired by some and despised by others for his supposed "transcendence" of race. Building on success (and brushing aside protests from the NCAA), ABC and the NFL inaugurated "Monday Night Football" in the fall of 1970. The show changed the rhythm of the week. "Movie attendance nose-dived," marveled historian Benjamin Rader, "hookers left the streets, restaurants closed their doors, and bowlers rescheduled their leagues." The show's aggressively self-centered host, Howard Cosell ("a legend in his own mind") led the polls as best-liked and also as least-liked sports commentator. Between them, Rozelle and Arledge created an electronic equivalent to the Roman arena, which is, no doubt, why Super Bowls are numbered in Roman numerals.[115]

———— Country Clubs

The Book of Sport, published in New York in 1901, is an encyclopedic tome, lavishly illustrated, containing essays on golf, court-tennis, racquets, squash hand-fives (a form of racquet-less squash), squash, lawn-tennis, polo, foxhunting, yachting, and coaching. These sports are similar to those pursued by Europe's *noblesse.* The book is unintentional evidence for Thorstein Veblen's contemporary argument that the sports of the leisure class satisfied the "requirements of substantial futility." What these sports have in common, quite obviously, is that they provide splendid opportunities for "conspicuous consumption." Of "coaching," that is, driving about the countryside in horse-drawn carriages, Oliver H. P. Belmont opined, "No sport which requires the perfection of skill and dash and the exercise of nerve will ever be abandoned by Americans."[116] Within a decade, however, wealthy Americans were, in fact, abandoning their coaches and transforming their stables into garages to house their fancy new automobiles. Neither Belmont nor any of the other men and women quoted in *The Book of Sport* showed much interest in the sports favored by less affluent Americans. There is no chapter on baseball and none on any other team sport.

At the turn of the century, younger men of means did play football at Ivy League colleges, and their sisters passed (but did not dribble) basketballs at Smith and Mount Holyoke. After graduation, there were fewer opportunities for sports participation. One could summer at Newport, Rhode Island, where financier J. Pierpont Morgan decreed that mere merchants—like Thomas Lipton—were to be snubbed. "You can do business with anyone, but you can go sailing only with a gentleman." One could also join an urban athletic club, many of which accepted women. New York's Berkeley Athletic Club, for instance, spent a hefty $200,000 to provide its female members with "a gymnasium, a swimming pool, a private dressing room furnished with maids, reception rooms and a female physican." But the preferred option for men and for women was to join a country club.[117]

Brookline's Country Club, commonly identified as the first of its kind, was begun in 1882 by Boston Brahmins from the Adams, Bowditch, Cabot, Lowell, Peabody, and Saltonstall families. Shinnecock Hills, which drew its members from the suburbs of New York, followed in 1891. The founders, Duncan Cryder and Edward S. Mead, were inspired by the golfers they had observed in Biarritz. They had the means to construct the first American golf course "that looked like a golf course."[118]

Polo, a satisfyingly aristocratic sport, was a hallmark of the first country clubs. (George Bellows depicted the game in *Polo at Lakewood,* which he painted in 1910.) Polo had a major drawback. It requires physical vigor beyond that of the average desk-bound corporate executive. Tennis and golf eventually supplanted polo as the archetypical country-club sports. Many suburban golf and tennis clubs reorganized as multisport country clubs.[119]

The country club's golf course was "an asymmetrical garden, a manicured landscape with a clubhouse that substituted for a British manor house." Specialists in the construction of these artificially natural landscapes and architects skilled in the design of clubhouses—men like Robert Trent Jones and Stanford White—were in great demand. A round of golf offered fewer opportunities for courtship than a tennis match, but the game had other merits. The fairway was, for instance, a pleasant place to tighten professional bonds or to close a lucrative business deal. The typical golfer was an older married man. If women were allowed the privileges of full membership, which was not invariably the case, they were customarily restricted to times that men found inconvenient.[120]

Tennis was especially attractive to younger members who wanted something less strenuous than a track-and-field meet but more invigorating than an amble down the fairway. On the clubs' courts women were free to swing a racquet without risking what Henry Slocum called "insinuations of rompishness." Tennis also offered the erotically charged possibility of mixed doubles that evolved into advantageous marital matches. In an article published in 1894, Elizabeth Cynthia Barney bragged, in reference to the Philadelphia Country Club, that "all of our finest lady tennis players belong to the best families."[121] What more was there for a young fellow to desire?

Twentieth-century eulogists have praised country clubs as democratic institutions, but they discriminated against Jews and against the rare African American who could afford membership. The emergent African-American middle class created its own small network of country clubs from which uneducated, working-class blacks were excluded. And German-American Jews, like those who established Chicago's Homewood in 1901, tended to shun the Yiddish-speaking *Ostjuden* newly arrived from Poland and Russia. There was a partial exception to the social exclusiveness of the country club. Caddies who showed a talent for driving and putting were sometimes offered club membership. They gave sound advice to addled duffers, and their prowess in national competition added to the club's prestige. Slowly, during the first half of the twentieth century, then more quickly during the second half, country clubs democratized in the sense that many of them accepted African-American and Jewish members—if they were educated and affluent.[122]

——— Playgrounds and Little Leagues

As thousands of men and women of the leisure class withdrew behind the hedges and fences of their spatially secluded country clubs, a number of their more progressive social peers concluded that it was better to Americanize than to flee from the immigrants who constituted the majority of the urban lower classes. To accomplish this arduous task, sports—especially team sports—were thought to be the ideal means. In 1898, Charles Stover, Jacob Riis, Lillian Wald, and a number of other reformers organized New York's Outdoor Recreation League, which opened Seward Park in 1899 and Hamilton Fish Park in 1900. There were running tracks, lockers, showers, and—at Fish Park—tennis courts. In 1906, the Playground Association of America began its campaign to bring team sports to immigrant children. The PAA's founder, Henry Curtis, had been a student of G. Stanley Hall, whose psychological theories formed the intellectual framework of the playground movement. (Hall envisioned sports as an antidote to the hormonal upheavals of adolescence.) Curtis had support from Jane Addams, nationally famous for her philanthropic work in Chicago's slums, and from Joseph Lee, founder of the Massachusetts Civic League. When the PAA began its work, the nation had a total of 87 playgrounds scattered through 24 cities. A decade later, 481 cities operated 3,940 urban playgrounds.[123]

The luster of this achievement fades somewhat when one learns that, in 1920, only 3 percent of America's playgrounds were open to African Americans. New York in the 1930s constructed 255 new playgrounds, of which just two were in black neighborhoods. Gender inequality was less evident. Benjamin Rader has argued that none of the reformers "perceived an urgent need for adult-managed sports for girls," but he seems to have overlooked considerable activity. The Young Women's Hebrew Association sponsored a number of sports. New York's Public Schools Athletic League (1903) offered girls' basketball and track-and-field as well as folk dancing. Chicago's parks provided space for over two thousand girls' basketball and softball teams.[124]

Historians distrustful of the reformers' motives see the PAA as an organization that imprisoned the children of Polish and Italian immigrants in "the iron cage of military and industrial disciplines." Dominick Cavallo's less cynical view is that team sports were "seen by reformers as an ideal means of integrating the young into the work rhythms and social demands of a dynamic and complex urban-industrial civilization." To Cavallo's assessment one should add that reformers such as Luther Gulick and Joseph Lee perceived sports as a socializing agent for *all* youths going through what the latter called the "Big Injun" stage of undisciplined adolescent self-assertion.[125]

The PAA was consciously reformist. The same cannot be said of the adult-organized children's leagues that now enroll nearly every middle-class child. These leagues were not created by philanthropists, social workers, or educators but by ordinary citizens. They are the functional equivalent—for American children—of Europe's network of government-subsidized private-sector clubs providing sports to members who range in age from children who are barely able to walk to the elderly who are barely able to walk.

Pop Warner Football began in 1929 when Joseph Tomlin, a Philadelphia stockbroker, formed a league named in honor of the legendary football coach at the Carlisle Indian School. A half century later, some 175,000 boys aged seven to fifteen played on 5,700 teams in 39 states and Mexico. More successful still was Little League Baseball, inaugurated in 1939 by Carl Stotz of Williamsport, Pennsylvania. By 1974, over 2 million boys and girls played in a network of 8,500 leagues that spanned the United States and a number of foreign countries. Today, children's football and baseball are less popular than soccer, the stereotypical suburban sport, sustained by "soccer moms" driving their sons and daughters from their schools to their practices and then—home at last!—to their microwaved TV dinners.[126]

That daughters now play Little League Baseball is the result of a series of lawsuits brought by their parents. Through the 1970s, spokesmen for LLB argued vehemently that a boy's sense of his masculinity identity might be damaged if, for instance, a girl hit his best pitch. They also expressed concern for the safety of girls who might be—in their telling words—"tagged out on the boobs." State and federal courts ruled against LLB, and Congress, in 1975, reworded the organization's charter to read "young people" rather than "boys."[127] Other court cases opened other children's leagues to girls' participation.

Children's sports programs have been controversial for reasons other than sexual discrimination. Critics like Edward C. Devereux have lamented the impoverishment of the repertory of traditional children's games and the loss of "informal peer group experiences." The colorful palette of games played by nineteenth-century children has indeed been replaced by the monochrome of one or two team sports. Although empirical studies have shown that children enter adult-organized sports programs with a preference for the simple pleasures of participation, although most volunteer coaches endeavor to teach the ethos of fair play, many children are taught by their coaches' attitudes and strictures to internalize a win-at-all-costs attitude. The longer children compete in adult-organized programs, the more likely they are to model themselves on professional athletes, which means that they are increasingly ready to cheat and to injure their opponents with "instrumental fouls."[128] A football coach who was criticized for administering drugs to a fourteen-year-old replied, "Let's face it, it's a competitive world, and football prepares kids for life." This approach to children's sports—and to life—is not limited to the United States. A Canadian hockey coach explained to the boys entrusted to his care, "If you can't skate with them, then the only way is to knock them down." Paul Breitner, one of Germany's greatest soccer players, maintained "that we must teach young people how to commit fouls!" A German coach had a terser comment: "Shit on fair play!"[129]

Critics appalled by the dishonesty and violence in and around children's sports blame parents as well as coaches. Fathers and mothers, experiencing anew their own childhood triumphs and expunging the memory of their own athletic failures, become obsessed with their children's sports careers. Parental obsession can produce superstars like Tiger Woods and Venus and Serena Williams; it can also lead to dysfunctional outbursts of uncontrollable rage. "After one [motorcycle] race," reported Ernest Havemann, "a father who thought his son had lost through a stupid mistake . . . was seen to vent his frustration by hitting the boy with a wrench." Other fathers have vented their frustration by berating and beating their children. The mayhem committed by disappointed parents has occasionally included murder.[130]

This is no doubt too dour a picture. Gary Alan Fine concluded a major sociological study of Little League Baseball with a defense of the enterprise: "The arguments of the critics of the program, although valid in individual cases, appear invalid generally." Sitting behind home plate, most parents, whether working- or middle-class, manage to exercise the virtue of disciplined self-control that they expect baseball to instill in their offspring. Parents instruct and encourage much more often than they berate their children.[131]

And the children? When offered a choice between playing on their own or in adult-organized leagues, most children choose the latter. The men and women who grieve that an insanely ambitious coach or parent robbed them of their childhood are greatly outnumbered by the millions of adults with positive memories. They recall that organized children's sports increased their confidence and self-esteem and taught them the virtues of fair play; they look back nostalgically on the day they scored the run that won the big game against the kids from the other side of town. It is also important to remember that children playing on their own do not always behave like Jean-Jacques Rousseau's Émile. A turn-of-the-century Boston lad offered Joseph Lee a good reason to avoid the unsupervised North End playground: "Oh, dere's a tough crowd down dere who would knock the stuffin out of yer."[132]

_____ Basketball: Invention and Diffusion

American football was invented only in the weak sense that men like Walter Camp suggested a number of rule changes that made the game increasingly unlike rugby. Basketball was invented in a much stronger sense of the process. It had no recognizable antecedents. It was tailor-made, cut from whole cloth in response to a specific request.

It happened in 1891, in Springfield, Massachusetts, at the School for Christian Workers (later renamed the International YMCA Training School and still later renamed Springfield College). Basketball's inventor was James Naismith, a thirty-year-old Canadian immigrant. The game was, in Naismith's words, "a modern synthetic product of the office. The conditions were recognized, the requirements met, and the rules formulated . . . before any attempt was made to test its value." Naismith had been given the task of inventing the game by Luther Gulick, who was then the school's superintendent. Gulick appealed to Naismith's ingenuity by arguing, with illustrations drawn from the chemistry of synthetic drugs and dyes, that novelty is merely the result of new combinations of known elements. Specifically, Gulick challenged the young instructor to devise a game complicated enough to maintain the interest of young men in their twenties and spatially confined enough to be played indoors when New England winters daunted faint-hearted Christians. Naismith tried prisoner's base, sailors' tag, rounders, town ball, battle ball, and leapfrog, but all failed the first criterion, that is, adults lost interest. He tried indoor baseball, football, soccer, and lacrosse, but all of them failed the second criterion, that is, they produced too many injuries when played in the confined space of a gymnasium. Whereupon the resourceful Canadian invented basketball. It was, in his own words, "a deliberate attempt to supply for the winter season a game that would have the same interest for the young man that football has in the fall and baseball in the spring."[133]

In an article published in the *American Physical Education Review* (1914) and in a book entitled simply *Basketball* (1941), Naismith reconstructed the sequence of logical steps he took as he reasoned his way to the solution of his problem. Perhaps the best indicator of his instrumental approach was the placement of the goal. Fearful of potential injury from balls hurled forcefully at a ground-level vertical goal (like soccer's), Naismith elevated the goal above the players' heads and designed it so that its aperture was horizontal and narrow. The ball *had* to be propelled gently—in those pre-dunk-shot days—if its arc was to pass through the center of the basket. Constructed rule by rule, basketball represented a rational design.[134]

The first game was played in the school's gymnasium on December 21, 1891, a date that anthropologists a millennium hence will undoubtedly recognize as the ritually significant winter solstice. The YMCA's *Triangle* published Naismith's original rules on January 15, 1892; the *New York Times* decided on April 26 that a description of the game was fit to print, and football coach Amos Alonzo Stagg obligingly introduced the rival game at the University of Chicago in 1893. Intercollegiate basketball began on February 9, 1895, when Hamline lost to the Minnesota State School of Agriculture. By the end of basketball's first decade, Columbia, Cornell, Harvard, Princeton, and Yale had organized the Intercollegiate League, while Amherst, Dartmouth, Holy Cross, Trinity, and Williams had joined together in the New England League.[135]

Trenton, New Jersey, seems to have produced the first professional players, in 1896–1897. Between then and 1922, there were at least a dozen "major" leagues, only one of which lasted for more than half a dozen years. The American Basketball League, founded in 1928, managed to survive, with interruptions, until 1953. The first "world championship" was contested in 1939 between two legendary African-American teams, New York's Renaissance Five and the Harlem Globetrotters (who were actually from Chicago). The Rens won. Additional excitement was generated that year by the NCAA tournament that was the forerunner of today's "March Madness."[136]

Women's basketball began at Smith College, only fifteen miles from Naismith's Springfield gymnasium. Senda Berenson, a graduate of the Boston Normal School of Gymnastics, altered the rules to make the game acceptable for young ladies. At first, the game was played as an intramural sport in which the seniors prepared the sophomores to encounter the "freshmen," who were coached by the juniors. "In order to protect the players from the embarrassment that might be caused either by the bloomers and black stockings that they wore . . . or by the nature of the exertion demanded in the game of basket ball, all men aside from President [L. C.] Seelye, who was expected to give the game an air of dignity, were barred from the gymnasium on the day of the game."[137]

Women's basketball spread almost as rapidly as the men's game. Within four years of the formulation of women's rules, on April 4, 1896, Stanford met the University of California. (Male spectators were not allowed to witness this bit of sports history.) A month later, the *New York Journal's* headline read: "Basket Ball—The New Craze For Athletic Young Women." The accompanying illustration showed Vassar girls "in their Field Day game of basket ball." In the midwest, the six-on-six game, sponsored by the Iowa Girls High School Athletic Union (1925), became the state's most popular spectator sport. "Gentlemen," said John W. Agans, one of the game's proponents, "If you attempt to do away with girl's [sic] basketball in Iowa, you'll be standing in the center of the track when the train runs over!"[138]

Berenson was not the only one to tinker with Naismith's rules. Basketball was continuously reshaped by various national and international organizations anxious to perfect the game and to enhance its attractiveness and profitability. One result of this instrumental approach to play is that the historian can chronicle the development of the rules in the minutest detail. The pivot was allowed in 1893, the dribble in 1896. At first, fouls were penalized by points, but the free throw was introduced in 1894 as an added element of suspense. Naismith began with nine players to a side (because his YMCA class consisted of eighteen men), but the AAU reduced teams to five in 1897. The peach-basket goals of the first game made retrieval of the ball something of an inconvenience; the problem-solvers knocked out the basket's bottom. The modern net, "basket" in name only, was introduced in 1906. The out-of-bounds rule was imposed in 1913, to end mad scrambles for loose balls, and the jump for the ball that followed every basket was eliminated in 1937, to quicken the pace of the game. With that innovation, the game assumed its fixed but by no means its final form.[139]

Like baseball, basketball has experienced ethnic succession in both its collegiate and its avowedly professional forms. In New York, Philadelphia, and other urban centers, the YMCA sought to introduce the game to the new immigrants from southern and eastern Europe. Distrusting the YMCA's muted Protestantism, young Roman Catholics hesitated before they embraced the game. They took eagerly to basketball as soon as parochial schools began to offer it. The Young Men's Hebrew Association made the game into a symbol of Jewish-American identity, but the *American Hebrew* for May 11, 1917, published some oddly pagan comments on the archetypical Jewish basketball player: "Two generations ago he cowered timidly in the ghettoes of the dark countries; now he leaps toward the light like a young god of the sun."[140]

At New York's City College, a secular school with a mostly Jewish student body, Nat Holman's teams were spectacularly successful. In 1938, sportswriter Paul Gallico marveled at the way that basketball "seems to appeal to the temperament of Jews . . . . Jewish players on the college teams around New York have had the game all to themselves." At that time, forty-nine of the American Basketball League's ninety players were Jews, but there was already an indication that African-American players were destined to replace Jews as the stereotypical players of "the city game." Abe Sapperstein, a Jewish promoter, took to the entertainment trail with the fabled Harlem Globetrotters. By the 1970s, allegations of a Jewish affinity for Naismith's invention disappeared, replaced by questionable genetic explanations for the dominance of black slam-dunkers ("White men can't jump").[141]

_____ Basketball: The Fall from Grace

In one of history's little ironies, the game invented by high-minded YMCA workers as a vehicle for "muscular Christianity" became a symbol of corruption in the 1950s. That gamblers bribed players in order to control the scores was common knowledge to basketball insiders. The sorry state of affairs became known to the wider public in 1951, when Junius Kellogg, a black Virginian who had been recruited to play for Manhattan College, was approached by a gambler, Henry Poppe, who offered him a bribe to restrain his scoring instincts. Kellogg reported the offer to his coach who reported it to President Bonaventure Thomas who reported it to the police. Poppe was arrested and persuaded to confess. The investigation that followed revealed a network of fixers who had successfully corrupted dozens of players at CCNY, Long Island University, Manhattan College, New York University, and a number of other schools. Thirty-five players were implicated for fixing eighty-six games during the 1947–1951 seasons. Ten years later, fifty players from North Carolina State and twenty-six other schools were implicated for fixing forty-four games played during the previous five years. Jack Molinas, who had acted as a middleman for the notorious gambler Aaron Wagman, was found guilty of gambling, conspiracy, and perjury. Molinas was sentenced to thirty-six years in prison, served a fraction of that time, was released on probation, and was murdered by an unidentified gunman. Wagman admitted, years later, that he had personally fixed more than a hundred games. The cozy relationship between gamblers and collegiate basketball players continued long after Wagman's day.[142]

The internal dynamics of basketball made it especially susceptible to manipulation. The point spread ("Massachusetts over Maryland by no more than ten points") allows honest bookmakers to quote odds closer to 50–50 (and thus to increase the volume of their business). The point spread also makes it easier for dishonest gamblers to seduce players: "No need lose the game or to look bad. Just make you sure you win by five points instead of ten."

Corruption is encouraged by the NCAA's refusal to admit the obvious: Many "student–athletes" are professionals in all but name. The NCAA's "package"—room, board, tuition, transportation to and from the university, and "laundry money"—is a ridiculously inadequate reward for athletes whose prowess generates millions of dollars in revenue. (Economists estimate that Patrick Ewing enriched Georgetown University by $12 million.) What is a "student–athlete" to think about the NCAA's rules when the NCAA sells the television rights to its annual basketball tournament for $6 billion, when the NCAA permits coaches to pocket hundreds of thousands of dollars from shoe manufacturers, when the NCAA then kicks up a fuss if a booster presents a player with a sports coat or treats him to a pizza?[143]

For a teenager from an economically and socially disadvantaged home, the temptation to break the rules is likely to be irresistible, especially when coaches give tacit approval to under-the-table payments. John "Hot Rod" Williams is an exemplary case. A marginal student from an impoverished family, Williams was courted by more than a hundred universities. He was given $10,000 for matriculating at Tulane University. In 1985 he was arrested and charged with manipulating the point spread in games against Southern Mississippi and Memphis State.[144] Why should he have been more honest than the genial crooks who handed him shoeboxes full of money?

The moral malaise of NCAA Division I basketball is not simply a question of dishonest coaches and athletes. The problem is systemic. Coaches who are under immense pressure to win games are tempted to do whatever they must in order to recruit talented athletes. In their eyes, it is plainly unfair for trustees or presidents to demand athletic success and then to hamper a coach in pursuit of it. At North Carolina State, Jim Valvano was indignant at the very thought of interference: "You think the chancellor is going to tell me what to do? Who to take into school or not to take into school? I doubt it." At Indiana University, Bobby Knight asked a similar rhetorical question: What made college presidents think they were "qualified to tell the athletic departments what the fuck to do?"[145]

It is naïve to expect that harried and harassed Division I coaches will admit to a phenomenally talented high school hoopster that the probability of his obtaining a bachelor's degree is approximately zero. In an exemplary analysis of a Division I basketball program, Patricia and Peter Adler reported that the players they studied arrived on campus with idealistic expectations. The players were assured by the recruiters that it was possible to excel as athletes and as students and simultaneously to enjoy the social amenities of undergraduate life. But it was not possible. The players were overwhelmed by the demands of Division I basketball. "They immersed themselves completely in the athletic role and neglected or abandoned their identities lodged in . . . other roles."[146]

The program that "engulfed" them was not unusual. A study of 644 basketball players from Divisions I–III found Division I players significantly more likely to have less demanding majors, to enroll in notoriously easy courses, to cut classes, to miss or to cheat on examinations, to have others write their papers, to hustle their professors, and—not surprisingly—to feel isolated from other students. That only 41 percent of all Division I basketball players graduate surprises no one who has studied intercollegiate sports. The figure for black players, in 1992, was 32 percent. There was a six-year stretch during which fifteen Division I universities failed to graduate a single male basketball player. Between 1972 and 1985, not one of Memphis State's African-American basketball players graduated. For most black basketball players, sports are—in the words of sociologist Harry Edwards—"a treadmill to oblivion." Nor should it surprise anyone that some disillusioned, frustrated, and embittered players have used illegal drugs, commited sexual assaults, or accepted bribes. "If General Motors or Exxon formed a cartel to treat their workers even half as badly as college athletes are treated," wrote economist Thomas Sowell, "there would be antitrust suits across the country and whole armies of executives would be led away in handcuffs."[147]

Paradoxically, the commercialization that has made intercollegiate sports vulnerable to corruption has apparently immunized the openly professional game. The astronomical salaries paid by the NBA have apparently put the players beyond the reach of gamblers. No one in his right mind jeopardizes a twenty-million-dollar contract in order to collect a ten-thousand-dollar bribe.

_____ The NBA, Nike, and the Black Superstar

Genetically favored or not, black basketball players overwhelmingly dominate the NBA. From its first season, 1949–1950, the NBA, which was formed by a merger between the National Basketball League (1937) and the Basketball Association of America (1946), recruited black players. During the 1960s, when basketball threatened baseball and football as the nation's premier spectator sport, the rivalry between Bill Russell (Boston Celtics) and Wilt Chamberlain (Philadelphia 76ers) thrilled the fans. Then came a period in which the NBA seemed to tailspin into a morass of violence and cocaine addiction. "The NBA was shunned by Madison Avenue," reported E. M. Swift in _Sports Illustrated,_ "because it was perceived as a league that was drug-infested, too black, and too regional." In 1983, ten NBA teams were in serious economic trouble. The owners found themselves a new commissioner, Daniel Stern, who responded to the crisis with a salary cap and a strict new drug policy. The match-ups between a white star—Larry Bird (Boston Celtics)—and a black one—Earvin "Magic" Johnson (Los Angeles Lakers)—seemed to revitalize the game.[148]

And then, in 1984, Michael Jordan joined the Chicago Bulls. With the support of a new owner, Jerry Reinsdorf, Jordan led the faltering Bulls to six national championships. Jordan was repeatedly and justly named as the league's most valuable player. Fabled for his apparently superhuman ability to hover in the air as he dunked the ball, he became a charismatic global icon, the world's most widely recognized person. (Pope John Paul II was second.) Thanks to Jordan, the "swoosh" on Nike shoes also became a global icon, familiar wherever basketball is played, which—in 2004—is nearly everywhere.[149]

Jordan's income from endorsements dwarfed his salary from the Bulls. His 1992 salary of $3.8 million was pocket money in comparison to the $100 million dollars a year that Jordan earned from corporate endorsements. Representatives from Nike, Gatorade, Sara Lee, Wheaties, Chevrolet, and McDonald's stood in line with unprecedented offers. In 1987, Nike offered $18 million for a seven-year contract. It was a good investment. Within two years Nike's sales doubled to $1.7 billion. It was not always a good deal for consumers. Inner-city teenagers unable to afford Air Jordan shoes sometimes murdered to wear them.[150]

Jordan has been treated, by Michael Eric Dyson and others, as "a seminal cultural text" and as a symbol of "fantasies of capital accumulation and material consumption." Critics of American society and culture have indicted Jordan, figuratively, for complicity in a long list of crimes. Some of the political and economic accusations are plausible. Jordan's refusal to endorse Harvey Gant's effort to unseat the notoriously reactionary Senator Jesse Helms (R–North Carolina) was indeed a betrayal of his home state's African-American community. Jordan's relationship with Nike does indeed implicate him in that company's policies and practices, including the construction of overseas factories where Asian workers are paid a small fraction of what American workers receive.[151]

Other accusations are more problematic. Cheryl Cole, David Andrews, and others have argued that the NBA and Nike have cynically exploited Jordan's real or fabricated good nature in order to reassure nervous white fans who might otherwise feel threatened by televised displays of physically aggressive black manhood. As "a floating racial signifier who, in Derridean terms, is constantly under erasure," Jordan allegedly offers "reconfigured racism" that allows his white admirers to see themselves, undeservedly, "as compassionate and ethical subjects."[152]

And still other accusations seem absurd. Mary G. McDonald faults Jordan because he is "marketed" as a married heterosexual and because his appearance in a coat and tie assuages "the cultural anxiety around black masculinity and sexuality." Cheryl Cole condemns Jordan for his complicity with Nike's P.L.A.Y. program, which donates some $10 million a year to provide children—especially black children—with "safe, clean, accessible facilities . . . and recreational opportunities." Cole sees the program as a clever strategy to deflect attention from the crimes committed by young blacks desperate to own Air Jordan shoes. Beneath the rhetoric of philanthropy, Cole detects a Jordan fronting for Nike in an insidious plot to "criminalize Black youth."[153] Jordan, the affable target of this critical barrage, seems to survive unscathed.[154]

LATIN AMERICA
THE *INGLESES* VERSUS THE *NORTEAMERICANOS*

_____ Pre-Columbian Prelude

When the Spanish arrived in the Americas, they confronted and conquered not only "primitive" tribes but also imperial civilizations—the Incan and the Aztec—with a degree of political and social organization comparable to their own. The ritual rubber-ball game played by the Aztecs (and by the other peoples of Mesoamerica) has attracted so much archeological and anthropological attention that it is now among the world's most studied sports—if it was a sport.

Closely related to the game was the myth of *Popol Vuh,* which told of twin brothers whose names appear in many different transliterations. The brothers left home in order to challenge the gods of the underworld to a game of football. They lost and paid the mythically predictable price of defeat—death. The head of one brother was placed in a tree, where a young girl happened upon it. From the mouth of the head spurted a stream of seeds that impregnated the girl. She bore sons who grew to young manhood and challenged the gods to a second game of football, which the young men won. Whereupon the heads of the twins rose to the heavens and became the sun and the moon.[1]

Ulmaliztil, the ball game that corresponded to this myth, was played on hundreds of courts, some I-shaped and some open-ended, located as far north as Arizona and as far south as Guatemala. The most impressive courts are the thirteen found at the Chichén Itzá temple complex in Yucatán. The largest of them measures 150 meters from end zone to end zone. On the basis of architectural and artistic remains, supplemented by the observations of the first Spanish explorers, most scholars agree that the balls were made of rubber, that they were propelled by the players' padded hips, buttocks, knees, and elbows, that one object of the game was to send the ball through a stone ring, and that some of the players, presumably the losers, were sacrificed to the gods. (This sort of "hard ball" comes grotesquely to mind when one reads that Saddam Hussein's son Uday imprisoned and tortured the Iraqi soccer players who lost a World Cup qualifier to Kazakhstan.)[2]

There is no consensus about the meaning of the Mesoamerican game. Some authorities, arguing that the ball symbolized the sun and the moon, believe the game was part of a divination cult. "The sacrifice of the sun (in the west) in the guise of a 'privileged' ballplayer helped to assure its successful underworld passage and ultimate transformation and rebirth (in the east)." Other scholars, calling attention to serpent–water–blood symbolism, believe the game was embedded in a fertility ritual. Still others see a political statement or "a substitute and a symbol for war." Spanish missionaries interpreted the game as pagan blasphemy.[3]

The Spanish banned the indigenous game and introduced the own sports: pelota, cockfights, horse races, the rodeolike *charreada,* and the *corrida de toros,* which was first performed in the seventeenth century. In colonial Mexico, as elsewhere in Hispanic America, bullfights were the bright center of the ludic spectrum—until modern sports dimmed their lustre.[4]

———— Soccer: "The Greatest Joy of the People"

Through most of South America, the word *deporte* (sport) refers first and foremost to soccer football. Renowned sociologists like Brazil's Roberto da Matta have sought to explain the continent's "football madness" by the game's intrinsic aspects. Soccer has clear rules and provides a sense of justice in societies where social justice is in short supply.[5] The rules are certainly clear, and a sense of justice may be present (despite screams of rage at the officials' bias), but soccer's success has less to do with its intrinsic aspects than with the fact that British economic and cultural capital dominated the continent through most of the nineteenth century.

In 1806, during a forty-five-day military occupation of Buenos Aires, British soldiers reduced the boredom of their duty with cricket matches. The troops left, and the merchants arrived. The wool trade brought Thomas Hogg, the energetic owner of a Yorkshire textile factory. Hogg helped to found a British commercial center, a British library, a British college, and, in 1819, a cricket club.[6]

Cricket became fashionable, but Hogg's sons turned to other sports. Tómas Hogg was a founder of the Dreadnought Swimming Club, which had its first contests in 1863. In 1866, he took up squash. With his brother James, he organized the Buenos Aires Athletic Society, which held its first track-and-field meet on May 30, 1867. At some point in the next decade, Tómas seems to have been responsible for Latin America's first golf club. He also participated in an inaugural rugby game played at the Buenos Aires Cricket Club on May 14, 1874. His brother James was on hand in 1880, when the recently invented game of lawn-tennis arrived in Argentina. It is impossible not to imagine Tómas, racquet firmly in hand, on the other side of the net.[7]

British sailors on shore leave had played some kind of football as early as 1840, at which time the local newspaper, *La Razón,* informed its readers that this odd pastime "consisted of running around after a ball." The next reference to the game seems to have come a generation later. When the Buenos Aires Football Club took to the field, on June 20, 1867, the ubiquitous Hogg brothers were the mainstay of one of the teams, while William Heald captained the other. According to *The Standard* for June 23, the Hoggs, wearing colored caps, defeated Heald's white-capped players four goals to none. The sport received a setback in 1874, when the members of the Buenos Aires Football Club voted, unanimously, to shift to rugby football. One of the two rugby teams was, inevitably, captained by "Señor Hogg."[8]

Soccer also flourished among the boys at British schools in Argentina, thanks largely to Alexander Watson Hutton. He arrived from Scotland in 1881 and joined the faculty of St. Andrew's College. Three years later, he established the Buenos Aires English High School, which offered a soccer pitch for the boys and tennis courts for the girls. When a shipment of regulation soccer balls ordered by Hutton arrived in Buenos Aires, puzzled customs officials did not know how to classify them and were said to have fabricated a new customs category: The leather objects were listed as "items for the crazy English." Hutton was undeterred by sarcasm. In 1893, he helped to launch the Argentine Association Football League.[9]

The year that Hutton introduced soccer in the Buenos Aires English High School, his colleagues did the same at British schools in Rosario and Santiago. At St. Andrew's, where the school club was founded in 1890, the Scottish headmaster, J. William Fleming, was notoriously strict about church attendance and soccer practice. Strictness paid. The boys from St. Andrew's defeated the "Old Caledonians" into win Argentina's first national soccer championship.[10]

Employees of British-owned railroads were also active in the diffusion of Argentine soccer. Famous clubs such as *Rosario Central* and *Excelsior* were founded by workers of the *Ferrocarril Central Argentino,* the *Ferrocarril Sud,* and other railroad companies. Between the railroad workers and the students at schools and colleges, challenges went back and forth. In Santiago, in 1890, the representatives of *Ferrocarril Nordeste Argentino* lost a famous 1–0 match against the youths of the *Colegio Nacional.*[11]

The British imprint on Argentine sport remained legible for decades. Reports of soccer matches were a monopoly of the English-language press until 1901, when a notice appeared in *El País.* It was not until 1905 that the name of the national soccer federation was given in Spanish. When *Racing Club de Buenos Aires* won the national soccer championship (1913), it was known as *el primer gran equipo criollo,* because all the players had Spanish or Italian names and none was associated with a British school. Even then, however, British names still outnumbered Spanish ones on many team rosters.[12]

By the time that the professional league was launched, in 1933, the problem was not the number of Britons in Argentina but rather the number of Argentines in Italy, where the rules of professional soccer allowed foreigners of Italian ancestry to be classified as *rimpatriato,* that is, "repatriated." Julio Libonatti left *Rosario Central* and signed with *Torino* in 1925. Dozens of other players followed him. The Argentine answer was to stiffen patriotism with pesos. Unfortunately, there were never enough pesos for Argentina to keep its greatest players. Alberto DiStefano reached the apogee of his career at *Real Madrid,* and Diego Maradona reached his in Barcelona and in Naples.[13]

By 1928, no one quarreled with *El Grafico*'s conclusion that football was "the collective sport of the *criollo,*" as deeply embedded in his psyche as the tango. Neither the *gaucho*'s traditional game of *pato,* nor Argentina's supremacy in international polo, nor the spectacular achievements of Formula I driver Juan Manuel Fangio, nor the radiant appeal of tennis star Gabriela Sabatini was able to distract the nation from its obsession with *fútbol.*

Journalists debated the merits of the "British" versus the "creole" style. The former, which emphasized passing the ball, was disciplined, mechanical, and efficient; the latter, which stressed dribbling, was inventive, artistic, an expression of the *alegría de la vida.* Intellectuals debated the deeper social significance of the game. Was enthusiasm for soccer a sad sign of "conformity with established society," as Juan José Sebreli insisted, or was it a statement of irrepressible individualism, which seems to have been the view of Eduardo Galeano.[14]

There was agreement on one fact. Football mattered. Defeat in the World Cup Final—like the humiliating 6–1 loss to Czechoslovakia in 1958—threw Argentine fans into a depression. Victory in the Final—like the one achieved against England in 1986, thanks to Maradona's "hand of God" goal—exhilarated them. In the ecstasy of *that* moment, few people fretted about the illegality of the goal or about Maradona's alcoholism, drug-addiction, and bad sportsmanship. Few cared that Maradona lived in Italy and played for Naples. *Argentina* had scored.[15]

In Chile as in Argentina, "English commercial houses and colleges were the great propagandists for the sport that, in time, became the passion of the multitude." The first club seems to have been the Valparaiso FC, created in 1889 by David N. Scott. Teams then sprang into life at English schools such as Mackay and Sutherland in nearby El Cerro Alegre and in firms such as *La Casa Rogers,* importers of White Rose Tea. By 1893, a few ethnic Chileans were also to be seen in the distinctive shorts and shirts worn by all self-respecting (and self-advertising) soccer players. That year also saw the first games between Valparaiso and Santiago as well as the first encounter with an Argentine team. The 1–1 tie between Chile and Argentina was less international than it seemed because all the players involved were either British-born or of British descent. The Football Association of Chile, chartered in 1895, was another organization dominated by *los ingleses.* Within a year, however, Santiago had its first purely Chilean clubs. Students at the *Instituto Nacional* and the *Escuela Normal de Preceptores* led the way to the "nationalization" of the game. The foundation of the *Associación de Fútbol de Chile,* in 1912, was a sign that the Chilean players were finally on their own.[16]

The Brazilian story was similar—except that football's position in Brazil is even more unchallenged than its place elsewhere in Latin America. Even more than in Argentina, the mood of the entire society seems to rise and fall with the fortunes of the national team. Luckily for the psychic health of the population, Brazil has qualified for every World Cup Final and has won five of them, more than any other nation.

The game began in the familiar way. In 1894, Charles Miller, born in São Paolo of English parents, returned from his studies in England and brought with him a pair of soccer balls. As Brian Glanville explained, "Soccer then—to [Miller's] surprise—was virtually unknown; even the resident British firms preferred to play cricket." Not at all discouraged, Miller promptly recruited players from the São Paulo Railway Company and other British-owned firms. The first game, the railroad workers versus employees of the municipal gas works, took place on the grounds of the local cycling club. Miller joined the São Paulo Athletic Club, which had been founded in 1878, and persuaded the cricket players to try the new game. (Their first opponents were the boys at Mackenzie College.) By 1902, São Paulo had a football league whose players—mostly British expatriates—were expert enough to trounce a visiting team composed of Britons who had settled in South Africa.[17]

Two years earlier, Oscar Cox, who had learned the game in Switzerland, recruited players from the Rio Cricket Association, which his father had founded, and created *Fluminense,* a socially exclusive soccer club destined to become one of the most illustrious in Brazilian history. In 1910, *Fluminense* invited its British counterpart, the strictly amateur Corinthians, to Rio de Janeiro. The visitors went on to São Paulo, where they inspired their hosts to create another of Brazil's most famous teams: the São Paulo Corinthians. Although most of Brazil's early players stemmed from the middle and upper classes, these new Corinthians did not; they—like Miller's first team—were recruited mainly from the employees of the São Paulo Railway Company. By 1914, Brazilian soccer had developed so rapidly that the national team was able to defeat Argentina in the first of their many bitterly fought encounters. In 1919, Brazil won the South American championship. A professional league was begun in 1933.[18]

Brazil's days of ludic glory began in earnest in 1958, when the national team won its first World Cup Final. Victories in 1962, 1970, 1994, and 2002 underlined the obvious fact that Brazil's national team has been the world's most successful. Home games were played in Maracaná Stadium, which holds 220,000 fans. (Brazil has eight of the world's nine largest stadia.) The stadium's layout tells a wordless story about the behavior as well as the size of Brazilian soccer crowds. Maracaná's playing field is surrounded by a ten-foot-deep moat and a ten-foot-high wire fence. Fans are fanatic. In her aptly titled *Soccer Madness* (1983), sociologist Janet Lever endorses the Brazilian conviction "that it was soccer, not coffee or samba, that put Brazil on the modern map." Identity is so intertwined with soccer in São Paulo that workers' productivity drops and workplace accidents increase whenever their favored team does poorly.[19]

Unlike the Argentines and the Chileans, most Brazilians can claim African origins. Not long after slavery was legally abolished in 1888, black Brazilians began to appear on the rosters of the smaller soccer clubs. They were not always welcome. When the America Football Club of Rio accepted its first black player, Arthur Friedenreich, a number of fans turned to *Fluminense* (which did not accept black players until the 1960s). When *Vasco da Gama's* racially integrated team entered the first division in 1923, a number of clubs quit rather than compete against African–Brazilian players. Responding to such manifestations of elitist racism, the city's poor created their own club, *Flamengo,* whose symbol is a black vulture. In time, of course, Brazilian soccer came to be dominated by mestizo or black players. Friedenreich became Brazil's first nationally celebrated sports hero. Active in the 1920s, he was outshone in the postwar years by Manuel Francisco dos Santos and Edson Arantes do Nascimento—star players better known simply as Garincha and

Pelé. Who dared to doubt Pelé, the idol of the Brazilian masses, when he informed the *Jornal do Brasil* that soccer is "the greatest joy of the people." In a society wracked by political, economic, and social problems, Brazilians are prone to remark that soccer is *"a única coisa que deu certa"* ("the only thing that has gone right").[20]

Throughout Latin America, soccer is a popular theater of macho masculinity. In the United States, it has become a showcase for female athleticism. At American colleges, women's soccer teams outnumber men's teams. In American high schools, over a quarter of a million girls play soccer. The final game of the 1999 Women's World Cup—the United States versus the People's Republic of China—was played in Pasadena's Rose Bowl before 90,185 hysterically enthusiastic spectators. The photograph of an exuberantly celebrating Brandi Chastain—in a black sports bra, with some remarkable abdominal muscles—is likely to remain one of the most widely recognized images of the twentieth century. The contrast between soccer in Latin America and in the United States proves conclusively that no sport is intrinsically masculine or feminine. Sports mean whatever they are made to mean.[21]

_____ *Béisbol*

Rafael Leónidas Trujillo Molina, the right-wing dictator of the Dominican Republic from 1930 to 1961, shared a passion for baseball with Fidel Castro, the left-wing dictator of Cuba from 1960 to who knows when. Nicaraguans who suffered under tyrannical Anastasio Somoza García credited him with one good deed. As a fan, a player, an umpire, and—eventually—as an owner of the *Cinco Estrelles,* Somoza promoted *béisbol.*[22] One indicator of the more or less nonpartisan popularity of Caribbean baseball is the number of Hispanic players who have had major-league careers in the United States. Cuba's Saturnino Orestes Arrieta "Minnie" Minoso Armas, Puerto Rico's Roberto Clemente, the Dominican Republic's Juan Marichal, Mexico's Fernando Valenzuela, and Venezuela's Omar Vizquel are just five selected at random from the long list of Hispanic players who achieved stateside stardom in the major leagues.

Cubans were apparently the first Caribbeans to catch the baseball virus from the *Norteamericanos,* and they were certainly active in spreading the fever. Nemesio Guilló claimed, in 1924, to have introduced baseball to Havana in 1864, after he returned from studying in the United States. He remembered a game in 1868 against the crew of an American ship docked in Matanzas. The first historically attested game took place in 1874, when the *Habana Base Ball Club* met the *Matanzas Base Ball Club.* Reporting Havana's 51–9 victory, *El*

Artista sprinkled English nouns among its Spanish verbs. Cuban teams were numerous enough by 1878 for Havana's Emilio Sabourín to organize the *Liga de Béisbol Profesional Cubana.* An 1887 tour by the Philadelphia Athletics helped to popularize the game.[23]

The first *aficionados* had to deal with the disapproval of the Spanish authorities, who preferred that the fans devote themselves to the gymnastic exercises brought home from France in 1842 by José Rafael de Castro. Drill seemed more compatible with good discipline than the exuberant disorder of a ball game. The colonial administration also suspected, quite correctly, that sports had political implications. Opposition to Spanish rule came largely from upper-class nationalists who looked to the United States for their sports as well as for political ideals and funds. Wencelas Gálvez y Delmonto was certain that modernity's game, baseball, would surpass bullfighting and cockfighting, traditional pastimes imported from Spain. In 1895, when armed resistance to Spanish rule brought an array of repressive countermeasures, baseball was banned.[24]

Sabourín, the organizer of the *Liga de Béisbol,* personified the intimate connection between sports and politics. He was part of an underground organization that collected and repaired weapons discarded by the Spanish troops. The weapons were then smuggled to the insurgent forces in the countryside. Sabourín was arrested in 1895, convicted of subversive activities, and exiled to a prison in Spanish Morocco. A fellow prisoner, Juan Gualberto Gómez, remembered him as a patriot and as "an enthusiastic partisan of this 'sport' that regenerates the human organism." Sabourín was devoted to *"el Base-Ball, su Familia y su Patria."*[25]

When the island passed from Madrid's rather ineffectual rule to Washington's oppressive "protection," Cuban baseball, together with North American economic investment, "took off." A viable amateur league was formed in 1914 and a viable professional one in 1917. There was soon international two-way traffic in ballplayers. Rafael Almeida and Armando Marsans were signed by the Cincinnati Reds in 1911. (They were not the first to go north: Estéban Bellán played for the Troy Haymakers in 1869.) In 1922, an entire team, the Cuban Stars, joined the Negro National League. A generation later, the best of the island's professional teams, Roberto Maduro's Havana Sugar Kings, joined the International League and competed in the United States (1954–1960). Meanwhile, a number of *yanquís* who failed to make major-league rosters in the United States tried their luck on the island. Some major-leaguers supplemented their salaries by playing "winter ball" in Cuba.[26]

The money and the climate were not the only attractions. In the days of dictator Fulgencio Batista, Havana was renowned for its nightclubs, casinos, racetracks, and brothels. And the Cubans' more relaxed attitudes toward racial differences made it possible for major-leaguers—all of whom at that time were white—to compete against Josh Gibson and other stars of the Negro National League.[27]

Professional sports were officially abolished in 1962, and Cuba's close ties with major-league baseball were severed, but baseball continued to be the island's (and its leader's) favorite sport. When baseball became a part of the Olympic program, a long-deferred dream was fulfilled. Cuba outscored the United States and won the gold.

Cricket seemed a more likely candidate than baseball for the title of Mexico's national game. British businessmen established the Mexican Cricket Club in 1827. Conditions were doubtlessly primitive in the early years of play, but amenities did follow. In the 1860s, the club "arranged special trolley service [from the capital] to its pitch at Napolés." A formal breakfast was served between innings—at one o'clock in the afternoon. The club had at least one Mexican player, M. J. Trigueros, a student at the *Escuela de Artes y Oficios.* Trigueros was also the prime mover of the Victoria Cricket Club, which he formed from the ranks of his fellow students.[28]

By the time that American investors in the Mexican economy surpassed British entrepreneurs in the value of their holdings, which occurred in 1890, baseball had already made an appearance. "Yankee employees of the Mexican National and the Mexican Central railroads . . . organized company teams in the summer of 1882 to play scrimmage games." In a match that pitted the National Baseball Club against players representing the Telephone Company, the railroad men prevailed by a score of 31–11.[29]

The first Mexican teams were formed no later than 1886, when a game was played at Corazón de Jesus to collect funds for the city's poorhouse. By 1895, Mexican players in the capital were skillful enough to win the city's baseball championship against the American Base-Ball Club and a British cricket team whose players "adjusted more or less successfully to American rules."[30]

In 1904, Mexican teams established two leagues. The first, for amateurs, played during the summer months; the second, for the semiprofessionals, had a winter season. *El Record,* the winners of the 1906–7 season, had their moment of glory when they competed against the visiting Chicago White Sox, the first major-league team to conduct spring training outside the United States. Although the Mexicans, whose team included two Americans, lost by a score of 12–2, local fans were nonetheless proud of them. After all, the White Sox had won the 1906 World Series against the favored Chicago Cubs.[31]

A passion for American sports became a sign of Mexican modernity. In the years that led to the Mexican Revolution of 1910–1911, there was "a rush to accept European, and especially American, activities . . . . Baseball particularly reflected the growing influence of the United States."[32] Like the Cubans, who saw baseball as a counter to a detested Spanish culture, many Mexicans saw the game as an implicit protest against the oppressive rule of Porfirio Díaz, the country's homegrown dictator.

In 1910, when protest took the more serious form of armed social revolution, Mexican attention turned to graver matters than a three–two count with the bases loaded. When the spasms of political unrest became less severe, in 1920, baseball revived. In 1925, Alejandro Aguilar Reyes established a five-team professional league. At first, the *Liga Mexicana* was a ragtag affair with erratic play and a chaotic schedule, but the league was stable and strong enough in the 1940s to cause a crisis in north-of-the-border baseball. Jorge Pasquel, the wealthy president of the *Liga,* decided to mount a real challenge to the *gringos.* Since a number of Mexican players had had successful careers in the United States, Pasquel concluded that turnabout was fair play. Aided by his four brothers and a willingness to pay players two or three times what they earned north of the Río Grande, Pasquel began to raid not only the Negro National League, which had always been easy prey for Hispanic talent-hunters, but also the major leagues. Pasquel recruited stars such as the Brooklyn Dodgers' Mickey Owen and expanded the *Liga* from six teams to eight. Commissioner Albert "Happy" Chandler blacklisted the "jumpers" but was unable to dam the southward flow of players or entice the defectors to return.[33]

Unfortunately for the ambitious Pasquel brothers, Mexico's largest stadium held only 22,000 fans. Too few tickets were sold to pay the recklessly inflated salaries, and there were no television networks then to offer multi-million-dollar contracts. When the Pasquels began to cut costs and eliminate entire teams, the "jumpers" begged Chandler to take them back, and he did, after a legal challenge to his blacklist threatened baseball's antitrust exemption.[34]

After Jorge Pasquel's death in 1955, Alejo Peralta, a wealthy and influential entrepreneur, became president of the *Liga Mexicana.* He treated the players "more as expendable entertainers than as workers," which motivated the players, in 1981, to form a union and then—like the American players in 1890—to create a rival league. Thanks in part to his connections with Mexico's governing party and with its labor unions, Peralta was able to cripple the eight-team *Liga Nacional* and drive it from field. The resulting system may not be democratic, but it is at least stable.[35]

Despite the importance of the game in Cuba and in Mexico, the Dominican Republic has become the center of gravity for Caribbean *béisbol.* The game came early to the island. Cuban patriots who had fled their homes after the failure of their first war for independence (1868–78) sought solace in baseball during their exile in Santo Domingo. The first Dominican clubs to enjoy more than an ephemeral existence were formed in 1891 by Ignacio and Ubaldo Alomá, ironworkers from Cuba. The clubs were officially entitled *Cervecería* (from the local beer) and *El Cauto* (from the local river), but fans referred to them by the colors of their uniforms, the *Rojos* and the *Azules*.[36]

In 1907, a group of mostly upper-class schoolboys organized *Licey,* which became one of the island's most successful teams. The capital city of Santo Domingo held its first championship in 1912, a year after *Licey* defeated a team from San Pedro de Macorís in one of the island's first interurban encounters. Santo Domingo also produced the first team to vanquish a visiting American nine. In 1914, Dominicans rejoiced as Enrique Hernández of the *Nuevo Club* pitched a no-hit, no-run game against a team of sailors from the cruiser *Washington.*[37]

From 1916 to 1924, the United States carried out one of its periodic military occupations of the Dominican Republic. Even before the Marines landed, James Sullivan, the American ambassador, saw that baseball might pacify the natives. The game "satisfies a craving in the nature of the people for exciting conflict, and [it] is a real substitute for the contest in the hillsides with rifles." Ignoring the ambassador's sage counsel, the State Department refused to make the diffusion of baseball a matter of public policy, but the game flourished without official support. American popular culture became so pervasive that two cricket teams in the town of Consuelo were renamed the Twentieth Century Fox and the Metro Goldwyn Mayer.[38]

Cubans continued to serve as conduits for American influence. When *Licey* imported several Cuban players to Santo Domingo, its crosstown rival *Escogido* responded by bringing in a real star, Martin Dihigo, who may be the only player enshrined in the Halls of Fame of Cuba, Mexico, and the United States. The desire to recruit Cuban stars became so frantic that the *Estrellas Orientales* of San Pedro de Macoris fielded only three Dominican players. Thanks to its imported talent, the *Estrellas* won the championship. This was too severe a blow to the prestige of President Trujillo. He forcibly merged *Licey* and *Escogido* into a new club privileged to bear his own name. He then stocked *Ciudad Trujillo* with eight African Americans from the Pittsburgh Crawfords and the Homestead Grays. Trujillo not only paid Josh Gibson, "Cool Papa" Bell, and the other black stars far more than they were able to earn in the United States, he also let them know that he expected great things from them. He is said to have ordered Satchel Paige "to pitch a shutout or face a firing squad." According to another anecdote, "When Trujillo's team lost a series to Santiago, his players returned to their hotel to discover a squad of angry militiamen . . . firing their rifles in the air. 'You know you are playing for El Presidente,' they shouted, and more shots rang out." The stories may be apocryphal, but the team did win the island's championship in 1937.[39]

After World War II, the flow of baseball players reversed direction. American players continued to be actively recruited for the island's teams, but they were outnumbered by the Dominicans who sought fame and fortune on the mainland. The first of many hundreds was Ozzie Virgil, imported by the New York Giants in 1956.[40] A number of factors combined to tighten the bonds between the island and major-league baseball. The racial integration of American baseball, which had begun in 1947, opened doors for Dominicans of African ancestry. After 1960, when contacts between the United States and Castro's Cuba ceased, the Dominican Republic became major-league baseball's Caribbean cornucopia.

Relations between the islanders and the mainlanders moved into a new phase when free agency came to major-league baseball in 1976. A year after the restrictions of the "reserve clause" were finally loosened by a combination of legal action and labor–management negotiations, the Toronto Blue Jays opened a Dominican baseball camp run by Epifanio "Epy" Guerrero, a former major-leaguer. By 1989, fifteen other major-league franchises had followed Toronto's lead and established "academies" on the island.[41]

The most elaborate "academy"—*Campo Las Palmas*—was operated by the Los Angeles Dodgers. Dreams of glory pulled and desperate poverty pushed young Dominicans to the gates of the camp. From the hundreds of youths who aspired to play in the United States, a few were selected to spend thirty days at *Las Palmas,* after which the best of them were signed for a bonus of $4,000 to play for six months in the island's minor leagues (for $700 a month). The best of *these* players advanced to the *Estrellas Orientales* or another of the island's six major-league teams. Those who moved on to play in the United States were numerous enough for San Pedro de Macorís to claim proudly that it is, on a per-capita basis, the world's leading source of baseball talent. At the start of 1987 season, this city of 130,000 had thirteen players on major-league rosters.[42]

Although young men continue to arrive at the camps, not everyone is happy with them. They have been characterized by Alan Klein as "the baseball counterpart of the colonial outpost, the physical embodiment overseas of the parent franchise." John Krich has called them "as recognizable a mark of foreign domination as the sugar mill."[43]

Yankee exploitation of Hispanic talent has not, however, diminished the

Hispanic love for *béisbol.* The attitude of many of the Caribbean's *fanaticos* was well represented by the Dominican journalist Pedro Julio Santana in an interview with Rob Ruck: "You must understand that baseball is not thought of as the sport of the Yankee imperialists. . . . Baseball is the national sport of the Caribbean. [The Americans] have not given us anything else that, in my opinion, is of any value."[44]

CONTINENTAL EUROPE
IMPORTS AND EXPORTS

"In the years after 1880," writes Ruud Stokvis, "English sports were adopted on the European continent by young members of the elite and the upper middle class."[1] The sequence of adoption took the form that geographers describe as the "S-curve pattern": Innovations of all kinds are initially slow to spread among a population; then there is a phase of rapid adoption; next, a long period follows during which the laggards are gradually won over to the new technique or mode of behavior.[2] On the continent, it was the anglophile segments of the upper class that responded initially to soccer football, the middle classes that quickly spread the word, and the workers and peasants whose tardy arrival at the soccer pitch completed the process of diffusion. Once *they* began to kick the ball about, players from the upper and middle classes dropped their gear and moved on to greener and more exclusive ludic pastures.

Soccer Football

There has been some confusion about who first brought football to the European continent. According to Eugen Weber, the first clubs were Swiss: *La Chatelaine* of Geneva (1869), the St. Gallen Football Club (1879), and the Grasshoppers of Zurich (1886). They were the combined work of English boys attending Swiss private schools and Swiss graduates of English universities.[3]

In fact, the Swiss may have been anticipated by boys at a Jesuit school in the Belgian town of Melle (near Ghent). At the *Maison de Melle,* which catered to sons of the upper and upper-middle classes, soccer was introduced in 1863 by Cyril Bernard Morrogh, an Irish pupil from Killarney. According to a memoir published by Jules Dubois in 1923 in the *Blad van de Vereniging der Oud Mellisten,* enthusiasm for the new game was so great and play was so wild that the ball soon "exhaled a resounding 'pouf,' its last sigh." Thomas

Savage brought a new one from London, play resumed, and the Belgian boys quickly learned a version of English "more useful than the beautiful poetry of Shakespeare that they pounded into us in the classroom."[4]

The games played at the *Maison de Melle* were, however, an isolated phenomenon. It was not until 1880 that expatriate Britons organized the Antwerp Football and Cricket Club. That same year, Father Germain Hermans, returning to Belgium after a year at St. George's College in Croyden, introduced soccer to his pupils at the *Collège de Saint-Stanislaus* in Tirlemont. In 1885, students at the *Sint-Francis-Xavier Instituut* joined forces with students from the *Koninklijk Atheneum* to challenge the Red Caps of the English College of Brussels. Six years later, students at the *Collège Saint-Bernard,* aided by some local Britons, founded the Brussels Football Club. The common thread was that "English students or employees set the ball to rolling, frequently to the astonishment of passing observers."[5]

Shared love of the game impelled Belgium's soccer players to join together as members of the *Union Belge des Sociétés de Sports Athlétiques* (1895), but Belgium's endemic ethnic conflict eventually led to the separate organization of French (1912) and Flemish (1930) soccer federations.[6]

The Dutch pattern was a variant of the Belgian—minus the ethnic tension. "The introduction of sports such as cricket, football, and tennis and the establishment of clubs to practice them . . . was the work of Englishmen resident in the Netherlands and of the Dutch who had been to England." C. H. Bingham, a cycling enthusiast who became the first director of the *Nederlandsche Vélocipèdisten Bond* (1883), was British. J. R. Dickson Romijn, founder of Deventer's *Utile Dulce Cricket Club* (1875) was educated in England. (Three years later, Romijn's father, who had been a Dutch consul in England, founded the *Haagsche Cricket Club*.)[7]

Maarten van Bottenburg has discovered that soccer was played in the port of Antwerp in the 1870s by dockworkers who learned the game from British seamen, but their teams "played irregularly under changing names and without having club houses, standardized uniforms or fixed playing fields." The future belonged to fourteen-year-old Pim Mulier. In 1883, after studying at an English boarding school, Mulier came home to Haarlem and persuaded the *Haarlemsche Football-Club* (1879) to switch from rugby to soccer. An admiring schoolmate said of him, "He was older than we and had the aura of his time in England."[8]

Unlike their Belgian counterparts, Dutch educators looked to Germany for models of physical education. They were firmly committed to noncompetitive gymnastic exercises of the sort that Germans called *Turnen*. They condemned Holland's emergent sports clubs as "a cancer" afflicting the nation's youth. In vain. The young, unimpressed by the regimented exercise advocated by their elders, took their cues from England. At the turn of the century, in Amsterdam as elsewhere in the Netherlands, "the game of football was limited to a small group of young students from well-to-do families," but the game spread from school to school and then took hold among Dutch workers. In 1887, Pim Mulier—now a twenty-two-year-old football veteran—organized the *Nederlandsche Voetbalboond.* Soccer overtook *Turnen* and became the country's most popular sport.[9]

German physical educators were no more able than their Dutch admirers to dampen the fire of the *Fußballmanie* that raged in their schools. Boys who were bored by the deadly routines of *Schulturnen* (educational calisthenics) responded eagerly to the excitement of football. Konrad Koch, an eighteen-year-old student at Braunschweig's *Gymnasium Martino-Catharineum,* introduced rugby in 1874. The six middle classes of the school formed a team in 1875. Some of the older students worried about a loss of dignity and resisted the lure of the rough-and-tumble game. Their teachers, realizing that boisterous outdoors play was preferable to unruly outbursts in the classroom, sternly ordered the reluctant youths to go out and have a good time.[10]

The teachers at Koch's school were unusually tolerant. Most educational authorities were initially hostile to rugby and to soccer. Their undeterred pupils formed "wild" teams for out-of-school play. Pastors and prelates were no happier about the teenage football fad than teachers were. One Lutheran minister urged a young Berliner to abandon his football club for the church's youth group, only to be told, in Berliner dialect, *"Wenn ick aus der Borussia raus muß, wat hab' ick denn noch vom Leben? Denn schieß' ick mir lieber tot"*: If I have to leave *Borussia,* what's left of life? I'd rather shoot myself.[11]

Throughout the commercial centers of northern Germany, young Germans of the mercantile and professional classes were inspired by British friends and colleagues to form soccer clubs. Bremen and Hamburg had theirs in 1880; Hannover and Berlin had theirs in 1881 and 1885. Five years later, the *Bund Deutscher Fußballspieler* united Berlin's British and German clubs in a single league. Elsewhere in Germany, sixteen-year-old Walter Bensemann founded clubs in Karlsruhe, Strassburg, and Munich. In their folkways, many of these early clubs mimicked the fraternities that were prominent at German universities. Football clubs took Latin names, e.g., *Borussia* instead of *Preu-ßen,* and went in for caps and banners and other paraphernalia of student life.[12]

After a number of failed attempts to found a national organization, eighty-six mostly middle-class delegates, including the indefatigable Bensemann, met in Leipzig on January 28, 1900, to form the *Deutscher Fußball-Bund*

(DFB). A tournament to determine the national champion took place three years later.[13]

A quarter century after Koch introduced football at his *Gymnasium,* working-class players were still few and far between. When football's attraction became too strong for the working class to resist, it was—once again—children who led the way to the playing field. Located in the heart of the heavily industrialized Ruhr Valley, *Schalke 04,* is one of Germany's most famous professional teams. It traces its origins back to May 4, 1904, when fifteen-year-old Heinrich Kullmann and fourteen-year-old Gerhard Klopp organized a group of their friends into a "wild" club that they named *Westfalia Schalke.* It was not long before the boys' fathers—miners and steel workers—noticed what their sons had done. One can imagine Herr Kullmann and Herr Kloop pausing on their way home from work, putting down their lunch pails, and joining the game. If they did not, other industrial workers did. In the first ten years of its existence, *Schalke* had forty-four members whose occupational status is known to us. Half of them were miners and fifteen others were factory hands or artisans. Soccer became, in Germany as in England, a basic constituent of working-class culture, part of what it meant to be *ein guter Kumpel* ("a good fellow worker").[14]

German soccer may have regained some of its erstwhile middle-class supporters on July 4, 1954, when Helmut Rahn and his teammates upset Ferenc Puskas and the heavily favored Hungarian team in the World Cup Final. The game was played in Bern. Germans following it on radio experienced a pivotal moment in their history as Rahn's ball flew into the goal *(das Tor)* and the announcer, Herbert Zimmermann, screamed: *"Toooorrrr!"* Peco Bauwens, the head of Germany's soccer federation, thanked Wotan, the Teutonic god of war, but it seemed to Zimmermann's excited audience that the war that mattered, the real war that had left Germany in ruins and in disgrace, was finally over. It was time to exult in the present and look to the future.[15]

The immediate future of German soccer was, however, rather grim. Despite the national team's World Cup victory, German clubs did poorly in European competition. In the first decade of the European Cup, initiated in 1956 by Gabriel Hanot, *Real Madrid* won five times, Portuguese and Italian teams also won five times, and *Frankfurt Eintracht* was the only German team to make it to the finals. In large numbers, Germany's best players were lured to the openly professional foreign leagues. The result of the exodus was the induced birth, in 1960–61, of the professional *Bundesliga.* Money was the magic force that brought the players home and kept them there.[16]

The *Bundesliga* survived a nasty scandal in 1971 (veteran players fixed a number of games), and the national team became a perennial contender for the World Cup, which Germany won in 1974 and again in 1990. Germany's brightest star, Franz Beckenbauer, was recognized (and revered) by tens of millions of Germans who had never heard of Nobel Prize–winner Heinrich Böll. As for those who *had* heard of the novelist, they, too, seemed to have become soccer fans. In the last decades of the century, soccer attracted so many German businessmen, professionals, academics, and intellectuals that *Fußballmania* ceased to be an unambiguous marker of working-class status.[17]

The *"invention britannique"* arrived in France no later than 1872, when the British residents of Normandy, led by F. F. Langstaff of the South Western Railway, formed the Havre Athletic Club. A rival claim to priority has been made by the Breton town of St. Servan. Joseph Gemain, who was one of the early players, testified that soccer came to Brittany with the English tourists who arrived in droves after the Southampton-St. Malo steamship line was inaugurated in 1864. The first team was called *Les Anglais de Saint Servan.*[18]

Like many of the early enthusiasts for football, the members of the first French clubs were often unsure about exactly which kind of football they wanted to play. On November 18, 1884, ten members of the Le Havre's club voiced a preference for soccer, two were for rugby, and twelve members—resolutely undecided—voted for a combination of both games. Eventually, around 1891, the club divided into soccer and rugby sections.[19]

Britons living in Paris formed a short-lived Paris Football Club in 1879. Schoolboys back from England or inspired by expatriate Britons founded *Le Racing-Club de Paris* (1882) and *Le Stade Français* (1883), both of which offered athletics as well as football. Pupils at the *Lycée Condorcet* created the *Lutèce FC* in 1884. Their peers at the *École Monge* followed suit after an Easter visit to Eton. The British in Paris tried again with the International Athletic Club (1887), the Football Association Club (1887), the White Rovers (1891), and the Standard Athletic Club (1892). In 1894, Standard won France's first national football tournament with a team of ten British and one French player. Four Frenchmen wore the colors of *Le Racing-Club de Paris* in 1906, when the "home team" lost to the Richmond Town Wanderers by a score of 15–0.[20]

By the turn of the century, there were football clubs in most French cities. Paris alone had twenty-five. In the south of France, many of the football clubs—rugby and soccer both—were born from cycling clubs that had already begun to wean the French from *boules* and other traditional games. Throughout the *fin de siècle,* nearly all French soccer players came from the anglophile urban bourgeoisie. In fact, in these early years, the game was so closely identified with the British that casual spectators listening to the players' excited exclamations often assumed that the *écoliers* were British lads with an admirable command of colloquial French.[21]

Neither in the south and southwest, where peasants preferred the rough-and-tumble of rugby, nor in the industrial centers of the north did the French working class take to soccer. As an essentially middle-class sport, soccer was able to attract only some two thousand spectators to a 1903 match for the national championship. Comparisons with Britain and Germany are telling. Two years earlier, a hundred thousand Britons had jammed London's Crystal Palace for the Football Association's Cup Final. Although Germany's *Fußball-Bund* was formed in 1900, it was not until 1919 that the *Fédération Française de Football Association* was constituted.[22]

Despite the relative backwardness of French soccer, there were a number of women's teams. The first important manifestations of women's soccer came during and immediately after World War I. As a curtain-raiser to a 1918 contest between the French and Belgian national teams, two teams from the Parisian club *Fémina Sport* played an intraclub match. That same year, Alice Milliat, dominant figure in the *Fédération Féminine et Sportive de France* (1917), inaugurated a national championship for female players.[23]

In the *entre-deux-guerres* period, dishonest football "amateurs" were regularly paid by their dishonest club managers and coaches. There was a scandal in 1926, when the treasurer of Montpellier's team, who had been fired, published the club's payroll. Gabriel Hanot spoke the plain truth to those who thought these payments corrupted working-class morals: "You cannot prevent those who struggle simply to get by from making the most of their natural talents." Industrialist Jean-Pierre Peugeot, the man behind *FC Sochaux* (1925), cut hypocrisy's Gordian knot. Admitting that he paid his players to kick goals rather than build automobiles, he persuaded the *Fédération Française de Football Association* to accept open professionalism, which the FFFA Council did on January 17, 1932.[24]

Although soccer has never been as popular in France as in Great Britain and Germany, the game has served the French well as a vehicle of acculturation and ethnic integration. The national federation has always fielded a higher percentage of foreign professionals than its European counterparts have. From the 1930s to the 1980s, about 20 percent of France's players were foreigners. When Larbi Ben Barek was recruited to *Olympique de Marseille* in 1938, he was one of 147 Africans in the French league's top two divisions. In the postwar period, the Casablanca-born star was followed by hundreds of other North African players.[25]

In these years, the league went—inexorably—through the same phases as other leagues in other countries. The owners held salaries to the lowest possible level and denied players the chance to move from team to team. Raymond Kopa, one of the game's brightest stars, complainted bitterly, "Today, in the middle of the twentieth century, the professional football player is the only man who can be bought and sold without even asking his opinion."[26] The players unionized and went on strike. Restraints on movement were reduced and salaries were increased.

The millions paid to Michel Platini and other stars came largely from the television networks. TFI and Canal Plus paid 621 million francs for the 1996–1997 rights. Corporate sponsors were a second source of revenue, national and local governments a third. (All cities with first-division teams provide direct or indirect subventions.) Some teams flourished (*Olympique de Marseille*) and some staggered under a heavy burden of debt *(FC Mulhouse),* but the level of play rose to the point where the French national team achieved the success that had long eluded it. In 1998, they won the World Cup Final. That the team was a "rainbow coalition" of ethnically diverse players was taken by many as an additional reason for celebration.[27]

Italian students played a lesser role in the adoption of soccer than did the schoolboys of northern Europe. British sailors introduced the game in the 1880s, when they docked and went ashore in Genoa, Leghorn, Naples, and other peninsular ports. British residents of Turin and Milan, the industrial and financial centers of northern Italy, organized most of the teams destined to dominate Italian football. "With remarkable precision," remarked Antonio Papa, "the map of soccer retraces the map of foreign capital in the peninsula." With some help from Swiss nationals working in Milan, Naples, and Bari, both maps were drawn by the British.[28]

Edoardo Bosio is usually considered to be the founder of Italian soccer. In March of 1887, returning to Turin from a business trip to England, he carried a soccer ball and some lively memories. Recruiting the employees of his firm, he arranged for a game. In 1891, his group fused with a team that had begun to play two years earlier. The result was the *Football Club Torinese.* In Genoa, it was British businessmen and consular officials who took the initiative, in 1896, and added soccer to the array of sports offered by their four-year-old Cricket and Athletic Club. Soccer quickly became so popular that the members renamed themselves the Genoa Football Club. A year later, British expatriates founded the famed Juventus Football Club of Turin. Englishmen and Italians joined forces in 1899 to create yet another club prominent in the history of the game: the Milan Cricket and Football Club. Still another collaboration gave birth in 1900 to the Anglo-Palermitan Athletic and Football Club.[29]

On April 15, 1898, clubs from Genoa and Turin, rejecting any impulse to think in small terms, created the *Federazione Italiana del Football*. The president was an Italian, the secretary an Englishman. Two months later, the infant seven-club association sponsored its first "national championship." Genoa, which fielded a rugged team bolstered by five foreigners, won this and five of the next six championships. In 1908, the federation decided to bar foreign players from its annual tournament, but a boycott by the powerful clubs from Genoa, Milan, and Turin led to a quick reversal of the rule. Nationalism did score a point in 1909, however, when the federation changed its name to the *Federazione Italiana Gioco del Calcio* (the Italian Federation for the Game of Football). [30]

In order to become truly popular, Italian soccer had to overcome the widespread (and correct) perception that modern sports in general and soccer in particular had been imported from a predominantly Protestant culture. Giovanni Semeria cleared the way for hesitant Roman Catholics by obfuscating the issue. Belittling the English origins of soccer, he explained that the relationship of the captain to his obedient teammates is analogous to the position of the pope in relation to the great mass of faithful believers. Semeria's ingenious argument seems to have cleansed soccer "from the taints of both Protestantism and 'modernity.'"[31]

Early in the twentieth century, Italy's industrial workers took to soccer and greatly increased the options available to the selectors of the national team, which made its debut May 15, 1910, in Milan's *Arena Civica*. The team was strong enough to defeat the French visitors by a score of 6–2. Italian soccer moved into a new era in the 1920s when the economically stressed directors of *Juventus* of Turin went to Fiat-manufacturer Eduardo Agnelli for succor. Agnelli transferred the team's amateurs to Fiat's payroll and propelled the team toward global glory.[32]

Italian soccer reached a zenith of sorts during the Fascist era (1922–1944), when the national team won two World Cup Finals (1934, 1938) and an Olympic title (1936). Antonio Ghirelli's account of the postwar years is a lively story of regional rivalry (industrial North versus rural South) and a sorry tale of pervasive corruption. The regional rivalry culminated in 1987, when Argentine-born Diego Maradona, whom Naples had acquired with a transfer payment of $7.5 million, led the club to its first national championship. The corruption appeared mainly in the form of officials who were biased or incompetent and players who were frequently bribed and occasionally drugged. In 1980, for instance, the president of the Milan FC, a referee, and players from thirteen different clubs were arrested in a bribery scandal. The courts acquitted everyone involved, the *Federazione* punished those whom it thought guilty, and the next scandal—an illegal betting system—involved twelve clubs and sixty-two players.[33]

Hungarians, many of them assimilated Jews, were especially receptive to the appeals of football. Charles Löwenrosen, a schoolboy whose parents had emigrated from Hungary to England, brought a soccer ball with him when he visited Budapest in 1896. Impressed by his tales of British sport, Löwenrosen's friends formed Hungary's first football team. By 1910, when the Hungarians hosted the Italians in Budapest, their game was so far advanced that they trounced the visitors by a score of 6–1. A professional league was inaugurated in 1924, nearly a decade before French professionalism. In the late 1940s and early 1950s, the Hungarian team, led by Ferenc Puskas, was the world's strongest. The team dealt the English their first defeat at Wembley Stadium and they should have won the 1954 World Cup, for which they were odds-on favorites. Hungarian hegemony was ended by the failed anti-Soviet revolution of 1956, which sent most of the national team into voluntary exile. Hungarian soccer never recovered. The level of play declined, and fixed games were so common in the 1980s that league championships resembled an auction. The end of Communism released a generation of Hungarian players to seek their fortunes in Germany and points west.[34]

It seems ironic, when one considers the leading role of Great Britain in the diffusion of soccer football, that the impetus for global organization came from France. In 1903, Robert Guérin, a leader in the *Union des Sociétés Françaises de Sports Athlétiques* (USFSA), suggested to Frederick Wall, secretary of England's powerful Football Association (FA), that an international federation be formed to propagate the game. To his chagrin, Guérin discovered that neither Wall nor any other English official was interested in the idea. "The Council of the Football Association," he was informed, "cannot see the advantages of such a Federation, but on all such matters upon which joint action [is] desirable they would be prepared to confer." Guérin characterized his efforts to persuade the British as "like beating the air." Undeterred, Guérin went ahead with his plans. On May 21, 1904, representatives of France, Belgium, Denmark, Holland, Spain, Sweden, and Switzerland met at the headquarters of the USFSA and formed the *Fédération Internationale de Football Association* (FIFA). With over two hundred members, FIFA is now the largest and most important of all the international sports federations.[35]

The four British soccer federations, whose members far outnumbered those of any continental nation, refused to join the new organization, a haughty attitude typical of Britons who felt that their invention of a game gave them patent rights to it. The four British federations did join FIFA in 1906, but they twice departed in fits of principle; first in 1920, when the federation declined to expel its German and Austrian members for their role in World War I, and again in 1928, when FIFA allowed "broken-time" payments to remunerate amateur players who missed work in order to compete in matches. Asked about the effects of British aloofness on the future of the game, Charles Sutcliffe, an official of Football League snapped, "I don't care a brass farthing about the improvement of the game in France, Belgium, Austria or Germany." Disapproval of the International Olympic Committee's interpretation of amateurism motivated the FA to boycott the 1924 and 1928 Olympics.[36]

Although the British were boycotting when FIFA launched its quadrennial world championship in 1930, the Uruguayan hosts invited them to participate. Secretary Wall replied tersely that the FA had received the hosts' letter and that he was "instructed to express regret at our inability to accept the invitation." English arrogance cleared the way for Uruguay, whom José Leandor Andrade had already led to Olympic victories in 1924 and 1928, to win FIFA's first World Cup Final. The glory of the third achievement was slightly dimmed by the weak field. Only four European teams undertook the long voyage to Montevideo: Belgium, France, Romania, and Yugoslavia.[37]

During their years of relative isolation from developments abroad, most British managers were resolutely amateur in their approach to strategy and tactics. "If a manager did dabble in 'method,'" lamented Stephen Wagg, "he was liable to be opposed either by directors or by players."[38] The "chalk talks" common in American sports seemed as ludicrous to the British as the German determination to make football *wissenschaftlich* ("scientific"). When the British competed for the first time in FIFA's World Cup, in 1954, they realized how far they had fallen behind. The Hungarian team that Germany defeated in the final had trounced England at Wembley by a score of 6–3. Twelve years of hard work were required before manager Alf Ramsey led England to its first (and only) world championship.

FIFA's organization, like the organization of the Olympic movement, has become extremely complicated. FIFA members are divided among six regional confederations. The *Confederación Sudamericana de Fútbol* began the process in 1916, and the Oceania Football Confederation finished it in 1966. The *Union Européene de Football Association* (1954) has the largest number of members, the largest number of football clubs, and the most organizational clout. The six confederations play an extremely important role because they are the basis for the allocation of places on the Executive Council and for the World Cup Finals.[39]

The confederations are also crucial in the struggle for the presidency of FIFA. British postwar leadership within FIFA was successfully ended by

Brazil's João Havelange in 1974, when he defeated an overly confident Stanley Rous in a bitterly contested presidential election. It may or may not have been true, as an embittered Keith Botsford remarked, that "small brown envelopes [went] into large black hands," but Havelange did garner the votes of the *Confédération Africaine de Football* (1957). In office, he made good on his promise of an expanded World Cup, which allowed more Asian and African finalists. The number of teams invited to the final was increased from sixteen to twenty-four (and increased again in 1994 to thirty-two). Havelange worked closely (some say hand in glove) with Adidas-owner Horst Dassler, the chief stockholder in the powerful marketing firm, International Sport and Leisure, founded in 1983. Havelange's power was sufficient for him to handpick his successor. In 1998, Switzerland's Joseph "Sepp" Blatter defeated Sweden's Lennart Johansson by 111 to 80. It was rumored that votes were changed at the last minute by the transfer of considerable cash. Most of Africa's 44 votes went to Blatter, although Johansson had the strong support of Issa Hayatou, president of the *Confédération Africaine de Football.*[40]

PRESIDENTS OF FIFA[41]

Robert Guérin	France	1904–1906
Daniel Woolfall	England	1906–1918
Jules Rimet	France	1921–1954
Rodolfe Seeldrayers	Belgium	1954–1955
Arthur Drewry	England	1956–1961
Stanley Rous	England	1961–1974
João Havelange	Brazil	1974–1998
Joseph Blatter	Switzerland	1998–

——— Basketball

In the summer of 1896, Ernst Herrmann, director of physical therapy at the Massachusetts Hospital for Dipsomaniacs, paid a visit to his father, who was a physical-education teacher at the *Martino–Katharineum–Gymnasium* in Braunschweig. Among the American novelties in his luggage was a basketball. August Herrmann and his colleague, Konrad Koch, the man who had introduced football to Germany more than twenty years earlier, were enchanted by the game, which they then introduced to their physical-education classes. F. W. Fricke, who taught at nearby Hannover, did the same. Unlike the YMCA workers who had invented the sport a mere five years earlier, Most Germans saw basketball as a girls' game. The rules they published in 1901 were apparently based on those that Senda Berenson had devised at Smith

College. Players were limited to three dribbles; the court was divided into three zones, each of which contained three players who were not allowed to move from one zone to another. The game did not prosper.[42]

Basketball fared somewhat better in Britain. In 1895, at the Hampstead Physical Training College, Swedish-born Martina Bergman-Osterberg experimented with the rules of women's basketball. The result was netball, which proved to be mildly successful in British and Australian schools. At the first major international athletic meet for women, the *Olympiades Féminines* held in Monaco in the spring of 1921, netball skills enabled the English team to win the basketball tournament, defeating *les françaises* by a score of 8–7. Despite this success, despite the support of the YMCA and the YWCA, despite the formation of an Amateur Basketball Association (1936), there were still, forty years after the arrival of the game, only thirty-four basketball clubs in all of England and Wales.[43]

Since basketball was invented under YMCA auspices, it was appropriate that powerful propagating impulses came from that organization. Elwood S. Brown, the YMCA activist who had organized the first Far Eastern Games (1913), was named as director of athletics for the American Expeditionary Force that President Wilson dispatched to France in 1917. Barely a month after the Armistice that ended the bloodshed, Brown wrote to Colonel Bruce Palmer, a member of General John Pershing's staff, and suggested that an athletic festival might do wonders to bring people together and thus cement the wartime alliance. Headquarters approved, the *Stade Pershing* was constructed in the *Bois de Vincennes,* and some fifteen hundred soldiers from eighteen different nations gathered in the summer of 1919 for the Inter-Allied Games. A basketball tournament was included in the program although its outcome was a foregone conclusion. In the third and last of the three games played, American servicemen defeated the hapless French by a score of 93–8.[44]

It may have been prophetic that the Italians also defeated the French (by the somewhat less alarming score of 15–11). Within two years of the Inter-Allied Games, Italian players joined the Swiss as the principal sponsors of the *Fédération Internationale de Basketball Amateur.* The FIBA's Italian vice-president, Giorgio Asinari di San Marzano, led a long campaign for recognition by the International Olympic Committee. His goal was reached when the 1936 Olympics included an official basketball tournament, won, to no one's surprise, by the United States.[45]

When German basketball finally took root, it was watered by some oddly indirect sources. Hugo Murero, a German army officer, heard of the game while on detached duty in Italy. Returning to the army's school at Wünsdorf, near Berlin, he became the *Referent für Basketball*. In 1935, his men took on a team from the University of Berlin, where Chinese and Japanese students had introduced the new game in 1927. When noncommissioned officers at the *Luftwaffe* school in Spandau joined in the fun, Germany had the critical mass for a national tournament. The unlikely town of Bad Kreuzbach was chosen as the tournament site because a member of the local gymnastics club had taught at a German school in Turkey and had been converted to basketball by American missionaries teaching at Istambul's Robert College.[46]

Markedly more rapid European growth came after 1945, when American popular culture began to wash over the continent in successive waves. The British, who had been largely immune to basketball fever, began to weaken, but amateur teams proliferated slowly until the creation of the National Basketball League (1972). Beginning with six amateur teams, the NBL grew, in its first sixteen years, to fifty-two teams, some of them professional. By century's end, teams that had struggled along with small subsidies from local businessmen were signing sponsorship contracts with Fiat, Sharp, and other multinational corporations. American influence was obvious in the campaign to publicize the game in the print media and to package it for television audiences. Spokesmen for the NBL admitted that they had modeled their league on the NBA and the NFL. American influence also accounted for the bouncy, bosomy cheerleaders and the Disney-inspired courtside mascots. If players dribbled, passed, and shot like Americans, one reason was that 30 percent of them, including all ten of the top scorers, had been born in the United States.[47]

Basketball has been more of a success on the continent. Michael Jordan and other American stars are "lionized in Italy, Spain and France, where glossy magazines with names like *Maxi-Basket* (published in Le Mans), *Nuevo Basket* (Barcelona) and *Super Basket* (Milan) keep almost breathless tabs on every aspect of the NBA." In Italy, the Roman Catholic Church has actively promoted basketball as a morally preferable alternative to soccer. Amateur players are numerous, and the professional game has attracted millions of *tifosi* (fans; literally, "those infected with typhus"). Since 1987, basketball has been the nation's second-most popular spectator sport. Italy's thirty-two-team professional league draws two million fans to its games; 25 percent of the television audience follows the championship race. The Italian league is backed financially by some of the country's wealthiest men. Rome's *Il Messaggero,* named for the city's leading newspaper, is owned, together with the newspaper, by Raul Gardini, a financier whom *Sports Illustrated* portrayed as the head of "a $22 billion conglomerate that does business on six continents."[48]

Throughout Europe, easy access to telecasts of American games has contributed to basketball's unprecedented popularity. NBA games are sure to remain a staple of European television as long as American corporations continue to invest in overseas mass media. As American economic power expands into eastern Europe, basketball is likely to become as popular there as it is in Italy.

American Football

Basketball gained ground in Europe (and in Asia) thanks largely to the missionary efforts of YMCA workers motivated by evangelical zeal. American football has been sold to European consumers by the NFL, an organization driven by more mundane ambitions. Despite the millions of dollars that the league has spent in promoting the game, football has been a much harder sell.

According to Joseph Maguire, the NFL's aggressive campaign aimed at "the cultural marginalization of soccer" began in 1982, the year in which the UK's Channel 4 telecast seventy-five minutes a week of NFL football. With American models in mind, Cheerleader Productions—a British company—provided Channel 4 with edited videotapes of regular-season play, complete with colorful graphics and a lively rock 'n' roll soundtrack. These NFL-inspired innovations persuaded the producers at the BBC and Independent Television to "Americanize" their sports coverage. As Garry Whannel noted, they adopted "some of the characteristics of what some call postmodern culture—disjointed juxtapositions, a focus on surface appearances, and a tendency for form to subsume content." And, of course, a tendency for faces in the crowd to draw attention away from inaction on the field.[49]

Additional publicity was generated in the summer of 1986, when the Dallas Cowboys were scheduled to play the Chicago Bears on the hallowed ground of Wembley Stadium. The British took note. For this encounter, which American Express, Budweiser, and TWA sponsored, eighty thousand tickets were sold in only seven days.[50] Subsequently, the average weekly viewership for the first season's telecasts, which had been slightly more than a million, rose to 3.7 million. The NFL's Super Bowl XXII, carried live, drew more than 6 million British viewers. This may not seem like a large audience compared to the audience of 12 million soccer fans who followed the telecast of the FA Cup Final, but American football had already become more popular with British viewers than such archetypically British sports as cricket and rugby. This was especially true for younger Britons, 26 percent of whom told surveyors that they enjoyed watching the American sport. It may have been competition from the United States that impelled RFU in the 1990s to accept protective gear, tactical substitution, cheerleaders, halftime shows, and Sunday games—innovations that make rugby more like the American game.[51]

Almost simultaneous with the appearance of the Dallas Cowboys and other NFL teams on "the telly" was the birth in 1983 of the first English team, the London Ravens. A year later, two leagues were formed: the British American Football Federation and the American Football League U.K. They merged in 1985 to become the thirty-eight-team British American Football League. (Was the acronym—BAFL—a cockney comment on the game's mysteries?) At this point, Anheuser-Busch, which had underwritten Channel 4's production costs for telecasts of NFL games, entered the fray and organized the semi-professional Budweiser League. Many of the teams—such as the Dunstable Cowboys—sported American names. For sponsors, clubs in the Budweiser League enlisted multinational corporations such as Johnson & Johnson, American Express, Toshiba, Minolta, and Hitachi.[52]

NFL Productions, a subsidiary which licenses the use of the organization's name and logo, also elbowed its way into the British market. Among the products touted are clothing for adults and children, watches and clocks, coffee mugs, books, magazines, calendars, posters, stickers, jigsaw puzzles, painting-by-numbers sets, playing cards, skateboards, rollerskates, beanbags, cookies, chocolate bars, and bubble gum. A 1988 Gallup Poll found that 91 percent of Britain's sixteen-to-twenty-five-year-olds considered NFL-licensed products to be as good as or better than the competition's brands.[53]

The NFL's efforts to bring American football to Britain were part of a grand strategy to diffuse the game throughout the European continent. NFL games began to appear on Scanset in Scandinavia, on Tele 5 in Germany and Austria, on Canal Plus in France and Belgium, and on other channels the length and breadth of the continent. They prepared the way for the World League of American Football that was launched in 1991 with NFL-sponsored franchises in Barcelona, Frankfurt, London, Montréal, and six American cities. In their first season, the London Monarchs had an average home-game crowd of more than 40,000. Midway in the second season, the Frankfurt Galaxy was drawing an average of 34,495 fans—more fans than attended the home games of *Frankfurt Eintracht,* the city's entry in Germany's *Bundesliga.* Despite this turnout, despite an initial NFL investment of $28,000,000, despite a television contract for $14,500,000, the World League suffered a cash-flow crisis and had to be bailed out by the parent organization. When this failed to stanch the deficits, the NFL closed its European shop.[54]

But not, it seems, permanently. Undaunted by its initial failure, the NFL revived the World League as a purely European operation. And then? "Ultimately," explained Roger Goodell to *Sports Illustrated*, "we'd like to expand to the Far East and Latin America."[55] It may be that the intrinsic characteristics of the game—its complexity, for instance, or its extraordinary level of physical violence—will limit the proposed expansion, but the NFL seems determined to continue playing the globalization game.

Ironically, in its campaign of global conquest, American football now faces "Americanized" competition from the game from which it originally evolved. When rugby promoters launched a ten-team European Super League in 1996, they marketed an "overall entertainment package" with pop concerts, cheerleaders, mascots, and fireworks. The league had big plans. Today Europe, tomorrow the world.[56]

TECHNOLOGICAL SPORTS

_____ Cycling

Cycling is one of the few sports with technical terms taken from French rather than English—*peleton, dérailleur, domestique*—because cycling is one of the few modern sports with French rather than British or American origins. The distant ancestor of the modern bicycle was, however, German. Baron Karl-Friedrich von Drais invented a two-wheeled wooden contraption that was propelled by the rider's feet pushing against the ground. He took his invention to Paris and patented it in 1818. The fad was short-lived.[1]

Pierre Michaux and his son Erneste began to produce a more practical vehicle—*le vélocipède*—in 1866. It was driven by a pedal attached to the axis of the front wheel. (Pierre's son Henri has been credited with the idea.) A year later the Michaux family exhibited their product at the *Exposition Universelle,* an appropriate venue because—in the poetic language of French historians—the bicycle, "daughter of technology, expresses the values of industrial society." One of the Michaux company's three hundred employees, Pierre Lallement, went to the United States, formed a partnership with James Carroll, and patented the Michaux design. A young Englishman, Rowley Turner, bought a French bicycle—presumably one manufactured by Michaux—and inspired his uncle, who was the manager of the Coventry Sewing Machine Company, to begin to manufacture the French invention. Coventry became the center of the British bicycle industry.[2]

In France, cycling became a craze. In 1868, there were races for young men (and young women) in Paris and in Bordeaux. The pace quickened the next year. The Olivier brothers, to whom the Michaux family sold their business, increased their output to two hundred cycles a day. Their state-of-the-art product had rubber tires and metal-spoked wheels. In conjunction with a new journal, *Le Vélocipède Illustré,* Oliver sponsored a Paris-to-Rouen race for *mesdames et messieurs.* Although French riders frequently dominated British races, James Moore, a friend of Erneste Michaux, won this one, speeding to victory at an average velocity of 7.5 mph. In this *annus mirabilis* of cycling, ten thousand spectators gathered at the Pré Catalan to watch three hundred cyclists race for prizes offered by the *Véloce-Club de Paris*.[3]

In the winter of 1876, at the Café Vercingétorix in the rue de Rennes, Henri Pagis brought the cycling clubs of the capital together in the *Union Véloci-pédique Parisiènne*. Touring clubs and specialist journals like *Sport Vélocipé-dique* (1880) sprang up throughout Europe and the Americas. During the late 1870s and early 1880s, national federations were formed. The British Bicycle Union (1878) was followed by the League of American Wheelmen (1880). French cyclists formed their national federations in 1881, the Belgians had theirs in 1883 and the Germans followed in 1884. In cycling as in soccer football, the French led the way to the next level of bureaucratic organization, establishing the *Union Cycliste Internationale* in 1900.[4]

The bicycle became a practical means of transportation when Henry Lawson invented the chain drive (1880) and John Dunlop began to produce rubber tires for same-size front and rear wheels (1888). Cycle manufacturer Peugeot opened a huge retail store on the Avenue de la Grande Armée, and Parisian department stores such as Bon Marché devoted whole sections of their catalogues to the bicycle. In 1899, France was dotted with more than three hundred built-to-purpose velodromes, symbols of the *belle époque*. Among them was the famed *Vélodrome Buffalo*, owned by the director of the *Folies Bergère*, managed by Tristan Bernard, and frequented by Bernard's artist friend Henri Toulouse-Lautrec (who picked up a few extra francs painting bicycle advertisements).[5]

Testing the limits of endurance (and avoiding desecration of the sabbath), nineteenth- and early twentieth-century European and American cyclists, female as well as male, competed in six-day races. "When the Harlem cabarets closed for the night," remarked Peter Nye, "the jazz bands and combos would head for the action of [Madison Square] Garden's six-day." It was at the Garden in 1914 that Australian cyclists Alf Goullet and Alford Grenda set a six-day record, which still stands, of 2,759 miles. In the long run, however, road races (favored by the Europeans) were a more viable form than indoor competitions (which enthralled nineteenth-century North Americans).[6]

Bicycles were clearly less expensive than carriages with a brace of horses. Ordinary men and women rushed to acquire them. The British Bicycle Union dropped the infamous "mechanics" clause that barred the working class from many amateur sports federations. As Wray Vamplew remarked, "The Union was . . . the first national sports authority to define amateurism without any reference to social status." Workers were now welcome, but for some the Bicycle Union's egalitarian gesture was insufficient. Radical members of Birmingham's Labour Church organized the National Clarion Cycling Club (1895). Their socialist counterparts in Germany formed *Solidarität* (1896), a national federation for working-class cyclists. By 1928 it had 320,00 members. Cycling was also the first modern sport to attract large numbers of Austrian workers. Italian socialists, meeting in Imola, formed a federation of *Cicilisti Rossi* in 1912, one day after the national congress of Young Socialists in nearby Bologna.[7]

European and North American entrepreneurs took notice and scrambled for shares in an exponentially expanding market. The United States had seventeen bicycle factories in 1890 and three hundred in 1895. Prices dropped, ownership rose. In the 1890s, millions of working-class men and women took to the roads with alacrity and celerity, spatially mobile as never before. "If cycling represented adventure for men," wrote Eugen Weber, "for women it represented the beginnings of emancipation." An anonymous Frenchwoman writing in 1897 put it more poetically: "The bicycle has given us wings; it is the first realization of the dream of Icarus."[8]

The hallelujah chorus had some sour notes. "You cannot serve God," intoned an American preacher, "and skylark on a bicycle." Piety was affronted by Sabbath-breakers, especially when they were indecently dressed, scandalously unchaperoned females. "When games and clothes conflicted," comments Jihang Park, "women unhesitatingly abandoned or altered games, not vice versa." The evidence indicates the contrary. For the many women who dared to flout convention, the bicycle became a pretext to dress as they never had before. Impractically full, dangerously fluttering skirts were replaced by simpler outfits less likely to become entangled in the gears. Bloomers were not common, but divided skirts were. Some men were upset by the adoption of "rational dress," but Charles Dana Gibson and other turn-of-the-century artists and photographers produced countless celebratory images of the "New Woman" in clothes designed for active sports.[9]

Dress was not the only problem. When women raced to the point of exhaustion and beyond, moralists like Miss T. R. Coombs were unable to "admire a girl, however beautiful she may be, whose face is . . . streaming with perspiration, whose hair is hanging in a mop about her ears, whose hairpins are strewn along the race-course, and whose general appearance is dusty, untidy and unwomanly." And some horrified German observers suspected that women mounted bicycles in order to experience the forbidden pleasures of masturbation. The French reacted more calmly to the sight of women on wheels. When garishly colored posters appeared with the female cyclist depicted as a bare-breasted goddess, as an Amazon, or even—alluding to the intrepid Gaul who fought against Julius Caesar—as a "female Vercingétorix," Frenchmen "found the women . . . seductive rather than menacing."[10]

Hardy young European women like Hélène Dutrieu, Amélie LeGall, Johanne Jørgenson, and Susanne Lindberg were undeterred by those who threw stones and cast allegations. They competed in grueling six-day races and they strained to set records. On August 27, 1893, for instance, Dutrieu covered 31.437 kilometers in an hour. For the most part, however, women toured rather than raced. In New Zealand, the women of Christchurch's Atalanta Cycling Club (1892) had to deal with men who pelted them with stones and thrust sticks into their spokes. They bravely persevered in their tours, but they meekly added that the thought of women who competed in cycling races filled them with "no small amount of disgust."[11]

When invention of the automobile threatened to displace the bicycle as sports equipment, the serious cyclist's response to the challenge was the Tour de France (1903), which was and still is the sport's most important competition. The Tour was the inspired invention of Henri Desgrange, cyclist, velodrome manager, sports journalist, and editor-in-chief of *L'Auto*. (The jersey worn by the leader of the race is yellow because that was the color of the newspaper's cover.) The inaugural tour, which lasted nineteen days, consisted of "only" six stages and a mere 2,408 kilometers. The weary victor, Maurice Garin, pocketed 6,125 gold francs. The circulation of *L'Auto* more than doubled, to 65,000 a day.[12]

During the 1920s and 1930s, the relatively peaceful period that the French know as *entre deux guerres,* the Tour became the nation's most important sports event, promoted by its sponsors not only as the ultimate endurance contest but also as a kind of rolling pilgrimage through the lovely landscapes and historical sites of France. In 1930, nationalism was accentuated by grouping the contestants into five national teams of eight riders each. The Tour continued on this basis during the first postwar years, but the dictates of global commerce were impossible to ignore. The riders have been reorganized into teams sponsored by Crédit Lyonnais, Deutsche Telekom, Nike, and other multinational corporations.[13]

Within their corporate teams, riders are divided into two unofficial groups: the stars *(videttes),* who vie for first place, and the *domestiques,* who support and assist them. While the emaciated losers of the Tour are pitied as *forçats de la route* (galley slaves of the highway), the winners are hailed as national heroes. Jacques Anquetil and Bernard Hinault, both of whom were five-time winners, achieved iconic status, worshiped by their countrymen as mythic figures who were sacrificed on their cycles as Jesus was on the Cross.

As Philippe Gaboriau observed, the cyclist who wears the yellow jersey is "a human god [*un homme-dieu*] who each year dies and is reborn." But not, however, in American eyes. The German champion Michael Schumacher is "one of the most famous athletes in the world," but he "remains a dark and distant mystery to most Americans. American winners—Lance Armstrong, for example—may appear on the cover of *Sports Illustrated,* but they cannot hope for the apotheosis that awaits the next French victor.[14]

Entrerpreneurs impressed by the Tour de France inaugurated similar tours in Belgium (1908), the Netherlands (1909), and Germany (1911), but none of these contests was as successful as Italy's great annual cycling event, the *Giro d'Italia,* which began in 1909. The leader wears a rose-colored jersey because the *Gazzetta dello Sport* (1896), which sponsored the *Giro,* appeared on rose-colored paper. Fausto Coppi and Gino Bartali were two stars of the *Giro* who shone even more brightly after their triumphs on the Tour de France. As Neville Chamberlain and Edouard Daladier flew to Munich in 1938 in a vain attempt to appease Adolf Hitler, anxious Europeans sought distraction by listening intently to radio reports of Bartali's triumph in the Tour. Ten years later, Bartali's head-to-head against France's Louison Bobet captivated Italians to the point where they seemed ready to ignore elections, strikes, and even an attempt to assassinate the head of Italy's Communist Party. In 1949, Bartali's great rival, Fausto Coppi, won both the Tour and the *Giro,* but his place in the Italian pantheon was jeopardized by an affair with a married woman and by his leftist politics. Bartali's place, on the other hand, was secured by membership in *Azione Cattolica.* He was venerated as *il salvatore della patria.* The word "savior" was not used lightly here.[15]

Control of the Tour de France is now in the hands of the *Société du Tour de France,* an independent corporation with its own PR staff, bank, hospital, and weather station. The *Société* controls media access and does its best to manage narratives of the Tour. In 1998, however, the *Société* lost control. The rewards of victory had become so immense and the physical demands of the Tour had become so inhumane that the temptation to cheat was irresistible and many if not most—some said *all*—cyclists were using drugs. The problem was not exactly new. Cyclists had for decades experimented with caffeine, nitroglycerine capsules, heroin, and cocaine. (The first recorded drug-related death—from trimethyl—occurred in 1886 during a race from Bordeaux to Paris.) During his glory days, in the 1960s Jacques Anquetil refused to be tested for drugs, but he came clean, after his retirement, "Everyone in cycling dopes himself and those who claim they don't are liars." His words were vividly illustrated during the 1967 Tour by the English cyclist Tommy Simpson, who died of an overdose of amphetamine.[16]

The difference, in 1998, was the publicity and the intervention of the government. Shortly before the start of the tour, French police arrested Willy Voet, a *soigneur* (trainer) employed by the Festina team, for possession of 250 batches of anabolic steroids and 400 ampoules of erythropoeitin (EPO), the hormone that stimulates the body's production of red cells. More banned drugs were found at Festina's headquarters in Lyon. After the Festina team was suspended, Alain Vandenbossche, a Belgian champion, revealed that he and others on the TVM team also used EPO. The police investigated and discovered drugs in one of TVM's automobiles and at their hotel. The entire TVM team tested positive. Before the Tour de France ended, police had found drugs in the vehicles or the hotels of two more teams. In all, six of the twenty-two teams withdrew from the race or were expelled.[17]

Why was drug use so prevalent? Chris Boardman explained that the conditions of the Tour forced the contestants to resort to drugs. "It's painful, it's dangerous, and it goes on a long time." Without drugs, it is literally impossible to cycle that far that fast. What this means is that the internal logic of modern sports—*citius, altius, fortius*—is changing peoples' minds about performance-enhancing drugs just as it changed peoples' minds about the ethos of amateurism. The American team at the 1983 Pan-American Games was decimated by drug-related disqualifications and by the panicky flight of athletes who feared detection and disqualification. The public barely noticed. Revelations about drugs in major-league baseball are met with a shrug. After the 1998 Tour, Festina went on to compete in Spain, Portugal, and Switzerland—with enthusiastic roadside support from the fans. None of the riders suspended from the 1998 Tour was barred from the 1999 *Giro d'Italia*. In time, the public will accept "cyborgs created by technology." If instrumental rationality produces "mortal engines," then mortal engines will be our heroes.[18]

_____ **Automobile Racing**

In an exemplary study entitled *L'Histoire en mouvements* (1992), Ronald Hubscher, Jean Durry, and Bernard Jeu pointed out that *fin de siècle* sportsmen, "always alert to technological innovations, became—in succession—cyclists, motorcyclists, automobile drivers, and then airplane pilots."[19] Very true. The invention of the internal-combustion engine led, inexorably, to a whole new set of races for vehicles as different as motorboats and snowmobiles. Automobile races have been the most important.

Although the United States may be more in love with motorcars than any other nation, enthusiasm for officially organized automobile races has probably been more a European than an American phenomenon. To meet the whims of the rich, turn-of-the-century manufacturers such as Adolphe Clément shifted gears in order to produce automobiles rather than bicycles. The first big motorcar race, sponsored in 1894 by *Le Petit Journal,* was from Paris to Rouen. A year later, a pair of French counts formed the *Automobile-Club de France* and staged the first Paris–Bordeaux–Paris automobile competition, sending a wave of excitement across the continent. Within a few years, there were races from Paris to Amsterdam, Madrid, Berlin, and Vienna.[20]

James Gordon Bennett Jr., the heir to a newspaper fortune, a leisured barbarian who indulged himself in steam-yachting, polo-playing, and urinating into fireplaces, found automobiles irresistible. He initiated a series of competitions among nations, the first of which took place in France in 1899. Thanks to Bennett's membership on the organizing committee of the 1900 Olympics, there were sixteen events for automobiles and motorcycles. One of them was a race from Paris to Toulouse and back, a distance of 1,347 kilometers. After *Le Matin* sponsored a Paris-to-Peking race, in 1907, automaker Henry Ford decided, in the summer of 1909, to introduce the public to his Model T by sponsoring a transcontinental New York-to-Seattle race. Ford No. 2 covered the 4,106-mile journey in twenty-three days.[21]

The Belgians seem to have been the first to race over a bounded track, six times around an 85-kilometer route at Ardennes. More famous tracks were built by the French at Le Mans (1906) and by the British at Brooklands (1907). For a brief time, Savannah, Georgia, strove for the lead in international racing. In May of 1908, 30,000 spectators crowded around the city's 9.8-mile course to watch drivers from France, Italy, and Germany, in vehicles produced by Fiat and Benz, race against a half-dozen American entries. Savannah was soon eclipsed, however, by Indianapolis. The Indy 500, which dates from 1911, began with 75,000 spectators enthralled by forty-four drivers racing two hundred times around the track for a purse of $75,000.[22]

The Indy 500, which Charles Edgley characterized as "a blue-collar Kentucky Derby," has become a mammoth event that draws hundreds of thousands of spectators every year, but Americans, generally, prefer their own personal, lovingly retooled "hot rods" to Europe's high-tech, corporate-owned, advertisement-covered Formula I racing cars. Germans idolized Rudolf Caracciola in the prewar years and Michael Schumacher in the postwar period; Juan Manuel Fangio and Sterling Moss became household names in Argentina and in the United Kingdom; but hardly an American can recognize the name of Grand Prix–winner Philip Hill. Americans have driven, figuratively, down the do-it-yourself highway. "We take pride," boasted an editorial in *Hot Rod Monthly*, "in the fact that we possess great mechanical know-how."[23]

The hot-rod craze was an only-in-America phenomenon because European teenagers seldom owned automobiles and there was no place to race them if they had. In the 1920s, if not earlier, youths all over the United States modified Detroit's assembly-line-produced vehicles and tested them on city streets. Age rather than social class determined the hot-rodder. The "drag race" was a mass phenomenon based on the adolescent male's obsession with the automobile as a symbol of rebellion.[24] The danger to the driver was part of the thrill. Film-star James Dean became the mythic representation of the hot-rodder when he played the hero in *Rebel without a Cause* (1955). Life's script came to an unexpected, cognitively dissonant end when Dean was killed in an off-the-set automobile crash—in a Porsche.

A generation earlier, Californians raced on Muroc Dry Lake, a hundred miles from Los Angeles. The lake was ten miles wide and twenty-two miles long, which allowed as many as twenty cars to roar off in a cloud of dust and a fog of fumes. It was a chaotic affair without rules or regulations. The days of romantic anarchy lasted until 1931, the year of the first organized hot-rod meet. The Southern California Timing Association was formed in 1937. One of its functions was to delineate classes of competition. The SCTA spawned *Hot Rod,* which began publishing in 1948 and quickly attained a monthly circulation of two hundred thousand. The magazine's editor, Wally Parks, presided for twenty years over the National Hot Rod Association (1951). An August 1956 editorial in *Hot Rod Monthly* was a clear statement of purpose and policy. The NHRA described its mission as the promotion of "hot rodding as an amateur sport . . . concentrated on *fun*—it is a recreational hobby based upon safety and accomplishment." Committed to amateurism and to a libertarian political stance, the NHRA initially refused to allow its members to accept cash prizes and resisted the Clean Air Act and every other attempt at government regulation.[25]

The National Association for Stock Car Auto Racing (1948) can be seen as hot-rodding with a Southern accent, the favorite sport of "good old boys." Although Virginia and the Carolinas are hotbeds of stockcar passion, NASCAR's first signature event was a "Speedweek" held at Daytona Beach, Florida. Cynics insinuate that the unacknowledged thrill most avidly desired is the sight of a fiery collision, but fans deny this: "They don't come to see blood and wrecks and fire and death," explained Giles Tippette. They come to see men (and women like Shirley Muldowney) cheat death of a sure thing. "It makes them feel good and hopeful about their own desperate race." Tributes to drivers killed in fatal crashes—Dale Earnhardt Sr., is a recent example—resemble the homage paid to ancients gods sacrificed in the rites of spring.[26]

_____ Flying

Asked about the history of aviation, Americans with a head for dates are likely to recall that the first airplane was flown by the Wright brothers at Kitty Hawk, North Carolina, in 1903; that heroic Charles Lindbergh made the first transatlantic solo flight in 1927; and that Amelia Earhart disappeared somewhere over the Pacific in 1937. The French focus on Louis Blériot's flight across the English Channel on July 25, 1909, a time when France led the world in aviation. Germans think of Otto Lilienthal's nineteenth-century experiments or of Marga von Etzdorf's eleven-day flight from Berlin to Tokyo in 1931.[27]

Flyers can set records in three ways: for speed, for altitude, and for distance. With all three possibilities in mind, James Gordon Bennett Jr., the playboy–publisher who loved to sponsor automobile races, financed a grand international aerial competition at Rheims in August of 1909. An American, Glenn Curtiss, posted an average speed of 47.65 mph, bested his four European rivals, and collected a cash prize and a trophy. In the contests for altitude and distance, France's Hubert Letham flew highest (503 feet) and Britain's Henry Farman went farthest (112 miles).[28]

Between the wars, aeronautical contests continued to be popular in the United States and in western Europe. In addition to the absolute records (fastest, highest, farthest), there were records to be set in point-to-point races (from coast to coast or from one side of the Atlantic to the other). In these races, female flyers were not at all physically disadvantaged in comparison to male pilots. (Their lighter weight was actually an advantage.) The most successful of the women, Jacqueline Cochran, won races, set records, and became president of the *Fédération Aéronautique Internationale*. The most famous of the female pilots was also the most foolish. On June 30, 1937, Amelia Earhart and her navigator took off from New Guinea on a flight to tiny Howland Island, 2,556 miles away. They had no flares and no emergency portable radio. They did not inform anyone of their radio frequency, and they did not realize that Howland Field had a high-frequency direction finder. Midway in their flight, they radioed the Coast Guard cutter *Itasca* that they were encountering overcast skies. Another message was picked up six hours later: "We are on a line of position 157 dash 337. Will repeat this message on 6210 kilocycles. We are running north and south." Then there was silence. What happened to them no one knows.[29]

Airborne sports were suspended during World War II. The National Air Races, which the National Aeonautics Administration had first organized in 1926, resumed in 1946 with contests for piston-engine and jet airplanes, but the public's attention shifted to the almost unimaginable triumphs and the almost unbearable catastrophes of space exploration.[30] NASA spokesmen sometimes describe their project as if they were involved in a race—to the moon, to Mars—but the "race" is not a sports event, and the astronauts, strapped to their seats or floating about in their tiny, instrument-packed space capsules, cannot be classified as athletes.

MODERN SPORTS IN ASIA

China

Modern sports came to China toward the end of the nineteenth century. Britons resident in the "Middle Kingdom" established football clubs in Tientsin (1884) and Shanghai (1887), but Americans, especially those working under the auspices of the YMCA, were far more important players in the game of ludic diffusion. In its early years, Chinese basketball was nurtured almost exclusively by the YMCA. Dr. Willard Lyon, who opened the Tientsin YMCA in 1895, was a typical activist. He was not content to limit his attention to the young Chinese who frequented the YMCA. "As early as 1896," wrote Jonathan Kolatch, "the Tientsin YMCA embarked on a program of promoting athletic competition in [Chinese] schools." In 1902, when C. H. Robertson arrived to assume responsibilities in Tientsin, he followed Lyon's path and spent part of his time in the local Chinese schools. He also arranged for an American teacher of physical education to be employed, at YMCA expense, in the school system. To stimulate interest on the part of the Chinese, the Americans resident in Tientsin organized an annual athletic meet for students at the local schools.[1]

Although the YMCA never had more than fifteen or twenty "physical secretaries" for all of China, those few were amazingly influential as coordinators of programs in Chinese and mission schools, as promoters of athletic meets, as trainers of native sports administrators, and as propagandists for increased support of physical-education programs. Basketball was, as those familiar with the game's origins might have guessed, the YMCA's favored sport. Dr. Lyon had introduced it in Tientsin, but the most energetic promoters of the game were located in Shanghai, where Dr. Max J. Exner arrived in 1908 as the Chinese YMCA's first National Physical Director.[2]

When the YMCA organized China's first national athletic meet, at Nanking in October of 1910, basketball was part of the program (along with track and field, tennis, and soccer). Although the officials were Americans, all the athletes on the one hundred forty competing teams were Chinese. A symbolic moment occurred during the meet when high-jumper Sun Baoqing snipped off the queue of hair that had knocked the crossbar from its support and made his first attempt a failure. He tried again, shorn, and became the national champion.[3]

The YMCA was also responsible for the inauguration of the Far Eastern Championship Games, the first of which were held in Manila in February of 1913. The principal organizer of these games was Elwood S. Brown, an active and effective physical director who served in the Philippines from 1910 to 1918. Within a year of his arrival with equipment for baseball and volleyball, Brown had organized the Philippine Amateur Athletic Association. When Filipino government clerks complained about the heat, even at the summer capital in the mountains, Brown concluded that these pampered white-collar workers had been spoiled by the indolent Spaniards and needed nothing quite so much as a strong dose of physical exercise. He took action against idleness, and the natives began to play ball (in how many senses?) with the Americans. Brown invited China to participate in the Far Eastern Games. How else was he to bring traditionally hostile peoples together in a spirit of unaccustomed mutual respect?[4]

International athletic meets were not a high priority of the Republic of China, which was then a mere two years old, but J. H. Crocker and other American YMCA workers in China acceded to Brown's request and arranged for a team to be present at the games. Forty Chinese athletes joined twenty from Japan and seventy from the hosting Philippines. Since the Philippines were then under American rule and far more influenced by American sports than the Chinese or the Japanese, it was hardly a surprise that the home team won most of the events, including the basketball championship. Despite the drubbing, the Chinese—or their American mentors—volunteered to host the Second Far Eastern Games, which were held in Shanghai in 1915. The 298-member Chinese team was larger than the contingents from Japan and the Philippines and was also more successful. China's president expressed pleasure and astonishment that "the medium of athletics had induced Chinese from such politically hostile districts as Canton, Shanghai and Peking to stand shoulder to shoulder as the champions of a common China."[5]

In 1915, the Chinese government requested that the YMCA organize departments of physical education at five universities, which the YMCA was happy to do. Three years later, the YMCA opened its own normal school in Shanghai in order to train Chinese physical educators. The overly ambitious project failed. The school closed its doors a year later, undone by financial problems, by the unfortunately timed furloughs of key American personnel, and by a rising tide of anti-American sentiment that drastically reduced the scope and effectiveness of all the YMCA's programs. After J. H. Gray returned to the United States in 1927, the YMCA was no longer a key player in Chinese sports and physical education. The determination of the Chinese to forge their own national destiny did not, however, mean an exclusive commitment to traditional sports such as archery or *chuiwan* (a game similar to golf). Basketball remained among the sports actively promoted by both the Nationalists and the Communists throughout the decades of their struggle for power and by the Communists after their victory in 1949.[6] It is appropriate that the first Chinese citizen to play a starring role in American professional sports is a basketball player, 7 foot 6 inch Ming Yao, signed by the Houston Rockets for the 2002 season.

During the republican period, from 1912 to 1949, the Confucian scholarly disdain for the merely physical waned, and Western sports increasingly influenced the behavior of Chinese men, especially those of the urban middle and upper classes. The effects on women's lives were even greater. At the third National Athletic Meet (1924), female athletes exhibited their prowess in basketball, softball, volleyball, and gymnastics; at the fourth meet (1930), their events were a part of the official program. In the course of the twentieth century, images of the ideal female changed radically from the delicately immobile court lady barely able to hobble on her deformed feet to the robustly active young girl racing up and down a basketball court. Female athletes have become "icons of desirable sexuality." From a liberal–feminist perspective, modern sports have been emancipatory.[7]

From the third National Athletic Meet until the seventh (1948), Chinese sports administrators—not foreign missionaries—were in charge. Although these national sports festivals were an increasingly salient aspect of Chinese culture, the nation's athletic elite did poorly in international competitions. China's National Olympic Committee was not officially recognized until 1931, nearly twenty years after Japan's. At the 1932 Olympic Games, where Japanese swimmers astonished the world by winning eleven of the sixteen medals in the men's competition, sprinter Li Changchun was the lone Chinese representative. He was eliminated in the heats. The sixty-nine person team sent to Berlin for the 1936 Olympics included female athletes, among them the champion swimmer Yang Xiuqiong, a beauty whom Fan Hong sees as "the perfect image of modern femininity for Nationalist China."[8]

The low level of elite sports (and the generally unhappy state of Chinese physical education) from the 1920s to the 1950s can be explained by the trauma of civil war and foreign invasion. Communist victory in 1949 heralded the transformation of Chinese sports as well as the rest of Chinese culture. Mao Zedong had written in 1917 that physical education is "more important than intellectual and moral education," but resources were scarce in 1949 and progress was slow. Radio gymnastics, introduced in 1951, was an inexpensive way to enhance the nation's fitness. The interrupted sequence of national sports festivals was resumed in 1959.[9]

In the first decades of the People's Republic of China (PRC), sports and physical culture were centrally controlled by a number of governmental commissions and ministries that changed their names and their bureaucratic structures in accordance with changes in the Communist Party's ideological position. During the first years of Communist rule, the emphasis was on national defense. The government's physical-culture initiatives were closely modeled on the USSR's program (from which it took its name: Ready for Labor and Defence). Young Chinese were trained and tested in conventional track-and-field sports. They also acquired proficiency in firing rifles and in charging with bayonets. The definition of sports was expanded to include parachute jumps and drills to protect oneself against chemical warfare. Girls as well as boys were instructed in weaponry. In 1958, for instance, Han Juyuan outperformed other young women and set a national record for tossing hand grenades.[10]

Although the regime's avowed aim was to promote fitness and sports for the masses, China's leaders recognized that athletes who broke world records and won international championships contributed to their country's prestige. Limited government support for elite sports bore early fruit in the 1950s. Weightlifter Chen Jingkai set a world's record in the bantamweight class. High-jumper Zeng Fengrong and table-tennis player Rong Guotuan became world champions. Unfortunately, quarrels with the International Olympic Committee over the status of Taiwan culminated in 1958 with the PRC's resignation from the committee. At the same time and for the same reason, China withdrew from the international federations for soccer and other sports.[11] The PRC did not make its debut as an Olympic power until 1984.

Spokesmen for the regime attempted to balance competing interests by proclaiming, in 1960, that sports and physical culture must "walk on two legs." There was to be simultaneous development of elite sports and recreational physical culture. Special schools were established to nurture potential champions, but there were also workplace sports clubs (with the same names as their Soviet counterparts) and mass nationwide competitions for tens and even hundreds of millions of ordinary Chinese.[12]

During the years when the Communists boycotted the Olympics, the Republic of China (Taiwan) continued to send teams to the games. It was one way for the diplomatically besieged state to maintain its presence on the international stage. The islanders did well. In the 1960 games, held in Rome, Yang Zhuanguang barely lost the decathlon to his close friend, the American Rafer Johnson.

The drive for international athletic supremacy was halted in 1966 when the "Great Cultural Revolution" drastically altered the regime's approach to sports. Chairman Mao's motto was "Friendship first, competition second." Accordingly, sports contacts were limited to friendly nations such as North Korea. The Ministry of Sport was identified as "a black headquarters of capitalists and revisionists."[13] Institutes were closed. Sports facilities were demolished. Athletes and coaches who had had international experience were suspect. Were they truly committed to Maoism? Some athletes, like Zhung Zedong, the world champion in table tennis (1961–1966), shared the fate of ideologically suspect artists and intellectuals. They were sent to prison or to labor camps. Others, like table-tennis stars Rong Guotan and Fu Qifang, committed suicide. At the elite level, Chinese sports were devastated.

While the PRC experienced ten years of political turmoil, athletes representing the Republic of China scored some notable successes. One of the island's sprinters, Ji Zheng, was third in the 80-meter hurdles at the 1968 Olympics in Mexico City. Two years later, she set world records in the 100-meter and 200-meter sprints (11.0 and 22.4 seconds) and in the 100-meter hurdles (12.8 seconds).[14]

When the policy of the PRC veered again, in 1971, the new initiatives were called "ping-pong diplomacy" (because the first sign of detente came when an American table-tennis team was invited to Beijing and warmly greeted by Premier Zhou Enlai). Two years later, swimmer Zen Guiying broke a number of national records and was celebrated as a heroic model for Chinese women. After Deng Xiaoping's accession to power, in 1978, a new motto was proclaimed: "Break out of Asia and advance on the world." One of the first signs of the breakout was the women's volleyball team's victory in the 1981 world championships. The game was telecast, its exciting images enhanced by Song Shixiong's dramatic play-by-play commentary. The victory thrilled China's television viewers and inspired renewed pride after the "demoralization [of] the last years of the Cultural Revolution."[15]

In pursuit of its ambitious goals, the government invested heavily in sports infrastructure. Physical education was required in all schools, and athletes once again received special attention (and extra rations of food). According to Dong Jinxia, the government, while continuing to proclaim the importance of recreational sports for the masses, dedicated two-thirds of its sports budget to the training of fewer than twenty thousand athletes, the pool from which Olympic champions were likely to emerge. For these elite athletes, the network of special sports schools, closed during the "cultural revolution," was reconstituted. By 1990, there were one hundred fifty such schools (while the Soviet Union had a mere forty-six). Large sums were allocated to build new sports facilities. Research into sports physiology and sports psychology was strongly supported at Beijing University.[16]

The National Games of 1987 were the odd outcome of Deng Xiaoping's effort to combine an authoritarian polity with a market economy, to mix Marxist "body culture" with capitalist "consumer culture." Pepsi-Cola was among the many foreign sponsors of the event. Tickets were quite expensive by Chinese standards. Coaches and athletes were offered substantial economic incentives to do well. The choreographers who planned the opening ceremony were tempted to emulate the show-biz pyrotechnics of the Los Angeles Olympics, but they decided to stay with traditional dancing dragons and the meticulously organized placard displays that are a trademark of Communist ritual.[17]

In the 1990s, the tempo of change accelerated. Teams in China's professional soccer league, which began operations in 1993, were sponsored by Panasonic and other multinational corporations. Players imported from Brazil raised the level of competition and gave further evidence of China's new openness. The income of "amateur" athletes and coaches became a function of their athletic performance, and those who prevailed in international competition were rewarded with bonuses, private apartments, ample food, and special medical attention. Thirteen-year-old Olympic diver Fu Mingxia, for example, received 80,000 yuan from the government and an additional 463,000 yuan from her sponsors. The total was three hundred times the annual salary of a teacher. Four years later, Chinese winners at the "Centennial Olympics" in Atlanta received "about 1,000,000 yuan from various sponsors and media agencies."[18]

Athletes became role models. Among young people, there was a new conception of the ideal body. Photographs of the physically hobbled aristocratic lady were replaced by images of ruggedly athletic girls of peasant stock. Calendars featuring "Western sportswomen or Chinese gymnasts in various athletic poses were popular fixtures on household walls." Charting these cultural changes, Susan Brownell observed that photographs of female bodybuilders began to appear as pinups.[19]

The return to the global sports arena had its risks. There were a number of defections to the West, like that of tennis star Hu Na, but the losses were few compared to the mass flight from East Germany. By and large, the system worked, and the regime basked in the glory of its representatives' spectacular achievements. Thanks in part to the substantial government investment in sports infrastructure and to the relatively generous subsidies to individual athletes and coaches, the Chinese began to win international championships. At the 1982 Asian Games in New Delhi, Chinese athletes won sixty-one events, ending thirty-one years of Japanese domination. Two years later, Chinese Olympians returned from Los Angeles with fifteen gold, eight silver, and nine bronze medals.[20]

To ensure Olympic success at Seoul in 1988, the PRC spent over a quarter of a billion dollars, more than fifty million dollars for each gold medal earned. When the results—measured in the number of medals—fell short of expectations, Minister of Sports Li Menghu was replaced by Wu Shaozu, a man whose career in the military promised greater success.[21]

Although very few Chinese women were involved in recreational sports, the government worked hard to find and train prospective champions. In the 1990s, female runners like Wang Junxia set new world records by astonishing margins. Her time over 3,000 meters—8:06.11 minutes—was an unprecedented improvement of 3.28 percent over the old record held by Norway's Ingrid Kristiansen in 1986. (No previous track record had ever been lowered by more than 2.51 percent.) At the 1994 world's swimming championships in Rome, Chinese women won twelve of a possible sixteen gold medals. In response to the suspicion that such performances were drug-enhanced, Chinese coaches referred to hard training and the ability of peasant women to "eat bitterness." It was probably true that Chinese athletes trained harder than their Western counterparts, but it was also true that Chinese men trained hard and still failed to achieve such stellar performances. Western suspicions were vindicated when a large number of female athletes tested positive for anabolic steroids. Between 1972 and 1994, ten of the world's elite swimmers had failed drug tests. Between 1990 and 1998, twenty-eight Chinese swimmers tested positive. In 1994 alone, eleven Chinese swimmers were disqualifed for the use of banned substances. The Chinese authorities acted forcefully to purge the system of performance-enhancing drugs. They were presumably successful, but they paid a price. At the 2000 Olympics in Sydney, there were no medals for Chinese swimmers and only one for the track-and-field athletes.[22]

In 1993, the desire to "break out of Asia and advance on the world" also motivated the government to modify its ban on openly professional sports and to launch a twenty-four-team soccer league (soon followed by leagues for basketball and volleyball). In keeping with the regime's new openness to capitalist development, soccer teams paid their players ten times the salary of the average Chinese worker. Transfer payments were allowed and foreign players were lured with bonuses. After the Physical Culture and Sports Committee was replaced, in 1998, by the All-China Sports Federation, large sums of money came to China from multinational corporate capitalist sponsors such as Hyundai, Samsung, Panasonic, and Pepsi-Cola. Chinese capitalism has matured to the point where Lenova, the PRC's number-one computer-maker, has joined the select group of multinational corporations paying tens of millions of dollars to sponsor the Olympic Games through the IOC's "TOP VI" (discussed in chapter 21). "China, which Mao once taught to despise bourgeois values, now has . . . fashion shows, stock exchanges and soccer hooligans."[23] The sports of the People's Republic seem more and more like the sports of Europe and North America, a tendency that will doubtless be accelerated as Beijing prepares to host the 2008 Olympic Games.

_____ India

South Asian cricket may be the most remarkable example of sports as cultural imperialism. "Cricket," writes Mihir Bose, "that very English game, is now one of the most prized of Indian institutions." Arjun Appadurai makes the same point with a sly allusion to a classic of English poetry: "There is a part of Indian culture today that seems forever to be England, and that is cricket." In order for this "most powerful condensation of Victorian elite values" (Appadurai's phrase) to have become the subcontinent's culturally dominant sport, cricket had to prevail over precolonial India's highly complex ludic forms. With permissible hyperbole, Ashis Nandy wrote, "Cricket is an Indian game accidently discovered by the English."[24]

There was little reason to believe, at the time of the Great Mutiny (1857), that a game played on the verdant lawns of English country houses was destined to become an Indian addiction. After all, the Indians already had a ballgame of their own, one that they played in their own distinctive way. "In the unruly indigenous game [of polo], an indeterminate number of riders on tiny ponies propelled a ball nearly randomly and generally chaotically around a loosely defined field." British officers stationed in India borrowed the "unruly indigenous game" and modernized it. The Indian elite turned to cricket.[25]

Although seamen employed by the East India Company played at Cambay in 1721 and the Calcutta Cricket Club was in existence by 1792, the first indigenous Indian club, the Orient, was not founded until 1848. The founders were Parsees, and for decades this religious minority produced the most ardent and successful Indian cricketers. When a Parsee eleven toured England in 1886, the first Indian team to do so, *Cricket Chat* was quick to see the political utility of the game. Pompous prose compensated for the magazine's slangy title: "Anything which can tend to promote an assimilation of tastes and habits between the English and the native subjects of our Empress-Queen cannot fail to conduce to the solidity of the British Empire."[26] This was not the opinion of the average Anglo-Indian player, who hindered rather than abetted the spread of the game among the native peoples. The British in India considered it quite cricket to ridicule native players.

H. T. Wickham, stationed in northern India from 1904 to 1922, was especially contemptuous of the local ruler. According to Wickham, it was the Maharajah's custom to arrive when the match was already in progress. He made his way "to a special tent where he sat for a time, smoking his long water pipe." Eventually, he decided to bat. "It didn't matter which side was batting, his own team or ours. He was padded by two attendants and gloved by two more, somebody carried his bat and he walked to the wicket . . . with an enormous turban on his head." He played poorly, but errors committed by the Maharajah were overlooked. For the prince who refused to make even this token effort, British officers like Charles Kincaid had only contempt.[27]

How then did this unlikely English game become India's most popular spectator sport? Largely, it seems, through the strenuous efforts of a series of British viceroys. Government policy, set in London, no more envisaged sports as a form of anglicization than did the average member of the officer's club in Madras or Calcutta, but Lord Harris, governor of Bombay, was from childhood an avid cricket player. During his tenure, he encouraged the construction of cricket grounds and the organization of native teams. In 1892, he inaugurated an annual tournament between Bombay's resident Britons and the city's Parsee minority, a series that in time came to include Hindu (1907) and Muslim (1912) teams. At an 1892 match in Poona between a British and a Parsee side, Harris actually invited the Indians to lunch. This was considered by many to be a reckless act of excessive good will. When Harris retired in 1895, he returned to England and became president of the Marylebone Cricket Club. He continued his efforts to foster Indian cricket. Thirty-one years later, as president of the Imperial Cricket Conference (the sport's highest administrative body), he disregarded the rules and insisted that the ICC accept two Indian representatives, named by him with his usual insouciance.[28]

Unlike the extreme conservatives, whose motto was "divide and conquer," Harris hoped that the game might bond India's religiously, linguistically, and ethnically diverse population. "You do well to love [cricket]," he intoned on his eightieth birthday, "for it is more free from anything sordid, anything dishonourable, than any game in the world." Fully sharing this idealism, Sir Stanley Jackson, governor of Bengal from 1927 to 1932, urged Hindus and

Muslims to play on the same teams. Lord Bradbourne, who served as governor of Bombay (1933–37) and Bengal (1937–39), was another idealist who imagined that cricket bats might level the barriers that separated Indians from one another. Bradbourne especially lamented the segregation of the spectators on the basis of religion. (In Bombay, for instance, the stands included officially designated sections for Hindus, Muslims, Parsees, and Roman Catholics.)[29]

In their campaign to enlighten the natives about the virtues of cricket, the viceroys had considerable help from British teachers whose educational kit included bats and balls. During Lord Curzon's tenure as viceroy, he established Mayo College (1872) and four other "public schools" whose aims included the transformation of physically timid high-caste lads into manly equivalents of the Etonians and Harrovians who ruled the subcontinent.

It was not easy to persuade the pampered sons of Indian princes to exert themselves in strenuous activities—running, rowing, and lifting—that were normally performed by members of the lower castes. C. E. Tyndale-Biscoe's experiences were probably typical. He was a blindly ethnocentric, ruthlessly stubborn dogmatist who was genuinely concerned to provide for what he conceived to be the welfare of the Kashmiri boys entrusted to his care. He lived and breathed the moral certainties of the "games ethic" and strove to introduce these certainties into "a culture whose religious, social and sexual mores ran directly contrary to much of what he represented and advocated." In his rush to propagate his educational ideals, Tyndale-Biscoe ran headlong into the Brahmin conviction that muscular development was a stigma of lower-caste birth. In the face of resistance, Tyndale-Biscoe persevered. At one point he thrust two of his native assistants into a boat and ordered them to row. In this manner, he proudly recalled in *Character-Building in Kashmir,* they "made a beginning in making that low-caste stuff commonly called muscle."[30]

By 1901, T. L. Pennell was able to assert that "the simpler natives [*sic*] games are gradually giving place to the superior attractions of cricket and football." At Mayo College, Herbert Sherring was pleased to observe that cricket "was apparently . . . played every day of the week including Sundays." A famous photograph from 1906 shows the elegantly uniformed cricket team, complete with proudly worn turbans and a proudly held athletic trophy. As adults, graduates of Mayo College and similar schools became the mainstay of Indian cricket.[31]

Prince Bhupendra Singh, the Sikh ruler of the mostly Hindu and Muslim state of Patiala, was enthralled by the game. Cricket historian Mihir Bose was enthralled, or at least amazed, by the prince: "In the grounds of his palace, which also housed three hundred wives and concubines and a scented swimming pool, there was a cricket field . . . in an area larger than Lord's and with facilities that rivalled the best of country-house cricket available . . . in England. Elephants were sometimes used to roll the wicket." Although the prince's love of cricket was never in doubt, he, like the British whom he emulated, used the game to make a political point about the need for Patiala's mutually hostile religious communities to overcome their animosities and to work together. He fielded religiously mixed elevens whose Hindu, Muslim, Parsee, and Christian players bowled and batted for the same team. As president of both the Board of Control of the Cricket Club of India and the Indian Olympic Association, Bhupendra used his wealth and status to promote cricket. He organized, financed, and captained a team that toured the British Isles (1911). He selected and coached the first official team sent to England (1932) and he paid the bills for an Australian eleven to tour India (1935–36). His son, Yadavendra Singh was simultaneously an active cricket player and a steadfast supporter of Gandhi and Nehru in their struggle for Indian independence. Yadavendra captained the Indian team that visited Australia in 1935–36, chaired the All-India Council of Sports, and founded the Asian Games Federation.[32]

The most famous of all Indian cricketers was K. S. Ranjitsinhji (1872–1933). Although "Ranji," as he was known to cricket fans, claimed to have been a prince, he was actually the grandson of a cousin of the ruler of Nawanagar. At the age of fifteen he was sent to England to be educated. He won his "blue" batting for Cambridge and went on to play for Sussex. Selected many times to represent England in Tests against Australia, he won the admiration of England's premier cricket writer. "When he batted," wrote Neville Cardus, "a strange light was seen for the first time on English fields." It was "a lovely magic . . . not prepared for by anything that happened in cricket before Ranji came to us."[33] In 1907, after the Jam Sahib of Nawanagar died without an heir, Ranji returned to India as the prince he had always pretended to have been.

His love of England inspired him to deny cultural difference: "I do not consider myself a foreigner in Cambridge." In 1897, he averred that he was proud "to know that, while he was playing cricket against Australia, a relative—and a dear one, his uncle—was fighting for his Queen on the frontier in India." Cricket, he averred, was "among the most powerful of the links which keep our Empire together." Moved by Ranji's devotion to their game and their empire, British writers seldom dwelled on his refusal to pay his creditors or to repay those from whom he borrowed large sums.[34]

After partition and independence, the commercial metropolis of Bombay became the center of Indian cricket. Newspapers, banks, and other corporations replaced British officials and Indian princes in the role of cricket promoters, but the game's corporate sponsors continued the British (and Gandhian) opposition to religiously divisive communal cricket. The official emphasis has been on cricket as a symbol of national unity. When India defeated England, in 1971, a celebratory crowd of a million and a half met the team upon its return to Bombay. Drawing attention away from the deep divisions of religion and caste that have plagued Indian democracy, cricket—like the English language—is one of the few things shared over the length and breadth of the subcontinent. Whether the shared love of cricket ameliorates or worsens relations between India and Pakistan is an unanswered question. Appadurai suggests the latter when he refers to their matches as "a star-studded simulacrum of warfare."[35]

Football was a harder sell than cricket. The redoubtable Tyndale-Biscoe had only limited success in his efforts to bring his reluctant pupils to the game. In fact, the Hindus among his pupils were horrified when he showed them a football and informed them that it was made of leather. In a panic, they shouted to him that he should take it away because it was *jutha* ("unholy"). His response to their religious objections is perhaps the best example ever of self-righteous cultural imperialism. In his *Autobiography,* he recalled that

> I called the teachers together and explained to them my plans for the afternoon. They were to arm themselves with single-sticks, picket the streets leading from the school to the playground, and prevent any boys from escaping en route . . . I brought up the rear with a hunting-crop. . . . We shooed them down the streets like sheep on their way to the butchers. Such a dirty, smelling, cowardly crew you never saw.

Explaining that it was a chilly afternoon and that the boys carried fire-pots under their cloaks, Tyndale-Biscoe went on: "We dared not drive them too fast for fear of their tripping up (as several of them were wearing clogs) and falling with their fire-pots, which would have prevented their playing football for many days to come." When the herded boys refused to begin the game, the teachers menaced them with their sticks and forced them to commence. A "player" who had become polluted when struck in the face by the ball was rushed to a nearby canal where he was washed and purified. There were other problems. "The bearded centre forward who first kicked the ball was forbidden to return to, and thus defile, his home. He went to live with relatives."[36]

While cricket took root in Kashmir and the Punjab, football flourished in Bengal. The Indian Football Association, which the British had founded in 1893, agreed in 1909 to allow native clubs to participate in its annual tournament. At first, the native clubs were outclassed by regimental teams, but Calcutta's Mohan Bagan FC reached the tournament's finals in 1911. When this happened, *The Englishman* reported (July 19, 1911) that "Bengali Calcutta has gone football mad." In the culminating match, Mohan Bagan defeated the East Yorkshire Regiment. Bengali men, who had long been scorned by the British as weak, effeminate, and unfit for military service, gloried in their triumph. Three years later, Mohan Bagan became the first native club admitted to membership in the Calcutta Football League. Although it now faces strong competition from the East Bengal FC, beloved of migrants from Bangladesh, and from Salgoacar SC, based in the former Portuguese enclave of Goa, Mohan Bagan continues to play a major role in the drama of Indian football.[37]

The drama is notably tempestuous. According to Novy Kapadia, Indian football is certainly chaotic and possibly corrupt. The All India Football Federation has been crippled by match-fixing and by "inept marketing, inadequate resource mobilization and [the] lack of a proper calendar of events." Chaos and corruption may or may not be the reason, but football had made few inroads beyond Bengal and Goa. Answering a poll about their sports preferences, 82 percent of Indian boys named cricket and a mere 3 percent opted for soccer. Badminton was most popular among the girls.[38]

Not all of India's modern sports have British provenance. The traditional Indian form of wrestling known as *bharatiya kushti* is still practiced in the north of the subcontinent. Devotees of this sport commit themselves wholeheartedly to the quest for a holy life. The wrestlers' exercises, which include swinging 80-kilogram "Indian clubs," are supervised by a guru whose word is law. He instructs his disciples in *pranayama* (controlled breathing) as well as in exercises familiar to Western athletes. Familiar exercises are, however, done with a difference. When the wrestlers do their kneebends and pushups, they recite mantras. In accordance with the devout Hindu's unremitting struggle against pollution, the wrestlers must strictly control their diet, their sexual habits, the way they breathe, even their urination and defecation. Within the wrestler's world, there are, however, some surprising departures from orthodox belief and behavior. Caste, which is otherwise a basic fact of Hindu life, is ignored. Acts normally perceived as polluting are acceptable. Brahmins who have just been initiated into the practice of *bharatiya kushti* might, for instance, massage the feet of an experienced lower-caste wrestler. When wrestlers meet in actual competition, they seem to enact an unconscious inversion of "normal" Hindu life. "In a world of strict rules of body purity, wrestlers enact a ritual of physical contact saturated in sweat, mucus, and occasionally blood."[39]

Kalarippayattu, which has been practiced in Kerala since at least the twelfth century, is unique to that southwestern coastal region. Less obsessed with purity and pollution than *bharatiya kushti,* the sport has attracted Muslims and Christians as well as Hindus. In their search for physical health and spiritual enlightenment, the practitioners of *kalarippayattu* combine karate-like exercises with yogalike positions. When students master these exercises and positions, they are allowed to practice with weapons, advancing with increasing proficiency from long staves to short sticks and then to the curved *otta* (which resembles an elephant's tusk) and to daggers, swords, maces, and spears. Competition plays a more important role in *kalarippayattu* than it does in *bharatiya kushti.*[40]

As early as 1915, Indian nationalists seeking an indigenous alternative to cricket and other modern sports revived the traditional children's game of *kabaddi.* They envisioned the game as a weapon in their struggle against colonial rule. The game resembles "Red Rover," but the raiders who rush to seize and subdue an opponent must hold their breath and chant rhymes that include the word *kabaddi.* Promoting *kabaddi,* Ajay Bhalla claims that the game became India's national sport when Indians overcame "the depravities of Western civilization." *Kabaddi* is strongly favored by the militantly Hindu political organization *Rashtriya Swayamesevak Sangh* (National Volunteer Corporation). Government claims to the contrary, the sport has *not* surpassed cricket in popularity.[41]

If *kabaddi* is to become India's national sport, it will have to overcome not only British imports such as cricket and soccer but also the American sports—basketball, volleyball, softball—that have been identified by some as harbingers of India's postcolonial future. YMCA workers, like Henry Gray and Harry Crowe Buch, were responsible for the introduction of American sports. This occurred when India was still under British rule, "the jewel in the crown." In Madras in 1920, Buch founded the National YMCA School of Physical Education, an immensely influential institution. Missionary efforts to involve Indian girls in sports were, however, mostly in vain. After independence in 1947, the government began a series of national sports festivals for girls and women, but female athletes are still drastically underrepresented in Indian sports.[42]

Darabji Tata and A. G. Neohren officially inaugurated the Indian Olympic Association in 1927, a full seven years after the former had led a four-man team of Indian athletes to its debut at the Antwerp games. Olympic success has come mostly in the form of gold medals for field hockey, three of which came in 1928–1936. Thanks largely to the efforts of G. D. Sondhi, who served on the International Olympic Committee from 1932 to 1966, New Delhi was chosen to host the first Asian Games, which took place in 1951.[43]

——— Japan

On July 8, 1853, Commodore Matthew Perry arrived at the port of Uraga with a letter to the Tokugawa shogun from President Franklin Pierce. The Japanese were informed that the United States expected them to open their islands to trade and to provide humane treatment for shipwrecked American seamen. Reluctantly, after a second visit by Perry, Japan complied. Among the unforeseen consequences was the "Meiji Restoration" of 1868, in which the shogunate was toppled and the emperor restored, not as an absolute ruler, but as a figurehead for modernizers determined to acquire Western science, technology, and weaponry.

Mercantile motives brought Perry to Japanese shores, but sports still played a small part in his initial interactions with his reluctant hosts. In addition to a minstrel show, Perry's sailors put on a display of manly fisticuffs. The Japanese answered with an exhibition of *sumō*. Neither party was properly impressed by the other. The Americans were disgusted by the beefy wrestlers, "over-fed monsters," who glared "with brutal ferocity at each other, ready to exhibit the cruel instincts of a savage nature." The Japanese, for their part, produced a woodblock print that shows "bulky sumo wrestlers delivering the shogun's gift of bales of rice to the scrawny American sailors."[44]

Steamships, telegraph lines, and coastal artillery were very much on the modernizers' minds, not cricket bats, soccer balls, or rowing shells, but it proved impossible to acquire the first items without the second. In the course of the Meiji period (1868–1912), an array of modern sports was introduced to Japan. British influence was paramount for several decades but gradually gave way to sports from the United States. Analyzing global sports participation in the 1980s and 1990s, Maarten van Bottenburg observed that the percentage of the population participating in sports of American origin is higher in Japan than in any European country (42 percent), while the percentage participating in sports of British origin is lower (23 percent). The reason is clear. "The British may have been dominant in commerce [in the Meiji period], but the Americans were more influential in the educational and cultural spheres."[45]

For a brief time, it seemed that France was to play a major role in the modernization of Japanese sports. Between 1867 and 1880, a French contingent at the Toyama Military School instructed Japanese officers in gymnastics and taught them how to ride and fence in the European manner.[46] In the dissemination of modern sports, however, French officers were soon supplanted by British businessmen and diplomatic officials and by American educators and advisers to the Japanese government.

Despite the fact that Japanese terrain was seldom suitable for cricket, British bowlers and batsmen refused to deny themselves the pastoral pleasures of their favorite game. On October 16, 1869, eleven Britons resident in the port city of Kobe met a team from H. M. S. *Ocean.* A cricket club was organized three days later, thanks largely to the initiative of businessman Arthur Hesketh Groom. Shortly thereafter, the Yokohama Cricket and Athletic Club was founded by the British in that harbor town (where occasional matches between the garrison and visiting naval personnel had taken place as early as 1864). Although a few Japanese tried their hand at cricket, the sport never became popular.[47] The *Kodansha Encyclopedia of Japan* does have an entry under "cricket": it provides information on insects of the order Orthoptera.

Soccer football was introduced to Japanese naval personnel in 1873 by Major Archfield Douglas, but the game failed to gain much of a foothold until the early twentieth century. In 1917, Japan sent a soccer team to the third YMCA-organized Far Eastern Games. A national soccer federation, established in 1921, was recognized by FIFA in 1929. The national team qualified for several World Cup Finals and won a bronze medal at the 1968 Olympics. A Japanese Soccer League was formed in 1965 from company teams, many of which were simply rebaptized when the professional "J-League" was launched in 1993.[48]

The J-League was unlike other Japanese sports organizations in that the directors insisted that teams identify themselves by locale rather than by corporate sponsor, e.g., the Urawa Reds rather than Mitsubishi Heavy Industries. In addition, by asking its teams to encourage the development of local sports clubs, the J-League sought to make active sports participation an aspect of everyday life. The league was also innovative in its marketing. The *Financial Times* described its stadia as discolike venues with "lots of vivid color, lights, fashion, music." The J-League allowed its players to express their individuality with long hair and short tempers, with designer jeans and fast cars. Uninhibited soccer players such as Miura Kazuyoshi were showcased like rock stars. Young Japanese, turning their backs on baseball, flocked to the game.[49]

Despite the marketers' inventiveness, rugby remains the more popular of the two football "codes." Like soccer, rugby began in the Meiji period. In 1890, only a year after Cambridge graduate E. B. Clarke introduced the game, students at Keiō University played against British members of the Yokohama Athletic Club. In the Kansai area, which includes Kobe, Osaka, and Kyoto, Dōshisha University emerged as a rugby power. In 1927, Keiō, Dōshisha, and Waseda joined with the nation's most prestigious public universities (Tokyo and Kyoto) to form a rugby federation. In Japan, as elsewhere, rugby was perceived as an ideal sport for young men to persuade themselves that sedentary study had not robbed them of their masculinity.[50]

Track-and-field events were introduced as part of the *undōkai* (sports days) at various schools, but interest in athletics remained minimal until the initiatives taken in 1883 by Frederick W. Strange, an Englishman teaching at Tokyo's prestigious First Higher Middle School (usually abbrevated as *Ichikō*). Imbued with the Victorian conviction that sports are the proper antidote for excessive cogitation, Strange staged a historic track-and-field meet for students at *Ichikō* and the nearby college that eventually became Tokyo University. A 300-yard bamboo-fenced track was laid out on the college grounds. All the customary running, jumping, vaulting, and throwing events were included, along with running a three-legged race and hurling a cricket ball. For the shot-put and the hammer-throw, Strange made do with whatever equipment was available. School benches did double duty as hurdles. "Instead of a pistol shot, [starts were] signaled by swinging down a folded Western-style umbrella."[51]

Japan's first track-and-field star appeared at an *undōkai* in the fall of 1902 at Tokyo University. Fujii Minoru was timed in the 100-meter at 10.24 seconds, an astonishing feat. The president of the university, Hamao Arita, proudly announced a world record, and *Spalding's Athletic Almanac* listed it as such. Four years later, Fujii was said to have pole-vaulted 3.9 meters, nearly half a meter better than the official world record.[52]

Apart from Fujii, whose achievements were less than completely credible, Japanese sprinters have never done very well in international competition. In 1912, for instance, when the 100-meter record was 10.6 seconds, Mishima Yahiko held the Japanese title with the unimpressive time of 12.0 seconds. (By then, the Japanese no longer credited Fujii's time of 10.24.) Itō Kōji, the first Japanese sprinter to run 100 meters in less than 10 seconds, achieved this breakthrough in 1999, thirty years after James Hines broke the 10-second barrier.[53]

Japanese runners preferred long-distance races and were better at them. In March 1909, the *Osaka Mainichi* newspaper sponsored a 20-mile "Kobe to Osaka Marathon Race." Kenko Chōnosuke won in 2 hours, 10 minutes, and 54 seconds. In 1917, Tokyo's *Yomiuri* newspaper sponsored a 300-mile relay race from Kyoto's Sanjō Bridge to Tokyo's Ueno Park. Still another newspaper, the *Hōchi Shimbun,* invited students from Keiô, Waseda, and other universities to participate in an *ekiden* (long-distance relay race) from Tokyo to the resort town of Hakone and back, a distance of over a hundred miles. Ten thousand spectators watched the first race on February 11, 1920.[54]

The most successful Japanese track-and-field athlete of the early Shōwa period (1925–30) was a young woman, Hitomi Kinue. After her 1926 graduation from what is now Tokyo Women's College of Physical Education, she was hired as a journalist by Osaka's *Mainichi Shimbun.* At that year's track-and-field championships, she competed so impressively that she was chosen to be Japan's lone representative at the second quadrennial International Women's Games sponsored by the *Fédération Sportive Féminine Internationale.* Traveling alone, the nineteen-year-old journeyed to Gothenburg, Sweden. She won the standing and the running long jump, was second in the discus and third in the 100-yard dash. Her 5.5 meters in the running long jump set a world's record. Two years later, at the Olympic Games in Amsterdam, she was second in the first-ever 800-meter race for women. When the International Women's Games were held in Prague, in 1930, she competed in several events and won the long jump with a spectacular leap of 5.9 meters—despite the fact that she was suffering from a sore throat and a fever. After the games, the Japanese team went on to dual meets in Warsaw, Berlin, Paris, and Brussels. Although Hitomi was exhausted and required almost daily injections, she competed in all these meets. She never recovered her health. In the spring of 1931, she began to cough blood. She died that summer.[55]

Fishermen and others who rowed and sailed on Japan's lakes, rivers, and coastal waters had always had informal boat races. Western-style aquatic sports began in 1861 when Nagasaki hosted an outlandish regatta for Japanese sampans, four-oared gigs, and houseboats. Kobe's British residents founded a Regatta and Athletic Club in 1870, and another major step was taken at Tokyo University in 1884, when Frederick W. Strange—the British track-and-field enthusiast—started a boat club modeled on those at Oxford and Cambridge. In 1887, the club organized intercollegiate races on the Sumida River, which flows through Tokyo. Providing Japanese students with an equivalent to the Henley Regatta was among the last of Strange's many contributions to Japanese sports. He died suddenly of a heart attack in 1889—he was only thirty-five.[56]

In 1878, Amherst College's George A. Leland introduced lawn tennis to the students of Tokyo University, but the game failed to stir much interest. Kobe's socially exclusive Lawn Tennis Club was not opened until 1900, and the *Mainichi Shimbun,* ordinarily eager to increase circulation by promoting sports events, waited until 1910 to sponsor its first tennis tournament. Students and graduates of Keiō University were as prominent in the diffusion of tennis as they were in the spread of other modern sports, but their tennis team was not organized until 1913. Despite Japan's rather hesitant acceptance of the game, Kumagai Kazuya took a silver medal in men's singles at the Olympic Games in Antwerp in 1920. Teamed with Kashio Seiichirō, he won a second silver in the doubles competition. Kumagai was one of a handful of Japanese players to reach the top ranks in tennis.[57]

Although the residents of Kobe's British colony skied and skated, winter sports were more popular in the central mountains and on the northern island of Hokkaido than in the Kansai area. In January of 1911, on snowy slopes near the town of Takeda in Niigata Prefecture, Theodor von Lerch, an Austrian officer, taught the men of the 58th Infantry Regiment how to ski. The following year, students at the national university in Sapporo founded an Alpine club to promote their favorite activity, mountain climbing, only to discover that it was more fun to glide swiftly down a slope than to clamber laboriously up one. Sapporo students also led the way in another winter sport. Their cross-country skiing club, founded in 1916, formed the nucleus of the *Zen Nihon Sukî Renmei* (All-Japan Ski Federation), founded in 1925.[58]

Baseball came to Japan through the good offices of Horace Wilson, a teacher at what was to become Tokyo University. He introduced the game in 1873. Students returning from the United States continued Wilson's work. Railroad engineer Hiraoka Hiroshi was another who learned the game in the United States, where he studied from 1871 to 1877. During his stay, he met A. G. Spalding, baseball's chief publicist, who presented him with an official rulebook and some baseball gear. In 1882, Hiraoka put together a team among employees of the Shimbashi Railroad.[59]

Initially, the expansion of baseball was haphazard and games occurred at whim. "Informal and unskilled players," writes Kusaka Yuko, "sought only sporadically the ephemeral enjoyment of these unorganized games."[60] The game seemed to spread faster than a good grasp of its complicated rules. Japanese players had many questions: How many balls for a walk? Was the pitcher required to hurl the ball where the batter wanted it?

Rules were one problem. Equipment and facilities were another. To play baseball one needs a ball, a bat, and an open space. Gloves and mitts and catchers' masks were not really necessary, but baseball simply was not baseball if it wasn't played in proper uniforms. As can be seen in nineteenth-century photographs, Japanese players quickly exchanged their *hakima* (split skirts) for baseball togs.

For more than a decade after its construction in 1882, the Shimbashi Athletic Club's baseball field was a unique facility. Then, around the turn of the century, elite schools began to construct more or less adequate baseball grounds. *Ichikō* constructed its first field in 1899, Keiô in 1903, Waseda in 1908, and Meiji in 1909. In the 1920s and the 1930s, a number of large baseball stadia were constructed, the most famous of which was Kōshien Stadium near Osaka, completed in 1924. The stadium was the site, from 1925 on, of the passionately contested final rounds of the national middle-school baseball tournament sponsored by Osaka's *Asahi* newspaper.

For many Japanese, the mere word "Kōshien" can induce a cloud of memories. The word "*Ichikō*" has the same narcotic effect. That school's baseball club began in 1886 under the eye of the indefatigable Frederick W. Strange. After his premature death, the gospel of athleticism was preached by Kinoshita Hiroji, who served as *Ichikō*'s headmaster from 1889 to 1897. While studying in Europe, Kinoshita had been immensely impressed by the Henley Regatta and by the high-minded ethos of fair play, which he saw as the equivalent of the Japanese tradition of *bushidō* (the warrior's path). If *Ichikō* were to produce sturdy young men devoted to national service, sports had to play the role they played at Eton and Harrow. And they did. "From sunup to sundown—before, between, or after classes—the crack of bamboo swords and baseball bats filled the air."[61]

Springtime races on the Sumida River replicated those at English "public schools," but *Ichikō*'s baseball players far outnumbered the oarsmen. Proudly claiming to practice harder than any other baseball team, the players became Japan's dominant schoolboy team. Between 1895 and 1902 they compiled a 56–10 won–lost record. By 1891, they were ready to take on the Americans at the Yokohama Athletic Club. After five years of frustrating negotiations, a match was finally arranged for May 23, 1896.[62]

The atmosphere was tense. Illusions about good sportsmanship vanished as the members of the Yokohama Athletic Club jeered on the arrival of the neatly uniformed *Ichikō* students and taunted them as they warmed up for the game. The arrogant Americans, who had anticipated an easy victory, suffered a humiliating defeat. The schoolboys smashed stereotypes and won by the lopsided score of 29–4. "While gloom pervaded Yokohama, *Ichikô* athletes returned home to a rousing welcome marked by *banzai* chants, choruses from the national anthem, and overflowing cups of *sake*." The unexpected victory occasioned a national celebration, but the *Japan Weekly Mail* was careful not to brag: "School-boys with their daily opportunities for practice, their constant matches, and *sparer figures* have always the advantage over a team of grown men . . . who have not played together."[63]

Ichikō's thrilling success contributed to the diffusion of baseball, which became wildly popular in secondary schools and colleges. When Nels Norgren of the University of Chicago led a collegiate team to Japan in 1922, he reported in amazement that baseball "is more the national sport of Japan than it is of America." Norgren, who spent more time with the educated elite than with the nation's rice farmers and factory hands, overstated the popular appeal of the game, but it was definitely an important part of campus life and it was soon to become a national passion. Beginning in 1927, *Nihon Hōsō Kyokai* (NHK) made it possible for fans to hear play-by-play radio broadcasts of intercollegiate and interscholastic baseball games. By 1932, 37.5 percent of those who had radios were tuning in to sports broadcasts, baseball games foremost among them.[64]

Donald Roden has suggested that baseball "caught on" in Japan because it seemed familiar, emphasizing "precisely those values that were celebrated in the civic rituals of state: order, harmony, perseverance, and self-restraint." The Japanese have, indeed, often described baseball as if it were the inculcator of these virtues, but there was no need to discover them in baseball when Japanese archery and the other martial arts had been around for centuries. Although it is certainly possible that the Japanese sought familiar values in baseball, it is more likely that they seized upon the game because it represented values that were *not* traditionally Japanese. The American game, which Roden described as an enactment of self-restraint, Mark Twain characterized as "the outward and visible expression of the drive and push and rush and struggle of the raging, tearing, booming nineteenth century." Twain was surely right. Baseball symbolized not tradition but modernity. Like the telegraph, the telephone, and many other technological marvels of the era, the ludic import bore the magical stamp: "Made in America."[65]

Japan's first professional team was formed in 1921 by the Japan Sports Association. It expired almost immediately and has long since been forgotten. In 1931, Shōriki Matsutarō, owner of Tokyo's *Yomiuri* newspaper, enticed Philadelphia Athletics owner Connie Mack to tour Japan with an all-star team. Mack returned in 1934 with a team that included Babe Ruth. Despite the right-wing government's hostility to Western sports, a hundred thousand Japanese fans lined Tokyo's streets to welcome the American visitors and another hundred thousand "pushed and shoved their way" into Tokyo's Meiji Stadium.[66]

It was obvious to Shōriki that these fans were primed for the professional game. When he launched the Japan Professional Baseball League in 1936, financial backing for the seven teams was provided by three railway companies and four newspapers. It was entirely appropriate that Japan's emblematically modern sport was sponsored by enterprises symbolizing modern transportation and communication. Technology also figured in coverage of the league. In addition to extensive newspaper accounts, there were radio broadcasts to spread the word. According to a national survey of listener preferences, 63.8 percent of those who owned radios said they tuned in to baseball games. (Sumō followed with 55.5 percent.)[67]

Despite its popularity, baseball suffered the stigma of American origins at a time when Japan's military leaders were about to lead the country into war with the United States. Baseball was tolerated by the government, but the use of English terms was prohibited. Instead of shouting *seifu!* (safe), the umpire announced his decision with a loud *yoshi!* (good). After the attack on Pearl Harbor, the mere substitution of Japanese words for English ones was insufficient. Xenophobia—and the material damage done by American bombers—forced the league to shut down in November 1944.[68]

Three months after the end of the war, representatives of seven professional baseball teams met in Tokyo to discuss the future. They managed to gather enough former players for two teams. The first postwar professional baseball game was played at Tokyo's Jingū Stadium on November 23, 1945, in front of a crowd of 5,878. In 1948, a new professional baseball league was born. In 1950, it split into two divisions: the Pacific League and the Central League. The latter, with the Yomiuri Giants (Tokyo) and the Hanshin Tigers (Osaka), has always been more popular.[69]

Among the Giants were the two brightest stars of postwar Japanese baseball. Oh Sadaharu joined the team in 1959. From 1962 to 1974, he led the league in home runs. He won two successive triple crowns: in 1973, he hit 51 home runs, batted .355, and drove in 114 runs; the 1974 numbers were 49, .332, and 197. Oh's lifetime total of 868 home runs eclipsed Hank Aaron's 755. Japanese ballparks are smaller than American stadia, but this advantage is balanced by the fact that the Japanese season lasts for only 130 rather than 162 games.[70]

The only baseball player to rival Oh as a national hero was his teammate Nagashima Shigeo. Robert Whiting, whose books on "samurai baseball" are not noted for understatement, called Nagashima "the best loved, most admired, and most talked about figure in the history of sport." The *Asahi Shimbun* was more reserved, calling Nagashima "the brightest star of postwar sports." He had his grandest moment on June 26, 1959, when the Emperor attended his—the Emperor's—first baseball game. Playing against the Yomiuri Giants' archrivals, the Hanshin Tigers, Nagashima won the game with a bottom-of-the-ninth *sayōnara* (game-winning) home run. He also earned three straight batting crowns and contributed immensely to the Giants' unprecedented streak of nine consecutive championships (1965 through 1973).[71]

Nagashima, however, lacked Oh's highly public identification with Japanese tradition. Most Japanese fans were unbothered that Oh's father was Chinese. His mixed ancestry may even have been an attraction for those whose sense of identity was "learned, incomplete, painful, vulnerable." Except for the most xenophobic fans, ethnic origins counted for less than spiritual orientation. Oh's mentor Arakawa Hiroshi introduced him to the mysteries of Zen Buddhism and the esoteric doctrines of *aikidō*. In 1962, while Arakawa and Oh were learning how to tap the mystic energy of *ki*, Arakawa had an epiphany that transformed his protégé's career. To perfect his batting, to become infused with *ki*, Oh needed to raise his right foot and adopt a "flamingo stance." It seemed foolish, and Oh certainly looked odd in comparison to batters who had been drilled in the "correct" stance, but it worked. What Zen and *aikidō* had begun, *kendô* concluded. Arawaka studied that discipline and told Oh to practice the swordsman's moves, but Arawaka decided that real *kendô* matches were too risky. It was Oh's destiny to wield a bat rather than a bamboo sword. In short, Oh Sadaharu had the "stats" required to gain entry into the record books, and he embodied the spirit of the samurai. He symbolized modernity, and he symbolized tradition. Small wonder that he became a hero.[72]

Early in the century, Tobita Suishū had dreamed of Japanese baseball players meeting American major-leaguers on equal terms. No student of the game thinks that that day has arrived, but Nomo Hideo was its harbinger. His 1995 acquisition by the Los Angeles Dodgers and his subsequent American success signaled a new trend in international sports relations. Nomo and the Japanese who joined him in the major leagues may play in Yankee Stadium and other American ballparks, but their figurative cosmopolitan home is the global sports arena.

A century before Nomo's arrival, at a time when Hiraoka Hiroshi was teaching baseball to the employees of the Shimbashi Railroad, Kanō Jigorō was busy with another ludic experiment destined to play a crucial role in the global sports arena. Like basketball and volleyball, *jūdō* was a consciously *invented* sport. Its creation was the result of instrumental rationality. Its techniques were scientifically designed to enable a smaller, weaker person to overcome a larger, stronger, less skillful opponent. Kanō was quite aware of what he had done. He averred that he had followed "the scientific method . . . and constructed a new system which is most suited to today's society."[73]

A year after his graduation from college, Kanō converted a room at Tokyo's Eishōji temple into a *dōjō* (exercise hall). There, in May 1882, he began to offer instruction in the martial arts. At first he simply combined techniques from the schools with which he was already familiar, but it was clear from the start that Kanō had more in mind than "an art of attack and defense." He sought "a way of life," which is why he called his martial art *jūdō* (soft path) rather than *jūjutsu* (soft technique). The name of his school—the *Kōdōkan*— was formed from three Chinese characters that can be translated as "the hall where the Way is taught and learned."[74]

Writing about "the invention of the martial arts," Inoue Shun has stressed that Kanō's *jūdō* was a modernization of *jūjutsu*. Without abandoning the traditional Japanese master–disciple relationship, Kanô incorporated elements of Western pedagogy in his teaching. "While the older schools disregarded verbal instruction in the belief that the [martial] arts were learned directly by experience and observation of the master, Kanô attached much importance to verbal explanation and comprehension." Kanō's willingness to experiment led him to shift the emphasis from the repetition of *kata* (set forms) to the more flexible practice of *randori* (sparring).[75]

The Kōdōkan began with only nine students. Five years later, there were nearly five hundred, attracted not only by Kanō's ethical principles but also by the efficacy of *jūdō* as a combat sport. Kanō's disciples dominated the tournaments sponsored by the Tokyo Metropolitan Police Bureau. Kanō's account of their feats was modestly subdued: "Whenever the Police Bureau hosted big competitions, the Totsuka school and the Kōdōkan competed. At one contest in 1888, each sent fourteen or fifteen contestants. . . . Surprisingly, two or three matches ended in a tie, with the Kōdōkan winning all the rest. Kōdōkan pupils had greatly improved, but I never dreamed that their skills had progressed to the point that they could achieve such results."[76] The victory was a public-relations triumph. The police began to hire Kanō's students as instructors and the Kōdōkan siphoned students and teachers from other versions of the martial arts.

Thanks in part to Kanō's position as a prominent educator, *jūdō* spread quickly through Japan's system of military and civilian colleges and universities. Enthusiastic reception at home encouraged Kanō to spread the good news abroad, which he did in eight overseas journeys. His efforts to internationalize *jūdō* were especially successful in Europe, where a *jūdō* federation was founded in 1932. In 1964, *jūdō* became the first Olympic sport of Asian origin. Success has had its downside. With globalization came "sportification." Gradually divested of its ethical content, Kanō's inspired "soft path" has become—for many if not most of its devotees—just another combat sport.[77]

Kanō's innovations included the acceptance of women at the *Kōdōkan*. He was bolder than other educators. At women's colleges, the progress of sports—as opposed to noncompetitive physical education—lagged far behind the pace set at the men's schools. The protracted debates over sportswear were symptomatic. Everyone recognized that it was difficult to do calisthenics in an *obi* (the tight sash worn with the kimono) and nearly impossible to run in *geta* (Japanese clogs). The kimono's long, fluttering sleeves were an additional hinderance. Reform-minded Inokuchi Akuri, who had studied at Smith College, returned to Japan in 1903 and prescribed blouses, bloomers, and skirts for her physical-education classes. In 1915, Nikaidō Tokuyo experimented with the simple tunics that she had observed while studying in England. Neither effort at dress reform was very successful. It was not until the 1920s that Western sports clothes became standard for female physical education.[78]

The annual "sports day" at Japanese schools was a good indicator of prevalent attitudes. At the middle school affiliated with Tokyo's Normal School for Female Teachers, the 1904 *undōkai* included four footraces and two tug-of-war contests, but there were six dances and ten displays of drill and calisthenics. The same day, the boys at the middle school affiliated with the Normal School for Male Teachers played football, wrestled, and competed in ten footraces.[79]

At schools founded by or under the influence of Protestant missionaries, programs in female physical education were somewhat more ambitious. At Dōshisha Women's College, for instance, lawn tennis was played as early as 1879. Tennis was, then as now, considered an appropriately "feminine" sport, but what does one make of this entry in the diary kept in the 1890s by a student at Meiji Girls' School? "Every day early in the morning I go to the kendō hall to practice kendō, and then attend morning service. Getting in a sweat and bracing up my spirits, I feel very refreshed. Then I find myself ready to meet my God within."[80] Notable here is not the combination of piety and athleticism but rather a girl's commitment to a martial art that had been a samurai marker.

Meiji's muscular Christian was exceptional. Resistance to women's sports continues to be greater in Japan than in the West. Although German women explain that pain from sore muscles is part of the joy of sports, Japanese women complain bitterly if their fitness trainers urge them to exert themselves. The trend, however, is for increased sports participation. Pollsters inform us that 45 percent of Japanese women do sports (loosely defined) at least twice a week, and Saeki Toshio asserts—not very credibly—that 24.2 percent of all Japanese women are joggers or marathoners. In Japanese high schools, girls are now some 40 percent of the *kendô*-club members. The number of older women in the nation's "Mama-San" volleyball leagues is estimated at two to three million.[81]

Japanese women are also keen on golf, a game that has moved from the margins to the center of Japanese culture. Although Japanese terrain is utterly unsuitable for golf, that game is now the preferred sport of the Japanese corporate elite. Golf was introduced in 1901 by Arthur Hesketh Groom, the same British merchant who established Kobe's cricket club. In 1903, a four-hole course was constructed at Mount Rokkō, near the port city, and the Kobe Golf Club was founded. Its Yokohama counterpart followed in 1906. The first national championship was held in 1907, and the *Nihon Gorufu Kyōkai* (Japanese Golf Association) was formed in 1924.[82]

Today, corporate executives and even the ordinary *sararīman* ("salary man," i.e., white-collar employee) are "golf crazy." A modicum of ability with driver and putter is essential for advancement in the corporate hierarchy. Although some 1.25 percent of the nation's land is occupied by golf courses, supply cannot keep up with the demand generated by an estimated twelve million golfers, 15 percent of whom are said to be women.[83]

Golf courses require extensive tracts of level or moderately hilly land and the supply–demand equation makes the acquisition of such land extremely expensive (as well as environmentally destructive). Ironically, the scarcity of usable land in Japan makes golf especially attractive to those who can afford to play the game because "the sheer physical size of the space this sport occupies may be seen as a measure of the social space occupied by its players." Confronted by this shortage of suitable space, golf clubs scramble to rent or buy space wherever they can. On the northwest edge of Kyoto, monks in their *kesa* and *geta* (Buddhist robes and wooden sandals) share the temple grounds of Shōdenji with businessmen nattily attired in their imported golfing togs. Another solution to the lack of space has been the purchase or construction of golf courses in Scotland, the United States, and Australia.[84]

Wherever the game is played, it requires a hefty commitment in time and money. Golfers who insist on a full eighteen-hole course must "book rounds months in advance, often drive for several hours to get to the courses, pay heavy user fees, and purchase memberships at prices commonly in excess of . . . $400,000." To become members of the socially exclusive Koganei Country Club, near Tokyo, affluent golfers allegedly paid three million dollars. Before the bursting of Japan's hyperinflationary "bubble economy," the fee for a single round of golf was as much as $300. Those who cannot afford club membership make do with second best. In downtown Tokyo, they stand shoulder to shoulder with dozens of other resentful enthusiasts, driving buckets of balls into a net. The prestige accrued is hardly worth the effort.[85]

Widespread active and passive participation in modern sports has not meant the disappearance of traditional sports. The Japanese who pack Kōshien Stadium to cheer for their favorite baseball team are often found, the next afternoon, at a sumō tournament. Sumō *did* suffer a crisis during the early Meiji period, when people were infatuated with foreign ways, and "things Japanese" were often shunned as "uncivilized." The solution to the crisis was the simultaneous modernization and "retraditionalization" of sumō.[86]

During the Tokugawa and Meiji periods, sumô was held outdoors, and temporary wooden stands were constructed for each tournament and dismantled afterward. The day's matches were postponed in the event of rain, and there were occasions when an entire month was required to complete ten days of matches. In 1909, a permanent, roofed, ferro-concrete building, the *Kokugikan* (National Sports Hall) was constructed. From that point on, sumō was free from the vagaries of the weather.

The organizational changes that sumō underwent in the Meiji period were less immediately visible than the *Kokugikan,* but they were extremely important. They culminated, in 1926, in the establishment of a national federation to govern professional sumō (now named the Japan Sumō Association). The association set about to modernize the sport. One accomplishment of the association was the completion of the long process that culminated in the championship system: "It has always been obvious, in Japan as elsewhere, that some athletes are better than others. In Japan as in the West, the traditional way to determine a champion was for claimants to the title to issue challenges. Like baseball and other modern sports, sumō evolved from such more or less impromptu challenges to modernity's rationalized format of regularly scheduled competitions specifically designed to identify the best athlete or team."

From the middle of the eighteenth century, four regularly scheduled tournaments per year, each lasting approximately ten days, were staged in Edo (modern Tokyo), Osaka, and Kyoto. Before the nineteenth century, sumō fans seem not to have compared one wrestler's past performance with another's. In the Meiji period, they began to compare performances over the ten-day course of an entire tournament. This interest took the material form of trophies presented to undefeated wrestlers. It was not uncommon, however, for several wrestlers to finish a tournament without a defeat, in which case each received a trophy.

The next stage in the evolution of the system came in 1900 when Osaka's *Mainichi Shimbun* offered to award a *keshōmawashi* (ornamental apron) to the tournament champion. If two or more men were undefeated, then the prize was given to the man who defeated the greatest number of higher-ranked opponents. (All wrestlers are ranked in eleven categories, from *mae-*

zumō to *yokozuna*.) If no wrestler survived the tournament undefeated, the apron went to the wrestler with the fewest losses. If two or more men tied for that honor, then the prize was to be given to the man who defeated the greatest number of higher-ranked opponents. This elaborate system, relying on rank-order rather than a point system, yielded a single tournament champion.

The electronic media have also played an important role in the modernization of sumō. When radio broadcasting began in 1925, stations expressed an immediate interest in broadcasting sumō tournaments. The leaders of the Sumō Association, however, were leery of the new medium. Why should fans pay good money to crowd into the *Kokugikan* if they could sit comfortably at home and listen to the radio? Broadcasters persisted, and the association reluctantly agreed to allow radio coverage on a trial basis for the January tournament of 1928. Contrary to the association's fears, radio seemed to increase rather than decrease the desire to be present at the bouts. The stadium was packed, and radio broadcasts became a regular feature.

To accommodate the new medium, however, there had to be adjustments in the traditional way that the matches were held. Before each match, the two wrestlers perform *shikiri,* the long ritual preparation for what often proves to be very short bout. During *shikiri,* they crouch in the center of the ring, glare at one another, stand, return to their corners for another handful of purifying salt, move back to the center of the ring, strew the salt, and crouch again for more baleful glaring. Traditionally, *shikiri* continued until both men were ready to charge and grapple. Radio broadcasts, however, have an allotted time span. To ensure that the day's matches finished before the end of the broadcast, wrestlers were told to limit *shikiri* to ten minutes, which—with a glare at the broadcaster—they did.

Although one might have expected that the arrival of television in the 1950s would make it possible to return to longer *shikiri,* which are certainly more interesting to watch than to hear, this was not the result. The time limit for the upper division was reduced to four minutes, and the Sumō Association smoothly manages the progression of matches so that they end a few minutes before the 6:00 p.m. conclusion of the day's telecast. Ritual has become routine, the match begins when it is supposed to, and *shikiri* tends to be, for the wrestlers and spectators alike, mere posturing.

The modernization of sumō is far from complete. There are, for instance, no weight classes. Although the wrestlers are officially divided into eleven ranks, promotion to the top rank—to *yokozuna*—depends as much on the wrestler's character as on his performance. He must be a good representative of "Japanese-ness." This explains why the Sumō Association hesitated for years before accepting Hawaii-born Akebono as its first non-Japanese *yoko-zuna*.

And then there is the "retraditionalization" of sumō. In the midst of Japan's rapid modernization, when many Japanese nationalists experienced an uneasy sense that Japan's traditional culture was about to disappear in a haze of smoke and steam, *sumō* was especially valued as a symbol of what it meant to be Japanese. In 1909, the referee was stripped of his modern garb and anachronistically attired in Heian-period kimono and headgear. In 1931, amid the chauvinism characteristic of military regimes, the roof above the sumō ring was redesigned to conform to the architectural style of the sacred Shinto shrine at Ise. Performing *shikiri* while surrounded by officials in eleventh-century attire, stamping and strewing salt under an architectural allusion to Shinto, the mighty *yokozuna* is a reminder of the ineffable in the midst of the impersonal objectivity of quantifiable achievement.

_____ Islamic Asia

Throughout the Islamic regions of Asia, traditional sports have been marginalized if not wholly replaced by modern sports introduced from Europe and the United States, but the process was neither swift nor easy. The government of Ottoman Turkey strongly resisted the introduction of modern sports. In 1896, when the wrestler Koç Mehmet applied to the Sultan for permission to participate in the first Olympic Games of the modern era, he was sent to prison for his audacity. When a Turkish group organized a soccer team in Constantinople in 1899, nine years after British seamen and diplomats had begun to play the game at Izmir, the Sultan ordered the team dissolved. They were allowed to watch British residents in Constantinople play, but they were warned by the police not to mingle with foreign spectators. In 1905, the Sultan gave reluctant permission for his subjects to form what became Turkey's most famous soccer club—*Galatasary*. In 1910, two years after a revolution restricted the Sultan's authority, the city had its first soccer league. In the 1920s, Mustafa Kemal Atatürk's secular government was far more positive about Western ways, and by the time of Atatürk's death in 1938, soccer had become a major sport.

Conceptualized in symbolic contrast to traditional sports, soccer becomes an emblem of modernity. "Choosing to identify with football means presenting oneself as a modern European sophisticate." In Turkish popular culture, wrestlers appear as oafish toughs while soccer players are celebrities who consort with film stars and political leaders. The picture may be somewhat overdrawn, but there is no doubt about the popularity of soccer football. In 1986, nearly half of all Turkish sports-club members played the game. Whether or not the recent political shift toward Islam reduces the popularity of soccer remains to be seen. If the Iranian experience is any indication, it will not.[87]

Soccer football in Iran was played as early as 1898, when British residents of Isfahan played a team of Armenians, but the continuous history of the game began in 1916 during the British occupation of territory wrested from Turkish rule. Officers of the South Persia Rifles played the game and taught it to native troops. A national soccer federation was established in 1919 by James McMurray, British director of the Imperial Bank of Iran, and A. R. Neligan, a medical doctor who treated British diplomatic personnel. British employees of the Anglo-Persian Oil Company were another conduit for the game. Soccer players were soon as numerous as the wrestlers who had for centuries been the typical Iranian athletes. The game received additional impetus in 1936, when the crown prince, Muhammad Reza Pahlavi, returned from schooldays in Switzerland, where he had captained the football team. Three years later, Iranian teams competed in a championship tournament. The national soccer team experienced a severe setback in 1947, when the Turkish team overwhelmed them, in Teheran, by a score of 10–1. The sport recovered from this humiliating defeat and became truly a mass phenomenon in 1968. The proximate cause of the recovery was Iran's defeat of Israel in the final game of the Asian Nations Cup.[88]

Until the Islamic revolution of 1978, modern sports of all kinds were promoted by Shah Muhammad Reza Pahlavi and his brother Gholam Reza, head of Iran's National Olympic Committee. Throughout the Shah's reign, however, there was considerable resistance from clerical leaders who saw modern sports as an affront to Islam. Fundamentalists were irate that soccer matches were allowed on Friday, the Muslim sabbath, and that they were broadcast on state-run television. Clerics found women's sports to be especially objectionable, and they were infuriated when the Shah's wife appeared on television—shamelessly unveiled—as a swimmer and a water-skier. Religious opposition to sports that were meant to modernize Iranian culture (and prop an unstable regime) contributed to the monarchy's downfall. Once the Islamic Revolution had taken place, however, the Ayatollah Khomeni was ready to accept most modern sports for men and even for women—if the women were properly dressed and carefully protected from the violating gaze of male spectators. In 1988, the Ayatollah authorized television coverage of men's sports if viewers were "without lust." Male voyeurism was not a problem at the women's events of the First Islamic Countries' Sports Solidarity Games (1993), because there were no male spectators. Although clerical opposition to football has not entirely disappeared, the game gained a modicum of legitimacy in Islamic eyes when the Iranian team outscored the American team in the 1998 World Cup.[89]

In Olympic and other international competition, Turks and Iranians have been especially successful in weight lifting and wrestling, two sports traditionally associated with the "houses of strength." The greatest hero of modern Iranian sports is the Olympic wrestler (silver in 1952, gold in 1956) Gholamreza Takhti, a man in whom one can see a successful fusion of traditional and Western influences.[90]

Modern sports have flourished in Pakistan. Although traditional forms of polo are still played in remote villages where cairn pillars serve as goals, the game's modern form, introduced in the Punjab by British soldiers, is more familiar to urbanites (who follow it on television). Since its independence in 1949, Pakistan has also produced some of the world's best field-hockey teams. Even greater has been the nation's success in squash rackets. Between 1950 and 1995, four Pakistani players—Hashim Khan, Azam Khan (Hashim's younger brother), Jahangir Khan, and Jansher Khan—won the British Open, which serves as the game's unofficial world championship, twenty-seven times. Since its recognition by the International Cricket Conference in 1952, Pakistan has also become a major power in that sport. Tests against India are followed as if they determined the fate of the nation. Unlike their brethren in Iran and in Taliban-ruled Afghanistan, Pakistan's Muslim clerics have been ineffective in their opposition to modern sports. World-class cricket players such as Imran Khan are national heroes, and clerical criticism has failed to stop the annual polo tournament in Shandur, a major event on government-owned television and the nation's most popular tourist attraction.[91]

The Islamic peoples of Southeast Asia have been, on the whole, somewhat less receptive to soccer and cricket than their coreligionists in the Near East and South Asia, but the proponents of modern sports have had their successes.

British military and diplomatic personnel planted grass and played cricket and tennis in climates where none but "mad dogs and Englishmen" ventured into the noonday sun. Few members of the native elites of Singapore and Penang were inspired to join them, but the milder pleasures of golf lured some to an international tournament held in Penang in 1888. Golf spread rapidly among the native elites. Missionary teachers such as Mabel Marsh and Josephine Foss used badminton, tennis, netball, and basketball as instruments to emancipate Asian women from the restrictions of domesticity, but they made more converts (to sports) among the peninsula's Chinese and Indian girls than among the mostly Muslim Malay girls.[92]

The first prime minister of the independent state of Malaysia, Tunku Abdul Rahman, was a soccer enthusiast who had played the game at Cambridge. Under his leadership, the government invested in a splendid new stadium and soccer flourished. Malaysian athletes have also been among the world's best badminton players, but other modern sports have had a precarious postcolonial existence.

Dutch colonists in what is now Indonesia made an effort to promote *korfball,* a Dutch variant of basketball, but they failed. Pim Mulier was more sucessful. Ruud Stokvis wrote of him, "The man who, as a boy, founded the first soccer club in Holland, in 1879, later, when he worked in the Dutch Indies, initiated soccer in that region of the world." The seeds fell on fertile ground. The *Padangsche Voetball Club* began play in 1901, and *Voetball* leagues ramified throughout Sumatra and Java. An Indonesian team of mixed ethnicity reached the 1938 World Cup Final but was eliminated in the first round. Basketball and volleyball were promoted here, as in the rest of Asia, by YMCA workers. Indonesia sent three men—a high-jumper, a swimmer, and a weight lifter—to Helsinki for the 1952 Olympics, but Indonesian athletes have seldom fared well in international competition—except in badminton. In that sport they have surpassed their Malaysian relatives and completely outclassed Western players. In 1996, eight of the world's twenty best players were Indonesians. The Indonesian badminton team took five Olympic medals in 1992 and four in 1996.[93]

Modern sports have not, however, eliminated traditional games. In Indonesia, Malaysia, and the Philippines traditional sports may be an endangered species, but they have managed to survive. Among them are *sepak raga, sepak takraw,* and *silat. Sepak raga* is similar to the ancient Japanese game of *kemari* in that the players, using any part of the body except the forearm and the hand, strive to keep the ball in the air. Like many traditional Asian games, *sepak raga* emphasizes harmony of movement, which is abetted by flute, gong, and drum music. *Sepak takraw,* which is played in one form or another throughout Southeast Asia, is closer to volleyball. Instead of using their hands, however, a trio of players use their feet or their heads to propel the hollow rattan ball over the net. Competition is keen. *Silat* is a fiercely cut-string competitive form of kite-flying.[94]

One reason for *sepak takraw*'s survival in Indonesia, in Malaysia, and among the Muslim minority in the Philippines is that it has become, in many ways, a modern sport. To save the game from extinction, players from throughout the region organized the Asian Sepak Takraw Federation, agreed upon a common set of rules, and campaigned for the acceptance of the sport in the Asian Games, a goal achieved when the eleventh Asian Games took place in Beijing in 1990.

Although Turkey's Selim Sirry Bey was the first Asian to join the International Olympic Committee, in 1908, the Islamic nations of Asia have encountered and caused difficulties in international competition. For decades after the establishment of Israel, many Islamic states refused to compete against what they termed the "Zionist entity." Israel was not invited to the Mediterranean Games when these games were held in Beirut (1959). In response to this and other acts of discrimination and exclusion, many international sports federations arranged for Israeli teams to participate in European rather than in Asian competitions. One consequence of this "pragmatic" solution was that Maccabi Tel Aviv won the European Club Championship in basketball in 1977, 1981, and 2001.[95]

The International Olympic Committee was made of sterner stuff than the *Fédération Internationale de Basketball Amateur.* When the Indonesian government decided to exclude Israel (and Taiwan) from the Fourth Asian Games, which were scheduled to take place in Jakarta in 1962, the IOC protested vigorously. The Indonesian government remained obdurate even after the IOC dispatched an emissary to Jakarta in an attempt to mediate the dispute. G. D. Sondhi, the IOC's distinguished Indian member, was forced to abandon his mission and flee the city in haste when a mob attacked his hotel. The IOC's response to this afront was to suspend Indonesia from the Olympic movement. In defiance, and with much political fanfare, Indonesia's President Sukarno then launched the Games of the New Emerging Forces. Sukarno's organization was intended as an alternative to the IOC. Forty-eight nations, mostly Asian and African, sent teams to the first GANEFO, in 1963, after which the organization "died a quiet death."[96]

Indonesia was not the only Islamic nation to cross swords with the IOC. A number of Islamic states boycotted the 1956 Olympics (to protest the British-French-Israeli invasion of Egypt) and the 1980 Olympics (to protest the USSR's invasion of Afghanistan). There has also been significant tension over Islamic reluctance to send female athletes to the games. The IOC considers the exclusion of women as a violation of the Olympic Charter and has threatened to bar nations that persist in the practice. Considering the IOC's reluctance to enforce its own rules, one has to take the threat with a grain of salt.

"OUR FORMER COLONIAL MASTERS"
AFRICAN SPORTS

In the course of the nineteenth century Africa became the most colonized of continents. In the race to acquire colonies, protectorates, and spheres of influence, the British were remarkably successful. The British were also principal agents in the diffusion of modern sports "from Capetown to Cairo." Africans were especially receptive to soccer, a receptivity that a German researcher has explained by asserting that Africans are "fascinated by whatever is round and bouncy." British success certainly had more to do with colonial policy than with the shape and elasticity of the soccer ball. There was a "sharp contrast between the role of sport in the ethos and make-up of the British colonial administrator on the one hand and his colonial counterparts from other European countries."[1]

The contrast between the British and the Germans was especially sharp. In German-ruled Africa, which was actually a large part of the continent before World War I, *Turnen*—noncompetitive gymnastics embued with nationalistic ardor—was the preferred form of physical recreation. Every self-respecting gymnastics club celebrated an annual *Turnfest,* usually on the Kaiser's birthday. German colonizers discouraged the spread of modern sports among the indigenous population.[2]

The French boasted of their *mission civilisatrice,* but they tended to see literature rather than sports as the appropriate civilizing vehicle. While claiming concern for physical education as a means to improve the health of the native population, French officials allocated less than 3 percent of their educational budget to physical activities. The French discouraged rather than promoted native involvement in organized sports. At best, the French "remained reticent about promoting sports in their colonies." At worst, they felt "a veritable psychosis . . . about the subversive potential of sports activities." When the French government, upset by the relatively poor performance of the national team at the 1928 Olympic Games, looked to the African colonies for "a reservoir of athletes," the army, which was in charge of colonial physical education, sabotaged the government's efforts to recruit native athletes.[3]

_____ British Africa

Behind the success of the British and the relative failure of the French in bringing modern sports to Africa was—quite simply—the British mania for athleticism. Sports were essential to the ideology of empire. When the Reverend J. E. C. Welldon announced his belief that "England has owed her sovereignty to her sports," he was by no means an unusual or eccentric spokesman.[4] It was widely assumed that sturdy shoulders were needed to bear what Rudyard Kipling—imperialism's poet laureate—called "the white man's burden." If Britannia were to rule the savannahs and the rain forests as well as the waves, one had to rely on sports—especially team games—to create the kind of character needed to meet extreme physical and mental challenges and to impose European civilization upon "lesser breeds without the law" (another phrase from Kipling). If French and German colonizers were far less obsessive in their approach to sports, it was not from a lack of concern for _ordre administratif_ or _Ordnung und Disziplin;_ it was rather that the French and the Germans were less certain than their British rivals that modern sports created moral fiber along with muscle mass.

From 1910 to 1948, British men recruited for administrative work by the Tropical African Service were selected with an eye to "character," and character was equated with the athletic ability demonstrated by the candidate at a "public school." Between 1899 and 1952, for instance, Eton, Harrow, Winchester, and the other elitist schools supplied more than 90 percent of all the officers in the Sudan Political Service. The administrative attention paid to sports was extreme. R. D. Furse, an Oxford-educated sports fanatic, printed application forms with a special section for sports. His Cambridge-educated colleague, R. E. H. Baily, circulated "a leather-bound book among his staff every morning, in which they were expected to indicate against their names the particular form of exercise they would be taking that afternoon." The men who had won their "colours" at Oxford and Cambridge were so prominent in the Sudan Political Service that wits spoke of "the Land of Blacks ruled by Blues." The situation was not appreciably different in other British colonies. Of the 216 officers sent to Kenya between 1890 and 1959, 76 percent had attended an elite secondary school and 77 percent had studied at Oxford or Cambridge.[5]

In Kenya, the colonizers "built up a sport culture . . . which was a copy of the one in Britain. . . . Even the smallest European community had its own club house, golf course, swimming pool, and tennis and squash courts. Where there were sufficient numbers, team games like rugby, cricket and field hockey were also played." Difficult circumstances were overcome by pluck. Nairobi's golfers, for example, persisted, although it was not unknown for players to be mauled by lions.[6]

No matter what the sport, colonial officers, military as well as civilian, preferred to compete among themselves and occasionally to indulge their more athletic wives and daughters in a game of field hockey, golf, or tennis. Although Kenya was certainly not the only colony where most natives were excluded from the attempts to replicate British culture in the tropics, there were exceptions to the rule. African soldiers and policemen were introduced to modern sports as part of their fitness programs, and children educated at missionary schools were taught to compete in athletics and to play cricket, rugby, and soccer.

The latter exception was especially important because these church-run schools trained the boys—and to a lesser extent the girls—who became the new native elite. Some colonial administrators left the missionaries to their own devices. Others, like Sir Frederick Lugard, the governor-general of Nigeria, went beyond a *laissez-faire* attitude. He actively encouraged the churches to include sports in the missionary schools they established throughout the colony. In these clerical schools for native children, Lugard hoped that soccer and other sports might serve as a means to achieve "the inculcation of a high moral standard." Postcolonial defenders of "Afrocentric culture" have sought, with little success, to break the spell that soccer has cast over young Nigerians.[7]

The masters of institutions like Nairobi's Alliance School and the Church Missionary Society Grammar School of Freetown, Sierra Leone, were physically energetic men who took sports seriously. Headmaster Francis Carey of Alliance School recalled that "Christianity and games were only a part of the life of the school but were indeed its most important elements." A former student of the Freetown School in Sierra Leone remembered that "games were compulsory . . . We played cricket in the dry season, and football in the rainy season, under the supervision of the appropriate master." According to Sev A. Obura, the General Secretary of the Uganda Olympic Committee, soccer was brought to the natives of Kampala in 1910 "by missionaries from the United Kingdom, our former colonial masters." These missionaries seem to have been anticipated by another man of the cloth, A. G. Fraser, who carried a soccer ball to Uganda in 1900 and, four years later, laid out a soccer field at King's School in Budo, a school established for the sons of Ugandan chiefs. When Fraser moved on to Achimota College in the Gold Coast, in 1927, he arranged for students there to have the civilizing benefits of two cricket ovals and four football fields. In Nigeria, too, British educators emphasized modern sports as instruments of acculturation.[8]

It was not just school*masters* who spread the gospel of modern sports. Marion Stevenson, a Scottish missionary at Tumutumu in Kenya, "played her small part in the diffusion of British games—in the interests of discipline and purity." Soccer, she alleged, distracted the boys from dances and fistfights. The girls were not similarly "distracted," because the girls were seldom encouraged to engage in modern sports of any kind.[9]

It should, however, be emphasized that missionary schools staffed by games-mad British teachers catered to the sons (and occasionally the daughters) of tribal leaders. Church-related schools were never meant to provide for every child. Throughout British-ruled Africa, ordinary people were not, as a rule, encouraged to abandon their traditional sports (except those that were "indecent" or too intimately a part of pagan ritual). Modern sports festivals, like Empire Day, first celebrated in Nigeria in 1893, gradually supplanted traditional games, but the organization of regular out-of-school ballgames came very slowly. It was, for instance, not until 1922 that the Football Association of Kenya, which may have been the first African sports federation for black players, was founded. Although a version of football was played in Nigeria long before the arrival of British colonizers, the modern game developed slowly. The first recorded soccer game was played at Lagos in 1914, and the Nigeria Football Association did not come into existence until 1945.[10]

Enthusiasm for soccer did not mean the total abandonment of tradition. The promoters of modern sports have had to reconcile themselves to the persistence of what seemed to them incongruous animist beliefs and behaviors. Decades after the introduction of soccer, magic continues to play a role. In Cameroon, where native teams were formed as early as 1927, Thomas Reefe reported that players were said to "kick up the ground around their opponent's goal in an effort to uncover the magic that keeps the ball from going in, and the magician's salary is a normal operating expense for many Kenyan soccer teams." In South Africa and Tanzania, a goat buried under the surface of the pitch is guaranteed to jinx the visiting team. Among the Zulu, scarification by a ritual adept (an *inyanga*) is a pregame ritual. (American athletes who wear the same tattered, grass-stained shirt for months "to keep the streak alive" have no right to dismiss African customs as "superstitions.")[11]

In any account of the diffusion of modern sports throughout Africa, Egyptian sports must figure as a special case. As early as 1895, Alexandria, which had for millennia been a European enclave, had a club for the practice and promotion of modern sports. This club, like the one opened in Cairo in 1907, was the work of German residents, but the strongest force behind the development of modern sports in Egypt was Angelo Bolanaki, an ethnic Greek from Alexandria whom Pierre de Coubertin chose, in 1910, as the first African member of the IOC. Bolanaki had organized a national athletics championship in 1908 and had already begun to dream of *Jeux Africains* that might bring together athletes from the entire continent. In anticipation of these games, he persuaded the city of Alexandria to construct a modern stadium. Coubertin's newly designed five-ring Olympic flag was raised there on April 5, 1914, in conjunction with a grand sports festival, but Bolanaki's dream of Pan-African Games was not realized until after World War II.[12]

During the British Protectorate (1914–1922), cricket, soccer, field hockey, and tennis spread among the Europeans resident in Egypt. The American College and the YMCA, both located in Cairo, introduced basketball and volleyball in 1925. Of all these sports, soccer was the most popular among young (male) Egyptians. In early Olympic competition, Egyptian athletes were more successful than other Africans (but not at soccer). At the 1928 Olympics in Amsterdam, Ibrahim Mustafa and Said Nasser won gold medals in wrestling and weight lifting, two sports traditionally popular in the Islamic world.[13]

At the other end of the continent, South Africa was another special case in that European settlers and their descendents formed a much larger percentage of the population than in the rest of sub-Saharan Africa. Of the sports of the first Dutch settlers—the Boers—we know very little, but the British played cricket as early as 1808, and Port Elizabeth had a cricket club in 1843. That cricket attracted very few Boers did not distress the British. As Will Whittam explained in 1884, "No German, Frenchman, or Fijee can ever master cricket, sir. Because they haven't got the pluck to stand before the wicket, sir." It happened that the Boers, whom Whittam hadn't mentioned, had pluck enough to hold the British at bay for three years of war (1899–1902). Ironically, it was as British prisoners of war that the Boers learned about and converted to modern sports.[14]

Missionary zeal led to the formation of an African cricket club in Port Elizabeth in 1869, and contests between black and white teams were not unusual in pre-apartheid South Africa. They were, indeed, "a feature of imperial public holidays . . . in the late nineteenth century." Black teams "regularly beat white sides on the special occasions, usually public holidays, when they played together." Early in the twentieth century, these contests were abandoned.[15]

By that time, Coloured (i.e., mixed race) cricketeers had also taken to the game. Port Elizabeth's South End CC dates from 1876. That did not mean acceptance on the part of those whom they emulated. The Coloured bowler

Krom Hendricks was not—despite his obvious talent—selected for the team that ventured to England in 1894. A South African Coloured Cricket Board was established in 1902, but, as late as 1913, the Wanderers Cricket Club of Johannesburg refused to set aside an area for Coloured spectators.[16]

Tennis was another sport favored by white South Africans, one that attracted women as well as men. Durban had its first tournament in 1881, a mere seven years after Walter Wingfield invented the game. Three years later, E. L. Williams reached the doubles finals at Wimbledon. Port Elizabeth, which became a hotbed of tennis, hosted the first national championships in 1891. A national federation was formed in 1903.[17]

Golf was played almost exclusively by whites, some of whom, like Gary Player, were world-class competitors. A partial exception to the rule was South African–born Papwa Sewgolum, winner of the Dutch Open in 1959 and 1960. When he played in the 1963 Natal Open, the South African Broadcasting Corporation canceled its coverage of the tournament. Sewgolum won and was compelled to receive his trophy outside rather than inside the Royal Golf Club. Rain drove the officials indoors, and Sewgolum was handed his trophy through a window. When he repeated his victory in 1965, the club repeated its rudeness.[18]

Canon George Ogilvie, headmaster of Cape Town's Diocesan College, introduced Winchester School's version of soccer football to the colony, and the first recorded match, between fifteen soldiers and fifteen civil servants, was played on August 23, 1862. The first stable club, Pietermaritzburg County, was formed in 1879. The sport was not immediately popular. South Africa's whites-only African Football Association was not established until 1892. It did not prosper. One reason for this is that soccer was promoted among the black population, not only by British educators but also by *Afrikaner* entrepreneurs like the De Beers Companie. In time, soccer came to be seen as *the* sport of the nonwhite majority while white South Africans turned increasingly to rugby.[19]

The first recorded rugby match seems to have been in Natal in 1870, when Maritzburg College met Hermannsburg School. Two years later, Bishop's College played Hilton College in Pietermaritzburg. Cape Town established its first clubs—Hamilton and Villagers—in 1879, Stellenbosch followed in 1883, and the South African Rugby Board was formed in 1889. In Durban, during the 1880s, the "Cape Coloureds" created a number of Muslim, Hindu, and Tamil rugby teams. They were notorious for rough play and close ties with urban gangs.[20]

The team nickname cherished by white South Africans, "Springboks," dates from the 1906–1907 rugby tour to England by a team that included both Boers and players of British descent. In the 1920s and 1930s, Boers, many of whom had learned the game at the University of Stellenbosch, flocked to rugby. It became a potent vehicle of male *Afrikaner* identity, providing young men with "a model of masculinity." Along with the Dutch Reformed Church and the Nationalist Party, the Springbok rugby team has been "the highest expression . . . of the *Afrikaner* spirit."[21]

When the *Afrikaner*-led Nationalist Party came to power in 1948, the full power of the state was used to give legal force to the customary racial and ethnic divisions of South African sports. Opposition to segregated sports was led—in exile—by the South African Sports Association (1958), and then by the South African Non-Racial Olympic Committee (1962). The opposition's most eloquent leader, Dennis Brutus, was banned, arrested, shot when he sought to escape his captors, and left to die on the sidewalk after the ambulance called to the scene refused to take him to a hospital. He lived, served an eighteenth-month prison sentence, and returned to the struggle.[22]

Controversy over apartheid failed to halt tours to South Africa by New Zealand's rugby team, but those who called for an end to sports contacts with South Africa won a series of victories. FIFA expelled the South African Football Association in 1964, and most of the other international sports federations followed suit. South Africa was not allowed to particpate in the 1964 or 1968 Olympics, and the South African National Olympic Committee, which stubbornly refused to resist the government's racist policies, was expelled in 1970. The IOC's final vote was 35–28–3.[23]

That same year a well-organized protest campaign—combined with vandalism—persuaded England's Test and County Cricket Board first to scale back and then to cancel its plans to host a South African tour. In the course of this controversy, England's most respected cricket reporter, John Arlott, announced that he would not cover the tour. Queen Elizabeth, who almost never intervened in political disputes, indicated her decision to stay away. Bad news of this sort seemed not to change minds in South Africa. Minister of the Interior Marias Vijoen explained, "We know . . . that the people behind the Olympic decision are the same Communist-inspired and Communist-paid agents who are behind the agitation in England to wreck the cricket tour." Although Prime Minister B. J. Vorster did not imply that the Queen was a Communist, he took the same hard line and was equally adamant about apartheid at home: "I want to make it quite clear that from South Africa's point of view no mixed sport between Whites and non-Whites will be practised locally."[24]

Defiant words, but they disguised some considerable anguish. "The sports boycott," noted Douglas Booth, "was the only anti-apartheid strategy that adversely touched the lives of ordinary white South Africans." In time, white South Africans found their role as pariahs unsustainable. The restrictions were relaxed. In 1979, for instance, Minister of Sport F. W. de Klerk announced that national sports federations would be given a degree of autonomy. White-only federations were urged to affiliate with black and Coloured federations. In 1990, speaking to parliament in his role as prime minister, de Klerk announced a new policy, one that led to the end of apartheid, to the election of Nelson Mandela as president of a reconstituted Republic of South Africa, and to the return of South Africa to the global sports arena. Apartheid was abandoned. The IOC readmitted South Africa's National Olympic Committee on July 9, 1991—in time for the Barcelona Olympics. Speaking for the IOC, Juan Antonio Samaranch gave Mandela a cordial welcome: "We've been waiting for you for a long time."[25]

Rugby's role as an expression of *Afrikaner* nationalism made the 1995 Rugby World Cup a moment of extraordinary historical signficance. Three years earlier, at a Test match against the New Zealand All-Blacks, *Afrikaner* fans, who were asked to observe a minute of silence, shouted "Fuck the ANC!" and sang "Die Stem," the anthem of *Afrikaner* nationalism. Mandela kept his cool. Before the 1995 World Cup, he was conciliatory, authorizing retention of the sacred Springbok emblem and logo. For their part, the Springboks and the South African Rugby Football Union adopted the slogan, "One Team, One Country." Mandela went beyond what was expected of him. He met with the team before the final game against New Zealand. During the game, he wore a Springbok jersey and cap and he cheered loudly for "his" team. These gestures of reconciliation—combined with the exhilaration of a three-point overtime victory—seem truly to have made a difference. Bitterness lingers, but the future of South African sports has never seemed brighter.[26]

───── **Francophone Africa**

The British were the principal actors in the drama of African sports diffusion, but they were certainly not alone upon the imperialist stage. In the years just before World War I, Roman Catholic missionaries introduced soccer into what was then the Belgian Congo and is now—after some decades as Zaire—the Democratic Republic of the Congo. In post–World War I Léopoldville (now Kinshasa), Père Raphaël de la Kethulle de Ryhove founded the *Fédération Sportive Conglolaise*. From Léopoldville, soccer and other modern sports were propagated throughout the colony. After 1919, when French colonists organized a Europeans-only soccer team in Brazzaville (French Congo), the Belgians and the French competed against one another.[27]

On Bastille Day, 1930, the players of Léopoldville's *Mutuelle* crossed the Congo River to challenge Brazzaville's *L'Étoile*. A year later, Brazzaville's authorities created a sports federation that included native as well as European teams. The colonial government's commitment to African sports was, however, less than whole-hearted. Watchful European volunteers acted as coaches, trainers, and officials. Most of the available funds were allocated to the European members of the *Club Athlétique Brazzavillois*. Interracial matches were discouraged. When they did occur, the colonial administration dictated that the Africans play in bare feet—to prevent savage injury to civilized shins. In response to this last indignity, some disaffected natives left the government-sponsored federation and joined the *Fédération Athlétique Conglolais*, which the Roman Catholic Church had established in 1933.[28]

At Conakry (capital of Guinea), a *Union Artistique, Sportive et de Tir* was organized in 1905. Among the sports practiced were not only the archery referred to in the club's name but also soccer, rugby, cycling, and tennis. By 1913, when the French in Senegal established the *Union Sportive et Artistique de Dakar*, sporting passions moved ahead of artistic enthusiasm in the organization's name if not in its activities. By 1934, Dakar was clearly the sports center of French West Africa. The city had three soccer clubs and two each for rugby and athletics. Dakar also boasted the colony's first *piscine* for swimmers who preferred artificial pools to coastal waters.[29]

When black Africans were accepted into Senegalese sports clubs, they were generally confined to separate sections and not allowed to compete against white athletes. The most famous Senegalese athlete of the period, the boxer Amadou Fall, better known as "Battling Siki," evaded this restriction by turning professional and moving to France, where, in 1922, he dethroned the popular light-heavyweight champion, Georges Carpentier. Like Jack Johnson, "Battling Siki" loved to taunt white opponents and to defy convention. "He walked the streets [of Paris] with a pet lion on a leash. . . . He was . . . fond of drinking, flashy clothes, and white women." He was vilified by the French press. He moved to the United States and became involved with the sport's criminal element. He was murdered in 1925.[30]

At roughly the same time that "Battling Siki" was flaunting his defiance of the French, a handful of more respectable Senegalese seem to have been accepted as members of *Le Racing-Club Dakarois*, which included soccer among its sports. In the 1930s, at a time when the colonial authorities were scouting unsuccessfully for African track-and-field talent, a number of Senegalese formed their own soccer clubs in the cities of Dakar, Saint-Louis, and Bamako. During most of World War II, French Equatorial Africa and French West Africa were controlled by the Vichy government, whose governor-general, Pierre Boisson, was an enthusiastic patron of indigenous sports. In 1942, a soccer tournament in Dakar was contested by seventy-eight teams.[31]

Modern sports radiated somewhat more quickly throughout French-ruled North Africa, where the French army's role was less prominent than in the sub-Saharan colonies. There were two reasons for this quick diffusion. Morocco, Algeria, and Tunisia had relatively large European populations, and Islamic culture was somewhat more receptive to modern sports (for men) than were the indigenous cultures south of the Sahara. An additional reason for the comparatively rapid adoption of modern sports throughout North Africa was the early realization on the part of Arab nationalists that sports clubs provided excellent cover for clandestine political organization.[32]

In Algeria, which had been seized by the French in 1830, the colonists formed clubs for marksmen, for gymnasts, and—eventually—for rugby and soccer players. Youssef Fates asserted that "the practice of sports and related physical activities was strictly reserved for Europeans," but there were exceptions to the rule of exclusion. Boughèra El Ouafi, competing as a member of the French team, won the marathon at the 1928 Olympics in Amsterdam. More important, when Oran, Algiers, and Constantine formed urban soccer leagues in 1919 and 1920, native teams were included. Cyclists made less headway, but *Vélo Sport Musulman* (1936) was a haven for North Africans determined to pedal their way through unendurable heat.[33]

In the course of the 1920s, with the rise of anticolonialist nationalism, sports became, according to Youssef Fates, "a phenomenon of appropriation. That which was not freely offered by the colonizer was seized from him." In 1926, Arab nationalists in Algiers organized the *Étoile Nord-Africaine* as a center for sports and politics. A scant two years later, Algerian soccer had become a predominantly Arab sport with unmistakable anticolonial overtones. In the FLN's struggle for Algerian independence, soccer became, in the words of Bernadette Deville-Danthu, "an instrument of sedition." In 1958, the FLN ordered Algerian players to leave France and form an *équipe national* in Tunis, which they did. After independence was achieved, one of these players, Rachid Mekhloufi, returned to France to captain the French team and was received warmly by Charles de Gaulle. "*La France,*" intoned the oracular general, "*c'est vous.*"[34]

In Tunisia, which became a French protectorate in 1881, soldiers rather than settlers were initially responsible for "the eruption . . . of western sports," but the colonists who crossed the Mediterranean from France and Italy to make their homes in Tunisia soon established a civilian network of sports clubs. In 1921, the *Ligue Tunisien de Football* brought together a medley of ethnically based sports organizations: *Jeune France* (for the French), *Stella d'Italia* (for Italian immigrants), *Le Foot-ball Club Sionniste* (for Jews), and *La Musulmane* (for Muslims). Ethnicity and religion had political implications of which everyone was keenly aware. "Every Tunisian sports victory against the European sports organizations," wrote Ben Larbi Mohamed and Borhane Erraïs, "contributed to the destruction of the myth of colonial power."[35]

The Moroccan story was similar. In 1913, when Europeans organized the *Union Sportive Marocaine,* they made no attempt to recruit Arab members. In 1938, when Islamic sports enthusiasts organized their own club in Casablanca, it quickly became "a symbol of resistance and struggle. . . . Each of its victories was felt to be a victory over colonialism."[36]

After the final victory, after the achievement of independence, the leaders of Africa's postcolonial regimes continued to instrumentalize sports for political purposes. Events such as the Africa Cup of Nations inaugurated in Khartoum (1957) and the *Jeux de l'Amitié* celebrated at Dakar (1963) were conceived as occasions for the continent's diverse peoples to forge new bonds. The high hopes for amity were often disappointed. When Gabon defeated the Congo in the final game of the *Coupe des Tropiques,* there were riots in the Congolese town of Libreville in which nine Gabonese were killed. Three thousand Congolese were then expelled from Gabon, after which, in retaliation, the hated *Gabonais* were driven from Brazzaville.[37]

The failure of sports to achieve pan-African unity did not dissuade African leaders from their belief in the power of sports to bridge differences. Postcolonial governments promoted sports as a means to foster commitment to an "imagined community" that members of tribal societies found difficult otherwise to imagine. Sports teams were sent to compete abroad as representatives of national rather than tribal identity. (Some of these teams were remarkably successful: In 1974, Zaire's soccer team was the first African squad to qualify for the World Cup Final; in 1990, Cameroon's team qualified and reached the quarter-final round.) Postcolonial governments constructed gigantic football stadia as symbols of national independence and staged national sports festivals as a way to encourage a common habitus. Nigeria, where the Yoruba, the Ibo, and other peoples found it difficult to live in peace, was typical. J. A. Adedeji noted optimistically that "modern stadia are being built in some state capitals and the idea of sports festivals is selling like a hot cake." If Adedeji was right, if the expensive new stadia have become sites for sports festivals that bring his people together emotionally as well as physically, then economic madness has, for once, been political wisdom.[38]

WINTER SPORTS

The Norse god Uller and his wife Skadi ski their way through the pages of Snorri Sturluson's thirteenth-century *Edda,* and there are scattered written references to hardy Scandinavian skiers, and to occasional skiing contests, in the centuries that follow. A pair of skiers appeared, in woodcut form, in the *Historia de Gentibus Septentrionalibus* (History of Northern Peoples), a chronicle of Scandinavian life published in 1555 by Olaus Magnus.[1] His Dutch contemporary, Pieter Brueghel the Elder was among the first to portray happy skaters—male and female—on Holland's frozen canals. Genre pictures of winter sports were brought to perfection a few years later by Hendrik Avercamp. In many of the latter's pictures, we can see men playing *kolf,* a game ancestral to both golf and ice hockey.

____ Curling

If curling is defined simply as a contest to see who can send a stone across a sheet of ice to rest closest to some kind of marker, then it is impossible to say when or where the sport began. Its documented history goes back at least as far as 1541, when the game was recorded at Paisley, Scotland. Numerous curling clubs were founded in the eighteenth century, when Alexander Pennicuik sang, "To Curle on the Ice does greatly please / Being a Manly *Scottish* Exercise." Historians of the game have demonstrated that curling, not golf, was the most popular Scottish game before the nineteenth-century arrival of soccer football. Scotland's nobility strongly favored curling over lawn bowls. The Grand Caledonia Club, founded in 1838, formalized the rules of the sport and promoted it throughout Scotland. Emigrants carried curling to Canada, where, in 1807, they founded the Montreal Curling Club.[2]

Like many early sports organizations, Montreal's club was renowned for its dinners, at which losers paid "for a bowl of whisky toddy, to be placed in the middle of the table for those who may chuse it." The sport's ethnic roots were revealed by clubs named The Thistle (1843) and The Caledonian (1850). A generation later, as Scottish immigrants settled the prairie regions of Manitoba, Saskatchewan, and Alberta, they made the most of level land and long, cold winters. Curling was probably the region's most popular sport until the 1920s. Winnipeg, which now claims to be the "curling capital of the world," became home to the Granite Curling Club in 1881. The city's first bonspiel (a match between curling clubs) took place in 1889. Until well after World War II, the Canadian version of the game was so informal that curlers competed on a bring-your-own rock basis.[3]

In 1966, curling federations from Europe and North America formed the International Curling Association. By this time, Canadian curlers, the Richardson family foremost among them, were so far ahead of other curlers that they had thousands of avid admirers back home in Scotland. In 1998, at Nagano, curling began its career as an official Olympic sport.[4]

_____ Skiing and Skating

A number of Norwegian towns claim to be the birthplace of modern winter sports. They agree that the happy delivery occurred in the middle of the nineteenth century. Among the notable early events were the Telemark race in Sauland in 1867 and the construction of the Holmenkollen ski jump in 1875. Another milestone was passed in 1901, when Norwegian and Swedish skiers and skaters met in Stockholm to celebrate the first quadrennial Nordic Games. These games, which included pageantry, theatrical productions, musical performances, and much folkloric festivity, contributed strongly to a sense of common Scandinavian identity. (Not enough, however, to halt the Norwegian drive for independence, which culminated in 1906.)[5]

The International Olympic Committee made room for figure skaters in the 1908 Olympics in London, but they were given a chilly reception. When Italy's Eugene Brunetta D'Usseaux proposed that winter sports be included at the next summer games, Sweden's Viktor Balck—the man most responsible for promoting the Nordic Games—strenuously opposed the suggestion. The skaters were back at the first postwar summer games because Antwerp happened to have an attractive _Palais de Glace._ Sweden's Magda Julin-Mauroy figure skated to a gold medal but not to the music she had originally chosen. In the immediate aftermath of World War I, Belgians were not yet ready to hear Johann Strauss's "Blue Danube."[6]

When the IOC met again, a year later, France's Melchior de Polignac, seconded by his Swiss and Canadian colleagues, proposed separate winter games, to be held the same year and in the same country as the summer games. Motivated mainly by a desire to keep winter sports for themselves, the IOC's Scandinavian members were opposed to the plan, but they were outnumbered. Chamonix, in the French Alps, was chosen to host the first winter games (because it had excellent rail connections). To mollify its Scandinavian minority, the IOC initially classified the event as an "International Winter Sports Week." There were competitions in speed skating, figure skating, cross-country skiing, and ski jumping (but not in Alpine skiing). Comforted to know that they were not considered Olympians, Norwegian skiers took part and won all their races. After Chamonix, the IOC voted to acknowledge the events, retroactively, as the first Winter Olympics. The Norwegian ski federation was annoyed, but it reluctantly agreed, by a vote of 29–27, to send a team to the 1928 Winter Olympics in St. Moritz.[7]

One reason for Scandinavian acquiescence was the recognition that Scandinavian no longer had a monopoly on winter sports. Cross-country skiing had spread quickly throughout northern Europe after the Norwegian explorer Fridtjof Nansen published a dramatic account of his 1888 trek across Greenland. Nansen detested modern sports, preferring traditional Norwegian *idraet* (body culture), but he inspired a generation to practice what he steadfastly refused to preach. The urge to buckle on skis and glide across the snow was so widely felt that German, Austrian, and American ski federations were founded almost simultaneously—in 1905. The Swiss beat them to it by a year. In 1908, when the Norwegians finally got around to creating the *Norges Skiforbund,* nearly two hundred special trains a year were already carrying tens of thousands of German skiers from Munich south to Garmisch.[8]

Norway's influence on North American cross-country skiing and ski jumping was pervasive. Nineteenth-century skiers were likely to be Norwegian-speakers who flew Norwegian flags and sang Norwegian folk songs. In Minnesota—pronounced "Minnesooota"—one of the earliest ski clubs was *Den Norske Turn og Skiforening* of Minneapolis, founded in 1885. Three years later, in Northfield, Minnesota, Norwegian-American students at St. Olaf's College founded the nation's first collegiate ski club. Of the seven men who began the Minnesota-based National Ski Association (1905), six were Norwegian Americans. In the popular mind, cross-country skiing was clearly associated with Norway. In California's Sierra Nevada, the *Marysville Daily Appeal* commented, "Nothing on a bright shiny morning can be more graceful and beautiful . . . than a fair young lassie" as she glides, sylphlike, "on her Norwegian shoes."[9]

Downhill skiing was another story, one with British rather than Norwegian characters. Although the British Isles can offer downhill skiers relatively few snow-covered mountain slopes, Alpine skiing—like the sport of mountain climbing—owes more to vacationers from London than to the Germans, Austrians, Italians, and Frenchmen who actually lived in the Alps. Arnold Lunn, an Englishman living in Mürren, Switzerland, invented the slalom on January 6, 1922, and promoted downhill skiing at the famed Kandahar Ski Club, which he founded in 1924. Lunn was also, for many years, a major non-Norwegian force within the *Fédération Internationale de Ski,* which he helped to establish in 1924. (That year was clearly skiing's *annus mirabilis.*)Together with the famed Austrian ski instructor Hannes Schneider, Lunn launched the Arlberg–Kandahar Downhill Race in 1928. Lunn's obdurate advocacy helped persuade the IOC to add Alpine contests—for men and women—to the 1948 winter games celebrated at St. Moritz.[10]

The British origins of Alpine skiing explain the early lead taken in the sport by Dartmouth and other New England colleges and universities. (It helped that New England—unlike Minnesota—had mountains.) The first American slalom course was built at Dartmouth in 1925, and annual races began in 1927. Although the National Ski Association was unhappy about this departure from Norwegian traditions, Dartmouth sponsored a national downhill championship in 1933, a few years before Sun Valley, Idaho, and Aspen, Colorado, opened their ski resorts.[11]

The post–World War II revival of the Olympics coincided with a significant increase in the number of the world's skiers and in nonskiers' awareness of their exploits. Austrian, French, and Italian Olympic champions such as Tony Sailer, Jean-Claude Killy, and Alberto Tomba became international celebrities. With the exception of Norway's Johan Koss, the cross-country champions have never attained quite the fame and fortune of the downhill stars. Endurance athletes suffering horribly from exhaustion are apparently less captivating than downhillers risking death in a spectacular, tumbling, spinning, high-speed crash.[12]

Women took to the ski slopes as quickly as men did. Mathias Zdarsky, the inventor of the Lilienfeld technique, acknowledged that women were as capable as men when it came to recreational skiing. Zdarsky drew the line at contests for female skiers, but there was no way to stop competitive women like Mizzi Angerer. In 1893, she won the first Mürzzschlag downhill race against a mixed field of male and female skiers. Other German women were among the founders of the famed *Oberharzer Skiclub* (1896), and women's journals such as *Die Radlerin* and *Die Deutsche Turnzeitung für Frauen* strongly recommended winter sports. By the turn of the century, affluent young Europeans and North Americans had come to consider winter holidays as occasions not only for competition but also for courtship. Damsels lingered by the ski lodge's wood fire, but athletic women skied side-by-side with the men.[13]

A century later, skiers number in the millions rather than the thousands, and ski slopes are badly stressed by overuse. Forests have been destroyed to make room for ski lodges and chairlifts. Snow machines lengthen the season for skiing and shorten it for vegetation. Mountains of trash present an ironic parallel to Alpine vistas.[14] North American skiers who venture by air into the remote backcountry, where they can glide through an unspoiled environment, accept the risk of an avalanche as the price that must be paid for solitude.

While intrepid skiers were scouting about for wilderness, the skaters moved indoors. In the commercial rinks constructed on both sides of the Atlantic in the last quarter of the nineteenth century, female skaters were generally as welcome as male if they paid the price of admission. In 1871, when the newly founded Copenhagen Skaters Association declared itself ready to accept female members, 875 of them arrived with their skates and their membership fees.[15] Commerce motivated the promoters. As for the motivation of the skaters, it is impossible to disentangle competition from courtship.

When cameramen replaced painters as the prime source of images in the age of mechanical reproduction, figure skaters such as Norway's Sonja Henie became international idols. Combining athletic talent with blonde hair and a pretty face, she skated her way from Chamonix to Hollywood, gathering three Olympic medals on the way (1928, 1932, 1936). After a number of girl-next-door Olympic champions such as Barbara Ann Scott, Peggy Fleming, and Dorothy Hamill, came Katarina Witt, whose blatantly sexual dance to music from *Carmen* made it impossible to pretend that a figure skater's athleticism is purely athletic or that aesthetic responses are wholly separate from erotic ones.[16]

Sexuality has also been a factor in the relative lack of appeal of men's figure skating. A number of male skaters have wavered between disguising and flaunting their homosexuality. If they pretend to be heterosexual, they can be accused of deception; if they are open about their preferences, they are liable to be perceived as discordant partners in pairs competition. Whatever the reason, most of the divinities in figure-skating's pantheon are female.

In 1994, Tonya Harding's rivalry with Nancy Kerrigan became *the* focus of media attention and public fascination after Harding conspired with her ex-husband to arrange a physical attack on Kerrigan that very nearly robbed her of the opportunity to compete in the Lillehammer games. (Kerrigan recovered and finished second to the Ukraine's Oksana Baiul; Harding came in eighth.) The television ratings for the climax of their competition were the sixth-highest in the history of the medium. Before, during, and after the Lillehammer Olympics, mainstream journalists scripted a melodrama in which

Kerrigan and Harding acted the parts of Virginal Beauty and Tough Girl. In post-Olympic analysis, Kerrigan and Harding were appropriated by "postmodern" feminists as examples of a "preferred text" (the willowy Kerrigan) versus a "subversive text" (the oaken Harding). Mass-media valences were reversed. Kerrigan was read as "the perfect slavegirl," as a pathetic woman complicit in her own subjugation, as a docile creature "willing to display her body for the sexual enjoyment of the onlooker." Harding, whom the mass media had vilified as "the Trash Queen," was admired for her "full round thighs and strong spade of a back" and for her scorn for the sport's bureaucratic establishment. Taken together, Kerrigan and Harding were "phantoms from the cold war that waft through the psychic territory of the fantasized white nation." Finding your way through the thicket of these analyses depends on your ability to read the map of postmodernist feminist scholarship.[17]

_____ Ice Hockey

Canada was the birthplace of ice hockey, and ice hockey has grown to become Canada's most popular participant and spectator sport. (Ice hockey did not become a part of Sweden's Nordic Games until 1922.)[18] Ice hockey is the only Canadian sport to be broadly popular with both of the nation's largest ethnic groups. Anglophones have had to acknowledge the greatness of Maurice Richard, while francophones have been forced to admit that Bobby Hull and Gordie Howe were also _formidable._

Several cities claim to have had the first hockey club or to have hosted the first contest. The first game played with a puck and by more or less modern rules seems to have been that contested at Montréal's Victoria Skating Rink in 1875. Four years later, at McGill University, W. F. Robertson and R. F. Smith codified the rules: nine players to a side, two-hour games, no body-checking, no forward-passing, and a face-off every time the puck went behind the goal. Clubs were formed at McGill (1881) and the Victoria Skating Rink (1882). Montreal's clubs then joined with those from Québec, and Ottawa to form the Amateur Hockey Association of Canada (1886). Québec's earliest clubs were formed by English-speakers. French Canadians got into the game in 1894 when _Le National_ was organized.[19]

Governor-General Frederick Arthur Stanley gave a kind of official imprimatur to the sport when his "hockey-crazed" sons persuaded him to build a rink at the Governor-General's residence and to donate the Stanley Cup as a material symbol of the Canadian championship. When Stanley returned to England in 1895, his sons and daughters taught the game to the young royals at Buckingham Palace. A five-club English league was launched in 1903, but ice hockey has never achieved mass appeal in the UK. A climate strong on fog and weak on ice offers, no doubt, part of the explanation for the slow growth of the game.[20]

The game's growth in Canada was rapid and disorganized. During the first quarter of the twentieth century, amateur and professional hockey leagues came and went in a confused sequence. While upper-class Canadians upheld the British tradition of amateur sports, the working class turned to American models of commercial entertainment. The openly professional International Hockey League began play in the fall of 1904. Ambrose O'Brien's National Hockey Association (NHA) entered the competition in 1909, followed in 1911 by the Pacific Coast Hockey League (PCHL), established by Vancouver millionaires Frank and Lester Patrick. In an effort to maximize profits, O'Brien and the Patricks sought to rationalize the sport. The former's NHA reduced teams from seven players to six, put identifying numbers on their backs, and divided the game into three periods with ten-minute breaks. In marketing the PCHL, the Patrick brothers were also quite innovative. They introduced the penalty shot and the penalty box, both intended to reduce mayhem on the ice, and they allowed the goalie to fall to the ice to block a shot. They also began to count "assists."[21]

The NHA was transformed into the National Hockey League, in 1917, but the PCHL offered stiff competition until 1925. When it collapsed, some of its teams were absorbed, as expected, into an expanded NHL. In a dramatic reversal of the usual vectors of ludic diffusion, the NHL began in 1925 to place franchises in the United States. Within two years, the NHL had teams in Boston, Chicago, Detroit, New York, and Pittsburgh, many of them owned by boxing promoters such as Tex Rickard and James Norris. For a venture in the entertainment industry, the NHL was remarkably stable. In 1966, on the eve of another spasm of expansion, every team in the league had been in the same city for at least forty-one years.[22]

That kind of stability indicates a reliable product and a considerable degree of customer loyalty. The NHL produced a spectacle characterized by swiftness, agility, dexterity, grace, and violence. The last characteristic has been taken for granted by the players and extolled by NHL officials. Stan Fischler, who seems to have assisted half of the NHL's stars in their production of tell-it-all autobiographies, comments, "Violence has been a part of the woof and warp of hockey since the first game was played in Montréal on March 3, 1875." John Mehlenbacher, a former NHL refereee, was more blunt: "The big wheels of the NHL figure they have to have blood to fill the arenas."[23] Fortunately for the owners and for the "goons" whose role is to intimidate and attack opposing players, Canadian and American judges and juries are extremely reluctant to consider violence committed in the course of a hockey match (or any other sports event) as criminal behavior.

Canadians followed the game in their daily newspapers, in hockey journals, and then, from 1923, via the newest medium of communication: radio. Beginning in 1931, there were Saturday-night radio broadcasts of games played by the Toronto Maple Leafs. General Motors, which sponsored the show, also bought the rights to broadcast games by the Montréal Canadiens and the Montreal Maroons. Two years later, station CKAC (Montréal) began broadcasts in French. By the end of the decade, two million Canadians tuned in to "Hockey Night in Canada," sponsored by Imperial Oil. Radio also brought Canadians news of their team's triumphant skate to Olympic gold at St. Moritz in 1928. (They won the final three games by scores of 11–0, 14–0, and 13–0!)[24]

Television merely tightened the hold that hockey had on the Canadian imagination. The CBC began to telecast NHL games in 1952. A decade later, over 80 percent of Canadian homes had a television set, and "Hockey Night in Canada" was the nation's most popular show, watched not only by three and a half million anglophone Canadians but also by two million *Canadiens*.[25]

Ice hockey is quite obviously the capstone in the arch of Canadian masculinity. The game offers young men an opportunity to demonstrate strength, speed, and—most important—toughness. NHL players, coaches, managers, and executives accept a level of physical violence unknown in the tamer version of hockey played in Europe. The spectacle of violence brings working-class fans to the arena and motivates the wealthy to rent Maple Leaf Gardens skyboxes for $175,000 a season. Body-checking at high speed, slamming an opponent against the boards, dropping the stick in order to throw (mostly ineffectual) punches—these maneuvers "bring crowds to their feet."[26]

That ice hockey is a theater of masculinity has made the game attractive for women who want to "deconstruct" gender stereotypes, but female participation on the ice is not exactly new. Young women were playing the game in the 1890s, and the University of Toronto had a women's team in 1901. To play the game was, even then, to make a political statement about girls' right to participate in boys' sports. To play the game today is to demonstrate that female hockey players can be almost (but not quite) as aggressive, competitive, and violent as their male counterparts. The truly revolutionary thing about Canadian women's hockey is that it is now accepted by most Canadian men.[27]

Less acceptable is the threat of "Americanization." After the expansion of the NHL in the 1920s, there was some flux among the franchises, followed by a long period of stability during which the NHL consisted of six teams: Boston, Chicago, Detroit, New York, Montréal, and Toronto. Then, over the next thirty-five years, the NHL sent teams south into the "Sun Belt." By 2002, twenty-four of the league's thirty teams were located in the United States. Québec City and Winnipeg were among the teams that moved. The relocation of the game struck Canadians with maximum impact in 1988, when Peter Pocklington of the Edmonton Oilers sold Wayne Gretzky to Bruce McNall's Los Angeles Kings for $15 million. Gretzky, who had set sixty-one NHL records, who had helped win four Stanley Cups, who had been nine times named the league's MVP, was an icon of Canadian identity. His engagement to an American actress, Janet Jones, added tremors to the cultural shock of his departure.[28]

There have been other instances of what some perceive as the American appropriation of Canadian identity. After the NHL hired him as its first American commissioner, in 1993, Gary Bettman negotiated a five-year, $155-million contract with Fox television. Among the innovative gadgetry installed to please the network were electronic transmitters inserted into hockey pucks to make the game "viewer-friendly." (The pucks glowed with highly visible colored halos as they streaked across the television screen.) Canadian fans were outraged, and this bit of "Americanization" was quickly abandoned.[29]

THE MODERN OLYMPIC GAMES

_____ Origins

The modern Olympic Games began as a European phenomenon, and non-Western peoples must still participate on Western terms. In the terminology of Talcott Parsons, there was from the very start a contradiction between universalistic ideals, which called for participation by "the youth of the world," and particularistic forms, which are unquestionably those developed in the West.

Although a number of nineteenth-century Europeans had endeavored to revive the ancient games, none of their efforts bore much fruit. An Englishman, Dr. W. P. Brookes, inaugurated a series of annual "Olympian Games" in Shropshire in 1849. They were purely local affairs in which rural folk participated in traditional games. In 1859, the Greeks made the first of several attempts to resuscitate the athletic contests that had expired some fifteen hundred years earlier. Their games, local and limited to ethnic Greeks, went largely unnoticed by the rest of the world. In 1891, John Astley Cooper boldly proposed a grand Pan-Britannic and Anglo-Saxon Festival, to which athletes from the British Empire and the United States were to be invited. His intention was to celebrate Anglo-Saxon superiority and to strengthen the bonds of ethnic solidarity. It was not until 1930 that his dream was partially realized in the form of the British Empire Games (subsequently rebaptized the Commonwealth Games).[1]

Baron Pierre de Coubertin, who possessed a more inclusively cosmopolitan vision and greater organizational skills than any of his predecessors, succeeded where they had failed. One factor in his success was his willingness to instrumentalize hallowed memories of the ancient games for some distinctly modern ends. Schooled in the classics, like every educated European, he exploited the aura of antiquity in order to further his avowedly political goal—international peace and reconciliation. His motivation was more than political. He was obsessed with a vision of "Olympism" as a secular faith. In a radio speech broadcast on the eve of the 1936 Olympics, he avowed, "The first essential characteristic of ancient as of modern Olympism is that it is a religion."[2]

On the eve of a congress convened at the Sorbonne in 1894, ostensibly to discuss amateurism, Coubertin published an essay in the *Revue de Paris* in which he eloquently advocated the revival of the Olympic Games. When the seventy-eight delegates from nine nations met, they were seated in a grand auditorium whose walls were decorated with neoclassical murals by Pierre Puvis de Chavannes. The delegates were aurally seduced by the ancient "Hymn to Apollo," discovered the previous year at Delphi, translated into French by Théodore Reinach, set to music by Gabriel Fauré, and sung by Jeanne Remacle and the chorus of the *Opéra français*. In this heady atmosphere of philhellenic high culture, the delegates applauded Coubertin's suggestion that an International Olympic Committee be organized to revive the ancient games. Coubertin picked the members, about a third of whom were peace activists.[3]

Coubertin chose a Greek scholar then resident in Paris, Demetrios Bikelas, to be the first IOC president. (He served until 1896, after which Coubertin took the office and served until 1925).[4] Appropriately, the first games of the modern era were celebrated in Athens in 1896. Consciously Hellenizing, Coubertin arranged for the Olympic program to include contests in hurling the javelin and the discus—two ancient events that had not been a part of modern track-and-field matches. Greek history inspired one of Coubertin's friends, Michel Bréal, to donate a trophy to be given to the winner of a twenty-two-mile race beginning at the site of the battle of Marathon and ending in the Olympic stadium. The present marathon distance—26.2 miles—was set in 1908, when the race began at Windsor Palace, as a favor to the British royal family, and ended in the stadium at Shepherd's Field, London.

Coubertin, however, was no antiquarian pedant. To the first modern games he invited not only track-and-field athletes and wrestlers but also swimmers and weight lifters, fencers and gymnasts, none of whose events had been a part of the ancient games. In other contests, oarsmen, cyclists, sharpshooters, and tennis players used equipment unknown before the nineteenth century.

Ecumenical Gestures

There were other indications that Coubertin's philhellenism had its limits. When the Greeks themselves, initially quite reluctant to sponsor the modern games, took full credit for their success, Coubertin resented the snub from those "who no longer needed me."[5] When the ingrates then announced their intention to keep the quadrennial celebrations in Greece, Coubertin was adamant. He insisted that the games be peripatetic in order to demonstrate the universality of his ideal. At each successive site, the spirit of Olympism was to be rekindled. Following the initial success in Athens, the world's athletes were called to Paris, to St. Louis, to London, and to Stockholm (after which the games were interrupted by World War I). It was not until 1956, however, that the games were celebrated outside Europe or the United States—and Melbourne was hardly a hotbed of non-Western culture. Tokyo and Mexico City, hosts for the Olympics of 1964 and 1968, were chosen in part to realize, belatedly, Coubertin's aspirations to universality. The choice of Moscow for the 1980 games and Beijing for those of 2008 was similarly motivated.

What of Africa? Although he was far more cosmopolitan than most of his countrymen, Coubertin, like most French patriots, believed that France had a "civilizing mission" in Africa. Sports were one instrument toward accomplishing that mission. Involving the African continent in the Olympic movement was, in his words, "the final battle . . . in sport's conquest of the world."[6] Early in 1923 he appointed a committee to investigate ways to bring modern sports to Africa. This *Commission d'Afrique* recommended two concurrent series of biennial regional games—one for indigenes and the other for European residents. The first regional games were planned for Algiers in 1925, but they were shifted to Alexandria, postponed until 1929, and then canceled. The Egyptians asserted that the IOC had been uncooperative, which it may have been. A more important reason for the cancelation was the "reticence [*sic*] of the colonizers to promote sports in their colonies."[7] Regional games took place only after decolonization.

Although modern sports came to British-ruled Africa before the French propagated them in their colonies, France took the lead in the 1960s in encouraging sports competitions among the newly independent states. The first important international athletic meet, the *Jeux de la Communauté,* was held at Tananarive (now Antananarivo), Madagascar, in April of 1960. These games were followed by the *Jeux de l'Amitié* at Dakar (1963) and then by the *Jeux Africains* at Brazzaville (1965). These last games, which Jean-Claude Ganga described as the "decisive departure" of African sports, had the strong support of IOC President Avery Brundage, a man often vilified as an out-and-out racist.[8]

Africa's Anglophone elites organized the African Games in 1973, held in Lagos in the former British colony of Nigeria. That year, the IOC established Olympic Solidarity, an organization that distributes economic and technical aid to the National Olympic Committees of Third World nations. This aid has accelerated the diffusion of modern sports throughout the continent, but no African city has ever been entrusted with the Olympics, and it is extremely unlikely that any will be in the foreseeable future—with the possible exception of Capetown.

As the games evolved, one form of parochialism faded away. Christian worship, which was introduced in 1908 and conducted in the stadium as a part of the opening ceremony in 1912, became peripheral in 1928, when the Dutch concluded that Protestant services were inappropriate at a festival to which athletes of every religion were invited. The secular symbolism of the interlaced rings of the Olympic flag flown at the 1920 games in Antwerp was designed by Coubertin to symbolize the unity of the globe's five continents. The baron noted proudly that the colors of the rings represented those of all the world's national flags. The ceremonial lighting of the Olympic flame, first ignited at Amsterdam in 1928, drew upon the universal symbolism of fire. The torch relay, introduced at the Berlin games of 1936, was a reminder of the pagan origins of the Olympics.

In 1964, at the first Olympics to be celebrated in a non-Western nation, the Japanese introduced their own identifying logo, and every subsequent host has done the same. In general, the culturally particularistic elements of the opening ceremony—Gershwin's music in Los Angeles in 1984, a tae kwan do display in Seoul in 1988, flamenco in Barcelona in 1992—have become increasingly prominent, even threatening to overwhelm the universalistic symbolism. As John J. MacAloon remarked, with the 1988 games in mind, "The processes of global interconnection and cultural differentiation occur everywhere simultaneously."[9]

And what of the athletes whose physical presence is the *sine qua non* of the games? The IOC summoned the "youth of the world" to friendly competition, but there was a proviso. They had to be amateurs. Coubertin thought that the amateur rule was an anachronism, a burdensome "mummy" that was lugged from one Olympic congress to the next, but he had to work with men who took their privileges seriously. The class bias of the IOC was blatant. The delegates to the 1894 Sorbonne conference exempted equestrians and yachtsmen, i.e., themselves, from the ban on valuable prizes. For nearly a century, prolonged disputes over the amateur rule and futile efforts to enforce it distracted the IOC from more important matters. It was not until 1991 that an amended Olympic Charter transferred the question of eligibility from the IOC to the international sports federations, most of which opted for "open" Olympics.[10]

There was another limitation to the universality of the Olympic ideal. The call to the "youth of the world" was more audible in some quarters than in others. At the first games, Australia's Edwin Flack and Chile's Luis Subercaseaux were alone among the 381 contestants in that they were neither European nor North American. In fact, references to "Europe" are imprecise; athletes from Eastern Europe played a negligible role in the early decades of the Olympic movement. The first Czech athletes competed in 1900, the first Poles in 1924. Although General A. D. Butowsky was a member of the original IOC, Czarist Russia did not send a team until 1908. The 5 Russians who competed at these games were scarcely noticed; their British hosts fielded a team of 710 athletes.[11]

The first African Olympians were two marathoners from South Africa, Len Tau and Jan Mashiani, who competed in St. Louis in 1904 as members of the British team. (They finished ninth and twelfth.) The three Africans who sailed to London for the 1908 games and nineteen of the twenty-one present in Stockholm in 1912 were white South Africans. At the Amsterdam games (1928), three Africans won gold medals: the Greco-Roman wrestler Ibrahim Mustafa (Egypt), the weight lifter Said Nasser (Egypt), and the marathon runner Borghèra El Ouafi (Algeria). As noted earlier, El Ouafi competed as a member of the French team.[12]

It was not until after World War II that African athletes made more than a token presence at the Olympic Games. It was 1960 before the first black African was awarded a gold medal; Abebe Bikila of Ethiopia achieved this honor when he won the marathon. At the 1968 games (Mexico City), Kenya burst upon the scene as a track-and-field power. Kipchoge Keino defeated world-record-holder Jim Ryun in the 1,500-meter race and came in second over 5,000-meters. Amos Biwott and Naftali Temu won gold medals in the 3,000-meter steeplechase and the 10,000-meter run. Kenya's 4 × 400-meter relay runners triumphed in their event. Wilson Kiprugut and Benjamin Kogo took silver medals in the 800-meter race and in the steeplechase. Bronze medals in the 5,000-meter race (Naftali Temu) and in featherweight boxing (Philip Waruinge) completed the harvest. As late as 1988, however, African athletes received only about one percent of the medals awarded at the Olympics.[13]

At the first Olympic Games (1896), Chile's Subercaseaux was—as noted above—the lone Latin American athlete. Subsequently, Chileans managed to win silver medals at the games of 1928, 1952, and 1956, but only two Latin American nations can boast of a significant number of Olympic victories. Between 1908 and 1976, Argentina's flag was raised for thirteen gold, eighteen silver, and thirteen bronze medals. (The first golds came in 1924, with a victory by the polo team, and in 1932, when Juan Zabala finished first in the marathon.) In 1976, Argentine athletes were surpassed by the Cubans, who returned from Montréal with six gold, four silver, and three bronze medals.

The Cubans had starred as fencers in 1904, when they won five of six possible medals, but it was Fidel Castro's Communist regime that made Olympic victory a national priority.[14]

Japan, the first Asian nation to undergo the process of modernization, was also the first to send athletes to the Olympics. Two runners competed in 1912. Mishima Yahiko, a 100-meter sprinter, tied his personal record and finished last in his heat. Kanaguri Shizō, a marathoner, succumbed to tiredness, fell asleep, and failed to finish the race. Japan's first gold medal came in Amsterdam (1928), where Oda Mikio won the triple jump at the games, but 1932 was the time and Los Angeles the place of the Asian athletic miracle. In every one of the men's swimming races, three Japanese reached the finals; they won eleven of the sixteen medals. Baron Nishi Takeichi added a twelfth in the equestrians' *Prix des Nations*.[15]

Female athletes, whose participation Coubertin deemed *impratique, inintéressante, inesthétique et incorrecte,* overcame his opposition and made their appearance in 1900 as golfers and tennis players, in 1904 as archers, in 1912 as swimmers and divers, and in 1928 as gymnasts and track-and-field athletes. In order to compete, these women, nearly all of whom were from Europe, North America, or Australia, had to deal with considerable resistance from other women as well as from conservative members of the IOC. While Sarah "Fanny" Durack and Wilhelmina Wyle were preparing for the 1912 Olympics, Rose Scott, president of the New South Wales Ladies' Amateur Swimming Association, tried to block them, announcing that it was "disgusting" that men were allowed to observe women's swimming and diving. "We don't want to return to the primitive state of the blacks."[16]

In the United States, Elizabeth Stoner of Mills College was horrified by what she heard of the *Olympiques Féminines,* staged by Alice Milliat in Paris in the summer of 1922. Stoner was appalled by the "feverish excitement based on the sex instinct." She disapproved of the male spectators who paid "an undue amount of attention . . . to the girls at the end of their events." Women who shared Stoner's views created a new organization—the Women's Division of the National Amateur Athletic Federation—and expressed adamant opposition to women's participation in the Olympics. The Women's Division, which was committed to noncompetitive physical education, was also vehemently opposed to national championships for women.[17]

Although the Women's Amateur Athletic Association of Canada was also opposed to national and international competition, five female Canadian track-and-field athletes and one swimmer made their way to Amsterdam for the 1928 Olympics. The track-and-field team won the women's 4 × 100-meter relay and the high jump and came in second and third in the 100 meters. Germany and Poland also sent strong teams. Amsterdam's demonstration of female athleticism was, however, spoiled when sportswriter John R. Tunis falsely described the 800-meter finalists as "eleven wretched women, five of whom dropped out before the finish, while five collapsed after reaching the tape." (All *nine* women finished the race and were no more exhausted than their male counterparts after their races.) The IOC, in a panic, dropped the 800-meter race from the program for Los Angeles. This retrograde movement did not go far enough for the Women's Division, which petitioned the IOC to omit women's athletics from the 1932 games. The IOC refused. Women competed in Los Angeles (and they received much more attention from the press—proportionally—than the men did).[18]

Mainstream American female physical educators were so adamantly opposed to Olympic competition that they refused to allow their students to try out for the team. The most successful female track-and-field athletes came from the industrial leagues (e.g., Mildred "Babe" Didrikson: two gold medals and a silver at the 1932 games), or from black colleges such as Tennessee State (e.g., Wilma Rudolph: three gold medals at the 1960 games).[19] The Women's Division—consistent to the end—was also opposed to women's participation in the industrial leagues.[20]

Latin American women were even slower to take advantage of Olympic opportunities. Maria Lenk, a Brazilian swimmer whose parents emigrated to Brazil in 1912, participated in the 1932 and 1936 games. In 1948, Argentina's Noemi Simonetto won a silver medal in the long jump. Eight years later, Chile's Marlene Ahrens was second in the javelin. Their achievements were surpassed at the Moscow games in 1980, when Cuba's María Caridad Colón won the javelin competition. Between then and 1996, when Costa Rica's Claudia Poll swam to victory in the 200-meter freestyle, Latin America's female Olympians were rare phenomena.[21]

Women from sub-Saharan Africa also mounted Moscow's victory platform. Zimbabwe's field-hockey team was memorable both for its victory at the games and for its postgames reward; to each member of the team, an ox was presented upon her return. Islamic women have been the last to ascend Olympic heights. Nawal El Mouawakie, competing for Morocco, broke the barrier in 1984, when she finished first in the 400-meter hurdles. That year, Islamic women were a mere 4 percent of their nations' Olympic teams. They can hardly be faulted for their tardy appearance and small numbers. As late as 1992, Algeria's Hassiba Boulmerka, winner of the 1500-meter race, had not only to outrun her rivals but also to surmount the psychological barrier of Islamic-fundamentalist death threats. It was not competition per se that bothered the fundamentalists—they were distressed because "young women are no longer ashamed of their bodies."[22]

One reason for the paucity of African, Asian, and Latin American men in the early annals of Olympic history was the requirement that athletes be selected and sent to the games by National Olympic Committees officially recognized by the IOC. The dates when each of the world's NOCs was granted official recognition by the IOC reveals the familiar pattern of ludic diffusion. Almost all of Europe was represented in the Olympic movement by 1920. Argentina, Uruguay, and Mexico formed NOCs in 1923. Bolivia, Chile, Brazil, Venezuela, and Colombia followed in the 1930s. The smaller Latin American republics were brought into the fold between 1945 and 1960. Most of Asia and Africa followed during the period of postwar decolonization, that is, between 1950 and 1980. The NOCs of Britain's former colonies achieved IOC recognition in the 1950s, France's colonies somewhat later, and Portugal's colonies last of all. During the next twenty years, the number of NOCs soared as the IOC granted quick recognition to committees from a number of dependent ministates (such as American Samoa and the British Virgin Islands) and from the successor states that were created as a result of the political disintegration of the Soviet Union, Yugoslavia, and Czechoslovakia.

The IOC and the NOCs—like the constituent parts of other organizationally complex international entities—are often at loggerheads. Some of the most serious clashes have been over the IOC's universalistic attempts to *include* athletes whom the NOCs wished to *exclude*. The controversy over the exclusion of Israel and Taiwan from the Asian Games wracked the Olympic movement, but the most protracted and divisive controversy was over South Africa's policy of apartheid, which clearly violated the Olympic Charter. The suspension and subsequent expulsion of the South African National Olympic Committee (SANOC) was the IOC's reluctant response to the *Afrikaner*-dominated South African committee's refusal to take a stand against its government's policy of strict racial segregation in sports.[23]

There were other destructive controversies in which NOCs fought the IOC or one another. After a representative team of New Zealand's rugby players toured South Africa, a number of African NOCs demanded that New Zealand's Olympic team be expelled from the 1976 games in Montréal. When the IOC refused to comply, arguing that it had no control over non-Olympic sports, twenty-eight African teams were ordered home by their governments. A more damaging boycott occurred in 1980. Desperate to respond in some nonmilitary way to the USSR's invasion of Afghanistan, President Jimmy Carter ordered the U.S. Olympic Committee to boycott the Moscow games.

His command was in ironic contradiction to the recently issued report of his *Commission on Olympic Sports* (1977). The Commission had deplored "the actions of governments which deny an athlete the right to take part in international competition." The USOC defiantly proclaimed its political independence and then cravenly complied with the government's demands. Intense diplomatic pressure brought the Canadian, German, and Japanese governments to heel, and they, in turn, forced their NOCs to spurn the invitation to Moscow. In solidarity with their fellow Muslims in Afghanistan, the Islamic world joined the boycott. The most remarkable stand was that taken by the NOCs of Western Europe. Nearly all of them defied their governments and sent teams to Moscow, where they competed under the Olympic banner rather than their national flags. (The British Olympic Association rejected the American initiative with a lapidary remark: "In this country Magna Carta rules, not Jimmy Carter.") In all, eighty-one NOCs sent teams to Moscow and sixty-two did not. The USSR proclaimed that the diminished games were an unprecedented success and then, four years later, retaliated with its own tit-for-tat boycott. Thirteen other Communist states stayed away from Los Angeles, but Romania broke ranks. When the Communist government of North Korea called for a boycott of the 1988 Olympics in Seoul (South Korea), Juan Antonio Samaranch's skillful diplomacy limited the damage. Of the six NOCs that answered Pyongyang's call to boycott, Cuba's was the only one whose absence altered the outcomes in the stadia.[24]

Throughout the "era of the boycott," the IOC remained a restricted club (to which women—Venezuela's Flor Isava Fonseca and Finland's Pirjo Haggman—were first admitted in 1981). The IOC's composition is an even better indicator of Western hegemony than the percentage of European and American athletes or the dates of recognition of the NOCs. The original IOC was as demographically narrow as the contingent of athletes at the first games. Twelve of the original fifteen IOC members were Europeans. The others were Professor William Milligan Sloane of Princeton University, Argentina's José Zubiaur (who never attended an IOC session), and Leonard A. Cuff of New Zealand (who never attended an IOC session). Having chosen a coterie of men, most of whom were titled or wealthy or both, Coubertin sought to enlarge the committee and to extend its geographical and cultural influence by having it elect members to serve as delegates to nations that had not sent athletes to the 1896 games. (The fiction that the members are delegates *to* rather than representatives *of* their nations was maintained until after World War II.)[25]

Latin America was an obviously fallow field upon which to sow the seeds of Olympism. Miguel de Beistegui, a Mexican, was tapped for the IOC in 1901.

The IOC extended its influence into the non-Western world when Turkey's Selim Sirry Bey joined the ranks in 1908. A year later, Kanō Jigorō was elected to the IOC in recognition of his roles as the founder of the *Dai Nippon Taiiku Kyōkai* (Greater Japan Physical Education Association) and as the inventor of *jūdō*. The first men to represent Africa were Angelo Bolanaki, the ethnically Greek Egyptian, and Sydney Farrar, a South African of British descent. They joined the IOC in 1910 and 1913. Delegates to India and China entered the Olympic fold in 1920 (Dorabji J. Tata) and 1922 (C. T. Wang). Despite these gestures toward universalism, the IOC remained an overwhelmingly European organization for another generation. At the start of the twenty-first century, Europeans and North Americans continue to dominate the IOC.[26]

IOC MEMBERS BY REGION

Area	1894	1954	2002
Africa	0	2	13
America	2	16	22
Asia	0	10	27
Europe	12	39	56
Oceania	1	3	6

That the IOC became a truly international organization in the postwar years is due largely to the efforts of Avery Brundage, the crusty, opinionated, obdurate Chicago businessman who was elected to the committee in 1936 and served as its president from 1952 to 1972. Although he was often insensitive to calls for racial equality and ambivalent about female athletes (runners, yes; shot-putters, no), Brundage was much more ecumenically disposed than Coubertin's first two successors, Henri Baillet-Latour, a Belgian count, and Sigfrid Edström, a Swedish industrial entrepreneur. Brundage was especially eager to discover Latin American sportsmen who might proselytize in an area not yet embued with Olympism. Writing to R. C. Aldao of Argentina in 1945, Brundage, who was then IOC vice-president, noted that the committee had no members from Bolivia, Chile, Colombia, Ecuador, Paraguay, Venezuela, or any of the Central American states. Could Aldao suggest qualified people? Names were supplied. Enrique O. Barbosa Baeza (Chile) and Miguel Ydigoras Fuentes (Guatamala) were elected to the IOC in 1948.[27]

Brundage's ecumenicism was strong enough to overcome his lifelong personal hostility to Communism. He made it part of his mission to convert the followers of Marx, Lenin, and Mao to the tenets of Coubertin. To accomplish this, he had to close his eyes to the Soviet Union's egregious violations of the amateur rule and the rule against governmental control of NOCs. Ingenuously explaining to his anti-Communist critics that the Russians had assured him of their faithful adherence to the Olympic Charter, Brundage—joined by all but three of the IOC's members—voted in May of 1951 to recognize the USSR's government-controlled NOC. Brundage was asked to swallow a harder pill when the Kremlin demanded the right to name its own representatives to the IOC. Edström and Brundage complained bitterly about this violation of the rules, but they eventually acquiesced in the infraction, and Konstantin Andrianov took his seat among the princes, the generals, and the millionaires of the IOC.

_____ Particularistic Universality

After his election as president of the IOC, Brundage—aided by such influential members as the Marquess of Exeter (UK), Jean de Beaumont (France), and Giulio Onesti (Italy)—actively recruited representatives of sub-Saharan Africa. In 1963, Adetokunbo Ademola, a British-educated Nigerian jurist, became the first black member. Nine years later, when Brundage passed the Olympic torch to Ireland's Michael Morris (Lord Killanin), there were four black Africans on the IOC (and four new members from North Africa). Killanin and his successor, Spain's Juan Antonio Samaranch, continued the search for non-Western IOC members. By 1993, 16.5 percent of the committee members came from Asia and 17.6 percent from Africa. Europeans and North Americans, however, continue to control the IOC. When Samaranch retired, Belgian's Jacques Rogge took his place, which meant that every IOC president—except Brundage—has been a European.

IOC PRESIDENTS

Demetrios Bikelas	Greece	1894–1896
Pierre de Coubertin	France	1896–1925
Henri de Baillet-Latour	Belgium	1925–1942
Sigfrid Edström	Sweden	1942–1952
Avery Brundage	United States	1952–1972
Michael Morris (Lord Killanin)	Ireland	1972–1980
Juan Antonio Samaranch	Spain	1980–2001
Jacques Rogge	Belgium	2001–

The enlargement of the committee did not automatically mean its democratization. Many European and North American nations had two or three representatives on the IOC; many Third World states had none at all. Andrianov and his colleague Aleksei Romanov, the second Russian to be elected to the

IOC, were determined to transform the committee and make the Olympic movement more globally representative. They argued forcefully in 1959 for a complete restructuring of the sixty-four-member committee. In order for the Olympic movement to become truly global, they argued, each of the NOCs and each of the twenty-five international sports federations had to have representation on the IOC. The effect of this scheme in practice would have been to triple the size of the IOC and to increase enormously the influence of the Communist bloc and the Third World. The plan was clearly analogous to Nikita Krushchev's nearly simultaneous proposal that the United Nations adopt a "troika" arrangement to allow executive power to be shared among that body's Communist, non-Communist, and nonaligned factions. The IOC members from Western Europe and North America were adamantly opposed to the Soviets' initiative. When the question came to a vote in 1961, the reformers were defeated 35–7.[28]

After this rebuff, Italy's resourceful Giulio Onesti tried a flanking maneuver. He invited representatives of the NOCs to meet among themselves to consider whether or not they should form a permanent organization. Representatives from sixty-eight committees caucused in 1965 and established the Study and Co-Ordinating Committee of the National Olympic Committees.

Brundage fought this initiative tooth and nail because he was vehemently opposed to any reform that institutionalized one-country–one-vote rule. He thought it absurd that Dahomey, Mongolia, and Panama should have the same weight in Olympic affairs as the United States, Great Britain, and the Soviet Union. Brundage's opposition failed to thwart Onesti, whose proposals had widespread support among Europeans as well as Asians, Africans, and Latin Americans. A Permanent General Assembly of National Olympic Committees (PGA) was created at Mexico City in 1968—at a time when "Black Power" protests at the games signaled deep dissatisfaction with the IOC's leadership. Brundage remained adamant, insisting that the upstart PGA "must be buried NOW," but his successors were more conciliatory. When Killanin followed Brundage, in 1972, one of his first moves was to establish a Tripartite Committee to regulate relationships among the IOC, the NOCs, and the international sports federations. Samaranch completed the work of organizational reform. Today, the PGA, renamed the Association of National Olympic Committees (ANOC), is recognized as an integral part of the Olympic movement, but it is not yet the case that every NOC entitled to de jure representation on the IOC.[29]

In 1967, at the same time that the NOCs were clamoring for a louder voice in the Olympic movement, a General Assembly of the International Federations (GAIF) was founded. Unlike the PGA, the GAIF was not formed to enhance the influence of sports administrators from the Communist bloc and the Third World. The GAIF was led by Australia's Berge Phillips (representing the swimmers and divers of the *Fédération Internationale de Natation Amateur*) and France's Roger Coulon (representing the wrestlers of the *Fédération Internationale de Lutte Amateur*). They and their supporters demanded that the IOC consider the international sports federations as partners rather than as minions. Brundage was unsympathetic; Killanin and Samaranch listened. The federations are now heard, but their relative empowerment has done little to diminish Western hegemony within the Olympic movement. In 1999, Senegal's Lamine Diack became the head of the International Amateur Athletic Federation, but the overwhelming majority of the international sports federations are still controlled by Europeans.[30]

The most important consequence of European hegemony has been that all the sports included in the Olympic program either have their origins in the West or are represented in the distinctly modern forms developed in Western culture. Archery, for instance, has prehistoric origins on every continent, but the bows used in Olympic contests are those developed by modern science and technology, and the targets, unlike the mimetic ones of early Islamic or premodern European archery, consist of regularly spaced concentric circles whose geometric configuration precisely determines the points awarded for each shot.

With its power to determine the athletic program of the games, the IOC can withhold or confer a kind of ludic legitimacy. Accordingly, its sessions are frequently prolonged wrangles over the inclusion or exclusion of particular sports. As early as 1930, the prestige of the Olympic Games was so great that representatives of the international federations for baseball, billiards, canoeing, lacrosse, pelota, and roller-skating vainly petitioned for IOC recognition of their sports. Volleyball can illustrate the process that leads, if successful, to inclusion in the Olympic program. During the 1950s, Armand Massard (France) and Vladimir Stoytchev (Bulgaria) waged a prolonged campaign on its behalf. They were repeatedly rebuffed. After a testy debate in Melbourne, in 1956, they lost by a vote of 19–13, but they achieved their goal in 1964 when volleyball was played at the Tokyo Olympics. (The Japanese hosts were gratified when their women's volleyball team upset the favorites from the USSR and won the gold.)[31]

Jūdō was the first non-Western sport to crash the Olympic party.[32] Olympic judo is, however, shorn of most traces of its Japanese origins (including its diacritical marks). Like the kayakers, whose sport derives from the pre-Columbian cultures of North America, judokas have increasingly adapted their martial art to the dictates of modern sports. As Michel Brousse has noted, "Modern judo has little resemblance to the judo of the Jigoro Kano." In judo as in other Olympic sports, "traditions have retreated in the face of modernity."[33] Perhaps it was an omen that a Dutch heavyweight, Anton Geesink, defeated Japan's star, Kaminaga Akio, at the Tokyo games.

The Olympic program remains a text written by Europeans and North Americans. "The universalism of the Olympic Games is a Western universalism."[34] Although it is undeniably true that African and Asian athletes participate, they compete on Western terms in sports that either originated in or have taken their modern forms from the West. The catalogue of Olympic sports continues, inexorably it seems, to lengthen, but traditional games and dances survive—at the Olympics—as a marginal folkloric phenomenon.

Mildred "Babe" Didrikson at the 1932 Olympics in Los Angeles.
Photograph from the collection of Ronald Smith.

Amelia Earhart, 1937.
AP/Wide World Photos.

Jesse Owens at the 1936 Olympics in Berlin. Library of Congress,
Prints and Photographs Division.

Joe DiMaggio in Yankee Stadium. © Bettman/CORBIS.

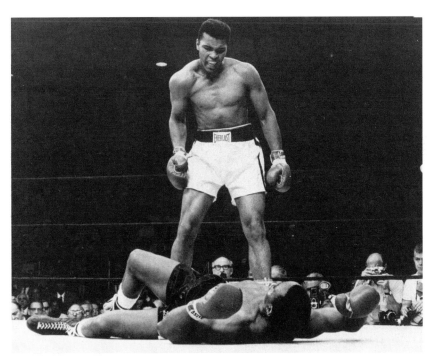

Muhammad Ali (then Cassius Clay) versus Sonny Liston, May 25, 1965.
© Bettmann/CORBIS.

Jean-Claude Killy (France) at the 1968 Winter Olympics in Grenoble.
International Olympic Committee.

Pelé in action, September 1968. AP/Wide World Photos.

Billie Jean King, ca. 1965. Paul DeLuca.

The 1958 Tour de France passes through Villedieu. Collection of Andrew Ritchie.

Ludmila Tourischeva on the balance beam at the 1972 Olympics in Munich.
Colorsport.

Vasily Alexeev at the 1972 Olympics in Munich. International Olympic Committee.

Mark Spitz at the 1972 Olympics in Munich. AP/Wide World Photos.

Hassida Boulmerka (Algeria) winning the 1,500-meter race at the 1991 World
Track and Field Championships in Tokyo. © Bettmann/CORBIS.

Zola Budd (South Africa) and Mary Decker Slaney (USA) vie in the 3,000-meter
race at the 1984 Olympics in Los Angeles. © Bettmann/CORBIS.

Katarina Witt (Germany) at the 1988 Winter Olympics in Calgary.
Nationales Olympisches Komitee der DDR

Konishiki versus Tereo, 1986. © Bettmann/CORBIS.

Gregg Louganis, ca. 1984. Neil Leifer.

Silken Lauman (Canada) at the 1992 Olympics in Barcelona.
AP/Wide World Photos.

Johan Koss (Norway) at the 1994 Winter Olympics in Lillehammer.
© Bettmann/CORBIS.

Michael Jordan, ca. 1995. © Bettmann/CORBIS.

American football at London's Webley Stadium.
Sean Ryan/National Football League.

Richard Cronk, *Venus on the Half Shell*. Mural, Venice Beach, California, 1981.
Photograph from the collection of Peter Kühnst.

RESISTANCE TO MODERN SPORTS

RESISTANCE TO MODERN SPORTS

_____ Gymnastics

The most stubborn opposition to the diffusion of modern sports came from a distinctively German form of gymnastic exercise that its adherents called *"Turnen."* Although the mainstream of *Turnen* was intensely romantic, its eighteenth-century sources were the humanistic and scientific approach to physical education advocated by a group of men known as the *Philanthropen.*

In the tiny German village of Schnepfenthal, in 1784, Christian Gotthilf Salzmann opened a school for middle-class children. Physical education was the responsibility of Johann Christoph GutsMuths, a man whose mania for quantified achievement amazed Salzmann: "Herr GutsMuths entered all these exercises in a table that indicated to the fraction of an inch what each pupil was able to achieve and how far he progressed from week to week."[1] GuthsMuths recorded—and subsequently published—names, dates, weather conditions, laps, distances, and times.

From attitudes like his, modern sports might have evolved, but Friedrich Ludwig Jahn—revered by his followers as *Turnvater* Jahn—took the movement in a diametrically opposed direction. Jahn was a fiery romantic teacher who led his pupils out of the classroom and into the woods. In the fields near Berlin, in 1811, he constructed a *Turnplatz* with towers, platforms, ropes, and rings. His example and his publications inspired others, and *Turnen* spread throughout Germany.[2]

Jahn was motivated by more than a desire to amuse his students. Like many nineteenth-century educators, he believed that strenuous exercise in the open air deflected young men from the horrors of masturbation. There was also a political motive. Jahn's passion for gymnastic exercises was driven by his fanatical hatred of the French who had, under Napoleon, occupied much of politically divided Germany. Intensely nationalistic, Jahn saw the *Turner* as the core of the army needed to drive the French back across the

Rhine. Many young *Turner* were, in fact, among the troops that eventually liberated Germany from French rule.[3]

Although Jahn abhorred the liberal principles of the French Revolution, he was nonetheless too much of an egalitarian for the reactionary regimes that returned to power after the Congress of Vienna in 1815. (The *Turner,* for instance, wore simple gray uniforms and addressed one another with the familiar *Du* rather than the formal *Sie.*) Jahn's defiant opinions and wildly unpredictable behavior aroused such animosity and fear in Prussia's autocratic rulers that they imprisoned him, in 1819, and outlawed *Turnen.*

When the Prussian ban was lifted, in 1842, the *Turner* entered their most liberal phase. In the eyes of the young revolutionaries who hoped to bring constitutional government to a land still ruled by hereditary monarchs, Jahn, who hated *"Junker, Juden und Pfaffen"* (gentry, Jews, and clerics), was an uneasy ally. When a number of *Turner* fought in the abortive revolution of 1848, Jahn condemned them and was then dismissed by them as an eccentric embarrassment. After the liberals' failure to bring constitutional government to Germany, the most radical *Turner* fled to America. Those who remained became increasingly conservative. While the emigrants volunteered almost en masse to fight for the Union in the Civil War, those who stayed behind founded the *Deutsche Turnerschaft* (in 1868) and became chauvinistic supporters of the German empire created in the aftermath of the Franco-Prussian War. In the course of the next fifty years, the *Deutsche Turnerschaft* became an enormously important institution. At their grand gymnastic festivals *(Turnfeste),* the *Turner* marched, performed mass gymnastic exercises, listened to patriotic orations, and pledged allegiance to their *Kaiser* and to German *Kultur.*[4] They also welcomed delegations of *Turner* who represented miniature versions of Germany in Africa and in the Americas.[5]

Simultaneous with the institutionalization of *Turnen* in thousands of private clubs from Aachen to Königsberg came the *Verschulung* ("scholastification") of German gymnastics. Guided by the writings of Adolf Spiess, German educators transformed Jahn's boisterous open-air activity into an indoor routine closely akin to military drill. Spiess published a widely used instructional text in which he described and categorized all the imaginable ways to march, hang from a bar, move one's arms, bend from the waist, and otherwise exercise the body. Three pages of this two-volume tome were devoted to games children might play if they were not paralyzed by boredom. German schools, where rows and columns of children moved in synchronized response to barked commands, became a means for the authorities to inculcate the political virtues of discipline and unquestioning obedience to authority.[6]

Conservatism dominated the clubs as well as the classrooms. It was an article of faith for the *Deutsche Turnerschaft* that modern sports were an alien import from Germany's most dangerous rival in the struggle for global political and economic dominance. "It is no accident," wrote Edmund Neuendorff, national leader of the *Deutsche Turnerschaft,* that *Turnen* was "born in the land of Goethe and Schiller, Kant and Fichte, Beethoven and Wagner, nor is it an accident that sports originated in England, a land without music or metaphysics." What else, asked Neuendorff, was to be expected from "the classical land of materialism"? Small wonder, then, that gymnastics journals cautioned against modern sports and the "rabid anglomania that is now horribly infecting a part of our people." The English were not the only culprits. Speaking for the *Deutsche Turnerschaft,* Ferdinand Goetz spurned French plans to revive the Olympic Games as an affront to German sensibility.[7]

The *Turner* drew up a root-and-branch indictment of modern sports. There were aesthetic and hygienic complaints. The *Turner* rejected the "one-sided-ness" (*Einseitigkeit*) of sports, which resulted in asymmetrical and unhealthy physiques. Soccer football, for instance, was ridiculed by Karl Planck as a barbaric and unhealthy pastime whose most characteristic physical motion resembled kicking the dog (*der Hundstritt*). Such ridicule was not motivated simply by envy. In 1910, the *Deutsche Turnerschaft* had one million members, twelve times the eighty-two thousand soccer players enrolled by the *Deutscher Fußballbund.*[8]

There were moral complaints. Neuendorff denigrated modern sports because they allegedly encouraged "pride" and "egoism" and destroyed "what the *Turner* have dedicated themselves to creating: a national community" *(Volksgemeinschaft).* In Wilhelm Angerstein's fevered eyes, modern sports threatened the destruction of the gymnasts' noble efforts to promote the moral development of the German people.[9]

There was also a profoundly romantic quarrel with the formal–structural characteristics of modern sports. Neuendorff judged the instrumental rationality characteristic of sports to be no better than "Taylorism" (a reference to efficiency expert Frederick W. Taylor's famous time-and-motion studies). Neuendorff also raged against the "loathesome sensationalism of seconds and millimeters." Other *Turner,* like Harro Hagen, urged renunciation of "concrete stadium, cinder track, tape-measure, stop-watch, manicured lawn, and track shoes. . . . In their place comes the simple meadow, open air." That the quantification characteristic of modern sports enticed athletes to quest for records was another occasion for wrath. In an 1897 article published in the *Deutsche Turnzeitung,* Ferdinand Schmidt thundered that it "cannot be our wish to post notices on our grounds of . . . records made possible by one-sided

. . . training aimed exclusively at lowering times by fractions of a second or lengthening distances by a centimeter."[10]

The contrast between *Turnen* and modern sports was, in short, a parallel to the eighteenth-century contrast between geometric *measure* and arithmetic *measurement*. As Hans Bonde phrases the difference, *Turnen* and other kinds of gymnastics are typically about "the collective control over *space*" while modern sports are typically about "the individual fight against *time*."[11]

With the passage of time, however, gymnasts at home and abroad experienced an erosion of support, especially among the young. Compromises were made and some contests were deemed acceptable—if the competition was not excessive. As early as 1880, the *Deutsche Turnerschaft* grudgingly made room for some strictly limited track-and-field competition at its Frankfurt *Turnfest*.[12] Ball games followed, but the *Turner* continued to favor the mass displays of cadenced movement that were the centerpiece of every gymnastics festival.

Physical educators to the west and south of Germany were strongly influenced by German *Schulturnen* (educational gymnastics). In Belgium, for instance, the German system was modified by J. J. Happel and propagated by Jahn's disciple and editor, Carl Euler, who settled in Brussels in 1860. A Belgian, Nicolaas Jan Cupérus, led the way in the formation of a national gymnastics federation in 1865 and a European one in 1881. His antipathy to modern sports was vehemently expressed in an 1894 letter to Pierre de Coubertin: "My federation has always believed and still believes today that gymnastics and sports are contrary things, and we have always combatted the latter as incompatible with our principles."[13]

Before his move to Belgium, Euler had been active in Holland, where he was the first teacher of gymnastics at the Royal Normal School in Haarlem. Inspired by Euler and other Germans, Dutch teachers of physical education formed a national association in 1862. Looking as they then did to Germany for their model, they founded gymnastics clubs with names like *De Germaan*, *Keizer Otto*, and *Adolf Spiess*. Like their German mentors, Dutch educators attempted vainly to construct an ideological dike against the successive waves of modern sports that emanated first from England and then from the United States.[14]

In northern Switzerland, an area of almost unadulterated Germanic culture, gymnastics clubs appeared as early as 1820, and a gymnastic federation was formed in 1869. The dominant personality was Adolf Spiess. In 1833, after study in Halle and Giessen, he settled in the small Swiss town of Burgdorf. Eleven years later he moved to Basel, where he taught physical education.

There he developed the techniques of *Schulturnen* that were eventually to sweep through the entire German educational system. Gymnastics became such an important element in Swiss culture that the development of soccer football was long delayed. The *Turner* of the German-speaking cantons "despised [soccer] and at the same time felt threatened by it." As late as 1978, Swiss gymnastics clubs still counted more members than the national soccer federation.[15]

Turnen reached Italy in the person of a Swiss expatriate, Rodolfo Obermann, who instituted a course in military gymnastics in Turin in 1833. Encouraged by Minister of Education Francesco de Sanctis, Obermann began to train civilian teachers in 1861. His normal school and that of Emilio Baumann, begun in 1877, were supposed to provide the personnel to implement the 1878 law mandating physical education for all of Italy's schools. The law was more or less a dead letter. Some teachers managed to introduce an occasional hour of calisthenics into the curriculum, but funds were scarce and reasons to divert the funds were plentiful. Young Italians were no more enamoured of gymnastic drill than their coevals to the north.[16]

Except in Alsace, where a gymnastics club was founded at Guebwiller in 1860, French pedagogues tended to shun *Turnen* in order to follow the variant of gymnastic drill devised early in the century by Francisco Amoros, director of the *Gymnase Normal Militaire*. The expatriate Germans of the *Société gymnastique de Lyon* (1844) inspired few Frenchmen. In the wake of France's humiliating defeat in the Franco-Prussian War, however, patriotic gymnastics clubs proliferated throughout the republic. "Feelings of revenge and the fear of renewed German aggression were reflected in the names of many of the newly founded gymnastics clubs: *La Revanche, La Patriote, La Régénératice, La France!*" The motto of the gymnastics union founded in 1873 was *Patrie–Courage–Moralité*. "Gymnasts will stand for the Republic," promised patriotic orators, "like blocks of granite and will be the instrument of revenge." Traditions inherited from Amoros were modified, and the parades, pageantry, speeches, and gymnastic exercises of these chauvinistic clubs increasingly mirrored the practices of the hated enemy across the Rhine. "From 1879 to 1914, French gymnastics practice developed in the shadow of political power. . . . Gymnastics [were] politics continued by other means."[17]

The gymnastics movement was also strong in the "ABC" countries of Latin America. Leopold Böhm seems to have taken the lead in Buenos Aires, where a *Turnverein* (gymnastics club) was organized in 1855. According to the *Deutsche Turnzeitung* for November 1, 1862, Brazil's first gymnastics club was founded in Rio de Janeiro in 1859. This club quickly expired, but another was formed in 1869 by J. A. Friedrich in Pôrto Alegre, the capital of the province of Rio Grande do Sul. In 1895, the nine clubs of that province formed the *Deutsche Turnerschaft von Rio Grande do Sul*. The first Chilean gymnastics clubs, also the work of German immigrants, seem to date from 1864 (Santiago) and 1871 (Valparaiso). A national gymnastics festival was held in Concepción in 1897. By the early twentieth century, there were also clubs in Mexico City, Caracas, and Montevideo, but Argentina, Brazil, and Chile were the only Latin American nations with sufficient German immigrants to support a really vigorous gymnastic movement. Although they were relatively few in number, the *Turner* shaped the contours of Latin American physical education.[18]

The roots of physical education in the United States can be traced back to 1825, when a twenty-seven-year-old *Turner* named Karl Beck became a teacher at the Round Hill School that George Bancroft and Joseph Cogswell had founded two years earlier in Northampton, Massachusetts. Bancroft and Cogswell were both familiar with the German *Philanthropen* and their enlightened ideas about the importance of physical education. Cogswell had visited Salzmann's school at Schnepfenthal. He and Bancroft were delighted to have hired Beck, whom they titled "a pupil and friend of Jahn, the greatest modern advocate of gymnastics." After Harvard College tried and failed to entice Jahn himself to become a member of its faculty, the college hired another of Jahn's disciples, Karl Follen, to set up a program of physical education. Follen wrote Beck on April 5, 1826, "I have commenced gymnastic exercises with the students. . . . At present I use one of the dining halls. All show much zeal."[19]

Follen constructed a regular *Turnplatz* modeled on Jahn's, but the students' zeal waned. Once the aura of novelty faded, gymnastic drill seemed unutterably dreary. Diocletian Lewis devised an American version of gymnastics, but young Americans were reluctant to perform the recommended exercises. Critics worried about young men's "pallid effeminacy" [*sic*] (A. A. Livermore), about "paste-complexioned youth" (Oliver Wendell Holmes), and about "the muscular feebleness of most American women" (Orson Fowler). Few young people listened.[20]

As it happened, Beck and Follen were a mere vanguard. Between 1840 and 1849, 385,434 Germans entered the United States. In the next five years, another 654,291 arrived. Of course, only a minority of these immigrants were *Turner,* but many of the others became involved in gymnastics once in the New World: it was one way to remain German. Friedrich Hecker founded Cincinnati's *Turngemeinde* (gymnastics association) in 1848; the New York

Turngemeinde followed one week later. Within three years, the clubs had their own newspaper, *Die Turnzeitung*. Since many of the new German Americans had been members of the radical *Demokratischer Turner-Bund* formed in Hanau in 1848, it was hardly a surprise when the New Yorkers joined nine clubs from Boston, Brooklyn, Philadelphia, and Baltimore to create the *Sozialistischer Turnerbund*, a radical organization that allied itself with the Free Soil Party in the election of 1852. At their Buffalo convention in September of 1855, the *Turner* created a political platform for the national elections of 1856. Over the objections of delegates who lived in the South, the majority voted their condemnation of chattel slavery. Clubs from Mobile, Savannah, Augusta, and Charleston were among the twenty-three that then withdrew from the organization in protest. When war came, *Turner* from the North rushed to defend and preserve the Union. One of them, Carl Schurz, rose to the rank of general and served after the war in the United States Senate and in President Grant's cabinet.[21]

The politics of the postwar *Turner* were liberal rather than radical, but their national organization, the *Nordamerikanischer Turnerbund* (NAT), continued to support such reforms as a shorter workday and the end of child labor. The *Turner* also argued forcefully for compulsory physical education in the schools. Since they had a coherent argument based on decades of discussion and experience, their influence in this matter was disproportionate to their very modest numbers.[22]

The membership of the NAT peaked in 1893, when the organization was able to count more than 40,000 *Turner*. Its decline can be attributed, in part, to the members' successful Americanization and, in part, to their stubborn refusal to come to terms with modern sports. As late as 1896, the organization's leaders continued to prize their German above their American identity. "The pole around which the future of German *Turnen* rotates," proclaimed that year's *Turner-Kalendar*, "is to be German and to act like Germans." As long as the maintenance of ethnic culture was paramount to German Americans, the *Turnverein* functioned well. Uniforms, a parade (accompanied by a stirring drum-and-fife unit), a mass demonstration of disciplined physical strength and agility, a banquet, speeches *auf Deutsch*, the singing of German *Lieder*— these elements sufficed to produce a powerful sense of communal solidarity. But, once the immigrants' children and grandchildren began to think of themselves as Americans, they deserted the cause of German culture, allowed their membership in the local *Turnverein* to lapse—and seized the opportunity to play baseball. Stripped of the emotional prop of nationalistic fervor, *Turnen* was never a match for modern sports.[23]

Gymnastics in Scandinavia

German cultural influence guaranteed Scandinavian interest in gymnastics. German-born Joseph Stockinger founded a *Turnverein* in Oslo in 1855. Scandinavian physical educators did not, however, remain satisfied with an imitation of German institutions. They created alternatives to *Turnen*. Per Henrik Ling, the revered founder of Swedish gymnastics, was more influenced by GutsMuths than by Jahn. Scornful of the rings, ropes, bars, and beams that were hallmarks of *Turnen*, Ling elaborated his own system, which his followers fiercely defended as the only "scientific" one. To propagate his version of gymnastic exercises, Ling established Stockholm's Central Institute of Physical Education (1814). Across the Kattegat in Denmark, the poet N. F. S. Grundtvig led a romantic back-to-the-land movement that included rural schools where young people quickened their spirits with folk songs and tautened their muscles with gymnastic exercises.[24]

The French showed some interest in Ling's ideas (because almost any form of physical education was better than the German brand), but the Swedish system was never as popular in France as in England. From Stockholm's *Centraal Institut*, young Martina Bergman-Osterberg journeyed to London, where she became Superintendent of Physical Education for London's schools (in 1881) and founder of the Hampstead Physical Training College (in 1885). Her influence on the physical education of British girls was immense. Although disputes among the followers of Jahn, Amoros, Ling, and other theorists of physical education were impassioned and—to an outsider—arcane, the variants of European gymnastics seem only marginally different from one another when one compares all of them with the modern sports that all of them opposed.[25]

The Sokol Movement

From the thirteenth century, when Russia's Alexander Nevsky repelled the invasion of the Teutonic Knights, to the twentieth, when the Soviet Union managed to survive the onslaught of Hitler's *Wehrmacht*, Germans and Slavs contended for political, economic, and cultural domination of Eastern Europe. In the last decades of the nineteenth century, *Turnen* figured prominently in the cultural struggle because Czechs, Slovaks, Poles, and Hungarians appropriated German gymnastics to use in their struggle for national liberation. The irony, of course, was that the Slavs resorted to a product of German culture in their efforts to liberate themselves from the political shackles of German and Austrian rule.

The two men who first realized *Turnen's* revolutionary potential for Slavic Europe, Jindrich Fügner and Miroslav Tyrs, were middle-class Czechs with complicated relationships to the hegemonic culture. Fügner's response to dual identity was to repudiate his German ancestry. His daughter Renata, who married Tyrs, quoted her father: "I was never a German. I am a citizen of Prague, a German-speaking citizen of Prague."[26] His friend and then son-in-law, born into a family that had forgotten its Czech antecedents, reversed the process of assimilation and changed his baptismal name—"Friedrich Tirsch"—to its original Slavic form.

Young Tyrs, a student of philosophy, took the lead in founding the first *Sokol* (Falcon) in February of 1862, a year after his graduation from Prague's Charles University. Fügner, who sold insurance, was the club's first president. Originally, the rank-and-file members were middle-class, white-collar workers and the officials were property-owners or educators, but the number of members who were manual workers rose above 50 percent by the end of the century. Whatever the members' social status, the political direction of the *Sokol* movement was never in doubt. Both of the founders were members of the executive council of the Young Czechs, a wing of the Czech National Party. The members of the *Sokol* wore red shirts, an allusion to Giuseppe Garibaldi's successful campaign to free northern Italy from Austrian rule. The rest of their uniform was based on traditional Slavic dress. In accord with their name, *Sokol* members wore jaunty hats with falcon feathers. From the beginning, Tyrs gave the movement a paramilitary emphasis. "Only a healthy nation," he wrote, "is an armed nation. A weapon in every fist!"[27]

Despite harassment from the authorities, the *Sokol* movement spread rapidly. In 1871, Tyrs began to edit a journal, also called *Sokol,* to propagate his message. A decade later, thousands of Czechs and Slovaks assembled in Prague to celebrate a grand *Turner*-style gymnastics festival. The Bohemian Sokol Union was formed in 1889, the Czech Sokol Union in 1896. They merged in 1908. Shortly before the outbreak of World War I, the Prague "nest," which had begun with 73 members, had 128,000 "falcons." In 1915, the Austrian government banned the clubs, but they were revived after the war. By 1937, shortly before the *Sokol* movement was destroyed by Nazi Germany, it counted over 800,000 members.[28]

Czechs and Slovaks were by no means the only ones to transform German gymnastics into an instrument of Slavic nationalism. A year after the birth of Prague's first club, the Slovenes of Liubliana founded the *Juzni Sokol* (Southern Falcon). The Poles of Lvov and Kraków organized their clubs later in the decade. In the western half of Poland, then a part of Germany, Slavic clubs were tolerated, but Poles who lived under Russian rule had a more difficult time. They were not allowed to parade in their *Sokol* uniforms or to display their organization's symbols. When the Czarist police discovered that a number of Poles living in Odessa had dared to form a *Sokol,* the offenders were hustled off to Siberia. Russian authorities were somewhat more permissive after the Revolution of 1905, and Polish "Falcons" were free to meet in Warsaw and found a national organization.[29]

In the Balkans, as in Czechoslovakia and Poland, there were numerous *Turnvereine* dedicated to the preservation of German culture, but, in the last quarter of the century, Slavic clubs sprang up all around them. Influenced by the Slovenes to the north of them, the Croats, Serbs, and Bosnians founded their own clubs in Zagreb (1874), Belgrade (1882), and Sarajevo (1903).[30]

In 1879, only one year after Bulgaria broke away from the Ottoman Empire, a pair of Czech brothers, Irgi and Georg Proschek, planted a *Sokol* in Sofia. It seems symbolically appropriate in light of the city's history of successive conquests that the club members performed their nationalistic gyrations in an abandoned mosque that had been erected on the site of a Byzantine church.[31]

While the Slavic gymnasts were unified in their opposition to German culture, each ethnic group emphasized its own language and literature, its own music, its own costume, and—unfortunately—its own grievances. A Slavic Sokol Association was founded in 1912, but the polyglot group was never as united in politics and purpose as the *Deutsche Turnerschaft.*[32]

The Slavic clubs also differed from the *Turner* in that their antipathy to modern sports was considerably less extreme. There *were* divisions between the proponents of gymnastics and the enthusiasts for sports. Budapest's premier athletic club, founded by Count Miksa Esterházy in 1875, split apart in a bitter quarrel over the two modes of physical culture. The Czech *Sokol* movement was initially reluctant to send its gymnasts to the Olympics, which its leaders deemed "useless" competition. On the whole, however, Slavic gymnasts were less likely than the *Turner* to fight tooth and nail against the import of soccer and other modern sports.[33]

_____ Workers' Sports

Resistance to modern sports led also to the establishment of an international workers' sports movement that was remarkably successful in Central Europe in the 1920s and 1930s. The movement began in Germany with the establishment in 1893 of the *Arbeiter Turnerbund* (Workers' Gymnastic Union), and German workers were—until Adolf Hitler destroyed their organization—the most important supporters of the Lucerne Sport International (LSI) that was formed in 1920 by the Socialist International. At its peak, in 1927, the organization claimed 1,300,000 members in eighteen countries, but 913,786 of them were in Germany and another 144,016 in Austria (where *Sportblatt* appeared daily with news of workers' sports). In Central Europe the LSI was a strong force in the class struggle; elsewhere branches of the organization struggled to survive. The French movement for *le sport ouvrier* was repeatedly splintered by political divisions.[34]

These divisions widened when the Soviet Union created the Red Sport International (RSI) in 1921. Endeavoring to disrupt where they could not dominate, the Communists fought the Socialists' LSI more fiercely than they fought the "bourgeois" sports organizations. After French Socialists and Communists joined forces in 1934 to form the *Fédération sportive et gymnastique du travail* (FSGT), the merged organization encompassed 103,420 members, a tenth as many as the German federation that Hitler had just destroyed. The British Workers' Sports Federation (1923) had even fewer members than the FSGT. Although the British federation obtained the support of the Trades Union Council, it could claim only 13,000 members at its peak in 1936. On the margins of American sports stood the Labor Sports Union (1927), attracting mostly Finnish-speaking members of the Communist Party. In 1932, a small number of these radical workers staged "counter-Olympics" in Chicago. The *Daily Worker*'s coverage of the event was "spasmodic at best." In 1936, the Workers Sports League of America organized a second protest that brought several hundred American athletes to an ambitiously titled "World Labor Athletic Carnival" on New York's Randall's Island. There was also a small, schism-wracked workers' sports movement in Argentina.[35]

Despite their rhetoric of equality, none of these workers' sports federations made a serious effort to recruit female members. Germany's *Arbeiter Turn- und Sportbund* had 95,000 female members, which was about 17 percent of the total membership. Only one-seventh of them were married women. The workers' cycling federation, *Solidarität,* had a similar percentage of female members. At approximately the same time, however, women comprised a third of the membership of the "bourgeois" *Deutsche Turnerschaft* and 38 percent of the *Makkabikreis* (the sports federation of German Zionists). In the struggle for sexual equality, French *ouvriers* did no better than German *Arbeiter.* The FSGT managed to send twenty-four young Frenchwomen to the Workers' Olympics in Antwerp in 1937, but the men's team numbered one hundred sixty-eight. Socialist attitudes, expressed in an article that appeared in a 1921 issue of *Freie Turnerin,* were scarcely different from "bourgeois" attitudes: "Nature has given woman the highest and most beautiful vocation: the reproduction of humankind."[36]

Initially, as its original name implies, the *Arbeiter Turnerbund* was committed to noncompetitive *Turnen* and opposed to modern sports, which the organization's leaders saw as a ludic analogue to capitalist competition. This was not simply a German view. In a 1910 article entitled "Sports, Youth, and Revolutionary Consciousness," the Italian socialist Angelica Balabanoff condemned sports as distracting and divisive.[37]

By the 1920s, however, the leaders of the workers' sports organizations had bowed to their members' demand that their athletic festivals include real sports competitions. Germany's *Arbeiter Turnerbund* (ATB) reluctantly authorized football sections in 1909 and changed its name, ten years later, to *Arbeiter Turn- und Sportbund* (ATSB).[38] The series of quadrennial "Workers' Olympics" that began in Frankfurt (1925) and concluded in Antwerp (1937) was fabricated from a broad tapestry of modern sports woven together with pageants, parades, speeches, and mass gymnastic exhibitions. The grand Antwerp extravaganza, which attracted 27,000 athletes, was, however, a proletarian swan song.[39]

THE SURVIVAL OF TRADITIONAL SPORTS

There is, of course, is no such thing as a "traditional society," perfectly static and exempt from the processes of historical change. All cultures evolve as a result of internal interactions, and even the most isolated peoples—the Inuit of the Arctic, the Chambri of Papua New Guinea—have slowly but surely been drawn into what many social scientists refer to as the "world system." The paradigmatic dichotomy between traditional and modern sports must be understood as a contrast between two "ideal types," neither of which is perfectly instantiated in the "real world."

Although there are exceptions to the rule, cultural change in the realm of sports is usually in one direction—from traditional to modern forms. Wherever traditional sports survive, they tend either to take on some of the characteristics of modernity or to persist in the form of what Raymond Williams termed "residual" (as contrasted to "emergent") culture. The religious significance of the contest wanes away to a token acknowledgment of the gods in whose honor and for whose favor the wrestlers or archers or stickball players once competed. The equipment and the facilities are rationalized to maximize performance. Players are ranked and winners are determined by objective measurements or on the basis of a point system. A bureaucratic organization emerges to administer regularly occurring tournaments and continually to adjust the rules and regulations. The transformed sport is marketed via television to spectators who have never witnessed the contest in any guise but its modern one.

Every step on the road to modernity is contested by traditionalists who see, rightly, that a succession of minor adjustments culminates eventually in a major transformation. Should the bat used to play *tsan,* a ballgame unique to the tiny Alpine valley of Aosta, be fabricated by a machine, which is easier and cheaper, or be carved by hand, which is the way it has always been done? How indispensable are the traditional (and no longer intelligible) verses chanted as Turkish wrestlers prepare to grapple? How necessary are the songs that accompany the Brazilian *capoeira,* songs now deemed "useless" and "effeminate" by younger *capoeiristas* who are "focused on the agonistic interchange and how they might defeat some opponent"? Should the Denendeh Traditional Games Association, a Canadian organization committed to the survival of indigenous sports, allow its "First People" members to compete in Kevlar canoes? Those who cherish traditional sports are constantly harassed by such questions. Like environmentalists who fear that a single adverse decision can irrevocably extinguish an endangered species or irreparably damage a delicately balanced ecosystem, the advocates of traditionalist physical culture are haunted by the sense that all innovations are irreversible.[1]

——— Bullfighting

Although speculation has linked the bullfight with prehistoric fertility rites and with the ancient religion of Mithraism, brought to Spain by Roman legions that had been stationed in the East, the sport as we know it took shape in the eighteenth century. At that time, the focus of attention shifted from the aristocrats who had fought the bulls from horseback to their unmounted assistants. Thanks in large part to the efforts of Francisco Romero, bullfights, which had been staged to celebrate a marriage, the birth of an heir, or the canonization of a saint, were reconceptualized as autotelic exhibitions of courage and skill. By the end of the nineteenth century, they were throughly commercialized and professional *matadores* earned as much in a day as the ordinary worker in a year.[2]

The traditional elements of the *corrida de toros* are so obvious that it is easy to overlook the fact that the *matador* now performs his fancy footwork in a highly rationalized ludic environment. "The history of bullfighting," concludes Timothy Mitchell, "is the history of the development of ever more efficient techniques for controlling the animal raw material." The traditional elements of the sport that excite—and sometimes horrify—the tourist are what the ethnographically inclined observer notices first. How can one not focus, when introduced to the *corrida de toros,* upon the colorful entrances and exits, the capes and costumes, the repertory of stylized motions, everything, in short, that makes bullfighting a travel-poster symbol of Spanish culture?

Bullfighting is an "archaic folk ritual," but it is also the consequence of "the slow but steady rationalization of the various ways that the peoples of Spain have played with bulls." Unlike the traditional elements that make the *corrida* a colorful spectacle that is superficially intelligible even to the tourist, the modernization of the sport is visible only to the informed eye. If one investigates, however, evidence of rationalization is plentiful. Matadors are registered nationally in the *Sector Taurino del Sindicato Nacional de Espectáculo.* Although the procession of matadors, picadors, *banderilleros,* and others enters the arena in the traditionally prescribed order, the *matadores* now compete in an order of seniority determined by the date of their official promotion from *matador de novillos* to *matador de toros.* They are supported by two *picadores* whose horses have been given tranquillizers to suppress their understandable nervousness. Each bull is supposed to have thirty minutes in the arena before the kill. Once the matador has entered the arena, he or she has exactly fifteen minutes to dispatch the bull.[3] The arena must be no more than 70 and no less than 45 meters in diameter. It is ringed by a barrier that is supposed to be precisely 1.7 meters high. The wall that separates the arena from the seats is 2.2 meters high.

The *corrida* itself, an artfully choreographed dance of death, has resisted quantification. The achievements of a matador are best described not by the statistics that have been employed to quantify baseball but rather by the lyricism of an Ernest Hemingway or Henry de Montherlant. Brilliant performances are rewarded with the presentation of one ear, two ears, or two ears and a tail. The crowd decides whether or not the first ear should be granted. The *Presidente,* who is the Director General of Security when the *corrida* takes place in Madrid and the Civil Governor when the event occurs in the provinces, determines whether or not to award greater honors. Their judgments are, quite obviously, subjective (and frequently met by jeers from those who judged differently). As the ritualized contest comes to an end, the medical experts who examined the bulls before they were allotted to the matadors return to inspect them once again and to certify that no one had tampered with them. To the *aficionado,* the weave of traditional and modern threads is seamless.[4]

The problem for the *aficionado* is that fewer and fewer of his countrymen share his passion for the *corrida.* In 1890, Guillermo Sundheim, a mining engineer, constructed a soccer pitch in the town of Huelva, near the Rio Tinto copper mines, where British engineers were playing cricket, soccer, and tennis. The Huelva Recreation Club was followed by Atlético de Bilbao (1898), FC Barcelona (1899), and Real Madrid (1902). These three great football clubs, which represented Basque, Catalan, and Spanish ethnicity, still dominate the Spanish game. Rivalry among these clubs has always been heated, but it blazed with special intensity during the decades of Francisco Franco's dictatorship—when the Fascist regime in Madrid sought to suppress Catalan and Basque aspirations for autonomy. Tourists may see the *corrida* as the romantic embodiment of Hispanic culture, but the average *hombre sur la strada* is more likely to be a football fan.[5]

───── *Capoeira*

Brazilian *capoeira* is a combat sport, a musical performance, and a dance. Although there are regional variations, the agonistic elements of *capoeira*are somewhat similar to those of Japanese *sumô*. The rules call for a player to force his opponent from the ring or to immobilize him. Players can kick and trip and use their hips as well as their hands and feet, but they are not allowed to strike with the fist. The music is provided by a number of distinctive instruments: the *berimbau,* constructed from a single metal string and a sounding gourd; the *pandeiro* (tambourine); *agogo* (clapperless bell); *reco-reco* (notched bamboo scraper); and *atabaque* (large drum). The songs that are an integral part of *capoeria* take the call-and-response form. The movements of the players are rhythmical—as if the combat were a dance.[6]

Capoeira has its roots in the nation's colonial past, in the culture of the Yoruba and other West African peoples transported to Brazilian plantations by Portuguese slave ships. (Many *capoeira* terms are derived from the Yoruba language.) *Capoeira* was a form of deep play that expressed the desire for "a liberation from slavery, from class domination, from the poverty of ordinary life, and ultimately even from the constraints of the human body." After the abolition of slavery in 1888, *capoeira* developed in the cities. It was forbidden in Rio de Janeiro and Recife but survived in Bahia. In 1927, Manoel dos Reis Machado founded a *Centro de Cultura Fisca e Capoeira.* He and a succession of *mestres* modernized *capoeira,* introducing exams, diplomas, and colored belts to signify levels of skill. Modernization failed, however, to expunge *capoeira*'s religious associations. As one *mestre* explained to an inquisitive anthropologist, the wood for the musical instruments "must be cut from a live tree in the forest on the right day and under the proper moon." Component parts of musical instruments are thought to correspond to Yoruba gods. The gods are also evoked in the lyrics of the songs that accompany *capoeira.*[7]

While older *capoeiristas* are serious about the music, the dance, and the ethical implications of their sport, younger players are "focused on . . . how they might defeat some opponent." To them, the traditional songs seem "effeminate" and out of place in the performance of masculinity. Some players seek to intimidate and humiliate their opponents although others profess a more chivalric code: "A great player should . . . bring out the potential for greatness in his opponent and should [also] manifest his atunement to the music." Originally an expression of an enslaved people yearning for liberation, *capoeira* is now—in the hopeful estimation of an anthropolgical admirer—part of the "struggle against the ravages of industrialization and ecological destruction."[8]

Endangered Species

In 1884, Archbishop Thomas Croke condemned the Irish penchant for English sports and defended "hurling, foot-ball kicking, according to the Irish rules, casting, leaping in various ways, wrestling, handy-grips," and other Hibernian sports. Hurling, which involves throwing and hitting a hard ball with an open-faced wooden club, was said to have been played in Ireland thousands of years ago by Cuchulain and other mythic heroes. It was surely a more authentic expression of Irish identity than cricket, which was first played in 1792 by the English garrison in Dublin. Michael Davitt wrote to his nationalist ally Michael Cusack and asked, "Why should we not have our athletic festivals like other people?" Why not? Cusack met with six other likeminded Irish nationalists at Hayes Hotel in Thurles, November 1, 1884, and founded the Gaelic Athletic Association. To no one's surprise, Croke and Davitt were among the GAA's patriotic sponsors. According to the journal *United Ireland,* the GAA's ideal was an independent nation "dotted all over with miniature armies of hurlers, bowlers, jumpers, weight-throwers, merry dancers and joyous singers." Athletes who played modern games were not allowed to join the Hibernian fun. Religious affiliation determined the *when* as well as the *what.* "Sunday afternoons after mass became the sacred time for GAA sport," noted Michael Mullen, "while Saturday venues for sporting matches defined them as Protestant."[9]

Within a few years, however, Cusack and his allies lost control of the organization to the radicals of the Irish Republican Brotherhood. The radicalized GAA became intensely political, denying membership to soldiers, sailors, policemen, and members of the Royal Irish Constabulary. The Catholic Church withdrew its support when the GAA refused to repudiate Charles Stewart Parnell, a spokesman for "Home Rule," whose love of Kitty O'Shea violated another man's home. The GAA experienced a deeper crisis in 1916, when Padraig Pearse and other members turned to violence. In the aftermath of the "Easter Uprising," the British arrested thousands of GAA members. In 1920, after Republicans assassinated a number of British agents, British soldiers stormed Croke Park in the middle of a GAA-sponsored game between Dublin and Tipperary, and killed thirteen people, including Michael Hogan, captain of the Tipperary side.[10]

After London recognized Irish independence (except in Ulster), the GAA continued the struggle for cultural autonomy (in Scotland as well as in the Republic of Ireland). The GAA routinely refused to share grounds with soccer clubs, and its Ulster Board continued to conduct business in Gaelic. Irish sports were, however, a hard sell. At the 1924 *Aonach Tailteann*—the revived form of an ancient Irish festival—a mere hundred Dubliners turned out to watch the traditional Irish stickball sport of *camogie* while twenty thousand of them thronged Phoenix Park to gape at an airplane race. In the long run, the effort to preserve traditional Irish sports is probably doomed. The Republic's soccer team, managed by Jack Charlton, an Englishman, reached the finals of the World Cup in 1990 and 1994. Football has become far more popular than hurling or handy-grips.[11]

The Arab governments of North Africa have made it a matter of public policy to ensure that *their* traditional games survive as a form of resistance to neocolonialism. Although they have demonstrated no desire to withdraw from the global sports arena, the governments of Morocco, Algeria, and Tunisia have encouraged their people simultaneously to preserve traditional sports such as *al kora* (a ball game) and *haih a deux* (similar to prisoner's base). Some regimes have gone further. The *Comité Militaire du Salut National* that ruled the Islamic Republic of Mauritania decreed, in 1980, that it was "indispensable . . . to rehabilitate and develop traditional sportive activities: foot races, horse races, camel races, target archery, and wrestling." Spokesmen for the regime condemned the International Olympic Committee for its false claim "to represent the world of sports." Borhane Erraïs, a Tunisian Marxist, summed up Arab antipathies in a sentence: Modern sports, he averred, are tantamount to *"génocide culturel."* North African intransigence seems, however, to be the exception that proves the rule. Islamic writers who begin by expressing pride in traditional sports almost invariably conclude by boasting of medals won at the Olympic Games or the *Jeux Africains.*[12]

Not everyone has abandoned the quest for an alternative to modernity. Henning Eichberg has published many books and articles condemning the artificiality of modern sports and praising the spontaneity and vitality of traditional pastimes.[13] He has taken a strong stand against the rationalized segmentation (*Parzellierung*) of ludic space. He has contrasted the fields and streams that were once the natural landscape of play with the "inhumane" steel, concrete, glass, and plastic venues of modern team games. In Eichberg's eyes, the stadia that dominate modern cities are the ludic equivalent of the "panoptic" prisons described by Michel Foucault. Instead of modernity's linear "functionalist container," Eichberg calls for ludic architecture that mimics the snail's shell and other natural forms. An alternative to modernist functionalism can be seen at the Danish *folkshøjskole* ("people's high school") in Gerlev, where Eichberg lives and works. In this buccolic environment, students and faculty combine sports with dancing, juggling, clowning, folk games, and "the popular culture of laughter." The untended elliptical running track is abandoned to its occasional use by American visitors.[14]

Eichberg has written enthusiastically of the Inuit peoples of the Arctic. Typical of their ludic culture is the drum–dance, a combination of sports, grotesque physical contortions, laughter, music, dance, poetry, shamanism, magic, and communal ecstasy. In the era of Danish colonization, this culture was threatened with extinction. The colonizers attempted "to forbid the drum–dance as something heathen. The drums were gathered and burned or delivered to museums." In place of the drum dance's ecstatic chaos, Europeans imposed "the disciplined practice . . . of Danish-Swedish gymnastics." The colonizers failed, however, to extinguish the "culture of laughter." In the era of decolonization, the Inuit Circumpolar Conference revived the drum–dance and other indigenous folkways of Greenland, Canada, Alaska, and Siberia.[15]

Eichberg is an eloquent spokesman. Other scholars, alarmed at the "collective amnesia that some have called modernity," have joined together to found the *Vlaamse Volkssport Centrale* (Flemish Center for People's Sports) and a number of similar organizations dedicated to the preservation and revival of traditional recreation. Conferences like the one held in Brittany in the spring of 1990 have opened up lines of communication among those who work actively for a *renaissance des jeux populaires*.[16]

Enthusiasts for traditional sports have not been content merely to publish newsletters such as the *Nieuwsbrief van het Sportmuseum Vlaanderen* or to read papers at academic symposia. In 1975, after a hiatus of nearly six hundred years, Venice revived the colorful regatta that weds the city to the Adriatic Sea. In a single year, 1985, the *Jeux des Petits États d'Europe* were celebrated in San Marino, the First Inter-Island Games took place on the Isle of Man, and athletes from Brittany, Cornwall, and other areas of suppressed ethnicity came together in the First Eurolympics of the Small Peoples and Minorities. In 1990, the Canadian city of Edmonton hosted the First North American Indigenous Games. In 1995, the People's Republic of China brought 3,300 athletes from 55 ethnic minorities to Kunming (in Yunnan), where they competed in traditional games.[17]

Rejoicing in this "subversive tendency toward multiplicity," Eichberg has optimistically predicted that the "age of Western colonial dominance is coming to an end—and with it the predominance of Olympic sports." He believes that modern sports will become less popular, that they will linger as "a sort of circus, show business, and media attraction," while "the masses in different cultures, nations, and regions will have their own festivals revealing their own patterns, their own traditions." Perhaps. One should, however, keep the numbers in mind. In 1995, the *Fédération Française de Football* had 2,055,610 members; the national federation for *balle au tambourin* had 720.[18] The eddies swirl, and time will tell which way the currents flow.

INSTRUMENTALIZED SPORTS

Throughout the 1920s and 1930s, liberal–democratic governments remained relatively indifferent to the success or failure of their athletes in international competition, and sports administrators were happy to be free of governmental interference. Communist, Fascist, and Nazi regimes had a different view of the relationship of politics to sports.[1] They programatically instrumentalized sports as a means to demonstrate national revitalization and to symbolize ideological superiority. These regimes—and those of Vichy France and Falangist Spain—varied in the specifics of their ideology, but all of them subordinated individual athletes to the state.[2]

Fascism

In Fascist Italy, men's sports were restructured along paramilitary lines. Landro Ferretti, the Fascist chairman of the National Olympic Committee (CONI), announced in 1928 that sport was "a school of determined effort which will provide Fascism with aware citizens in peacetime and courageous soldiers in wartime." Women's physical education was conceptualized within the framework of eugenics. Moderate exercise was essential if a woman was to achieve "her natural and primary mission: maternity. Saturday afternoons became the "Fascist sabbath," when all Italians were to devote themselves to physical fitness. Benito Mussolini—*Il Duce*—led the way, literally embodying the Fascist ethos in "his impressive torso, his athletic arms." How different, explained Sisto Favre in *Lo Sport Fascista,* from egoistic British nonsense about sports as a source of "purely personal satisfaction."[3]

The intellectual inspiration for the Fascist program came from the poet Filippo Tommaso Marinetti and the *Futuristi* whom he inspired. Marinetti called for "pride in one's own body, in one's physical health, in one's beautiful musculature." After Mussolini's seizure of power in 1922, the state acted to institutionalize Marinetti's ideas about fitness and sports. A solid basis for the regime's sports program was established in 1926 with the creation of the *Opera Nazionale Balilla*. This national organization for young Italians was named for the patriotic boy Giovanni Battista "Balilla" Perasso, who stoned a group of Austrian soldiers and thereby ignited the rebellion, in 1746, that freed the city of Genoa from foreign rule. The ONB offered extracurricular physical education and sports for boys and girls from six to seventeen. Membership in the ONB was a prerequisite for joining a sports club and for competing under the auspices of CONI. The ONB's role was enhanced a year later when the regime disbanded the sports organizations sponsored by the Roman Catholic Church, the YMCA, and the Boy Scouts. The ONB was suppressed in 1937 and replaced as the regime's youth organization by the *Gioventu Italiana del Littorio*. The GIL, which included sports among its sponsored activities, was mandatory for boys and girls aged six to seventeen. Once the "New Italians" were embarked on their careers, responsibility for their physical fitness was entrusted to *Opera Nazionale Dopolavoro* (1926), which provided "after-work" recreational opportunities, including sports.[4]

Driven by a cult of youthful athleticism, the regime invested heavily in sports for university students. With undisguised satisfaction, Mussolini witnessed the triumph of Italian students in the international games held in Turin (1933) and in Vienna (1939). Even more satisfying was the Italian performance at the Los Angeles Olympics (1932), where the team was second only to the Americans, returning in triumph with twelve gold, twelve silver, and eleven bronze medals. Two years after that, Italian soccer players defeated Czechoslovakia in the final game of the World Cup. At the 1936 Olympics, Italian athletes were outpaced by their German and American opponents, but they still managed to win nine gold, nine silver, and five bronze medals.[5]

The influential Fascist official Augusto Turati attempted in 1928 to popularize a newly invented ball game whose "vigorous vitality" was praised in *La Gazzetta dello Sport* as *italianissimo*. The rules of *volata* were similar to those of soccer except that the players were allowed to handle the ball and to restrain their opponents. The international success of Italy's soccer team doomed Turati's initiative.[6]

When it came women's sports, the regime was ambivalent and conflicted. The Roman Catholic Church was on the whole hostile to the idea. *L'Osservatore Romano* worried that sports might "distract woman from her reproductive mission" and "bring indecency into the stadium." And yet, in their quest for athletic glory, Fascist leaders trumpeted the message that *Il Duce* wanted female athletes. The regime lauded the aristocratic aviatrix Carina Negrone when she set an altitude record of 39,741 feet. Fascist spokesmen proclaimed that athleticism did not detract from femininity or damage a woman's reproductive organs; it enhanced her *bellezza*. There is no reason, wrote Turati in *La Scuola Fascista,* girls should not experience "the joy of running with bare legs and trying to go faster." Other Fascist leaders disagreed. Women such as Ondina Valla, who won the 80-meter hurdles at the 1936 Olympics, should be admired for their "moral force" rather than for their "robust muscles."[7]

_____ Nazism

The National Socialist approach to "physical culture" was equally confused and contradictory. The Nazis were fanatical proponents of an irrational *Weltanschauung* that affirmed the absolute importance of *Blut und Boden* ("blood and soil"). Ideologically, the Nazis were much closer to *Turnen* than to modern sports. Before they came to power in 1933, Nazi theorists condemned the openness and internationalism of modern sports. Bruno Malitz, for instance, expressed outrage that "Jewish Negroes" had competed "on German tracks, had played football on German fields, had swum in German pools. . . . Whatever a Jew praises is poison for us." Alfred Bäumler condemned both the ubiquitous quantification of modern sports and the "madness of records" (*"Rekordwahn"*). Hitler had words of praise for Max Schmeling and other boxers, but he himself was notoriously unathletic.[8]

Immediately after Hitler came to power, the gymnasts of the *Deutsche Turnerschaft* rushed to pledge their allegiance. Edmund Neuendorff assured the *Führer* in a letter (May 16, 1933) that the *Turner* were eager to march under Hitler's leadership, "shoulder to shoulder" with the Storm Troopers, "into the Third Reich." Neuendorff invited Hitler to address the *Deutsche Turnerschaft* at its 1933 *Turnfest* in Stuttgart. Hitler complied.[9]

Germany's sports federations hurried to purge their rolls of Jewish members—months *before* they were ordered to by the regime. Felix Linneman of the *Deutscher Fußballbund* and Georg Hax of the *Deutscher Schwimmverband* were especially eager to please Germany's new leader. The *Deutscher Reichsausschuß für Leibesübungen* (DRA), which was an umbrella organization for many different sports federations, groveled. Forgetting their stirring rhetoric about sports as a school of courage, the DRA's leaders begged Hitler to become their honorary president. He ignored the request, and the subservient DRA fared no better than the workers' *Arbeiter Turn- und Sportbund.* Both were abolished in the spring of 1933. The Lutheran and Roman Catholic sports federations were eliminated in 1935. Passionate declarations of devotion to Hitler failed to save the *Deutsche Turnerschaft.* Neuendorff was forced to resign in 1934, and the hallowed organization voted its own dissolution on

April 18, 1936. Germany's National Olympic Committee managed to preserve a measure of independence until the Berlin games of 1936, after which it, too, was reorganized under Nazi control.[10]

The sports federations that survived the first months of Nazi rule were compelled to join the *Deutscher Reichsausschuß für Leibesübungen* (DRL), headed by *Sportführer* Hans von Tschammer und Osten, whom Hitler had appointed on April 28, 1933. In 1938, the DRL was brought into full conformity with Nazi ideology. It was then renamed the *Nationalsozialistischer Reichsbund für Leibesübungen* (NSRL).[11]

The regime also created a gamut of sports programs outside the jurisdiction of the NSRL. For boys and girls there were the *Hitler Jugend* (Hitler Youth) and the *Bund Deutscher Mädel* (Union of German Maidens). The schools surrendered control of sports to these organizations. In 1936, membership became obligatory for all "Aryans" aged ten to eighteen. Adults participated in sports under the auspices of *Kraft durch Freude* (Strength through Joy), established in 1933 in imitation of Italy's *Opera Nazionale Dopolavoro*.[12] There were also programs for sports participation in the military and in the storm troopers paramilitary ranks. German Jews were, of course, expelled from all Nazi sports organizations, but they were permitted to join the clubs of the Zionist *Makkabi* movement and those of the assimilationist *Schild* federation. Ironically, both federations, which had been quite marginal in pre-Nazi Germany, expanded with the influx of Jews forced out of the mainstream sports organizations.[13]

During the twelve years of Nazi rule, there was considerable confusion about who was responsible for what. There was also ideological conflict. Girls and women were required to participate in *nationalsozialistische Leibesübungen,* but what exactly was meant by "national-socialist physical activities"? Granted that young women needed regular and fairly strenuous exercise if they were to fulfill their destiny of "healthy motherhood." Did they also need sports competition? Some Nazi theorists were convinced that they did not. Sports were strictly a *Männersache* ("a men's affair"). Others thought that German women ought to be serious athletes and they won most of the arguments. Between 1930 and 1939, the number of girls and women in German sports clubs rose from 5.8 percent to 14.4 percent of all members. The guidelines for required physical education at the university level specified the creation of "strong-willed" women. The female members of the German Olympic team were praised as Nordic heroines whom ordinary women ought to honor and to emulate. "Blond . . . Olympic victors, their hands raised in the Nazi salute, appeared on all the magazine covers." No fewer than forty-five medals were awarded to Germany's female athletes at the 1936 Olympics.

(One of them went to Helene Meyer, a "half-Jewish" fencer brought home from the United States in order to persuade the IOC that the Nazis had not broken their promise to allow Jews to compete for Germany.) [14]

That there *was* to be a German Olympic team was not at all predictable when Hitler was named chancellor. Although the Nazis' most authoritative newspaper, *Der Völkische Beobachter,* had moderated its stridently anti-Olympic tone, merely demanding that Jews and blacks be barred from the 1936 games, many Nazis assumed that Germany was at last to be cured of the international plague of modern sports. At the *Deutsche Hochschule für Leibes-übungen* (German University of Physical Education), Nazi students planted oak saplings on the tennis courts and dug trenches in the running track. Several months later, when Theodor Lewald and Carl Diem—the president and the general-secretary of the organizing committee for the 1936 Olympics—went to discuss plans with Hitler, they were quite pessimistic about the future. To their astonishment, Hitler offered them practically unlimited funds and urged them to stage the grandest possible games. There was, it seems, no better way to demonstrate Nordic superiority. Vocal opposition to the 1936 games came not from Hitler but from foreign sports administrators—mostly American—who doubted that the Nazis were ready to abide by the Olympic Charter and to field a team that included German Jews. [15]

Although the International Olympic Committee was assured by Hitler's *Sportführer* that Jews were eligible for the German team, it was obvious to every informed observer that they were not. Shortly before the games, Gretel Bergmann, a Jewish high jumper, cleared 1.6 meters, only to be told by Tschammer und Osten that she was not good enough for the team. Elfriede Kahn, whose best was 1.54 meters, was selected instead of Bergmann. When reports of the Nazis' failure to keep their promise reached the United States, there were calls for a boycott. Avery Brundage, head of the American Olympic Committee, stubbornly refused to believe the evidence of deception. Using every trick in the trade, he managed, narrowly, to frustrate the boycott movement. His reward was election to the IOC to replace Ernest Lee Jaencke, the only member who had argued for a change of venue. There were also boycott movements in Canada and in western Europe, but they were minor affairs compared to the battle in the United States. [16]

Whether the 1936 games were the fulfillment of Coubertin's dream (Brundage's view) or a nightmarish travesty (the view of many sports historians), they were unquestionably impressive. The torch relay that brought the Olympic flame from Olympia to Berlin, the immense stone stadium, the grandiose opening and closing ceremonies, the record-breaking performances of Jesse Owens and dozens of other athletes—all combined to make the 1936 games the modern era's most memorable as well as its most controversial. A good deal of what happened in 1936 was staged for the benefit of Leni Riefenstahl's monumental two-part film, *Olympia,* an overwhelmingly powerful documentary that has been as controversial as the games.[17]

If the number of medals won is an accurate measure of athletic success, Germany was able to claim victory (despite American superiority in the track-and-field contests). And if the recollections of ordinary men and women matter to historians—as they should—most Germans were pleased by the opportunities for sports participation provided by the Nazi regime. In the German peoples' day-to-day experience, sports were—according to Christiane Eisenberg—*less* militaristic than they had been in the 1920s, when the German army, limited by the Treaty of Versailles to a mere 100,000 men, infiltrated civilian sports with paramilitary drills and exercises. Under the Nazis, the military was unfettered, camouflage was unnecessary, and the sports clubs were free to play football rather than to prepare their members for war. Amid the horrors of the Nazi dictatorship, sports provided many Germans with "an enclave of normality." There was a great deal of ideological indoctrination, but most Germans ignored the racist rant. "We were simply doing sports," recalled one woman in a postwar interview. "Nothing was said about politics." That, at least, is what "Elise E." now remembers.[18]

Communism: The USSR

Czarist Russia was an athletic backwater, where the first recognizably modern sports organization was the Imperial Yacht Club (1846), comprised of one hundred fifty noblemen. The first national federation was the similarly elitist All-Russia Association of Rowing and Yachting Clubs (1898). Middle-class merchants and professional men formed a gymnastics federation in 1883. (Anton Chekhov, a medical doctor as well as a writer, was among the founders.) Russian peasants, who were the vast majority of the population, competed among themselves in running, jumping, and wrestling as well as in the bat-and-ball game of *lapta.*[19]

Soccer seems to have arrived in Odessa and St. Petersburg in the 1870s, but the implant took roots only in 1894, when Harry Charnock introduced the game to workers at the Morozov textile mills near Moscow. That same year, *FC Viktoria* was organized by British and German residents of St. Petersburg. Three clubs—all for foreigners—began a city championship series in 1901. The first Russian team, *Sport FC,* joined the competition in 1902—and lost every game of its initial season. The players must have been apt students, for *Sport FC* took the St. Petersburg championship in 1908, a year after the inauguration of matches against Moscow. A national federation followed in 1912, but the level of competition was still far below international standards.[20]

With the exception of wrestlers like Georgi Hakkenschmidt and skaters like A. P. Lebedev and Nikolai Panin, pre–World War I Russian athletes generally performed poorly against foreign competition. From the 1912 Olympics in Stockholm, the two-hundred-man team managed to bring home only four silver medals and two bronze. The soccer match against Germany was a debacle—the Russians lost 16–0.[21]

Communist rule, established by the Bolshevik Revolution of 1917, transformed Russian sports. This transformation did *not* take the form of an accelerated diffusion of modern sports. Quite the contrary. The Central Board of Universal Military Training (*Vsevobuch* in its Russian abbreviation) that Lenin established in May of 1918 was much more concerned with physical fitness than with modern sports. In October 1920, the Communist Party's influential youth organization *Komsomol* warned against the revival of "bourgeois" sports clubs. The reasoning behind this stand was that sports contests "bred, in some people's minds, attitudes alien to socialist society." Soccer players competing to score goals looked too much like capitalists competing to control markets.[22]

Through the 1920s, there were debates between the "hygienists," who were influenced by the nineteenth-century medical theorist Pyotr Lesgaft, and the "proletcultists," who wanted—as their name implies—to promote proletarian physical culture. "While the 'hygienists' admitted the possibility of the usefulness of some 'bourgeois' sports," explained James Riordan, "the 'Proletkul'tists' made no such concessions."[23] They concentrated on *Sokol*-style gymnastics, mass displays, pageants, and excursions. They invented new games with ideologically suggestive titles like "Rescue from the Fascists."

The "proletcultists" were a strong force in the early 1920s, but they failed to win Lenin's approval, which meant, ultimately, that they could not prevail. The Communist Party decided at its Twelfth Congress (1923) to establish clubs that provided not only physical training but also opportunities for sports participation. If the mode of production determines the shape of society, it was only natural that these new clubs be organized at the workplace. Comrades engaged in transportation became members of *Lokomotiv,* while employees of producers' cooperatives joined *Spartak.* The most powerful of these clubs, all of which had branches throughout the Soviet Union, were *TsSKA* (for the army) and *Dinamo* (for the secret police and border guards). It was difficult, if not outright dangerous, for a talented athlete to refuse an offer to transfer from *Lokomotiv* or *Spartak* to either of these clubs.[24]

The Communist regime continued to proclaim the importance of physical fitness, but the drive for some kind of noncompetitive physical education appropriate to proletarian culture was more or less ended in 1925, when A. A. Zigmund was removed from his post at Moscow's State Institute of Physical Culture. During Stalin's notorious "purges," Zigmund and other prominent "proletcultists" were arrested, tried, convicted, and executed. (Their radical ideas were revived, in the 1970s, by French and German Neo-Marxists whose call for the abolition of sports was ridiculed by Soviet theorists as infantile, left-wing deviationism.)[25]

Having silenced the opposition (by murder), the regime promoted the "correct" approach to physical culture: All Soviet citizens should participate in sports. The keystone in the arch of mass participation was the quadrennial "Spartakiad," the first of which occurred in August of 1956. These mammoth affairs were meant to involve and inspire the entire able-bodied population of the USSR. The government claimed, unconvincingly, that over eighty million Soviet citizens participated in the 6th Spartakiad (1974–1975). Nearly all of those who did indeed participate were eliminated in the preliminary rounds (e.g., out-of-shape office workers who ran 100 meters in 15 seconds), but thousands of elite athletes competed in the finals, which were held at Moscow's huge Lenin Stadium. At each Spartakiad, the finalists—there were over eleven thousand of them in 1967—were said to have set hundreds of Soviet and world records.[26]

Another block in the grand arch was *Gotov k trudu I oborone* (Ready for Labor and Defense), inaugurated in 1931. GTO's purpose was to promote "speed, agility, strength, endurance and general military aptitude."[27] On the basis of the guidelines established for sports performance, participants in GTO were awarded achievement badges and given certificates of rank. The highest of the four ranks was "Master of Sport."

Did the system do what it was supposed to do? In 1981, N. I. Ponomaryov maintained that "work and sport are harmoniously combined" in Soviet society and that they "mutually supplement and enrich one another." According to the government's reports, the Soviet Union's sports program was so attractive that a third or more of the ten-to-sixty-year-old population was regularly active. It was so egalitarian that Soviet women were said to be 40 percent of all sports-club members (at a time when West German women comprised only 31 percent of the *Deutscher Sportbund*). The claims were dubious. In fact, sociologists from Eastern Europe now admit that the falsification of statistics on sports participation was the rule rather than the exception. Local studies by V. Artemov and other Soviet sports sociologists revealed, even in the 1960s and 1970s, that only a small minority of industrial workers, and an even smaller minority of agricultural workers, participated actively in sports. Participation was skewed; professional men and women were far more likely than unskilled laborers to be club members and to participate actively in sports. Gender inequality prevailed at every level. In 1965, for example, there were 4,678 "Masters of Sport," but only 1,052 of them were female. Ordinary women had access to sports facilities at their place of work, but after work they were expected to shop, cook dinner, and care for the children while their husbands played soccer. It was finally admitted, in the relatively open era of *perestroika,* that only 8 percent of Soviet men and 2 percent of Soviet women engaged regularly in sport.[28]

For the minority of Soviet citizens who did participate, soccer was the game of choice (for men). One of the first actions of the All-Union Committee established in 1936 was to create an amateur soccer league. Most of the players were authentic amateurs, but the pressures of competition pushed ambitious clubs to stockpile talented players and to reward them for their achievements. In Odessa, for instance, the state-run steamship line bankrolled a club—*Chernomorets*—that did more than pay its players handsome salaries. The company constructed for their exclusive use a million-ruble, out-of-town training center with three football pitches, a swimming pool, a luxury hotel, garages, and many other amenities. The city of Odessa itself had poor sports facilities and no public pool.[29]

Soccer was also the most popular spectator sport. Indeed, the unspoken justification for privileged athletes in an economy of scarcity was that they provided entertainment. "For some workers," wrote Robert Edelman, "their identity as followers of a team became more important than their identity as proletarians." Sports became the opiate of the workers, a relatively inexpensive compensation for "the long-neglected consumer sector." Soviet sociologists put the relationship more positively. They affirmed the social importance of spectatorship. N. I. Ponomaryov argued that it created an "emotional symbiosis" that bonded the spectators with the athletes who incorporated the virtues of Soviet society. In fact, big matches, like those between *Spartak* and *Dinamo,* were occasions for gleeful festivity and drunken hooliganism. After a notable riot in Leningrad, in 1937, soldiers were used to control soccer crowds. In the years of *perestroika,* when the Soviet Union was relatively receptive to Western influences, soccer hooligans appeared in the required leather jackets and torn jeans.[30]

According to Edelman, soccer fans had good reason to be dissatisfied. Local party bosses, plant managers, union officials, military officers, and the secret police all interfered with the game. They "sought to dismiss coaches at a whim, dictate lineups, determine tactics, buy players, bribe referees, and fix games."[31] Ice hockey, the second most popular spectator sport, told a somewhat happier story. The USSR won every world championship from 1963 through 1971. The game was relatively honest, and the fans were mostly nonviolent. In the 1970s, Vladislav Tretiak, who played for the army's team, became a popular icon.

Disparities between elite and recreational sports widened after World War II, when Stalin decided that the USSR should enter the "bourgeois" sports arena and prove the athletic superiority of the "New Soviet Man." On October 22, 1945, *Pravda* announced cash rewards for world records—up to 25,000 rubles. The Central Committee of the Communist Party proclaimed the goal of athletic supremacy. The number of special schools for athletically talented children, the first of which were built in 1934, was expanded until there were, in 1975, 4,938, with a total enrollment of 1,633,132 children.[32]

Universities opened institutes for the study of sports. At the pinnacle was the Moscow State Institute for the Study of Sports, founded in 1919, admission to which was granted only to certified Masters of Sport. Scientifically trained coaches utilized the results of physiological and psychological research to prepare athletes for the Olympics and other international competitions. At the regime's peak, in the 1980s, the USSR was represented at home and abroad by some ninety thousand state-supported "amateurs" who expected to be rewarded for their victories with dollars as well as with rubles.[33]

News of the spectacular achievements of Soviet athletes was a staple of *Sovietskii Sport,* which was said to have twenty million readers. The journal was also said, by Soviet scholars, to provide a "fully objective and unbiased treatment of the international sports movement." An example of its unbiased treatment was the coverage of the 1980 Olympics, which the United States and scores of other countries boycotted. The journal landed the games as "a striking affirmation" of the Soviet Union's love of peace.[34]

Afghans may have doubted the love of peace, but the superiority of the Olympic team was unquestionable. Between 1952 and 1992, teams from the USSR and the USA met at nine summer Olympics. Except for 1968 (Mexico City), the Soviet team outscored the American team. Domination of the winter Olympics, where East Germany was the USSR's chief rival, was almost as complete.[35]

Some of this athletic superiority can be explained by the use of anabolic steroids, which especially advantaged the Soviet Union's female athletes. After the disintegration of the USSR, a number of sports administrators and coaches confessed that drugs figured in their phenomenal success. "From

1974 all Soviet swimmers were using banned substances," admitted one of the USSR's top swimming coaches. "I've personally administered the drugs and advised swimmers individually on how to avoid getting caught." (We should not, however, assume that the Soviets were alone in their use of drugs. The American weightlifter Ken Patera was ready to compete pill-for-pill against his Russian rival: "Then we'll see which is better, his steroids or mine.")[36]

Drugs were not the whole story. A great deal of the USSR's athletic superiority resulted from the regime's centrally directed diversion of scarce material resources from recreational to elite sports. This allocation meant, inevitably, that ordinary citizens had few chances, during their schooling or afterward, to participate in sports. There was, however, at least one compensation for this deprivation. Ivan and Tatiana may have been too exhausted by their assembly-line jobs to use the factory's inadequate sports facilities, but they were offered the opportunity to cheer for and to identity with Olympic champions such as Anatoly Tarasov (soccer player), Valery Borzov (sprinter), Vasily Alexeev (weight lifter), and Ludmila Tourischeva (gymnast). Whether it was worth it, only Ivan and Tatiana can say.

_____ The German Democratic Republic

Sports in the German Democratic Republic (DDR) were what they would have been in the USSR if Russians had been as methodical and efficient as Germans. Like the USSR, the DDR proclaimed in its constitution, "Physical culture, sports, and tourism, as elements of socialist culture, serve the all-round physical and spiritual development of the citizenry." To achieve its goals, the DDR developed a centralized Soviet-style governmental bureaucracy that invested $2 billion a year in sports at a time when the Federal Republic of Germany (BRD), four times the size of the DDR, spent a mere $70 million. In the BRD, there was one coach for every 20 athletes; in the DDR, one for every 2.5 athletes.[37]

Committees for *Sport und Körperkultur* were formed, shifted from one sector of the government to another, reorganized, renamed, and replaced. Policies were unchanged. The system was designed, like that of the Soviet Union, to prepare the citizenry for "work and defense." And the regime was as serious about defense as it was about work. Articles in the academic journal *Theorie und Praxis der Körperkultur* warned readers to be on their guard against the imperialist plotters in Bonn and Washington. Among the sports promoted for young people of both sexes, aged fourteen to twenty-four, were gliding, flying, parachuting, motorcycling, orienteering, and shooting.[38]

The DDR's most important sports organization was the *Deutscher Turn- und Sportbund* (1957). Its most important administrator was Manfred Ewald, who headed the DTSB from 1961 to 1988. He was also in charge of the National Olympic Committee. His youthful membership in the Nazi party was not held against him.[39]

The DTSB, which enrolled 14.3 percent of the DDR's population of seventeen million, provided sport for the masses through nationally organized clubs with branches at workplaces.[40] The system was so closely modeled on the USSR's that the names of the clubs were, for the most part, identical. The most important clubs were *Dynamo* (for civilian security personnel, including the secret police), *Vorwärts* (for military personnel), and *Lokomotiv* (for transport workers). The majority of the nation's elite athletes belonged officially to *Dynamo* or *Vorwärts*. In the DDR as in the USSR, these were clubs whose blandishments it was unwise to spurn. As president of the DTSB, Manfred Ewald decided who did what in East German sports, "with the exception of what happened within *Dynamo* and *Vorwärts*."[41]

Beginning in 1966, the government staged Soviet-style *Spartakiaden,* grand sports festivals designed to involve the entire population of the DDR. Spokesmen for the regime boasted of the opportunities for participation enjoyed by ordinary citizens, but, in fact, workplace facilities were poor, and the rate of participation was much lower than in the BRD, where sports were organized mainly on the basis of private clubs. The dream of a classless society was not achieved. "To a greater degree than the Federal Republic," wrote Dieter Voigt, "the DDR's sports participants came from society's middle and the upper echelons." East German women, nearly all of whom were employed outside the home, rarely found time for sports participation and they were almost totally excluded from sports administration. (Despite the gender discrimination that drastically limited their opportunities, most East German women seem now to be nostaglic about their brief careers as schoolgirl athletes.)[42]

While failing to provide opportunities for participation to its "workers and peasants," the DDR was phenomenally successful in the production of elite athletes. As early as 1952, the regime established special schools to nurture athletic talent. In these *Kinder- und Jugendsportschulen,* thousands of children five to ten years old spent up to sixty hours a week at sports. Specialization in sports was also manifest in the centralized research facilities that were constructed at Leipzig. These facilities, some of which engaged in secret research, were nested within the *Deutsche Hochschule für Körperkultur* (1950), a university devoted entirely to the scientific study of sports. From Leipzig, coaches and trainers throughout the DDR received meticulous instructions. Unlike their American counterparts, who pride themselves on instinctive "know how" and "hands-on" experience, German coaches and trainers listened to what the scientific experts said and did as they were told. Günter Erbach announced at an international conference that "the athletes themselves . . . work out, discuss, agree upon and finally realize their plans and intentions for the . . . development of sporting activities."[43] Conference participants who believed him also believed that the Berlin Wall was erected to block an invasion from the West.

From the 1960s until the collapse of the regime, medical personnel administered anabolic steroids and other drugs to elite athletes (who did not always know what "medicine" they were being given). These steroids improved the performance of the DDR's male athletes, but the enhancement was minimal compared to what the male hormones did for female athletes, who won the majority of the DDR's Olympic medals. The steroid dosage given to sprinters Bärbel Wöckel and Marita Koch was nearly twice that taken by the detected and disgraced Canadian sprinter Ben Johnson.[44]

The DDR's spectacular athletic achievements became much more visible in 1972 when—for the first time—the two German states fielded separate Olympic teams. In 1976, East German athletic superiority became even more obvious. In the women's events, the DDR won 45.4 percent of all possible medals. Kornelia Ender defeated the favored American swimmers in three individual races (and added a fourth gold in the 4 x 100-meter relay). Ender and her teammates swam to victory in eleven of thirteen races. In response to Shirley Babashoff's bitter remark about her rivals' suspiciously deep voices, the East Germans cleverly replied, "They came to swim, not to sing."[45]

The swimmers were not the only East German athletes to astonish the world with a series of world-record performances. Shot-putter Ilona Slupianek's career was illustrative. At the 1977 European championships, she tested positive for anabolic steroids. She was banned for a year. One year and sixteen days later, she won the European championship, tested postive for anabolic steroids, and was disqualified for the second time. She returned to competition in the 1980 Olympics, where she won the gold medal. This time, like every other tested athlete at the Moscow games, she passed the drug test.[46]

The ruthless, obsessive production of champions continued unabated until the 1989 demise of the DDR. In its last Olympic appearance, at Seoul in 1988, the DDR—with a population of only sixteen million—outscored the United States and finished second to its "big brothers" in the Soviet Union.

Two years later, the Berlin Wall had come down and the system had fallen apart. Of the DDR's ten thousand coaches, three thousand were forced to find a new profession and over five thousand were unemployed.[47]

_____ Cuba

Two years after Fidel Castro overthrew the dictatorship of Fulgencio Batista, an *Instituto Nacional de Deportes, Educación Física y Recreación* was established. The institute's announced goal was to provide every citizen with the opportunity to do sports. The government's 1985 claim of 100 percent sports participation was not credible, but the facilities provided for ordinary Cubans were undoubtedly far better than they had been. Sports participation was more widespread than under Batista. The regime's emphasis, however, was like the emphasis in the USSR and the DDR. Special schools were built to nurture the talents of a male and female athletic elite. Younger children were trained at *Escuelas de Iniciación Deportiva Educacional.* The most gifted went on to the *Escuelas Superiores de Perfeccionamiento Atlético.* By the end of the 1980s, these schools had enrolled some forty thousand students.[48]

The results were impressive. Boxers like Teófilo Stevenson and runners like Alberto Juantoreno became idols of the nation, and the Olympic team became one of the world's most powerful. At the Barcelona games (1992), the Cuban team—with fourteen gold medals—ranked fifth. Female athletes have been much less successful than male athletes—Roman Catholic attitudes toward women's roles have lingered on—but María Caridad Colón offered Cuban girls a model of hitherto unknown possibility in 1980, when she hurled her javelin 68.4 meters and became the first Latin American woman to win an Olympic gold medal.[49]

Cuban superiority was especially evident in the Pan-America Games, once overwhelmingly dominated by the United States. In 1991, Cuban athletes won more events than the Americans—140 to 130—"and did so in the sports that really matter: basketball, baseball, boxing, and track and field."[50]

The regime paid a price for its victories abroad. Lured by the prospect of political freedom and material prosperity, many of Cuba's athletic elite have defected. In 1993, at the Central American and Caribbean Games in San Juan, Puerto Rico, forty team members sought asylum. The urge to flee to greener pastures intensified when Soviet economic aid evaporated, and Cuba's infrastructure deteriorated. Older idols, such as Stevenson and Juantoreno, resisted tempting offers from American sports promoters, but younger athletes, such as the star pitcher Orlando "El Duque" Hernández, have been deaf to Castro's eloquent appeals to stay home and help Cuba weather the crisis.[51]

21 MODERN SPORTS AS A GLOBAL PHENOMENON

Generalizations about billions of people are bound to have millions of exceptions, but comments on broad trends (the currently fashionable term is *longue durée*) are, nonetheless, still appropriate.

——— Participation

When sociologists began to study modern sports, one of the first things they noticed was that the advantaged always seemed to participate in sports, actively and passively, more than the disadvantaged. This generalization held no matter how one defined advantage. Much of the empirical research confirmed common knowledge: men did more sports than women, the young more than the old, the healthy more than the sickly. In other instances, however, the data confounded expectations. Marxists who had condemned "bourgeois" sports as a mechanism invented by capitalists to control, exploit, and "dehumanize" their workers were forced to admit that, contrary to theory, the rich did more sports than the poor, managers more than factory hands, the employed more than the unemployed, and the highly educated more than those with a grade-school or high-school education. In Europe and North America, racial and ethnic majorities were, on the whole, more likely to participate in sports than racial and ethnic minorities.[1]

There were, of courses, differences in the kinds of sports practiced. The very wealthy, for example, were likely to be yachtsmen and polo players; the very poor were wrestlers and weight lifters (if male) or bowlers (if female). Women's sports were, for the most part, not sports at all; they were noncompetitive physical activities like calisthenics or a day at the seashore. When women's sports really *were* sports (e.g., basketball and volleyball), they tended to be played much less competitively than the men's version of the game. When older people continued to participate actively, they turned from strenuous team games like football (of all kinds) to the less arduous pleasures of golf and shuffleboard. Ethnic minorities frequently played the games popular in their homelands—like *bocce*—rather than those of the people among whom they lived. And there were, of course, cultural differences that dictated, for instance, that American and Japanese sports were played mostly within the educational system, while French and German sports were played mostly in state-subsidized private clubs.

All this has changed. The modern world is obviously not an egalitarian society in which sports participation is unrelated to demographic differences, but the tendency is clearly toward convergence. To take the most obvious (and most studied) example: There has been a boom everywhere, even in the Islamic world, in the number of girls and women who do sports—true sports—and a dramatic increase in the intensity of their participation. Between 1973 and 1998, for example, the number of American women engaged in intercollegiate sports increased by 112 percent, while men's participation decreased by 11 percent. Everywhere in the modern world, the ratio of men's to women's sports participation has shifted toward—although it has not yet reached—parity. And, to take a rather less obvious example, it is much farther from the truth now than it once was that "sports culture and consumer culture are wholly united . . . in regarding old, weak, handicapped, ill, and unhealthy bodies as an anathema." The Paralympics and the proliferation of sports programs for the elderly are two examples of altered attitudes.[2]

The tendency toward convergence, however, is only a tendency. Demographic factors continue to predict who does what in the domain of sports. In Northern Ireland, for instance, social class, religion, and gender interact to steer middle-class Protestant boys into rugby and cricket, while working-class Roman Catholic girls show their stuff in rugged games of *camogie* (the distinctively Irish stickball game).[3]

Exceptions aside, the tendency toward convergence has resulted in a world characterized, simultaneously, by sameness and difference, by homogeneity and heterogeneity. The sameness is obvious. The global diffusion of modern sports has meant that people everywhere are familiar with and able to participate in the same sports (which are, of course, never *exactly* the same because they are always inflected by culture). Global diffusion has also meant that people can choose from an immense array of modern (or premodern) sports. The palette of possibilties from which they choose this sport or that one is far more varied and colorful than in the past. Extreme cases still attract media attention—Fiji Islanders who ski are newsworthy—but there really is no reason, today, for anyone to be surprised at anyone else's involvement in one sport rather than another. I may yet take judo lessons. My friend Higuchi-*sensei* may yet join one of Kyoto's tennis clubs.

Hooligans at Home and Abroad

"The discussion of spectatorship," wrote a trio of American social psychologists, "amounts to a nearly universal condemnation of the phenomenon." Much of the condemnation is based on the false assumption there is an inverse relationship between doing sports and watching them. Research proves the contrary. There is actually a strong positive correlation between active and passive sports participation. Dozens of empirical studies of European and American sports fans have demonstrated that approximately two-thirds of all *in situ* spectators are active in sports. Two examples should suffice: 63 percent of the baseball fans at Boston's Fenway Park described themselves as active athletes; 63 percent of the soccer fans at a game in Cologne reported that they played the game.[4] Much of the condemnation of spectatorship is, however, based less on scorn of the proverbial "couch potato" than on the fear of the equally proverbial "football hooligan."

The phrase "football hooliganism" calls to mind an image of drunken skinheads waving the Union Jack, chanting obscenities, and assaulting fans whose main offense was that they were not English. There is some truth to the image. English supporters, who are mostly young working-class males, have clashed famously with the fans (and the police) of nearly every country in the European Union. The 1985 attack of Liverpool supporters against *Juventus* fans in Heysal Stadium (Brussels) probably did more than any other atrocity to propagate the image of English hooligans as a deadly menace. Thirty-nine Italian *Juventus* fans were killed, and English teams were, for several years, barred from European venues.[5]

English fans have the worst reputation, deserved or not, but hooliganism is a global phenomenon. European fans have also managed to cause considerable disorder. For many young Belgians who have left school for dead-end jobs or none at all, life centers on football games and the opportunity they afford for verbal and physical violence. Among these Belgians, the exchange of Nazi symbols is common. Dutch skinheads are notorious for similar attitudes. When *Feyenrood* (Rotterdam) plays *Ajax* (Amsterdam) at home, one of the loudest chants is "Hamas, Hamas, Jews to the gas chamber." (In the pre-war period, Amsterdam's Jews supported *Ajax,* which had several Jewish players.) West German hooligans are part of a youth culture that defined itself against *das Bürgerliche* by provocation, that is, by smoking, drinking, wearing outlandish makeup, riding the subway without paying, and shouting Nazi slogans. Prominent among German hooligans are the "Ossies" ("Easterners") from what was the German Democratic Republic. They have been described as "skinheads who use football matches to scream their hatred of the world, brandishing swastikas and reviving memories of the pogroms." Their slogans—"Send Schalke [fans] to Auschwitz!"—are certain to upset respectable middle-class fans even when the youths who shout the slogans have very little idea of what they mean. The young, working-class hooligans—mostly but not entirely male—from Bologna, Lazio, and a number of other Italian cities demonstrate their anti-Semitism with an array of Fascist symbols. Slavic fans have a similar reputation for horrendous behavior. In fact, some have argued that the epidemic of "virulent ethnic hatred" that ravaged Croatia, Bosnia, Serbia, and Kosovo "appeared first among soccer fans."[6]

Latin America, too, has experienced football hooliganism. In Peru, supporters of *Alianza Lima* have organized themselves into a number of militant groups, one of which signals its ferocity by likening its activities to genocide. In Argentina, where hooligans have been extensively studied, the *barras bravas* (die-hard fans) are known for racist and homophobic chants characterizing Brazilian fans as "all niggers" and "all queer." Among the chants of Boca supporters is one that goes like this:

> *Hinchada, hinchada, hinchada—hay una sola*
> *Hinchada es la de Boca que le rompe el culo a todas.*
> [Fans, fans, fans—the only real fans are
> Boca's, who tear the ass-holes of all the others.]

Verbal violence begets physical violence. Between 1958 and 1992, at least one hundred and eighteen people were killed in Argentina in clashes among fans and between fans and the police. In the 1990s, soccer-related deaths averaged about five a year.[7]

North American hooligans are equally capable of repulsive behavior, but their demographic profile is somewhat different. They are to be found on college campuses as well as among the urban underclass. To unnerve a basketball player whose father had been assassinated in Beirut, students at Arizona State University taunted him with cries of "PLO! PLO!" When American hooligans regress from verbal to physical violence, they are likely to engage in a celebratory riot in which goalposts are torn down, shop windows smashed, and automobiles torched. In the wake of a championship, cities like Chicago or Detroit are liable to experience an alcohol-abetted rampage by "feral packs of kids and criminals who loot, shoot and leave their hometowns awash in blood, bullets and broken glass."[8]

In short, the socially acceptable polarities of a sports event—it's by definition "us against them"—provides society's outsiders with a pretext for the expression of their frustrations, disappointments, alienation, and anger. For the socially estranged, violence is the game within the game. As a "hard" supporter of Leeds FC remarked of a good brawl, "Fighting's entertainment, 'owt else."[9]

Can we, therefore, speak of sports-related hooliganism as an instance of globalization? To the degree that bands of young men on the European continent or in Latin America consciously imitate English "hard ones," we certainly can, but European and Latin American youths have modified the patterns of spectatorship in accordance with local culture. They have, in many instances, decided consciously *not* to imitate the English. Italian fans, equipped with drums, witty songs, gigantic banners, and color-coded scarves, have created a oppositional form of spectatorship in which cynical humor substitutes for physical violence. Despite extremes of verbal violence, Italian fans have been far more pacific than England's football hooligans. Scotland's "Tartan Army" and Denmark's *Danske Roligans* (*rolig* = "peaceful") are both ventures in the propagation of a jolly carnivalesque form of spectatorship. Norwegian followers of British football have formed a *Supporterunionen for Britisk Fotball*. They demonstrate that it is possible to support Liverpool or Millwall without xenophobia. The history of Indian cricket forces another modification of the generalizations about sports-related hooliganism and its demographic profile. Some of worst disorders have occurred in conjunction with cricket matches, and some of the worst offenders have been privileged youths from an "affluent, educated, upper-caste elite" that has "monopolized cricket grounds in post-independence India." In short, the globalization of sports spectatorship has meant not only sameness but also difference.[10]

A final happy note on hooliganism. The truly violent "aggro"-seekers have shown no inclination to organize globally for international demonstrations of transgressive protest. For this boon, ordinary sports spectators, most of whom are timid blokes, can be grateful.

_____ The Mass Media

The sports fans who paint their faces orange and shriek for Holland or parade about in kilts to demonstrate their Scottish loyalties perform as much to attract the television cameras as to boost the morale of the players. The globalization of the mass media has drastically altered the world of sports. The overwhelming majority of the world's sports fans follow their favorites by means of newspapers, radios, television sets, and computer screens.

Sports journalism, which began in the eighteenth century with monthly periodicals such as *The Sporting Magazine* (1792), now offers thousands of specialized daily, weekly, monthly, and annual publications. The British were, as expected, much quicker than continental Europeans to develop a sporting press. The *London Morning Herald* introduced its sports pages in 1817, and the *Times* began a regular sports section in 1819. The Manchester-based weekly, *Athletic News,* began publishing in 1875. Holland's economic and cultural ties to England were so close that the first continental journal devoted to modern sports—*Nederlandsche Sport*—appeared only five years later. Belgium's *La Chronique* followed in 1891, but Flemish-speakers had to wait until 1912, when *Sportwereld* was first published, for sports journalism in their own language. Although German gymnasts had an *Allegemeine Turn-Zeitung* in 1842, modern sports were not regularly covered in the German press before 1886, when Munich's *Neueste Nachrichten* began a daily section. William Randolph Hearst added a sports section to the *New York Journal* in 1895. Italian and Spanish fans began to follow modern sports—mostly soccer—in the *Gazzetta dello Sport* (1896) and *El Mundo Sportivo* (1906).[11]

A 1937 survey found that British newspapers allotted 11.4 percent of their Tuesday-through-Saturday space to sports while 17.7 percent of the Sunday issue covered sports (mostly soccer). By 1955, 46 percent of the *Daily Mail* was devoted to sports, but the demand for statistics and trivia was insatiable. Today, sports dailies like *L'Équipe* (Paris) sell millions of copies. Moscow's *Sovietskii Sport* and *Futbol* have been replaced by an active sports press driven by economics rather than by ideology. The same transition to market-driven sports journalism has occurred in Bucharest, Budapest, and other metropolises of the now-defunct Warsaw Pact.

Radio sportscasting began on July 2, 1921, when RCA's WJZ broadcast the heavyweight match between Jack Dempsey and Georges Carpentier from Boyle's Thirty Acres in Jersey City, N.J. In 1925, German radio broadcast coverage of the Münster Regatta and a soccer game (*Armenia Bielefeld* vs. *Preußen Münster*). Beginning in 1927, *Nihon Hôsô Kyôkai* (NHK) made it possible for Japanese fans to hear play-by-play broadcasts of baseball games. That same year, the British Broadcasting Corporation covered the Oxford–Cambridge Boat Race, the Grand National Steeplechase, Wimbledon, and the Football Association Cup Final. For rights to the last event, the BBC donated £100 to charity. Radio reinforced the public perception of these fixtures as annual celebrations of nationhood. In 1929, French fans were able to follow the Tour de France on radio.[12]

Although the marriage between television and sports was not consummated until the postwar period, courtship began in the 1930s. In August 1936, flickering images of the Olympic Games were transmitted to twenty-seven *Fernsehstuben* (television locales) scattered throughout Berlin. Over one hundred and fifty thousand Germans gathered to watch them. After experimenting with the Oxford–Cambridge boat race, in 1937, the BBC persuaded the somewhat apprehensive Football Association to allow transmission of the 1938 Cup Final (Huddersfield Town versus Preston North End). American television followed, a year later, with NBC's coverage of an intercollegiate baseball game (Columbia versus Princeton).[13]

To say that World War II interrupted the progress of sports television is to look through the wrong end of the telescope, but there was, in fact, an interruption. When progress resumed, the British government allowed the BBC to telecast the 1947 Cup Final to the UK's 30,000 television sets—despite a severe shortage of electricity. The 1948 Olympics, held in London, were the first "mega-event" of postwar sports. The BBC paid £1,500 for the right to telecast the games, a feat accomplished with only nine cameras (compared to the hundreds that are now standard). At that point, fewer than 2 percent of British households owned a television set; ten years later, 82 percent did. In 1954, Eurovision was created, which enabled forty-five stations in eight countries to telecast FIFA's 1954 World Cup Final. Football League was initially hesitant to allow live telecasts of its game, but the BBC was permitted to show five-minute snippets from seventy-five games of the 1955–1956 season.[14]

When cable television came on the scene, Parliament declared that the Oxford–Cambridge boat race, Wimbledon tennis, the World Cup Finals, and a number of other events were part of Britain's national heritage. Parliament mandated that they be telecast "free to air." Canadians were also reluctant to permit a laissez-faire market in sports television. In 1962, Ottawa decreed that football's Grey Cup Final was "an instrument of national unity" that must be telecast jointly by CBC and CTV.[15]

In the United States, capitalism was given a freer hand. In the early postwar years, when the owners of professional baseball, basketball, and football teams were fearful that fans might prefer to loll before a television set rather than to push their way through the stadium's turnstiles, all four television networks offered a seemingly endless round of boxing matches. Once the marriage of team sports and television was consummated, the giddy carousel of marketplace competition began to revolve, and the rights to cover professional sports leagues rotated among the major commercial networks. By 1983, the cost of coverage was so great than ABC and NBC shared it, paying $1.2 billion for six years' broadcasting of major-league baseball. This fee was in addition to the considerable sums paid for local rights, sums that tended to increase the gap between the most successful and the least successful teams. Although the income from national television is divided among all the teams in major-league baseball, which to some degree counters the economic advantage of teams in the nation's largest metropolitan areas, the revenue from local television broadcasting flows directly into the coffers of the local team. This means, for instance, that the New York Yankees can count on $50 million a year from local telecasts, while the Seattle Mariners must make do with a tenth of that.[16]

The $1.2 billion paid by ABC and NBC was only a beginning. Following the 1995 season, Fox TV, NBC, and ESPN paid $1.7 billion for five years of baseball. Football rights were even more expensive and required even more in the way of corporate cooperation. For the NFL rights from 1994 through 1997, ABC, ESPN, Fox TV, NBC, and Turner Network Television paid a total of $4.38 billion. The figures for 1998–2005 have to be read and reread before one can grant even provisional credulity. The numbers are in billions of dollars.

ESPN	Sunday and Thursday night games	4.8
ABC	Monday night games plus three Super Bowls	4.4
Fox	National Football Conference plus three Super Bowls	4.4
CBS	American Football Conference plus two Super Bowls	4.0

The total is $17.6 billion, or $73 million per team per year. In comparison, CBS's $6.2 billion contract for eleven years of the (non-profit) NCAA's basketball tournament has to be considered a real bargain.[17]

Beginning in 1955, the BBC had to face the sort of competition that characterized American television before competition became too ruinous to pursue. Regional television was linked to form ITV. The competition was intense. The BBC's multisport "Grandstand," which began in 1958, was overtaken by ITV's "The World of Sport." Eventually, British television solved the problem of competition just as their American counterparts had. In 1979, the rival networks agreed to share delayed-telecast rights to Football League games. For four years' rights, they paid £9.2 million (plus £800,000 for overseas film rights). When FL allowed live coverage, in 1983, BBC and ITV together bought two years of rights to ten matches a season for £5.2 million. Rupert Murdoch's BSkyB outbid them for football rights in 1992. BSkyB paid £191.5 million and renewed the contract in 1997 for £670 million. Both contracts allowed telecasting sixty games a season. (Five clubs—Arsenal, Chelsea, Leeds, Liverpool, and Manchester United—receive over 30 percent of this bounty, a share that clearly advantages them in the quest for football talent.)[18]

Satellite transmission, which began in the 1960s, eventually transformed the Olympic Games and the World Cup Finals into spectacles witnessed by billions of viewers. Estimates of the exact number of viewers vary. The Atlanta Olympics (1996) were said to have been seen by 19.6 billion people, which averages to approximately a billion a day. Viewership for the final game of the 1998 World Cup (France versus Brazil) was estimated at 1.7 billion, making the event "the biggest shared experience in human history." Although Britain's 20-team Premier League was unable to promise BSkyB a viewership of quite this magnitude, the numbers reached by satellite transmission justified a deal of over £1 billion for three seasons of play (2004–2007).[19]

During the last quarter of the century, the proliferation of profit-oriented satellite and cable television networks eliminated what was left of the monopoly that noncommercial state-run or state-subsidized television networks had once enjoyed. Privately owned corporations joined the competition for the right to telecast nonprotected mega-events (and to reach all those billions of potential customers). The predictable consequence was a dizzy escalation in the cost of television rights. For the American rights to the Olympic Games of 2004–2006–2008 (Athens, Turin, Beijing), NBC committed itself to pay $2.3 billion. This was nearly *four thousand* times the $600,000 that NBC had paid for the right to telecast the 1964 games via satellite from Tokyo. The cost to European and Japanese networks was once negligible in comparison to what the American networks were forced to pay, but the IOC no longer heeds their plea of poverty. The Europeans and the Japanese now contribute their billions to Olympic coffers.[20]

If FIFA imitates the IOC in economic behavior as well as in the concoction of telegenic spectacles, one reason is that both organizations did business with and through a Lucerne-based marketing firm, International Sport and Leisure (ISL). For the global rights to the 2002 and 2006 World Cup Finals, excluding the United States, ISL teamed with the German firm Kirch Media and agreed to pay FIFA $2.2 billion. When ISL's parent company went bankrupt, in 2001, Kirch Media bought ISL's share and resold the rights to various networks around the world.[21]

Understanding the organizational chart of the international mass-media industry is a challenge best met by professional accountants. Historians can only make do with suggestive examples. In 1995, the Walt Disney Company paid $19 billion to acquire Capital Cities/ABC, which owns ABC television and ESPN (United States) and 50 percent of The European Sports Network (TESN) and 25 percent of Canal Plus. ESPN also owns 33 percent of the Eurosport Consortium. TESN operates in Germany as *Sport Kanal,* in France as *TV Sport,* in the Netherlands as *Sportnet,* and in the UK as Screensport. The international media empires of men such as Rupert Murdoch, Kerry Packer, Ted Turner, Silvio Berlusconi, and Bernard Tapie are maddeningly complex. A team of sociologists has diagrammed the "global sport mass media oligopoly." The graphs are not incomprehensible.[22]

Conflicts among media giants are as hard to follow as the exploits of Renaissance *condottieri*. In the 1995–1996 battle for television rights to a projected Super League of Australian rugby, Kerry Packer and Rupert Murdoch both courted the Australian Rugby League, bid competitively, traded insults, sued one another, appealed adverse judicial verdicts, and then settled for a division of the spoils, in which Packer's Channel 9 was to air two games a week and Murdoch's Foxtel five. A short time after the settlement, it came undone and Packer emerged—for the moment—victorious.[23]

The relentless commercialization of these mega-events has had some predictable consequences. A detailed study of the 1992 Olympics illustrates some of the results of coverage by commercial television. Although state-run networks—the BBC, Japan's NHK, Germany's ARD and ZDF—managed to provide more or less uninterrupted coverage of the opening ceremony, NBC, Canada's CTV, and Australia's Channel 7 all interrupted the flow with advertisements. NBC's ninety-seven commercials required over an hour of airtime. Small wonder that Americans, polled in 1995, were more likely to recognize McDonald's golden arches than Pierre de Coubertin's Olympic rings. It was an additional insult to viewers of the opening ceremony that NBC's commentators ignored the arrival of the Olympic torch and seemed baffled by the symbolic choreography of "Mediterranean Sea, Olympic Sea." Eurosport's Archie MacPherson also found the symbolism "a little bit heavy." French and German commentators were better informed and more informative.[24]

There is another aspect of the relationship between global television and global sports that needs to be discussed. Who calls the shots? The evidence is clear. Australian rugby and basketball games are divided into quarters rather than halves to allow for more advertisements. The NBA and the NFL have special television time-outs to accommodate commercials. In 1998, the NFL agreed to increase their number to twenty per game. As television executive William MacPhail cheerfully explained, "A man just waves his hand at the referee when we need a commercial. Nobody cares." The NBA introduced the 24-second rule (1954) and the 3-point rule (1982) in order to accelerate the action and make the game more "TV-friendly." The same motive dictated archery contests with fifteen arrows per contestant (rather than one hundred forty-four) and tennis matches that end with a tie-breaker (instead of eight games to six). Events at the Olympic Games are frequently scheduled to appear on prime time in the United States even if athletes must compete early in the morning or late in the evening. Olympic figure skaters no longer do compulsory figures because television viewers dislike them. In return for the $456 million it received from NBC for the Atlanta Olympics, the IOC moved the opening ceremony from Saturday to Friday, thereby providing an extra day of competition. The agreement also brought a brand new Olympic sport, beach volleyball, that seemed made to order for viewers who were nostalgic for "Bay Watch."[25]

It is not just the rules that have been altered. Mohammad Ali's fights against grotesquely inferior opponents went on much longer than they should have. Was it to allow the commercials—sold in advance—to be aired between rounds? David Lacey's comment on soccer is probably true of most spectator sports: "English football is now handcuffed to television and nobody can doubt which of the two is under arrest."[26]

Complaints of this sort are ungenerous. NBC and the other commercial networks do perform technological wonders as they telecast the marvels of athletic performance for a viewership of billions. It is, however, hard to be properly grateful when the final moments of one's favorite sport are omitted to make room for a Gatorade advertisement.

Global Sponsorship

In the last decades of the century, sports sponsorship was restructured on the basis of a partnership between multinational corporations and international nongovernmental sports organizations. The IOC, which had become uneasy about its economic dependence on the sale of television rights, forged an alliance with ISL, the Lucerne-based multinational corporation owned jointly by Horst Dassler, who owned Adidas, and the Japanese advertising agency Dentsu. The IOC's initial agreement with ISL, signed in 1985, had generated $95 million by the end of 1988. The nine multinational corporations that participated in what came to be called TOP I (The Olympic Program I) grew to twelve for TOP II. Eight of the original nine continued as "worldwide sponsors" (Coca-Cola, Kodak, Visa, *Time,* Matsushita, Brother, Philips, and 3M), one dropped out (Federal Express), and four corporations joined the program (UPI, Bausch & Lomb, Mars, Ricoh). TOP II raised some $175 million. TOP III reduced the number of "worldwide sponsors" to ten but added four "official suppliers" (John Hancock, Lufthansa, Mercedes, Ricoh). TOP IV, which carried the program through the year 2000, brought in sponsorship revenues in excess of $350 million, a figure likely to be surpassed by the eleven TOP V sponsors.[27]

Economic dependence on the sale of television rights threatened FIFA's freedom of action just as it had threatened the IOC's. The solution to the problem was the same: diversify the sources of income. For the 1998 World Cup Final, ISL secured twelve multinational corporate sponsors, each of which was willing to pay FIFA £12.5 million. The lucky sponsors for the 1998 extravaganza in France formed a familiar cast of characters: American (Budweiser, Coca-Cola, Gillette, McDonald's, MasterCard, Snickers), Dutch (Philips), German (Adidas, Opel), and Japanese (Canon, Fuji, JVC). In return for their money, the international and national sponsors received 350,000 tickets to Olympic events in addition to the right to exploit Olympic symbolism (the rings, the torch, etc.).[28]

Sponsorship of the Olympic Games and the World Cup Finals was economically rational. The sponsors counted on an increase in the sales of their goods and services. They also counted on an increase in their share of the market. They were guided by their experience in domestic sales. In the 1980s, one of FIFA's sponsors, the brewers of Budweiser beer, sponsored no fewer than seventy-two professional baseball, basketball, football, and soccer teams—in addition to more than three hundred intercollegiate teams. Between 1976 and 1986, Budweiser's share of the national market bounded from 22 percent to 40 percent, despite increased competition from imported brands of superior quality.[29]

Sports' dependence on sponsorship has had countless consequences, some obvious, some not. An example of the former is banning the use of American Express credit cards at the Olympics—of which Visa is an official sponsor. An example of the latter is the outcome of the 240-kilometer cycling race at the Sydney Olympics. Germany's Jan Ullrich finished first. Andreas Klöden, also representing Germany, allowed Alexander Vinokourov, representing Kazakhstan, to take the silver medal that he—Klöden—might easily have taken. The explanation for this sudden burst of altruism is that all three riders compete on the professional circuit as part of Team Telekom. Mario Kummer, *directeur sportif* for the German media giant, had orchestrated the outcome of the Olympic race.[30]

———— The Global Labor Market

Throughout the nineteenth century, British residents abroad created hundreds of sports teams in places as far from home as Buenos Aires, Capetown, and Melbourne. And the British were not the only ones who happened to play sports while employed abroad in one or another occupational capacity. Americans who did business in Japan played baseball at the Yokohama Athletic Club, and Swiss citizens who happened to be in Italy, France, or Spain founded soccer clubs in Turin, Marseille, and Barcelona. The novelty is that the global market for "sports labor" now employs thousands of men (and hundreds of women) who go abroad primarily in order to engage in sports. In the past, a small number of professional athletes moved from place to place, but very few of them went back and forth across international borders as today's nomadic athletes routinely do.[31]

Cricket players are drawn from place to place, but soccer football is the stongest magnet. In 1938, one hundred forty-seven Africans played in the First and Second Divisions of the French soccer league. Over a span of fifty years, foreign players comprised approximately 20 percent of the league. Nearly 40 percent of Spain's *Prima Liga* and Germany's *Bundesliga* are foreign nationals. The percentage of foreign players was even higher in the North American Soccer League, which, in the 1980s, consisted almost entirely of fading stars at the end of their careers, men like Germany's Franz Beckenbauer and Brazil's Pelé. When the dam of Soviet power was broken, a flood of East European soccer players flowed west. In 1988, a transfer fee of £3.2 million sent Alexander Zavarov from the Ukraine (*Dynamo* Kiev) to Italy (*Juventus* Turin). In 1990, seventeen of the twenty-two members of the Czech national team moved west. In 1998, there were more than two thousand Yugoslav sports professionals playing abroad. Inevitably, westward emigration lowered the level of play in eastern Europe. "I am not fool," lamented a fan in Budapest, "I can see what I see, the game is shit."[32]

Rules and regulations restricting the number of foreign players on a national team can be evaded. In 1984, Zola Budd became a British subject much more quickly than South Africans who were less fleet of (bare) foot. In 1998, Japanese authorities, who are notoriously reluctant to grant citizenship to foreign residents, hustled Brazil's W. A. Lopes through the bureaucratic labyrinth in time for soccer's World Cup Finals. Latin American soccer players of remote Italian ancestry have been welcomed home for national and international play. Most league-imposed impediments to movement across the national borders of the European Union were removed by the European Court in 1995, when it ruled that neither UEFA nor the Belgian national soccer federation had the authority to block Jean-Marc Bosman's transfer from Liège to Dunkerque. The court interpreted the Treaty of Rome to mean that transfer fees are legal only for the duration of a player's contract. Movement accelerated.[33]

Within Europe, Dutch and Scandinavian migrants are especially prized for their ability to speak English and to adapt culturally. German professionals are also known as "good Europeans." Half of Germany's 1990 World Cup Finals team played for foreign clubs. Outside of Europe, the pattern of movement has been—in Immanuel Wallerstein's terms—from the "periphery" to the "core." African football players from former French and Portuguese colonies tend to accept offers to play in France or Portugal, where the language and culture are not quite so foreign as they would be in Germany or

Scandinavia. The migration out of Africa has been massive. Not a single member of Nigeria's team at the 1998 World Cup Finals was then playing for a Nigerian club. It is rare for a truly successful soccer player to stay with the club that nurtured him as a junior. As a professional, Diego Maradona played for clubs in Argentina (Boca), Spain (Barcelona), Italy (Naples), Spain (Seville), and Argentina (Newall's Old Boys).[34]

Soccer players are the most numerous migrants, but basketball players from the United States—the most famous of whom may be Bill Bradley—have dribbled, passed, and dunked in European leagues. In 1986, foreign players made up a third of the top division of the English Basketball League. The influx of baseball players from Latin America to the United States has been so great that a third of all major-leaguers are now foreign-born. Hundreds of Canadian hockey players are to be found on European ice (not to mention those playing in the American franchises of the NHL). Competing to join Western European teams, Canadian skaters are likely to cross sticks with players from Russia and the Czech Republic.[35]

There has also been a kind of Brownian movement in track-and-field sports—except that the movement is far from random. Innumerable African athletes have been recruited to run for American universities. In 1981, for instance, the University of Texas at El Paso won the NCAA track-and-field championships with a team well stocked with African athletes. Without them, El Paso would not have been among the top six teams. The grants-in-aid offered by American colleges and universities have transformed many NCAA track-and-field meets into international confrontations. John Bale described a 1983 NCAA regional championship in which "the men's 400 meters was won by a Jamaican, the 800 meters by a Brazilian, the 1,500 meters by an Irishman, the 5,000 and 10,000 meters by a Tanzanian, the 400-meter hurdles by a Swede, the pole vault by a Swiss, the triple jump and hammer throw by Englishmen, and the javelin throw by an Icelander." Foreign athletes also won four of the women's events. Some of the thousands of foreign athletes in the United States may have been motivated mostly by their desire to obtain an education, but it is doubtful that they were recruited and given scholarships solely for their intellectual promise.[36]

Global mobility is the *sine qua non* of today's golf and tennis worlds. Golfers and tennis players "are the nomads of the sports labour migration pattern." Small wonder that they are well represented among the international clients of Mark McCormack's International Management Group (IMG). Among the constellation of stars whom McCormack has represented are golfers (Arnold Palmer, Jack Nicklaus, Norman Player), tennis players (Chris Evert), track stars (Sebastian Coe), skiers (Jean-Claude Killy), automobile racers (Jackie Stewart), and boxers (Mohammad Ali). E. M. Swift notes, moreover, that it is "more or less routine for athletes represented by IMG to play in IMG-promoted tournaments that are sponsored by corporations to which IMG serves as consultant." The tournaments are then the stuff of a weekly sports round-up, "Trans World Sports," which a subsidiary of IMG telecasts to sixty-one countries in fifteen different languages. It is understandable that *Sports Illustrated* deemed McCormack "the most powerful man in sports."[37]

The product lines endorsed by elite athletes are as international as McCormack's clientele. Australian golfer Greg Norman earned roughly 90 percent of his income—some $5 million a year in the 1980s—from endorsements of Qantas, Hertz, Daikyo, Swan Lager, Reebok, Akubra, Epson, and other multinational firms. British soccer player Kevin Keegan had contracts with Nabisco, Fabergé, and at least nine other British and American corporations. After his harvest of medals at the 1968 Winter Olympics in Grenoble, French skier Jean-Claude Killy signed contracts with Head skis, Wolverine gloves, Breckenridge & LaDaille resorts, United Air Lines, Bristol-Myers, Chevrolet, and a long list of other corporations. He was surpassed by Swedish tennis star Bjorn Borg, who had more than forty simultaneous endorsement contracts. And Borg, in turn, was eclipsed by Michael Jordan. In the fall of 2003, before he had played a single game for the Cleveland Cavaliers, LeBron James was reported to have more than $100 million in endorsement deals to supplement his paltry annual salary of $10.8 million. Among female athletes, Anna Kournikova has been spectacularly successful as a product endorser, but she—as countless feminists have glumly noted—has been marketed more for her looks than for her ability as a tennis player.[38]

POSTMODERNISM AND
LES SPORTS CALIFORNIENS

There is a rough consensus about the characteristics of modern sports but no agreement about what is meant by "postmodern sports." The reason for this situation is that postmodern sports may be an animal found only in the imaginary zoo of sociological speculation.[1]

Some scholars see postmodernism exemplified in the career of flamboyant athletes such as British soccer star Paul "Gazza" Gascoigne. Richard Giulianotti and Michael Gerrard see Gascoigne as a "carnival of colourful signifiers [that] has no . . . existential depth." His "postmodern stardom embraces all ungrounded signifiers." Other scholars, taking "the linguistic turn," see postmodern sports spectacles as texts or as "pre-texts" for the spectators to focus upon themselves. Another way to understand postmodernism in the domain of sports—one that I prefer—is to look for "family resemblances" (Wittgenstein's term) among a set of activities that French sociologists call *les sports californiens,* sports that represent a regrettable submission to American cultural influence. (It is especially annoying that skateboarders speak of *mon skate* instead of *ma planche à roulettes.*)[2]

Among the most frequently cited of these "Californian" sports are the activities of motorcyclists, skateboarders, rollerbladers, hang gliders, windsurfers, snowboarders, acrobatic skiers, and other nonconformist adventurers. What these sports seem to have in common is that most of them began as informally structured, individual activities that took place in urban or natural space (rather than in the specialized, built-to-order venues of most modern sports). They rely on new technologies and call for acrobatic moves. They attract young people of both sexes. (Asked for his opinion of basketball star Shaquille O'Neal, eleven-year-old Miles Messner was scornful: "Shaquille O'Neal is *nothing* compared to [skateboarder] Tony Hawk!") These "Californian" sports also offer a *frisson* of risk. As Alain Loret notes, these new sports renounce measurement and "valorize delirium." He and Iain Borden see them as transgressive statements. Skateboards, for instance, are like litter and graffiti in that they leave "a counter-inscription" on the cityscape.[3]

These new sports do seem to be ubiquitous. Tourists traversing the square between Cologne's cathedral and its Römisch–Germanisches Museum are imperiled by teenaged Germans on skateboards. Austrian skiers have to share Alpine slopes with snowboarders. Windsurfers have flocked to Baltic beaches and Australia's "Sunshine Coast." Hang gliders have invaded the skies above America's national parks. Must we conclude that we live in the era of post-modern sports?

Perhaps not. We should recall that many of the novel characteristics of post-modern sports are not all that novel. Consider the automobile races of the *fin de siècle*. They relied on technologically sophisticated equipment; their heady velocity offered the vertiginous pleasures of risk; and they were especially attractive to young people. There is another reason to be skeptical about the claim that we have moved into postmodernity. We should note another "family resemblance" among "Californian" sports: Most of them have made—or seem about to make—the familiar transition from more or less spontaneous play to the rules and regulations of an institutionalized sports contest. There has, admittedly, been ambivalence about commercial sponsorship, about the formation of bureaucratic organizations, and about participation in national and international championships. Terje Haakonsen, for instance, refused to compete in the Olympic halfpipe snowboard competition. He balked—but his peers accepted the invitation, and the snowboard competition was staged as a globally televised performance for which the winners received their medals on the basis of quantified achievement. If William of Occam's razor is as sharp now as when he honed it in the fourteenth century, there is no need to create a new category of sports. Without the pretentious descriptors borrowed from Roland Barthes and Jean Baudrillard, postmodern sports look suspiciously like modern sports.[4]

If the adjective "postmodern" has any usefulness, it is in reference to the experience of the spectator rather than to the formal–structural characteristics of the sports. One way to explain this point is to look closely at a painting by the California artist Richard Cronk.[5] *Venus on the Half Shell* (1981) evokes a medley of associations. Cronk's title is a clever example of incongruous intertextuality. It refers, of course, to Sandro Botticelli's famous Renaissance recontextualization of ancient myth in *The Birth of Venus*. Botticelli's Venus is borne by a floating clamshell. Nude except for her long blonde hair, the goddess stands between a pair of hovering angels and a human attendant who rushes to clothe her in a robe. Cronk's title is a playful reference not only to

Botticelli but also to a popular way of serving seafood. His Venus is modestly dressed in shorts and a tank top—a typically Californian outfit—as she roller-skates by a tennis court, weaving her way among strollers and shoppers. *Venus on the Half Shell* is a typically postmodern pastiche of cultural disjunctions. Cronk relied upon the viewer's ability to combine images of daily life in modern California with recollections of Botticelli's vision.

The viewers' experience vis-à-vis *Venus on the Half Shell* is a clue to the sports spectators' experience in front of their television screens. Watching Manchester United or the Chicago Bulls or the Yomiuri Giants on television, fans see the game from as many different perspectives as there are cameras at the site. Commentators not only tell the viewers what the viewers have just seen, they chatter constantly about the past lives and future prospects of the players. When the game is telecast by a commercial network, which is now typically the mode, the dramatic action on the field of play is obscured by network logos and interrupted by advertisements, most of which are constructed from a collage of images presented in rapid sequence. Now and then, the viewers' television screens show the stadium's giant television screen. The fragmentation of experience is less extreme for *in situ* spectatorship, but loudspeakers and electronic scoreboards and the transistor radio that one needs in Fenway Park to follow the action in Yankee Stadium do make a difference.

Spectatorship—the *consumption* of sports spectacles—has in fact become sufficiently discordant to warrant references to "the postmodern condition," but the *production* of sports spectacles continues to be relentlessly modern. Sports spectators may demonstrate a "postmodern sensibility." They may be unaware of the "grand narratives" of history and they may be prone to "deconstruct" the significance of whatever they observe. They may revel in the fragmentation of experience. But they can do as little to alter the institutional structures of globally organized modern sports as they can to reform the institutional structures of multinational corporate capitalism. Marxist critics are wrong to assert that sports and capitalism are structurally identifical, but the two now interact on the global stage in a complicated drama of instrumental rationality.[6] For sports spectators dreaming of an idyllic past in which amateur athletes played for the fun of it and never kept score, this is not a happy message, but there are no signs on the horizon of a return to that mostly imaginary past. Sports spectators still have an option. They can shift from passive to active participation. They can switch roles and actually *play* the old ball game. When they do, however, they will reveal how thoroughly they have internalized the habitus of modern sports. For better or for worse.

NOTES

Abbreviations used in the notes

BJSH	*British Journal of Sport History*
CJHS	*Canadian Journal of History of Sport*
CSS	*Culture, Sport, Society*
ESHR	*European Sport History Review*
EWS	*Encyclopedia of World Sport*
GL	*Geschichte der Leibesübungen*
IEWS	*International Encyclopedia of Women and Sport*
IJHS	*International Journal of the History of Sport*
IRSS	*International Review of Sport Sociology*
JSH	*Journal of Sport History*
JSSI	*Journal of Sport and Social Issues*
SHR	*Sport History Review*
SI	*Sports Illustrated*
SPEC	*Sport and Physical Education in China*
SZGS	*Sozial- und zeitgenössische Geschichte des Sports*
WGWT	*Winter Games, Warm Traditions*

Introduction: Rules of the Game

1. Chris Gratton and Peter Taylor, *Economics of Sport and Recreation* (London: Spon, 2000), p. 69.
2. Roger Caillois, *Les Jeux et les hommes* (Paris: Gallimard, 1958), p. 7.
3. John M. Roberts, Malcolm J. Arth, and Robert R. Bush, "Games in Culture," *American Anthropologist,* 61:4 (August 1959): 597–605.
4. David Belden, *L'Alpinisme* (Paris: L'Harmattan, 1994); Linda J. Borish, "'A Fair, Without *the* Fair, Is No Fair at All,'" *JSH,* 24:2 (Summer 1997): 155–76. The main focus of my own history of women's sports is on sports that are played by both men and women; see *Women's Sports* (New York: Columbia University Press, 1991).
5. Bernard Suits, *The Grasshopper* (Toronto: University of Toronto Press, 1978), p. 146.
6. These are among the motives named by athletes studied in Michel Bouet's unsurpassed study, *Les Motivations des sportifs* (Paris: Éditions universitaires, 1969).
7. Bernard Jeu, "Toute-puissance et immortalité . . . ," *Ethno-Psychologie,* 27:1 (March 1972): 20; see also his, *Le Sport, la mort, la violence* (Paris: Éditions universitaires, 1972); Michel Bouet, *Signification du sport* (Paris: Éditions universitaires,

1968), pp. 211, 214; Ommo Grupe, *Vom Sinn des Sports* (Schorndorf: Karl Hofmann, 2000); Gunter Gebauer, "Wettkampf als Gegenwelt," in *Aktuelle Probleme der Sportphilosophie,* ed. Hans Lenk (Schorndorf: Karl Hofmann, 1983), p. 345; F. J. J. Buytendijk, *Das Fußballspiel* (1952; Würzburg: Werkbund–Verlag, n.d.), pp. 19–20. In response to Buytendijk, see Hannelore Ratzeburg, "Fußball ist Frauensport," in *Frauen Bewegung Sport* (Hamburg: VSA, 1986), pp. 85–94.

8. I refer to "exemplary sports" because histories are different from encyclopedias. Readers curious about *midwam, milakia,* and the many other sports that I have not mentioned can consult the English translation of the *World Sports Encyclopedia,* edited by Wojciech Liponski, (St. Paul, Minn.: MBI, 2003), which includes entries for more than three thousand sports.

9. Allen Guttmann, *From Ritual to Record* (New York: Columbia University Press, 1978), pp. 15–55.

10. Rick Reilly, "Unsynchronized Swimming," *SI,* 93 (October 18, 2000): 34.

11. Max Weber, *Wirtschaft und Gesellschaft,* 2 vols. (1920; Cologne: Kiepenheuer & Witsch, 1964); Georges Vigarello, *Une Histoire culturelle du sport* (Paris: Robert Laffont, 1988).

12. Richard D. Mandell, "The Invention of the Sports Record," *Stadion,* 2:2 (1976): 250–64.

13. André Obey, *L'Orgue du stade* (Paris: Gallimard, 1924), p. 35.

1. Preliterate Peoples

1. Carl Diem, *Die Olympische Flamme,* 3 vols. (Berlin: Deutscher-Archiv Verlag, 1942), 1:86.

2. Wolfgang Eichel, quoted in Horst Ueberhorst, "Ursprungstheorien," in *GL,* ed. Horst Ueberhorst, 6 vols. (Berlin: Bartels & Wernitz, 1972–1989), 1:17; see also Dieter Voigt, *Soziologie in der DDR* (Cologne: Verlag Wissenschaft & Politik, 1975), pp. 29–31.

3. Carl Diem, *Weltgeschichte des Sports,* 3rd ed., 2 vols. (Frankfurt/Main: Cotta, 1971), 1:3. Bernard Jeu went beyond Diem. He asserted that, in all sports, "there is undeniably something sacred"; see his *Analyse du sport* (Paris: PUF, 1987), p. 9.

4. Stewart Culin, *Games of the North American Indians* (Washington: U.S. Government Printing Office, 1907), p. 34; see also Joseph B. Oxendine's *American Indian Sports Heritage* (Champaign, Ill.: Human Kinetics, 1988), p. xiii; Kendall Blanchard and Alyce Cheska, *The Anthropology of Sport* (South Hadley, Mass.: Bergin & Garvey, 1985).

5. Wanni Wibulswasdi Anderson, "Sport in Thailand," in *Sport in Asia and Africa,* ed. Eric A. Wagner (Westport, Conn.: Greenwood Press, 1989), p. 126.

6. Thomas Vennum Jr., *American Indian Lacrosse* (Washington: Smithsonian Institution Press, 1994); Kendall Blanchard, *The Mississippi Choctaws at Play* (Urbana: University of Illinois Press, 1981); James Mooney, "The Cherokee Ball Play," *American Anthropologist,* 3:2 (1890): 105–32.

7. Morris Edward Opler, "The Jicarilla Apache Ceremonial Relay Race," *American Anthropologist*, 46:1 (January–March 1944): 75–97.

8. Karl Weule, "Ethnologie des Sports," in *Geschichte des Sports aller Völker und Zeiten*, ed. G. A. E. Bogeng, 2 vols. (Leipzig: E. A. Seemann, 1926), 1:8.

9. Arthur E. Grix, "Die Indianerläufer," in *Sportgeschichte aus erster Hand*, ed. Hilde Barisch (Würzburg: Arena Verlag, 1977), pp. 133–42.

10. Käthe Hye-Kerkdal, "Wettkampfspiel und Dualorganisation bei den Timbira Brailiens," *Die Wiener Schule der Völkerkunde Festschrift* (Vienna: Ferdinand Berger, 1956), pp. 504–33; Jürgen Dieckert and Jakob Mehringer, "Mit 147 Kilogram durch die Savanne," *Sportwissenschaft*, 21:1 (1991): 48–61; Jakob Mehringer and Jürgen Dieckert, "Running to Keep the World Going," *Journal of Comparative Physical Education and Sport*, 19:2 (1997): 85–95.

11. Leni Riefenstahl, *The Last of the Nuba* (New York: Harper & Row, 1973), pp. 130, 134.

12. Ibid., pp. 130, 132.

13. Ibid., pp. 133–34.

14. Leni Riefenstahl, *A Memoir* (New York: St. Martin's, 1992), p. 557; see also Rolf Husmann and Christoph Meier, "Nuba-Ringen in Khartum," in *Tradition, Migration, Notstand*, ed. Bernhard Streck (Göttingen: Edition Re, 1990), pp. 69–84.

15. Sigrid Paul, "The Wrestling Tradition and Its Social Functions," in *Sport in Africa*, ed. William J. Baker and J. A. Mangan (New York: Africana Publishing Co., 1987), pp. 23–46.

16. John Bale, *Imagined Olympians* (Minneapolis: University of Minnesota Press, 2002), p. xx (for quotation).

17. Allen Guttmann, *A Whole New Ball Game: An Interpretation of American Sports* (Chapel Hill: University of North Carolina Press, 1988), p. 22.

2. Before the Greeks

1. P. S. Vermaak, "The Contest Theme in the Seals from Mesopotamia," in *Actas del Congreso Internacional ISHPES*, ed. Roland Renson, Teresa González Aja, Gilbert Andrieu, Manfred Lämmer, and Roberta Park (Madrid: Instituto Nacional de Educación Física de Madrid, 1993), pp. 47–69; Vermaak, "Sulgi as Sportsman in the Sumerian Self-Laudatory Royal Hymns," *Nikephoros*, 6 (1993): 7–21; Robert Rollinger, "Aspekte des Sports im alten Sumer," *Nikephoros*, 7 (1994): 7–64.

2. Wolfgang Decker, *Sport und Spiel im alten Aegypten* (Munich: C. H. Beck, 1987), pp. 35–37.

3. Allen Guttmann, *Women's Sports* (New York: Columbia University Press, 1991), p. 11 and plate 1.

4. Decker, *Sport und Spiel*, pp. 27, 67, 175; Wolfgang Decker, *Quellentexte zu Sport und Körperkultur im Alten Aegypten* (Sankt Augustin: Hans Richarz, 1975), pp. 49–52.

5. Decker, *Quellentexte*, p. 60; Decker, *Sport und Spiel*, p. 65; Wolfgang Decker, "Der unbesiegbare Pharao," *Anno Journal*, 85 (1981): 44–48.

6. Decker, *Quellentexte,* p. 82; Scott T. Carroll, "Wrestling in Ancient Nubia," *JSH,* 15:2 (Summer 1988): 121–37.

7. E. Norman Gardiner, *Athletics of the Ancient World* (Oxford: Clarendon Press, 1930), p. 6.

8. Decker, *Sport und Spiel,* pp. 99–102.

9. Michael Herb, *Der Wettkampf in den Marschen* (Hildesheim: Weidmann, 2001).

10. Luigi Moretti, *Olympionikai: I Vincitori negli antichi Agoni Olimpici* (Rome: Accademia Nazionale dei Lincei, 1957); Ludwig Koenen, *Eine agonistische Inschrift aus Aegypten und frühptolemäische Königsfeste* (Meisenheim am Glan: Anton Hain, 1977); Decker, *Quellentexte,* pp. 96–97.

11. Gunter Gebauer and Hans Lenk, "Der erzählte Sport," in *Körper- und Einbildungskraft,* ed. Gunter Gebauer (Berlin: Dietrich Reimer, 1988), pp. 146–47.

12. Jaquetta Hawkes, *Dawn of the Gods* (New York: Random House, 1968), pp. 121–24; Hans Peter Dürr, *Sedna* (Frankfurt: Suhrkamp, 1984), pp. 175–84; Wolfgang Decker, "Zum Stand des 'Stierspiels' in der alten Welt," in *Altertumswissenschaften im Dialog,* ed. Reinhard Dittmann, Christian Eder, and Bruno Jacobs (Münster: Ugarit, 2003), pp. 31–79.

13. Thomas F. Scanlon, "Women, Bull Sports, Cults and Initiation in Minoan Crete," *Nikephoros,* 12 (1999): 50.

14. Arthur Evans, *The Palace of Minos,* 4 vols. (London: Macmillan, 1921–1935): 3:227; Wolfgang Decker, *Sport in der griechischen Antike* (Munich: C. H. Beck, 1995), pp. 26, 67; J. K. Anderson, *Hunting in the Ancient World* (Berkeley: University of California Press, 1985), p. 13. See also Colin Renfrew, "The Minoan–Mycenaean Origins of the Panhellenic Games," in *The Archaeology of the Olympics,* ed. Wendy J. Raschke (Madison: University of Wisconsin Press, 1988), pp. 14–25.

3. Greek Athletic Festivals

1. Bronislaw Bilinski, *L'Agonistica sportiva nella Grecia Antica* (Rome: Angelo Signorelli, 1961), p. 18; Allen Guttmann, *Sports Spectators* (New York: Columbia University Press, 1986), p. 14; see also Eugenio Polito, "Competizione e Vittoria," in *Nike: Il Gioco e la Vittoria,* ed. Adriano La Regina (Milan: Mondadori Electa, 2003), pp. 13–23.

2. Massimiliano Papini, "Ginnasio, Nudità atletica e posizione sociale degli Agonisti," in *Nike,* p. 50; see also H. W. Pleket, "Sport und Leibesübungen in der griechischen Welt des hellenistisch-römischen Zeitalters," in *GL,* ed. Horst Ueberhorst, 6 vols. (Berlin: Bartels & Wernitz, 1972–1989), 2: 282–86; Willy Zschietzschmann, *Wettkampf- und Uebungsstätten in Griechenland,* 2 vols. (Schorndorf: Karl Hofmann, 1960–1961): 2:14–15; Walter W. Hyde, *Olympic Victor Monuments and Greek Athletic Art* (Washington: Carnegie Institution, 1921).

3. Stephen V. Tracy, "The Panathenaic Festival and Games," *Nikephoros,* 4 (1991): 133–53; Massimiliano Papini, "Santuari e Giochi Panellenici," in *Nike,* 24–49; Allen Guttmann, *The Erotic in Sports* (New York: Columbia University Press,

1996), pp. 15–29; Thomas F. Scanlon, *Eros and Greek Athletics* (New York: Oxford University Press, 2001).

4. Nigel Crowther, "Visiting the Olympic Games in Ancient Greece," *IJHS*, 18:4 (December 2001): 37–52; Joachim Ebert, "Neues zum Hippodrom . . . ," *Nikephoros*, 2 (1989): 89–107.

5. Ludwig Deubner, *Kult und Spiel im alten Olympia* (Leipzig: Heinrich Keller, 1936), p. 5; Ulrich Popplow, *Leibesübungen und Leibeserziehung in der griechischen Antike* (Schorndorf: Karl Hofmann, 1959), p. 60; Michael B. Poliakoff, *Combat Sports in the Ancient World* (New Haven: Yale University Press, 1987), p. 149. See also Ludwig Drees, *Olympia,* trans. Gerald Onn (New York: Praeger, 1968); Christoph Ulf and Ingomar Weiler, "Der Ursprung der antiken Olympischen Spiele in der Forschung," *Stadion,* 6 (1980): 1–38.

6. M. I. Finley and H. W. Pleket, *The Olympic Games* (New York: Viking, 1976), p. 57; see also Manfred Lämmer, "Zum Verhalten von Zuschauern bei Wettkämpfen in der griechischen Antike," in *Sport zwischen Eigenständigkeit und Fremdbestimmung,* ed. Giselher Spitzer and Dieter Schmidt (Bonn: Institut für Sportwissenschaft und Sport, 1986), pp. 75–85.

7. Pausanias, *Description of Greece* [V, vi, 7], trans. W. H. S. Jones, 5 vols. (London: Heinemann, 1935), 2:411, 413. Pherenike is sometimes called Callipateira.

8. For the debate on origins, see Hugh M. Lee, "The 'First' Olympic Games of 776 B.C.," in *The Archaeology of the Olympics,* ed. Wendy J. Raschke (Madison: University of Wisconsin Press, 1988), pp. 110–18; John Mouratidis, "The 776 B.C. Date and Some Problems Connected with It," *CJHS,* 16:2 (December 1985): 1–14; Benny Peiser, "The Crime of Hippias," *Stadion,* 16:1 (1990): 37–65; Christian Wacker, "The Record of the Olympic Victory List," *Nikephoros,* 11 (1998): 39–50; Ronald Bilik, "Die Zuverlässigkeit der frühen Olympionikenliste," *Nikephoros,* 13 (2000): 47–62.

9. Wolfgang Decker believes the first contest may have been a chariot race; see *Sport in der griechischen Antike* (Munich: C. H. Beck, 1995), p. 67.

10. Popplow, *Leibesübungen und Leibeserziehung in der griechischen Antike,* p. 71.

11. Historians disagree about some of these dates; see Julius Jüthner, *Die athletischen Leibesübungen der Griechen,* 2 vols. (Vienna: Hermann Böhlaus Nachfolger, 1965): 2:73; Drees, *Olympia,* pp. 31–32.

12. Roberto Petrucco, *Lo Sport nella Grecia Antica* (Florence: Leo S. Olschki Editore, 1972), p. 217; Joachim Ebert, *Olympia* (Vienna: Edition Tusch, 1980), pp. 59–60 (for the pentathlon) and 57–59 (for the pankration).

13. Hans-Volkmar Herrmann, *Olympia* (Munich: Hirmer, 1972), p. 124; Joachim Ebert suggests a somewhat different conjectural, five-day sequence; see his *Olympia,* pp. 45–46.

14. H. W. Pleket, "Zur Soziologie des antiken Sports," *Mededelingen Nederlands Instituut te Rome,* 36 (1974): 60; Ebert, *Olympia,* p. 57; Bronislaw Bilinski, "Un pescivendolo olimpionico," *Nikephoros,* 3 (1990): 157–75; Carmine Catenacci, "Il Tiranno alle Colonne d'Eracle, l'agonistica e le tirannidi archaiche," *Nikephoros,* 5 (1992): 34; Decker, *Sport in der griechischen Antike,* pp. 135–36.

15. David C. Young, "First with the Most," *Nikephoros,* 9 (1996): 175–97. Finley and Pleket comment that "there was no way even to say in Greek 'to set a record' or 'to break a record'", in *Olympic Games,* p. 22. Julius Jüthner, listing discuses that weighed as little as 1.268 kg. and as much as 6.63 kg., illustrates the problem; see his *Die athletischen Leibesübungen der Griechen,* 2:239–41.

16. E. Norman Gardiner, *Athletics of the Ancient World* (Oxford: Clarendon Press, 1930), p. 52; Ulrich Sinn, "Ein bedeutsamer Befund bei den Ausgrabungen in Olympia," *Nikephoros,* 7 (1994): 313–14; Gerhard Lukas, *Die Körperkultur in frühen Epochen der Menschheitsentwicklung* (Berlin: Sportverlag, 1969), pp. 169–70; Karl Lennartz, *Kenntnisse und Vorstellungen von Olympia und den olympischen Spielen in der Zeit von 393–1896* (Schorndorf: Karl Hofmann, 1974), pp. 13–17.

17. Herrmann, *Olympia,* p. 14.

18. Gardiner, *Athletics of the Ancient World,* p. 103; H. A. Harris, *Greek Athletes and Athletics* (London: Hutchinson, 1964), p. 42; Ebert, *Olympia,* p. 71.

19. Sarah B. Pomeroy, *Spartan Women* (New York: Oxford University Press, 2002), p. 12; Xenophon, *The Constitution of the Spartans* [1.4], trans. H. G. Daykyns, in *The Greek Historians,* ed. F. R. B. Godolphin, 2 vols. (New York: Random House, 1942), 2:658–59; Plutarch, *Lives of Illustrious Men* [Lycurgus 14.2–3], trans. John Dryden et al., 3 vols. (Chicago: Bedford, Clarke, n.d.), 1:79–80. I have modernized the translation.

20. Giampiera Arrigoni, "Donne e Sport nel Mundo Greco," in *Le Donne in Grecia,* ed. Giampiera Arrigoni (Bari: Editori Laterza,1985), pp. 65–95; Thomas Scanlon, "Virgineum Gymnasium," in *Archaeology of the Olympics,* p. 201.

21. Anne Ley, "Atalante—Von der Athletin zur Liebhaberin," *Nikephoros,* 3 (1990): 31–72.

22. Thomas F. Scanlon, "Race or Chase at the Arkteia of Attica?" *Nikephoros,* 3 (1990): 74; see also Lilly Kahil, "L'Artémis de Brauron," *Antike Kunst,* 20 (1977): 86–98; Paula Perlman, "Plato *Laws* 833C-834D and the Bears of Brauron," *Greek, Roman and Byzantine Studies,* 24 (1983): 115–30; Hans Langenfeld, "Griechische Athletinnen in der römischen Kaiserzeit," in *The History, the Evolution and Diffusion of Sports and Games in Different Cultures,* ed. Roland Renson, Pierre Paul De Nayer, and Michel Ostyn (Brussels: Bestuur voor de Lichamelijke Opvoeding, de Sport en het Openluchtleven, 1976), pp. 116–25; Arrigoni, "Donne e Sport nel Mundo Greco," in *Le Donne in Grecia,* pp. 95–101; Hugh M. Lee, "Sig3 802," *Nikephoros,* 1:1 (1988): 103–17.

23. Pausanias, *Description of Greece* [V, xvi, 1–4], 2:473.

24. Erwin Mehl, "Mutterrechtliche Reste in der olympischen Festordnung," in *Carl Diem,* ed. Werber Körbs, Heinz Mies, and Klemens C. Wildt (Frankfurt: Wilhelm Limpert, 1962), p. 76.

25. Manfred Lämmer, "Eine Propaganda–Aktion des Königs Herodes in Olympia," *Kölner Beiträge zur Sportwissenschaft,* 1 (1972): 160–73; Lämmer, "Griechische Wettkämpfe in Jerusalem. . . ," *Kölner Beiträge zur Sportwissenschaft,* 2 (1974): 182–227; H. A. Harris, *Greek Athletics and the Jews* (Cardiff: University of Wales Press, 1976).

4. Roman Sports

1. Jean-Paul Thuillier, *Les Jeux athlétiques dans la civilisation étrusque* (Rome: École française de Rome, 1985), pp. 51–79.

2. Ibid., pp. 460, 491.

3. Ibid., 339–40; see also Walter Burkert, *Homo Necans,* trans. Peter Bing (Berkeley: University of California Press, 1983).

4. Thuillier, *Les Jeux athlétiques dans la civilisation étrusque,* pp. 246; see also Jean-Paul Thuillier, "Les réprésentations sportives dans l'oeuvre du peintre de Micali," *Spectacles sportifs et scéniques dans le monde étrusco-italique* (Rome: École française de Rome, 1993), pp. 32–43; Francesca Boitani, "Lo Sport in Etruria," in *La Sport nell'Italia Antica,* ed. Anna Maria Moretti (Rome: Ingegneria per la Cultura, 2003), pp. 6–21.

5. Jacques Heurgon, *Daily Life of the Etruscans,* trans. James Kirkup (London: Weidenfeld & Nicolson, 1964), p. 206; Thuillier, *Les Jeux athlétiques dans la civilisation étrusque,* pp. 617–19, 622–23.

6. Athenaeus, *The Deipnosophists* [12.517d], trans. Charles Burton Gulick, 7 vols. (London: Heinemann, 1927–1941), 5:329.

7. Georges Ville, *La Gladiature en Occident des origines à la mort de Domitien* (Rome: École française de Rome, 1981), pp. 2–8; Thuillier, *Les Jeux athlétiques dans la civilisation étrusque,* pp. 338–40; John Mouratidis, "On the Origin of the Gladiatorial Games," *Nikephoros,* 9 (1996): 111–34; Jean-René Jannot, "Phersu, Phersuna, Persona," in *Spectacles sportifs et scéniques dans le monde étrusco-italique,"* p. 290.

8. Horace, *The Satires and Epistles,* trans. Smith Palmer Bovie (Chicago: University of Chicago Press, 1959), p. 104.

9. H. A. Harris, *Sport in Greece and Rome* (Ithaca: Cornell University Press, 1972), p. 80. On Roman ball games, see also Peter McIntosh, "Physical Education and Recreation in Imperial Rome," in *Landmarks in the History of Physical Education,* ed. Peter McIntosh, 3rd ed. (London: Routledge & Kegan Paul, 1981), pp. 48–49; Siegfried Mendner, *Das Ballspiel im Leben der Völker* (Münster: Aschendorff, 1956), pp. 91–93.

10. Frank Bernstein, *Ludi Publici* (Stuttgart: Franz Steiner, 1998), pp. 51–78; Augusta Hönle and Anton Henze, *Römische Amphitheater und Stadien* (Zurich: Atlantis, 1981), pp. 85–88; see also Richard C. Beacham, *Spectacle Entertainments of Early Imperial Rome* (New Haven: Yale University Press, 1999), pp. 1–44.

11. J. P. V. D. Balsdon, *Life and Leisure in Ancient Rome* (London: Bodley Head, 1969), p. 247; Bernstein, *Ludi Publici,* pp. 335–39.

12. Ludwig Friedländer, *Roman Life and Manners under the Early Empire,* trans. J. H. Freese and Leonard A. Magnus, 4 vols. (London: George Routledge & Sons, 1908–1913), 2:11–12; Hönle and Henze, *Römische Amphitheater und Stadien,* p. 86.

13. Friedländer, *Roman Life and Manners,* 2:11–12.

14. Barbara Rieger, "Die Capitolia des Kaisers Domitian," *Nikephoros,* 12 (1999): 171–203.

15. Beacham, *Spectacle Entertainments,* pp. 245–49. For a kinder view of Nero as an athlete, see John Mouratidis, "Nero," *JSH,* 12:1 (Spring 1985): 5–20.

16. Balsdon, *Life and Leisure,* p. 291; Patrizia Sabbatini Tumolesi, *Gladiatorum Paria: Annunci di Spettacoli Gladiatorii a Pompei* (Rome: Edizioni di Storia e Letteratura, 1980), 147–49; Dio Cassius, *Roman History,* trans. Earnest Cary and H. B. Foster, 9 vols. (New York: Macmillan, 1914–1927), 9:93–115 [on Commodus].

17. Roland Auguet, *Cruelty and Civilization* (London: Allen & Unwin, 1972), p. 95.

18. Carlin A. Barton, *The Sorrows of the Ancient Romans* (Princeton: Princeton University Press, 1993), pp. 12, 47–49, 65–66, 79–81; Michael Grant, *Gladiators* (London: Weidenfeld & Nicolson, 1967), p. 96; Juvenal, *Satires,* trans. Rolfe Humphries (Bloomington: Indiana University Press, 1958), p. 67.

19. Keith Hopkins, *Death and Renewal* (Cambridge: Cambridge University Press, 1983), p. 24; however, Balsdon (*Life and Leisure,* p. 302) is skeptical about manumission after a fixed number of years.

20. Auguet, *Cruelty and Civilization,* pp. 19–21; Thomas Weidemann, "Das Ende der römischen Gladiatorenspiele," *Nikephoros,* 8 (1995): 159.

21. Beacham, *Spectacle Entertainments,* p. 44.

22. Ville, *La Gladiature en Occident,* pp. 129–73; Balsdon, *Life and Leisure,* pp. 307–8.

23. Friedländer, *Roman Life and Manners,* 2:62; George Jennison, *Animals for Show and Pleasure in Ancient Rome* (Manchester: University of Manchester Press, 1937), pp. 47, 73; Ville, *La Gladiature en Occident,* p. 52.

24. Auguet, *Cruelty and Civilization,* p. 73; Hönle and Henze, *Römische Amphitheater und Stadien,* pp. 20–27.

25. Donald Kyle, *Spectacles of Death in Ancient Rome* (London: Routledge, 1998); the quotation is from p. 250.

26. Hönle and Henze, *Römische Amphitheater und Stadien,* pp. 48, 55–59; see also Alex Scobie, "Spectator Security and Comfort at Gladiatorial Games," *Nikephoros,* 1:1 (1988): 191–243.

27. Suetonius, *The Lives of the Caesars* [Aug. 44–45], trans. J. C. Rolfe, 2 vols. (Cambridge, Mass.: Harvard University Press, 1979), 1:195, 197; Balsdon, *Life and Leisure,* pp. 259–60; Traugott Bollinger, *Theatralis Licentia* (Winterthur: Hans Schellenberg, 1969), pp. 6, 19; Alan Cameron, *Circus Factions* (Oxford: Clarendon Press, 1976), pp. 176–77.

28. Seneca, *Ad Lucilium Epistulae Morales,* trans. Richard. M. Gummere, 3 vols. (London: Heinemann, 1917–25), 1:30–31; Cicero, cited by Hönle and Heinze, *Römische Amphitheater und Stadien,* p. 20; Ovid, *The Art of Love,* trans. Rolfe Humphries (Bloomington: Indiana University Press, 1957), pp. 164; Tertullian, *De Spectaculis,* trans. T. R. Glover (London: Heinemann, 1931), pp. 271–73.

29. Georges Ville, "Les Jeux des gladiateurs dans l'Empire chrétien," *Mélanges d'archéologie et d'histoire de l'école française de Rome,* 72 (1960), pp. 288–89; Michael B. Hornum, *Nemesis* (Leiden: E. J. Brill, 1993); Werner Weismann, *Kirche und Schauspiele* (Würzburg: Augustinus, 1972), pp. 57–58; Novatian, *De Spectaculis,* ed. G. F. Diercks (Turnholt: Brepols, 1972), p. 171.

30. Augustine, *Confessions,* trans. E. B. Pusey (London: J. M. Dent, 1907), pp. 106–7; Georges Ville, "Les Jeux des gladiateurs dans l'Empire chrétien," pp. 326–31.

31. John H. Humphrey, *Roman Circuses* (London: B. T. Batsford, 1986), p. 126; Harris, *Sport in Greece and Rome,* p. 198.

32. The eggs were raised and lowered; the dolphins swiveled; see Humphrey, *Roman Circuses,* pp. 260–65.

33. Ibid., pp. 132–74; Harris, *Sport in Greece and Rome,* pp. 198–99.

34. Friedländer, *Roman Life and Manners,* 2:26.

35. Humphrey, *Roman Circuses,* pp. 91–95; Hönle and Henze, *Römische Amphitheater und Stadien,* p. 184.

36. Gerhard Horsmann, *Die Wagonlenker der römischen Kaiserzeit* (Stuttgart: Franz Steiner, 1998), pp. 19–25, 153–54, 194–98; see also Friedländer, *Roman Life and Manners,* 2:22–23; Wolfgang Decker, "*Furor circensis,*" *Journal of Roman Archeology,* 14 (2001): 499–511.

37. Alan Cameron, *Porphyrius the Charioteer* (Oxford: Clarendon Press, 1973), p. 150.

38. Cameron, *Circus Factions,* p. 231.

39. Ovid, *Art of Love,* p. 69; Juvenal, *Satires,* p. 35; Balsdon, *Life and Leisure,* p. 253.

40. Bollinger, *Theatralis Licentia,* p. 71; C. R. Whittaker, "The Revolt of Papirius Dionysius A.D. 190," *Historia,* 12 (1964): 348–69.

41. Sotiris G. Giatsis, "The Massacre in the Riot of Nika . . . ," *IJHS,* 12:3 (December 1995): 141–52.

42. Cameron, *Circus Factions,* pp. 20, 284, 311, 101 (in the order of quotation).

43. Ammianus, quoted in Harris, *Sport in Greece and Rome,* pp. 221–22; Balsdon, *Life and Leisure,* p. 314; Pliny, *Letters,* trans. Betty Radice (Harmondsworth, U.K.: Penguin, 1963), p. 236.

44. Suetonius, *The Lives of the Caesars* [Dom. 4.1], 2:347; Statius, *The Silvae* [I, 6], trans. D. A. Slater (Oxford: Clarendon Press, 1908), pp. 73–74; Ville, *La Gladiature en Occident,* pp. 263–64; T. T. Duke, "Women and Pygmies in the Roman Arena," *Classical Journal,* 50 (1955), 223–24; the stele is illustrated in Louis Robert, *Les Gladiateurs dans l'Orient Grec,* 2nd ed. (Amsterdam: Hakkert, 1971), pp. 301–2; Petronius, *Satyricon* [xlv.7], trans. William Arrowsmith (Ann Arbor: University of Michigan Press, 1959), p. 43; Juvenal, *Satires* [6.268–82], p. 18.

45. Hugh Lee, "Athletics and the Bikini Girls from Piazza Armerina," *Stadion,* 10 (1984): 45–76; Martin Dolch, "Wettkampf, Wasserrevue oder diätische Übungen?" *Nikephoros,* 5 (1992): 553–81.

5. Traditional Asian Sports

1. Michael Kolb, "Taijiquan (T'ai Chi Chuan) und die chinesische Kultur," *Sport Bewegung Kultur,* ed. Edgar Beckers and Hans Georg Schulz (Bielefeld: Mane Huchler, n.d.), 128–55.

2. Confucius, quoted by Mike Speak, "Recreation and Sport in Ancient China," in *SPEC,* ed. James Riordan and Robin Jones (London: E & FN Spon, 1999), p. 28;

see also Fan Hong, *Footbinding, Feminism and Freedom* (London: Frank Cass, 1997), pp. 21–22.

3. Speak, "Recreation and Sport in Ancient China," in *SPEC*, p. 28.

4. Mike Speak, "The Emergence of Modern Sport," in ibid., p. 49.

5. Li Yu, quoted in Speak, "Recreation and Sport in Ancient China," in ibid., p. 33.

6. Silvia Freiin Ebner von Eschenbach, "Das Spiel in der chinesichen Literatur," *Nikephoros*, 9 (1996): 11; Hans Ulrich Vogel, "Homo ludens sinensis," in *Über Fußball*, ed. Werner Schlicht and Werner Lang (Schorndorf: Karl Hofmann, 2000), pp. 7–41 (quotation, p. 25).

7. *Chūgoku kodai no supōtsu* (Tokyo: Baseball Magazine Co., 1985), pp. 153–60.

8. Speak, "Recreation and Sport in Ancient China," in *SPEC*, pp. 33, 48.

9. Speak, "The Emergence of Modern Sport," in ibid., p. 54.

10. Ibid., p. 64.

11. Carl Diem, *Asiatische Reiterspiele* (Berlin: Deutscher Archiv-Verlag, 1942), p. 143. Unless otherwise indicated, information on Chinese polo is taken from Diem (pp. 138–64) and James T. C. Liu, "Polo and Cultural Change," *Harvard Journal of Asiatic Studies*, 45:1 (June 1985): 203–24. The quoted phrase is from Liu (p. 214).

12. Li Guo and Wang Jian, quoted in Diem, *Asiatische Reiterspiele*, pp. 145–46. The photographs appear on pp. 147–51.

13. Ibid., p. 160; Liu, "Polo and Cultural Change," pp. 215, 219.

14. Diem, *Asiatische Reiterspiele*, pp. 152–56.

15. Herbert A. Giles, "Football and Polo in China," *The Nineteenth Century*, 59 (March 1906): 511–12.

16. Liu, "Polo and Cultural Change," pp. 208, 218, 222.

17. This and the next four paragraphs are drawn from Allen Guttmann, "Sports— India," in *Encyclopedia of Modern Asia,* ed. David Levinson and Karen Christensen, 6 vols. (New York: Scribner, 2002), 5:304–5.

18. Abu l-Fazl Allami, *The Ain-i Akbari,* trans. H. Blochmann (Delhi, New Taj Office, 1989), pp. 309–10.

19. Diem, *Asiatische Reiterspiele,* pp. 212, 218–19; Norah M. Titley, *Sports and Pastimes* (London: The British Library, 1979), p. 5.

20. Jörg Möller, *Spiel und Sport am japanischen Kaiserhof* (Munich: Iudicium, 1993), pp. 34–41.

21. Patricia Cuyler, *Sumo* (Tokyo: Weatherhill, 1985), pp. 28–30, 90–92.

22. Lawrence Bickford, *Sumo and the Woodblock Print Masters* (Tokyo: Kodansha International, 1994).

23. Cuyler, *Sumo,* p. 81.

24. Watanabe Tōru, "Kemari no tenkai ni tsuite no ichikôsatsu," *Taiikugaku kiyô,* 3 (1966): 13–22; Watanabe Tōru and Kuwayama Kōnen, *Kemari no kenkyū* (Tokyo: University of Tokyo Press, 1994), pp. 5–25.

25. Möller, *Spiel und Sport,* p. 41; Koyama Takashige, "Nihon kyōdō gairon," in *Gendai kyūdō kōza,* ed. Uno Yōzaburô (Tokyo: Yūzankaku, 1970), pp. 11–12; G. Cameron Hurst III, *Armed Martial Arts of Japan* (New Haven: Yale University Press, 1998), pp. 103–5.

26. Hurst, *Armed Martial Arts*, p. 110; Möller, *Spiel und Sport*, p. 10.

27. Hurst, *Armed Martial Arts*, pp. 41–45.

28. Ibid., pp. 116; Imamura Hiroyuki, *Nihon taiiku shi* (Tokyo: Fumaidô, 1970), p. 89.

29. Hurst, *Armed Martial Arts*, pp. 123–27, 174–75; see also Allen Guttmann and Lee Thompson, *Japanese Sports* (Honolulu: University of Hawaii Press, 2001), pp. 53–54.

30. Guttmann and Thompson, *Japanese Sports*, pp. 56–64.

31. Musashi Miyamoto, *A Book of Five Rings*, trans. Victor Harris (Woodstock, N.Y.: Overlook Press, 1974), pp. 46, 95.

32. Hurst, *Armed Martial Arts*, pp. 83–87 (quotation, p. 83); see also Imamura, *Nihon taiiku shi*, p. 161.

33. Hurst, *Armed Martial Arts*, p. 73.

34. Ibid., p. 80.

35. Ibid., p. 98.

36. Joachim Heim, "Bogenwerk und Bogensport bei den Osmanen," *Der Islam*, 14 (1925): 289–360; Paul E. Klopsteg, *Turkish Archery and the Composite Bow* (Evanston, Ill.: P. Klopsteg, 1934), pp. 72–79.

37. *The Book of Dede Korkut*, trans. Geoffrey Lewis (London: Penguin Books, 1974), p. 64.

38. Reza Arasteh, "The Social Role of the *Zurkhana* . . . ," *Der Islam*, 36 (February 1961): 256–59; Hans-Peter Laqueur, *Zur kulturgeschichtlichen Stellung des Türkischen Ringkampfs einst und jetzt* (Frankfurt: Peter Lang, 1979), p. 10; Philippe Rochard, "The Identities of the Iranian *Zûrkhânah*," *Iranian Studies*, 35:4 (Fall 2002): 313–40.

39. Marius Canard, "La Lutte chez les Arabes," in *Cinquantenaire de la Faculté des Lettres d'Alger* (Algiers: n.p., 1932), p. 183.

40. G. Whitney Azoy, *Buzkashi* (Philadelphia: University of Pennsylvania Press, 1982).

41. Kai Kâ'ûs ibn Iskandar, *A Mirror for Princes: The Qâbû Nâma*, trans. Reuben Levy (London: Cresset Press, 1951), p. 86; Richard N. Frye, *Bukhara* (Norman: University of Oklahoma Press, 1965), p. 88.

42. Annemarie Schimmel, *A Two-Colored Brocade*, (Chapel Hill: University of North Carolina Press, 1992), p. 286.

43. Hafiz (Shams al-Din Muhammad Shirazi), quoted by Diem, *Asiatische Reiterspiele*, p. 188.

44. Paul Horn, "Roß und Reiter im Sahnâme," *Zeitschrift der Deutschen Morgenländischen Gesellschaft*, 51:4 (1907): 837–49; Nejim M. Sehrewerdi, "Al-Kura Wal-Sawlajan," in *The History, the Evolution and Diffusion of Sports and Games in Different Cultures*, ed. Roland Renson, Pierre Paul De Nayer, and Michel Ostyn (Brussels: Bestuur voor de Lichamelijke Opvoeding, de Sport en het Openluchtleven, 1976), pp. 18–29; Schimmel, *Two-Colored Brocade*, pp. 284–85.

45. Norah M. Titley, *Persian Miniature Painting* (Austin: University of Texas Press, 1983), p. 97 (Pl. 13).

46. Diem, *Asiatische Reiterspiele*, pp. 173–74, 178.

6. European Sports from the Middle Ages to the Renaissance

1. Jean J. Jusserand, *Les Sports et jeux d'exercice dans l'ancienne France* (Paris: Plon, 1901), pp. 18, 87; Paul Meyer, ed., *L'Histoire de Guillaume le Maréchal,* 3 vols. (Paris: Renouard, 1891–1901), 3:374; Richard Barber, *The Knight and Chivalry* (Ipswich: Boydell Press, 1974), pp. 189, 193; Noel Denholm-Young, "The Tournament in the Thirteenth Century," in *Studies in Medieval History,* ed. R. W. Hunt, W. A. Pantin, and R. W. Southern (Oxford: Clarendon Press, 1948), pp. 262, 238; Maurice Keen, *Chivalry* (New Haven: Yale University Press, 1984), pp. 85–87.

2. *Statuta,* quoted in Francis Henry Cripps-Day, *History of the Tournament in England and France* (London: Bernard Quaritch, 1918), Appendix 3, p. xxv; Thomas Zotz, "Adel, Bürgertum und Turnier in deutschen Städten vom 13. bis 15. Jahrhundert," in *Das ritterliche Turnier im Mittelalter,* ed. Josef Fleckenstein (Göttingen: Vandenhoek & Ruprecht, 1985), pp. 473–74; Klemens C. Wildt, *Leibesübungen im deutschen Mittelalter* (Frankfurt: Wilhelm Limpert, 1957), p. 28; Walter Schaufelberger, *Der Wettkampf in der alten Eidgenossenschaft* (Bern: Paul Haupt, 1972), p. 46; see also Denholm-Young, "The Tournament," in *Studies in Medieval History,* pp. 257–62.

3. Sabine Krüger, "Das kirchliche Turnierverbot im Mittelalter," in *Das ritterliche Turnier im Mittelalter,* pp. 401–22; Juliet R. V. Barker, *The Tournament in England* (Woodbridge, Suffolk: Boydell Press, 1986), p. 83; Thomas Szabó, "Das Turnier in Italien," in *Das ritterliche Turnier im Mittelalter,* pp. 344–70; Barber, *The Knight and Chivalry,* p. 191.

4. Cripps-Day, *History of the Tournament in England and France,* p. 29; Sidney Painter, *William Marshal* (Baltimore: Johns Hopkins University Press, 1933), p. 38.

5. Arthur B. Ferguson, *The Indian Summer of English Chivalry* (Durham: Duke University Press, 1960), p. 14; see also Jusserand, *Les Sports et jeux d'exercice,* p. 73; Sydney Anglo, *The Great Tournament Roll of Westminster,* 2 vols. (Oxford: Clarendon Press, 1968), 1:19–40; and his *Spectacle, Pageantry, and Early Tudor Policy* (Oxford: Clarendon Press, 1969); Maurice Keen, "Huizinga, Kilgour and the Decline of Chivalry," *Medievalia et Humanistica,* new series, 8 (1977): 1–20.

6. Joachim K. Rühl, "Wesen und Bedeutung von Kampfansagen und Trefferzahlskizzen . . . ," in *Sport zwischen Eigenständigkeit und Fremdbestimmung,* ed. Giselher Spitzer and Dieter Schmidt (Bonn: Institut für Sportwissenschaft und Sport, 1986), pp. 86–112; and Rühl, "Measurement of Individual Sport-Performance in Jousting Combats," in *Actas del Congreso Internacional ISHPES,* ed. Roland Renson, Teresa González Aja, Gilbert Andrieu, Manfred Lämmer, and Roberta Park (Madrid: Instituto Nacional de Educación Física de Madrid, 1993), pp. 226–38.

7. Jean Froissart, *Chronicles,* trans. John Bourchier, 4 vols. (London: J. Davis, 1814–16), 4:51–60; Anglo, *Great Tournament Roll,* 1: 28; Jean Verdon, *Les Loisirs en France au moyen age* (Paris: Jules Tallandier, 1980), p. 179.

8. John Hutton to Lord Lisle, March 5, 1538, *The Lisle Letters,* ed. Muriel St. Clare Byrne, 6 vols. (Chicago: University of Chicago Press, 1981), 5:46.

9. At a time when a warship cost £260, the tournament cost nearly £4,400; see Anglo, *Great Tournament Roll,* p. 16 n. 2. Anglo's second volume is a facsimile of the entire roll.

10. Philippe, quoted in Philippe Contamine, "Les Tournois en France à la fin du moyen âge," in *Das ritterliche Turnier im Mittelalter,* p. 432; Martin Hahn, *Die Leibesübungen im mittelalterlichen Volksleben* (Langensalza: Hermann Beyer und Sohn, 1929), pp. 56, 58; Martin Vogt, "Der Sport im Mittelalter," in *Geschichte des Sports aller Völker und Zeiten,* ed. G. A. E. Bogeng, 2 vols. (Leipzig: E. A. Seemann, 1926), 1:172; Joachim K. Rühl, "German Tournament Regulations of the 15th Century," *JSH,* 17:2 (Summer 1990): 163–82.

11. Lilian M. C. Randall, *Images in the Margins of Gothic Manuscripts* (Berkeley: University of California Press, 1966), figs. 706, 708–10, 719; Werner Körbs, *Vom Sinn der Leibesübungen zur Zeit der italienischen Renaissance* (Gräfenhainchen: Schultze, 1938), pp. 23, 62.

12. Roy Strong, *Splendor at Court* (Boston: Houghton Mifflin, 1973).

13. Alan Young, *Tudor and Jacobean Tournaments* (Dobbs Ferry, N.Y.: Sheridan House, 1987), p. 74; R. Coltman Clephan, *The Tournament* (London: Methuen, 1919), pp. 76–78; Jusserand, *Les Sports et jeux d'exercice,* pp. 149–54; on the death of Henri, see also John McClelland, "Le Tournoi de juin 1559 et les deux François de Guise," in *Le Mécénat et l'influence des Guises,* ed. Yvonne Bellenger (Paris: Honoré Champion, 1997), pp. 177–85.

14. Kenneth Grant Tremayne Webster, "The Twelfth-Century Tourney," *Anniversary Papers* (Boston: Ginn, 1913), p. 230; Larry D. Benson, "The Tournament in the Romances of Chrétien de Troyes & [*sic*] *L'Histoire de Guillaume Le Maréchal,*" *Chivalric Literature,* ed. Larry D. Benson and John Leyerle (Kalamazoo: Western Michigan University Press, 1980), pp. 1–24; des Champs, quoted in Jusserand, *Les Sports et jeux d'exercice,* p. 141.

15. Josef Fleckenstein, "Das Turnier als höfisches Fest im hochmittelalterlichen Deutschland," in *Das ritterliche Turnier im Mittelalter,* p. 246; Keen, *Chivalry,* p. 91; Louisa Olga Fradenburg, *City, Marriage, Tournament* (Madison: University of Wisconsin Press, 1991), pp. 212, 223; Werner Rösener, "Ritterliche Wirtschaftsverhältnisse und Turnier im sozialen Wandel des Hochmittelalters," in *Das ritterliche Turnier im Mittelalter,* p. 333.

16. Angela Teja, "Les Fêtes du Carnaval Romain dans le Moyen Age et la Renaissance," in *Proceedings of the XIIth HISPA Congress,* ed. Manfred Lämmer, Roland Renson, and James Riordan (Sankt Augustin: Academia Verlag, 1989), pp. 63–72; Michael Hörrmann, "Ringrennen am Stuttgarter Hof," *SZGS,* 3:1 (1989): 50–69; Georges Vigarello, "De la Force à la prestance," in *La Naissance du mouvement sportif associatif en France,* ed. Pierre Arnaud and J. Camy (Lyon: Presses universitaires de Lyon, 1986), pp. 29–46.

17. Silver, quoted in Christina Hole, *English Sports and Pastimes* (London: B. T. Batsford, 1949), p. 68.

18. Henning Eichberg, *Leistung, Spannung, Geschwindigkeit* (Stuttgart: Klett-Cotta, 1978), p. 66.

19. Peter Kühnst, *Sport,* trans. Allen Guttmann (Dresden: Verlag der Kunst, 1996), p. 63, pl. 65.

20. For Gaston III and John I, see John Cummins, *The Hound and the Hawk* (New York: St. Martin's Press, 1988), pp. 1–2; Law of 1390, quoted by Roger Longrigg, *The English Squire and His Sport* (New York: St. Martin's Press, 1977), pp. 26–27; see also P. B. Munsche, *Gentleman and Poachers* (Cambridge: Cambridge University Press, 1981); Richard Thomas, "Hunting," in *The Politics of Sport,* ed. Lincoln Allison (Manchester: University of Manchester Press, 1986), p. 179.

21. Don Morrow, "Sport as a Metaphor," *Aethlon,* 5:2 (Spring 1988): 122; Longrigg, *The English Squire and His Sport,* p. 46.

22. Léon Gautier, *La Chevalerie,* ed. Jacques Levron (Paris: Arthaud, 1959), p. 170; Joseph Strutt, *The Sports and Pastimes of the People of England,* 3rd ed. (London: Thomas Tegg, 1838), p. 13.

23. Randall, *Images in the Margins of Gothic Manuscripts,* figs. 714, 716; Jean Longnon, ed., *The Très Riches Heurs of Jean, Duke of Berry,* trans. Victoria Benedict (New York: George Braziller, 1969), pl. 9.

24. Annick Davisse, Léo Lorenzi, and Jane Renoux, *Olympie* (Paris: La Courtille, 1980), p. 27.

25. Marcia Vale, *The Gentleman's Recreations* (Cambridge: D. S. Brewer, 1977), p. 28, fig. 5; White, quoted in Kathleen McCrone, *Playing the Game* (Lexington: University Press of Kentucky, 1988), p. 3; Dudley, quoted in Elizabeth Burton, *The Elizabethans at Home* (London: Secker & Warburg, 1958), p. 190.

26. Strictly speaking, animal "sports" are not really sports (as I have defined the term), but they were definitely included in older usage, to which I briefly defer here.

27. Thomas Platter, *Beschreibung der Reisen durch Frankreich, Spanien, England und die Niederlande, 1595–1600,* ed. Rut Keiser, 2 vols. (Basel: Schwabe, 1968), pp. 793–95; Strutt, quoted in Henry Alken, *The National Sports of Great Britain* (London: Methuen, 1903), no pagination; John Nichols, *The Progresses and Public Processions of Queen Elizabeth,* 3 vols. (London: John Nichols & Son, 1823), 1:438 n. 2; C. L. Kingsford, "Paris Garden and the Bear-Baiting," *Archaelogia,* 70 (1920): 168. Kingsford indicates that Sundays were the day of closure for London's theaters.

28. England's first guild was not formed until 1538; see Theo Reintges, *Ursprung und Wesen der spätmittelalterlichen Schützengilden* (Bonn: Ludwig, Röhrscheid, 1963), pp. 54, 65, 68. Much later, after the founding of the Toxophilite Society (1781), sport archery became a vogue among the aristocracy; see E. G. Heath, *A History of Target Archery* (Newton Abbot, U.K.: David & Charles, 1973).

29. Reintges, *Ursprung und Wesen,* p. 287; L. A. Delaunay, *Étude sur les anciènnes compagnies d'archers, d'arbalétriers et d'arquebusiers* (Paris: Champion, 1879), pp. 19–20.

30. Roland Renson, "Leibesübungen der Bürger und Bauern im Mittelalter," in *GL,*

ed. Horst Ueberhorst, 6 vols. (Berlin: Bartels & Wernitz, 1972–1989), 3:105–11; Hermann Goja, *Die österreichischen Schützengilden und ihre Feste* (Vienna: Verlag Notring der wissenschaftlichen Verbände Oesterreichs, 1963), pp. 123–24.

31. Reintges, *Ursprung und Wesen,* p. 287; Arnold Wehrle, *500 Jahre Spiel und Sport in Zürich* (Zurich: Berichthaus, 1960), p. 7; Kusudo Kazuhiko, *Doitsu Chūsekōki no Supôtsu* (Tokyo: Fumaidô, 1998), pp. 245–322; Klaus Zieschang, *Vom Schützenfest zum Turnfest* (Ahrensburg: Czwalina, 1977), pp. 80–82; Erik De Vroede, "Het Spel van Trou-Madame," *Nieuwsbrief van de Vlaamse Volkssport Centrale,* 8:2 (1988): 20–23.

32. Goja, *Schützengilden,* pp. 45–84; Wehrle, *500 Jahre Spiel und Sport in Zürich,* p. 17.

33. Delaunay, *Étude sur les anciènnes compagnies d'archers, d'arbalétriers et d'arquebusiers,* p. 247; Erik De Vroede, "Popinjay Shooting in Flanders," *Spiele der Welt im Spannungsfeld von Tradition und Moderne,* ed. Gertrud Pfister, Toni Niewerth, and Gerd Steins, 2 vols. (Sankt Augustin: Academia Verlag, 1996): 1:157–63; Joseph Casier, *Chef-Confrérie Royale et Chevalière de St. Michel* (Ghent: Venderporten, 1921), p. 46; Maurits Sacre and Aime de Cort, *Volkspelen en Volksvermaken in Vlaamsch Belgie* (Merchtem, Belgium: Sacre-De Buyst, 1925), p. 116; Josee Moulin–Coppens, *De Geschiedenis van het Oud Sint-Jorisguilde Te Gent* (Ghent: Hoste Staelens, 1982, pp. 173–74; Eugeen Van Autenboer, "De Vrouw in de Gilde" (unpublished paper, Leuven, 1985), pp. 12, 15.

34. Hans Germann, *Der Ehrenspiegel deutscher Schützen* (Leipzig: Thankmar Rudolph, 1928), p. 59; Kusudo, *Doitsu Chûsekôki no Supôtsu,* pp. 248–49.

35. Kusudo, *Doitsu Chûsekôki,* pp. 303–5.

36. Thomas Schnitzler, "Die Kölner Schützenfeste des 15. und 16. Jahrhunderts," *Jahrbuch des kölnischen Geschichtsvereins,* 63 (1992): 137; see also Michael Hörrmann, "Leibesübungen in der höfischen Gesellschaft," *Sportwissenschaft,* 19:1 (1989): 36–51; Thomas Schnitzler, "Zur Leistungsquantifizierung im spätmittelalterlichen Schützenwesen," *Brennpunkt der Sportwissenschaft,* 4:2 (1990): 243–56.

37. Germann, *Der Ehrenspiegel deutscher Schützen,* pp. 87–101; Fritz Pieth, *Sport in der Schweiz* (Olten: Walter Verlag, 1979), p. 109; Anne Braun, *Historische Zielscheiben* (Leipzig: Edition Leipzig, 1981), pp. 109–10.

38. Robert W. Henderson, *Ball, Bat and Bishop* (New York: Rockport Press, 1947), pp. 47–48; Jean-Michel Mehl, "Le Jeu de Paume," *Sport/Histoire,* 1 (1988): 19–30; and his *Les Jeux au royaume de France* (Paris: Fayard, 1990), pp. 31–48.

39. Thierry Depaulis, "Héroard et les jeux 'oisifs' du petit Louis XIII," in *Jeux, sports et divertissements au moyen âge et à l'âge classique,* ed. Jean-Michel Mehl (Paris: Éditions du Comité des Travaux Historiques et Scientifiques, 1993), p. 113; Siegfried Mendner, *Das Ballspiel im Leben der Völker* (Münster: Aschendorff, 1956), p. 73; Jean Le Floc'hmoan, *La Genèse des sports* (Paris: Payot, 1962), pp. 46–48.

40. John Twigg, "Student Sports . . . ," *IJHS,* 13:2 (August 1996): 83; Robert Ashton, "Popular Entertainment and Social Control in Later Elizabethan and Early Stuart London," *London Journal,* 9:1 (Summer 1983): 8; Earle on tennis, quoted in

Derek Birley, *Sport and the Making of Britain* (Manchester: Manchester University Press, 1993), p. 81; Earle on bowling, quoted in Dennis Brailsford, *Sport and Society* (London: Routledge & Kegan Paul, 1969), p. 116.

41. Stefano Privato, "Le Ballon avant le football," *Sport et Histoire,* new series, 1 (1992): 16; Günther G. Bauer, "Das . . . Salzburger Hofballhaus, 1620/25–1775," *Homo Ludens,* 6 (1996): 107–48.

42. Jean-Paul Callède, "Basque Pelota in the European Space," *IRSS,* 28:2–3 (1993): 223–41.

43. Teresa McLean, *The English at Play in the Middle Ages* (Shooter's Lodge, Windsor Forest: Kensal Press, 1983), p. 8; Eric Dunning and Kenneth Sheard, *Barbarians, Gentlemen and Players* (Oxford: Martin Robertson, 1979), p. 28.

44. Francis Peabody Magoun, *History of Football* (Bochum–Langendreer: Heinrich Pöppinghaus, 1938), pp. 99–138; Francis P. Magoun Jr., "Scottish Popular Football, 1424–1815," *American Historical Review,* 37:1 (October 1931): 1–13; Hole, *English Sports and Pastimes,* pp. 50–59; Roger Chartier and Georges Vigarello, "Les Trajectoires du sport," *Le Débat,* 19 (February 1982): 37; Jusserand, *Les Sports et jeux d'exercice,* p. 282.

45. Bouet, *Signification du sport,* p. 257; Dunning and Sheard, *Barbarians, Gentlemen and Players,* pp. 23–25; Robert Favreau, "Fêtes et jeux en Poitou à la fin du moyen âge," in *Jeux, sports et divertissements,* p. 37; Joël Guibert, *Joueurs de boules en pays nantais* (Paris: L'Harmattan, 1994), p. 16.

46. Elyot, quoted in Percy M. Young, *A History of British Football* (London: Arrow Books, 1973), pp. 48; Philip Stubbes, *Anatomy of Abuses,* ed. Frederick J. Furnivall (London: Trübner, 1877–79), p. 184; James I, quoted in Young, *History of British Football,* p. 58; Overbury, quoted in Magoun, *History of Football,* p. 38.

47. FitzStephen, quoted in David C. Douglas and George W. Greenaway, eds., *English Historical Documents 1042–1189* (London: Eyre & Spottiswoode, 1953), p. 960; Dennis Brailsford, *A Taste for Diversions* (Cambridge: Lutterworth Press, 1999), p. 40.

48. Print, reproduced in William Heywood, *Palio and Ponte* (New York: Hacker Art Books, 1969), facing p. 170; de' Bardi, quoted, in ibid., pp. 166–67; Martin Dolch, "Vom Ursprung des Luftgefüllten Lederballs," *Stadion,* 7:1 (1981): 58.

49. De' Bardi, quoted in Heywood, *Palio and Ponte,* pp. 166–67; Horst Bredekamp, *Florentiner Fußball* (Frankfurt: Campus, 1993), p. 89; see also Theodor Mommsen, "Football in Renaissance Florence," *Yale University Library Gazette,* 16 (1941): 14–19.

50. Bredekamp, *Florentiner Fußball,* p. 42.

51. Heywood, *Palio and Ponte,* p. 150; Robert Davidsohn, *Geschichte von Florenz,* 4 vols. (Berlin: E. S. Mittler & Sohn, 1927), 4:284–86; Körbs, *Vom Sinn der Leibesübungen zur Zeit der italienischen,* pp. 13–15.

52. Robert C. Davis, *The War of the Fists* (New York: Oxford University Press, 1994). Neighborhoods—*contadini*—also formed the organizational basis for a somewhat less hazardous sport. Siena's *palio* was a race in which splendidly dressed horsemen risked their lives in a mad gallop around the city's main piazza. Col-

orful banners declared that the contest was in honor of the Virgin, who rescued the city from the Florentines in 1260, but—if today's Sienese are at all like their Renaissance ancestors—the riders provoked the passions of the crowd because each was seen as the representative of a *contadina*. See Alan Dundes and Alessandro Falassi, *La Terra in Piazza* (Berkeley: University of California Press, 1975).

53. Henri, quoted in Davis, *The War of the Fists*, p. 47; Robert Muchembled, "Les Jeunes, les jeux et la Violence en Artois au XVIe Siècle," in *Les Jeux à la renaissance*, ed. Philippe Ariès and Jean-Claude Margolin (Paris: Vrin, 1982), p. 570.

7. *"Made in England"*

1. Henning Eichberg, "Auf Zoll und Quintlein," *Archiv für Kulturgeschichte*, 56 (1974): 141–76; André Obey, *L'Orgue du stade* (Paris: Gallimard, 1924), p. 17.

2. Robert W. Malcolmson, *Popular Recreations in English Society, 1700–1850* (Cambridge: Cambridge University Press, 1973), p. 19; Parkyns, quoted in ibid., p. 55; see also Joachim K. Rühl, "Religion and Amusements in Sixteenth-and Seventeenth-Century England," *BJSH*, 1:2 (September 1984): 125–65.

3. Herbert Schoeffler, *England: Das Land des Sportes* (Leipzig: Tauchnitz, 1935); Christian Graf von Krockow, *Sport und Industriegesellschaft* (Munich: Piper, 1972); Henning Eichberg, *Der Weg des Sports in die industrielle Zivilisation* (Baden-Baden: Nomos, 1973); Richard D. Mandell, *Sport* (New York: Columbia University Press, 1984), pp. 132–57.

4. Bernard Gillet, *Histoire du sport* (Paris: Presses universitaires de France, 1970), p. 55; Edmund Neuendorff, *Geschichte der neueren deutschen Leibesübungen vom Beginn des 18. Jahrhunderts bis zur Gegenwart*, 4 vols. (Dresden: Limpert Verlag, 1934), 1:105; Watzdorf, quoted by Christiane Eisenberg, *"English Sports" und Deutsche Bürger* (Paderborn: Ferdinand Schöningh, 1999), p. 89.

5. Roland Renson, "Play in Exile," in *HISPA*, ed. G. Curl (Dartford: Dartford College of Education, 1977), pp. 507–20; Samuel Pepys, *Diary*, ed. Robert Latham and William Matthews, 11 vols. (Berkeley: University of California Press, 1970–1983), 5:4; Douglas Phillips-Birt, *The History of Yachting* (New York: Stein & Day, 1974), p. 15; *The Loyal Protestant* (July 23, 1681; September 21/25, 1682; March 13, 1683), quoted in Maria Kloeren, *Sport und Rekord* (Leipzig: Tauchnitz, 1935), pp. 23, 30, 36; Richard Ford, *This Sporting Life* (London: New English Library, 1977), p. 27; Roger Longrigg, *The English Squire and His Sport* (New York: St. Martin's Press, 1977), pp. 138–39.

6. Henning Eichberg, *Leistung, Spannung, Geschwindigkeit* (Stuttgart: Klett-Cotta, 1978), p. 33; André Stegmann, "La Naissance de l'art équestre en France," in *Les Jeux à la renaissance*, ed. Philippe Ariès and Jean-Claude Margolin (Paris: Vrin, 1982), p. 127.

7. Carl B. Cone, ed., *Hounds in the Morning* (Lexington: University Press of Kentucky, 1981), pp. 93–94 (on *Eclipse*); Longrigg, *The English Squire and His Sport*, pp. 139, 143–44; Eichberg, "Auf Zoll und Quintlein," p. 160.

8. Laura Thompson, *Newmarket* (London: Virgin, 2000), pp. 55–56; Derek Birley

dates the *Racing Calendar* from 1769; in *Sport and the Making of Britain* (Manchester: University of Manchester Press, 1993), p. 136.

9. Dennis Brailsford, *Sport and Society* (London: Routledge & Kegan Paul, 1969), p. 216.

10. Longrigg, *The Enqlish Squire and His Sport*, pp. 163–64; Caroline Ramsden, *Ladies in Racing* (London: Stanley Paul, 1973), p. 151.

11. Wray Vamplew, *The Turf* (London: Allen Lane, 1976), pp. 80–93, 116–17; Mike Huggins, *Flat Racing and British Society: 1790–1914* (London: Frank Cass, 2000), p. 188; Christopher R. Hill, *Horse Power* (Manchester: Manchester University Press, 1988).

12. Stephan Oettermann, *Läufer und Vorläufer* (Frankfurt: Syndikat, 1984); Alan Tomlinson, "Speculations on the Body and Sporting Spaces," *American Behavioral Scientist,* 46:11 (July 2003): 1579; Dennis Brailsford, *A Taste for Diversions* (Cambridge: Lutterworth Press, 1999), pp. 201–2.

13. Kloeren, *Sport und Rekord,* 240; Peter F. Radford, "Women's Foot-Races in the 18th and 19th Centuries," in *Spiele der Welt im Spannungsfeld von Tradition und Moderne,* ed. Gertrud Pfister, Toni Niewerth, and Gerd Steins, 2 vols. (Sankt Augustin: Academia Verlag, 1996): 2:61; Brailsford, *A Taste for Diversions,* p. 153; *Stirling Journal,* quoted in Neil Tranter, "The Chronology of Organized Sport in Nineteenth-Century Scotland," *IJHS,* 7:2 (September 1990): 202 n. 11; see also Earl R. Anderson, "Footnotes More Pedestrian Than Sublime," *Eighteenth-Century Studies,* 14:1 (Fall 1980): 56–68.

14. *True Protestant Mercury,* quoted by Kloeren, *Sport und Rekord,* p. 35; Pierce Egan, *Boxiana,* 5 vols. (London: Sherwood, Nealy & Jones, 1829), 1:57–59; Dennis Brailsford, *Bareknuckles* (Cambridge: Lutterworth Press, 1988), p. 10.

15. Brailsford, *Bareknuckles,* pp. 8–9.

16. On Egan and his contemporaries, see John C. Reid, *Bucks and Bruisers* (London: Routledge & Kegan Paul, 1971). The name of the Duke's estate appears in several spellings.

17. Carl B. Cone, "The Molineaux–Cribb Fight, 1810," *JSH,* 9:3 (Winter 1982): 90; Cone, ed., *Hounds in the Morning,* p. 156.

18. Egan, *Boxiana,* 4: 365; 1: 280.

19. Ibid., 2:9; Brailsford, *Sport and Society,* p. 58; Zacharias Conrad von Uffenbach, *London in 1710,* trans. W. H. Quarrell and Margaret Mare (London: Faber & Faber, 1934), pp. 90–91; *Daily Post,* quoted in Kloeren, *Sport und Rekord,* p. 65.

20. Rowland Bowen, *Cricket* (London: Eyre & Spottiswoode, 1970), p. 29; Derrick, quoted in H. S. Altham, *A History of Cricket* (1926; London: George Allen & Unwin, 1962), pp. 21–22; Christopher Brookes, *English Cricket* (London: Weidenfeld and Nicolson, 1978), p. 24. See also Richard Holt, "Cricket and Englishness," *IJHS,* 13:1 (March 1996): 48–70.

21. Brookes, *English Cricket,* p. 50; Dominic Malcolm, "Cricket and Civilizing Processes," *IRSS,* 37:1 (March 2002): 37–57.

22. John Bale, "Cricket," in *The Theater of Sport,* ed. Karl B. Raitz (Baltimore: Johns Hopkins University Press, 1995), p. 70; Sackville, quoted in David Underdown, *Start of Play* (London: Penguin Books, 2001), p. 147. See also Keith A. P. Sandi-

ford, "Cricket and the Victorian Society," *Journal of Social History,* 17:2 (Winter 1983): 307–17.

23. *Daily Universal Register,* quoted in Neil Wigglesworth, *The Evolution of English Sport* (London: Frank Cass, 1996), p. 34; Brookes, *English Cricket,* p. 68; Underdown, *Start of Play,* pp. 152–76.

24. Jack Williams, "Cricket," in *Sport in Britain,* ed. Tony Mason (Cambridge: Cambridge University Press, 1989), p. 119.

25. Nyren, quoted in Brookes, *English Cricket,* p. 57. One definition of "public schools" is that they were the ones studied by the Clarendon Commission (1861): Eton, Winchester, Westminster, Charterhouse, St. Paul's, Merchant Taylors', Harrow, Rugby, and Shrewsbury.

26. Timothy J. L. Chandler, "Games at Oxbridge and the Public Schools, 1830–80," *IJHS,* 8:2 (September 1991): 175; Peter McIntosh, "Games and Gymnastics for Two Nations in One," in *Landmarks in the History of Physical Education,* ed. Peter McIntosh, 3rd ed. (London: Routledge and Kegan Paul, 1981), pp. 188, 191; see also Timothy J. L. Chandler, "The Development of a Sporting Tradition at Oxbridge," *CJHS,* 19:2 (December 1988): 1–29.

27. *Reading Mercury,* quoted in Nancy Joy, *Maiden Over* (London: Sporting Handbooks, 1950), p. 14; Rachel Heyhoe Flint and Netta Rheinberg, *Fair Play* (London: Angus and Robertson, 1976), pp. 14–15.

8. Cricket Follows the Flag

1. Warner, quoted in James Bradley, "The MCC, Society and Empire," *IJHS,* 7:1 (May 1990): 15.

2. Alan Metcalfe, *Canada Learns to Play* (Toronto: McClelland and Stewart, 1987), p. 83.

3. Ibid., pp. 22, 83; and his "Organized Sport and Social Stratification in Montreal, 1840–1901," in *Canadian Sport,* ed. Richard S. Gruneau and John G. Albinson (Don Mills, Ontario: Addison-Wesley, 1976), pp. 77–101; Paul R. Dauphinais, "A Class Act," *IJHS,* 7:3 (December 1990): 432–42. French Canadians were, in general, less enthusiastic about modern sports than British Canadians. They continue to be statistically underrepresented in modern sports; see Philip G. White and James E. Curtis, "Participation in Competitive Sport among Anglophones and Francophones in Canada," *IRSS,* 25:2 (1990): 125–38.

4. Don Morrow, "The Powerhouse of Canadian Sport," *JSH,* 8:3 (Winter 1981): 20–39; *Toronto Patriot,* quoted in Richard Gruneau, *Class, Sports, and Social Development* (Amherst: University of Massachusetts Press, 1983), p.104; Thring, quoted in David Brown, "Canadian Imperialism and Sporting Exchanges" *CJHS,* 18:1 (May 1987): 57; school paper, quoted in David W. Brown, "Imperialism and Games on the Playing Fields of Canada's Private Schools," in *Olympic Scientific Congress 1984,* ed. Norbert Müller and Joachim K. Rühl (Niedernhausen: Schors Verlag, 1985), p. 129; Nancy and Maxwell L. Howell, *Sports and Games in Canadian Life* (Toronto: Macmillan of Canada, 1969), pp. 42–43.

5. Cooper, "Canadians Declare 'It Isn't Cricket,'" *JSH,* 26:1 (Spring 1999): 75;

Villeneuve, quoted in Jean Harvey, "Sport and the Quebec Clergy, 1930–1960," in *Not Just a Game,* ed. Jean Harvey and Hart Cantelon (Ottawa: University of Ottawa Press, 1988), p. 74; Rose-Marie Lèbe, "The Evolution of Physical Education in Quebec," in *Old Borders, New Borders, No Borders,* ed. Jan Tolleneer and Roland Renson (Aachen: Meyer & Meyer, 2000), pp. 147–56; see also Dauphinais, "A Class Act," pp. 432–42; White and Curtis, "Participation in Competitive Sport among Anglophones and Francophones in Canada," pp. 125–38.

6. Alan Metcalfe, "Sport and Athletics," *JSH,* 3:1 (Spring 1976): 1–19; NLA Constitution, quoted in Don Morrow, Mary Keyes, Wayne Simpson, Frank Cosentino, and Ron Lappage, *A Concise History of Sport in Canada* (Toronto: Oxford University Press, 1989), p. 57; Howell and Howell, *Sports and Games in Canadian Life,* pp. 69–74; Alexander M. Weyand and Milton R. Roberts, *The Lacrosse Story* (Baltimore: H. & A. Herman, 1965), p. 55. See also Donald M. Fisher, *Lacross* (Baltimore: Johns Hopkins University Press, 2002).

7. Metcalfe, *Canada Learns to Play,* p. 26; *Montreal Gazette,* quoted in Howell and Howell, *Sports and Games in Canadian Life,* p. 82; Morrow et al., *A Concise History of Sport in Canada,* p. 128; Colin D. Howell, *Blood, Sweat and Cheers* (Toronto: University of Toronto Press, 2001), p. 41.

8. Bruce Kidd, "How Do We Find Our Own Voices in the 'New World Order'?" *SSJ,* 8:2 (June 1991): 183; see also Sean Hayes, "America's National Pastime and Canadian Nationalism," *CSS,* 4:2 (Summer 2001): 157–84.

9. Timothy Lockley, "'The Manly Game,'" *IJHS,* 20:3 (September 2003): 79; Rivington, cited by Foster Rhea Dulles, *America Learns to Play* (New York: D. Appleton-Century, 1940), p. 52.

10. William Byrd, *The Secret Diary of William Byrd of Westover, 1709–1712,* ed. Louis B. Wright and Marion Tinling (Richmond: Dietz Press, 1941), p. 144; Stephens, quoted in Lockley, "'The Manly Game,'" p. 79.

11. George B. Kirsch, *The Creation of American Team Sports* (Urbana: University of Illinois Press, 1989), pp. 21–49; Kirsch, "The Rise of Modern Sports," *New Jersey History,* 101 (Spring–Summer 1983): 57; Robert M. Lewis, "Cricket and the Beginnings of Organized Baseball in New York City," *IJHS,* 4:3 (December 1987): 315–32; Stephen Freedman, "The Baseball Fad in Chicago, 1865–1870," *JSH,* 5:2 (Spring 1978): 42–64.

12. Waller, quoted in J. Thomas Jable, "Latter-Day Cultural Imperialists," in *Pleasure, Profit, Proselytism,* ed. J. A. Mangan (London: Frank Cass, 1988), p. 175; see also J. Thomas Jable, "Social Class and the Sport of Cricket in Philadelphia, 1850–1880," *JSH,* 18:2 (Summer 1991): 205–23.

13. Lillywhite, quoted in Jable, "Latter-Day Cultural Imperialists," p. 179.

14. Ibid., pp. 175–92; see also George B. Kirsch, "American Cricket," *JSH,* 11:1 (Spring 1984): 28–50.

15. Brian Stoddart, "Cricket, Social Formation and Cultural Continuity in Barbados," *JSH,* 14:3 (Winter 1987): 318; Keith A. P. Sandiford and Brian Stoddart, "The Elite Schools and Cricket in Barbados," *IJHS,* 4:3 (December 1987): 347; see also Stoddart, "Cricket, Social Formation and Cultural Continuity in Barbados,"

317–40; and Dave Soares, "Cricket in Jamaica," *Jamaica Journal,* 22:2 (May–July 1989): 25–32.

16. Jeffrey Hill, "Cricket and the Imperial Connection," *The Global Sports Arena,* ed. John Bale and Joseph Maguire (London: Frank Cass, 1994), p. 57; see also Angus Calder, "A Man for All Cultures," *CSS,* 6:1 (Spring 2003): 19–42.

17. C. L. R. James, *Beyond a Boundary* (1963; New York: Pantheon Books, 1983), pp. 17, 33, 35, 51, 53; H. Addington Bruce, "Baseball and the National Life," *Outlook,* 104 (May 1913): 269.

18. James, *Beyond a Boundary,* pp. 248–52. Thomas Hughes was the author of the immensely popular novel of life at Rugby School, *Tom Brown's Schooldays* (1857). The term "muscular Christianity" first appeared in the *Edinburgh Magazine* for February 1858; see Henry R. Harrington, "Charles Kingsley's Fallen Athlete," *Victorian Studies,* 21:1 (Autumn 1977): 73–86.

19. Brian Stoddart, "Caribbean Cricket," *International Journal,* 43:4 (Autumn 1988): 618–42.

20. Brian Stoddart, "Gary Sobers and Cultural Identity in the Caribbean," *Sporting Traditions,* 5:1 (November 1988): 131; Orlando Patterson, "The Cricket Ritual in the West Indies," *New Society,* 23 (June 26, 1969): 988–89; see also Kevin A. Yelvington, "Ethnicity 'Not Out,'" *Arena Review,* 14:1 (May 1990): 1–12; Christine Cummings, "The Ideology of West Indian Cricket," ibid., 25–32.

21. Jay R. and Joan D. Mandle, *Grass Roots Commitment* (Parkersburg, Iowa: Caribbean Books, 1988), p. 66; see also their "Basketball, Civil Society and the Post Colonial State in the Commonwealth Caribbean," *JSSI,* 14:2 (Fall 1990): 59–75; and their "Failure of Caribbean Integration," *Studies in Latin American Popular Culture,* 13 (1994): 153–64.

22. Brian Stoddart, *Saturday Afternoon Fever* (North Ryde: Angus & Robertson, 1986), pp. 15–55.

23. Historians have paid little attention to the "primitive" sports of the continent's aborigines, but they have recently documented the aborigines' role in modern sports; see Douglas Booth and Colin Tatz, *One-Eyed* (St. Leonards: Allen & Unwin, 2000).

24. John A. Daly, *Elysian Fields* (Adelaide: John A. Daly, 1982), pp. 93–102.

25. Richard Cashman, *'Ave a Go, Yer Mug!* (Sydney: Collins, 1984), p. 26. See also Chris Harte, *A History of Australian Cricket* (London: André Deutsch, 1993), pp. 2–9.

26. Martin Crotty, "Manly and Moral," *IJHS,* 17:2–3 (June–September 2000): 11–30; John A. Daly, "A New Britannia in the Antipodes," in *Pleasure, Profit, Proselytism,* pp. 163–74; David W. Brown, "Muscular Christianity in the Antipodes," *Sporting Traditions,* 3:2 (May 1987): 173–87.

27. Ray Crawford, "Sport for Young Ladies," *Sporting Traditions,* 1:1 (November 1984): 67–68; Marion K. Stell, *Half the Race* (North Ryde: Angus & Robertson, 1991), pp. 14–16, 33–34; Richard Cashman and Amanda Weaver, *Wicket Women* (Kensington: New South Wales University Press, 1991), pp. 1–25, 37–38.

28. Cashman and Weaver, *Wicket Women,* pp. 1–3; Stell, *Half the Race,* pp. 14–15.

29. Richard Cashman, "Cricket," in *Sport in Australia,* ed. Wray Vamplew and Brian Stoddart (Cambridge: Cambridge University Press, 1994), pp. 60–61.

30. Eric Midwinter, *W. G. Grace* (London: George Allen & Unwin, 1981), pp. 41–75; Douglas Booth and Colin Tatz, *One-Eyed* (St. Leonards: Allen & Unwin, 2000), pp. 40–44; *Times,* quoted in Colin Tatz, *Obstacle Race* (Sydney: New South Wales University Press, 1996), p. 62. Aborigines had played the game from at least 1850, when Matthew Blagden Hale introduced it in Poonindie, South Australia; see Booth and Tatz, *One-Eyed,* p. 40.

31. Rowland Bowen, *Cricket* (London: Eyre & Spottiswoode, 1970), p. 286; John Arlott, *The Ashes* (London: Pelham Books, 1972). Less open-minded Britons complained that the Australians behaved like professionals; see James Bradley, "Inventing Australians and Constructing Englishness," *Sporting Traditions,* 11:2 (May 1995): 35–60.

32. William F. Mandle, "Cricket and Australian Nationalism in the 19th Century," *Journal of the Royal Australian Historical Society,* 59:4 (December 1973): 225–46.

33. Rockley Wilson, quoted in Ric Sissons and Brian Stoddart, *Cricket and Empire* (London: George Allen and Unwin, 1984), p. 10; Warner, quoted in Laurence LeQuesne, *The Bodyline Controversy* (London: Secker and Warburg, 1983), p. 34; MCC, quoted in Sissons and Stoddart, *Cricket and Empire,* p. 60. Although culturally as well as geographically quite close to Australia, New Zealand was colonized later enough for rugby—a product of the late nineteenth century—to become the national sport rather than cricket. See five essays by Scott A. G. M. Crawford: "Sport at the End of the World," in *GL,* ed. Horst Ueberhorst, 6 vols. (Berlin: Bartels & Wernitz, 1972–1989), 6:174–96; "Patterns of Leisure in Early Otago—New Zealand," *Stadion,* 5:1 (1979): 42–67; "'We Have Rough Labour, But We Can Afford a Day for Recreation Too,'" *Stadion,* 10 (1984): 95–133; "'Muscles and Character Are There the First Object of Necessity,'" *BJSH,* 2:2 (September 1985): 109–26; "Rugby in Contemporary New Zealand," *JSSI,* 12:2 (Spring–Fall 1988): 108–21.

34. Robin Grow, "From Gum Trees to Goalposts, 1858–1876," in *More Than a Game,* ed. Rob Hess and Bob Stewart (Melbourne: Melbourne University Press, 1998), pp. 4–43, quotation on p. 27; see also Bob Stewart, Rob Hess, and Chris Dixon, "Australian Rules Football," in *Sporting Immigrants,* ed. Philip A. Mosely et al. (Crows Nest, NSW: Walla Walla Press, 1997), pp. 185–98; Tatz, *Obstacle Race,* pp. 150–51; Russell Holmesby, "In a New League, 1925–1945," in *More Than a Game,* p. 154; Thomas V. Hickie, *They Ran with the Ball* (Melbourne: Longman Chesire, 1993), pp. 7–17. For the rules, see Maxwell Howell, "Football, Australian," in *EWS,* ed. David Levinson and Karen Christensen (Santa Barbara: ABC–CLIO, 1996), pp. 342–46.

35. Graeme Kinross-Smith, "Lawn Tennis," in *Sport in Australia,* pp. 133–53; Kevin Fewster, "Advantage Australia," *Sporting Traditions,* 2:1 (November 1985): 47–68. Australia's great female players—Margaret Smith Court and Evonne Goolagong—arrived in the 1970s; see Angela Lumpkin, *Women's Tennis* (Troy, N.Y.: Whitston, 1981).

36. Stell, *Half the Race,* p.119; Dennis Phillips, "Australian Women at the Olympics," *Sporting Traditions,* 6:2 (May 1990): 181–200.

37. Jennifer Hargreaves, *Heroines of Sport* (London: Routledge, 2000), p. 126; Toni Bruce and Christopher Hallinan, "Cathy Freeman," in *Sport Stars,* ed. David L. Andrews and Steven J. Jackson (London: Routledge, 2001), pp. 257–70.

38. Philip Mosely and Bill Burray, "Soccer," in *Sport in Australia,* pp. 213–30; Philip A. Mosely, "Soccer," in *Sporting Immigrants,* pp. 155–73; Rob Hay, "Croatia," *Immigrants and Minorities,* 17:1 (March 1998): 49–66; John Hughson, "The Croatian Community," ibid., pp. 50–62; John Hughson, "The Bad Blue Boys . . . ," in *Entering the Field,* ed. Gary Armstrong and Richard Giulianotti (Oxford: Berg, 1997), pp. 239–59; John Hughson, "The Boys Are Back in Town," *JSSI,* 24:1 (February 2000): 8–23.

39. Bruce Mitchell, "Baseball in Australia," *Sporting Traditions,* 7:1 (November 1990): 2–24.

40. Harry Clay Palmer, "The 'Around the World' Tour," in *Athletic Sports in America, England, and Australia,* ed. Harry Clay Palmer (Philadelphia: Hubbard Bros., 1889), pp.151–282; *Post,* quoted in Daniel Bloyce, "'Just Not Cricket,'" *IJHS,* 14:2 (August 1997): 215; see also Bruce Mitchell, "A National Game Goes International," *IJHS,* 9:2 (August 1992): 288–301.

41. Braham Dabscheck, "A Long Deep Drive into Centre Field?" *Australian Society for Sports History Bulletin* (March 1991): 14–19.

42. Stoddart, *Saturday Afternoon Fever,* p. 103; Richard Cashman, *Paradise of Sport* (Melbourne: Oxford University Press Australia, 1995), p. 197; Cashman, *'Ave a Go, Yer Mug!* pp. 153–66; Ian Harriss, "Packer, Cricket and Postmodernism," in *Sport and Leisure,* ed. David Rowe and Geoff Lawrence (Sydney: Harcourt, Brace & Jovanovich, 1990), pp. 109–21; Peter J. Sloane, *Sport in the Market?* (London: Institute of Economic Affairs, 1980), p. 62. Television also played a direct role in cricket's economic survival. When the government banned televised tobacco advertisements in 1976, Benson & Hedges promptly invested $800,000 (Australian) to sponsor cricket. When Gregory Matthews wrote an article *critical* of tobacco, the Australian Cricket Board fined him; see Bob Stewart, "Sport as Big Business," in *Power Play,* ed. Geoffrey Lawrence and David Rowe (Sydney: Hale & Iremonger, 1986), pp. 64–84; Cashman, *Paradise of Sports,* pp. 129–30.

9. The Institutionalization of Modern Sports in Great Britain

1. Of the rivalry between churches and public houses, as places for working men to seek recreation, Joseph Lawson said that "the former was seldom open while the latter was seldom closed"; quoted by Hugh Cunningham, *Leisure in the Industrial Revolution* (New York: St. Martin's Press, 1980), p. 84.

2. Richard Holt, *Sport and the British* (Oxford: Clarendon Press, 1989), p. 75; see also Eric Dunning and Kenneth Sheard, *Barbarians, Gentlemen and Players* (Oxford: Martin Robertson, 1979), pp. 50–52; W. David Smith, *Stretching Their Bodies* (Newton Abbot: David & Charles, 1974); Timothey J. L. Chandler, "Emergent

Athleticism," *IJHS*, 5:3 (December 1988): 312–30; and his "Games at Oxbridge and the Public Schools, 1830–80," *IJHS*, 8:2 (September 1991): 171–204.

3. Thring, quoted by J. A. Mangan, *Athleticism in the Victorian and Edwardian Public School* (Cambridge: Cambridge University Press, 1981), p. 47.

4. Ibid., p. 71.

5. Ibid., p. 48; James A. Mangan, "Social Darwinism, Sport and English Upper Class Education," *Stadion*, 7:2 (1981): 101; see also his *The Games Ethic and Imperialism* (New York: Viking Press, 1985), p. 21.

6. The irony is that both "vices" were fostered by these same-sex schools and that some of the masters, e.g., Harrow's C. J. Vaughan, were pedophiles; see Mangan, *Athleticism*, pp. 44, 277 n. 7; Holt, *Sport and the British*, p. 91.

7. Samuel Pepys, *Diary*, ed. Robert Latham and William Matthews, 11 vols. (Berkeley: University of California Press, 1970–1983), 7:246; John Evelyn, *Diary*, ed. E. S. de Beer, 6 vols. (London: Oxford University Press, 1955), 3:549; James Boswell, *London Journal*, ed. Frederick A. Pottle (New York: McGraw-Hill, 1950), p. 87.

8. Wesley, quoted in Dennis Brailsford, "Religion and Sport in Eighteenth-Century England," *BJSH*, 1:2 (September 1984): 175; Robert W. Malcolmson, *Popular Recreations in English Society, 1700–1850* (Cambridge: Cambridge University Press, 1973, pp. 127–35; Robert D. Storch, "The Policeman as Domestic Missionary," *Journal of Social History*, 9:4 (June 1976): 481–509. Respectable opinion failed to stop Billy the Dog, "whose specialty . . . was to kill a very large number of rats in a very few minutes"; he and other canines continued to perform in slum basements; see Dennis Brailsford, *A Taste for Diversions* (Cambridge: Lutterworth Press, 1999), p. 241.

9. Raymond Carr, *English Fox Hunting* (London: Weidenfeld & Nicolson, 1976), pp. 25, 33–86; Holt, *Sport and the British*, p. 52.

10. Henry Alken, *The National Sports of Great Britain* (London: Methuen, 1903), p. ix; Sutton, quoted in Carr, *English Fox Hunting* p. 115; Norbert Elias, "An Essay on Sport and Violence," in *Quest for Excitement*, ed. Norbert Elias and Eric Dunning (Oxford: Basil Blackwell, 1985), pp. 150–174. Pigeon-shooting, which the SPCA found equally abominable, also had strong Parliamentary support and survived until 1921; see Mark Alan Kellet, "The Power of Princely Patronage," *IJHS*, 11:1 (April 1994): 63–85.

11. Anthony Trollope, *British Sports and Pastimes* (London: Virtue, Spalding & Co., 1868), p. 12; Charles Dickens, *Uncollected Writings from HOUSEHOLD WORDS*, ed. Harry Stone, 2 vols. (Bloomington: Indiana University Press, 1968), 1:305; *Times*, quoted in Mike Huggins, *Flat Racing and British Society: 1790–1914* (London: Frank Cass, 2000), p. 121.

12. Roger Longrigg, *The English Squire and His Sport* (New York: St. Martin's Press, 1977), pp. 196–203; Brailsford, *A Taste for Diversions*, p.117. Osbaldeston's contemporary, John Mytton, was another madcap profligate; his sporting life cost him nearly £500,000; see Charles James Apperley, *Memoirs of the Life of the Late John Mytton, Esq.* (London: Edward Arnold, 1935).

13. Wray Vamplew, "The Sport of Kings and Commoners," in *Sport in History*, ed.

Richard Cashman and Michael McKernan (St. Lucia: University of Queensland Press, 1979), pp. 307–25; Huggins, *Flat Racing and British Society,* p. 27.

14. Wray Vamplew, "Unsporting Behavior," in *Sports Violence,* ed. Jeffrey H. Goldstein (New York: Springer Verlag, 1983), p. 22; and his "Horse-Racing," in *Sport in Britain,* ed. Tony Mason (Cambridge: Cambridge University Press, 1989), p. 219; Jean Sutherland Boggs, *Degas at the Races* (New Haven: Yale University Press, 1998).

15. Derek Birley, *Sport and the Making of Britain* (Manchester: University of Manchester Press, 1993), p. 303; Tod Sloan, *Tod Sloan, By Himself,* ed. A. Dick Luckman (1915; San Diego: San Diego University Press, 1988); John Dizikes, *Yankee Doodle Dandy* (New Haven: Yale University Press, 2000). Wealth was no guarantee of happiness: Archer was not yet thirty when he shot himself.

16. Edward Hotaling, *They're Off* (Syracuse: Syracuse University Press, 1995), p. 95; Wray Vamplew, *The Turf* (London: Allen Lane, 1976), pp. 69–72, 224–31; Roger Munting, "Social Opposition to Gambling in Britain," *IJHS,* 10:3 (December 1993): 295–312. Football pools were even more popular; in 1951, three-fourths of all British households participated in them; see Richard Ford, *This Sporting Life* (London: New English Library, 1977), p. 242.

17. Wray Vamplew, "Horse-Racing," in *Sport in Britain,* p. 228.

18. Dennis Brailsford, *Sport, Time, and Society* (London: Routledge, 1991), p. 92; Alan Lloyd, *The Great Prize Fight* (New York: Coward, McCann, & Geoghegan, 1977).

19. Birley, *Sport and the Making of Britain,* p. 286; John Sugden, *Boxing and Society* (Manchester: Manchester University Press, 1996), p. 50; Elliot J. Gorn, *The Manly Game* (Ithaca: Cornell University Press, 1986). In 1991, on average, there was a title bout every three days.

20. Timothy Chandler, "Games at Oxbridge and the Public Schools, 1830–80," *IJHS,* 8:2 (September 1991): 173; Christopher Dodd, *The Oxford and Cambridge Boatrace* (London: Stanley Paul, 1983); Neil Wigglesworth, *A Social History of English Rowing* (London: Frank Cass, 1992).

21. Christopher Dodd, "Rowing," in *Sport in Britain,* pp. 288–89.

22. *Gentlewomen's Book,* quoted in Wigglesworth, *A Social History of English Rowing,* p. 107; Currie, quoted in Dodd, "Rowing," in *Sport in Britain,* p. 298; Eric Halladay, *Rowing in England* (Manchester: Manchester University Press, 1990), p. 154.

23. Isthmian Club, quoted in Alan Tomlinson, "Speculations on the Body and Sporting Spaces," *American Behavioral Scientist,* 46:11 (July 2003): 1583; Richard Holt, "Amateurism and Its Interpretation," *Innovation,* 5:4 (1992): 19–31; *Times,* April 26, 1880, quoted in Peter Bailey, *Leisure and Class in Victorian England* (London: Routledge & Kegan Paul, 1978), p. 135; Wigglesworth, *A Social History of English Rowing,* p. 134; see also Martin Crotty, "'Separate and Distinct,'" *IJHS,* 15:2 (August 1998): 153–63. Barricades of exclusion were also constructed abroad. The anglophile oarsmen of Frankfurt's *Germania* rowing club, founded in 1869, explicitly barred manual workers from membership; see Edmund Neuendorff, *Geschichte der neueren deutschen Leibesübungen vom Beginn des 18. Jahrhunderts bis zur Gegenwart,* 4 vols. (Dresden: Limpert Verlag, 1934), 4:531.

24. Frank Cosentino, "Ned Hanlan—Canada's Premier Oarsman," *CJHS,* 5:2 (December 1974): 5–17; Andrea Brown, "Edward Hanlan," *CJHS,* 10:2 (May 1980): 1–44.

25. John Lowerson, *Sport and the English Middle Classes, 1870–1914* (Manchester: Manchester University Press, 1993), pp. 159–60; Daryl Adair, "Rowing and Sculling," *Sport in Australia,* ed. Wray Vamplew and Brian Stoddart (Cambridge: Cambridge University Press, 1994), p. 180; Wigglesworth, *A Social History of English Rowing,* pp. 132–33.

26. Henning Eichberg, "Sport im 19. Jahrhundert," in *GL,* ed. Horst Ueberhorst, 6 vols. (Berlin: Bartels & Wernitz, 1972–1989), 3:351–53; John Idorn, "History," in *Sport in Denmark* (Copenhagen: Det Danske Selskab, 1978), p. 21; Ryszard Wrocynski, Henryk Laskiewicz, and Kajetan Hadzelek, "Polen," in *GL,* 5:424; Peter Sendlak, "Leibesübungen und Sport in der Sowjetunion," in *GL,* 4:80.

27. Grant Jarvie, "Sport, Parish Life, and the Emigré," *JSH,* 25:3 (Fall 1998): 381–97; and Jarvie, "Highland Gatherings, Sport, and Social Class," *SSJ,* 3:4 (December 1986): 344–55. See also Gerald Redmond, *The Sporting Scots of Nineteenth-Century Canada* (Rutherford, N.J.: Farleigh Dickinson University Press, 1982).

28. John Bale, "Racing toward Modernity," *IJHS,* 10:2 (August 1993): 215–32; Roberto L. Quercetani, *A World History of Track and Field Athletics* (London: Oxford University Press, 1964), pp. 2, 94.

29. Montague Shearman, *Athletics and Football,* 4th ed. (London: Longmans, Green, 1894), pp. 51–55, 60–63, 219–20.

30. Gérard Bruant, *Anthropologie du geste sportif* (Paris: Presses universitaires de France, 1992), p. 82.

31. Shearman, *Athletics and Football,* p. 235; founders, quoted in David C. Young, *The Olympic Myth of Greek Amateur Athletics* (Chicago: Ares, 1984), p. 19.

32. Whigham, quoted in Eugene A. Glader, *Amateurism and Athletics* (West Point, N.Y.: Leisure Press, 1978), p. 16.

33. Alain Ehrenberg, *Le Culte de la performance* (Paris: Calmann-Lévy, 1991), p. 80; *Daily Mail,* quoted in Joseph Maguire, "Images of Manliness and Competing Ways of Living . . . ," *BJSH,* 3:3 (December 1986): 283.

34. Phil Vasili, *The First Black Footballer* (London: Frank Cass, 1998).

35. Ralph C. Wilcox, "The Shamrock and the Eagle," *Ethnicity and Sport in North American History and Culture,* ed. George Eisen and David K. Wiggins (Westport, Conn.: Greenwood, 1994), pp. 55–74; Dick Schaap, *An Illustrated History of the Olympics,* 3rd ed. (New York: Knopf, 1975), pp. 107–8; George R. Matthews, "The Controversial Olympic Games of 1908 . . . ," *JSH,* 7:2 (Summer 1980): 40–53; Pierre de Coubertin, *Une Campagne de vingt-et-un ans (1887–1908)* (Paris: Librairie de l'éducation physique, 1909), p. 201.

36. At the Women's World Games, held in London in the summer of 1934, Germany scored more points than the combined total of the next three teams; see Mary Henson Leigh, "The Evolution of Women's Participation in the Summer Olympic Games" (Ph. D. dissertation, Ohio State University, 1974).

37. Roger Bannister, *The Four Minute Mile* (New York: Dodd, Mead, 1955), p. 86.

38. Herbert Warren Wind, *The Story of American Golf,* 2nd ed. (New York: Simon &

Schuster, 1956), p. 18; Heiner Gillmeister, "A Tee for Two," *Homo Ludens,* 6 (1996): 17–36; see also Olive M. Geddes, "Golf," in *Sport, Scotland and the Scots,* ed. Grant Jarvie and John Burnett (East Linton: Tuckwell Press, 2000), pp. 105–27; Heiner Gillmeister, "Golf on the Rhine," *IJHS,* 19:1 (March 2002): 1–30.

39. William Baker, *Sports in the Western World* (Totowa, N.J.: Rowman & Littlefield, 1982), p. 90.

40. Kathleen McCrone, *Playing the Game* (Lexington: University Press of Kentucky, 1988), pp. 166–77.

41. Mike May, "The Athletic Arms Race," *Scientific American Presents,* 11:3 (Fall 2000): 74–79; Scott A. G. M. Crawford, "Golf," in *EWS,* ed. David Levinson and Karen Christensen (Santa Barbara: ABC–CLIO, 1996), pp. 383–84; John Bale, *Landscapes of Modern Sport* (Leicester: University of Leicester Press, 1994), p. 2.

42. John Lowerson, "Golf," in *Sport in Britain,* pp. 187–214.

43. Helen Walker, "Lawn Tennis," in *Sport in Britain,* pp. 245–75; Kathleen E. McCrone, "The 'Lady Blue,'" *BJSH,* 3:2 (September 1986): 195.

44. Gore, quoted in Walker, "Lawn Tennis," *Sport in Britain,* p. 260; Jennifer Hargreaves, *Sporting Females* (London: Routledge, 1994), p. 99; Manuela Müller-Windisch, *Aufgeschnürt und außer Atem* (Frankfurt: Campus Verlag, 1995), pp. 183–85.

45. Anne Marie Waser, "Tennis in France, 1880–1930," *IJHS,* 13:2 (August 1996): 166–76; Anne Marie Weser, "La Diffusion du tennis en France," in *Histoire des sports,* ed. Thierry Terret (Paris: L'Harmattan, 1996), pp. 101–33; Walker, "Lawn Tennis," in *Sport in Britain,* p. 264; Anais Lenglen, quoted by Larry Engelmann, *The Goddess and the American Girl* (New York: Oxford University Press, 1988), p. 37. Jean Borotra later served as the head of Vichy France's sports program; see Jean-Louis Gay-Lescot, *Sport et éducation sous Vichy (1940–1944)* (Lyon: Presses universitaires de Lyon, 1991).

46. McCrone, *Playing the Game,* pp.128–37 (quotation on p. 130); Kathleen E. McCrone, "Emancipation or Recreation?" *IJHS,* 7:2 (September 1990): 204–29.

47. McCrone, *Playing the Game,* p. 133; Roberta J. Park, "Sport, Gender and Society in a Transatlantic Victorian Perspective," *BJSH,* 2:1 (May 1985): 23.

48. Kathleen E. McCrone, "Play Up! Play Up! And Play the Game!" *Journal of British Studies,* 23 (1984): 125; and her "Class, Gender, and English Women's Sport . . . ," *JSH,* 18:2 (Spring 1991): 177.

49. Chesterton, quoted in McCrone, *Playing the Game,* p. 135; *Womanhood,* quoted in Catriona M. Parratt, "Athletic 'Womanhood,'" *JSH,* 16:3 (Summer 1989): 153.

50. Catherine Smith, "Control of the Female Body," *Sporting Traditions,* 13:2 (May 1997): 67; Mila C. Su, "Hockey, Field," in *IEWS,* ed. Karen Christensen, Allen Guttmann, and Gertrud Pfister (New York: Macmillan Reference, 2001), p. 514.

51. Tony Mason, *Sport in Britain* (London: Faber & Faber, 1988), p. 88; see also Midwinter, *W. G. Grace* (London: Allen & Unwin, 1981); Simon Rae, *W. G. Grace* (London: Faber & Faber, 1998).

52. John Bale, *Sport and Place* (Lincoln: University of Nebraska Press, 1982), p. 76; Wray Vamplew, "Playing for Pay," in *Sport, Money, Morality and the Media,* ed.

Richard Cashman and Michael McKernan (Adelaide: University of New South Wales Press, 1981), pp. 111–12.

53. Jack Williams, *Cricket and England* (London: Frank Cass, 1999), p. 1; Ric Sissons, *The Players* (London: Kingswood Press, 1988), pp. 167, 245 (the quotation from Lord Hawke, p. 253).

54. *Punch* and *Cricket,* quoted in McCrone, *Playing the Game,* pp. 143–44, 147–48; see also Joy, *Maiden Over,* pp. 14–16, 26–36, 84–140; Flint and Rheinberg, *Fair Play,* pp. 14–18; John Nauright and Jayne Broomhall, "A Woman's Game," *IJHS,* 11:3 (December 1994): 387–407.

55. Sissons, *The Players,* p. 268; Williams, "Cricket," in *Sport in Britain,* p. 122; Jack Williams, *Cricket and Race* (Oxford: Berg, 2001), p. 173. Tests are played against Australia (from 1877), South Africa (from 1889), the West Indies (from 1928), New Zealand (from 1930), India (from 1932), Pakistan (from 1952), Sri Lanka (from 1982), and Zimbabwe (from 1992).

56. Keith A. P. Sandiford, "The Professionalization of Modern Cricket," *BJSH,* 2:3 (December 1985): 270–89; Chris Gratton and Peter Taylor, *Economics of Sport and Recreation* (London: Spon, 2000), p. 172; Jack Williams, *Cricket and Race,* p. 93.

57. Percy M. Young, *A History of British Football* (London: Arrow Books, 1973), p. 113; Adrian Harvey, "'An Epoch in the Annals of National Sport,'" *IJHS,* 18:4 (December 2001): 53–87; Harvey, "Football's Missing Link," *ESHR,* 1 (1999): 92–116. Martyn Bowden, "Soccer," in *The Theater of Sport,* ed. Karl B. Raitz (Baltimore: Johns Hopkins University Press, 1995), pp. 111–12.

58. Young, *History of British Football,* p. 132; James Walvin, *The People's Game* (London: Allen Lane, 1975), p. 67; Harvey, "'An Epoch in the Annals of National Sport,'" pp. 53–87.

59. H. A. Harris, *Sport in Britain* (London: Stanley Paul, 1975), p. 110; Lyttleton, quoted in Tony Mason, *Association Football and English Society, 1863–1915* (Sussex: Harvester Press, 1980), p. 213.

60. Trollope, *British Sports and Pastimes,* pp. 2–3; Birley, *Sport and the Making of Britain,* p. 265; Tony Mason, "The Blues and the Reds," in *Die Kanten des runden Leders,* ed. Roman Horak and Wolfgang Reiter (Vienna: Promedia, 1991), pp. 173–75; Walvin, *The People's Game,* pp. 50–68.

61. Walvin, *The People's Game,* p. 74; Mason, *Association Football and English Society, 1863–1915,* pp. 21–68.

62. John Hargreaves, *Sport, Power and Culture* (New York: St. Martin's Press, 1986), p. 67.

63. Walvin, *The People's Game,* pp. 31–68; Mason, *Association Football and English Society, 1863–1915,* p. 33.

64. Wray Vamplew, *Pay Up and Play the Game* (Cambridge: Cambridge University Press, 1988), pp. 28, 38.

65. Ibid., p. 194. It should be noted that Scottish football remained a middle-class sport until the early twentieth century; see N. L. Tranter, "The Social and Occupational Structure of Organized Sport in Central Scotland during the Nineteenth Century," *IJSH,* 4:3 (December 1987): 301–14.

66. Steven Tischler, *Footballers and Businessmen* (New York: Holmes & Meier, 1981),

pp. 58–65; Alan Tomlinson, "North and South," in *British Football and Social Change,* ed. John Williams and Stephen Wagg (Leicester: University of Leicester Press, 1991), pp. 48–63; Tony Mason, "Football, Sport of the North?" in *Sport and Identity in the North of England,* ed. Jeff Hill and Jack Williams (Keele: Keele University Press, 1996), pp. 41–52; see also, in the same collection, Jeff Hill, "Rite of Spring: Cup Finals and Community in the North of England," pp. 85–111.

67. Lowerson, *Sport and the English Middle Classes, 1870–1914,* p. 23.

68. Charles Edwardes, "The New Football Mania," *Nineteenth Century,* 32 (October 1892): 627; Preston North End fan, quoted by Tony Mason, *Association Football and English Society, 1863–1915,* pp. 163–64; Neil Tranter, *Sport, Economy and Society in Britain, 1750–1914* (Cambridge: Cambridge University Press, 1998), p.17; Eric Dunning et al., "Football Hooliganism in Britain before the First World War," *IRSS,* 19:3–4 (1984): 229. For major contributions to the debates over sports-related spectator violence, see Peter Marsh, Elisabeth Rosser, and Rom Harré, *The Rules of Disorder* (London: Routledge & Kegan Paul, 1978); Eric Dunning et al., "The Social Roots of Football Hooligan Violence," *Leisure Studies,* 1:2 (1982): 139–56; Patrick Murphy, John Williams, and Eric Dunning, *Football on Trial* (London: Routledge, 1990); Gary Armstrong and Rosemary Harris, "Football Hooligans," *Sociological Review,* 39:3 (1991): 427–58; Eric Dunning, Patrick Murphy, and Ivan Waddington, "Anthropological versus Sociological Approaches . . . ," ibid., 459–78; R. W. Lewis, "Football Hooliganism in England before 1914," *IJHS,* 13:3 (December 1996): 310–39.

69. Nicholas Fishwick, *English Football and Society, 1910–1950* (Manchester: Manchester University Press, 1989), p. 150; Jeffrey Hill, "Cocks, Cats, Caps and Cups," *CSS,* 2:2 (Summer 1999): 13.

70. Fred Inglis, *The Name of the Game* (London: Heinemann, 1977), p. 35; Martyn Bowden, "Soccer," in *The Theater of Sport,* pp. 117–18; see also John Bale, *Sport, Space and the City* (London: Routledge, 1993); Harry Gee, *Wembley* (London: Pelham Books, 1972).

71. The Hillsborough match at which the catastrophe occurred was a semifinal between Liverpool and Nottingham Forest; see John F. Coghlan and Ida M. Webb, *Sport and British Politics since 1960* (London: Falmer Press, 1990), pp. 258–60; Niels Kayser Nielsen, "The Stadium in the City," in *The Stadium and the City,* ed. John Bale and Olof Moen (Keele: Keele University Press, 1995), p. 22; John Bale, *Landscapes of Modern Sport* (Leicester: University of Leicester Press, 1994), p. 174; see also Bruce Kidd, "Toronto's SkyDome," in *The Stadium and the City,* pp. 175–96.

72. Mason, *Association Football and English Society, 1863–1915,* pp. 38–39; see also Tischler, *Footballers and Businessmen,* pp. 51–87; Peter Douglas, *The Football Industry* (London: George Allen & Unwin, 1973).

73. Mason, *Association Football and English Society, 1863–1915,* pp. 42–44; Charles Korr, *West Ham United* (Urbana: University of Illinois Press, 1986), p. 54.

74. Rule 18, quoted in Steven Tischler, *Footballers and Businessmen,* p. 61.

75. Simon Inglis, *Soccer in the Dock* (London: Willow Books, 1985); Wray Vamplew, "Close of Play," *CJHS,* 15:1 (May 1984): 68.

76. Steven Tischler, *Footballers and Businessmen*, pp. 105–20; George W. Keeton, *The Football Revolution* (Newton Abbot: David & Charles, 1972), p. 131; Mason, *Association Football and English Society, 1863–1915*, p. 133 n. 141.

77. Wray Vamplew, *Pay Up and Play the Game*, pp. 77–111; Fishwick, *English Football and Society, 1910–1950*, p. 42; see also Peter J. Sloane, "The Economics of Professional Football," *Scottish Journal of Political Economy*, 18 (June 1971): 121–46. An indication of the decline of British influence upon Australian sports occurred when South Melbourne's Australian Rules Football team was bought and sold and moved to Sydney; see Bruce Wilson, "Pumping Up the Footy," in *Sport and Leisure*, ed. David Rowe and Geoff Lawrence (Marrickville: Harcourt Brace Jovanovich, 1990), p. 37.

78. Ian Taylor, "Professional Sport and the Recession," *IRSS*, 19:1 (1984): 19; Brian Holland, Lorna Jackson, Grant Jarvie, and Mike Smith, "Sport and Racism in Yorkshire," in *Sport and Identity in the North of England*, pp. 165–86.

79. Les Back, Tim Crabbe, and John Solomos, *The Changing Face of Football* (Oxford: Berg, 2001), p. 110; Martin Polley, *Moving the Goalposts* (London: Routledge, 1998), p. 135.

80. Witter, quoted in Les Back, Tim Crabbe, and John Solomos, "'Lions and Black Skins,'" in *"Race," Sport and British* Society, ed. Ben Carrington and Ian McDonald (London: Routledge, 2001), p. 90.

81. Gratton and Taylor, *Economics of Sport and Recreation*, pp. 200–3; Barrie Houlihan, *The Government and Politics of Sport* (London: Routledge, 1991).

82. Richard Holt and Tony Mason, *Sport in Britain, 1945–2000* (Oxford: Blackwell, 2000), pp. 81–88.

83. Chris Gratton, "The Economic Importance of Modern Sport," *CSS*, 1:1 (May 1998): 101–17; and his "The Peculiar Economics of English Professional Football," in *The Future of Football*, ed. Jon Garland, Dominic Malcolm, and Michael Rowe (London: Frank Cass, 2000), pp. 11–28; Rick Parry, "Liverpool FC in the Global Football Age," in *Passing Rhythms*, ed. John Williams, Stephen Hopkins, and Cathy Long (Oxford: Berg, 2001), pp. 215–27; John Williams, "English Football Stadiums after Hillsborough," in *The Stadium and the City*, pp. 230–31.

84. Arthur Hopcraft, *The Football Man* (Harmondsworth: Penguin Books, 1971), p. 30; Tony Mason, "Stanley Matthews," in *Sport and the Working Class in Modern Britain*, ed. Richard Holt (Manchester: Manchester University Press, pp. 159–78; Ford, *This Sporting Life*, p. 251; Richard Holt, *Sport and the British* (Oxford: Clarendon Press, 1988), pp. 315–17; Garry Whannel, "Punishment, Redemption and Celebration in the Popular Press, in *Sport Stars*, ed. David L. Andrews and Steven J. Jackson (London: Routledge, 2001), pp. 138–50; James Walvin, *Leisure and Society, 1830–1950* (London: Longman, 1978), p. 150. On Matthews, see also Garry Whannel, "From Pig's Bladders to Ferraris," *CSS*, 5:3 (Autumn 2002): 73–94. On Beckham, see also Ellis Cashmore and Andrew Parker, "One David Beckham?" *SSJ*, 20:3 (2003): 214–31. On increased social distance and the alienation of the fan, see Ian Taylor, "'Football Mad,'" in *Sport*, ed. Eric Dunning (London: Frank Cass, 1971), pp. 352–77; John Clarke, "Football and Working Class Fans," in *Football Hooliganism*, ed. Roger Ingham et al. (London:

Inter-Action, 1978), pp. 37–60. Hooliganism was simultaneously prevalent in Germany; see Rolf Lindner and E. Thomas Breuer, *"Sind doch nicht alle Beckenbauers"* (Frankfurt: Syndikat, 1978), p. 90.

85. Alan Bairner, "Football and the Idea of Scotland," in *Scottish Sport in the Making of the Nation,* ed. Grant Jarvie and Graham Walker (Leicester: University of Leicester Press, 1994), p. 10; Tranter, "The Social and Occupational Structure of Organized Sport in Central Scotland during the 19th Century," 301–14; Bill Murray, *The Old Firm* (Edinburgh: John Donald, 1984); Joseph M. Bradley, "Football in Scotland," *IJHS,* 12:1 (April 1995): 81–98; Joseph M. Bradley, "The Patriot Game," *IRSS,* 37:2 (June 2002): 177–97. Murray has been criticized for alleged anti-Catholic bias; see G. P. T. Finn, "Racism, Religion and Social Prejudice," *IJHS,* 8:1 (May 1991): 72–95; and his "Scottish Myopia and Global Prejudices," *CSS,* 2:3 (Autumn 1999): 54–99.

86. Mary H. Leigh and Thérèse M. Bonin, "The Pioneering Role of Madame Alice Milliat . . . ," *JSH,* 4:1 (Spring 1977): 72–83; Allen Guttmann, "Milliat, Alice," in *IEWS,* pp. 743–44; Alethea Melling, "Cultural Differentiation, Shared Aspiration," *ESHR,* 1 (1999): 27–53; Alethea Melling, "'Charging Amazons and Fair Invaders,'" *ESHR,* 3 (2001): 155–80.

87. K. G. Sheard and Eric G. Dunning, "The Rugby Football Club as a Type of 'Male Preserve,'" *IRSS,* 8:3–4 (1973): 5–21; Timothy J. L. Chandler, "The Structuring of Manliness and the Development of Rugby Football . . . ," in *Making Men,* ed. John Nauright and Timonthy J. L. Chandler (London: Frank Cass, 1996), pp. 13–31; Philip Dine, *French Rugby Football* (Oxford: Berg, 2001); Robert Morrell, "Forging a Ruling Race," in *Making Men,* pp. 91–120; Jock Phillips, "The Hard Man," in ibid., pp. 70–90; John Nauright, "Sport, Manhood and Empire," *IJHS,* 8:2 (September 1991): 239–55; Richard Light, "Learning to be a 'Rugger Man,'" *Football Studies,* 2:1 (1999): 74–89.

88. Dunning and Sheard, *Barbarians, Gentlemen and Players,* pp. 79–129.

89. Tony Collins, *Rugby's Great Split* (London: Frank Cass, 1998), pp. 97–98, 162; Eric Dunning and Kenneth Sheard, "The Bifurcation of Rugby Union and Rugby League," *IRSS,* 11:2 (1976): 51; see also K. G. Sheard, "'Breakers Ahead!' Professionalization and Rugby Union Football," *IJHS,* 14:1 (April 1997): 116–37.

90. Tony Collins, *Rugby's Great Split,* p. 173; see also Paul Greenhalgh, "'The Work and Play Principle,'" *IJHS,* 9:3 (December 1992): 356–77.

91. Dunning and Sheard, *Barbarians, Gentlemen and Players,* p. 177; Gareth Williams, "Rugby Union," in *Sport in Britain,* p. 313.

92. Dunning and Sheard, *Barbarians, Gentlemen and Players,* p. 265.

93. David Smith and Gareth Williams, *Fields of Praise* (Cardiff: University of Wales, 1980), pp. 2, 145, 284; see also Martin Johnes, "Eighty Minute Patriots?" *IJHS,* 17:4 (December 2000): 93–110; J. B. G. Thomas, *The Men in Scarlet* (London: Pelham Books, 1972); David L. Andrews, "Welsh Indigenous! and British Imperial?" *JSH,* 18:3 (Winter 1991): 335–49.

94. Alan Metcalfe, "Sport and Community," in *Sport and Identity in the North of England,* pp. 21–30; see also his "Organized Sport in the Mining Communities of South Northumberland, 1800–1889," *Victorian Studies,* 25:4 (Summer 1982):

469–95; and his, "'Potshare bowling' in the Mining Communities of East North-umberland, 1800–1914," in *Sport and the Working Class in Modern Britain,* pp. 29–44; see also, on the traditional working-class game of knur and spell, Alan Tomlinson, "Shifting Patterns of Working-Class Leisure," *SSJ,* 9:2 (June 1992): 192–206.

10. The Institutionalization of Modern Sports in the United States

1. Thomas Babington Macaulay, *History of England,* 6 vols., ed. C. H. Firth (London: Macmillan, 1913–15), 1:142.

2. Foster Rhea Dulles, *America Learns to Play* (New York: D. Appleton-Century, 1940), p. 20; see also Dennis Brailsford, "The Puritans saw their mission to erase all sport and play from men's lives," *Sport and Society* (London: Routledge & Kegan Paul, 1969), p. 141. For a more balanced view, see Joachim K. Rühl, "Religion and Amusements in Sixteenth- and Seventeenth-Century England," *BJSH,* 1:2 (September 1984): 125–65.

3. Court of Assistants, quoted in Nancy L. Struna, "Puritans and Sport," *JSH,* 4:1 (Spring 1977): 4; Connecticut law, quoted in Dulles, *America Learns to Play,* pp. 5–6; William Bradford, *Of Plimouth Plantation,* ed. Samuel Eliot Morison (New York: Alfred A. Knopf, 1952), p. 97; Samuel Sewall, *Diary,* ed. M. Halsey Thomas, 2 vols. (New York: Farrar, Straus & Giroux, 1973), 2:795.

4. Mather, quoted in Peter Wagner, "Puritan Attitudes toward Physical Recreation in 17th Century New England," *JSH,* 3:2 (Summer 1976): 144; Baxter, quoted in Robert W. Malcolmson, *Popular Recreations in English Society, 1700–1850* (Cambridge: Cambridge University Press, 1973), p. 89. See also Gerhard Schneider, *Puritanismus und Leibesübungen* (Schorndorf: Karl Hofmann, 1968); Erich Geldbach, *Sport und Protestantismus* (Wuppertal: Brockhaus, 1975); Hans-Peter Wagner, *Puritan Attitudes toward Recreation in Early Seventeenth-Century New England* (Frankfurt: Peter Lang, 1982).

5. Dunton, quoted in Dulles, *American Learns to Play,* p. 33; *Newsletter,* quoted in Struna, "Puritans and Sport," p. 19; Wagner, *Puritan Attitudes toward Recreation in Early Seventeenth-Century New England,* p. 31.

6. Bruce C. Daniels, *Puritans at Play* (New York: St. Martin's Press, 1995), p. 98.

7. William Elliott, *Carolina Sports by Land and Water* (New York: Derby & Jackson, 1859), p. 292; Jones, quoted in John Dizikes, *Sportsmen and Gamesmen* (Boston: Houghton Mifflin, 1981), p. 316 n. 22.

8. Brickell, quoted in B. W. C. Roberts, "Cock-fighting," *North Carolina Historical Review,* 42 (Summer 1965): 305; Philip Vickers Fithian, *Journal and Letters,* ed. Hunter Dickinson Farish (Williamsburg: Colonial Williamsburg, 1943), pp. 121, 128; Elkanah Watson, *Men and Times of the Revolution,* 2nd ed. (New York: D. Appleton, 1861), pp. 300–301; Richard E. Powell Jr., "Sport, Social Relations and Animal Husbandry," *IJHS,* 10:3 (December 1993): 377; see also Fred Hawley, "Cock-fighting in the Piney Woods," *Sport Place,* 1:2 (Fall 1987): 18–26.

9. Thomas Ashe, *Travels in America,* 3 vols. (London: John Abraham, 1808), 1:227; John Bernard, *Retrospections of America, 1797–1811* (New York: Harper & Broth-

ers, 1887), p. 154; Thomas Anburey, *Travels through the Interior Parts of America,* 2 vols. (Boston: Houghton Mifflin, 1923), 2:229; see also T. H. Breen, "Horses and Gentlemen," *William and Mary Quarterly,* 34:2 (April 1977): 239–57.

10. Dale A. Somers, *The Rise of Sports in New Orleans, 1850–1900* (Baton Rouge: Louisiana State University Press, 1972).

11. Nancy L. Struna, "The North–South Races," *JSH,* 8:2 (Summer 1981): 28–57.

12. David K. Wiggins, "Isaac Murphy," *CJHS,* 9:1 (May 1978): 15–32; Dizikes, *Sportsmen and Gamesmen,* p. 134.

13. John W. Loy, Barry D. McPherson, and Gerald Kenyon, *Sport and Social Systems* (Lexington, Mass.: Addison-Wesley, 1978), p. 310. In the 1990s, the availability of offtrack betting has drastically reduced the numbers of those who actually spend a day at the races; see Holly Kruse, "Social Integration, the Arrangement of Interior Space, and Racetrack Renovation," *JSSI,* 27:4 (November 2003): 330–45.

14. *Spirit of the Times,* quoted in Elliot J. Gorn, *The Manly Art* (Ithaca: Cornell University Press, 1986), pp. 58, 108; B. R. M. Darwin, *John Gully and His Times* (New York: Harper, 1935).

15. *Times,* quoted in Somers, *Rise of Sport in New Orleans,* p. 184; Ryan, quoted in Gorn, *The Manly Art,* p. 215; James J. Corbett, *The Roar of the Crowd* (Garden City, N.Y.: Garden City Publishing Co., 1926); see also Michael T. Isenberg, *John L. Sullivan and His America* (Urbana: University of Illinois Press, 1988).

16. Jeffrey T. Sammons, *Beyond the Ring* (Urbana: University of Illinois Press, 1988), pp. 39–40; Al-Tony Gilmore, *Bad Nigger!* (Port Washington, N.Y.: Kennikat Press, 1975); Randy Roberts, *Papa Jack* (New York: Free Press, 1983); Chris Mead, *Champion* (New York: Scribner's, 1985); Randy Roberts, *Jack Dempsey* (Baton Rouge: Louisiana State University Press, 1979); S. Kirson Weinberg and Henry Arond, "The Occupational Culture of the Boxer," *American Journal of Sociology,* 57 (1952): 460–69; Steven A. Riess, "A Fighting Chance," *American Jewish History,* 74:3 (March 1985): 223–54; Peter Levine, *Ellis Island to Ebbets Field* (New York: Oxford University Press, 1992), pp. 144–69; Allen Bodner, *When Boxing Was a Jewish Sport* (Westport, Conn.: Praeger, 1997); Steven A. Riess, ed., *Sports and the American Jew* (Syracuse: Syracuse University Press, 1998).

17. Ali's "autobiography," *The Greatest* (1975), is less factually reliable than David Remnick, *King of the World* (New York: Random House, 1998). For interpretation, see Elliott J. Gorn, ed., *Muhammad Ali* (Urbana: University of Illinois Press, 1995); Gerald Early, ed., *The Muhammad Ali Reader* (New York: William Morrow, 1998). On boxing's crookedness, see Barney Nagler, *James Norris and the Decline of Boxing* (Indianapolis: Bobbs-Merrill, 1964); Steven A. Riess, "Only the Ring Was Square," *IJHS,* 5:1 (May 1988): 29–52.

18. David K. Wiggin, "Victory for Allah," in *Muhammad Ali, the People's Champ,* pp. 88–116; Joyce Carol Oates, *On Boxing* (Garden City, N.Y.: Doubleday, 1987), p. 9; Gary Smith, "After the Fall," *SI,* 59 (October 8, 1984): 80.

19. George Moss, "The Long Distance Runners of Ante-Bellum America," *Journal of Popular Culture,* 8:2 (Fall 1974): 370–82. Stannard is quoted on p. 372.

20. John A. Lucas and Ronald A. Smith, *Saga of American Sport* (Philadelphia: Lea &

Febiger, 1978), pp. 97–98; Ted Vincent, *Mudville's Revenge* (New York: Seaview Books, 1981), pp. 34–53.

21. *Gazette,* quoted by Dahn Shaulis, "Pedestriennes," *JSH,* 26:1 (Spring 1999): 34.

22. Gerald Redmond, *The Caledonian Games in Nineteenth-Century America* (Rutherford, N.J.: Fairleigh Dickinson University Press, 1971), pp. 50–53, 83.

23. Richard G. Wettan and Joe D. Willis, "William Buckingham Curtis," *Quest,* 27 (Winter 1977): 28–37; Joe Willis and Richard Wettan, "Social Stratification in New York City Athletic Clubs, 1865–1915," *JSH,* 3:1 (Spring 1976): 45–63. A sanitized version of NYAC's history appears in Bob Considine and Fred G. Jarvis, *The First Hundred Years* (New York: Macmillan, 1969).

24. Joe D. Willis and Richard G. Wettan, "L. E. Myers, 'World's Greatest Runner,'" *JSH,* 2:2 (Fall 1975): 93–111.

25. Caspar W. Whitney, *A Sporting Pilgrimage* (New York: Harper and Brothers, 1895), p. 167.

26. Robert W. Wheeler, *Jim Thorpe,* rev. ed. (Norman: University of Oklahoma Press, 1979); Reet A. and Maxwell L. Howell, "The Myth of 'Pop Warner,'" *Quest,* 30 (Summer 1978): 19–27.

27. Unnamed reporter, quoted in Susan E. Cayleff, *Babe* (Urbana: University of Illinois Press, 1995), pp. 43, 64–65; William J. Baker, *Jesse Owens* (New York: Free Press, 1986), p. 50; Allen Guttmann, *The Olympics,* 2nd ed. (Urbana: University of Illinois Press, 2002), pp. 161–70.

28. Pamela Cooper, *The American Marathon* (Syracuse, N.Y.: Syracuse University Press, 1998).

29. Albert G. Spalding, *America's National Game* (New York: American Sports Pub. Co., 1911), p. 10. The standard histories of the game are Harold Seymour, *Baseball,* 3 vols. (New York: Oxford University Press, 1960–1990); David Quentin Voigt, *American Baseball,* 2 vols. (Norman: University of Oklahoma Press, 1966–1970). On the early years of the game, see George B. Kirsch, *The Creation of American Team Sports* (Urbana: University of Illinois Press, 1989); Warren Goldstein, *Playing for Keeps* (Ithaca: Cornell University Press, 1989). On Spalding, see Arthur Bartlett, *Baseball and Mr. Spalding* (New York: Farrar, Straus & Young, 1951); Peter Levine, *A. G. Spalding and the Rise of Baseball* (New York: Oxford University Press, 1985).

30. Harold Peterson, *The Man Who Invented Baseball* (New York: Scribner's, 1973), pp. 72–73; Melvin L. Adelman, "The First Baseball Game . . . ," *JSH,* 7:3 (Winter 1980): 132–35; see also Joel Zoss and John Bowman, *Diamonds in the Rough* (Chicago: Contemporary Books, 1996), pp. 51–62. The Knickerbockers played at Hoboken's "Elysian Fields," the estate of John Cox Stevens, the man who had founded the New York Yacht Club, the man whose *America* was soon to outsail the swiftest British vessels; see Adelman, *A Sporting Time* (Urbana: University of Illinois Press, 1986), p. 198–99.

31. Seymour, *Baseball,* 1:15.

32. "Baseball Fever", quoted in Benjamin G. Rader, *Baseball* (Urbana: University of Illinois Press, 1992), p. 5.

33. Steven A. Riess, *Touching Base* (Westport, Conn.: Greenwood Press, 1980); quotation, p. 66.

34. George B. Kirsch, *Baseball in Blue and Gray* (Princeton: Princeton University Press, 2003).

35. Riess, *Touching Base*, p. 19; William R. Hogan, "Sin and Sports," in *Motivations in Play, Games and Sports*, ed. Ralph Slovenko and James A. Knight (Springfield, Ill.: Charles C. Thomas, 1967), p. 129.

36. J. Thomas Jable, "Sport in Philadelphia's African-American Community, 1865–1900," in *Ethnicity and Sport in North American History and Culture*, ed. George Eisen and David Wiggins (Westport, Conn.: Greenwood, 1994), pp. 157–76; Frederick W. Cozens and Florence Scovil Stumpf, *Sports in American Life* (Chicago: University of Chicago Press, 1953), p. 299.

37. W. I. Harris, "Baseball," in *Athletic Sports in America, England, and Australia*, pp. 37–40; Eric M. Leifer, *Making the Majors* (Cambridge, Mass.: Harvard University Press, 1995), pp. 56–64; Bryan Di Salvatore, *A Clever Base-Ballist* (Baltimore: Johns Hopkins University Press, 2000), p. 88.

38. Leifer, *Making the Majors*, pp. 64–78.

39. On Ward and the Brotherhood, see Di Salvatore, *A Clever Base-Ballist*.

40. David Stevens, *Baseball's Radical for All Seasons* (Lanham, Md.: Scarecrow Press, 1998), p. 139.

41. Charles C. Alexander, *Our Game* (New York: Henry Holt, 1991), p. 62; James Quirk and Rodney D. Fort, *Pay Dirt* (Princeton: Princeton University Press, 1992), p. 297; see also Glenn Moore, "The Strong and Ungloved Hand," in *Polemics, Poetics and Play*, ed. Simon Creak et al. (Melbourne: University of Melbourne Press, 1997), pp. 71–102.

42. Steven A. Riess, *City Games* (Urbana: University of Illinois Press, 1989), p. 197; Bruce Kuklick, *To Every Thing a Season* (Princeton: Princeton University Press, 1991), pp. 11–30.

43. Eugene C. Murdock, *Ban Johnson* (Westport, Conn.: Greenwood, 1982), pp. 43–66.

44. Seymour, *Baseball*, 1:87; Alexander, *Our Game*, pp. 85–86; Charles C. Alexander, *John McGraw* (New York Penguin Books, 1989), pp. 109, 116–17.

45. Jules Tygiel, *Past Time* (New York: Oxford University Press, 2000), pp. 15–35.

46. *Spalding's Guide*, quoted in John Rickards Betts, *America's Sporting Heritage* (Reading, Mass.: Addison-Wesley, 1974), p.117; Seymour, *Baseball* 1:175; see also Marty Appel, *Slide, Kelly, Slide* (Lanham, Md.: Scarecrow Press, 1996).

47. Seymour, *Baseball*, 3:443–74; Sophia Foster Richardson, "Tendencies in Athletics for Women in Colleges and Universities," *Popular Science Monthly*, 50 (February 1897): 517; Gai I. Berlage, "Sociocultural History of the Origin of Women's Baseball at the Eastern Women's Colleges during the Victorian Period," in *Cooperstown Symposium on Baseball and the American Culture (1989)*, ed. Alvin L. Hall (Westport, Conn.: Meckler Publishing Co., 1991), pp. 108–9; see also Barbara Gregorich, *Women at Play* (New York: Harcourt, Brace, 1993); Lynn Embrey, "'Great Hit, Jo-Jo,'" *Sporting Traditions*, 14:1 (November 1997): 55–77.

48. In addition to Gregorich's, *Women at Play,* see Lois Browne, *Girls of Summer* (New York: HarperCollins, 1992); Gai Berlage, *Women in Baseball* (Westport, Conn.: Praeger, 1994); Susan E. Johnson, *When Women Played Hardball* (Seattle: Seal Press, 1994).

49. Richard F. Peterson, "'Slide, Kelly, Slide,'" in *The American Game,* ed. Lawrence Baldassaro and Richard A. Johnson (Carbondale: Southern Illinois University Press, 2002), pp. 55–67; Steven A. Riess, "Race and Ethnicity in American Baseball: 1900–1919," *Journal of Ethnic Studies,* 4:4 (Winter 1979): 43.

50. Arthur Judson Palmer, "Fastest Man on Wheels" [on Taylor], *SI,* 12 (March 14, 1960): E9–E16; David W. Zang, *Fleet Walker's Divided Heart* (Lincoln: University of Nebraska Press, 1991); Robert Peterson, *Only the Ball Was White* (Englewood Cliffs, N.J.: Prentice-Hall, 1970), p. 37; Michael E. Lomax, "Black Baseball's First Rivalry," *SHR,* 28:2 (1997): 134–45.

51. Larry R. Gerlach, "German Americans in Major-League Baseball," in *The American Game,* p. 29; Robert W. Creamer, *Babe* (New York: Simon & Schuster, 1974); Marshall Smelser, *The Life That Ruth Built* (New York: Quadrangle, 1975).

52. Eliot Asinof, *Eight Men Out* (New York: Holt, Rinehart & Winston, 1963); Jules Tygiel, *Baseball's Great Experiment* (New York: Oxford University Press, 1983), p. 31; J. G. Taylor Spink, *Judge Landis and Twenty-Five Years of Baseball* (New York: Thomas Y. Crowell, 1947), p.136; see also Kent M. Krause, "Regulating the Baseball Cartel," *IJHS,* 14:1 (April 1997): 55–77.

53. Ruth to President Calvin Coolidge, quoted in Voigt, *American Baseball,* 2:155; Ruth to brothel companions, quoted in Kal Wagenheim, *Babe Ruth* (New York: Praeger, 1974), p. 131; Henry Aaron and Lonnie Wheeler, *I Had a Hammer* (New York: HarperCollins, 1991).

54. Anthony A. Yoseloff, "From Ethnic Hero to National Icon," *IJHS,* 16:3 (September 1999): 1–20; Michael Altimore, "'Gentleman Athlete,'" *IRSS,* 34:4 (1999): 359–67; Richard Ben Cramer, *Joe DiMaggio* (New York: Simon & Schuster, 2000).

55. Rob Ruck, *Sandlot Seasons* (Urbana: University of Illinois Press, 1987), p. 156; Paige, quoted in William Brashler, *Josh Gibson* (New York: Harper & Row, 1978), p. 48.

56. Tygiel, *Baseball's Great Experiment,* pp. 48–49.

57. Roberto González Echevarría, *The Pride of Havana* (New York: Oxford University Press, 1999), pp. 288–90; see also Samuel O. Regalado, *Viva Baseball!* (Urbana: University of Illinois Press, 1998).

58. Gerald W. Scully, "Discrimination," in *Government and the Sports Business,* ed. Roger G. Noll (Washington: Brookings Institution, 1974), pp. 221–74; and his *Business of Major League Baseball* (Chicago: University of Chicago Press, 1989), pp. 171–81; Parbudyal Singh, Allen Sack, and Ronald Dick, "Free Agency and Pay Discrimination in Major League Baseball," *SSJ,* 20:3 (2003): 275–86.

59. John W. Loy Jr. and Joseph F. McElvogue [wrongly given as "Elvogue"], "Racial Segregation in American Sport," *SSJ,* 5 (1970): 5–23; Benjamin Margolis and Jane Allyn Piliavin, "'Stacking' in Major League Baseball," *IRSS,* 16:1 (1999): 16–34.

60. Lionel S. Sobel, *Professional Sports and the Law* (New York: Law–Arts, 1977),

pp. 1–4. For economic analysis of professional sports in the U.S., see Noll, ed., *Government and the Sports Business;* Scully, *The Business of Major League Baseball;* Quirk and Fort, *Pay Dirt;* Andrew Zimbalist, *Baseball and Billions,* 2nd ed. (New York: Basic Books, 1994); For the economics of European sports, see Chantal Malenfant-Dauriac, *L'Économie du sport en France* (Paris: Centre d'étude des techniques économiques modernes, 1977); Harald Fischer, *Sport und Geschäft* (Berlin: Bartels & Wernitz, 1986); Chris Gratton and Peter Taylor, *Economics of Sport and Recreation* (London: Spon, 2000).

61. Allen Guttmann, *A Whole New Ballgame* (Chapel Hill: University of North Carolina Press, 1988), pp. 67–68.

62. Scully, *The Business of Major League Baseball,* pp. 156–65; Zimbalist, *Baseball and Billions,* p. 21; see also James B. Dworkin, *Owners versus Players* (Boston: Auburn House, 1981), p.198.

63. John Wilson, *Playing by the Rules* (Detroit: Wayne State University Press, 1994), p. 109; Scully, *The Business of Major League Baseball,* p. 38.

64. Zimbalist, *Baseball and Billions,* pp. 25–26; Paul C. Weiler, *Leveling the Playing Field* (Cambridge: Harvard University Press, 2000), pp. 118–20; Quirk and Fort, *Pay Dirt,* p. 238; see also Rodney Fort, "Pay and Performance," in *Diamonds Are Forever,* ed. Paul M. Sommers (Washington: Brookings Institution, 1992), pp. 134–60.

65. Zimbalist, *Baseball and Billions,* p. xx.

66. Brian J. Neilson, "Baseball," in *The Theater of Sport,* ed. Karl B. Raitz (Baltimore: Johns Hopkins University Press, 1995), p. 59; Zimbalist, *Baseball and Billions,* p. 129; Michael N. Danielson, *Home Team* (Princeton: Princeton University Press, 1997), p. 242; Roger G. Noll and Andrew Zimbalist, "'Build the Stadium—Create the Jobs!'" in *Sports, Jobs, and Taxes,* ed. Roger G. Noll and Andrew Zimbalist (Washington: Brookings Institution, 1997), pp. 1–30; Hugh Dauncey, "Building the Finals," *CSS,* 1:2 (December 1998): 98–120; see also Charles C. Euchner, *Playing the Field* (Baltimore: Johns Hopkins University Press, 1993).

67. In a single year, 1960, Los Angeles, which already had major-league baseball and NFL football, acquired new franchises for baseball, basketball, football, and ice hockey; see Arnold Beisser, *The Madness in Sports* (New York: Appleton-Century-Crofts, 1967), pp. 126–27.

68. Robert A. Baade and Allen R. Sanderson, "The Employment Effect of Teams and Sports Facilities," in *Sports, Jobs, and Taxes,* pp. 92–118; Dennis Zimmerman, "Subsidizing Stadiums," ibid., pp. 119–45; Paul Lansing and James S. Casper, "The Costs and Benefits of Publicly-Funded Stadiums," *International Sports Journal,* 4:1 (Winter 2000): 60–79; George H. Sage, "Stealing Home," *JSSI,* 17:2 (August 1993): 110–24.

69. Zimbalist, *Baseball and Billions,* p. 69; Scully, *The Business of Major League Baseball,* p. 126. The New York Yankees, purchased by George Steinbrenner in 1973 for $10 million, were worth approximately $900 million in 1998; see "Scorecard: Statitudes," *SI,* 89:18 (November 2, 1998): 40.

70. Benjamin A. Okner, "Taxation and Sports Enterprises," in *Government and the Sports Business,* pp. 159–83; Zimbalist, *Baseball and Billions,* pp. 61–67.

71. Thomas A. Petty, "Baseball," in *Motivations in Play, Games and Sports*, pp. 413–14; see also Louis A. Zurcher and Earl Meadow, "On Bullfights and Baseball," in *The Sociology of Sport*, ed. Eric Dunning (London: Frank Cass, 1971), pp. 174–97.

72. See also Murray Ross, "Football Red and Baseball Green," *Chicago Review*, 22 (January–February 1971): 30–40; Peter Grella, "Baseball and the American Dream," *Massachusetts Review*, 16:3 (Summer 1975): 550–67; Ronald Story, "The Country of the Young," in *Cooperstown*, ed. Alvin L. Hall (Westport, Conn.: Meckler Press, 1991), 324–42; Bill Brown, "The Meaning of Baseball in 1992 . . . ," *Public Culture*, 4:1 (Fall 1991): 43–69.

73. Michael R. Real, "Super Bowl," *Journal of Communication*, 25 (1975): 35.

74. Steven M. Gelber, "Working at Playing," *Journal of Social History*, 16:4 (1983); 9; Roger Angell, *The Summer Game* (New York: Viking, 1972), p. 4. On numeracy, see Patricia Cline Cohen, *A Calculating People* (Berkeley: University of California Press, 1982).

75. *Yale Literary Magazine*, quoted in Stephen H. Hardy and Jack W. Berryman, "A Historical View of the Governance Issue," in *The Governance of Intercollegiate Athletics*, ed. James Frey (West Point, N.Y.: Leisure Press, 1982), p. 18; see also Steven Pope, *Patriotic Games* (New York: Oxford University Press, 1996); Gerald R. Gems, *For Pride, Profit, and Patriarchy* (Lanham, Md.: Scarecrow Press, 2000).

76. David Hackett Fischer, *Albion's Seed* (New York: Oxford University Press, 1989), p. 149; Homer's *Class Day at Harvard University* is reproduced in *Ballou's Pictorial Magazine*, 15 (July 3, 1858): 1; Parke H. Davis, *Football* (New York: Charles Scribner's Sons, 1911), pp. 35–37; Edwin Cady, *The Big Game* (Knoxville: University of Tennessee Press, 1978), p. 75. See also Michael Oriard, *Reading Football* (Chapel Hill: University of North Carolina Press, 1993).

77. Davis, *Football*, pp. 45–50, 62–66.

78. Ibid., pp. 69–70; Oriard, *Reading Football*, p. 26.

79. David Riesman and Reuel Denney, "Football in America," in *Individualism Reconsidered* (Glencoe, Ill.: Free Press, 1954), p. 250; Whitney, *A Sporting Pilgrimage*, p. 192; see also Mark Bernstein, *Football* (Philadelphia: University of Pennsylvania Press, 2001).

80. Oriard, *Reading Football*, p. 37.

81. Camp, quoted in Gems, *For Pride, Profit, and Patriarchy*, p. 17; Allen Sach, "American Business Values and Involvement in Sport," in *Women and Sport*, ed. Dorothy V. Harris (University Park: Pennsylvania State University, 1972), pp. 277–91; Benjamin G. Rader, *American Sports* (Englewood Cliffs, N.J.: Prentice-Hall, 1983), pp. 84–85; Allen L. Sack and Ellen J. Staurowsky, *College Athletes for Hire* (Westport, Conn.: Praeger, 1998), p. 31.

82. Ronald A. Smith, *Sport and Freedom* (New York: Oxford University Press, 1988), p. 160; Lucas and Smith, *Saga of American Sport*, pp. 246–47; Robin Lester, *Stagg's University* (Urbana: University of Illinois Press, 1995); Harper, quoted in Stephan Wassong, *Pierre de Coubertins US-amerikanische Studien . . .* (Würzburg: Ergon, 2002), p. 117.

83. White, quoted in Smith, *Sport and Freedom*, p. 74; Bascom, quoted in James M.

Pitsula, "Competing Ideals," *SHR,* 33:2 (November 2002): 61; McCosh, quoted in Rader, *American Sports,* p. 268.

84. *Wesleyan Christian Advocate,* quoted by Andrew Doyle, "'Foolish and Useless Sport,'" *JSH,* 24:3 (Fall 1997): 319–20; Walter Camp, "What Are Athletics Good For?" *Outing,* 63 (December 1913): 263; W. Cameron Forbes, "The Football Coach's Relation to the Players," *Outing,* 37 (December 1900): 339; Oriard, *Reading Football,* p. 146; Michael A. Messner, "Sports and Male Domination," *SSJ,* 5:3 (September 1988): 202.

85. John Sayle Watterson, *College Football* (Baltimore: Johns Hopkins University Press, 2000), p. 46.

86. Paul R. Lawrence, *Unsportsmanlike Conduct* (New York: Praeger, 1987), pp. 7–10; John Hammond Moore, "Football's Ugly Decades, 1893–1913," *Smithsonian Journal of History,* 2:3 (Fall 1967): 49–68; Ronald A. Smith, "Harvard and Columbia and a Reconsideration of the 1905–06 Football Crisis," *JSH,* 8:3 (Winter 1981): 5–19; see also Jack Falla, *The NCAA, the Voice of College Sports* (Mission, Kans.: NCAA, 1981); Arthur A. Fleisher III, Brian L. Goff, and Robert D. Tollison, *The National Collegiate Athletic Association* (Chicago: University of Chicago Press, 1992).

87. Roberta J. Park, "From Football to Rugby—and Back, 1906–1919," *JSH,* 11:3 (Winter 1984): 5–40; John S. Watterson, "The Gridiron Crisis of 1905," *JSH,* 27:2 (Summer 2000): 291–98.

88. Michael R. Steele, *Knute Rockne* (Westport, Conn.: Greenwood, 1983); quotation from O'Hara, p. 105. Reagan's devotion to Rockne took cinematic form in *Knut Rockne, All American* (1940).

89. Arnold Flath, "A History of the Relations between the National Collegiate Athletic Association and the Amateur Athletic Union of the United States, 1905–1963" (Ph.D. dissertation, University of Michigan, 1963); Fallsa, *NCAA;* Walter Byers and Charles Hammer, *Unsportsmanlike Conduct* (Ann Arbor: University of Michigan Press, 1995); Ying Wu, "Early NCAA Attempts at the Governance of Women's Intercollegiate Athletics, 1968–1973," *JSH,* 26:3 (Fall 1999): 585–601.

90. Mary A. Boutilier and Lucinda SanGiovanni, *The Sporting Woman* (Champaign, Ill.: Human Kinetics, 1983), p. 169; Ellen W. Gerber et al., *The American Woman in Sport* (Reading, Mass.: Addison-Wesley, 1974), pp. 236–37.

91. European governments passed similar laws at roughly the same time; see David McArdle, "Can Legislation Stop Me from Playing?" *CSS,* 2:2 (Summer 1999): 44–57; Gerd von der Lippe, "Frauensport in Norwegen," in *Frauensport in Europa,* ed. Christine Peyton and Gertrud Pfister (Ahrensburg: Czwalina, 1989), pp. 156–57.

92. James L. Shulman and William G. Bowen, *The Game of Life* (Princeton: Princeton University Press, 2001), pp. 125–56; Keith P. Henschen and David Fry, "An Archival Study of the Relationship of Intercollegiate Athletic Participation and Graduation," *SSJ,* 1:1 (1984): 52–56. On the AIAW, see also Elaine M. Blinde, "Contrasting Orientation toward Sport," *JSSI,* 10:1 (Winter/Spring 1986): 6–14; Elaine Blinde and Susan L. Greendorfer, "Structural and Philosophical Differences . . . ," *Journal of Sport Behavior,* 10:2 (June 1987): 59–72; Allen L. Sack,

"College Sport and the Student–Athlete," *JSSI,* 11:1–2 (Fall/Winter 1987–1988): 31–48.

93. Ying Wushanley, "Playing Nice and Losing" (Ph.D. dissertation, Pennsylvania State University, 1997); Ying Wu, "Margot Polivy, Legal Costs, and the Demise of the Association for Intercollegiate Athletics for Women," *SHR,* 30:2 (November 1999): 119–39.

94. George H. Sage, "The Intercollegiate Sport Cartel . . . ," *The Governance of Intercollegiate Athletics,* p. 133; Ronald A. Smith, *Play-by-Play* (Baltimore: Johns Hopkins University Press, 2001), p. 72.

95. Supreme Court, quoted in *New York Times,* June 28, 1984; Smith, *Play-by-Play,* pp. 143–76; Lawrence, *Unsportsmanlike Conduct,* pp. 94–110; Tom McMillen and Paul Coggins, *Out of Bounds* (New York: Simon & Schuster, 1992), p. 103.

96. James J. Duderstadt, *Intercollegiate Athletics and the American University* (Ann Arbor: University of Michigan Press, 2003), p. 133; John R. Thelin and Lawrence L. Wiseman, *The Old College Try* (Washington, D.C.: George Washington University School of Education and Human Development, 1989), p. 16; John F. Rooney Jr., and Audrey B. Davidson, "Football," in *The Theater of Sport,* pp. 217–18.

97. Henry S. Pritchett, "Preface," in Howard J. Savage et al., *American College Athletics* (New York: Carnegie Foundation, 1929), p. xv.

98. *Atlanta Constitution,* quoted in Michael Oriard, *King Football* (Chapel Hill: University of North Carolina Press, 2001), p. 107; A. Whitney Griswold, "College Athletics," *SI,* 3 (October 17, 1955): 44; John Underwood, *The Death of an American Game* (Boston: Little, Brown, 1979), p. 244. For a classic account of the universities' scramble to recruit functionally illiterate high school football stars, see Willie Morris, *The Courting of Marcus Dupree* (Garden City, N.Y.: Doubleday, 1983).

99. Andrew Zimbalist, *Unpaid Professionals* (Princeton: Princeton University Press, 1999), p. 12; Phil Taylor and Shelley Smith, "Exploitation or Opportunity?" *SI,* 75 (August 12, 1991): 47.

100. Abercrombie, quoted in Joan M. Chandler, *Television and National Sport* (Urbana: University of Illinois Press, 1988), p. 52–53; Donald Chu, *The Character of American Higher Education and Intercollegiate Sport* (Albany: SUNY Press, 1989), pp. 113–14; Ewald B. Nyquist, "The Immorality of Big-Power Intercollegiate Athletics," in *Sport and Higher Education,* ed. Donald Chu, Jeffrey O. Segrave, and Beverly J. Becker (Champaign, Ill.: Human Kinetics, 1985), p. 107; Vandiver, quoted by Douglas S. Looney, "Jackie Hits the Jackpot," *SI,* 56 (February 1, 1982): 29; Murray Sperber, *College Sports Inc.* (New York: Henry Holt, 1990), p. 165; William F. Reed, "What Price Glory?" *SI,* 73 (December 24, 1990): 34–39.

101. John R. Thelin, *Games Colleges Play* (Baltimore: Johns Hopkins University Press, 1994), pp. 52, 181; David Whitford, *A Payroll to Meet* (New York: Macmillan, 1989); Byers and Hammer, *Unsportsmanlike Conduct,* pp. 17–36; Zimbalist, *Unpaid Professionals,* p. 24.

102. David F. Salter, *Crashing the Old Boys' Network* (Westport, Conn.: Praeger, 1996), pp. 61–63.

103. Mary P. Koss and John A. Gaines, "The Prediction of Sexual Aggression . . . ,"
     Journal of Interpersonal Violence, 8:2 (March 1993): 94–108; Todd W. Crosset,
     Jeffrey R. Benedict, and Mark A. McDonald, "Male Student–Athletes Reported
     for Sexual Assault," *JSSI,* 19:2 (May 1995): 126–40; Jeff Benedict, *Public Heroes,
     Private Felons* (Boston: Northeastern University Press, 1997); and his *Athletes
     and Acquaintance Rape* (Thousand Oaks, Calif.: Sage, 1998).

104. Barry Switzer and Bud Shrake, *Bootlegger's Boy* (New York: William Morrow,
     1990), p. 16. *Sports Illustrated,* which has certainly contributed to the glorifica-
     tion of athletes, has regularly documented some of the abuses and perversions
     of interscholastic and intercollegiate sports; for example, Robert H. Boyle and
     Roger Jackson, "Bringing Down the Curtain," *SI,* 57 (August 9, 1982): 62–79;
     Jerry Kirshenbaum, "An American Disgrace," *SI,* 70 (February 27, 1989): 16–19;
     Rick Telander and Robert Sullivan, "You Reap What You Sow," ibid, 20–31; Rick
     Reilly, "What Price Glory?" ibid, 32–34; Sonja Steptoe and E. M. Swift, "Anatomy
     of a Scandal," *SI,* 80 (May 16, 1994): 18–28; Alexander Wolff, "Broken Beyond Re-
     pair," *SI,* 82 (June 12, 1995): 20–26; Michael Farber, "Coach and Jury," *SI,* 83 (Sep-
     tember 25, 1995): 31–34; Alexander Wolff and George Dohrmann, "School for
     Scandal," *SI,* 94 (February 26, 2001): 72–84.

105. Michael Oriard, *The End of Autumn* (Garden City, N.Y.: Doubleday, 1982),
     pp. 52–53.

106. In 1931, the question for the NCAA was whether or not there should be "inter-
     sectional or national championships in football"; the question today is how to
     identify an official undisputed champion; see Charles W. Kennedy, *Sport and
     Sportsmanship* (Princeton: Princeton University Press, 1931), p. 21.

107. John F. Rooney Jr., *The Recruiting Game* (Lincoln: University of Nebraska Press,
     1980); Rick Telender, *The Hundred Yard Lie* (New York: Simon & Schuster, 1989).

108. Gems, *Windy City Wars,* p. 67; Stephen H. Hardy, *How Boston Played* (Boston:
     Northeastern University Press, 1982), p. 112; Geoff Winningham, Al Reinert, and
     Don Meredith, *Rites of Fall* (Austin: University of Texas Press, 1979); Douglas E.
     Foley, "The Great American Football Ritual," *SSJ,* 7:2 (June 1990): 111–35.

109. Edwards, quoted in H. G. Bissinger, *Friday Night Lights* (Reading, Mass.: Addi-
     son-Wesley, 1990), p. 291. On the "myth of school sports," see Andrew W. Mira-
     cle Jr. and C. Roger Rees, *Lessons of the Locker Room* (Amherst, N.Y.: Prometheus
     Books, 1994), p. 21.

110. John Allen Krout, *Annals of American Sport* (New Haven: Yale University Press,
     1929), p. 257; John M. Carroll, *Red Grange and the Rise of Modern Football* (Ur-
     bana: University of Illinois Press, 1999), pp. 1–9 (Coolidge quotation, p. 114). See
     also Marc S. Maltby, *The Origins and Early Development of Professional Football*
     (New York: Garland, 1997); Robert W. Peterson, *Pigskin* (New York: Oxford Uni-
     versity Press, 1997).

111. The act protected NCAA games by forbidding Friday night and Saturday after-
     noon telecasts of NFL games. In 1973, Congress banned home-market blackouts
     if the game was sold out 72 hours before gametime. See also David A. Klatell and
     Norman Marcus, *Sports for Sale* (New York: Oxford University Press, 1988),
     p. 82. More generally, see Stephen R. Lowe, *The Kid on the Sandlot: Congress and*

Professional Sports (Bowling Green, Ohio: Bowling Green State University Popular Press, 1995).

112. Ron Powers, *Supertube* (New York: Coward-McCann, 1984), pp. 152–59; Phil Patton, *Razzle-Dazzle* (Garden City, N.Y.: Dial Press, 1984), pp. 86–99; Sheldon Gallner, *Pro Sports* (New York: Charles Scribner's Sons, 1974), p. 144.

113. Irsay, quoted in Danielson, *Home Team,* p. 67.

114. Maurice Roche, *Mega-Events and Modernity* (London: Routledge, 2000).

115. Leola Johnson and David Roediger, "'Hertz, Don't It?'" in *Reading Sport,* ed. Susan Birrell and Mary G. McDonald (Boston: Northeastern University Press, 2000), pp. 40–73 (on Simpson); Benjamin G. Rader, *In Its Own Image* (New York: Free Press, 1984), p. 115; Joan M. Chandler, "Sport as TV Product," in *The Business of Professional Sports,* ed. Paul D. Staudohar and James A. Mangan (Urbana: University of Illinois Press, 1991), pp. 48–60.

116. Monique de Saint Martin, "La Noblesse et les 'Sports Nobles,'" *Actes de la recherche en sciences sociales,* 80 (November 1989): 22–32; Thorstein Veblen, *The Theory of the Leisure Class* (New York: Macmillan, 1899), p. 259; Oliver H. P. Belmont, "Coaching," in *The Book of Sport,* ed. William Patten (New York: J. F. Taylor, 1901), p. 219.

117. Morgan, quoted in Donald J. Mrozek, *Sport and American Mentality, 1880–1910* (Knoxville: University of Tennessee Press, 1983), p. 123; Cindy L. Himes, "The Female Athlete in American Society: 1860–1940" (Ph. D. dissertation, University of Pennsylvania, 1986), p. 48. On the country club, see also "Robert Dunn, "Newport, the Blessed of Sport," *Outing,* 52:6 (September 1908): 689–99.

118. Hardy, *How Boston Played,* pp. 140–42; Wind, *The Story of American Golf,* p. 23; see also Richard J. Moss, *Golf and the American Country Club* (Urbana: University of Illinois Press, 2001).

119. James M. Mayo, *The American Country Club* (New Brunswick, N.J.: Rutgers University Press, 1998).

120. Ibid., quotation on p. 87.

121. Henry W. Slocum Jr., "Lawn Tennis as a Game for Women," *Outing,* 14 (July 1889): 289; Elizabeth Cynthia Barney, "The American Sportswoman," *Fortnightly Review,* 62 (August 1894): 267.

122. Gems, *The Windy City Wars,* p. 112.

123. Guttmann, *A Whole New Ball Game,* pp. 82–91. The American playground movement had immense influence in Germany; see Wolf-Dietrich Brettschneider and Hans Peter Brandl-Bredenbeck, *Sportkultur und jugendliches Selbstkonzept* (Weinheim: Juventa, 1997), p. 45.

124. Betts, *America's Sporting Heritage,* p. 338; Riess, *City Games,* pp. 148, 163; Rader, *American Sports,* p. 164; Linda Borish, "Jewish American Women, Jewish Organizations, and Sports, 1880–1940," in *Sports and the American Jew,* pp. 105–31; Gems, *Windy City Wars,* p. 149.

125. Stanley Aronowitz, "Foreword," to Cary Goodman, *Choosing Sides* (New York: Schocken Books, 1979), p. x; Dominick Cavallo, *Muscles and Morals* (Philadelphia: University of Pennsylvania Press, 1981), p. 2. Lee's ideas were set forth in

Play in Education (New York: Macmillan, 1915). Faith in youth sports as an antidote to adolescent deviance continues. See Margaret Gatz, Michael A. Messner, and Sandra J. Ball-Rokeach, eds., Paradoxes of Youth and Sport (Albany: SUNY Press, 2002).

126. Guttmann, A Whole New Ball Game, p. 91; James A. Michener, Sports in America (New York: Random House, 1976), pp. 93–119.

127. Sarah K. Fields, "Cultural Identity, Law, and Baseball," CSS, 4:2 (Summer 2001): 23–42.

128. Edward C. Devereux, "Backyard versus Little League Baseball," in Social Problems in Athletics, ed. Daniel M. Landers (Urbana: University of Illinois Press, 1976), p. 46; and Robert R. Faulkner, "Making Violence by Doing Work," in ibid., pp. 93–112.

129. Anonymous football coach, quoted in Michael Jay Kaufman and Joseph Popper, "Pee Wee Pill Poppers," Sport, 63 (December 1976): 151; anonymous Canadian coach, quoted in Edmund W. Vaz, The Professionalization of Young Hockey Players (Lincoln: University of Nebraska Press, 1982), p. 29; Breitner, quoted in Gunter A. Pilz, "Fußballsport und körperliche Gewalt," in Der Satz 'Der Ball ist rund' hat eine gewisse philosophische Tiefe, ed. Rolf Lindner (Berlin: Transit, 1983), p. 88; anonymous German coach, quoted in Gunter A. Pilz, "Performance Sport," IRSS, 30:3–4 (1995): 395. See also Robin Kähler and Meinhart Volkamer, "Einstellung von Schülern zu Regeln und Normen im Sport," in Sport und Gewalt, ed. Gunter Pilz et al. (Schorndorf: Karl Hofmann, 1982), pp. 163–90; Gunter A. Pilz, Wandlungen der Gewalt im Sport (Ahrensburg: Czwalina, 1982); Michael D. Smith, Violence and Sport (Toronto: Butterworth, 1983).

130. Ernest Havemann, "Down Will Come Baby, Cycle and All," SI, 39 (August 13, 1973): 49; William Nack and Lester Munson, "Out of Control," SI, 93 (July 24, 2000): 86–95; see also John Underwood, "Taking the Fun Out of a Game," SI, 43 (November 17, 1975): 86–98.

131. Gary Alan Fine, With the Boys (Chicago: University of Chicago Press, 1987), p. 221; Geoffrey G. Watson, "Games, Socialization and Parental Values," IRSS, 12:1 (1977): 17–47; Page B. Walley, George M. Graham, and Rex Forehand, "Assessment and Treatment of Adult Observer Verbalizations at Youth League Baseball Games," Journal of Sport Psychology, 4 (1982): 254–66.

132. Anonymous boy, quoted in Hardy, How Boston Played, p. 99. Marty Ralbovksy's Destiny's Darlings (New York: Hawthorne Books, 1974), a study of a championship Little League team, is an exemplary account of positive and negative memories.

133. James Naismith, "Basket Ball," American Physical Education Review, 19:5 (May 1914): 339–40; see also Bernice Larson Webb, The Basketball Man (Lawrence: University of Kansas Press, 1973); Keith Myerscough, "The Game with No Name," IJHS, 12:1 (April 1995): 137–52.

134. Basketball is the best but not the first example of a sport invented on request. In 1877, William Wilson, president of the Associated Swimming Clubs of Scotland, invented water polo in response to a request from Glasgow's Bon Accord

Swimming Club; see Thierry Terret, *Naissance et diffusion de natation sportive* (Paris: L'Harmattan, 1994), p. 117; Pascal Charroin and Thierry Terret, *Une Histoire du water-polo* (Paris: L'Harmattan, 1998), p. 28.

135. Neil D. Isaacs, *All the Moves* (Philadelphia: Lippincott, 1975), pp. 19–22.

136. Robert W. Peterson, *Cages to Jump Shots* (New York: Oxford University Press, 1990).

137. Catherine E. D'Urso, "A View of American Attitudes toward Femininity: The History of Physical Education for Women and Collegiate Women's Basketball" (unpublished essay, Amherst College, 1989), pp. 47–48. Berenson divided the court into three zones with two players per team in each of them. The players were not allowed to leave their zones, to dribble the ball, or to guard aggressively.

138. Lynne Emery, "The First Intercollegiate Contest for Women," in *Her Story in Sport*, ed. Reet Howell (West Point, N.Y.: Leisure Press, 1982), pp. 417–23; *New York Journal*, cited and illustrated in Martha Banta, *Imaging American Women* (New York: Columbia University Press, 1987), p. 90; Agans, quoted in Janice A. Beran, *From Six-on-Six to Full Court Press* (Ames: Iowa State University Press, 1993), p. 30.

139. Peterson, *Cages to Jump Shots*, pp. 24–27, 37–41, 81–93, 111–12, 176, 179–81.

140. *American Hebrew*, quoted in Levine, *Ellis Island to Ebbets Field*, p. 17.

141. Paul Gallico, *Farewell to Sport* (New York: Alfred A. Knopf, 1938), p. 325; Levine, *Ellis Island to Ebbets Field*, p. 66.

142. Charles Rosen, *Scandals of '51* (New York: Holt, Rinehart & Winston, 1978), pp. 15, 19; William H. Beezley, "The 1961 Scandal at North Carolina State and the End of the Dixie Classic," *Arena*, 7:3 (November 1983): 33–52; John Underwood, "The Biggest Game in Town," *SI*, 63 (August 26, 1985): 25–26; Albert J. Figone, "Gambling and College Basketball," *JSH*, 16:1 (Spring 1989): 44–61.

143. John Underwood, *Spoiled Sport* (Boston: Little, Brown, 1984); Fleisher, Goff, and Tollison, *The National Collegiate Athletic Association*, p. 93; Smith, *Play-by-Play*, p. 190; Ralph C. Wilcox, "Of Fungos and Fumbles," in *Sport in the Global Village*, ed. Ralph C. Wilcox (Morgantown, W.Va.: Fitness Information Technology, 1994), pp. 84–85.

144. Douglas S. Looney, "Big Trouble at Tulane," *SI*, 62 (April 8, 1985): 36–39. After a mistrial, Williams was retried and acquitted. He then signed with the Cleveland Cavaliers for $675,000; see Jamie Diaz, "A Quick Start for the Hot Rod," *SI*, 65 (November 10, 1986): 61.

145. Valvano and Knight: quoted in Sperber, *College Sports Inc.*, pp. 18, 339.

146. Patricia A. and Peter Adler, *Backboards and Blackboards* (New York: Columbia University Press, 1991), p. 27.

147. Wilbert M. Leonard II, "Exploitation in Collegiate Sports," *Journal of Sport Behavior*, 9:1 (March 1986): 11–30; Donald Siegel, "Higher Education and the Plight of the Black Athlete," *JSSI*, 18:3 (August 1994): 211–12; Sack and Staurowsky, *College Athletes for Hire*, pp. 103–9; Wilcox, "Of Fungos and Fumbles," in *Sport in the Global Village*, p. 79; Lionel C. Barrow, "Black Colleges

Not Sharing in the Gold," *Crisis,* 98:9 (1991): 15–19; Harry Edwards, "The Collegiate Athletic Arms Race," *JSSI,* 8:1 (Winter/Spring 1984): 14; Sowell, quoted in George H. Sage, *Power and Ideology in American Sport* (Champaign, Ill.: Human Kinetics, 1990), p. 186.

148. E. M. Swift, "From Corned Beef to Caviar," *SI,* 74 (June 3, 1991): 80; Bill Russell and William McSweeney, *Go Up for Glory* (New York: Coward-McCann, 1966); Bill Russell and Taylor Branch, *Second Wind* (New York: Random House, 1979); Wilt Chamberlain and David Shaw, *Wilt* (New York: Macmillan, 1973); Paul D. Staudohar, *The Sports Industry and Collective Bargaining* (Ithaca: Cornell University Press, 1986); Wilt Chamberlain, *A View from Above* (New York: Villard Books, 1991).

149. Jim Naughton, *Taking to the Air* (New York: Time Warner, 1992); Donald Katz, "Triumph of the Swoosh," *SI,* 79 (August 16, 1993): 54–73; Walter LaFeber, *Michael Jordan and the New Global Capitalism* (New York: Norton, 1999).

150. Rick Telander, "Senseless," *SI,* 72 (May 14, 1990): 36–38, 43–44, 49.

151. Michael Eric Dyson, "Be Like Mike?" Cultural Studies, 7:1 (1993): 64, 68; LaFeber, *Michael Jordan and the New Global Capitalism.*

152. David L. Andrews, "The Fact(s) of Michael Jordan's Blackness," *SSJ,* 13:2 (1996): 126; Cheryl L. Cole and Samantha King, "Representing Black Masculinity and Urban Possibilities," in *Sport and Postmodern Times,* ed. Geneviève Rail (Albany: SUNY Press, 1998), p. 54; see also David L. Andrews, ed., *Michael Jordan, Inc.* (Albany: SUNY Press, 2001); Mary G. McDonald and David L. Andrews, "Michael Jordan," in *Sport Stars,* ed. David L. Andrews and Steven J. Jackson (London: Routledge, 2001), pp. 20–35.

153. Mary G. McDonald, "Michael Jordan's Family Values," *SSJ,* 13:4 (1996): 355; Cheryl Cole, "American Jordan," ibid., 377, 382. (This entire *SSJ* issue is devoted to "deconstructing" Michael Jordan.) See also Ketra L. Armstrong, "Nike's Communication with Black Audiences," *JSSI,* 23:3 (August 1999): 266–86.

154. Ironically, Dennis Rodman, whose flaky behavior some see as the polar opposite of Jordan's bland conformity, has not fared much better. Rodman, whose antics include transvestite appearances, allegedly "maintains and reinscribes dominant modalities of masculinity, phallocentrism, heteronormativity, white supremacy and consumer capitalism"; see Mélisse Lafrance and Geneviève Rail, "Excursions into Otherness," in *Sport Stars,* p. 48. I can see the point about consumer capitalism.

II. Latin America

1. John W. Fox, "The Lords of Light versus the Lords of Dark," in *The Mesoamerican Ballgame,* ed. Vernon L. Scarborough and David R. Wilcox (Tucson: University of Arizona Press, 1991), pp. 213–38; Heidi Linden, *Das Ballspiel in Kult und Mythologie der Mesoamerikanischen Völker* (Hildesheim: Weidmann, 1993).

2. Ted J. J. Leyenaar and Lee A. Parsons, *Ulama* (Leiden: Spruyt, Van Mantgem & De Does, 1988); John Sugden and Alan Tomlinson, *FIFA and the Contest for World Football* (Cambridge: Polity Press, 1988), p. 168 (on Uday).

3. Leyenaar and Parsons, *Ulama,* p. 24; Eric Taladoire and Benoit Colsenet, "'Bois Ton Sang, Beaumanoir,'" in *The Mesoamerican Ballgame,* p. 174.

4. Kathleen M. Sands, "Charreada, in *Sport in Latin America and the Caribbean,* ed. Joseph L. Arbena and David G. LaFrance (Wilmington, Del.: Scholarly Resources, 2002), pp. 117–31; William H. Beezley, *Judas at the Jockey Club* (Lincoln: University of Nebraska Press, 1987), pp. 14–27.

5. Roberto da Matta, "Notes Sur le *futebol* brésilien," Le Debat, Nr. 19 (Feb. 1982): 68–76. Joseph A. Page, "Soccer Madness," in *Sport in Latin America and the Caribbean,* p. 37.

6. Enrique C. Romero Brest, Alberto R. Dallo, and Simón Silvestrini, "Los Deportes y la Educación Física en la República Argentina," in *GL,* ed. Horst Ueberhorst, 6 vols. (Berlin: Bartels & Wernitz, 1972–1989), 6: 847; Eduardo A. Olivera, *Origenes de los Deportes Britanicos en el Río de la Plata* (Buenos Aires: L. J. Rosso, 1932), pp. 11–12, 15.

7. Brest et al., "Los Deportes y la Educación Física," in *GL,* 6: 849, 866, 871–72, 876; Olivera, *Origenes,* pp. 61, 99–112.

8. *La Razón,* quoted in Brest et al., "Los Deportes y la Educación Física," in *GL,* p. 6: 866; Olivera, *Origenes,* pp. 30–34; Héctor Alberto Chaponick, *Historia del Fútbol Argentino,* 3 vols. (Buenos Aires: Editorial Eiffel, 1955), 1: 24–25, 44–46, 49–50; Horacio J. Spinetto, "Ciento Veinte Años de Rugby Argentino," *Todo Es Historia,* 25 (January 1992): 8.

9. Olivera, *Origenes,* pp. 30–34; Chaponick, *Historia,* 1:15, 17, 50–55; Brest et al., "Los Deportes y la Educación Física," in *GL,* 6:868–69.

10. Chaponick, *Historia,* 1:17, 51, 54, 59.

11. Ibid.,1:18, 23–24, 51–52.

12. Vic Duke and Liz Crolley, "Fútbol, Politicians and the People," *IJHS,* 18:3 (September 2001): 93–116; Chaponick, *Historia,* 1:27, 65–92; Eduardo P. Archetti, *Masculinities* (Oxford: Berg, 1999), pp. 54, 59; and his "Argentinient," in *Fußball, Soccer, Calcio,* ed. Christiane Eisenberg (Munich: DTV, 1997), p. 152; see also Osvaldo Bayer, *Fútbol Argentino* (Buenos Aires: Editorial Sudamericana, 1990), p. 20; Eduardo P. Archetti, "Nationalisme, Football et Polo," *Terrain,* 25 (September 1995): 73–90.

13. Pierre Lanfranchi and Matthew Taylor, *Moving with the Ball* (Oxford: Berg, 2001), pp 75, 91; Jimmy Burns, *Hand of God* (New York: Lyons Press, 1996); Eduardo P. Archetti, "'And Give Joy to My Heart,'" in *Entering the Field,* ed. Gary Armstrong and Richard Giulianotti (Oxford: Berg, 1997), pp. 31–51.

14. *El Grafico,* quoted by Archetti, *Masculinities,* p. 123; Juan José Sebreli, "Fútbol y Alienación," in *El Fútbol,* ed. Jean Cau et al. (Buenos Aires: Jorge Ávarez Editor, 1967), p. 125; Eduardo Galeano, *Soccer in Sun and Shadow* (London: Verso, 1999). In *pato,* mounted teams struggle for manual possession of the six-handled leather ball that has replaced the dead duck of earlier days; see Richard W. Slatta, "The Demise of the Gaucho and the Rise of Equestrian Sport in Argentina," *JSH,* 13:2 (Summer 1986): 104–5.

15. Burns, *Hand of God,* pp. 159–63.

16. Antonio Vera, *El Fútbol en Chile* (Santiago: Editoria Nacional Quimantú, 1973); quotation, p. 9.

17. Brian Glanville, *Soccer* (London: Eyre & Spottiswoode, 1969), p. 57; Antol H. Rosenfeld and Otto Zerries, "Formen traditioneller und moderner Bewegungskultur in Brasilien," in *GL,* 6:916; Ilan Rachum, "Futebol," *New Scholar,* 8:1–2 (1978): 185–86; Ulfert Schröder, "Fußball in Brasilien," in *Fußball-Weltgeschichte,* ed. Karl-Heinz Huba (Munich: Copress, 1992), pp. 61, 64.

18. Rachum, "Futebol," pp. 187–90; Glanville, *Soccer,* pp. 57–58; José Sergio Leite Lopes, "Successes and Contradictions in 'Multiracial' Brazilian Football," in *Entering the Field,* p. 53–86.

19. Martyn Bowden, "Soccer," in *The Theater of Sport,* ed. Karl B. Raitz (Baltimore: Johns Hopkins University Press, 1995), pp. 131–33; Janet Lever, *Soccer Madness* (Chicago: University of Chicago Press, 1983), p. 69; see also Cesar Gordon and Ronaldo Helal, "The Crisis of Brazilian Football," *IJHS,* 18:3 (September 2001): 139–58; Janet Lever, "Soccer," *Trans-Action,* 7:2 (1969): 36–43.

20. Lever, *Soccer Madness,* pp. 76, 130–31; Pelé, quoted by Philip Evanson, "Understanding the People," *South Atlantic Quarterly,* 81:4 (Autumn 1982): 400; Derek Pardue, "Jogada Lingüística," *JSSI,* 26:4 (November 2002): 374; see also José Sergio Leite Lopes and Sylvain Maresca, "La Disparition de 'La Joie du Peuple,'" *Actes de la recherche en sciences sociales,* 79 (September 1989): 21–36; Robert M. Levine, "The Burden of Success," *Journal of Popular Culture,* 14:3 (Winter 1980): 453–64.

21. Chuck Cascio, *Soccer U.S.A.* (Washington: Robert B. Luce, 1975); Jere Longman, *The Girls of Summer* (New York: HarperCollins, 2000); Allen Guttmann, "Maskulin oder Feminin? Die Entwicklung des Fußballs in den USA," in *Fußballwelten,* ed. Peter Lösche, Undine Ruge, and Klaus Stolz (Opladen: Leske+Budrich, 2001), pp. 205–18.

22. Wolf Krämer-Mandeau, "Ocupación, Dominación y Liberación—la Historia del Deporte en Nicaragua," in *GL,* 6:1043–46.

23. Roberto González Echevarría, *The Pride of Havana* (New York: Oxford University Press, 1999), p. 90; Edel Casas, Jorge Alfonso, and Albert Pestana, *Viva y en Juego* (Havana: Editorial Científico Técnica, 1986), pp. 7–10; Angel Torres, *Historia del Béisbol Cubano, 1878–1976* (Los Angeles: Angel Torres, 1976), pp. 11, 37.

24. Wolf Krämer-Mandeau *Sport und Körpererziehung auf Cuba* (Cologne: Pahl-Rugenstein, 1988), p. 18; Michael M. and Mary Adams Oleksak, *Béisbol* (Grand Rapids, Mich.: Masters Press, 1991), pp. 5–6; see also Louis A. Pérez Jr., "Between Baseball and Bullfighting," *Journal of American History,* 81:2 (September 1994): 493–517.

25. Gualberto Gómez, quoted in Casas et al., *Viva y en Juego,* p. 18.

26. Paula J. Pettavino and Geralyn Pye, *Sport in Cuba* (Pittsburgh: University of Pittsburgh Press, 1994), p. 26; Donn Rogosin, *Invisible Men* (New York: Atheneum, 1985), p. 61.

27. Rogosin, *Invisible Men,* p. 160; Pettavino and Pye, *Sport in Cuba,* p. 37. The milder climate did not, however, soften everyone. When Johnny Dunlap of the

Boston Braves invited Early Wynn to have a drink with him and Willie Wells, a black player, Wynn responded, "I don't drink with niggers," whereupon Dunlap broke Wynn's jaw; in ibid., pp. 162–63.

28. Beezley, *Judas at the Jockey Club*, p. 18.
29. Ibid., p. 19.
30. Ibid., p. 22. Yucatán was another baseball center; see Gilbert M. Joseph, "Forging the Regional Pastime: Baseball and Class in Yucatán," in *Sport and Society in Latin America*, ed. Joseph L. Arbena (Westport, Conn.: Greenwood, 1988), pp. 29–61.
31. Beezley, *Judas at the Jockey Club*, pp. 23–24.
32. William H. Beezley, "Bicycles, Modernization, and Mexico," in *Sport and Society in Latin America*, p. 25; see also Beezley, *Judas at the Jockey Club*, pp. 17–26.
33. Alan M. Klein, *Baseball on the Border* (Princeton: Princeton University Press, 1997), pp. 47, 66–79; Joseph L. Arbena, "Sport, Development, and Mexican Nationalism, 1920–1970," *JSH*, 18:3 (Winter 1991): 350–64.
34. M. and M. Oleksak, *Béisbol*, pp. 50–52.
35. David G. LaFrance, "Labor, the State, and Professional Baseball in Mexico in the 1980s," *JSH*, 22:2 (Summer 1995): 111–34.
36. Rob Ruck, *The Tropic of Baseball* (Westport, Conn.: Meckler, 1991), p. 5.
37. Alan M. Klein, *Sugarball* (New Haven: Yale University Press, 1991), pp. 16–17.
38. Sullivan, quoted in ibid, p. 110; Ruck, *Tropic of Baseball*, p. 136.
39. The first anecdote is from John Krich, *El Béisbol* (New York: Atlantic Monthly Press, 1989), p. 111; the second is from Rogosin, *Invisible Men*, p. 168; see also Klein, *Sugarball*, pp. 22–23.
40. Ruck, *Tropic of Baseball*, pp. 73–74.
41. Ibid, pp. 61–62.
42. Phillip M. Hoose, *Necessities* (New York: Random House, 1989), p. 117.
43. Klein, *Sugarball*, p. 42; Krich, *El Béisbol*, p. 156.
44. Ruck, *Tropic of Baseball*, p. 28; see also Alan M. Klein, "Sport and Culture as Contested Terrain," *SSJ*, 8:1 (March 1991): 79–85.

12. Continental Europe

1. Ruud Stokvis, "De populariteit van sporten," *Amsterdams Sociologisch Tijdschrift*, 15:4 (March 1989): 679.
2. John Bale, "The Adoption of Football in Europe," *CJHS*, 11:2 (December 1980): 56–66; and his "International Sports History as Innovation Diffusion," *CJHS*, 15:1 (May 1984): 38–63.
3. Eugen Weber, "Gymnastics and Sports in *Fin-de-Siècle* France," *American Historical Review*, 76:1 (February 1971): 84 n. 31.
4. Dubois, quoted by Robert Neirynck, "De Scholen der Jozefieten, Xaverianen en Benediktijnen en de Ontwikkeling van de Voetbalsport in Belgie (1863–1895)" (M.A. thesis, Catholic University of Louvain, 1985), p. 43.
5. Ibid., p. 177.
6. Vic Duke, "The Politics of Football in Belgium," *La Commune Eredità dello Sport*

   in Europa, ed. Arnd Krüger and Angela Teja (Rome: Scuola dello Sport–CONI, 1997), pp. 360–63.

7. Ruud Stokvis, *Strijd over Sport* (Devanter: Van Loghum Slaterus, 1979), pp. 47–48.

8. Maarten van Bottenburg, "The Differential Popularization of Sports in Continental Europe," *The Netherlands Journal of Social Sciences,* 28:1 (April 1992): 12; Stokvis, *Strijd over Sport,* p. 9; schoolmate, quoted in van Bottenburg, *Verborgen Competitie* (Amsterdam: Bert Bakker, 1994), p. 142.

9. Stokvis, *Strijd over Sport,* p. 73; Peter-Jan Mol, *Geschiedenis van de Sport in Amsterdam: 1918–1940* (Amsterdam: Peter-Jan Mol, 1998), p. 43.

10. Christiane Eisenberg, *"English Sports" und Deutsche Bürger* (Paderborn: Ferdinand Schöningh, 1999), p. 179; Wilhelm Hopf, "'Wie konnte Fußball ein deutsches Spiel werden?'" in *Fußball,* ed. Wilhelm Hopf (Bensheim: Pädagogischer Extra Buchverlag, 1979), pp. 69–70.

11. Roland Binz, *"Borussia ist stärker"* (Frankfurt: Peter Lang, 1988), p. 217.

12. Ibid., 176–78; Sportmuseum Berlin, ed., *Sport in Berlin* (Berlin: Dirk Nishen, 1991), p. 90; Christiane Eisenberg, "Fußball in Deutschland," *Geschichte und Gesellschaft,* 20:2 (1994): 181–210.

13. Ulfert Schröder, "Fußball in Deutschland," in *Fußball-Weltgeschichte,* ed. Karl-Heinz Huba (Munich: Copress, 1992), p. 70.

14. Christiane Eisenberg, "Football in Germany," *IJHS,* 8:2 (September 1991): 205–20; Siegfried Gehrmann, "Der F. C. Schalke 04," in *Fußball,* pp. 117–20; Siegfried Gehrmann, "Der F. C. Schalke 04—ein Verein und sein Nimbus," in *Die Kanten des runden Leders,* ed. Roman Horak and Wolfgang Reiter (Vienna: Promedia, 1991), pp. 45–54; Rolf Lindner and Heinrich Thomas Breuer, *"Sind Doch Nicht Alles Beckenbauers"* (Frankfurt: Syndikat, 1978).

15. Gert Auf der Heide, "Heldentat im 'Fritz-Walter-Wetter,'" *Bonner General-Anzeiger,* January 23, 1999; Arthur Feinrich, "The 1954 Soccer World Cup and the Federal Republic of Germany's Self-Discovery," *American Behavioral Scientist,* 46:11 (July 2003): 1491–1505. (Bauwens is quoted on p. 1495).

16. Rolf Lindner, "Die Professionalisierung des Fußballsports," in *Der Satz 'Der Ball ist rund' hat eine gewisse philosophische Tiefe,* ed. Rolf Lindner (Berlin: Transit, 1983, pp. 56–66; Siegfried Gehrmann, "Keeping Up with Europe," in *Sport in the Global Village,* ed. Ralph C. Wilcox (Morgantown, W.Va.: Fitness Information Technology, 1994), pp. 145–57.

17. Gerd Hortleder, *Die Faszination des Fußballspiels* (Frankfurt: Suhrkamp, 1974), pp. 35–49.

18. Alfred Wahl, *Les Archives du football* (Paris: Gallimard/Juillard, 1989), pp. 28–29; Weber, "Gymnastics and Sports," p. 84; Laurent Coadic, "Implantation et diffusion du football en Bretagne (1890–1925)," *Sport et Histoire,* new series, 1 (1992): 27–50.

19. Weber, "Gymnastics and Sports," p. 84; Wahl, *Les Archives du football,* pp. 30–31.

20. Richard Holt, *Sport and Society in Modern France* (London: Macmillan, 1981), pp. 65–69; Jacques Thibault, *Sport et éducation physique 1870–1970,* 2nd ed. (Paris: Vrin, 1979), p. 109; Ronald Hubscher, Jean Durry, and Bernard Jeu,

l'Histoire en mouvements (Paris: Armand Colin, 1992), pp. 143–48; Wahl, *Les Archives du football,* pp. 31–36; Tony Mason, "Some Englishmen and Scotsmen Abroad," in *Off the Ball,* ed. Alan Tomlinson and Garry Whannel (London: Pluto Press, 1986), p. 70.

21. Pierre Lanfranchi, "Rugby contro Calcio," *Ricerche Storiche,* 19:2 (May–August 1989): 1–13; Pierre de Coubertin, *Une Campagne de vingt-et-un ans (1887–1908)* (Paris: Librairie de l'éducation physique, 1909), p. 15; Wahl, *Archives du football,* pp. 37–56; Pierre Lanfranchi, "Apparition et affirmation du football en Langue-doc, 1900–1935," in *La Naissance du mouvement sportif associatif en France,* ed. Pierre Arnaud and Jean Camy (Lyon: Presses universitaires de Lyon, 1986), pp. 259–73.

22. Lanfranchi, "Rugby contro Calcio," 1–13; Wahl, *Archives du football,* p. 80.

23. Laurence Prudhomme, "Sex faible et ballon rond," in *Histoire du sport féminin,* ed. Pierre Arnaud and Thierry Terret, 2 vols. (Paris: L'Harmattan, 1996), 1:111–26.

24. Alfred Wahl and Pierre Lanfranchi, *Les Footballeurs professionels des années trente à nos jours* (Paris: Hachette, 1995), pp. 39–40; Hanot, quoted in Wahl, *Archives du football,* p. 241; Patrick Fridenson, "Les Ouvriers de l'automobile et le sport," *Actes de la recherche en sciences sociales,* 79 (September 1989): 50–62. Renault and Citroën also created sports clubs for their workers.

25. Pierre Lanfranchi, "The Migration of Footballers," in *The Global Sports Arena,* ed. John Bale and Joseph Maguire (London: Cass, 1994), pp. 63–77; Wahl and Lanfranchi, *Les Footballeurs professionels,* pp. 249–52; Paul Darby, "The New Scramble for Africa," *ESHR,* 3 (2001): 221–22.

26. Kopa, quoted in Wahl and Lanfranchi, *Les Footballeurs professionels,* p. 179.

27. John Marks, "The French National Team and National Identity," *CSS,* 1:2 (December 1998): 41–57; James Eastham, "The Organization of French Football Today," ibid., 58–78.

28. Antonio Papa, "Le Domeniche di Clio: Origini e Storia del Football in Italia," *Belfagor,* 2 (1988): 134; Pierre Lanfranchi, "Frankreich und Italien," in *Fußball, Soccer, Calcio,* ed. Christiane Eisenberg (Munich: DTV, 1997), pp. 45–48. The same pattern occurred in Spain, where soccer spread first among the resident British and the sons of the industrial bourgeoisie of Catalonia; see Gabriel Colomé, "Il Barcelona e la società catalana," in *Il Calcio e il suo Pubblico,* ed. Pierre Lanfranchi (Naples: Edizioni Scientifiche Italiane, 1992), pp. 59–65.

29. Antonio Ghirelli, *Storia del Calcio in Italia,* rev. ed. (Turin: Giulio Einaudi, 1990), pp. l9–22; Guido Panico, "Le origini del foot-ball in Italia," in *Il Calcio e il suo Pubblico,* pp. 49–55; Giovanni Albonago, "Fußball in Italien," in *Fußball-Weltgeschichte,* p. 88; Paul Gardner, *The Simplest Game* (Boston: Little, Brown, 1976), pp. 36–37.

30. Ghirelli, *Storia del Calcio in Italia,* pp. 25–48. On the mostly nonexistent relations between the Renaissance game and the modern one, see Stefano Pivato, "Il Pallone prima del Football," in *Il Calcio e il suo Pubblico,* pp. 19–30.

31. Stefano Pivato, "Soccer, Religion, Authority," *IJHS,* 8:3 (December 1991): 427.

32. Patrick Hazard and David Gould, "Three Confrontations and a Coda," in *Fear*

and Loathing in World Football, ed. Gary Armstrong and Richard Giulianotti (Oxford: Berg, 2001), p. 209.

33. Ghirelli, *Storia del Calcio in Italia,* pp. 179–311.

34. Ibid., pp. 41–42; József Vetö, *Sports in Hungary,* trans. István Butykay (Budapest: Corvina Press, 1965), p. 44; Pierre Lanfranchi, "Fußball in Europa 1920–1938," in *Die Kanten des runden Leders,* pp. 166–67; Michael Müller, "Dribbling in den Freien Markt," in ibid., pp. 104–10.

35. FA, quoted by Alan Tomlinson, "Going Global," in *Off the Ball,* p. 85; Guérin, quoted by Wahl, *Archives du football,* p. 98.

36. Sutcliffe, quoted in Pierre Lanfranchi and Matthew Taylor, *Moving with the Ball* (Oxford: Berg, 2001), p. 46; www.fifa.com.

37. Wall, quoted in Mason, "Football," in *Sport in Britain,* ed. Tony Mason (Cambridge: Cambridge University Press, 1989), p. 177; Franklin Morales, "Historia del Deporte del Uruguay," in *GL,* ed. Horst Ueberhorst, 6 vols. (Berlin: Bartels & Wernitz, 1972–1989), 6:980–83; Wahl, *Archives du football,* p. 98.

38. Stephen Wagg, *The Football World* (Brighton: Harvester Press, 1984), p. 31.

39. www.fifa.com.

40. Botsford, quoted in Paul Darby, *Africa, Football and FIFA* (London: Frank Cass, 2002), p. 83; John Sugden and Alan Tomlinson, *Great Balls of Fire* (Edinburgh: Mainstream, 1999); Alan Tomlinson, "FIFA and the Men Who Made It," in *The Future of Football,* ed. Jon Garland, Dominic Malcolm, and Michael Rowe (London: Frank Cass, 2000), pp. 55–71; Alan Bairner and Paul Darby, "The Swedish Model and International Sport," *IRSS,* 36:3 (September 2001): 337–59; Darby, *Africa, Football and FIFA,* pp. 136–60.

41. www.fifa.com. There was a three-year gap between Woolfall's death and Rimet's election.

42. Jürgen Ritterbach, "Die Geschichte des Basketballs in Deutschland von den Anfängen bis 1945" (Cologne: Deutsche Sporthochschule, 1988), pp. 6–25.

43. Hajo Bernett, "Die ersten 'olympischen' Wettbewerbe im internationalen Frauensport," *SZGS,* 2:2 (1988): 73; John Bale, *Sport and Place* (Lincoln: University of Nebraska Press, 1982), p. 137; Joseph Maguire, "The Commercialization of English Elite Basketball, 1972–1988," *IRSS,* 23:4 (1988): 310–11.

44. Bottenburg, "The Differential Popularization of Sports in Continental Europe," p. 20; Joseph Mills Hanson, ed. *The Inter-Allied Games* (Paris: The Games Committee, 1919), pp. 14–20, 88, 201–2; Elmer L. Johnson, *The History of YMCA Physical Education* (Chicago: Follett, 1979), p. 90; William Baker, *Sports in the Western World* (Totowa, N.J.: Rowman & Littlefield, 1982), p. 213.

45. Ritterbach, "Geschichte des Basketballs," p. 44. (In addition to Switzerland and Italy, FIBA's founding members represented Argentina, Portugal, Greece, Romania, Czechoslovakia, and Latvia.)

46. Ibid., pp. 28–42, 66–68.

47. Joseph Maguire, "American Labour Migrants, Globalization and the Making of English Basketball," in *The Global Sports Arena,* pp. 226–55; Maguire, "The Commercialization of English Elite Basketball, 1972–1988," in ibid., pp. 305–22. The modest success of British professional basketball had an effect on the amateur

game. According to Maguire ("American Labour Migrants," p. 238), the number of players in schools and clubs, which was 240,000 when the NBL was launched, had increased nearly fivefold in the course of the decade.

48. Jack McCallum, "Tomorrow the World," *SI,* 69:20 (November 7, 1988): 62; Paolo Cambone, *Storia Culturale dei Moderni Giochi Sportivi di Squadra* (Rome: Edizioni SEAM, 1996), p. 123; on Gardini, Curry Kirkpatrick, "Sitting Pretty in Rome," *SI,* 71:16 (October 9, 1989): 28; see also Harvey Araton and Filip Bondy, *The Selling of the Green* (New York: Harper/Collins, 1992), pp. 1–10.

49. Joseph Maguire, "More Than a Sporting Touchdown," *SSJ,* 7:3 (September 1990): 213–37; and his "American Football, British Society, and Global Sport Development," in *The Sports Process,* ed. Eric G. Dunning, Joseph A. Maguire, and Robert E. Pearton (Champaign, Ill.: Human Kinetics, 1993), pp. 207–29; Garry Whannel, *Fields in Vision* (London: Routledge, 1992), p. 102; see also Christopher R. Martin and Jimmie L. Reeves, "The Whole World Isn't Watching (But We Thought They Were)," *CSS,* 4:2 (Summer 2002): 213–36.

50. Maguire, "More than a Sporting Touchdown," p. 224.

51. In addition to articles cited in the previous two notes, see Steven Barnett, *Games and Sets* (London: British Film Institute, 1990), pp. 68, 100–101; Dominic Malcolm, Ken Sheard, and Andy White, "The Changing Structure and Culture of English Rugby Union Football," *CSS,* 3:3 (Autumn 2000): 63–87.

52. Maguire, "More Than a Sporting Touchdown," pp. 222–33; and his "American Football . . . ," pp. 213–14.

53. Maguire, "American Football . . . ," pp. 216–17.

54. Joseph Maguire, "The Media–Sport Production Complex," *European Journal of Communication,* 6 (1991): 315–36; Rick Reilly, "One to Remember," *SI,* 74:23 (June 17, 1991): 44–50; Christopher Davies, "A Jolly Good Show," ibid., 50; Peter King, "World Beater," *SI,* 76:20 (May 25, 1992): 42–44.

55. Goodell, quoted in Steve Rushin, "On the Road Again," *SI,* 79:7 (August 16, 1993): 20.

56. David Denham, "Modernism and Postmodernism in Professional Rugby League in England," *SSJ,* 17:3 (2000): 281.

13. Technological Sports

1. Gérard Salmon, "Une Histoire orpheline," *Sport et Histoire,* new series, 1 (1992): 51–65. *Peleton* refers to the group leading the race, *dérailleur* to the gear-shifting mechanism, and *domestiques* to the cyclists whose task is to support their team's best riders.

2. Ronald Hubscher, Jean Durry, and Bernard Jeu, *L'Histoire en mouvements,* (Paris: Armand Colin, 1992), p. 80; Andrew Ritchie, *King of the Road* (London: Wildwood House, 1975), pp. 53–58; and his article, "The Origins of Bicycle Racing in England," *JSH,* 26:3 (Fall 1999): 489–520.

3. Ritchie, *King of the Road,* pp. 59–61, 147–48; James McGurn, *On Your Bicycle* (New York: Facts on File, 1987), pp. 33–38.

4. Hubscher, Durry, and Jeu, *L'Histoire en mouvements,* p. 142; Wray Vamplew, *Pay Up and Play the Game* (Cambridge: Cambridge University Press, 1988), p. 189; McGurn, *On Your Bicycle,* pp. 51–73; Richard Holt, *Sport and Society in Modern France* (London: Macmillan, 1981), p. 86; Eichberg, "Sport im 19. Jahrhundert," in *GL,* ed. Horst Ueberhorst, 6 vols. (Berlin: Bartels & Wernitz, 1972–1989), 3:356–57; Maurice Verhaegen, "Belgien," in ibid., 5:137; Philippe Gaboriau, *Le Tour de France et le vélo* (Paris: L'Harmattan, 1995), pp. 105–6.

5. Gaboriau, *Le Tour de France et le vélo,* p. 105; Hubscher, Durry, and Jeu, *L'Histoire en mouvements,* pp. 81, 84; Holt, *Sport and Society in Modern France,* p. 87.

6. Liselott Diem, *Frau und Sport* (Freiburg: Herder, 1980), p. 29; Gerald R. Gems, "Working Class Women and Sport," *Women in Sport and Physical Activity Journal,* 2:1 (Spring 1993): 19; Peter Nye, *Hearts of Lions* (New York: Norton, 1988), p. 92; David N. Maynard, "The Divergent Evolution of Competitive Cycling in the United States and Europe," in *The Masks of Play,* ed. Brian Sutton-Smith and Diana Kelly-Byrne (New York: Leisure Press, 1984), pp. 78–87.

7. Vamplew, *Pay Up and Play the Game,* p. 189; Stephen G. Jones, *Sport, Politics and the Working Class* (Manchester: Manchester University Press, 1988), pp. 31–32; Arnd Krüger, "The German Way of Worker Sport," in *The Story of Worker Sport,* ed. Arnd Krüger and James Riordan (Champaign, Ill.: Human Kinetics, 1996), p. 16; Franz Thaller, "Leibesübungen im Mittelalter und in der frühen Neuzeit," in *Sport am Puls der Zeit,* ed. Franz Thaller and Josef Recla (Graz: Institut für Leibeserziehung der . . . Universität Graz, 1973), p. 69; Stefano Pivato, "The Bicycle as a Political Symbol," *IJHS,* 7:2 (September 1990): 179.

8. Glen Norcliffe, *The Ride to Modernity* (Toronto: University of Toronto Press, 2001), p. 112; Eugen Weber, "Prologue," to *La Naissance du mouvement sportif associatif en France,* ed. Pierre Arnaud and Jean Camy (Lyon: Presses universitaires de Lyon, 1986), p. 19; anonymous Frenchwoman, quoted in Pierre Arnaud, "Le genre ou le sexe?" in Pierre Arnaud and Thierry Terret, *L'Histoire du sport féminin* 2 vols. (Paris: L'Harmattan, 1996), 2:153.

9. Preacher, quoted in Foster Rhea Dulles, *America Learns to Play* (New York: D. Appleton-Century, 1940), p. 207; Jihang Park, "Sport, Dress Reform and the Emancipation of Women in Victorian England," *IJHS,* 6:1 (May 1989): 21; Gibson, illustrated in Martha Banta, *Imaging American Women* (New York: Columbia University Press, 1987), p. 89. On clothing as an issue in women's sports, see Manuela Müller-Windisch, *Aufgeschnürt und Außer Atem* (Frankfurt: Campus Verlag, 1995); Phillis Cunnington and Alan Mansfield, *English Costume for Sports and Outdoor Recreation* (London: Adam & Charles Black, 1969).

10. T. R. Coombs, quoted in Ritchie, *King of the Road,* p. 155; Heike Kuhn, *Vom Korsett zum Stahlroß* (Sankt Augustin: Academia, 1995), p. 78; Christopher Thompson, "Un troisième sexe?" *Le Mouvement Social,* no. 192 (July–September 2000): 35–36; see also Claire S. Simpson, "Respectable Identities," *IJHS,* 18:2 (June 2001): 54–77.

11. Allen Guttmann, *Women's Sports* (New York: Columbia University Press, 1991), p. 102; Kuhn, *Vom Korsett zum Stahlroß,* p. 45; Claire Simpson, "The Develop-

ment of Women's Cycling in Late Nineteenth-Century New Zealand," *Sport, Power and Society in New Zealand,* ed. John Nauright (Sydney: ASSH, 1995), p. 35.

12. Edouard Seidler, *Le Sport et la press* (Paris: Armand Colin, 1964), p. 48; Christopher Thompson, "Controlling the Working-Class Sports Hero in Order to Control the Masses?" *Stadion,* 27 (2001): 139–51; Holt, *Sport and Society in Modern France,* pp. 94–102; Hugh Dauncey and Geoff Hare, "The Tour de France," *IJHS,* 20:2 (June 2003): 1–29.

13. Christophe Campos, "Beating the Bounds," *IJHS,* 20:2 (June 2003): 149–74; Eric Reed, "The Economics of the Tour," ibid., pp. 103–27.

14. Christopher Thompson, "The Tour in the Inter-War Years," ibid., pp. 86–87; François Torbeen, *Les Géants du cyclisme* (Paris: Éditions mondiales, 1963), pp. 145–64; Gaboriau, *Le Tour de France et le vélo,* p. 84; Hugh Dauncey, "French Cycling Heroes of the Tour," *IJHS,* 20:2 (June 2003): 175–202; for Schumacher, see Jeff MacGregor, "International Man of Mystery," *SI,* 98:17 (April 28, 2003): 55; for Armstrong and his lack of popularity, see Ted M. Butryn and Matthew A. Masucci, "It's Not about the Book," *JSSI,* 27:2 (May 2003): 124–44. The first American winner was Greg LeMond. Although he made the cover of *Sports Illustrated,* few Americans noticed; see Nye, *Hearts of Lions,* pp. 277–83.

15. Andrew Ritchie and Rüdiger Rabenstein, "Mostly Middle-Class Cycling Heroes," *ESHR,* 4 (2002): 98. Hubscher, Durry, and Jeu, *L'Histoire en mouvements,* pp. 443–44; Georges Magnane, *Sociologie du sport* (Paris: Gallimard, 1964), pp. 108–9; Sandro Provvisionato, *Lo Sport in Italia* (Rome: Savelli, 1978), p. 50; see also Stefano Pivato, "Italian Cycling and the Creation of a Catholic Hero," *IJHS,* 13:1 (March 1996): 128–38; Dauncey and Hare, "The Tour de France," pp. 1–29.

16. Ludwig Prokop, "Zur Geschichte des Doping," in *Rekorde aus der Retorte,* ed. Helmut Acker (Stuttgart: Deutsche Verlags-Anstalt, 1972), p. 23; Anquetil, quoted in Tom Donohoe and Neil Johnson, *Foul Play* (Oxford: Basil Blackwell, 1986), p. 7. See also Catherine Palmer, "Spin Doctors and Sportsbrokers," *IRSS,* 35:3 (September 2000): 364–77.

17. John Hoberman, "A Pharmacy on Wheels," in *The Essence of Sport,* ed. Verner Møller and John Nauright (Odense: University Press of South Denmark, 2003), pp. 107–27; Patrick Mignon, "The Tour de France and the Doping Issue," *IJHS,* 20:2 (June 2003): 227–45; see also Benjamin D. Brewer, "Commercialization in Professional Cycling 1950–2002," *SSJ,* 19:3 (2001): 276–301; Patrick Trabal and Pascal Duret, "Le Dopage dans le cyclisme professional," *STAPS,* 60 (Winter 2003): 59–74.

18. Boardman, quoted in Ivan Waddington, *Sport, Health and Drugs* (London: E & FN Spon, 2000), p. 161; Craig Neff (on the Pan-American Games), "Caracas," *SI,* 48 (September 5, 1983): 18–23; Tom Verducci (on baseball), "Totally Juiced," *SI,* 96 (June 3, 2002): 34–48; Debra Shogan (on cyborgs), *The Making of High-Performance Athletes* (Toronto: University of Toronto Press, 1999), p. 73; John M. Hoberman, *Mortal Engines* (New York: The Free Press, 1992).

19. Hubscher, Durry, and Jeu, *L'Histoire en mouvements,* pp. 67, 440; Philippe Ga-

boriau, "L'Auto et le Tour de France," in *Histoire des sports,* ed. Thierry Terret (Paris: L'Harmattan, 1996), pp. 39–49.

20. Weber, "Prologue," *La Naissance du mouvement sportif associatif en France,* p. 22.

21. John A. Lucas and Ronald A. Smith, *Saga of American Sport* (Philadelphia: Lea & Febiger, 1978), pp. 162–67; Jeroen Heijmans, "Motorsport at the 1900 Paris Olympic Games," *Journal of Olympic History,* 10:3 (September 2002): 30–35; Hubscher, Durry, and Jeu, *L'Histoire en mouvements,* p. 442; Terrence M. Cole, "Ocean to Ocean by Model T," *JSH,* 18:2 (Summer 1991): 224–40.

22. Hubscher, Durry, and Jeu, *L'Histoire en mouvements,* p. 441; Julian K. Quattlebaum, *The Great Savannah Races* (Athens: University of Georgia Press, 1983); Richard Pillsbury, "Stock Car Racing," in *The Theater of Sport,* ed. Karl B. Raitz (Baltimore: Johns Hopkins University Press, 1995), pp. 273–74.

23. Charles Edgley, "Beer, Speed, and Real Men, *Sport Place,* 1:1 (Winter 1987): 21; Robert H. Boyle, *Sport—Mirror of American Life* (Boston: Little, Brown, 1963), pp. 135–79; Christine Peyton, "Karrieren auf den Rennpisten," *SZGS,* 2:3 (1988): 106–23; Garry Chick, "Formula 1 Auto Racing," in *EWS,* ed. David Levinson and Karen Christensen (Santa Barbara: ABC–CLIO, 1995), 1:354–58; *Hot Rod,* editorial, quoted in H. F. Moorhouse, *Driving Ambitions* (Manchester: University of Manchester Press, 1991), p. 175.

24. James P. Viken, March L. Krotee, and Gregory P. Stone, "Popular Culture and the Erosion of Class Distinctions in the Mass Sport of Drag Racing," in *The Dimensions of Sport Sociology,* ed. March L. Krotee (West Point, N.Y.: Leisure Press, 1979), pp. 127–40.

25. *Hot Rod Monthly,* quoted in Moorhouse, *Driving Ambitions,* p. 100.

26. John Bale, *Sports Geography* (London: E & F N Spon, 1989), p. 186; Richard Pillsbury, "Stock Car Racing," in *The Theater of Sport,* pp. 270–95; Giles Tippette, *The Brave Men* (New York: Macmillan, 1972), p. 41; Sam Moses (on Muldowney), "The Best Man for the Job Is a Woman," *SI,* 54 (June 22, 1981): 70–84. *Sports Illustrated* commemorated Earnhardt's death with a black-and-white cover photograph ("DEATH OF A CHAMPION") and an extended tribute by Mark Bechtel, "Crushing," *SI,* 94 (February 26, 2001): 36–44.

27. Hubscher, Durry, and Jeu, *L'Histoire en mouvements,* p. 447; Gertrud Pfister, *Fliegen—Ihr Leben* (Berlin: Orlanda, 1989), pp. 51, 91.

28. Stu Luce, "Air Racing," in *EWS,* p. 22.

29. Gregory Alegi, "Air Sports," in *IEWS,* ed. Christensen, Guttmann, and Pfister, p. 34; Earhart, quoted in Judy Lomax, *Women of the Air* (New York: Dodd, Mead, 1987), p. 82; see also George Palmer Putnam, *Soaring Wings* (New York: Harcourt, Brace, 1939); Mary S. Lovell, *The Sound of Wings* (New York: St. Martin's, 1989); Doris L. Rich, *Amelia* (Washington: Smithsonian Institution Press, 1989).

30. Alegi, "Air Sports," in *IEWS,* pp. 23–24.

14. Modern Sports in Asia

1. Bill Murray, *The World's Game* (Urbana: University of Illinois Press, 1996), p. 19; Jonathan Kolatch, *Sports, Politics, and Ideology in China* (New York: Jonathan

David, 1972), p. 9; see also Pao-Yin Shuy, "The Early Development of Modern Physical Education and Sports in the Ching Dynasty in China," in *The History, the Evolution and Diffusion of Sports and Games in Different Cultures,* ed. Roland Renson, Pierre Paul De Nayer, and Michel Ostyn (Brussels: Bestuur voor de Lichamelijke Opvoeding, de Sport en het Openluchtleven, 1976), pp. 339–44.

2. Kolatch, *Sports, Politics, and Ideology in China,* pp. 8–9.

3. Fan Hong and Tan Hua, "Sport in China," *IJHS,* 19:2–3 (June-September 2002): 197.

4. Elmer L. Johnson, *The History of YMCA Physical Education* (Chicago: Follett, 1979), p. 160; Janice A. Beran, "Physical Education and Sport in the Philippines," in *Sport in Asia and Africa,* ed. Eric A. Wagner (Westport, Conn.: Greenwood Press, 1989), pp. 151–52; Joseph Mills Hanson, ed., *The Inter-Allied Games* (Paris: The Games Committee, 1919), pp. 11–12.

5. Chinese president, quoted in Hanson, ed., *The Inter-Allied Games,* p. 13; Rolf von der Laage, *Sport in China* (Berlin: Bartels & Wernitz, 1977), pp. 46–47.

6. Kolatch, *Sports, Politics, and Ideology in China,* pp. 24–27.

7. Ibid., pp. 13–14; Fan Hong, *Footbinding, Feminism and Freedom* (London: Frank Cass, 1997), p. 275.

8. Kolatch, *Sports, Politics, and Ideology in China,* pp. 13–17; Susan Brownell, *Training the Body for China* (Chicago: University of Chicago Press, 1995), pp. 48–56; Mike Speak, "China in the Modern World," in *SPEC,* ed. James Riordan and Robin Jones (London: E & FN Spon, 1999), p. 86; Hong, *Footbinding, Feminism and Freedom,* p. 275.

9. Hong, *Footbinding, Feminism and Freedom,* p. 131; see also John R. Fairs, "Maoism, Puritanism, and Physical Education," *CJHS,* 15:1 (May 1984): 1–29.

10. Kolatch, *Sports, Politics, and Ideology in China,* pp. 135–65; Dong Jinxia, *Sport and Society in Modern China* (London: Frank Cass, 2003), p. 63.

11. Lu Xianwu and Lin Shuying, "Outstanding Athletes and their Coaches," in *Sport in China,* ed. Howard G. Knuttgen, Ma Qiwei, and Wu Zhongyuan (Champaign, Ill.: Human Kinetics, 1990), pp. 123–41; Brian B. Pendleton, "'The Mantis and the Chariot,'" *Arena Review,* 3:4 (October 1979): 15–26; Allen Guttmann, *The Games Must Go On* (New York: Columbia University Press, 1984), pp. 142–47.

12. Guttmann, *The Games Must Go On,* pp. 91–94; Wu Zhongyuan and Que Yongwu, "Organizational Structure of China's Physical Culture," in *Sport in China,* pp. 41–57; Roy A. Clumpner and Brian B. Pendleton, "The People's Republic of China," in *Sport under Communism,* ed. James Riordan (Montreal: McGill–Queen's University Press, 1978), pp. 103–40.

13. Fan Hong, "Not All Bad!" *IJHS,* 16:3 (September 1999): 48.

14. Gerald Lawson, *World Record Breakers in Track and Field Athletics* (Champaign, Ill.: Human Kinetics, 1997), pp. 311, 320, 379; David Levinson, "Chi Cheng," in *IEWS,* ed. Karen Christensen, Allen Guttmann, and Gertrud Pfister (New York: Macmillan Reference, 2001), pp. 220–21.

15. Fan Hong, "Not All Bad!, p. 63; Susan Brownell, "Representing Gender in the Chinese Nation," *Identities,* 2:3 (1996): 224; see also her "Cultural Variations in Olympic Telecasts," *Journal of International Communication,* 2:1 (1995): 26–41.

16. Jinxia, *Sport and Society in Modern China*, pp. 105–6. *Sport in China*, ed. Knutt-gen, Qiwei, and Zhongyuan, contains five essays on research into sports science, pp.145–203.

17. Brownell, *Training the Body for China*, pp. 49–119.

18. Robin Jones, "The Emergence of Professional Sport," in *SPEC*, pp. 185–201; James Riordan and Dong Jinxia, "Chinese Women and Sport," in ibid., p. 168; Fan Hong, "The Olympic Movement in China," *CSS*, 1:1 (May 1998): 162.

19. Brownell, *Training the Body for China*, p. 275.

20. Brian B. Pendleton, "Deuce or Double Fault?" in *Sport and Politics*, ed. Gerald Redmond (Champaign, Ill.: Human Kinetics, 1986), pp. 13–19. Hu Na's defection had caused the PRC to consider a boycott of the 1984 Olympics; see Dale P. Toohey, "The Politics of the 1984 Los Angeles Olympics," in ibid., pp. 161–69.

21. Riordan and Jinxia, "Chinese Women and Sport," in *SPEC*, pp. 167–68; Hong, "Making Sporting Heroines in Modern China," *Stadion*, 26:1 (2000): 121.

22. Amby Burfoot, "Can of Worms," *Runner's World*, 28:12 (December 1993): 60–69; Jinxia, *Sport and Society in Modern China*, pp. 143–54; James Riordan and Dong Jinxia, "Chinese Women and Sport," in *SPEC*, pp.159–61. On the participation rates of ordinary Chinese women, see Wang Zhen, Chen An-Huai, and Qian Yao-Ting, "Female Chinese Textile Workers," *IRSS*, 23:1 (1988): 43–50.

23. Robin Jones, "Ten Years of China Watching," in *Old Borders, New Borders, No Borders*, ed. Jan Tolleneer and Roland Renson (Aachen: Meyer & Meyer, 2000), pp. 105–15; "China's Lenovo joins Olympic sponsors club," *China Daily*, April 21, 2004; Hong, "The Olympic Movement in China," p. 163.

24. Mihir Bose, *A History of Indian Cricket* (London: Andre Deutsch, 1990), p. 16. Ar-jun Appadurai, "Playing with Modernity," in *Consuming Modernity*, ed. Carol A. Breckenridge (Minneapolis: University of Minnestoa Press, 1995), pp. 23, 25; Nandy, quoted by Richard Cashman, "Cricket on the Subcontinent," *Sporting Traditions*, 9:1 (November 1992): 108. The literary allusion is to Rupert Brooke's sonnet, "If I should die, think only this of me." On Indian sports, more generally, see Joseph S. Alter, *The Wrestler's Body* (Berkeley: University of California Press, 1992); Jeevanandam P. Thomas, "A Brief Historical Survey of Physical Educa-tion and Sports in India," in *GL*, ed. Horst Ueberhorst, 6 vols. (Berlin: Bartels & Wernitz, 1972–1989): 6:199–214.

25. Patrick McDevitt, "The King of Sports," *IJHS*, 20:1 (March 2003): 3.

26. *Cricket Chat*, quoted in Bose, *History of Indian Cricket*, p. 24.

27. Wickham, quoted in Richard Cashman, *Patrons, Players and the Crowd* (New Delhi: Longman Orient, 1980), p. 25; for Kincaid, see Simon Wilde, *Ranji* (Lon-don: Kingswood Press, 1990), p. 163.

28. Bose, *History of Indian Cricket*, pp. 27–33.

29. Cashman, *Patrons, Players and the Crowd*, pp. 11–18; Harris is quoted on p. 11. See also Ramachandra Guha, "Cricket, Caste, Community, Colonialism," *IJHS*, 14:1 (April 1997): 174–83; Boria Majumdar, "Cricket in Colonial India," *IJHS*, 19:2–3 (June–September 2002): 157–88.

30. J. A. Mangan, *The Games Ethic and Imperialism* (New York: Viking Press, 1985), pp. 178; Tyndale-Biscoe quoted, p. 183.

31. Pennell, quoted in J. A. Mangan, "Christ and the Imperial Games Fields," *BJSH*, 1:2 (September 1984): 188; Sherring, quoted in Mangan, *The Games Ethic and Imperialism*, p. 135; the photograph is reproduced in Allen Guttmann, *Games and Empires* (New York: Columbia University Press, 1994).

32. Bose, *History of Indian Cricket*, pp. 47–52; the quotation is from p. 49. See also Cashman, *Patrons, Players and the Crowd*, pp. 27–34.

33. Cardus, quoted in Cashman, *Patrons, Players and the Crowd*, p. 35.

34. Ranjitsinhji, quoted in Wilde, *Ranji*, p. 48, and in Cashman, *Patrons, Players and the Crowd*, p. 35.

35. Appadurai, "Playing with Modernity," in *Consuming Modernity*, p. 43.

36. Tyndale-Biscoe, quoted in Mangan, *The Games Ethic and Imperialism*, p. 186.

37. Tony Mason, "Football on the Maidan," *IJHS*, 7:1 (May 1990): 85–96; Paul Dimeo, "Football and Politics in Bengal," in *Soccer in South Asia*, ed. Paul Dimeo and James Mills (London: Frank Cass, 2001), pp. 57–74; Dimeo, "'Team Loyalty Splits the City into Two,'" in *Fear and Loathing in World Football*, ed. Gary Armstrong and Richard Giulianotti (Oxford: Berg, 2001), pp. 105–18; and Dimeo, "Colonial Bodies, Colonial Sport," *IJHS*, 19:1 (March 2002): 72–90.

38. Novy Kapidia, "Triumphs and Disasters," in *Soccer in South Asia*, p. 37; Mario Rodrigues, "The Corporates and the Game," in ibid., p. 121.

39. Alter, *The Wrestler's Body*, pp. 196–97.

40. Phillip B. Zarrilli, "Repositioning the Body," in *Consuming Modernity*, pp. 183–215.

41. Bhalla, quoted in Joseph S. Alter, "*Kabaddi*, a National Sport of India," in *Games, Sports and Cultures*, ed. Noel Dyck (Oxford: Berg, 2000), p. 97; Ian McDonald, "'Physiological Patriots'?" *IRSS*, 34:4 (December 1999): 343–58.

42. Thomas, "A Brief Historical Survey of Physical Education and Sports in India," in *GL*, 6:199–214.

43. Ibid., Xiaofei Liu, *Der Weg der Dritten Welt in die Olympische Bewegung* (Sankt Augustin: Academia, 1998), pp. 37, 66–68; Packianathan Chelladurai et al., "Sport in Modern India," *IJHS*, 19:2–3 (June–September 2002): 366–83.

44. Francis L. Hawks, *Narrative of the Expedition of an American Squadron to the China Seas and Japan* (New York: D. Appleton, 1857), p. 432; quoted from Francis Hall, *Japan through American Eyes*, ed. F. G. Notehelfer (Princeton: Princeton University Press, 1992), p. 127 n. 24; Patricia Cuyler, *Sumo* (Tokyo: Weatherhill, 1985), p. 11.

45. Maarten van Bottenburg, *Verborgen Competitie* (Amsterdam: Bert Bakker, 1994), pp. 132–33.

46. Kinoshita Hideaki, *Supōtsu no kindai Nihonshi* (Tokyo: Kyōrin Shoin, 1970), pp. 3–7.

47. Shinsuke Tanada, "Diffusion into the Orient," *IJHS*, 5:3 (December 1988): 372–76; Wolfram Manzenreiter, *Die soziale Konstruktion des japanischen Alpinismus* (Vienna: Abteilung für Japanologie/Institut für Ostasienwissenschaften, 2000), p. 53; Hugh Cortazzi, *Victorians in Japan* (London: Athlone, 1987), p. 293; Imamura Yoshio, *Nihon taiiku shi* (Tokyo: Fumaidô, 1970), p. 85; Edward Seidensticker, *Low City, High City* (New York: Alfred Knopf, 1983), p. 167.

48. Haruo Nogawa and Hiroka Maeda, "The Japanese Dream," in *Football Cultures*

and Identities, ed. Gary Armstrong and Richard Giulianotti (London: Macmillan, 1999), pp. 223–24; John Horne and Derek Bleakley, "The Development of Football in Japan," in *Japan, Korea and the 2002 World Cup,* ed. John Horne and Wolfram Manzenreiter (London: Routledge, 2002), pp. 89–105.

49. *Financial Times,* quoted by Jonathan Watts, "Soccer shinhatsubai," in *The Worlds of Japanese Popular Culture,* ed. D. P. Martinez (Cambridge: Cambridge University Press, 1998), p. 193; Nogawa and Maeda, "The Japanese Dream," in *Football Cultures and Identities,* pp. 223–33; Takayuki Yamashita and Natsuko Saka, "Another Kick Off," in *Japan, Korea and the 2002 World Cup,* pp. 147–61.

50. Imamura, *Nihon taiiku shi,* p. 331; Nogawa and Maeda, "The Japanese Dream," in *Football Cultures and Identities,* p. 223; Gareth Williams, "Rugby Union," in *Sport in Britain,* ed. Tony Mason (Cambridge: Cambridge University Press, 1989), p. 338; Tanaka Tokuhisa and Yoshikawa Kumiko, *Spōtsu* (Tokyo: Kintō, 1990), pp. 42–47; Kinoshita, *Supōtsu no kindai nihonshi,* p. 87. Richard Light dates the national rugby federation from 1926; see "A Centenary of Rugby and Masculinity . . . ," *Sporting Traditions,* 16:2 (May 2000): 93.

51. Teijirô Muramatsu, *Westerners in the Modernization of Japan* (Tokyo: Hitachi, 1995), pp. 221–25; quotation from p. 224. See also N. K. Roscoe, "The Development of Sport in Japan," *Transactions and Proceedings of the Japan Society,* 30 (1933): 54; Ikuo Abe and J. A. Mangan, "The British Impact on Boys' Sports and Games in Japan," *IJHS,* 14:2 (August 1997): 192; Abe and Mangan, "'Sportsmanship'—English Inspiration and Japanese Response," *IJHS,* 19:2–3 (June–September 2002): 99–128.

52. *Asahi Shimbun* (Tokyo), January 28, 1999; William R. May, "Sports," in *The Handbook of Japanese Popular Culture,* ed. Richard Gid Powers and Hidetoshi Kato (Westport, Conn.: Greenwood Press, 1989), p. 173. Gordon Daniels gives Fujii's vault as 3.424 meters and the world record as 3.427 meters, but vaulting records were not ordinarily measured to the millimeter; see "Japanese Sport," in *Sport, Culture, and Politics,* ed. J. C. Binfield and John Stevenson (Sheffield: Sheffield Academic Press, 1993), p. 178. Imamura Yoshio (*Nihon taiiku shi,* p. 423) gives Fujii's record as 3.66 meters.

53. Masujima Midori, *Samenai Yume* (Tokyo: Za masada, 2000), p. 36.

54. *Asahi Shimbun,* January 28, 1999; Imamura, *Nihon taiiku shi,* p. 424; Kinoshita, *Supōtus no kindai Nihonshi,* pp. 56–60; Tanaka and Yoshikawa, *Supōtsu,* p. 168; Mombushō kyōgi supōtsu kenkyūkai, ed,,"*Miru supōtsu" no shinkō* (Tokyo: Baseball Magazine, 1996), pp. 174–80.

55. Ohara Toshihiko, *Hitomi Kinue monogatari* (Tokyo: Asahi Shimbunsha, 1990).

56. Cortazzi, *Victorians in Japan,* pp. 19,164; Muramatsu, *Westerners in the Modernization of Japan,* p. 225; see also Kinoshita, *Supōtsu no kindai nihonshi,* pp. 21–22, 122–23; Imamura, *Nihon taiiku shi,* pp. 425–26.

57. Tanaka and Yoshikawa, *Supôtsu,* pp. 66–67.

58. Shinsuke Tanada, "Introduction of European Sport in Kobe . . . ," in *Civilization in Sport History,* pp. 68–76; Franz Klaus, "Gedenken an Generalmajor Theodor von Lerch," *Zdarksy-Blätter,* 35 (March 1986): 11–13; Sasase Masashi, "Hokkaidō Teikoku Daigaku Suki⁻-bu ni okeru tōzan to kyōgi . . . ," *Taiikushi kenkyû,* 11

(1994): 41–54; Manzenreiter, *Die soziale Konstruktion des japanischen Alpinismus,* p. 90.

59. Imamura, *Nihon taiiku shi,* pp. 331–32; Kinoshita, *Supōtsu no kindai nihonshi,* pp. 44–45.

60. Yuko Kusaka, "The Development of Baseball Organizations in Japan," *IRSS,* 22:4 (1987): 266.

61. Donald Roden, *Schooldays in Imperial Japan* (Berkeley: University of California Press, 1980), p. 113.

62. My main source for the game is Donald Roden, "Baseball and the Quest for National Dignity in Meiji Japan," *American Historical Review,* 85:3 (June 1980): 511–34.

63. Ibid., p. 524; *Japan Weekly Mail,* quoted in ibid., p. 525.

64. Norgren, quoted in Robert J. Sinclair, "Baseball's Rising Sun," *CJHS,* 16:2 (December 1985): 48; Kōzu Masaru, *Nihon kindai supōtsushi no teiryū* (Tokyo: Sōbun kikaku, 1994), pp. 241–50.

65. Roden, "Baseball and the Quest for National Dignity," p. 519; Mark Twain, quoted in Harry Clay Palmer, "The 'Around the World' Tour," in *Athletic Sports in America, England, and Australia,* ed. Harry Clay Palmer (Philadelphia: Hubbard Bros., 1889), p. 447.

66. Palmer, "The 'Around the World' Tour," pp. 205–7; Richard C. Crepeau, "Pearl Harbor: A Failure of Baseball?" *Journal of Popular Culture,* 15:4 (Spring 1982): 67–74; Edward Uhlan and Dana L. Thomas, *Shoriki* (New York: Exposition Press, 1957), p. 109.

67. Kiku Kōichi, *"Kindai puro supōtsu" no rekishi shakaigaku* (Tokyo: Fumaido, 1993), pp. 189, 233, 237–38; Hashimoto, *Nihon supōtsu hōsōshi* (Tokyo: Taishūkan shoten, 1992), p. 30.

68. Tanaka and Yoshikawa, *Supōtsu,* p. 37; Kōzu, *Nihon kindai supōtsu no teiryū,* pp. 327–28; Nakamura Toshio, Izuhara Yoshiaki, and Todoriki Kenji, *Gendai supōtsu ron* (Tokyo: Kyōrin shoin, 1970), p. 222.

69. Itō Kazuo, "Puro yakyū," in *Saishin Supōtsu daijiten,* ed. Kishino Yūzō (Tokyo: Taishūkan shoten, 1987), pp. 1126–35.

70. Sadaharu Oh and David Falkner, *Sadaharu Oh* (New York: Times Books, 1984).

71. Robert Whiting, *The Chrysanthemum and the Bat* (New York: Dodd, Mead, 1977), p. 100; *Asahi Shimbun,* March 14, 1999.

72. William W. Kelly, "Blood and Guts in Japanese Professional Baseball," in *The Culture of Japan as Seen through Its Leisure,* ed. Sepp Linhart and Sabine Frühstück (Albany: SUNY Press, 1998), p. 102; William W. Kelly, "Learning to Swing: Oh Sadaharu and the Pedagogy and Practice of Japanese Baseball," in *Learning in Likely Places,* ed. John Singleton (New York: Cambridge University Press, 1998), pp. 265–85.

73. Kanō, quoted by Inoue Shun, "Budō," in *The Culture of Japan as Seen through Its Leisure,* p. 85. Inoue offers a slightly different translation in "The Invention of the Martial Arts," in *Mirror of Modernity,* ed. Stephen Vlastos (Berkeley: University of California Press, 1998), p. 165.

74. Jigorō Kanō, *Kodokan Judo* (Tokyo: Kodansha International, 1986), p. 16.

75. Inoue Shun, "Budō," in *The Culture of Japan as Seen through Its Leisure*, p, 85.

76. Kanō, quoted by Inoue, "Invention of the Martial Arts," in *Mirror of Modernity*, p. 166.

77. Michel Brousse and David Matsumoto, *Judo* (Seoul: International Judo Federation, 1999).

78. Miyoko Hagiwara, "Japanese Women's Sports and Physical Education under the Influence of Their Traditional Costumes," in *Civilization in Sport History*, ed. Shimizu Shigeo (Kobe: Kobe University, 1987), p. 266; Nishimura Ayako, "Zenkoku kōtō jōgakkōchō kaigi ni mrareru kōtō jōgakko no taiiku mondai," *Taiiku shi kenkyū*, 5 (March 1988): 7–21; Yoshie Hata, "The Influence of Protestantism of [*sic*] Modern Physical Education in Japan," in *Civilization in Sport History*, p. 82.

79. Hiroko Seiwa and Chieko Onishi, "Women and Athletic Meetings in Japan" (unpublished paper, ISHPES Congress, Lyon, 1997).

80. Anonymous student, quoted in Hata, "The Influence of Protestantism of [*sic*] Modern Physical Education in Japan," in *Civilization in Sport History*, p. 79.

81. Knut Dietrich, "Fitneßsport als Teil der Großstadtkultur," in *Körperkulturen und Identität*, ed. Henning Eichberg and Jørn Hansen (Münster: LIT-Verlag, 1989), pp 107–12; Laura Spielvogel, *Working Out in Japan* (Durham: Duke University Press, 2003); Ryozo Kanezaki, "Sociological Considerations on Sport Involvement of Japanese Female Adults," *IRSS*, 26:4 (1991): 271–85; Toshio Saeki, "Sport in Japan," in *Sport in Asia and Africa*, pp. 52, 69; Yasuhiro Sakaue, "Kendo," in *EWS*, ed. David Levinson and Karen Christensen (Santa Barbara: ABC–CLIO, 1996), p. 549; Tanaka and Yoshikawa, *Supōtsu*, p. 65.

82. Tanaka and Yoshikawa, *Supōtsu*, pp. 80–81; Tanaka Yoshihisa, *Gorufu to Nihonjin* (Tokyo: Iwanami shinsho, 1992), pp. 70–73.

83. Ono Akira, *Gendai supōtsu hihan* (Tokyo: Taishūkan shoten, 1996), p. 94; Nelson H. H. Graburn, "Work and Play in the Japanese Countryside" in *The Culture of Japan as Seen through Its Leisure*, p. 202.

84. Eyal Ben-Ari, "Golf, Organization, and 'Body Projects,'" in *The Culture of Japan as Seen through Its Leisure*, p. 154; Brian Stoddart, "Wide World of Golf," *SSJ*, 7:4 (1990): 382; Peter J. Rimmer, "Japanese Investment in Golf Course Development," *International Journal of Urban and Regional Research*, 18 (1994): 234–55.

85. Ben-Ari, "Golf, Organization, and 'Body Projects,'" in *The Culture of Japan as Seen through Its Leisure*, p. 143.

86. The details of the rest of this account of sumô are taken from Allen Guttmann and Lee Thompson, *Japanese Sports* (Honolulu: University of Hawaii Press, 2001), pp. 181–88.

87. Martin Stokes, "'Strong As a Turk,'" in *Sport, Identity, and Ethnicity*, ed. Jeremy MacClancy (Oxford: Berg, 1996), p. 27; see also Philippe Rochard, "The Identities of the Iranian *Zûrkhânah*," *Iranian Studies*, 35:4 (Fall 2002): 313–40.

88. H. E. Chehabi, "Sport and Politics in Iran," *IJHS*, 12:3 (December 1995): 48–60; and his "Political History of Football in Iran," *Iranian Studies*, 35:4 (Fall 2002): 341–69.

89. In addition to the two essays by Chehabi, cited above, see Jennifer Hargreaves, *Heroines of Sport* (London: Routledge, 2000), p. 65.

90. In addition to the Chehabi essays cited above, see A. Reza Arasteh, "The Social Role of the *Zurkhana* (House of Strength) . . . ," *Der Islam,* 36 (February 1961): 256–59.

91. Peter Parkes, "Indigenous Polo and the Politics of Regional Identity in Northern Pakistan," in *Sport, Identity, and Ethnicity,* pp. 43–67.

92. Peter A. Horton, "'Padang or Paddock,'" *IJHS,* 14:1 (April 1997): 1–20; and his "Complex Creolization," *ESHR,* 3 (2001): 77–104; Janice Brownfoot, "Emancipation, Exercise and Imperialism," *IJHS,* 7:1 (May 1990): 61–84.

93. Ruud Stokvis, "The International and National Expansion of Sports," in *Sport in Asia and Africa,* p. 18; Freek Colombijn, "View from the Periphery," in *Football Cultures and Identities,* pp. 126–38; Kathleen M. Spence, "Badminton," in *EWS,* p. 68; see also Iain Adams, "*Pancasila,*" *IJHS,* 19:2–3 (June–September 2002): 295–318.

94. Stephan A. Douglas, "Sport in Malaysia," in *Sport in Asia and Africa,* pp. 165–82; Janice A. Beran, "Physical Education and Sport in the Philippines," in ibid., pp. 147–64; Thomas Smidt, "'Versportung' traditioneller Bewegungskultur in Indonesien," *Sportwissenschaft,* 15:3 (1985): 308–16; Alan Trevithick, "Takraw," in *EWS,* pp. 1010–14.

95. Yair Galily, "Playing Hoops in Palestine," *IJHS,* 20:1 (March 2003): 126–42.

96. Richard Espy, *The Politics of the Olympic Games* (Berkeley: University of California Press, 1979), p. 110; Swanpo Sie, "Sports and Politics," in *Sport and International Relations,* ed. Benjamin Lowe, David B. Kanin, and Andrew Strenk (Champaign, Ill.: Stipes, 1978), pp. 279–96; Allen Guttmann, *The Games Must Go On,* pp. 225–30; Xiaofei Liu, *Der Weg der Dritten Welt in die Olympische Bewegung,* pp. 71–103. The Indonesian historian Sukintaka describes Sondhi's mission as an attempt to "bust up" the Asian Games; see "History of Indonesian Sports," in *GL,* 6:716.

15. "Our Former Colonial Masters"

1. Holger Obermann,"Fußball als Exportartikel," in *Beiträge zur Zusammenarbeit im Sport mit der Dritten Welt,* ed. Rolf Andresen, Hermann Rieder, and Gerhard Trosien (Schorndorf: Karl Hofmann, 1989), p. 50; Anthony Kirk-Greene, "Badge of Office?" *IJHS,* 6:2 (September 1989): 236.

2. Peter Rummelt, *Sport im Kolonialismus—Kolonialismus im Sport* (Cologne: Pahl-Rugenstein, 1986), pp. 168–78; Floris J. G. van der Merwe, "A History of Sport and Physical Education in Southwest Africa/Namibia," in *GL,* ed. Ueberhorst, 6 vols. (Berlin: Bartels & Wernitz, 1972–1989), 6:532–35.

3. Bernadette Deville-Danthu, "Les jeux d'outre mer," in *L'Empire du sport,* ed. Daniel Hick (Aix-en-Provence: Centres des Archives d'Outre-Mer, 1992), p. 66; and her *Le Sport en noir et blanc* (Paris: L'Harmattan, 1997), pp. 33, 81; and also "La participation des sportifs indigènes à l'Exposition Coloniale Internationale

de Paris de 1931," *Sport et Histoire,* new series, 2 (1992): 9–26; Maarten van Bottenburg, *Verborgen Competitie* (Amsterdam: Bert Bakker, 1994), pp. 255–56.

4. Welldon, quoted in J. A. Mangan, *The Games Ethic and Imperialism* (New York: Viking Press, 1985), p. 36.

5. Ibid., pp. 76–79; Anthony Kirk-Greene, "Imperial Administration and the Athletic Imperative," in *Sport in Africa,* ed. William J. Baker and J. A. Mangan (New York: Africana, 1987), p. 99; and his "The Sudan Political Service," *International Journal of African Historical Studies,* 15:1 (1982): 22; John Bale and Joe Sang, *Kenyan Running* (London: Frank Cass, 1996), p. 76; see also Heather J. Sharkey, "Colonialism, Character-Building and the Culture of Nationalism in the Sudan, 1898–1956," *IJHS,* 15:1 (April 1998): 1–26.

6. George Godia, "Sport in Kenya," in *Sport in Asia and Africa,* ed. Eric A. Wagner (Westport, Conn.: Greenwood, 1989), p. 269; Bale and Sang, *Kenyan Running,* p. 70.

7. Lugard, quoted in Mangan, *Games Ethic and Imperialism,* p. 105; see also Phillip Vasili, "The Right Kind of Fellows," *IJHS,* 11:2 (August 1994): 191–211.

8. Carey and former student, quoted in James A. Mangan, "Ethics and Ethnocentricity," in *Sport in Africa,* pp. 147–48; Sev A. Obura to Allen Guttmann, October 29, 1980; Mangan, *Games Ethic and Imperialism,* pp. 175–77; Helen Osayimwen-Oladipo, "The Historical Development of Sport in Nigeria," in *GL,* 6:467; see also E. O. Ojeme, "Sport in Nigeria," in *Sport in Asia and Africa,* pp. 249–66.

9. Mangan, "Ethics and Ethnocentricity," in *Sport in Asia and Aafrica,* p. 152. Women are still drastically underrepresented in African sports; see Morenike Onanuga, "Frauensport in Afrika," in *Frauenleichtathletik,* ed. Norbert Müller, Dieter Augustin, and Bernd Hunger (Niedernhausen: Schors, 1985), pp. 457–65.

10. Godia, "Sport in Kenya," in *Sport in Asia and Africa,* p. 269; Ademola Onifade, "Historical Development of Amateur Sports and their Administrative Agencies in Nigeria," *CJHS,* 16:2 (December 1985): 33–43; Issac Olu Akindutire, "The Historical Development of Soccer in Nigeria," *CJHS,* 22:1 (May 1991): 20–31.

11. Thomas Q. Reefe, "The Biggest Game of All," in *Sport in Africa,* pp. 63–64; Cora Burnett, "The 'Black Cat' of South African Soccer and the Chiefs-Pirates Conflict," in *Fighting Fans,* ed. Eric Dunning, Patrick Murphy, Ivan Waddington, and Antonios Astrinakis (Dublin: University College Dublin Press, 2002), p. 188; Anne Leseth, "The Use of *Juju* in Football," in *Entering the Field,* ed. Gary Armstrong and Richard Giulianotti (Oxford: Berg, 1997), pp. 159–74; N. A. Scotch, "Magic, Sorcery and Football among the Urban Zulu," *Journal of Conflict Resolution,* 5 (1961): 70–70; Bea Vidacs, "Football in Cameroon," *CSS,* 2:3 (Autumn 1999): 100–117.

12. Rummelt, *Sport im Kolonialismus—Kolonialismus im Sport,* pp. 212–16, 221–24; Xiaôtèe Liu, *Der Weg der Dritten Welt in die Olympische Bewegung* (Sankt Augustin: Academia, 1998), pp. 23–30.

13. Leila Sfeir, "Sport in Egypt," in *Sport in Asia and Africa,* p. 190; Rummelt, *Sport im Kolonialismus—Kolonialismus im Sport,* pp. 123–24, 221–25; Allen Guttmann, *The Games Must Go On* (New York: Columbia University Press, 1984), pp. 230, 265.

14. Floris J. G. van der Merwe, "'Athletic Sports' and the Cape Town Society, 1652–1900," *CJHS*, 19:1 (May 1988): 28–39; Whittam, quoted in John Nauright, *Sport, Cultures and Identities in South Africa* (London: Leicester University Press, 1997), p. 28; Floris J. G. van der Merwe, "Sport and Games in Boer Prisoner-of-War Camps during the Anglo-Boer War, 1899–1902," *IJHS*, 9:3 (December 1992): 439–54; van der Merwe, "Sport as a Means of Securing Sanity and Health in Prisoner-of-War Camps during the Anglo-Boer War (1899–1902)," in *Sport et Santé dans l'Histoire*, ed. Thierry Terret (Sankt Augustin: Academia, 1999), pp. 149–56.

15. Nauright, *Sport, Cultures and Identities in South Africa*, p. 62; André Odendaal, "South Africa's Black Victorians," in *Pleasure, Profit, Proselytism*, ed. J. A. Mangan (London: Frank Cass, 1988), p. 199.

16. Robert Archer and Antoine Bouillon, *The South African Game* (London: Zed Press, 1982), p. 91; Douglas Booth, *The Race Game* (London: Frank Cass, 1998), p. 20; Rummelt, *Sport im Kolonialismus—Kolonialismus im Sport*, p. 133.

17. Nauright, *Sport, Cultures and Identities in South Africa*, pp. 43–44; Rummelt, *Sport im Kolonialismus—Kolonialismus im Sport*, p. 146.

18. Archer and Bouillon, *The South African Game*, pp. 104–5.

19. David R. Black and John Nauright, *Rugby and the South African Nation* (Manchester: Manchester University Press, 1998), pp. 29–30; Archer and Bouillon, *The South African Game*, pp. 98–101; Rummelt, *Sport im Kolonialismus—Kolonialismus im Sport*, pp. 144–45; Albert Grundlingh, "Playing for Power?" *IJHS*, 11:3 (December 1994): 408–30; Grant Farred, "Theatre of Dreams," in *Sport and Postcolonialism*, ed. John Bale and Mike Cronin (Oxford: Berg, 2003), pp. 123–45.

20. John Nauright, "Masculinity, Muscular Islam and Popular Culture," *IJHS*, 14:1 (April 1997): 184–90.

21. Nauright, *Sport, Cultures and Identities in South Africa*, pp. 39–43; Robert Morrell, "Forging a Rule Race," in *Making Men*, ed. John Nauright and Timothy J. L. Chandler (London: Frank Cass, 1996), p. 101; Chris Laidlow, *Mud in Your Eye* (London: Pelham Books, 1973), p. 187.

22. Peter Hain, *Don't Play with Apartheid* (London: George Allen & Unwin, 1971), pp. 56–57.

23. Richard Thompson, *Retreat from Apartheid* (Wellington, N.Z.: Oxford University Press, 1975); Guttmann, *The Games Must Go On*, pp. 232–40; Richard Edward Lapchick, *The Politics of Race and International Sport* (Westport, Conn.: Greenwood, 1975), pp. 191–96.

24. Vijoen, quoted in Lapchick, *Politics of Race and International Sport*, p. 179; Vorster, quoted in Archer and Bouillon, *The South African Game*, p. 209. See also Joan Brickhill, *Race against Race* (London: International Defence and Aid Fund, 1976).

25. Booth, *The Race Game*, pp. 80; Samaranch, quoted in Fernand Landry and Magdeleine Yerlès, *The Presidencies of Lord Killanin (1972–1980) and of Juan Antonio Samaranch (1980—)* (Lausanne: IOC, 1996), p. 219.

26. Black and Nauright, *Rugby and the South African Nation,* pp. 115, 124–26; see also Douglas Booth, "United Sport," *IJHS,* 12:3 (December 1995): 105–24; Albert Grundlingh, "From Redemption to Recidivism?" *Sporting Traditions,* 14:2 (May 1998): 67–86.

27. Diakabana N'Senga, "Genèse et Développement du Sport en République du Zaïre," in *GL,* 6:406–9; Bangela Lema, "Sport in Zaire," in *Sport in Asia and Africa,* pp. 232–33; Roland Renson and Christel Peeters, "Sport als Missie," in *Voor Lichaam en Geest,* ed. Mark D'Hoker, Roland Renson, and Jan Tolleneer (Leuven: Universitaire Pers Leuven, 1994), pp. 201–15; Phyllis M. Martin, "Colonialism, Youth and Football in French Equatorial Africa," *IJHS,* 8:1 (May 1991): 56–71.

28. Martin, "Colonialism, Youth and Football in French Equatorial Africa," pp. 56–71; Alfred Wahl, "Football et Jeux de Ballon," in *L'Empire du sport,* pp. 44–45.

29. Deville-Danthu, *Le Sport en noir et blanc,* pp. 51–53; Daniel Hick, "Les Sports et l'eau," in *L'Empire du sport,* p. 33.

30. Thomas Gerbasi, "Battling Siki," www.cyberboxingzone.com.

31. Deville-Danthu, *Le Sport en noir et blanc,* pp. 53, 71–72, 186; Alain Monsellier, "Histoire des activités physiques traditionelles et des sports modernes au Sénégal," in *GL,* 6:364; Bernadette Deville-Danthu, "Les premières tentatives d'encadrement des activités physique et sportives de la jeunesse en A.O.F. (1922–1936)," in *Les Jeunes en Afrique,* ed. Hélène D'Almeida-Topor et al. (Paris: L'Harmattan, 1992), pp. 448–62; Bernadette Deville-Danthu, "Note sur l'histoire du sport dans l'empire français," in *L'Empire du sport,* p. 11.

32. For the traditional sports of North Africa, see Louis Mercier, *La Chasse et les sports chez les arabes* (Paris: Marcel Rivière, 1927).

33. Youssef Fates, "Sport en Algérie," in *GL,* 6:301; Edward S. Goldstein, "Amsterdam 1928," in *Historical Dictionary of the Modern Olympic Movement,* ed. John E. Findling and Kimberly D. Pelle (Westport, Conn.: Greenwood, 1996), p. 70; Wahl, "Football et jeux de ballon," in *L'Empire du sport,* p. 44; Philip Dine, "Sport, Imperial Expansion, and Colonial Consolidation," in *Sport as Symbol,* ed. Floris van der Merwe (Sankt Augustin: Academia, 1996), p. 66.

34. Fates, "Sport en Algérie," in *GL,* 6: 301; Deville-Danthu, "Note sur l'histoire du sport dans l'empire français," in *L'Empire du sport,* p. 13; De Gaulle, quoted in Pierre Lanfranchi and Matthew Taylor, *Moving with the Ball* (Oxford: Berg, 2001), p. 174.

35. Ben Larbi Mohamed and Borhane Erraïs, "Un Siècle d'histoire du sport en Tunisie, 1881–1981," in *GL,* 6: 277, 283–84.

36. Karkoure M'Hamed, "Histoire du sport au Maroc," in ibid., 6:327.

37. Deville-Danthu, *Le Sport en noir et blanc,* pp. 436, 439; see also Désiré Malet, "Les Jeux Africains," in *Sport de France* (Paris: Service de Presse, 1971), pp. 503–7; Liu, *Der Weg der Dritten Welt in die Olympische Bewegung,* pp. 53–63; Jean-Claude Ganga, *Combats pour un sport africain* (Paris: L'Harmattan, 1979).

38. www.fifa.com; J. A. Adedeji, "Work and Leisure in Contemporary Nigerian Society," *IRSS,* 15:2 (1980): 125.

16. Winter Sports

1. Danièle Alexandre-Bidon, "Les Jeux et sports d'hiver au moyen âge et la renaissance," in *Jeux, sports et divertissements au moyen âge et à l'âge classique,* ed. Jean-Michel Mehl (Paris: Editions du Comité des Travaux Historiques et Scientifiques, 1993), p. 151.

2. Alexander Pennicuik, quoted in David B. Smith, "Curling," in *Sport, Scotland and the Scots,* ed. Grant Jarvie and John Burnett (East Linton: Tuckwell Press, 2000), p. 69; N. L. Tranter, "The Patronage of Organized Sport in Central Scotland, 1820–1900," *JSH,* 16:3 (Summer 1989): 234–35.

3. Montreal Curling Club Rules, quoted by Gerald Redmond, *The Sporting Scots of Nineteenth-Century Canada* (Rutherford, N.J.: Farleigh Dickinson University Press, 1982), p. 109; Don Morrow, Mary Keyes, Wayne Simpson, Frank Cosentino, and Ron Lappage, *A Concise History of Sport in Canada* (Toronto: Oxford University Press, 1989), pp. 1–4; Morris Mott and John Allardyce, "'Curling Capital,'" *CJHS,* 19:1 (May 1988): 1–14; Stephen G. Wieting and Danny Lamoureux, "Curling in Canada," *CSS,* 4:2 (Summer 2001): 140–53; Morris Mott, "Curling," in *EWS,* ed. David Levinson and Karen Christensen (Santa Barbara, Calif.: ABC-CLIO, 1995), pp. 226–31.

4. Mott, "Curling," in *EWS,* pp. 226–31.

5. Kristen Mo, "The Development of Skiing as a Competitive Sport," in *WGWT,* ed. Matti Goksøyr, Gerd von der Lippe, and Kristen Mo (Oslo: Norwegian Society of Sports History, 1997), pp. 182–91; Matti Goksøyr, "Phases and Functions of Nationalism," *IJHS,* 12:2 (August 1995): 125–46; Jens Ljunggren and Leif Yttergren, "The Nordic Games," in *Contemporary Studies in the National Olympic Games Movement,* ed. Roland Naul (Frankfurt: Peter Lang, 1997), pp. 117–36; Jens Ljunggren, "The Nordic Games, Nationalism, Sports and Cultural Conflicts," in *WGWT,* pp. 35–45.

6. Roland Renson, "Why Winter Sports at the Antwerp Olympic Games 1920?" in *WGWT,* pp. 141–53; Renson, *De Herboren Spelen* (Brussels: Belgisch Olympisch en Interfederaal Comité, 1995).

7. Arnd Krüger, "The History of the Olympic Winter Games," in *WGWT,* pp. 101–22; Matti Goksøyr, "Phases and Functions of Nationalism," *IJHS,* 12:2 (August 1995): 139.

8. Olav Bø, "Skiing throughout History," in *WGWT,* pp. 13–25; Matti Goksøyr, "Phases and Functions of Nationalism," p. 132; Carl J. Luther, "Geschichte des Schnee- und Eissports," in *Geschichte des Sports,* ed. G. A. E. Bogeng, 2 vols. (Leipzig: E. A. Seemann, 1926), 2: 497–557; E. John B. Allen, "The World Wide Diffusion of Skiing to 1940," in *WGWT,* p. 173.

9. Jack A. Benson, "Before Aspen and Vail," *Journal of the West,* 21:1 (January 1983): 52–61; *Marysville Daily Appeal,* quoted by E. John B. Allen, "Sierra 'Ladies' on Skis in Gold Rush California," *JSH,* 17:3 (Winter 1990): 349–50. See also E. John B. Allen, "The Land of Promise," *Stadion,* 18:1 (1992): 90–105.

10. Richard Holt, "An Englishman in the Alps," *IJHS,* 9:3 (December 1992): 421–32.

11. Allen, "The Land of Promise," pp. 90–105.

12. Gerd Hortleder and Gunter Gebauer, eds., *Sport–Eros–Tod* (Frankfurt: Suhrkamp, 1986); Suzanne Laberge and Mathieu Albert, "Sports à risque," in *Les Risques et la mort,* ed. Eric Volant and Joseph Lévy (Montréal: Méridien, 1996), pp. 79–105.

13. Gertrud Pfister, "Gracefully and Elegantly Downhill," in *WGWT*, pp. 223–39.

14. Otmar Weiss et al., "Ski Tourism and Environmental Problems," *IRSS,* 33:4 (1998): 367–79. Mountaineers also damage fragile ecosystems; see Lawrence C. Hamilton, "The Changing Face of American Mountaineering," *Review of Sport and Leisure,* 6:1 (Summer 1981): 14–36.

15. Else Trangbaek, "Gender and Skating," in *WGWT,* p. 240.

16. Bettina Fabos, "Forcing the Fairytale," *CSS,* 4:2 (Summer 2001): 185–212.

17. Pamela J. Creedon, "Women, Sport, and Media Institutions," in *MediaSport,* ed. Lawrence A. Wenner (London: Routledge, 1998), pp. 88–99; Gina Daddario, *Women's Sport and Spectacle* (Westport, Conn.: Praeger, 1998), pp. 105–28. Quotations are from articles in *Women on Ice,* ed. Cynthia Baughman (New York: Routledge, 1995): Abigail M. Feder, "'A Radiant Smile from the Lovely Lady'" (p. 37); Ellyn Kestenbaum, "What Tonya Harding Means to Me, or Images of Independent Female Power on Ice" (p. 65); Laura Jacobs, "Pure Desire" (pp. 49–50); and Zillah R. Eisenstein and Patricia R. Zimmermann, "The Polympics and Post–Cold War Femininities" (p. 260). See also, Stephanie Foote, "Making Sport of Tonya," *JSSI,* 27:1 (February 2003): 3–17.

18. Leif Yttergren, "The Nordic Games," *IJHS,* 11:3 (December 1994): 500.

19. Morrow et al., *A Concise History of Sport in Canada,* pp. 169–75; Donald Guay, "Les Origines du Hockey," *CJHS,* 20:1 (May 1989): 32–46; Neil D. Isaacs, *Checking Back* (New York: Norton, 1977); Michel Vigneault, "La Diffusion du Hockey à Montréal, 1895–1910," *CJHS,* 17:1 (May 1986): 60–74.

20. Morrow et al., *A Concise History of Sport in Canada,* p. 177; Garry Crawford, "Cultural Tourists and Cultural Trends," *CSS,* 5:1 (Spring 2002): 22.

21. Richard Gruneau and David Whitson, *Hockey Night in Canada* (Toronto: Garamond Press, 1993), pp. 85–92; Bruce Kidd, *The Struggle for Canadian Sport* (Toronto: University of Toronto Press, 1996), p. 210.

22. James Quirk and Rodney D. Fort, *Pay Dirt* (Princeton: Princeton University Press, 1992), pp. 35–38, 327–32.

23. Stan Fischler, *Slashing!* (New York: Thomas Y. Crowell, 1974), p. 4; Mehlenbacher, quoted in Richard B. Horrow, *Sports Violence* (Arlington, Va.: Carrollton Press, 1980), p. 41.

24. Gruneau and Whitson, *Hockey Night in Canada,* pp. 100–101; Donald C. Simmons Jr., "St. Moritz 1928," in *Historical Dictionary of the Modern Olympic Movement,* ed. John E. Findling and Kimberly D. Pelle (Westport, Conn.: Greenwood, 1996), p. 229.

25. Gruneau and Whitson, *Hockey Night in Canada,* p. 105.

26. Ibid., p. 175.

27. Kidd, *The Struggle for Canadian Sport,* pp. 102–3; Nancy Theberge, *Higher Goals* (Albany: SUNY Press, 2000).

28. Morrow et al., *A Concise History of Sport in Canada,* pp. 169–229; Quirk and Fort,

Pay Dirt, pp. 35–38; Daniel S. Mason, "'Get the Puck Outta Here'!" *JSSI,* 26:2 (May 2002): 140–67; Steven J. Jackson and Pam Ponic, "Pride and Prejudice," *CSS,* 4:2 (Summer 2001): 43–62.

29. Mason, "'Get the Puck Outta Here'!" pp. 148–62.

17. The Modern Olympic Games

1. Christopher R. Hill, *Olympic Politics* (Manchester: University of Manchester Press, 1992), pp. 9–15; David C. Young, *The Modern Olympics* (Baltimore: Johns Hopkins University Press, 1996), pp. 24–41, 81–95; Katharine Moore, "The Pan-Britannic Festival," in *Pleasure, Profit, Proselytism,* ed. J. A. Mangan (London: Frank Cass, 1988), pp. 144–62. See also David C. Young, *The Olympic Myth of Greek Amateur Athletics* (Chicago: Ares, 1984).

2. Pierre de Coubertin, *L'Idée olympique* (Cologne: Carl-Diem-Institut, 1966), p. 129; and *Une Campagne de vingt-et-un ans (1887–1908)* (Paris: Librairie de l'éducation physique, 1909); and also his *Mémoires olympiques* (Lausanne: Bureau international de pédagogie sportive, 1931); Marie-Thérèse Eyquem, *Pierre de Coubertin* (Paris: Calmann–Lévy, 1966); Louis Callebat, *Pierre de Coubertin* (Paris: Fayard, 1988).

3. Richard D. Mandell, *The First Modern Olympics* (Berkeley: University of California Press, 1976); John J. MacAloon, *This Great Symbol* (Chicago: University of Chicago Press, 1981); Dietrich Quanz, "Civic Pacifism and Sports-Based Internationalism," *Olympika,* 2 (1993): 1–23.

4. Andreas Morbach, *Dimitrios Vikélas* (Würzburg: Ergon, 1998).

5. Coubertin, *Une Campagne de vingt-et-un ans,* p. 125.

6. Coubertin, quoted in Bernadette Deville-Danthu, "Les jeux d'outre mer," in *L'Empire du sport,* ed. Daniel Hick (Aix-en-Provence: Centres des Archives d'Outre Mer, 1992), p. 61; see also Otto Mayer, *À Travers les anneaux olympiques* (Geneva: Cailler, 1960), pp. 103–4.

7. Deville-Danthu, "Les jeux d'outre mer," in *L'Empire du sport,* p. 66.

8. Jean-Claude Ganga, *Combats pour un sport africain* (Paris: L'Harmattan, 1979), p. 147; see also Achot Melik-Chaknazarov, *Le Sport en afrique* (Paris: Présence Africaine, 1970), pp. 143–45.

9. John J. MacAloon, "The Turn of Two Centuries: Sport and the Politics of Intercultural Relations," in *Sport, the Third Millennium,* ed. Fernand Landry, Marc Landry, and Magdeleine Yerlès (Sainte-Foy: Presses de l'Université Laval, 1991), p. 42.

10. Coubertin, *Mémoires olympiques,* p. 200; Norbert Müller, *Von Paris bis Baden-Baden* (Niedernhausen: Schors, 1981), p. 29.

11. Reet and Max Howell, *Aussie Gold* (Albion, Queensland: Brooks Waterloo, 1988), pp. 6–7; L. Chappelet, *Le Système olympique* (Grenoble: Presses universitaires de Grenoble, 1991), p. 99; Wojciech Liponski, "Sport in the Slavic World before Communism," *ESHR,* 1 (1999): 237–40; James W. Riordan, "Tsarist Russia and International Sport," *Stadion,* 14:2 (1988): 228–29. Estimates of the number of athletes at the first games vary.

12. Floris J. G. van der Merwe, "Africa's First Encounter with the Olympic Games
. . . ," *Journal of Olympic History,* 7:3 (September 1999): 29–34; Walter Abmayr,
"Afrika und Leichtathletik," in *Beiträge zur Zusammenarbeit im Sport mit der
Dritten Welt,* ed. Rolf Andresen, Hermann Rieder, and Gerhard Trosien (Schorn-
dorf: Karl Hofmann, 1989), p. 59. The names of these and other African athletes
are spelled in many different ways.

13. Ramadhan Ali, *Africa at the Olympics* (London: Africa Books, 1976), p. 67; Don
Anthony, "The North-South and East-West Axes of Development in Sport," in
Sport, the Third Millennium, p. 333.

14. Milton Coffré Iluffi, "Historia del Deporte y la Educación Física en Chile," in *GL,*
ed. Horst Ueberhorst, 6 vols. (Berlin: Bartels & Wernitz, 1972–1989), 6:944–46;
Brest et al., "Los Deportes y la Educación Física en la Republica Argentina," in
ibid., 6:873, 885; Wolf Krämer-Mandeau, *Sport und Körpererziehung auf Cuba*
(Cologne: Pahl-Rugenstein, 1988).

15. William R. May, "Sports," in *The Handbook of Japanese Popular Culture,* ed.
Richard Gid Powers and Hidetoshi Kato (Westport, Conn.: Greenwood Press,
1989), p. 174; Kokusai Bunka Shinkokai, *Sports* (Tokyo: Kokusai Bunka Shinkokai, 1939), p. 8; Allen Guttmann, *The Olympics,* rev. ed. (Urbana: University of
Illinois Press, 2002), pp. 51–52, 69.

16. Coubertin, quoted in Otto Mayer, *À Travers les anneaux olympiques,* p. 70; Scott,
quoted in Reet and Max Howell, *Aussie Gold,* p. 54.

17. Stoner, quoted in Karen V. Epstein, "Sameness or Difference," *IJHS,* 9:2 (August
1992): 281–82; Joan S. Hult, "American Sportswomen 'Go for the Gold'—1912–
1936," in *Olympic Scientific Congress 1984,* ed. Norbert Müller and Joachim K.
Rühl (Niedernhausen: Schors Verlag, 1985), pp. 30–43; Mayer, *À Travers les anneaux olympiques,* pp. 163–64.

18. Doris H. Pieroth, *Their Day in the Sun* (Seattle: University of Washington Press,
1996). Female athletes were 9 percent of the total and were featured in 16 percent of the newspaper articles and in 34.7 percent of the photographs; see David
B. Welky, "Viking Girls, Mermaids, and Little Brown Men," *JSH,* 24:1 (Spring
1997): 28.

19. Ronald A. Smith, "Women's Control of American College Sport," *SHR,* 29:1 (May
1998): 103–20. On the industrial leagues, see Steven A. Riess, *City Games* (Ur-
bana: University of Illinois Press, 1989), pp. 83–86; Gerald R. Gems, *The Windy
City Wars* (Lanham, Md.: Scarecrow Press, 1997), pp. 150–54; Lynne Emery,
"From Lowell Mills to the Halls of Fame," in *Women and Sport,* ed. D. Margaret
Costa and Sharon R. Guthrie (Champaign, Ill.: Human Kinetics, 1994), pp. 107–
21. On the black colleges, see Cindy Himes Gissendanner, "African-American
Women and Competitive Sport, 1920–1960," in *Women, Sport, and Culture,* ed.
Susan Birrell and Cheryl L. Cole (Champaign, Ill.: Human Kinetics, 1994),
pp. 81–92.

20. Cindy Himes [later Gissendanner], "The Female Athlete in American Society:
1860–1940" (Ph.D. dissertation, University of Pennsylvania, 1986), pp. 180–81.

21. Sebastião Votre and Ludmila Mourão, "Ignoring Taboos," *IJHS,* 18:1 (March
2001): 196–218; María Graciela Rodríguez, "Argentina," in *IEWS,* ed. Karen

Christensen, Allen Guttmann, and Gertrud Pfister (New York: Macmillan Reference, 2001), p. 59; Carlos Guerrero, *Grandes del Delporte* (Santiago de Chile: Editora Nacional Gabriela Mistral, 1975), pp. 7–9; Frank Giral, *María Caridad Colón* (Havana: Editorial Cientfico–Technica, 1986), p. 105. Swimmer Jeanette Campbell was second in the 100-meter freestyle in 1936, but she had just become an Argentine citizen.

22. Leila Sfeir, "The Status of Muslim Women in Sport," *IRSS,* 20:4 (1985): 287; Allen Guttmann, *Women's Sports* (New York: Columbia University Press, 1991), pp. 163–71, 186–88, 199–206, 243–50; William J. Morgan, "Hassiba Boulmerka and Islamic Green," in *Sport and Postmodern Times,* ed. Geneviève Rail (Albany: SUNY Press, 1998), pp. 345–65; Youssef Fates, "Sport en Algérie," in *GL,* 6:312; Sakina Bargach and Alain Moreau, "Les Activités physiques et sportives . . . ," in *Géopolitique du sport,* ed. Borhane Erraïs, Daniel Mathieu, and Jean Praicheux (Besançon: Université de Franche-Comte, 1990), pp. 149–50.

23. Allen Guttmann, *The Games Must Go On* (New York: Columbia University Press, 1984), pp. 227–30, 233–47.

24. *Commission on Olympic Sport,* quoted in James A. R. Nafziger, "Diplomatic Fun and the Games," in *The Olympic Games in Transition,* ed. Jeffrey O. Segrave and Donald Chu (Champaign, Ill.: Human Kinetics, 1988), p. 229; British Olympic Association, quoted by Christopher R. Hill, *Olympic Politics* (Manchester: University of Manchester Press, 1992), p. 125; Baruch Hazan, *Olympic Sports and Propaganda Games* (New Brunswick, N.J.: Transaction Books, 1980); Derick L. Hulme Jr., *The Political Olympics* (New York: Praeger, 1990); Rolf Pfeiffer, *Sport und Politik* (Frankfurt: Peter Lang, 1987); Bill Shaikin, *Sport and Politics* (New York: Praeger, 1988); Guttmann, *The Olympics,* pp. 141–63; Fernand Landry and Magdeleine Yerlès, *The Presidencies of Lord Killanin (1972–1980) and of Juan Antonio Samaranch (1980—),* (Lausanne: IOC, 1996), pp. 123–25. Sources vary about the numbers of boycotting and nonboycotting NOCs.

25. Karl Adolf Scherer, *Der Männerorden* (Frankfurt: Wilhelm Limpert, 1974); Cesar R. Torres, "Tribulations and Achievements," *IJHS,* 18:3 (September 2001): 61–64.

26. Guttmann, *The Games Must Go On,* pp. 263–71; Lamartine P. DaCosta, "The IOC Geopolitics in South America, 1896–1936," *Journal of Olympic History,* 10:3 (September 2002): 61–66; Ian Jobling, "In Pursuit of Status, Respectability and Idealism," *IJHS,* 17:2–3 (June–September 2000): 142–63.

27. Brundage to Aldao, October 29, 1945 (Avery Brundage Collection, Box 50, University of Illinois at Urbana). On Brundage's Olympic career, see Guttmann, *The Games Must Go On,* pp. 62–255.

28. "Plan for Reorganizing the International Olympic Committee . . . ," *Bulletin du CIO,* 67 (August 15, 1959); "Minutes of the 58th Session of the International Olympic Committee, Athens, June 19–21, 1961," *Bulletin du CIO,* 75 (August 15, 1961); see also Guttmann, *The Games Must Go On,* pp. 170–72.

29. CONI (Comite Nazionale Olimpico d'Italia) to NOCs, October 3, 1964; Giulio Onesti to Avery Brundage, March 20, 1965; Brundage to Onesti, September 14, 1965 (Avery Brundage Collection, Box 61); "Minutes 66th Session of the Interna-

tional Olympic Committee, February 2–5, 1968" (ibid., Box 93); Brundage to Vice-Presidents of the IOC, October 8, 1971 (ibid., Box 58); see also Guttmann, *The Games Must Go On,* pp. 173–86; Michael Morris (Lord Killanin), *My Olympic Years* (London: Secker & Warburg, 1983); Geoffrey Miller, *Behind the Olympic Rings* (Lynn, Mass.: H. O. Zimman, 1979); Chappelet, *Le Système olympique;* Landry and Yerlès, *The Presidencies of Lord Killanin (1972–1980) and of Juan Antonio Samaranch (1980—),* pp. 48–49.

30. Guttmann, *The Games Must Go On,* pp. 179–80; "Olympic News," *Journal of Olympic History,* 8:1 (January 2000): 52–59.

31. *Bulletin Officiel du CIO,* 5:16 (July 1930): 19; *IOC Newsletter,* no. 15 (December 1968).

32. Avery Brundage to Otto Mayer, February 4, 1961 (Avery Brundage Collection, Box 48).

33. Michel Brousse, "Du Samouraï à l'athlète," *Sport/Historie,* 3 (1989): 12, 21; see also B. C. and J. M. Goodger, "Judo in the Light of Theory and Sociological Research," *IRSS,* 12:2 (1977): 5–34; and their "Organisational and Cultural Change in Post-War British Judo," *IRSS,* 15:1 (1980): 21–47; Kevin Gray Carr, "Making Way, " *JSH,* 20:2 (Summer 1993): 167–88.

34. Thomas Alkemeyer, *Körper, Kult und Politik* (Frankfurt: Campus, 1996), p. 210.

18. Resistance to Modern Sports

1. Salzmann, quoted in Hajo Bernett, *Die pädagogische Neugestaltung der bürgerlichen Leibesübung durch die Philanthropen* (Schorndorf: Karl Hofmann, 1960), p. 75.

2. For Jahn's views, see his *Werke,* ed. Carl Euler, 2 vols. (Hof: Verlag von G. A. Grau, 1884–85). The literature on Jahn is enormous; see Horst Ueberhorst, *Zurück zu Jahn?* (Bochum: Universitätsverlag, 1969); Christiane Eisenberg, "Charismatic Nationalist Leader," *IJHS,* 13:1 (March 1996): 14–27.

3. Alfred Richartz, "Sexualität-Körper-Öffentlichkeit," in *Aspekte einer zukünftigen Anthropolgie des Sports,* ed. Thomas Alkemeyer (Clausthal–Zellerfeld: DVS, 1992), pp. 161–81.

4. Jahn, quoted in Edmund Neuendorff, *Geschichte der neueren deutschen Leibesübungen,* 4 vols. (Dresden: Limpert, 1934), 2:122; Robert Knight Barney, "German–American Turnvereins and Socio-Politico-Economic Realities . . . ," *Stadion,* 10 (1984): 135–81; Hans-Georg John, *Politik und Turnen* (Ahrensburg: Czwalina, 1976); Lorenz Peiffer, *Die Deutsche Turnerschaft* (Ahrensburg: Czwalina, 1976); Michael Krüger, *Körperkultur und Nationsbildung* (Schorndorf: Karl Hofmann, 1996); Lothar Wieser, "'Für die Freiheit Deutschlands ist jedes Mittel recht,'" *Sportwissenschaft,* 30:2 (2000): 141–55.

5. Peter Rummelt, *Sport im Kolonialismus—Kolonialismus im Sport* (Cologne: Pahl-Rugenstein, 1986), pp. 168–78; Horst Ueberhorst, *Turner unterm Sternenbanner* (Munich: Heinz Mos, 1978); Maik Temme, *Die Deutsche Turnbewegung in Chile, 1852–1945* (Würzburg: Ergon, 2000); Annette R. Hofmann, *Aufstieg und Niedergang des deutschen Turnens in den USA* (Schorndorf: Karl Hofmann, 2001).

6. Neuendorff, *Geschichte,* 3:194; Christa Kleindienst-Cachay, *Die Verschulung des Turnens* (Schorndorf: Karl Hofmann, 1980); Michael Krüger, "'Das Turnen als reaktionäres Mittel,'" *Sportwissenschaft,* 23:1 (1993): 9–34.

7. Neuendorff, *Geschichte,* 4:474; *Zeitschrift für Turnen und Jugendspiele,* quoted in Maarten van Bottenburg, "The Differential Popularization of Sports in Continental Europe," *Netherlands Journal of Social Sciences,* 28:1 (April 1992): 6; Goetz, quoted in Erke Hamer, *Willibald Gebhardt* (Cologne: Carl-Diem-Institut, 1971), p. 13.

8. Michael Krüger, "Ruhmsucht und Rekordfimmel," in *Für einen besseren Sport,* ed. Hartmut Gabler and Ulrich Göhner (Tübingen: Institut für Sportwissenschaft, 1990), pp. 383–95; Karl Planck, *Fußlümmelei* (Stuttgart: Kohlhammer, 1898), p. 6; Carl Diem, *Die Olympische Flamme,* 3 vols. (Berlin: Deutscher-Archiv Verlag, 1942), 2: 690.

9. Neuendorff, *Geschichte,* 4:486; Angerstein, quoted in Krüger, "Turnen als reaktionäres Mittel," p. 32.

10. Neuendorff, *Geschichte,* 4:485, 664; Hagen, quoted in Henning Eichberg, *Der Weg des Sports in die industrielle Zivilisation* (Baden-Baden: Nomos, 1973), p. 120; Schmidt, quoted in Neuendorff, *Geschichte,* 4:386.

11. Hans Bonde, "Farmers' Gymnastics in Denmark . . . ," *IJHS,* 10:2 (August 1993): 209.

12. Krüger, *Körperkultur und Nationsbildung,* p. 345.

13. Cupérus, quoted in Raymond Barrull, "L'Émergence de la gymnastique sportive à la fin du XIXe siècle et au début du XXe siècle," in *La Naissance du mouvement sportif associatif en France,* ed. Pierre Arnaud and Jean Camy (Lyon: Presses universitaires de Lyon, 1986), p. 65. See also Roland Renson, "'Le corps académique,'" *Stadion,* 17:1 (1991): 87–99; Thierry Terret, "A la recherche de l'identité Belge," *Sport/Histoire,* new series, 1 (1992): 81–101; Roland Renson, "Foreign Gymnasiarchs in Belgium 1830–1914," in *La Commune Eredità dello Sport in Europa,* ed. Arnd Krüger and Angela Teja (Rome: Scuola dello Sport–CONI, 1997), pp. 26–29.

14. Ruud Stokvis, *Strijd over Sport* (Devanter: Van Loghum Slaterus, 1979), pp. 65, 72; van Bottenburg, "Differential Popularization of Sports in Continental Europe," p. 17.

15. Arnold Wehrle, *500 Jahre Spiel und Sport in Zürich* (Zurich: Berichthaus, 1960), p. 64; Fritz Pieth, *Sport in der Schweiz* (Olten: Walter Verlag, 1979), pp. 44–46, 135; van Bottenburg, "Differential Popularization of Sports in Continental Europe," p. 24.

16. Michele Di Donato, "Italien," in *GL,* ed. Horst Ueberhorst, 6 vols. (Berlin: Bartels & Wernitz, 1972–1989), 5:242; Michele Di Donato, "Sport and Physical Education in Italy," in *Sport and Physical Education around the World,* ed. William Johnson (Champaign, Ill.: Stipes, 1980), pp. 354–70; Gigliola Gori, "Sports Festivals in Italy between the 19th and 20th Centuries," in *Contemporary Studies in the National Olympic Games Movement,* ed. Roland Naul (Frankfurt: Peter Lang, 1997), pp. 19–52.

17. Ronald Hubscher, Jean Durry, and Bernard Jeu, *l'Histoire en mouvements* (Paris:

Armand Colin, 1992), p. 139; motto, quoted in Jacques Thibault, *Sport et éducation physique, 1870–1970,* 2nd ed. (Paris: Vrin, 1979), p. 90; patriotic orators (in indirect quotation), Hubscher, Durry, and Jeu, *l'Histoire en mouvements,* p. 44; see also P. Chambat, "Les Fêtes de la discipline: Gymnastique et politique en France (1879–914)," in *La Naissance du mouvement sportif associatif en France,* p. 86; Pierre Arnaud, ed., *Les Athlètes de la République* (Toulouse: Editions Privat, 1987); Jacques Defrance, *L'Excellence corporelle* (Rennes: Presses universitaires de Rennes, 1987).

18. Lothar Wieser [wrongly given as "Wiese"], "Zur Geschichte des deutschen Turnens in Südamerika mit besonderer Berücksichtigung Brasiliens," in *GL,* 6:953–60; Wieser, "Zur Sozialgeschichte des Deutschen Turnens in Südamerika," *SZGS,* 2:2 (1988): 7–32; Maik Temme, *Die Deutsche Turnbewegung in Chile.* Wieser names the town of Joinville's club as Brazil's first by a year ("Zur Geschichte," p. 957).

19. Cogswell and Bancroft and Follen, quoted in Erich Geldbach, "Die Verpflanzung des Deutschen Turnens nach Amerika," *Stadion* 1:2 (1975): 337, 346; see also Bruce L. Bennett, "The Making of Round Hill School," *Quest,* 4 (April 1965): 53–63.

20. Livermore and Holmes, quoted in Roberta J. Park, "Biological Thought, Athletics and the Formation of a 'Man of Character': 1830–1900," in *Manliness and Morality,* ed. J. A. Mangan and James Walvin (New York: St. Martin's, 1987), p. 19; Fowler, quoted in Jan Todd, *Physical Culture and the Body Beautiful* (Macon, Ga.: Mercer University Press, 1998), p. 178.

21. Ueberhorst, *Turner unterm Sternenbanner,* pp. 44–51, 73–85, 127–32; Hannes Neumann, *Die deutsche Turnbewegung in der Revolution 1848/49 und in der amerikanischen Emigration* (Schorndorf: Karl Hofmann, 1968), pp. 63–117; Robert Knight Barney, "German Forty-Eighters and Turnvereine in the United States during the Antebellum Period," *CJHS,* 3:2 (December 1982): 62–79; and his "German-American Turnvereins and Socio-Politico-Economic Realities . . . ," pp. 135–81.

22. Ueberhorst, *Turner unterm Sternenbanner,* pp. 127–32.

23. *Turner-Kalendar,* quoted in ibid., p. 151.

24. Fridtjov Stene, "Norwegen," in *GL,* 5:68; Peter McIntosh, "Therapeutic Exercise in Scandinavia," in *Landmarks in the History of Physical Education,* ed. Peter McIntosh, 3rd ed. (London: Routledge & Kegan Paul, 1981), pp. 85–111.

25. Gilbert Andrieu, "L'Influence de la gymnastique suédoise sur l'éducation physique en France entre 1874 et 1914," *Stadion,* 14:2 (1988): 163–80; Sheila Fletcher, *Women First* (London: Athlone Press, 1984).

26. Fügner, quoted in Claire Nolte, "'Our Task, Direction and Goal,'" in *Die slawische Sokolbewegung,* ed. Diethelm Blecking (Dortmund: Forschungsstelle Ostmitteleuropa, 1991), p. 39. I have corrected Nolte's translation.

27. Ibid., pp. 37–51; Tyrs is quoted on p. 43.

28. In addition to the source cited in the previous two notes, see also Michal Teresch, "Der 'Sokol' bei den slawischen Nationen," in *Die slawische Sokolbewegung,* pp. 25–28; Frantisek Kratky, "Tschechoslowakei," in *GL,* 5:311–16.

29. Wolfgang Kessler, "Der Sokol in den jugoslawischen Gebieten (1863–1941)," in *Die slawische Sokolbewegung,* pp. 198–218; Ryszard Wroczynski, Henryk Laskiewicz, and Kajetan Hadzelek, "Polen," in *GL,* 5:421–22; Wojciech Liponski, "Sport in the Slavic World before Communism," *ESHR,* 1 (1999): 218–21; Przemyslaw Matusik, "Der polnische 'Sokol' zur Zeit der Teilungen und in der II. Polnischen Republik," in *Die slawische Sokolbewegung,* pp. 104–35; Wojchiech Liponski, "Still an Unknown European Tradition," *IJHS,* 13:2 (August 1996): 10–14.

30. Kessler, "Der Sokol in den jugoslawischen Gebieten," in *Die slawische Sokolbewegung,* pp. 198–218.

31. Losan Mitev, "Die Entwicklung der Turngesellschaften 'Sokol' und 'Junak' in Bulgarien bis zum Jahr 1914," in ibid., pp. 175–81.

32. Teresch, "Der 'Sokol' bei den slawischen Nationen," in ibid., pp. 33–34.

33. Józef Vető, *Sports in Hungary,* trans. István Butykay (Budapest: Corvina Press, 1965), pp. 21, 115–17; Jiri Kossi, "Sokol, Sport and Olympics," *Journal of Olympic History,* 11:3 (September 2003): 12–18.

34. Robert F. Wheeler, "Organized Sport and Organized Labour," *Journal of Contemporary History,* 13 (1978): 199; see also Horst Ueberhorst, *Frisch Frei Stark und Treu* (Düsseldorf: Droste Verlag, 1973); Hans Joachim Teichler and Gerhard Hauk, eds., *Illustrierte Geschichte des Arbeitersports* (Bonn: Dietz, 1987); Herbert Dierker, "Arbeitersport in Berlin," in *Sport in Berlin,* ed. Gertrud Pfister and Gerd Steins (Berlin: Forum für Sportgeschichte, 1987), pp. 159–84; André Gounot, "Sport réformiste ou sport révolutionnaire?" in *Les Origines du sport ouvrier en europe,* ed. Pierre Arnaud (Paris: L'Harmattan, 1994), pp. 219–45.

35. André Gounot, "Between Revolutionary Demands and Diplomatic Necessity, in *Sport and International Politics,* ed. Pierre Arnaud and James Riordan (London: E & FN Spon, 1998), pp. 184–209; David A. Steinberg, "The Workers' Sport Internationals, 1920–1928," *Journal of Contemporary History,* 13 (1978): 233–51; Pierre Arnaud, "Le Sport des ouvriers avant le sport ouvrier (1830–1908)," in *Origines du sport ouvrier,* pp. 45–85; Yvon Léziart, "Pratiques sportives et classes laborieuses," in ibid., pp. 111–27; William Murray, "The Worker Sport Movement in France," in *The Story of Worker Sport,* ed. Arnd Krüger and James Riordan (Champaign, Ill.: Human Kinetics, 1996), pp. 27–42; Murray, "Sport and Politics in France in the 1930s," *Studies in Sport History,* 2 (1987): 32–90; and his "The French Workers' Sports Movement . . . ," *IJHS,* 4:2 (September 1987): 203–30; André Gounot, "L'Internationale Rouge Sportive . . . ," *SHR,* 31:2 (November 2000): 152; Mark Naison, "Lefties and Righties," in *Sport in America,* ed. Donald Spivey (Westport, Conn.: Greenwood, 1985), pp. 129–44; William J. Baker, "Muscular Marxism and the Chicago Counter-Olympics of 1932," *IJHS,* 9:3 (December 1992): 400; Edward S. Shapiro, "The World Labor Athletic Carnival of 1936," *American Jewish History,* 74:3 (March 1985): 255–73; Cristina Mateu, "Política e Ideología de la Federación Deportiva Obrera, 1924–1929," in *Deporte y Sociedad,* ed. Pablo Alabarces, Roberto DiGiano, and Julio Frydenberg (Buenos Aires: Editorial Universitaria de Buenos Aires, 1998), pp. 67–86.

36. Sigrid Block, *Frauen und Mädchen in der Arbeitersportbewegung* (Münster: LIT,

1987), p. 275; Heike Egger, "Frauen und Arbeitersport in den 20er Jahren," *Stadion,* 26:1 (2000): 57; Christiane Eisenberg, "Massensport in der Weimarer Republik," *Archiv für Sozialgeschichte,* 33 (1993): 160; Gertrud Pfister and Toni Niewerth, "Jewish Women in Gymnastics and Sport in Germany, 1898–1938," *JSH,* 26:2 (Summer 1999): 298; André Gounot, "Sport ouvrier et communisme en France, 1920–1934," *Stadion,* 23 (1997): 83–111; Marianne Amar, "'La sportive rouge' (1923–1939)," in *Origines du sport ouvrier,* pp. 167–91; *Freie Turnerin,* quoted in Gabriela Wesp, *Frisch, Fromm, Fröhlich, Frau* (Königstein: Ulrike Helmer, 1998), p. 65.

37. Stefano Pivato, "Socialisme et antisportisme," *Origines du sport ouvrier,* p. 133.

38. Rolf Lindner, "Von Sportsmen und einfachen Leuten," in *Der Satz 'Der Ball ist rund' hat eine gewisse philosophische Tiefe,* ed. Rolf Lindner (Berlin: Transit, 1983), p. 31; Frank Filter, "Fußballsport in der Arbeiter- Turn- und Sportbewegung," *SZGS,* 2:1 (1988): 55–73. Christiane Eisenberg dates the soccer sections to 1907–1908; "Fußball in Deutschland," *Geschichte und Gesellschaft,* 20:2 (1994): 192.

39. Jürgen Fischer, "Die Olympiade der Sozialistischen Arbeitersportinternationale in Frankfurt 1925," in *Die Zukunft der Olympischen Spiele,* ed. Hans-Jürgen Schulke (Cologne: Pahl-Rugenstein, 1976), pp. 96–127; Wheeler, "Organized Sport and Organized Labour," pp. 191–210; Steinberg, "The Workers' Sport Internationals, 1920–1928," pp. 233–51.

19. The Survival of Traditional Sports

1. Anna Bianco Dettori, "Traditonelle Spiele im Aostatal," in *Körperkulturen und Identität,* ed. Henning Eichberg and Jørn Hansen (Münster: LIT-Verlag, 1989), pp. 25–30; Hans-Peter Laqueur, *Zur kulturgeschichtlichen Stellung des Türkischen Ringkampfs einst und jetzt* (Frankfurt: Peter Lang, 1979), pp. 26–28; J. Lowell Lewis, *Ring of Liberation* (Chicago: University of Chicago Press, 1992), p. 161; Audrey R. Giles, "Kevlar™, Crisco™, and Menstruation," *SSJ,* 21:1 (2004): 18–35.

2. William H. Desmonde, "The Bull-Fight as a Religious Ritual," *American Imago,* 9 (June 1952): 173–95; Adrian Shubert, *Death and Money in the Afternoon* (New York: Oxford University Press, 1999), pp. 6–9, 70–71; Timothy Mitchell, *Blood Sport* (Philadelphia: University of Pennsylvania Press, 1991); Garry Marvin, *Bullfight* (Oxford: Basil Blackwell, 1988).

3. Timothy J. Mitchell, "Bullfighting: The Ritual Origin of Scholarly Myths," *Journal of American Folklore,* 99, (October–December 1986): 394, 397, 406. Although a few women, such as Concita Citrón and Christina Sánchez, have had successful careers, most matadors are male; see Jeremy MacClancy, "Female Bullfighting, Gender Stereotyping, and the State," *Sport, Identity, and Ethnicity,* ed. Jeremy MacClancy (Oxford: Berg, 1996), pp. 69–85; Sarah Pink, *Women and Bullfighting* (Oxford: Berg, 1997).

4. Gerd Hortleder, "Fechten und Stierkampf," in *Sport–Eros–Tod,* ed. Gerd Hortleder and Gunter Gebauer (Frankfurt: Suhrkamp, 1986), pp. 233–53.

5. Duncan Shaw, *Fútbol y Franquismo* (Madrid: Alianza Editorial, 1987), pp. 19–20;

Carlos Fernández Santander, *El Fútbol durante la Guerra Civil y El Franquismo* (Madrid: Editorial San Martin, 1990); Teresa González Aja, "Spanish Sports Policy in Republican and Fascist Spain," in *Sport and International Politics,* ed. Pierre Arnaud and James Riordan (London: E & FN Spon, 1998), pp. 97–113.

6. My source for *capoeira* is Lewis, *Ring of Liberation.*

7. Ibid., pp. 2, 142.

8. Ibid., pp. 96, 161, 213; see also Greg Downey, "Domesticating the Urban Menace," *IJHS,* 19:4 (December 2002): 1–32.

9. Croke and Davitt, quoted by John Sugden and Alan Bairner, *Sport, Sectarianism and Society in a Divided Ireland* (Leicester: Leicester University Press, 1993), pp. 27–28; W. F. Mandle, "The I. R. B. and the Beginnings of the Gaelic Athletic Association," *Irish Historical Studies,* 20 (1976–1977): 418–38; Mike Cronin, *Sport and Nationalism in Ireland* (Dublin: Four Courts Press, 1999), pp. 80–82; *United Ireland,* quoted in W. F. Mandle, "Sport as Politics," in *Sport in History,* ed. Richard Cashman and Michael McKernan (St. Lucia: University of Queensland Press, 1979), pp. 99–123; Michael Mullan, "Opposition, Social Closure, and Sport," *SSJ,* 12:3 (1995): 271. See also Richard Davis, "Irish Cricket and Nationalism," *Sporting Traditions,* 10:2 (May 1994): 77–96.

10. Sugden and Bairner, *Sport, Sectarianism and Society in a Divided Ireland,* pp. 32–33; Paul Rouse, "The Politics of Culture and Sport in Ireland," *IJHS,* 10:3 (December 1993): 333–60.

11. Joseph M. Bradley, *Sport, Culture, Politics and Scottish Society* (Edinburgh: John Donald, 1998); Alan Bairner, "Sport, Nationality and Postcolonialism in Ireland," in *Sport and Postcolonialism,* ed. John Bale and Mike Cronin (Oxford: Berg, 2003), pp. 159–74; Mike Cronin, "Projecting the Nation through Sport and Culture," *Journal of Contemporary History,* 38:3 (July 2003): 395–411. When Northern Ireland qualified, the Irish Republican Army responded with a car bomb; see Martin Polley, *Moving the Goalposts* (London: Routledge, 1998), p. 62.

12. Henning Eichberg and Ali Yehia El Mansouri, "Sport in Libya," in *GL,* ed. Horst Ueberhorst, 6 vols. (Berlin: Bartels & Wernitz, 1972–1989): 6: 261–73; Michael Hirth, "Éducation physique et sport en République Islamique du Mauritanie," in ibid., 6:352, 354; Borhane Erraïs, "La Planète sportive," in *Sport, the Third Millennium,* ed. Fernand Landry, Marc Landry, and Magdeleine Yerlès (Sainte-Foy: Presses de l'Université Laval, 1991), p. 582.

13. From among Eichberg's many contributions to this theme, see the following: "Spielverhalten und Relationsgesellschaft in West Sumatra," *Stadion,* 1:1 (1975): 1–48; "Von der grünen Heide zur fensterlosen Halle," *Jahrbuch der Turnkunst,* 76 (1981–82): 73–85; "Leistung zwischen Wänden—die sportive Parzellierung der Körper," *Berliner Historische Studien,* 9 (1983): 119–39; "Zielgraden und Krumme Linien," *Stadion,* 10 (1984): 227–45; "The Enclosure of the Body," *Journal of Contemporary History,* 21 (1986): 99–121; *Leistungsräume Sport als Umweltproblem* (Münster: LIT-Verlag, 1988); "Von Tristram Shandy zu 'Marschall Vorwärts,'" *Sportwissenschaft,* 19:3 (1989): 272–96; "Trommeltanz der Inuit," in *Körperkulturen und Identität,* pp. 51–64; "Race-Track and Labyrinth," *JSH,* 17:2 (Summer

1990): 245–60; "Travelling, Comparing, Emigrating: Configurations of Sport Mobility," in *The Global Sports Arena,* ed. John Bale and Joseph Maguire (London: Frank Cass, 1994), pp. 256–80; "Die Ekstase des Körpers im Trommeltanz," *Stadion,* 25 (1999): 33–67.

14. Henning Eichberg, "New Spatial Configurations in Sport?" *IRSS,* 28:2–3 (1993): 247; see also John Bale, "The Spatial Development of the Modern Stadium," in ibid., pp, 121–32.

15. Eichberg, "Trommeltanz der Inuit," p. 59; Victoria Paraschak, "Variations in Race Relations," *SSJ,* 14:1 (1997): 1–21.

16. Jean-Jacques Barreau, "Traditions festives, activités ludiques et spectacle sportif," in *Éclipses et renaissance des jeux populaires,* ed. Jean-Jacques Barreau and Guy Jaouen (Brittany Conference Papers, 1990), pp. 17–26.

17. Lidia D. Sciama, "The Venice Regatta," in *Sport, Identity, and Ethnicity,* pp. 137–65; Eichberg, "A Revolution of Body Culture," in *Eclipses et renaissance des jeux populaires,* pp. 106–7; Dennis Whitby, "Elite Sport," in *SPEC,* ed. James Riordan and Robin Jones (London: E & FN Spon, 1999), p. 124.

18. Henning Eichberg, "Olympic Sport—Neocolonization and Alternatives," *IRSS,* 19:1 (1984): 102, 206; Laurent Pouquet, "De la compétition au sport-loisir," in *Le Sport,* ed. Lionel and Pierre Arnaud (Paris: Problèmes politiques et sociaux, 1996), p. 9.

20. *Instrumentalized Sports*

1. This chapter includes sections on the instrumentalized sports of Fascist Italy, Nazi Germany, the USSR, and Communist Cuba. Brief references to Japanese sports during the 1930s and 1940s and more extensive comments on the sports of Communist China appear in Chapter XIV.

2. On Vichy France, see Jean-Louis Gay-Lescot, *Sport et éducation sous Vichy* (Lyon: Presses universitaires de Lyon, 1991); on Spain, Duncan Shaw, *Fútbol y Franquismo* (Madrid: Alianza, 1987). More generally, see Juan José Sebreli, *Fútbol y Masas* (Buenos Aires: Editorial Galerna, 1981); and John M. Hoberman, *Sport and Political Ideology* (Austin: University of Texas Press, 1984). A special issue of the *IJHS* was devoted to Fascist body culture, 16:4 (December 1999). Studies specific to Fascist, Nazi, and Communist sports are cited below.

3. Ferretti, quoted in Angela Teja, "The Transformation of the National Olympic Committee during the Fascist Regime," in *Sport as Symbol,* ed. Floris van der Merwe (Sankt Augustin: Academia, 1996), p. 51; Rosella Isidori Frasca, *E il Duce le volle Sportive* (Bologna: Patròn Editore, 1983), p. 89; Mussolini, described by Felice Fabrizio, *Sport e Fascismo* (Rimini-Firenze: Guaraldi, 1976), p. 115; Favre, quoted in Gianni Rossi, "Alla Ricerca dell'Uomo Nuova," in *Atleti in Camicia Nera,* ed. Renato Bianda, Giuseppe Leone, Gianni Rossi, and Adolfo Urso (Rome: Giovanni Volpe Editore, 1983), p. 39.

4. Marinetti, quoted in Fabrizio, *Sport e Fascismo,* p. 13; Gigliola Gori, *L'Atleta e la Nazione* (Rimini: Panozzo Editore, 1996), pp. 99–102; Felice Fabrizio, *Storia della Sport in Italia* (Rimini–Firenze: Guaraldi, 1977), p.112; Gigliola Gori,

"Women's Physical and Sporting Education at School and University in the Years of Fascism," *Stadion*, 26:1 (2000): 69–98; Sandro Provvisionato, *Lo Sport in Italia* (Rome: Savelli, 1978), p. 27.

5. Fabrizio, *Sport e Fascismo*, pp. 58–68; Gori, *L'Atleta e la Nazione*, pp. 105–20.

6. *La Gazzetta dello Sport*, July 3, 1929, quoted in Sergio Giuntini, "Gioco, sport e nazionalismo in Italia dall'Ottocento al Fascismo," in *La Commune Eredità dello Sport in Europa*, ed. Arnd Krüger and Angela Teja (Rome: Scuola dello Sport–CONI, 1997), p. 399; Marco Impiglia, "The Volata Game," in ibid., pp. 420–26.

7. *L'Osservatore Romano*, quoted in Pierre Milza, "Sport et relations internationales," *Relations Internationales*, 38 (Summer 1984): 166 n. 43; Alegi, "Air Sports," in *IEWS*, ed. Karen Christensen, Allen Guttmann, and Gertrud Pfister (New York: Macmillan Reference, 2001), p. 36; Turati, quoted in Adolfo Urso, "Il Fascismo e I suoi Giovani," in *Atleti in Camicia Nera*, p. 98; Gori, *L'Atleta e la Nazione*, p. 152.

8. Malitz, quoted in Hajo Bernett, ed., *Der Sport im Kreuzfeuer der Kritik* (Schorndorf: Karl Hofmann, 1982), 218–19; Bäumler, quoted in Thomas Alkemeyer, *Körper, Kult und Politik* (Frankfurt: Campus, 1996), p. 251. See also Tara Magdalinski, "Beyond Hitler," *Sporting Traditions*, 11:2 (May 1995): 69.

9. Neuendorff, quoted in Horst Ueberhorst, *Edmund Neuendorff* (Berlin: Bartels & Wernitz, 1970), p. 70; Hajo Bernett, "Der deutsche Sport im Jahre 1933," *Stadion*, 7:2 (1981): 225–83.

10. Hajo Bernett, *Sportpolitik im Dritten Reich* (Schorndorf: Karl Hofmann, 1971); Bernett, *Der Weg des Sports in die Nationalsozialistische Diktatur* (Schorndorf: Karl Hofmann, 1983); and his "Die Zerschlagung des deutschen Arbeitersports . . . ," *Sportwissenschaft*, 13:4 (1983): 349–73.

11. Dieter Steinhöfer, *Hans von Tschammer und Osten* (Berlin: Bartels & Wernitz, 1973); see also Hans Joachim Teichler, *Internationale Sportpolitik im Dritten Reich* (Schorndorf: Karl Hofmann, 1991), pp. 53–77.

12. Hajo Bernett, "Nationalsozialistischer Volkssport bei 'Kraft durch Freude,'" *Stadion*, 5:1 (1979): 89–146.

13. Hajo Bernett, *Sportunterricht an der nationalsozialistischen Schule* (Sankt Augustin: Hans Richarz, 1985); Gernot Friese, *Anspruch und Wirklichkeit des Sports im Nationalsozialismus* (Ahrensburg: Czwalina, 1974); Hajo Bernett, *Der jüdische Sport im Nationalsozialistischen Deutschland 1933–1938* (Schorndorf: Karl Hofmann, 1978); Kurt Schilde, "Jüdischer Sport im 'Deutschen Wald,'" *SZGS*, 2:2 (1988): 44–58.

14. On women's sports, see Gertrud Pfister and Dagmar Reese, "Gender, Body Culture, and Body Politics in National Socialism," *Sport Science Review*, 4:1 (1995): 102; Christiane Eisenberg, *"English Sports" und Deutsche Bürger* (Paderborn: Ferdinand Schöningh, 1999), p. 400; Gertrud Pfister, "Weiblichkeitsideologie," *Beiträge zur historischen Sozialkunde*, 13:1 (January–March 1983): 23; Regina Landschoof and Karin Hüls, *Frauensport im Faschismus* (Hamburg: Ergebnisse Verlag, 1985), p. 67; Gertrud Pfister, "Mayer, Helene," in *IEWS*, ed. Christensen, Guttmann, and Pfister, pp. 710–11; see also Pfister, "Conflicting Femininities," *SHR*, 28:2 (1997): 89–107.

15. *Völkische Beobachter,* cited by Thomas Alkemeyer, in *Körper, Kult und Politik* (Frankfurt: Campus, 1996), p. 237; Eisenberg,*"English Sports" und Deutsche Bürger,* p. 366; Carl Diem, *Ein Leben für den Sport* (Ratingen: Henn, 1976), pp. 156–64; Arnd Krüger, *Theodor Lewald* (Berlin: Bartels & Wernitz, 1975), pp. 40–58.

16. On Bergmann, see Gertrud Pfister, "Bergmann, Gretel," in *IEWS,* ed. Christensen, Guttmann, and Pfister, pp. 123–24; Allen Guttmann, *Women's Sports* (New York: Columbia University Press, 1991), p. 65. On the boycott movement, see Arnd Krüger, *Die Olympischen Spiele 1936 und die Weltmeinug* (Berlin: Bartels & Wernitz, 1972); Allen Guttmann, *The Games Must Go On* (New York: Columbia University Press, 1984), pp. 62–81; Bruce Kidd, "The Popular Front and the 1936 Olympics," *CJHS,* 11:1 (May 1980): 1–18; Stephen R. Wenn, "A House Divided," *Research Quarterly,* 67:2 (June 1996): 161–71.

17. In addition to the texts cited above, see Richard D. Mandell, *The Nazi Olympics* (New York: Macmillan, 1971); Friedrich Bohlen, *Die XI. Olympischen Spiele Berlin 1936* (Cologne: Pahl-Rugenstein, 1979); Hajo Bernett, "Symbolik and Zeremoniell der XI. Olympischen Spiele . . . ," *Sportwissenschaft,* 16:4 (1986): 357–97; Hilmar Hoffmann, *Mythos Olympia* (Berlin: Aufbau, 1993); Susan D. Bachrach, *The Nazi Olympics Berlin 1936* (Boston: Little, Brown, 2000); Leni Riefenstahl, *Memoiren,* 2 vols. (Frankfurt: Ullstein, 1990–1992), 1: 257–85; Glenn B. Infield, *Leni Riefenstahl* (New York: Crowell, 1976); Cooper C. Graham, *Leni Riefenstahl and Olympia* (Metuchen, N.J.: Scarecrow Press, 1986); Jürgen Trimborn, *Riefenstahl* (Berlin: Aufbau–Verlag, 2002).

18. Christiane Eisenberg, *"English Sports" und Deutsche Bürger,* p. 441; "Elise E.," quoted by Landschoof and Hüls, *Frauensport im Faschismus,* p. 100.

19. Wolf Krämer-Mandeau, "Regionale Spiele und Sportarten . . . ," *Stadion,* 17:2 (1991): 245–77.

20. Jim Riordan, "Rußland and Sowjetunion," in *Soccer, Calcio, Fußball,* ed. Christiane Eisenberg (Munich: DTV, 1997), pp. 130–38; John D. Windhausen and Irina V. Tsypkina, "National Identity and the Emergence of the Sports Movement in Late Imperial Russia," *IJHS,* 12:2 (August 1995): 164–82; Peter A. Frykholm, "Soccer and Social Identity in Pre-Revolutionary Moscow," *JSH,* 24:2 (Summer 1997): 143–54. Alexander Sunik, "Russia in the Olympic Movement around 1900," *Journal of Olympic History,* 10 (September 2002): 46–60.

21. James Riordan, *Sport in Soviet Society* (Cambridge: Cambridge University Press, 1977), pp. 9–41. Unless otherwise indicated, the data on Czarist and Soviet sports are from this source.

22. Ibid., p. 83.

23. Ibid., p. 103.

24. Hart Cantelon, The Leninist/Proletkul'tist Culture Debates," in *Leisure, Sport and Working-Class Cultures,* ed. Hart Cantelon and Robert Hollands (Toronto: Garamond Press, 1988), pp. 77–97; Robert F. Baumann, "The Central Army Sports Club . . . ," *JSH,* 15:2 (Summer 1988): 151–66. The bureaucratic structures of Soviet physical culture changed frequently. The system established in 1936 was typical. Sports administration was the responsibility of the All-Union Com-

mittee for Physical Culture and Sport Affairs. This committee was attached to the Central Executive Committee of the USSR and was subject to the will of the Communist Party (which, of course, was subject to the will of Joseph Stalin).

25. For representative examples of the Neo-Marxist critique, see Bero Rigauer, *Sport und Arbeit* (Frankfurt: Suhrkamp, 1969); Jac-Olaf Böhme et al., *Sport im Spätkapitalismus* (Frankfurt: Limpert, 1972); Ginette Berthaud et al., *Sport, culture et répression* (Paris: François Maspero, 1972); Karin Rittner, *Sport und Arbeitsteilung* (Frankfurt: Limpert, 1976); Jean-Marie Brohm, *Sociologie politique du sport* (Paris: Jean-Pierre Delarge, 1976). For critiques of the critique, see Hans Lenk, *Leistungssport* (Stuttgart: Kohlhammer, 1972); and William J. Morgan, *Leftist Theories of Sport* (Urbana: University of Illinois Press, 1994).

26. James Riordan, *Sport in Soviet Society,* pp. 173–76, 248–53.

27. Ibid., p. 130.

28. N. I. Ponomarev, *Sport and Society,* trans. James Riordan (Moscow: Progress Publishers, 1981), p. 91; Andrzej Wohl, "The Phenomenon of Soviet Sport . . . ," *IRSS*, 18:3 (1983): 54–55; Gyöngyi Szabo Földesi, "From Mass Sport to the 'Sport for All' Movement in the 'Socialist' Countries of Eastern Europe," *IRSS*, 26:4 (1991): 247; V. Artemov, "Social Planning of Physical Education and Sports Activity," *IRSS*, 6 (1971): 103–12; Riordan, *Sport in Soviet Society,* p. 214. Female participation was especially low in the predominantly Muslim areas (where early advocates of women's sports were occasionally murdered); see Jim Riordan, "The Social Emancipation of Women through Sport," *BJSH*, 2:1 (May 1985): 56.

29. Riordan, *Sport in Soviet Society,* pp. 235–40.

30. Robert Edelman, *Serious Fun* (New York: Oxford University Press, 1993), pp. 15, 213; see N. I. Ponomarev [sic], "Sport as a Show," *IRSS*, 15:3–4 (1980): 73–78.

31. Edelman, *Serious Fun,* p. 178.

32. Riordan, *Sport in Soviet Society,* pp. 262, 337.

33. N. Norman Shneidman, *The Soviet Road to Olympus* (Toronto: Ontario Institute for Studies in Education, 1978), pp. 74–84; Victor Peppard and James Riordan, *Playing Politics* (Greenwhich, Conn.: JAI Press, 1993), pp. 128–29.

34. Oleg Milshtein, "Sport in Europe and the Helsinki Agreements," in *Sport and International Understanding,* ed. Maaret Ilmarinen (Berlin: Springer, 1984), pp. 82–91.

35. Peppard and Riordan, *Playing Politics,* p. 71.

36. Sergei Vaichekhovsky, quoted in Jim Riordan, "Rewriting Soviet Sports History," *JSH,* 20:3 (Winter 1993): 256; Ken Patera, quoted by Pat Putnam, in "Good Things Come in Large Packages," *SI,* 35 (1971): 21; see also Jim Riordan, "The Rise and Fall of Soviet Olympic Champions," *Olympika,* 2 (1993): 25–44.

37. Article 8, Section 3, quoted in Günter Erbach,"Körperkultur und Sport . . . ," in *Jugend und Sport,* ed. H. Groll and H. Strohmeyer (Vienna: Österreichischer Bundesverlag für Wissenschaft und Kunst, 1970), p. 86; Karin A. E. Volkwein and Herbert Haag, "Sport in Unified Germany," *JSSI,* 18:2 (May 1994): 185–86; see also Hermann Josef Kramer, *Körpererziehung und Sportunterricht in der DDR* (Schorndorf: Karl Hofmann, 1969).

38. David Childs, "The German Democratic Republic," in *Sport under Communism,* ed. James Riordan (Montreal: McGill–Queen's University Press, 1978), pp. 76–80; see also Günther Wonneberger et al., *Die Körperkultur in Deutschland von 1945 bis 1961* (Berlin [East]: Sportverlag, 1969); Peter Kühnst, *Der Mißbrauchte Sport* (Cologne: Sport & Wissenschaft, 1982).

39. Volker Kluge, "'Wir waren die Besten,'" in *Körper, Kultur und Ideologie,* ed. Irene Diekmann and Joachim H. Teichler (Bodenheim: Philo, 1997), pp. 169–216.

40. Dieter Voigt, *Soziologie in der DDR* (Cologne: Wissenschaft und Politik, 1975), p. 67. The Federal Republic had 16 percent of its 62 million people enrolled in the DSB, but the DSB, unlike the DTSB, continued to expand until, in 1987, it claimed 32.85 percent of the population; see Karl Heinz Gieseler, "Gründung, Entwicklung und Strukturen der Sportselbstverwaltung," in *Sport im Verein und Verband,* ed. Helmut Digel (Schorndorf: Karl Hofmann, 1988), pp. 35–39.

41. Kluge, "'Wir waren die Besten,'" in *Körper, Kultur und Ideologie,* p. 196.

42. Dieter Voigt, *Soziale Schichtung im Sport* (Berlin: Bartels & Wernitz, 1978), p. 7; Gertrud Pfister, *Frauen und Sport in the DDR* (Cologne: Sport + Buch Strauss, 2002), 208–41.

43. Willi Ph. Knecht, *Das Medaillenkollektiv* (Berlin: Holzapfel, 1978), pp. 94–95; Pfister, *Frauen und Sport in der DDR,* p. 90; Günter Erbach, "Physical Culture and Sport . . . ," in *Sport in the Modern World,* ed. Ommo Grupe et al. (Berlin: Springer, 1973), p. 415.

44. Gunter Holzweißig, *Diplomatie im Trainungsanzug* (Munich: Oldenbourg, 1981), pp. 131–53; Karin Volkwein, "Sport and Ethics in Unified Germany," in *Proceedings: First International Symposium for Olympic Research,* ed. Robert K. Barney and Klaus V. Meier (London: University of Western Ontario, 1992), pp. 55–66.

45. Andrew Strenk, "Diplomats in Track Suits," in *Sport and International Relations,* ed. Benjamin Lowe, David B. Kanin, and Andrew Strenk (Champaign, Ill.: Stipes, 1978), p. 361.

46. Tom Donohoe and Neil Johnson, *Foul Play* (Oxford: Basil Blackwell, 1986), pp. 1–17. The DDR was, of course, not the only anabolic steroid offender. Robert Voy, who served at the chief medical officer of the United States Olympic Committee from 1984 until his resignation in 1989, claimed that the USOC may have suppressed evidence of steroid use at the 1984 Olympics in Los Angeles. He asserted flatly that he had been told by his superiors in the USOC to "keep his f—-ing mouth shut"; see Robert Voy and Kirk D. Deeter, *Drugs, Sport, and Politics* (Champaign, Ill.: Human Kinetics, 1991), pp. 90, 157. See also Jean-Pierre de Mondenard, *Dopage aux Jeux Olympiques* (Paris: Amphora, 1996).

47. Victor Zilberman, "German Unification and the Distintegration of the GDR Sport System," in *Sport in the Global Village,* ed. Ralph C. Wilcox (Morgantown, W.Va.: Fitness Information Technology, 1994), p. 276.

48. Paula J. Pettavino and Geralyn Pye, *Sport in Cuba* (Pittsburgh: University of Pittsburgh Press, 1994), pp. 134–48; Wolf Krämer-Mandeau, "Batos, Mani, Corrida und Baseball," *Stadion,* 14:2 (1988): 181–220; see also Krämer-Mandeau, *Sport und Körpererziehung auf Cuba* (Cologne: Pahl-Rugenstein, 1988).

49. Frank Giral, *María Caridad Colón* (Havana: Editorial Cientfico-Technica, 1986), p. 105.

50. Pettavino and Pye, *Sport in Cuba,* p. 4.

51. Steve Fainaru and Ray Sánchez, *The Duke of Havana* (New York: Villard, 2001).

21. Modern Sports as a Global Phenomenon

1. These generalizations are based on hundreds of empirical studies, many of which I have cited in previous publications; see my *From Ritual to Record* (New York: Columbia University Press, 1978), p. 174; and "Translator's Introduction," in Bero Rigauer, *Sport and Work* (New York: Columbia University Press, 1981), p. 115. For a recent example, see Gertrud Pfister, "Doing Sport in a Headscarf?" *JSH,* 27:3 (Summer 2000): 497–524.

2. Daniel F. Mahony and Donna Pastore, "Distributive Justice," *JSSI,* 22:2 (May 1998): 127–52; Allen Guttmann, *Women's Sports* (New York: Columbia University Press, 1991), pp. 231–50; John Hargreaves, "The Body, Sport and Power Relations," in *Sport, Leisure and Social Relations,* ed. John Horne, David Jary, and Alan Tomlinson (London: Routledge & Kegan Paul, 1987), p. 152; Jennifer Hargreaves, *Heroines of Sport* (London: Routledge, 2000), pp. 174–214.

3. Karen Trew et al., "Young People's Participation in Sport in Northern Ireland," *IRSS,* 32:4 (1997): 419–31.

4. Dolf Zillmann, Jennings Bryant, and Barry S. Sapolsky, "The Enjoyment of Watching Sports Contests," in *Sport, Games, and Play,* ed. Jeffrey H. Goldstein (Hillsdale, N.J.: Lawrence Erlbaum, 1989), p. 302; data on Fenway Park collected by Terry Breen and Peter Roisman, Amherst College (Spring 1979); Hans J. Stollenwerk, "Zur Sozialpsychologie des Fußballpublikums," in *Fußballsport,* ed. Dirk Albrecht (Berlin: Bartels & Wernitz, 1979), pp. 203–4; see also Allen Guttmann, *Sports Spectators* (New York: Columbia University Press, 1986), pp. 150–53.

5. Eugene Trivizas, "Offences and Offenders in Football Crowd Disorders," *British Journal of Criminology,* 20 (1980): 276–88; Richard Giulianotti, "Social Identity and Public Order," in *Football, Violence and Social Identity,* ed. Richard Giulianotti, Norman Bonney, and Mike Hepworth (London: Routledge, 1994), p. 19.

6. Kris van Limbergen, Carine Colaers, and Lode Walgrave, "The Societal and Psycho-Sociological Background of Football Hooliganism," *Current Psychology,* 8 (1989): 4–14; *Feyenrood* fans, quoted in Simon Kupers, *Ajax, the Dutch, the War* (London: Orion, 2003), p. 223; Klaus-Jürgen Bruder et al., "Fankultur und Fanverhalten," in *Fanverhalten, Massenmedien und Gewalt im Sport,* ed. Erwin Hahn et al. (Schorndorf: Karl Hofmann, 1988), p. 16; Gunter A. Pilz, "Zur gesellschaftlichen Bedingheit von Sport und Gewalt," in *Gesellschaftliche Funktionen des Sports,* ed. Hannelore Käber and Bernhard Tripp (Bonn: Bundeszentrale für politische Bildung, 1984), p. 169; Antonio Roversi, "Football Violence in Italy," *IRSS,* 26:4 (1991): 311–30; Rinella Cere, "'Witches of Our Age,'" *CSS,* 5:3 (Autumn 2002): 182; Dubravko Dolic, "Die Fußballnationalmannschaft als Trägerin nationaler Würde?" in *Fußballwelten,* ed. Peter Lösche, Undine Ruge, and Klaus

Stolz (Opladen: Leske+Budrich, 2001), pp. 155–74; Udo Merkel, "Football Identity and Youth Culture in Germany," in *Football Cultures and Identities,* ed. Gary Armstrong and Richard Giulianotti (London: Macmillan, 1999), p. 63; Srdjan Vrcan and Drazen Lalic, "From Ends to Trenches and Back," ibid., pp. 177–78.

7. Aldo Panfichi and Jorge Thieroldt, "Barras Bravas," *Fighting Fans,* ed. Eric Dunning, Patrick Murphy, Ivan Waddington, and Antonios Astrinakis (Dublin: University College Dublin Press, 2002), p. 151; Eduardo P. Archetti, "Argentinian Football," *IJHS,* 9:2 (August 1992): 227; Marcelo Marió Suárez-Orozco, "A Study of Argentine Soccer," *Journal of Pschoanalytic Anthropology,* 5:1 (Winter 1982): 17; Vic Duke and Liz Crolley, "*Fútbol,* Politicians and the People," *IJHS,* 18:3 (September 2001): 106–14; Eduardo P. Archetti and Amílcar G. Romero, "Death and Violence in Argentinian Football," in *Football, Violence and Social Identity,* p. 49.

8. Steve Wulf, "Bad Mouthing," *SI,* 68 (March 14, 1988): 17; William Oscar Johnson, "The Agony of Victory," *SI,* 79 (July 5, 1993): 31.

9. Anonymous supporter, quoted in Dick Hobbs and David Robbins, "The Boy Done Good," *Sociological Review,* 39:3 (1991): 563.

10. Christian Bromberger, Alain Havot, and Jean-Marc Mariottini, "Allez l'O.M.! Forza Juve!" *Terrain,* 8 (April 1987): 8–41; Antonio Roversi and Roberto Moscati, "La violenza nel calcio in Italia," *Il Calcio e il suo Pubblico,* ed. Pierre Lanfranchi (Naples: Edizioni Scientifiche Italiane, 1992), pp. 274–84; Christian Bromberger, "Ciucco e Fuochi d'Artificio," *Micromega,* 4 (1990): 171–81; Christian Bromberger, Alain Hayot, and Jean-Marc Mariottini, *Le Match de Football* (Paris: Éditions de la Maison de l'Homme, 1995); Richard Giulianotti, "Scotland's Tartan Army," *Sociological Review,* 39:3 (1991): 502–27; Henning Eichberg, "Crisis and Grace," *Scandinavian Journal of the Medical Science of Sports,* 2 (1992): 119–28; Matti Goksøyr and Hans Hognestad, "No Longer Worlds Apart?" in *Football Cultures and Identities,* p. 206; Boria Majumdar, "Cricket in India," *CSS,* 6:2–3 (Summer–Autumn 2003): 169, 186–87.

11. Edouard Seidler, *Le Sport et la presse* (Paris: Armand Colin, 1964); Harald Binnewies, *Sport und Sportberichterstattung* (Ahrensburg: Czwalina, 1975), pp. 18–19; Siegfried Weischenberg, *Die Außenseiter der Redaktion* (Bochum: N. Brockmeyer, 1976), pp. 123–29; John M. Osborne, "'To Keep the Life of the Nation on the Old Lines,'" *JSH,* 14:2 (Summer 1987): 137–50; Herman van Pelt, "The Flemish Community . . . and Its Sports Journalism," *IRSS,* 17:1 (1982): 91–97.

12. Erik Barnouw, *A Tower in Babel* (New York: Oxford University Press, 1966), p. 80; Ron Powers, *Supertube* (New York: Coward–McCann, 1984), p. 37; Weischenberg, *Die Außenseiter der Redaktion,* pp. 141–44; Kōzu Masaru, *Nihon kindai supōtsu no teiryū* (Tokyo: Sōbun kikaku, 1994), pp. 244–50; Jeffrey Hill, "Cocks, Cats, Caps and Cups," *CSS,* 2:2 (Summer 1999): 11.

13. Weischenberg, *Die Außenseiter der Redaktion,* p. 145; Powers, *Supertube,* p. 33.

14. Richard Haynes, "A Pageant of Sound and Vision," *IJHS,* 15:1 (April 1998): 211–26; Garry Whannel, "The Television Spectacular," in *Five-Ring Circus,* ed. Alan Tomlinson and Garry Whannel (London: Pluto Press, 1984), pp. 30–43.

15. Steven Barnett, *Games and Sets* (London: British Film Institute, 1990), pp. 31–32, 103. In 1997, the European Commission ordered similar protection for sports

classified as part of a nation's cultural heritage; see Harry Arne Solberg, "Cultural Prescription," *CSS,* 5:2 (Summer 2002): 1–28.

16. Gerald Redmond, "Imperial Viceregal Patronage," *IJHS,* 6:2 (September 1989): 213; Jeff Neal-Lunsford, "Sport in the Land of Television," *JSH,* 19:1 (Spring 1992): 56–76; Gerald W. Scully, *The Business of Major League Baseball* (Chicago: University of Chicago Press, 1989), p. 31; Andrew Zimbalist, *Baseball and Billions,* 2nd ed. (New York: Basic Books, 1994), p. xix.

17. Robert V. Bellamy Jr., "The Evolving Television Sports Marketplace," in *MediaSport,* ed. Lawrence A. Wenner (London: Routledge, 1998), pp. 73–87; Eric M. Leifer, *Making the Majors* (Cambridge, Mass.: Harvard University Press, 1995), pp. 133–34; James P. Quirk and Rodney Fort, *Hard Ball* (Princeton: Princeton University Press, 1999), p. 39; Kevin Cook and Mark Mravic, "Scorecard: March to Madness," *SI,* 91 (November 29, 1999): 40. The CBS NCAA contract is for 2003–2013.

18. Garry Whannel, *Fields in Vision* (London: Routledge, 1992), pp. 105–6; Peter J. Sloane, *Sport in the Market?* (London: Institute of Economic Affairs, 1980), p. 44; John Williams, "The Local and the Global in English Soccer and the Rise of Satellite Television," *SSJ,* 11:4 (December 1994): 376–97; Chris Gratton and Peter Taylor, *Economics of Sport and Recreation* (London: Spon, 2000), pp. 203–4.

19. Amy Bass, *Not the Triumph but the Stuggle* (Minneapolis: University of Minnesota Press, 2002), p. 12; Geoff Hare, "Buying and Selling the World Cup," *CSS,* 1:2 (December 1998): 124; Wolfram Manzenreiter and John Horne, "Global Governance in World Sport . . . ," in *Japan, Korea and the 2002 World Cup,* ed. John Horne and Wolfram Manzenreiter (London: Routledge, 2002), p. 3; *Japan Times,* August 10, 2003.

20. Sally Jenkins, "Peacock Power," *SI,* 83 (December 25, 1995–January 1, 1996): 54; Bellamy, "The Evolving Television Sports Marketplace," in *MediaSport,* pp. 73–87.

21. John Horne and Wolfram Manzenreiter, "The World Cup and Television Football," in *Japan, Korea and the 2002 World Cup,* pp. 197–201.

22. Neil Blain, Raymond Boyle, and Hugh O'Donnell, *Sport and National Identity in the European Media* (Leicester: Leicester University Press, 1993), pp.18–36; Robert V. Bellamy Jr., "Issues in the Internationalization of the U.S. Sports Media," *JSSI,* 17:3 (December 1993): 171–72; Stephen Wagg, "Playing the Past," in *British Football and Social Change,* ed. John Williams and Stephen Wagg (Leicester: University of Leicester Press, 1991), pp. 220–38; Jim McKay and David Rowe, "Field of Soaps," *Social Text,* 15:1 (Spring 1997): 69–86; Werner Lang, "Der Fall Berlusconi," in *Über Fußball,* ed. Werner Schlicht and Werner Lang (Schorndorf: Karl Hofmann, 2000), pp. 126–51; Jean-François Bourg, *L'Argent fou du sport* (Paris: Table Ronde, 1994), pp. 21–37; Alan Law, Jean Harvey, and Stuart Kemp, "The Global Sport Mass Media," *IRSS,* 37:3–4 (September–December 2003): 279–302. The five diagrams in Law et al. depict Murdoch's News Corporation, Disney, AOL/Time Warner, Bertelsmann, and Vivendi/Universal.

23. McKay and Rowe, "Field of Soaps," pp. 69–86.

24. Miquel de Moragas Spà, Nancy K. Rivenburgh, and James F. Larson, *Television in*

the Olympics (London: John Libbey, 1995), pp. 96–97; Nancy K. Rivenburgh, "Images of Others," *Journal of International Communication,* 2:1 (1995): 6–25; Fernand Landry and Magdeleine Yerlès, *The Presidencies of Lord Killanin (1972–1980) and of Juan Antonio Samaranch (1980—)* (Lausanne: IOC, 1996), pp. 203–4; MacPherson, quoted in John Izod, "Television Sport and the Sacrificial Hero," *JSSI,* 20:2 (May 1996): 183.

25. Jack McCallum and Richard O'Brien, "Scorecard: Viewer's Guide," *SI,* 88 (January 26, 1998): 25–26; William MacPhail, quoted by William Johnson, "After TV Accepted the Call, Sunday Was Never the Same," *SI,* 32 (January 12,1970): 29; Jerry Kirshenbaum, "Scorecard: TV Friendly?" *SI,* 79 (August 9, 1993): 10.

26. Lacey, quoted in Barnett, *Games and Sets,* p. 141. See also Joseph Maguire, "The Media-Sport Production Complex," *European Journal of Communciation,* 7:2–3 (1990): 315–36.

27. Allen Guttmann, *The Olympics,* rev. ed. (Urbana: University of Illinois Press, 2002), pp. 173–74.

28. Gratton and Taylor, *Economics of Sport and Recreation,* p. 168; John Sugden and Alan Tomlinson, *FIFA and the Contest for World Football* (Cambridge: Polity Press, 1988), p. 93; Geoff Hare, "Buying and Selling the World Cup," pp. 126, 139. The corporations lined up for TOP V (2001–2004) are Coca-Cola, John Hancock, Kodak, McDonald's, Panasonic, Samsung, Schlumberger-Sema, Swatch, Time International, Visa, and Xerox; see www.olympics.org.uk.

29. John L. Crompton, "Sponsorship of Sport by Tobacco and Alcohol Companies," *JSSI,* 17:3 (December 1993): 161.

30. Annemarie Jutel, "Olympic Road Cycling and National Identity," *JSSI,* 26:2 (May 2002): 195–208.

31. Pierre Lanfranchi and Matthew Taylor, *Moving with the Ball* (Oxford: Berg, 2001), pp. 15–35.

32. Joseph Maguire and David Stead, "Far Pavilions?" *IRSS,* 31:1 (1996): 1–21; Paul Darby, *Africa, Football and FIFA* (London: Frank Cass, 2002), p. 15; Pierre Lanfranchi, "The Migration of Footballers," in *The Global Sports Arena,* ed. John Bale and Joseph Maguire (London: Frank Cass, 1994), p. 68; Vic Duke, "The Flood from the East?" ibid., pp. 153–67; Vic Duke, "Going to Market," in *Giving the Game Away,* ed. Stephen Wagg (Leicester: Leicester University Press, 1995), p. 94; Jonathan Magee and John Sugden, "'The World at their Feet,'" *JSSI,* 26:4 (November 2002): 422; Lanfranchi and Taylor, *Moving with the Ball,* p. 111; anonymous Hungarian fan, quoted in Gyöngi Szabó Földesi, "Social and Demographic Characteristics of Hungarian Football Fans . . . ," *IRSS,* 31:4 (1996): 422.

33. Naoki Chiba, Osamu Ebihara, and Shinji Morino, "Globalization, Naturalization and Identity," *IRSS,* 36:2 (June 2001): 214–15; Steve Greenfield and Guy Osborn, "From Feudal Serf to Big Spender," *CSS,* 1:1 (May 1998): 1–23.

34. Joseph Maguire and David Stead, "Border Crossings," *IRSS,* 33:1 (March 1998): 59–73; David Stead and Joseph Maguire, "'Rite de Passage' or Passage to Riches?" *JSSI,* 24:1 (February 2000): 36–60; Lanfranchi and Taylor, *Moving with the Ball,* pp. 1–13; Joseph Maguire and Robert Pearton, "Global Sport and the Migration Patterns of France '98 World Cup Finals Players," in *The Future of*

Football, ed. Jon Garland, Dominic Malcolm, and Michael Rowe (London: Frank Cass, 2000), pp. 175–89; Paul Darby, "The New Scramble for Africa," *ESHR*, 3 (2001): 217–44.

35. John Bale, *The Brawn Drain* (Urbana: University of Illinois Press, 1991), p. 4; Arturo J. Marcano and David P. Fidler, "The Globalization of Baseball," *Global Legal Studies*, 6 (1999): 511; Vic Duke, "Going to Market," in *Giving the Game Away*, p. 94. See also Vic Duke, "The Flood from the East?" in *The Global Sports Arena*, pp. 153–67; Joseph Maguire, "Blade Runners," *JSSI*, 20:3 (August 1996): 335–60.

36. Bale, *Brawn Drain*, pp. 70, 3 (in that order).

37. Joseph Maguire and John Bale, "Sports Labour Migration in the Global Arena," in *The Global Sports Arena*, p. 5; E. M. Swift, "The Most Powerful Man in Sports," *SI*, 72 (May 21, 1990): 101.

38. Daryl Adair and Wray Vamplew, *Sport in Australian History* (New York: Oxford University Press, 1997), p. 29; Whannel, *Fields in Vision*, pp. 70–74; Ronald Hubscher, Jean Durry, and Bernard Jeu, *l'Histoire en mouvements* (Paris: Armand Colin, 1992), p. 246; Jean-Claude Killy and Al Greenberg, *Comeback* (New York: Macmillan, 1974), p. 38; Jack McCallum, "You Gotta Carry That Weight," *SI*, 99:16 (October 27, 2003): 70.

Coda: Postmodernism and Les Sports Californiens

1. For attempts at the definition and analysis of postmodern sports, see Richard Giulianotti, *Football* (Cambridge: Polity Press, 1999); Robert E. Rinehart, *Players All* (Bloomington: Indiana University Press, 1998); Geneviève Rail, ed., *Sport and Postmodern Times* (Albany: SUNY Press, 1998); Bob Stewart and Aaron Smith, "Australian Sport in a Postmodern Age," *IJHS*, 17:2–3 (June–September 2000): 278–304.

2. Richard Giulianotti and Michael Gerrard, "Evil Genie or Pure Genius?" in *Sport Stars*, ed. David L. Andrews and Steven J. Jackson (London: Routledge, 2001), pp. 134–35; Gisèle Lacroix, "Le Look fun et ses enjeux," in *Géopolitique du sport*, ed. Borhane Erraïs, Daniel Mathieu, and Jean Praicheux (Besançon: Université de Franche-Comte, 1990), pp. 61–72; Claire Calogirou and Marc Touché, "Sport-passion dans la ville," *Terrain*, 25 (September 1995): 40.

3. Duncan Humphreys, "Snowboarders," *Sporting Traditions*, 13:1 November 1996): 3–23; Kristin L. Anderson, "Snowboarding," *JSSI*, 23:1 (February 1999): 55–79; Suzanne McDonald-Walker, *Bikers* (Oxford: Berg, 2000); Becky Beal, "Alternative Masculinity . . . in the Subculture of Skateboarding," *Journal of Sport Behavior*, 19:3 (August 1996): 204–20; Iain Borden, *Skateboarding* (Oxford: Berg, 2001); Ronald Hubscher, Jean Durry, and Bernard Jeu, *l'Histoire en mouvements* (Paris: Armand Colin, 1992), pp. 316–18; Miles Messner, quoted in Michael A. Messner, *Taking the Field* (Minneapolis: University of Minnesota Press, 2002), p. 80; Alain Loret, "Une Logique contestataire," in *Le Sport*, ed. Lionel and Pierre Arnaud (Paris: Problèmes politiques et sociaux, 1996), p. 21;

Borden, *Skateboarding*, p. 21. See also Alain Ehrenberg, *Le Culte de la performance* (Paris: Calmann-Lévy, 1991).

4. Duncan Humphreys, "'Shredheads Go Mainstream'?" *IRSS*, 32:2 (June 1997): 147–60; Rebecca Heino, "New Sports," *JSSI*, 24:2 (May 2000): 176–91.

5. Illustrated in Peter Kühnst, *Sport* (Dresden: Verlag der Kunst, 1996), p. 346.

6. David Denham, "Modernism and Postmodernism in Professional Rugby League in England," *SSJ*, 17:3 (2000): 287. Denham refers to "metanarratives" of "commodification and rationalization."

INDEX

Herrmann, Ernst, 190
Herrmann, Hans-Volkmar, 21
Hertz, 321
Heysal Stadium (Brussels), 36, 309
highjumping, 11
Highland Games, 97
Highland Society of New York, 125
Higuchi Hideo, 308
Hill, Philip, 202
Hillsborough Stadium (Sheffield), 110
Hilton College, 244
Hinault, Bernard, 199
Hinduism, 44
Hindus, as athletes, 214–16, 219
Hines, James, 222
Hippias of Elis, 20
hippodromes, 19, 25
Hiraoka Hiroshi, 224, 228
Hispanic Americans, as athletes, 136, 173
Histoire du Graal (Robert de Borron), 55
Histoire en mouvements (Ronald Hubscher
et al.), 201
Historia de Gentibus Septentrionalibus (Olaus
Magnus), 250
Hitachi, 194
Hitler, Adolf, 282–83, 295, 297
Hitler Jugend, 296
Hitomi Kinue, 223
Hoad, Lew, 87
Hobbs, Jack, 104
Hoboken 80, 124
hockey: field, 102–3, 220, 236, 241, 243, 265;
ice, 158, 255–59, 302, 320
Hockey Field, 103
"Hockey Night in Canada," 257
Hogan, Michael, 289
Hogg, James, 168–69
Hogg, Thomas, 168
Hogg, Tómas, 168–69
Holman, Nat, 162
Holmenkollen, 251
Holmes, Oliver Wendell, 137
Holmes, Oliver Wendell Jr, 278
Holy Cross College (Worcester), 160
Homây, 44
Homer, 17
Homer, Winslow, 142
Homewood Country Club (Chicago), 156
homosexuality, 310

Hoogerheyde, 61
hooligans, 112, 309–11
Hopcraft, Arthur, 113
Hopkins, Keith, 30
Hopman, Harry, 87
Horace, 28
horse races, 21, 41, 69–71, 92–94, 120–22, 168,
290, 312–13
Horsmann, Gerhard, 34
Hot Rod Monthly, 203
"hot rods," 202–3
houses of strength. *See zûrkhânah*
Houston, 138
Howell, Colin, 79
Hu Na, 211
Hubscher, Ronald, 201
Huddersfield Town (soccer club), 313
Huelva Recreation Club, 287
Hughes, Thomas, 82
Hulbert, William A., 130
Hull (rugby club), 115
hunting, 13, 15–16, 26, 43, 49, 57–59
hurling, 289–90
Hurst, Cameron, 46, 48
Hutton, Alexander Watson, 169
Hyde Park High School (Chicago), 151
Hye-Kerkdal, Käthe, 9
"hygienists," 299
Hyman, Dorothy, 99
"Hymn to Apollo," 260
Hyundai, 213

Ibrahim Pasha, 50
Ibrox Park (Glasgow), 114
ice skating. *See* skating, ice
Ichikō (Tokyo), 222, 225
Iliad, 17
Illinois Athletic Club (Chicago), 127
Illinois Sports Facilities Authority, 138
Illinois, University of, 152
IMG. *See* International Management Group
Imola, 198
Imperial Cricket Conference, 214
Imperial Oil, 257
Imperial Yacht Club (Russia), 298
Indian Football Association, 218
Indian Olympic Association, 216, 219–20
Indianapolis 500 (automobile racing), 3, 202
Indians, American, 126